Web Marketing

ALL-IN-ONE

FOR

DUMMIES®

2ND EDITION

Web Marketing
ALL-IN-ONE
FOR
DUMMIES®
2ND EDITION

**by John Arnold, Ian Lurie, Marty Dickinson,
Elizabeth Marsten, and Michael Becker**

WILEY

John Wiley & Sons, Inc.

Web Marketing All-in-One For Dummies®, 2nd Edition

Published by
John Wiley & Sons, Inc.
111 River Street
Hoboken, NJ 07030-5774
www.wiley.com

Copyright © 2012 by John Wiley & Sons, Inc., Hoboken, New Jersey

Published by John Wiley & Sons, Inc., Hoboken, New Jersey

Published simultaneously in Canada

For general information on our other products and services, please contact our Customer Care Department within the U.S. at 877-762-2974, outside the U.S. at 317-572-3993, or fax 317-572-4002.

For technical support, please visit www.wiley.com/techsupport.

Wiley publishes in a variety of print and electronic formats and by print-on-demand. Some material included with standard print versions of this book may not be included in e-books or in print-on-demand. If this book refers to media such as a CD or DVD that is not included in the version you purchased, you may download this material at http://booksupport.wiley.com. For more information about Wiley products, visit www.wiley.com.

Library of Congress Control Number: 2012941789

ISBN: 978-1-118-24377-0 (pbk); ISBN 978-1-118-28425-4 (ebk); ISBN 978-1-118-28167-3 (ebk); ISBN 978-1-118-28476-6 (ebk)

Manufactured in the United States of America

10 9 8 7 6 5

WILEY

About the Authors

John Arnold is the author of *E-Mail Marketing For Dummies* and the co-author of *Mobile Marketing For Dummies. He* is an engaging conference speaker, media contributor, and marketing consultant. He also spent 2 ½ years writing about marketing and answering reader-submitted marketing questions for Entrepreneur Magazine.

Ian Lurie is CEO of Portent, a digital agency he started in 1995. He is a long-time Internet marketing geek, with a blog, a book, and occasional speaking gigs on the subject. If you care about this kind of stuff, Ian's been interviewed and/or written for *The Seattle Times,* the *Puget Sound Business Journal, Direct Magazine,* DMNews, and *Visibility Magazine.*

Ian believes strongly that great marketing, online and off, relies on clarity and helps customers make good decisions about products, services, and people. His diverse background includes degrees in history and law; experience as an information designer, graphic designer, marketing copywriter, and programmer; two years working in a bicycle shop; and a brief stint as a political hack. As a child he used a TRS-80 Model One to print fliers advertising his lawn mowing business. The rest is history.

Ian has spoken at SMX Stockholm, SMX West, SEMpdx SearchFest, and the WSA, and he contributed to the most excellent book you have in your hands right now. Ian's blog, Conversation Marketing, is on Advertising Age's list of the top 150 marketing blogs. You can visit it at www.conversationmarketing. com. You can visit his company at www.portent.com.

Marty Dickinson launched his first website — MusicMates.com — in 1996 as a hobby. Today, Music Mates is one of the largest musician referral sites in the country. Marty soon began helping other business owners with their Internet strategies through services, writing, and workshop-style training.

Someone once asked him, "We'd like to hire you, but how do we know you will be around in six months?" So, Marty formalized his Internet marketing–services company by calling it HereNextYear, Inc. (www.HereNextYear.com). Since then, he has produced and managed nearly 100 of his own websites and has assisted with more than 200 client projects.

One of Marty's greatest enjoyments is to share his strategies through public speaking and writing. In particular, nontechnical business owners appreciate his ability to present complex subjects in an easy-to-understand language.

Elizabeth Marsten is the Director of Search Marketing at Portent Inc., a full-service Internet marketing agency based in Seattle, WA. She oversees the pay per click (PPC), search engine optimization (SEO), social media, link building, and copy staff and has spoken around the U.S., including SMX Advanced, Miva Merchant, PPC Hero, SMX East, SMX West, and Wappow! She is a regular contributor of PPC best practices on the Portent Inc. blog and the author of a PPC best practices ebook series.

Her PPC marketing experience started with an interview for office manager, which she didn't get but was instead offered the position of PPC specialist (which she initially thought was *pay per clip marketing* until she Googled it. Google asked her whether she meant *pay per click* marketing; she did. From there on, she has lived PPC every day, all day, and still pretty much does. Her detail-oriented skills and obsessive need for order and structure have served her and her clients well in their campaigns, which have ranged broadly from office furniture and wedding invitations to glue guns and salt.

Michael Becker is a leader in the mobile marketing industry, taking on the roles of industry practitioner, industry volunteer, and entrepreneur academic. Michael is co-founder of iLoop Mobile, Inc., a leading mobile marketing platform solutions provider and winner of the Mobile Marketing Association (MMA) Innovation of the Year Award (2007).

Michael sits on the MMA North American board of directors and global board of directors, founded and co-chairs the award-winning MMA Academic Outreach Committee, and founded and co-edits the award-winning MMA International Journal of Mobile Marketing, the world's leading academic journal focused on the use of the mobile channel for marketing. Also, Michael is a contributing author of *Mobile Internet For Dummies,* and the co-author of *Mobile Marketing For Dummies.* He supports the Direct Marketing Association Mobile Council, has written numerous articles on mobile marketing, and is winner of the MMA Outstanding Individual Achievement Award (2007).

Dedications

John Arnold: To the One who causes all things to work together for good and reminds me that marketing is not the most important thing in life

Ian Lurie: To my family, who make me want to be a better person, every day

Elizabeth Marsten: my new husband, Ken

Marty Dickinson: For my family, who has always inspired me to live a life of service to others, and my many business mentors who have shown me how

Michael Becker: To all those looking to establish and develop flourishing intimate, interactive, relationships through a new, exciting, and rapidly maturing medium: the mobile channel

Authors' Acknowledgments

John Arnold: I would first like to thank my wife and kids for being my cheering section. Everyone should be so fortunate to have a tireless team of supporters under their own roof.

Next, I would like to thank Matt Wagner for running the ideal literary agency. This book wouldn't have been possible without his experience and guidance, and nor would any others.

Finally, thanks to the outstanding team of authors who contributed to the content in this book. Thanks for loving your customers more than your technical prowess, and thanks for your technical prowess. Thanks especially to Ian, who contributed nearly half of this book's page count.

Ian Lurie: I'd be nuts if I didn't first thank my wife and kids, too. My wife Dawn put the kids to bed many more times than normal while I sat, typing frantically to meet deadlines. My son Harrison and daughter Morgan put up with me constantly multitasking, recording, or scribbling notes while I helped them with their homework.

Thanks to John Arnold, too, for being a very tolerant and helpful editor and advisor while I peppered him with first-timer questions. Everyone at Wiley I've never met face-to-face but who gave me such great advice during this process: Thanks for giving me such a fantastic opportunity.

Finally, thanks to everyone at my company and to my clients. Your boss/consultant was very distracted during the writing of this book, and you all kept things running regardless. You've all taught me a lot in the past ten years. I couldn't have written a word without those lessons.

Elizabeth Marsten: Thanks to Ian Lurie for hiring me and bringing me on board in the first place and to John Arnold for keeping us organized and on schedule. Thanks to my parents (who got the 1st edition dedicated to them), for paying for the college education that laid the groundwork for my acquiring some sort of writing skills. And much thanks to my new husband, Ken, who supports me in everything, all the time, no matter how annoying.

Thanks big time to the team at Portent Inc., who all contributed in some way or another.

Marty Dickinson: My first thank you goes to John Arnold for extending the invitation to me for being a part of this important and timely work. Secondly, I'd like to thank Wiley Publishing for their process as a whole. The format in which we were to submit book content has made me a better communicator in anything I write or present on stage.

My clients and customers deserve some gratitude, too, for it is you who continue to give me the incentive to try new business-building strategies and share with you the ones that work.

And, finally, special appreciation goes to my loving wife Sue, my princess Jessica, and son Douglas for keeping my feet to the fire to meet writing deadlines. I love you all.

Michael Becker: I'd like to acknowledge the everlasting and loving support of my wife and kids, who have put up with countless late nights and travel over the years as I've pursued my dreams. They're incredibly dear to me, and I would be nowhere without them.

I'd also like to extend my appreciation to a number of my industry colleagues, including my co-workers at iLoop Mobile: especially Matt Harris, who has demonstrated incredible leadership; Mike Ricci for his tireless creativity and edits; Chris Wayman for his pursuit of excellence; and the rest of the iLoop Mobile team. I couldn't find a better group of people to work with. I would be remiss in not recognizing my associates at the Mobile Marketing Association, including Laura Marriott for her support over the years. I also want to extend my thanks to Michael O'Farrell, Executive Director of the dotMobi Mobile Advisory Group, who invited me to contribute to the group. I'd also like to recognize the team at the Direct Marketing Association, including Paul McDonnough, Lori An Pope, Ken Ebeling, Julie Hogan, and Ramnath Lakshmi-Raton, who have all given me the opportunity to contribute to the DMA's efforts in helping the industry embrace the mobile channel for marketing.

Finally, I'd like to extend my thanks to John Arnold, who invited me to contribute this effort and guided me through the entire process. His contributions to the work have been invaluable.

Publisher's Acknowledgments

We're proud of this book; please send us your comments at http://dummies.custhelp.com. For other comments, please contact our Customer Care Department within the U.S. at 877-762-2974, outside the U.S. at 317-572-3993, or fax 317-572-4002.

Some of the people who helped bring this book to market include the following:

Acquisitions and Editorial

Project Editor: Rebecca Senninger
   (Previous Edition: Rebecca Huehls)

Executive Editor: Steven Hayes

Copy Editor: John Edwards

Technical Editor: Michelle Oxman

Editorial Manager: Leah Michael

Editorial Assistant: Leslie Saxman

Sr. Editorial Assistant: Cherie Case

Cover Photo: © iStockphoto.com /
   Cary Westfall

Cartoons: Rich Tennant (www.the5thwave.com)

Composition Services

Project Coordinator: Patrick Redmond

Layout and Graphics: Jennifer Creasey,
   Lavonne Roberts

Proofreader: Cynthia Fields

Indexer: BIM Indexing & Proofreading Services

Special Help
   Amanda Graham

Publishing and Editorial for Technology Dummies

   Richard Swadley, Vice President and Executive Group Publisher

   Andy Cummings, Vice President and Publisher

   Mary Bednarek, Executive Acquisitions Director

   Mary C. Corder, Editorial Director

Publishing for Consumer Dummies

   Kathleen Nebenhaus, Vice President and Executive Publisher

Composition Services

   Debbie Stailey, Director of Composition Services

Contents at a Glance

Table of Contents

Introduction

If your business, organization, or association needs to reach people who use computers or mobile devices for shopping, browsing the Internet, or interacting with others, you need web marketing. And if you need web marketing, you need this book.

Here are some reasons why.

Successful web marketing requires you to place and maintain your messages on multiple Internet mediums because your prospects and customers use those same Internet mediums to help them look for products and services. You don't have to be a technical expert to reap the rewards of web marketing, but you do need to understand how people behave when they fire up their Internet browser, e-mail program, or mobile device; that way, your marketing messages are always top-of-mind when customers are ready to make a purchase.

Because people search for products and services online, you need a web presence that can be found easily via search engines. People are more likely to do business with companies that stand out among the competition, so you need online advertising and pay per click (PPC) to attract interest.

The millions of folks who interact socially online act as an influence to others who share their interests and preferences. Thus, your marketing messages need to find their way to social media networks, blogs, podcasts, and viral communities. You need to be able to communicate with your prospects and customers when you have timely information, which means using effective e-mail marketing, really simple syndication (RSS), and mobile messaging.

To keep track of which marketing strategies get you closer to your goals, you need analytics and tracking. The rapid adoption of mobile devices with web capabilities means that your marketing messages need to be available to folks with a smartphone or tablet so they can find your offers anytime and almost anywhere.

The breadth of topics covered in this book, combined with easy-to-follow tips, make this book perfect for your business, organization, or association. Keep this book on a nearby bookshelf or on your desk so you can reference it often. That way, you can allow the combined experience of these five seasoned authors — all experts in their own niche of web marketing — to guide your plans and decisions to more successful outcomes.

About This Book

You're busy. After all, you're trying to market a business (or are just getting started), right? With that in mind, this book is for time- and value-conscious people who are in charge of marketing a small-to-medium–sized business, organization, or association. If that sounds like you, you've been using or exploring web-marketing tactics. And if you haven't, you're in the right place.

No matter what your level of experience, you'll find this task-oriented reference book as your guide to the entire web-marketing process step by step. This book is also a great resource for you if you're searching for a career in web marketing or a web marketing–related field.

What's in This Book

This book is really eight minibooks, each covering a topic related to web marketing. Each minibook covers a topic in its entirety, so each is a concise — yet comprehensive — path to learn about the web marketing topics you need to know about.

The content in each minibook and each chapter stands alone, so you don't have to read all the minibooks — or even all the chapters — in order. You can use this book like an entire series of books on the subject of web marketing. Scan through the table of contents to find a single topic to refresh your memory or to get a few ideas before beginning a task, or you can read an entire chapter or a series of chapters to gain understanding and gather ideas for executing one or more parts of an entire web-marketing campaign. When a topic is mentioned that isn't covered in depth in that chapter, you'll find a cross-reference to another minibook and chapter where you can find the details.

The following sections offer a quick overview of what each minibook contains.

Book 1: Web Presence

The "Build it, and they will come!" days of the Internet are long gone. With literally billions of web pages online, according to Google, competition for customers online is fierce. Most successful business owners have turned to using multiple outlets to promote their products and services through the Internet. And many have outsourced teams of helpers to implement integrated, Internet marketing campaigns. How can you compete?

This minibook introduces you to the Internet marketing process of today: a step-by-step sequence to follow for using the Internet to its fullest potential for your business. Whether your business has reached a growth plateau or is just starting, simply locate where you are in the process and plug in!

Best of all, you don't need to be a web designer or a programmer to put this section to immediate use for your business. Focus on understanding "the process" so you can find the right helpers to help establish — and explode — your online presence. This minibook shows you how.

Book II: Search Engine Optimization

Building a web site is pointless if no one can find it, and three-quarters of everything that happens on the Internet starts with a hit on a search engine. *Big takeaway:* Ignore search engines, and you might as well turn away three of every four customers who ask for help.

The good news? A high ranking in organic, unpaid search results can drive thousands or even tens of thousands of customers to your site. The bad news? You can't bribe or buy your way to the top. You have to get there by building a site that's attractive to search engines and customers alike.

And that's the art of search engine optimization (SEO). Don't get rattled by the term: SEO isn't a black art. It's nothing but a series of steps and little things you do to move up in the rankings. This minibook walks you through the steps, getting you started on your way up the search result rankings.

Book III: Web Analytics

Web marketing is unique: You can track the performance of every ad, page, and product; measure the return generated by your marketing efforts; and quickly adjust your site and advertising to get the best result.

To do all that, though, you need web analytics. This minibook starts with the general principles of traffic reporting and analytics — and the difference between the two. Then it demonstrates setting up traffic reporting and analyzing the data you collect.

Book IV: Online Advertising and Pay Per Click

Pay-per-click advertising can be a very complex — yet simple — medium to conquer. The concept itself is simple. You post an ad, someone clicks it, and you pay a fee for every time someone clicks. Where it gets complex is in the management of those ads, keywords, and budgeting. This minibook helps walk you through the most necessary concepts that you need to know to have a successful pay per click account.

Pay per click is a great way to get a spot for your website on the front page of search results and to get in front of people who are specifically looking for what you have to offer. If you're working on organic search engine rankings but just aren't there yet, pay per click is just one of the resources you should consider using for getting your message to an interested audience.

Book V: E-Mail Marketing

Every successful marketing strategy entails cutting through the clutter, and few places are more cluttered than the average consumer's e-mail Inbox.

E-mail marketing represents an opportunity to experience both the thrill of increased customer loyalty and steady repeat business as well as the agony of bounced e-mail, unsubscribe requests, and spam complaints. Whether you find thrill or agony in your e-mail marketing strategy depends on your ability to effectively deliver valuable and purposeful e-mails to prospects and customers who need your information.

This minibook combines time-tested marketing strategies with consumer preferences and best practices to help you develop and deliver professional-looking e-mails that your prospects and customers look forward to receiving. Additionally, this minibook shows you how to turn your prospects into loyal customers who make more frequent purchases.

Book VI: Blogging and Podcasting

Everyone's talking about blogging, to the point where it's hard to know what's truth and what's myth. When you look past the hype, though, you can see that blogging is a powerful business tool.

Using a blog helps you reach new customers, connect with influencers, tell the story behind your product or service, and build your site's SEO potential.

This minibook explains what blogs are and why they matter, how to set up a blog, principles for writing blog posts, and how to reach out to other bloggers to build traffic.

Book VII: Social Media Marketing

Social media is a buzzphrase that's used to describe a wide array of conversational tools in use on the Internet, including Facebook, Twitter, LinkedIn, and Google+. These tools help web users connect, converse, and make better use of the resources they find online.

Social media is also a business opportunity. You can reach customers, find new audiences, and talk to existing ones in more ways than ever.

This minibook explains social media; separates truth from fiction; and then demonstrates specific business strategies for major social media outlets.

Book VIII: Mobile Marketing

The mobile phone is no longer simply a phone: It's evolved into a smartphone with access to the web, newspapers, maps, a camera, radio content, video — and yes, it's still a phone, too. Tablets, such as the iPad, are also breaking new ground for connecting consumers with your marketing.

In this minibook, you find the information you need to integrate mobile marketing successfully into your marketing plans. You find what mobile marketing is, the mobile marketing ecosystem, best practices, the myriad paths that make up the mobile channel, and a plethora of applications you can use to communicate, deliver, and exchange value with your audience. After you read this minibook, you'll have a strong grasp of the practice of mobile marketing and will be ready to engage your audience.

Icons Used in This Book

The Tip icon marks tips (duh!) and shortcuts that you can use to make web marketing easier.

Remember icons mark the information that's especially important to know. To siphon off the most important information in each chapter, just skim through the paragraphs marked with these icons.

The Technical Stuff icon marks information of a highly technical nature that you can normally skip.

The Warning icon tells you to watch out! It marks important information that may save you headaches.

Information highlighted with this icon points out how a technique or tool works in the real world. We might recount something from our experiences or share something we've seen or heard. Nothing speaks louder than history, so don't skip these nuggets of web marketing in action.

Where to Go from Here

For even more web marketing information, check out this book's cheat sheet at www.dummies.com/cheatsheet/webmarketingaio. We'll occasionally have updates to this book as well, which you can find at www.dummies.com/go/webmarketingaioupdates.

Book I

Web Presence

The 5th Wave   By Rich Tennant

"So far our web presence has been pretty good. We've gotten some orders, a few inquiries, and nine guys who want to date our logo."

Contents at a Glance

Chapter 1: Internet Business Basics

In This Chapter

✔ Understanding the Internet marketing process

✔ Creating a website plan

✔ Knowing who your customers are

✔ Setting goals for your website

✔ Calculating your website promotion budget

✔ Deciding what to do yourself and when to hire an expert

*I*f you're just getting started on the Internet, you may feel like you have a daunting task in front of you. Experienced Internet marketers feel similar stress in that they get so distracted with whatever new technology is released, they lose focus on the core components that have made their businesses thrive for so many years.

The good news for both groups is that the actual process for succeeding online hasn't changed. Sure, more tools are available online today than there were in 1996, but all of those technological advances have been created to simply help you through the web marketing process.

This chapter is meant for business owners, website designers, programmers, and other providers of Internet services alike. First, you get an overview of today's Internet marketing process. By understanding the process, you know the right time and sequence of steps to apply any strategy you glean from this book, such as having various website components in place before launching a Google AdWords campaign, or knowing your conversion rates before attempting to recruit affiliates to promote your product. You then assemble a realistic plan that will enable you to use the Internet to its fullest.

Understanding the Internet Marketing Process

Today's entrepreneur finds success by following a step-by-step process to grow and run his company via the Internet. The following sections outline this process for you.

Step 1: Get in control

The success or failure of your Internet marketing strategy determines whether food appears on your table next month and whether your bills get paid. You must be in control of any process that affects your lifestyle. Basic components you should be in control of include

+ **Original website design files, including images, photos, and logos:** In the event that your designer suddenly becomes unavailable through other employment, discontinued interest in your project, or even death, having access to the originals will allow you to transition easily to another service provider.

+ **Website hosting logins:** Every website needs a website hosting location where all the files are stored and accessed on the Internet. You should always choose your own hosting company and pay for that service directly to the hosting company. Any login usernames and passwords supplied by that hosting company should be in your name and in your control. You might very well provide access to your website to designers, programmers, and Internet marketers, but the only way you'll have the ability to change passwords in the event you want to change personnel is if you are in charge of your hosting account.

+ **Backups of all content, pages, and HTML code:** In the event that you need to change website hosting companies or if you decide to fire your copywriter or administrative staff who might supply or maintain your website content, always have a current backup of your website's pages. That way, if your hosting company pulls the plugs on its servers and goes out of business, you could still be up and running with another hosting provider within a matter of hours — *if you have good backups of your content.* Otherwise, if you don't have access to those pages, you would need to create all those documents from scratch. Not good.

+ **Domain name logins and registrations in your name:** If the website is the heart of your online efforts, your domain name is the brain. It is the most critical piece of your identity that displays who you are and what your business is about. As the business owner, you *must* own your domain name, have it registered in your name, and have exclusive rights to maintain it. Never let your designer, administrative assistant, or even your mother register your domain name for you. A domain name such as *YourBusinessName*.com is tied to the web server where your website resides. If you decide to change hosting companies, the only way to change where the domain name points to is by logging into your *domain name registrar* (the company where you registered your domain name) and changing the appropriate settings. This is something only you should have control over.

✦ **Additional logins or passwords:** Beyond the basic website level, a variety of usernames and passwords will be issued to you. These could include a Google AdWords account, article directory submission logins, visitation statistics reporting access, YouTube video accounts, social networking logins (as presented in Book VII), and third-party e-mail management systems (see Book V), to name a few. When you're implementing your own Internet marketing campaigns, be sure to have all account registrations in your name, using your e-mail address. That way, you always retain administrative rights to those promotional outlets.

Try KeePass (`http://keepass.info`), a free tool for storing all your usernames and passwords on your desktop computer. All you have to remember is one main password, and then you'll have access to them all.

However, if you choose to outsource the more time-intensive Internet marketing functions (such as Google AdWords, as an example), be open to the idea of a professional organization having the exclusive right to that account. After all, there is a great deal of magic that skilled Google AdWords managers will be reluctant to hand over to you should you choose to cut your ties with their services. In cases like these, you really are still in control: That is to say (cough), you are in control of whether you will pay that service provider for additional services next month. Make sure that your service provider supplies you with routine progress reports so that you can make that assessment accurately.

Getting your site files via FTP

If you use a web designer outside your company, you can easily transfer copies of all your current HTML files, images, and photos by transferring your files with File Transfer Protocol (FTP) software. Here are the steps, but you should have your hosting company or designer walk you through the backup process if this is your first time:

1. **Download the free (LE) version of Core FTP at** `www.coreftp.com/download.html` **(Windows) or Cyberduck at** `http://cyberduck.ch`, **which is also free.**

2. **After the program downloads, click Open to begin the setup wizard.**

   The screen defaults to the Site Manager.

3. **In the Site Manager, enter a title related to your site.**

4. **Fill in the Host, Username, and Password fields as supplied by your hosting company.**

5. **Click Connect.**

   You see all your website files on the right and your computer files on the left.

6. **Click the main directory on the right side; when you see an arrow pointing left, click it.**

   Your website files begin transferring to your computer.

Step 2: Establish your products and services for sale

If you have a business, money needs to eventually transact, or you won't be in business for long. Part of the Internet marketing process is identifying what products your market wants, how or whether your competition offers anything similar, and what online methods you will use to transact that sale online and deliver the goods. The rest of the chapters in this minibook offer an introduction to strategies that help you accomplish this step.

Step 3: Communicate your solution

Your future customers will visit your website with a problem to solve. And, they're hoping you have the solution! Before launching any traffic-building campaign, assure that your website provides what your visitors expect to see when they arrive. Test and tweak your graphics, offers, and content to assure that you have the highest potential conversion rate.

A *conversion* is the point at which a website visitor takes the next desired step with your business, for example, buying a product, subscribing to your newsletter, or picking up the phone to get more information. The percentage of visitors that convert — the *conversion rate* — is one of the most critical numbers to keep track of on a weekly, or even daily, basis.

See the upcoming section "Create traffic and conversion what-if scenarios" for more about the importance of conversion rates. Book III offers more nitty-gritty details about setting and meeting conversion rate goals.

Step 4: Build traffic to your website

After your website is converting on a small scale, the next step is to increase visitation. This is where press releases, search engine optimization, articles, and podcasting (to name a few campaigns) come into play. Your job is to research each type of traffic generator and decide which outlets are good fits for your budget and desired speed to market. Each minibook in this book provides detailed steps toward implementing the most impactful traffic builders used today on the Internet. Master those first — such as search engine optimization (Book II), pay-per-click advertising (Book III), and social networking (Book VII) — and you will naturally graduate to other traffic-building opportunities over time.

For more information on how to get more traffic to your website, see `http://herenextyear.com/help-topics/get-more-web-site-traffic.php`.

Step 5: Become the recognized expert in your field

People buy online from other people who they know, like, and trust. The web is a tremendous tool for achieving all three, and in a short amount of time, often on a shoestring budget. You become the expert by sharing what

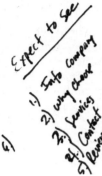

you know about your industry. The blog is one of the greatest inventions in recent years for developing a following and becoming a perceived leader in your field. A blog is, by definition, a website like any other. It contains graphics, content, and formatting just like all traditional websites. However, a blog has additional firepower that, if used correctly, can automate almost the entire publicity distribution process for you, giving you the opportunity for near-immediate visibility (see Book VI).

Another essential, and often overlooked or misused, component to becoming a recognized authority in your field involves using e-mail (see Book V).

Step 6: Create a virtual sales force

After you have traffic and proven conversion rates, you can recruit people to promote your products and services to others. These virtual ambassadors (most of whom you will never meet in person) are *affiliates*.

You don't have to pay affiliates until they sell something, but having even just four or five eager affiliates could easily double or triple your revenue inside one month's time. Without an affiliate program, you would be missing out on one of the greatest opportunities on the web: letting others sell your products and services for you. The next chapter of this minibook covers affiliate marketing in more detail.

Step 7: Power-partner with others for exponential sales growth

Also known as a *joint venture, power-partnering* is similar to having an affiliate program but on a much larger level, both financially and personally. The process involves finding one very special person who's of high stature in an industry and then convincing that person to recommend your product or service to his very large sphere of influence. The results could mean literally thousands of sales for you within as short as one week's time.

Moving ahead with the process

The great thing about this Internet marketing process is that it works for every business type, large or small. The unfortunate stories you've heard from other business owners about their painful online experiences is probably because they didn't work the process. That process includes asking for help from people who have demonstrated Internet marketing skills and paying for such services in your annual marketing budget.

Going forward — seeing as how you now know the process — you can probably figure out where your business fits in. Maybe you have plenty of traffic, but your website isn't converting as many visitors to customers as you want. In that case, go to Step 3 in the process. Or, you're getting traffic and sales, but you're experiencing an unusual amount of returns. Go to Step 2 and build a better product or service. Conversely, after you make it through the sequence and you're now becoming a recognized expert in your field, you want to set your sights on creating an affiliate program because a virtual sales force and ultimately a joint venture opportunity will be right around the corner.

With the Internet marketing process in hand, you can take a fresh and honest approach to creating your plan.

Planning Your Website Strategy

Just as the Internet marketing process is a sequence, developing your online strategy is much the same. For example, you must know your customers and how much they're willing to spend before you can create goals for how much you can sell. You need to know your own capabilities and interests as well as how much you want to be involved with the mechanics of the project before you can determine your budget.

Placing importance on your website

Authors and marketing educators alike will tell you to stop putting so much emphasis on your website and put all your efforts into social networking. But your website is important, because it's the only thing you can control. Facebook, Twitter, Google+, and LinkedIn all have the right to pull the plug on your account whenever *they feel* you've breached their terms of service. Instead, you should be using social media to inspire people you connect with to visit your website.

If anything, your website is now so vitally important that it can be thought of as the very heart of everything you do on the Internet, including all of the following:

✦ **Most cost-effective sales vehicle:** You can accept orders 24 hours a day, 7 days a week without the need for employees to process the order by phone or in person.

✦ **Ultimate lead generator:** Even the smallest businesses can be in competition with the largest companies for attracting new customers worldwide.

✦ **E-mail list builder:** Inspiring visitors to give you their e-mail address for something they will get in return (such as a newsletter, a free report, or coupons) allows you the opportunity to make routine contact with prospects so that you can earn their trust over time.

✦ **Publisher:** Write or record content of value and push it to thousands of viewers on your social networks automatically.

✦ **Market research spy:** Use online tools to find out what your competition is doing to promote products and services on the Internet to help you make your own decisions of how and where to promote.

✦ **Fast market tester:** Make changes to prices and sales copy as often as you'd like and the changes happen immediately, usually with no cost associated (unlike print marketing).

✦ **Collections agent:** Credit cards are automatically charged at the point of purchase before the product is shipped or services are delivered.

✦ **Communications vehicle:** Company developments can be announced to a mass audience within a few hours or even minutes.

✦ **Support department:** The Internet offers one person the ability to provide immediate assistance to multiple customers at the same time by displaying FAQs and offering personalized attention with online chat and e-mail support.

✦ **Product delivery truck:** The Internet allows new product forms to be developed that require no shipping, such as e-books and MP3 audio downloads.

Defining your target customers and competition

Many business owners create a product first and then try to figure out who they can sell to. This method isn't optimal, though, because it doesn't offer a predictable outcome. Always be aware of who needs your product or service and your competition. These are your two keys to success, and you can do much of your research to gain this knowledge on the Internet.

If you already have a website up and running, identifying the most popular groups visiting your website is easy. Just look at the visitation statistics for the pages of your website to see the popular topics your audience is interested in.

However, if you're just in the development phase of your website, find an industry-specific forum (a web-based discussion board) to find out what questions people are asking about your industry. The most popular topics and discussions in those forums will help you identify most popular needs — and, therefore, the most probable categories of people who will be visiting your website.

Going beyond your website

How have times have changed since 2007? Big companies are hiring savvy marketing staff to conduct Facebook contests and reply to Twitter tweets. QR codes are appearing on T-shirts, ties, and bumper stickers. Application development companies can't hire good programmers fast enough to produce the next viral iPhone games. YouTube gets more searches per day than Google, Yahoo!, and Bing combined! A new page of an ordinary website can now get displayed at the top of Google's search results in less than 5 seconds!

1. **Document three categories of needs.**

   At least three main groups of people will always visit your website in search of a solution. For example, if you were a doctor, you could know from history that new patients come to you because they

   - Have an insurance change and are forced to find a new doctor
   - Aren't getting their needs met with a former doctor and are looking for someone new
   - Are unhappy with the doctor staff or surroundings

2. **Identify competition.**

   Using Google.com, search for specific keyword phrases to see what competition might be present in your area of focus. For example, if you were a doctor with a specialty in dealing with stroke victims, you would want to search Google for *stroke doctor,* followed by your city or even your state.

3. **Spy on your competition by pointing your browser to Quantcast (`www.quantcast.com`) (see Figure 1-1) and entering the URLs of competing sites in the search box.**

   Continuing with the doctor scenario, you could look for the following pointed results:

   - Average number of visits per month
   - Average age
   - Percentage of male versus female visitors

4. **Estimate revenue potential.**

   Verify whether enough business exists to make that product worthwhile.

5. **Calculate potential market share.**

   List the number of competitors and potential customers by region.

Developing your website goals and budget

After you're confident that you have a product or service that's in demand, you can begin to develop the goals for your website. Here's a list of what you need to calculate those goals:

- ✦ How much profit do you need per month for your business to grow?
- ✦ How many new customers do you need each month to achieve that revenue level?
- ✦ What is the average sale quantity needed to accomplish your goals?

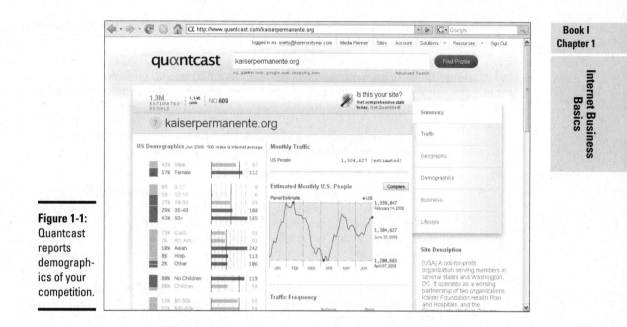

Figure 1-1:
Quantcast
reports
demograph-
ics of your
competition.

Too often, a business owner will create her operating budget from the ground up. First, she accumulates costs involved with setting up an office. Then, advertising costs are calculated. Business cards and brochures are quoted. At the end of the day, a required monthly sales revenue requirement is generated to assure a certain amount of growth per month or year for a start-up company. This approach is reversed when it comes to using the Internet to build a business. The following sections outline a better process to follow when establishing a budget for web marketing.

Start with your financial goals

Many proven models are available for building businesses online so that you have no reason to "pick numbers out of a hat" any longer. In fact, you can pick virtually any financial number you want to receive per month or per year and have a very close idea of what kind of budget will be required to get you there. Use this formula to determine your own online marketing budget:

1. **Determine your desired annual gross revenue.**

In other words, decide how much money you want to make by the end of a 12-month period. For this example, use the number that seems to be in everyone's sights these days: $1 million in gross annual revenue.

2. **Calculate your average sales value (ASV).**

An *average sales value* is the total dollars received for all purchases within a given time frame divided by the number of purchases made. It is neither cost related nor profit oriented. Average sale value is simply a number for you to use as a marker to help determine how many overall sales of all products combined you need in the future to reach a desired gross revenue.

You might have only one product or service to sell right now — and that's okay. You can work on that later! Maybe you've been in business for years, with multiple product lines, a variety of pricing, and a number of purchases for each price point per month. In any case, you need an average sale value to work with to determine your Internet marketing budget. For the following example, keep it simple and say that you have an average sale value of $27 for an e-book you created.

3. **Project your required sales per day.**

   Create a basic spreadsheet showing common average sale values and how many sales per year you would need to arrive at $1 million in gross revenue. In the following formula, DR is desired revenue, ASV is average sale value, and SPY is number of sales per year:

   ```
   DR / ASV = SPY
   ```

Continuing with the $27 e-book example, you need 37,037 sales of your e-book over one year's time; see Figure 1-2. Broken down further, that translates to an average of 3,086 orders per month, or 102 orders per day. Remember that is *on average*. So, the first few months could be considered ramp-up time during a new product launch phase, and you could still hit that number by the end of the 12 months if you play the numbers.

Figure 1-2: Annual, monthly, and daily sales needed for revenue goal.

# of Sales Needed for $1,000,000 in Gross Revenue per Year			
Average Sale Value	# Sales/Year	# Sales/Month	# Sales/Day
$10	100,000	8333	274.0
$27	37,037	3086	101.5
$100	10,000	833	27.4
$200	5,000	417	13.7
$500	2,000	167	5.5
$1,000	1,000	83	2.7
$5,000	200	17	0.5

These are simple calculations to make, but sometimes you don't really see it until you truly *see it* on paper.

The numbers you calculate here are starting points. In Chapter 2 of this mini-book, you find out how to turn a simple $27 sale into a $100 sale or more by using upselling, cross-selling, and back-end selling techniques. Then, if every $27 sale turns into a $100 sale, you would need only 27 sales per day (versus 102) on average or 833 sales per month (versus 3,086) to arrive at your desired $1 million revenue goal.

With a better idea of how many sales you're after per year, month, and day, read on to discover how to calculate the website visitation rate you need to arrive at those numbers.

Create traffic and conversion what-if scenarios

Next, create a similar spreadsheet to show how improving your conversion rates can reduce the amount of traffic you need to make the same revenue as well as the amount of sales per month. (If you're unfamiliar with conversion rates, refer to the section "Understanding the Internet Marketing Process," earlier in this chapter.)

To determine your required visitations per month to meet your sales revenue goals, use the following formula, where S is the number of sales you need, C is the conversion rate (which is a percentage), and V is the number of website visitors needed to produce those results:

```
S / C = V
```

Adding this formula to a spreadsheet (see Figure 1-3) is not only critical to your creation of a budget and overall Internet marketing plan, but it also enables your ability to dream a bit as well. Although 1 percent is a good starting point and maybe .5 percent is even more realistic as an average, why not triple the number displayed in the sales column or double your conversion rate to see how that reduces the number of visitors you need to acquire? Go ahead; no one is watching. It's okay to dream!

Figure 1-3:
Website visitor traffic needed per month.

# of Visitors per Month Needed to Achieve Monthly Sales Goal of 3086 at $27 Each		
Monthly Sales Desired	Conversion Rate	Monthly Visitation Required
3,086	0.10%	3086000
3,086	0.50%	617200
3,086	1.00%	308600
3,086	1.50%	205733
3,086	2.00%	154300
3,086	3.00%	102867
3,086	5.00%	61720
3,086	10.00%	30860

Continuing with the $27 e-book example and the goal of making $1 million in revenue by the end of a year, the formula would look like this:

```
3,086 / 0.01 = 308,600
```

Or, in simple language:

> 3,086 (sales per month) divided by .01 (a 1% conversion rate) = 308,600 visitors needed per month to reach your goal

Notice how much the needed monthly visitation drops with each small increase in conversion rate. Many marketers have proven that spending your efforts testing ways to increase conversion rates — rather than focusing solely on increasing traffic — is far easier (and certainly less expensive).

Here are a few significant insights for analyzing information like this:

✦ **Predictability:** You can predict how much revenue your business will see next month — and over the coming months — based on the traffic you generate over just one week's time.

✦ **Reactivity:** When you recognize that visitation decreases suddenly or your conversion rates drop, you have the opportunity to investigate why — and make immediate changes. A shift of even one-quarter of a percentage rate increase or decrease could mean the difference of thousands of dollars.

✦ **Testability:** One of the greatest features of the web is that practically anything online can be changed. Gone are the days when you have to pay a designer to build your website once and never get to change anything. Today's tools allow you to constantly test, tweak, and try new things to increase conversion rates and visitation. You don't have to wait until you see a severe drop in visitors or sales to do something about it. You can always be working toward increasing those results!

You can easily see the importance of continually monitoring visitation and conversion rates. Such good practices make up the basic fabric from which you make all online promotion decisions going forward.

Book III goes in depth into web analytics tracking setup and strategies.

More than half of prospective clients who seek Internet strategy help don't know their visitation or conversion rates. Get the answers before you call a service provider for help. The provider's first two questions will be to ask you those rates.

Calculate how much to spend per visitor

After you determine how many sales you need to meet your goals and how much traffic you need to generate your desired sales volume, the next logical step is to calculate how much money you can afford to spend to get the traffic. You can use a basic spreadsheet to do this job, as shown in Figure 1-4.

Figure 1-4:
Expense
allowance
per visitor.

	# of Visitors per Month Needed to Achieve Monthly Sales Goal of 3086 at $27 Each					
Monthly Sales Units Desired	Total Monthly Sales at $27	Conversion Rate	Monthly Visitation Required	Cost Per Visitor Break-Even	Cost Per Visitor at 20% Net	
3,086	$ 83,322	0.10%	3086000	$ 0.03	$ 0.02	
3,086	$ 83,322	0.50%	617200	$ 0.14	$ 0.11	
3,086	$ 83,322	1.00%	308600	$ 0.27	$ 0.22	
3,086	$ 83,322	1.50%	205733	$ 0.41	$ 0.32	
3,086	$ 83,322	2.00%	154300	$ 0.54	$ 0.43	
3,086	$ 83,322	3.00%	102867	$ 0.81	$ 0.65	
3,086	$ 83,322	5.00%	61720	$ 1.35	$ 1.08	
3,086	$ 83,322	10.00%	30860	$ 2.70	$ 2.16	

This number is significant for your operating budget process because it allows you to create a specific marketing projection based on predicted results. For example, you could have 20 percent of your budget allocated to organic search engine optimization services, 10 percent toward your continued learning, 50 percent going to Google AdWords, and 20 percent allocated toward offline marketing efforts. Simply change the numbers in the formula to create your own instant what-if scenarios.

Knowing your limits

Many of us start a business because we want to be our own boss: to make all the decisions and be responsible for all functions. By the time the business is up and running, though, you've likely discovered just how many decisions need to be made and how many functions you have to do — and how much time they all consume. For example, using the Internet to bring leads and sales to your business can easily be a full-time job for three or four people, let alone you by yourself. Even the most cutting-edge online strategies won't move forward until you turn the keys in the ignition.

Answer these questions to help you decide how much you want to be involved with the day-to-day operations of a website strategy:

✦ What are you really, *really* good at?

✦ Which skills make sense for you to improve, and for what tasks should you hire someone who already has the necessary skill set?

✦ What do you enjoy doing that you could do all day long and not require payment?

✦ What type of work do you absolutely despise?

Use Table 1-1 to rate your ability and willingness to perform the following functions (rank from 1–5, where 1 = low and 5 = high). Then add each line for your total.

Table 1-1   **Rating Yourself on Key Web Marketing Tasks**

Task Description	Ability	Interest	Total
Website design	1 ②3 4 5	1 2③4 5	5
Programming	①2 3 4 5	①2 3 4 5	2
Web server administration	1 2 3 4 5	1 2 3 4 5	0
Content writing	1 2 3 4 5	1 2 3 4 5	4
Customer service	1 2 3 4 5	1 2 3 4 5	10
Technical support	1 2 3 4 5	1 2 3 4 5	✓
Copywriting	1 2 3 4 5	1 2 3 4 5	
Social networking	1 2 3 4 5	1 2 3 4 5	✓
Publicity	1 2 3 4 5	1 2 3 4 5	
Accounting	1 2 3 4 5	1 2 3 4 5	✓
Sales	1 2 3 4 5	1 2 3 4 5	✓
Training	1 2 3 4 5	1 2 3 4 5	✓
Research	1 2 3 4 5	1 2 3 4 5	✓
TOTAL			

For any task where your total is less than 6, it would likely be in your best interest of time to pay someone to perform that role for you. Anything for which you score an 8 or higher, you might find total enjoyment from performing that task on your own. The middle ground offers opportunity for learning and growth.

Nearly everyone who's truly successful on the Internet has a team of people who bring special skills to the table. The web changes so quickly that any one person keeping up with everything is impossible, especially after you have a successful selling product or service on your hands. Start now to be open to the idea of building your own team of helpers or paying an existing team to handle the tasks you do not want to deal with. Turn to Chapter 7 in this minibook for help building your team.

(handwritten at top: (Kevin) Web Developer → Marketing Advertisement)

Chapter 2: Making Money Online

In This Chapter

✔ **Identifying the components of accepting a sale online**

✔ **Turning one sale into two or more**

✔ **Building traffic for free and for a fee**

✔ **Recruiting and training a virtual sales force**

(handwritten: Teach for a fee)

Making money on the Internet is like panning for gold: Your fortune can be made instantly, or you can spend a lifetime chasing the dream. Had a gold panner in the late 1800s known what we know about the Internet today, he would've realized that directly panning for gold to feed his family wasn't his only income opportunity. For example, he could have also rented his spot on the creek, or sold drinking water to other panners [or taught beginners his secrets of gold panning for a small fee] And after he had a proven claim, he could've recruited others to pan for him or paid others to sell usage of his claim.

When you think of making money from the Internet, what's the first thing that comes to mind? Selling your own product through your website is probably at the top of the list. Or, maybe you offer a service and want people to pay online so that you can help them. Both of those, of course, are relevant ways to make a sale on the Internet — but several others exist.

This chapter exposes you to a variety of ways to make money online, including the tools and tactics to help you mine online for traffic and revenue.

Discovering the Ways to Make Money on the Internet

The many ways to make money by using the Internet fall into three main categories:

✦ Promoting affiliate products or services

✦ Monetizing traffic

✦ Selling your own product

The following sections take a look at each more closely.

Promoting affiliate products

An *affiliate product* is an item that someone else produces, delivers, and supports. All you have to do is recommend that others visit that company's website. When someone makes a purchase through that website as a result of your recommendation, you get paid a sales commission. Affiliate programs don't usually require you to create a website to promote them. They are also commonly free to join.

A domain name at www.bestdomainplace.com is an example of an affiliate product (see Figure 2-1). Whenever someone buys a domain name or any of the other Internet services offered, you get a small commission on the sale. The product is then delivered and supported by the main company. All you have to do is supply some customizations and the traffic.

This is how an affiliate program works:

1. **Find an affiliate product.**

Your first step is to find a product that you're interested in recommending. Your interest can stem from a topic that your customers have shown interest in that you don't offer, or maybe a trend you recognize in your industry. For example, if you see too many business owners with domain names registered by their web designers — meaning that the business owner didn't truly own his own domain name — you can refer them to a domain name registrar that you're affiliated with.

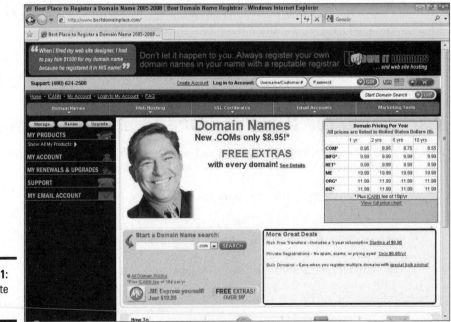

Figure 2-1:
An affiliate product.

Your first affiliate products of interest will likely come from items you've already used and are impressed with, such as a good e-book, a software program, or maybe a CD set. And, affiliate programs can be quite lucrative — offering more than $1,000 per sale — so you don't have to settle only for small-dollar-value products.

Here are two main ways to find affiliate programs to consider:

- *Search on a search engine.* To find an affiliate product on a search engine, search for an industry-specific topic or an exact product, followed by the words [affiliate program].

- *Use an affiliate aggregator,* such as ClickBank (www.clickbank.com) or Commission Junction (www.cj.com), where all the money and affiliate payments are handled. Simply create a new account for yourself and search available products to promote.

2. **Access your unique affiliate link.**

   Visit the company's website and add an affiliate account there. You will be directed to an administration area, where you can find a link to use in your promotions, as shown in Figure 2-2.

   When people click your affiliate link and make a purchase, you get credit for sales that originate with your recommendation.

3. **Promote your affiliate link or banner.**

   After you have the link to promote, copy and paste it for use in your e-mails and on your website.

Take the extra step to always register a domain name to forward to your unique affiliate link. That way, you don't have to remember a long string of numbers and letters every time you want to promote your link to someone. Plus, promoting an affiliate product verbally is a lot easier if you have people visit a domain name that's tied to the affiliate link. That way, you still get credit for the sale.

Visit the administration area frequently because that's where you find important statistics related to your affiliate product, such as the number of visitors to your affiliate link, the number of sales per month, the conversion rates, and most importantly, the dollar figure you can expect to receive in your bank account for those referred sales.

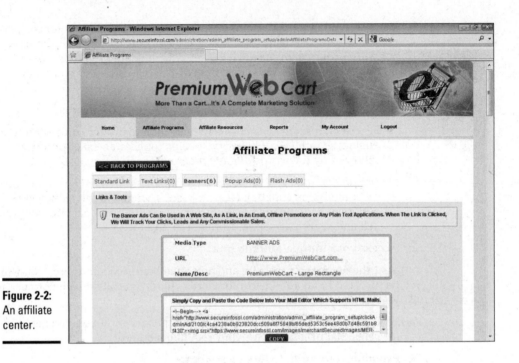

Figure 2-2:
An affiliate
center.

Monetizing traffic

If you can attract website visitors, you can turn that traffic into money —
monetize — without promoting affiliate products or attempting to sell your
own. Here are a few examples of monetizing traffic:

+ **Google AdSense ads:** AdSense is still one of the most popular methods of
  advertising on the Internet today. Within a few minutes, Google supplies a
  bit of code that you add to your site, and you begin making money immediately when someone clicks the provided links. Google makes it especially
  easy for you by instantaneously figuring out what ads to display on your
  page that have the most potential of being clicked. Get started by adding a
  Google AdSense account at `www.google.com/adsense`.

  AdSense ads don't typically produce large revenue for small websites with
  low visitation. So, to make any real money with AdSense, be prepared to
  build a site with lots of pages like the example at `www.leadership`
  `articles.net`, where literally hundreds of pages have been optimized
  for high search engine–results positioning. Notice the Google ads at the top.

  The whole intention with AdSense ads is to drive your traffic to other
  people's websites. So, it's usually not a good idea to display AdSense
  ads on pages where you're attempting to sell your own product!

✦ **Traditional banner advertising:** When you work directly with an advertising client to display her ads on your website, you're using traditional banner advertising. Traditional banner ads on your site include

- *Cost per click (CPC):* When you use this method, it's up to you to track how many times visitors to your website click an ad's link. Google Analytics is free statistics-tracking software that allows you to track what are called *banner ad exits,* appropriately named because visitors will be exiting your website through the banner ad. To get an in-depth explanation of how to use Google Analytics to track banner ad usage, go to

```
http://support.google.com/googleanalytics/bin/
          answer.py?hl=en&answer=55526
```

Then, you report that number of clicks to your advertising client and charge her accordingly. You decide the amount you charge per click. You can have this type of advertising prepaid; for example, 3 cents per click for an inventory of 10,000 clicks, for a total of $300.

If your advertising client wants to produce her own ad (which is usually the case), you'd better hope that she creates an ad that attracts clicks, or her ad will just be taking up space on your website. Be a coach to your advertising client by offering ideas for how to best promote to your website traffic.

Wondering about the difference between cost per click (CPC) and pay per click (PPC)? Technically, when the money comes from the bank account, there is no difference between PPC and CPC. Your perspective in the transaction may influence how you see things, however. Certainly the easier of the two to understand is "pay" per click, meaning as the business owner, you will "pay" every time someone clicks your ad. On the other hand, "cost" per click is accurate too because, to the one who actually "pays" for the clicks, a higher or lower "cost" per click can be experienced based on how you create your ad, the landing page, and so on.

- *Cost per 1,000 page views (CPM):* With this method, you don't rely on the quality of ads for you to get paid. An advertiser simply pays you in advance to showcase his ad on a page of your website for a certain number of times that the web page is accessed by visitors. Typically, CPM rates range between $4 and $10 per 1,000 page views, but prices can easily be higher for niche audiences.

If you intend to sell traditional advertising on your website, be prepared to show advertisers detailed reports of page view visitation and click-through rates. A *click-through* occurs when a visitor to your website clicks the ad you're promoting and is brought to another web location. Your advertiser will expect to see proof that he got what he paid for, or he could ask for his money back. See Book III, Chapter 2 for information about how to track traffic volume.

The Interactive Advertising Bureau (IAB) website at www.iab.net/ iab_products_and_industry_services/1421/1443/1452 provides a display of the most common banner ad sizes. With IAB media company members being responsible for almost 90 percent of all online advertising in the United States, this resource is certainly the industry standard for banner ad best practices.

- *Pay per call and pay per lead:* These methods of advertising have been gaining popularity over the past couple of years and are usually managed by third-party companies, such as Ingenio Pay Per Call (http://paypercall.ingenio.com), and might include using banner or text ads to get your visitors to take action with their promotions. The great appeal with a company such as Ingenio is that you don't pay a dime until you get a phone call from a lead.

- *Call per action (CPA):* With this method, the advertiser has to pay only when a sale is made. This is the ultimate form of paid advertising because the pressure is really on the promotional agency to close the deal so that its efforts get rewarded. Actually, CPA advertising is a lot like having your own affiliate program because the third party is paid only when you get a sale.

Selling your own products and services

Creating and selling your own products and services online can be a very profitable venture. After all, you get to keep all the money after paying your costs.

With affiliate programs, proven content is normally already provided for you, so ramp-up time is fast and your investment is low. With monetizing traffic, the ads on your pages are commonly already tested and proven to work.

Selling your own products and services can prove to be the most challenging because you have so much work to do before you can begin selling. However, there is no substitute for creating your own product if you want creative control and long-term growth potential.

You don't even need your own product; you can offer a service. Consider Marriage Counselors Hub (www.marriagecounselorshub.com), as shown in Figure 2-3. It's a directory that builds and features profiles that give professionals web exposure.

Figure 2-3:
A website
that offers
a service
rather than
a product.

Here are some guidelines to follow when offering your own products and services for sale online:

✦ **Information products are still king.** An information product — which can be as simple as a how-to book or an e-book — is still the easiest and least expensive product to produce and deliver. Virtually anyone with a computer can use a word processing program to write a how-to book and then convert it to a PDF (Portable Document Format) file. You can use a free, online PDF converter at www.pdfonline.com/convert_pdf.asp.

✦ **Audio is queen.** If typing isn't your forte or style, buy recording equipment and talk into a microphone to create 30- to 40-minute MP3 audio files to sell. For as little as $75, you can buy a digital recording device with a lapel microphone for hands-free recording. Or, make a complete CD set showcasing your knowledge. After you get started with audio, you will quickly realize the unlimited opportunity potential available by producing recorded products and promotional content.

Another great use of audio would be to interview an expert the next time you attend a conference. Host a short ten-minute Q&A, add the sound file to your blog, and send a notice to your opt-in list that you added the recording for their review.

✦ **Video is HOT, HOT, HOT.** Every website can enhance the buyer's experience by offering video, especially when you have a product for sale. Software can be demonstrated, shoes can be modeled, e-books can be featured, and services can be displayed. Video sells online, and video products sell, too. Professional video can now be produced in your own home for a one-time purchase of just a few hundred dollars in software and equipment.

✦ **Webinars continue to be the ultimate education tool.** A *webinar* is an online session in which you walk through a presentation or training session on your computer while an audience views your presentation online and hears your voice from their computer. The best part about webinars is that they can be recorded and offered as a product for sale. Microsoft's webinar service at www.gotowebinar.com — owned and operated by Citrix — has video and audio recording built in to its webinar tools.

✦ **Create a whole product line.** For every information product you produce, you can create an entire product line by offering the nearly identical product in e-book form, MP3 audio recording, video, webinars, and in-person seminar training.

The following sections in this chapter focus on the tools needed to accept and promote online sales of your own product. Of course, many of the techniques described here can be applied to promoting affiliate products and monetizing traffic, but the examples shown are more directed toward selling products online.

Assembling an Internet-Based Buying Process That Converts

Sure, you must have a website that's graphically satisfying to visitors to entice them to become interested in — and find — your offer (as discussed in Chapter 3 of this minibook). Of course, you must have promotional copy that inspires a prospect to take action with your offer (see Chapter 5 of this minibook). Perhaps the most important component of all is the actual buying process you provide. Without a smooth buying process, you could lose not just some sales but all your sales potential. The following sections walk you through the elements of online transactions and offer tips to ensure that customers who buy your products have a positive experience on your site.

These sections focus on marketing. If you're building a site yourself or need to work directly with a technical team, you likely need to understand at least some technical aspects of web design, site organization, and security as you move from marketing concepts to actually implementing your buying process. For help, check out *Building Web Sites All-in-One For Dummies* by Doug Sahlin (published by John Wiley & Sons, Inc.).

Defining the components of an online transaction

Every online transaction has three main components: the transaction page, the merchant account, and the payment gateway. The following sections introduce each component and offer tips for getting started.

The transaction page

The *transaction page* is where buyers enter their contact information and credit card number. For the transaction page, you use a formal shopping cart or a custom form:

✦ **Shopping cart:** The most popular way to sell products and services is through an Internet-based ordering system known as a *shopping cart.* You're probably familiar with the system through your own online shopping: Just as you use a cart to shop in a grocery store — picking certain items off the shelf, adding them to your shopping cart, and then proceeding through the checkout lane — a website visitor clicks an Add to Cart button for purchasing items online. The difference is that an online shopping cart system allows you to set up your entire store on the Internet, complete with products, services, categories, sale discounts, and of course, a transaction page where visitors see credit card payment types accepted, fields to enter their billing information, shipping, and tax. See the section "Shopping cart setup secrets," later in this chapter, for tips on working with shopping carts.

✦ **Custom form:** Not all transaction models can fit into the mold of a pre-packaged shopping cart;, some require a custom form instead. A custom form allows you to have any combination of product purchases on the same page. The downside is that custom forms take a lot more work to create and integrate with the payment gateway.

See www.thunderridgeski.com for a good example where a season-pass purchaser might also buy a pass for his wife and two children, along with a locker. The form allows the transactions to take place all on the same customized, secure page, as shown in Figure 2-4.

Whether you choose to use a third-party shopping cart like Premium Web Cart versus a custom order system will largely be based on cost and turn-around time. When you use a commercial shopping cart, you can be selling your product within just a few hours, provided that you already have an Internet-capable merchant account and gateway. Custom secure ordering systems require more planning and programming. You may even experience time delays waiting for secure server–related items to be ordered like an SSL (Secured Socket Layer) certificate, static IP address, or setup of a dedicated server.

Figure 2-4:
A custom
order form.

The merchant account

You must have an arrangement with a company to accept credit card information for your online transactions, using an Internet-capable merchant account. This special kind of merchant account is designed to accept and track credit card transactions over the Internet. This Internet-capable merchant account could be PayPal, or you could get your own through a bank.

To set up your own merchant account, check out Lew Kelly with Expedient Financial Services, Inc. Lew has been selling merchant accounts for more than ten years. His phone number is 303-256-7501. He gives a free consultation by phone if you're out of state, or an in-person visit if you're within metro Denver and the Front Range of Colorado. For more information about merchant accounts, go to `http://herenextyear.com/help-topics/best-merchant-account.php`.

Using only PayPal at the beginning for accepting payments online is a good idea while you get your feet wet with online transactions. As soon as possible, though, get your own merchant account. Some website visitors may simply not buy from you if you accept payments only through PayPal. Some might be fearful of being the victim of PayPal's next hacking, while others will question whether you're really an established business. To be fair, if you don't offer a PayPal payment option, some potential customers may not buy from you, either, because they pay for everything online via PayPal.

The payment gateway

A *payment gateway* is a tool that ties the transaction page with the merchant account. Authorize.Net is an example of a payment gateway and is a great choice for accepting orders through the Internet. Authorize.Net (`www.authorize.net`) is also the only gateway that allows custom forms.

Shopping cart setup secrets

From a revenue standpoint, it is absolutely critical to set up your shopping cart to sell — and sell well. Table 2-1 outlines actions to take as you set up your shopping cart and explains the benefit of each action.

Table 2-1	Shopping Cart Setup Secrets
Shopping Cart Setup Action	*Benefit*
Customize the look of the order page to match the appearance of the rest of your website.	Users aren't distracted by an abrupt change in look and feel.
Assure that all images are uploaded to a secure directory.	An error message won't display when visitors click from your sales page to the order page.
Display the item description, quantity being ordered, and price on the order page.	Buyers are assured that they're paying for only what they want.
Display that either credit cards or PayPal (or both) can be used as the payment source.	You show willingness to accommodate customers' preferences.

(continued)

Table 2-1 *(continued)*

Shopping Cart Setup Action	Benefit
Remove all navigation buttons from the order page.	This prevents tempting the buyer to exit the purchasing process.
Create a custom Thank You page for each individual product sold.	This gives you the possibility for cross-selling.
Create an autoresponder for each product, which is an e-mail or sequence of e-mails automatically sent to a customer upon purchase.	You can add a customer to a specific list to market later with back-end sales offers.

Premium Web Cart (www.premiumwebcart.com) is a good choice for a shopping cart. It's one of the few shopping cart systems offering free technical support by telephone. Features of Premium Web Cart include

+ **Ease of use:** You can easily add to and maintain product items in the shopping cart without having to pay a designer or programmer.

+ **Feature-rich:** No other package at this price level offers the cart, affiliate program, e-mail broadcasting, membership, customer relation management program, project tracking, and inventory. Start small and grow!

+ **Premade graphics:** The system creates attractive Add to Cart buttons for you: Just copy and paste the code to your website.

+ **Customizability:** The capability to make your order pages look just like the rest of your website.

+ **Payment options:** These enable you to offer payments through PayPal, your merchant account, or both.

+ **Coupons:** Using coupons enables you to run specific promotions and to track their effect on sales.

+ **Custom Thank You pages:** This is one of the rarest features of low-end shopping carts and one of the most important for increasing sale value per customer. When folks make a purchase through your shopping cart, they already have their credit card on the table. This is the best time to get them to buy more. Only through the use of a custom Thank You page can you make that special offer while their credit card is still out of their pocket and you have their undivided attention.

+ **Built-in affiliate program:** You don't need to find a third-party, affiliate-tracking system to manage your shopping cart. It's all integrated already. (The section "Promoting affiliate products," earlier in this chapter, introduces third-party affiliates.)

+ **Digital download capable:** If you have an e-book or MP3 audio files, you can set them up in the system to be downloaded upon purchase instead of hosting the files on your own server.

✦ **Built-in autoresponders and mailing system:** An *autoresponder* is an automated system that sends a message (that you create) to someone that requests information from you. You'll find a direct correlation between folks receiving automated or routine e-mails from you and their willingness to purchase your products or services.

Any sales trainer will tell you that you need to be in communication with a prospect at least seven times before he is willing to buy from you. On the web, this number is typically even higher because everyone is skeptical online. So, you must prove over time that you are worthy of doing business with. Setting up automated responses gives you the opportunity to gain trust from your prospects so that they will buy from you. A great way to attract your audience to join your autoresponder list is to offer opt-in forms on your website to download free reports. When someone buys your product, he can automatically be moved to a customer list and be removed from the prospect list.

✦ **Payment Card Industry Data Security Standard (PCI DSS) Compliance:** Premium Web Cart satisfies all testing requirements for keeping your transactions secure from hackers. It invests thousands of dollars each year to maintain compliance so you do not have that added expense to pay yourself.

✦ **Free telephone technical support:** This is the most important feature, as well as the hardest to find these days. If you choose to sell products online, it's only a matter of time before you need some help. Never subscribe to a shopping cart system that doesn't offer support when you need it.

Premium Web Cart is a great solution for all levels of marketers and companies. With the increase of penalties for PCI Compliance violations, you should always use a third-party company to host the online transaction process. Simply buying your own SSL certificate for your shared hosting account at GoDaddy is not enough anymore!

Answering important questions

Before someone takes the final step and uses a credit card to make a purchase through your ordering system, a series of questions go through his mind within a matter of minutes. Many of these questions can and should be addressed in your sales letter or on your product sales page (as described in Chapter 5 of this minibook). But, these questions must also be addressed during the checkout process, or it could kill the sale.

People want to buy from you. After all, your offer is the solution to their problem. All you have to do is not stand in their way. Too often, webmasters put too much effort into graphics instead of paying attention to writing copy that sells, or to the shopping cart itself, which provides a smooth order process. By human nature, your audience consciously or unconsciously looks for reasons to not buy from you. Your job is to minimize those obstacles by providing the information they need to make an informed decision to buy while at the same time providing an easy buying procedure.

Here are just some of the questions your website visitors will be asking themselves before placing an order:

✦ **How do I get what I ordered?** Clearly describe your delivery method. Will you offer an immediate digital download link, or will purchasers be required to drive somewhere for pickup?

✦ **How long will it take to get what I ordered?** Mention whether you have the items in stock or whether a fulfillment house needs to burn a series of CDs that will be sent in the next three weeks, for example.

✦ **Is this site secure?** Make a statement to your prospects that invites them to look for an image of a closed padlock in their browser while on your order page.

✦ **Is this company legitimate, or did it make an outlandish offer it can't really fulfill?** Use testimonials to prove that you can do what you say you can do.

✦ **Did I make the right decision?** Assure buyers that their purchasing choice was a good one by offering a follow-up e-mail.

✦ **What will be done with my contact information after the order?** Assure your customers that their contact and billing information is held strictly confidential.

✦ **Who do I contact if I have a problem with my order?** Provide a phone number or an e-mail address where people can get in touch with you if they have any questions. Respond promptly to these communications.

✦ **Where do I go to get a refund?** Mention this in your guarantee. (See Chapter 4 of this minibook.)

✦ **Did I get everything I was supposed to?** Provide a checklist of all items that are to be received so that your customer can cross-check what arrived.

✦ **Should I expect more communication from the seller?** If your product offer includes more communication from you — such as weekly coaching, a bonus e-course, or ongoing support, for example — be sure to state what to expect in the offer.

✦ **When will my credit card be charged?** It has become more common to have a statement in the header of the shopping cart that requires people to agree to payment terms such as "I understand and authorize that upon purchase, my credit card will be charged $975 payable to HereNextYear, Inc."

✦ **Am I ordering the right product?** Reassure the buyer that this product is right for him. A popular way to do this is in the postscript statements at the bottom of the page. For example

> *P.S. Remember, if your company has experienced more than a 2% turnover in the past six months, this team-building program is tailor-made for you!*

✦ **Am I getting the best price possible for this purchase?** Another element of effective copywriting (as discussed in Chapter 5 of this minibook) is to tell your readers that you have scoured the web and have found that no one has what you're selling, for the price you're offering.

✦ **Have I completed the sales process yet, or do I have something more to do?** If three steps are involved in the buying process, mention that to your customer. When the final step is complete, display on-screen that the visitor has completed the process.

✦ **Is it really worth the price?** Reassure the buyer that your product is worth not only the price you're charging but also a whole lot more as well. Back up that statement with real reasons to increase the value of the purchase. Assemble your product offers so that the buyer gets at least 15 times the price in value.

Doubling or Tripling Your New Customer Revenue

Doubling or tripling the initial sale amount for new customer purchases begins with having more products to offer. These can be your own products or affiliate items. Make a list of all the products you could possibly promote, and you're on your way to maximizing every new customer sale.

The next step is to think about your range of products and their cost. Every business should have products for sale with multiple price levels, known as *price points*. A consultant, for example, could feature products ranging from free to several thousand dollars, as shown in Table 2-2.

Table 2-2	A Consultant's Possible Price Points
Product Type	*Price Point*
Industry report	Free
E-book	$27
2-hour seminar	$50
3-CD set with training manual	$97
Silver-level coaching program	$149 per month
1-day boot camp workshop	$250
5-week live webinar training course	$497
Gold-level coaching program	$300 per month
Platinum-level coaching program	$997 per month
One-on-one consulting on-site	$4,500 per day

With your product range and price points in place, you can upsell, cross-sell, and back-end sell your products to existing customers. Although it's no secret that the easiest people to sell to are your existing customers, a point often overlooked is that people always want more. They will pay for an initial problem to be fixed and then pay more for related issues to be addressed. Your task is to simply inform them that "more" is available and give them an incentive to take advantage of it. That's where upselling, cross-selling, and back-end selling come into play, as you discover in the following sections.

Upselling

Upselling is nothing more than convincing someone to buy a more expensive version of what he already decided to buy. You've likely been asked, "Would you like cheese on that? Fries with that?" Or, if you've ever ordered a gin and tonic, you were probably asked whether you preferred a name-brand gin versus the house stuff. Sure, the bartender was trying to be a good host, but he was also trying to make a better sale. Using the earlier example of selling an e-book, an upsell opportunity is when someone buying the e-book for $27 gets to the order page and is made a special offer to purchase a 3-CD set with training manual instead, for $97.

Cross-selling

Cross-selling is most easily defined as promoting accessories during the purchase process. Say that someone buys an e-book for $27. Then, the Thank You page features a special offer that the purchaser can add the 2-hour seminar CD set to her purchase. That's cross-selling.

Cross-selling can occur before or after the initial sale is made — and sometimes in both instances! You really have to know your audience, though, when trying to cross-sell. If you offer too many accessories before the point of purchase, the buyer may get distracted, confused, or just plain annoyed by feeling pushed to buy more. Overzealousness can kill a sale.

Always go after the initial sale, and then offer additional options immediately after that first purchase is complete. The promotion is made on a custom Thank You page. If you've ever bought something on the Internet, you eventually get to a page that reads `Thank you for your order. Please print this page for your records`. This is the page that you want to customize to maximize your potential for increasing your initial purchases from one dollar value to the next.

Figure 2-5 shows a Thank You page, where the reader is given an incentive to buy two training manuals at one, low cost. By the time the customer gets to this Thank You page, he has already spent $27. By inspiring him to take immediate action and spend another $70, the total transaction becomes $97.

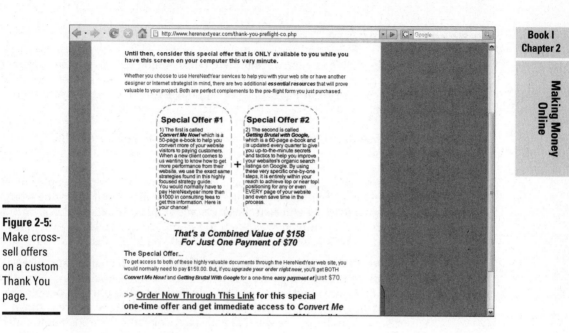

Figure 2-5:
Make cross-
sell offers
on a custom
Thank You
page.

Back-end selling

When people become associated with your business, whether as customers or even just as newsletter subscribers, you have the opportunity to offer solutions to them. *Back-end selling* is promoting products on the "back end" of an action they took with you. You can find so many giveaways of information and tangible items on the Internet today that could otherwise be sold for money because of this simple reason: More value is often found in the back-end sale.

Here are some simple examples of back-end selling:

✦ An e-mail newsletter promoting a new product release offered only to current customers

✦ A follow-up phone call or in-person meeting with a customer two weeks after the product has been received

✦ A personalized letter sent by postal mail addressed specifically to the person who purchased your product

If you have enough affiliate products in your arsenal, you can pick the perfect moment to suggest a recommendation for purchasing.

Generating Traffic

Generating traffic to your website requires spending your own time to attract visitors, paying for visitors directly, or hiring helpers to do the work required to get the visitors. Getting a top spot on Google isn't free — even your time has value.

Having said that, here are seven core categories to generate traffic to your website:

✦ **Free search:** With all the hype suggesting how much time people spend tweeting on Twitter or posting on Facebook, just about everyone who uses the Internet still searches for something on Google, Yahoo!, or Bing every day. Creating new content for your website weekly or even daily needs to be a primary focus of your traffic-building plan.

Although time and effort have a cost, many search engines and directories don't require you to pay a fee to get listed. Google, Bing, Yahoo!, and dmoz are good examples. Simply find out what phrases people are searching for, and then add content to your website to address those issues. Search engines will find your pages of content through automated processes developed by the search engine companies.

By getting new pages of your website visible on the preceding search engines alone, you have the potential of being in front of more than 80 percent of all search engine traffic. Optimizing your site content can help you appear higher in search engine results, as Book II explains.

✦ **Using other people's traffic:** After you've had some experience creating content for your own website and getting some search engine positioning for those pages or blog posts, you're ready to make use of one of the hottest ways to build targeted traffic to your website: Write a guest blog for a business that complements yours, but doesn't compete with it (see Figure 2-6). See Book VI for the ins and outs of blogging.

Always include a link to your own website as part of the blog post and follow up with comments.

One of the hot traffic generators of today is to take guest blog posting to a higher level by conducting a blog tour. Line up 10, 15, or 50 blog dates so that readers can sequentially follow you from blog to blog. The blog owners all benefit from the shared traffic from other blogs and your own promotions.

✦ **Paid search:** With the growth in development of measurement tools (such as Google Analytics, for example), paid search has become an essential form of promotion for nearly every product or service. A few of these methods are discussed earlier in this chapter in the "Monetizing traffic" section — CPC, CPM, PPC (call, not click), PPL, and CPA. Each applies to how you can pay to receive targeted traffic as well.

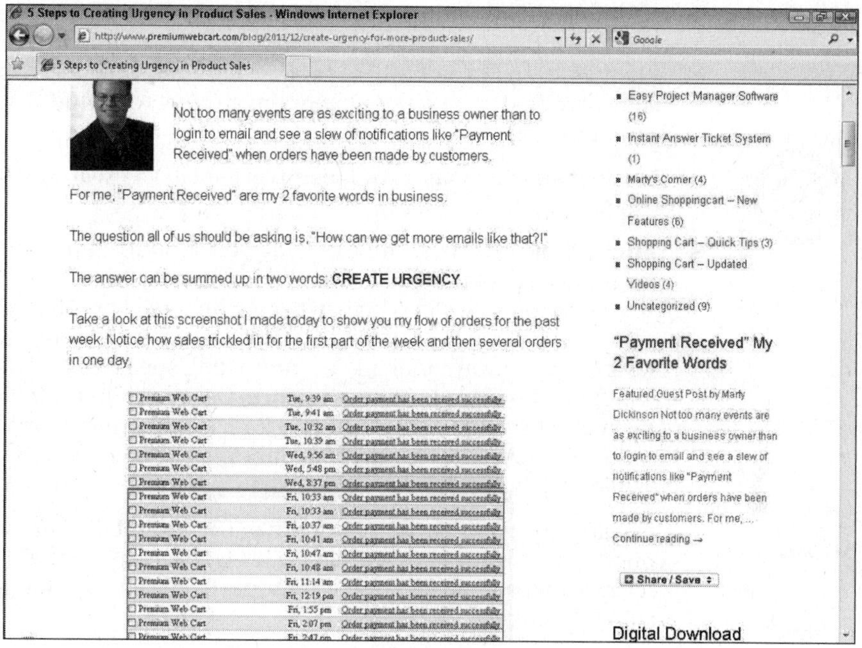

Figure 2-6:
Generate
traffic
to your
business
by writing
guest blog
posts.

✦ **Social networking:** Participating in discussions on Twitter, Facebook, Google+, and LinkedIn are proven website traffic-generating processes. Remember to always link to your website. Figure 2-7 shows this process in action on Facebook. Internet users will always search for and exchange content. You just have to find out what they're searching for and supply them with unique content. More on this topic can be found in Chapter 5 of this minibook.

Twitter, Facebook, Google+, and LinkedIn

Figure 2-7:
Driving
traffic from
a Facebook
post to a
website.

✦ **Face-to-face networking:** Some people still enjoy meeting face to face for their networking. Meetup (www.meetup.com) helps with the organizing, scheduling, and promoting of such groups. So, you can easily find many niche or industry-targeted networking groups to attend that meet regularly in person.

Consider starting your own Meetup group! It's a great way to network with potential customers.

✦ **Other offline efforts:** Don't overlook your opportunities to use offline resources to promote your website. Radio talk shows are always looking for guest experts. Offer a giveaway to listeners every time you're on the radio. Networking events, associations, leads groups, and schools and churches are always looking for interesting speakers to deliver short, 30-minute messages to their audience. Deliver content-rich information and suggest a visit to your website for a free download or for more information about your company. And, always provide the opportunity for people to be added to your e-mail list.

Joe Sabah has appeared on more than 650 radio talk shows around the country, most by never even leaving his home. He produces a handy contact list and program at www.sabahradioshows.com for getting on radio talk shows.

✦ **Referrals:** Of course, no one is a higher-quality visitor than a personal referral. Referrals will spend more time on your website and are much more likely to buy from you because they have reached a certain level of trust in you because of the referral.

Whether referrals come from offline or online, always strive to increase visitors who are referred by someone else. One of the great ways to do just that is to start your own affiliate program, which is discussed in the next section.

Creating Your Own Affiliate Program

Not long after you gather some experience as an affiliate promoting other people's products you start to imagine how you would benefit from having others promote your products and services. Plus, you will discover things they're doing right as well as what needs improvement when it comes to helping you sell their products. Use these experiences and incentives to create your own affiliate program so that others can sell your products and services for you. Even a moderately successful affiliate program can quickly propel your business to a new level that would've been impossible (or at least extremely difficult) to attain on your own.

Setting up affiliate tracking

All web-based affiliate programs require three essential components:

✦ **An affiliate center:** This is where affiliates can add an account for them-selves, check their sales, and get links, ads, and scripts to promote.

✦ **A reliable, integrated connection to the product being sold:** Don't allow an affiliate to promote your products with links that don't work! Best case, you'll be embarrassed. Worst case, your affiliate will likely never promote your products again.

✦ **A payment-tracking system:** To stay on an affiliate's good side, you need a mechanized way to determine when and how much you need to pay each affiliate.

Fortunately, Premium Web Cart offers all these features rolled into one, which is why it's a good choice to use as an affiliate program. See the section "Shopping cart setup secrets," earlier in this chapter, for details on Premium Web Cart.

Register for your own affiliate program so that you can identify areas of the sign-up process that need improvement.

Attracting affiliates

After your affiliate center is complete, announce to your clients that you're looking for people to recommend your products and services to others and that you pay referral fees. The easiest people to recruit for promoting your products to others are those who have used your products and services. Your customers often become your best salespeople.

Send a letter to your client lists announcing any products that are part of your affiliate program for them to market.

Training affiliates

Having a small network of affiliates will bring in some additional sales, but the general rule is that you will need 20 affiliates for everyone who produces any measurable sales. That means to have 50 producers, you would need to have more than 1,000 registered affiliates. This ratio can be greatly reduced through continuous opportunities for training. Here are some ways you can train your affiliates:

✦ **Conduct a weekly conference call.** Keep this call short, say, no more than 40 minutes. And always have someone on the call who is being interviewed — maybe an industry expert or a sales trainer. Conference calls where one person talks the whole time are boring and are usually long-winded and disorganized. Create an agenda for what will be covered on the call and follow it. Always start on time and end on time.

Try Free Audio Conferencing (www.freeaudioconferencing.com) for your conference calls. It allows you to have as many as 85 people on a call.

✦ **Record the conference calls.** Most conferencing systems provide a means for recording your calls at the press of a button. Send an e-mail to your affiliate list with a link to the recorded call immediately after the call is complete so that any affiliate can listen to it again and share it with others. And, if some folks missed the call, you can give a little promotion in the e-mail about what was covered and why they should listen.

✦ **Provide one-on-one assistance.** Until your affiliate group gets too large to manage by phone, provide some individual coaching to each new affiliate beginning right after a member signs up.

✦ **Provide the tools to use in their promotions.** Most of your affiliates won't want to write their own sales copy and pay a designer to create banner ads for your products. So be willing to provide the sales copy, images, promotions, audio, and even potentially video for your affiliates to use in their efforts to promote your products.

Joint Venturing for Exponential Sales Growth

Joint ventures are different from affiliates: They're more involved, yet often far more lucrative. You must follow certain rules, though, and a protocol.

For example, if you are a motivational speaker, you can set up your own workshop and have your affiliates sell your workshop. That's an affiliate. Or, you can partner with another expert to set up the workshop and sell it to his customers. He provides the customers; you provide the expertise. That's a joint venture.

The following sections explain how to pursue a joint-venture relationship to potentially double or triple your business in size, stature, and sales volume within a matter of a few months.

Getting your facts straight

Compared with affiliates, which are quick to promote products to their lists and to people they know, joint-venture hosts are very selective. Notice that emphasis on *host* instead of *partner*. That's because a joint-venture host is more like the master of ceremonies at a seminar than a true business partner. Joint-venture hosts don't care about looking at your accounting books or having an influence on who you hire as employees. They just want to sell your product in mass quantities and get a big check in the mail from you! It's the host's job to give you a raving recommendation to his multitudes of followers, and your task is to provide the goods to the host's followers. Before you approach a potential host for a joint venture, you must have all your ducks in a row, including

✦ **Sales:** Documented proof of your success selling your own products and services.

✦ **Visitation and conversion rates:** Documentation of how many people visit your website per month and also how many of those visitors convert to customers resulting from your website, sales copy, and shopping cart. If your host drives 50,000 visitors to your sales page tomorrow, what kind of sales could be expected? In Book III, you can read all about using web analytics tools to capture these numbers.

✦ **Affiliate performance:** How many affiliates you have. And, how many sales your affiliates have produced for you so far as well as your affiliates' conversion rates.

Affiliates will typically get better conversion rates than even you (as the website owner) because the visitors are coming as a result of a personal referral. Conversion rates from a joint-venture host can be even higher because the receiving audience knows that the host's high-profile recommendation is at stake. If they're recommending it, it *must* be good!

✦ **Fulfillment:** How many orders you could fill in a week's time. For example, imagine if Mark Victor Hansen (of *Chicken Soup for the Soul* fame) were to send a recommendation out to his entire list (more than 1 million people!) and had 50,000 orders to fill in 24 hours. How many mailers could you stuff in a week's time? Know your delivery capabilities before you even start talking to a joint-venture host.

Finding a joint-venture host

One of the problems with joint venturing is that it's not new anymore. Internet-based joint ventures started as far back as 1995. Today, anyone with a substantial list and a visible profile probably has 50 to 100 people per month or more clamoring after him to do a joint venture. Even if you can get in the door to talk to the golden goose of your industry, you'll probably be met with a response like, "Who the heck are you, and why should I be listening to you?"

Start with smaller joint ventures. Follow these simple guidelines to locate joint-venture partners, and you will have plenty of opportunities to go after the big guys after you build a track record:

✦ **Attend networking events, seminars, and association meetings.** You need to meet people and let them know you're looking for joint-venture hosts to help take your product to new levels. Create a 20-second *elevator pitch* that announces what your product is, the conversion rates you're getting from your website, and how much a potential joint-venture host might make with a list of 10,000 or more subscribers that you both would be promoting, too. Numbers talk, and joint-venture hosts listen to numbers.

✦ **Participate in online forums.** You probably won't find T. Harv Ecker or Anthony Robbins participating in online forums much, but you'd be surprised how many multimillionaires do spend an hour or more daily offering advice online (anonymously, of course). Add a signature line (as shown in Figure 2-8) in your forum bio stating that you're seeking joint-venture hosts, add a link to your website, and start participating in forum discussions.

✦ **Ask your affiliates and clients for referrals.** Your affiliates and clients likely know someone who could be a possible joint-venture host for you. Ask them what vendors they use who might be able to roll out your product or service as a value-added offer to their customers.

Finding joint-venture hosts isn't really difficult. You'll discover that just by using the three preceding resources alone. The trick is to convince the right hosts to do business with you and make things happen. You need to have a plan and present it well.

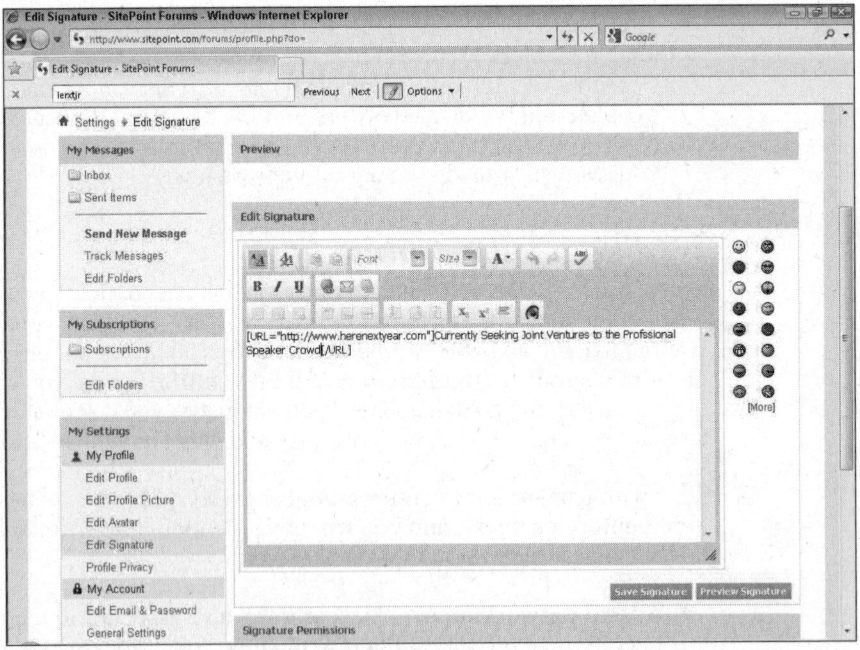

Figure 2-8:
Add a
signature
line in
a forum
posting.

Presenting your plan

Depending on the size of the host's company, you might be expected to conduct a formal presentation to a group of staff with your plan. If you start small, however, many joint ventures can be assembled over a cup of coffee at your local coffeehouse or sometimes even via a phone call. Use your instincts to read how formal the meeting should be. But be assured that the more professional, organized, and successful you appear, the more seriously your project will be considered. The following sections help you put together your materials and make your pitch to a potential host.

Gather your presentation materials

The first step is putting together a nice iPad or PowerPoint presentation (or binder with printed pages) with materials that your host will likely want to see. Be sure to include the following:

✦ Printout of the sales volume you're experiencing

✦ One-page report of your affiliates and how much they make by selling your product

✦ Visitation statistics report showing how many people visit your website on a monthly basis and where those visitors are coming from

✦ Full copy of your sales letter or product sales page

✦ List of testimonials from happy customers

✦ Report of returns and refund requests

✦ Photos of you with high-profile experts in the industry (if you have them)

✦ Sample joint venture host agreement, which typically includes

• *The terms of the revenue sharing:* What percentage of the sale are you willing to offer your host, and how long after the promotion occurs are you willing to pay commissions for sales generated? For example, if you get a phone call from someone a year from now who saw a promotion run by your host offering a special price, will you accept the sale? Will you pay your host the due commission for that sale?

You have to promise a high-enough percentage to attract the attention of a good host in the first place: 50, 60, and sometimes even 100 percent of the revenue is given to the host for his support of your product.

• *The expectations for each involved:* Because you know your products, offer to write sales copy. Add a sentence in the agreement that the host will "use my promotions as written or slightly modified to meet her natural speaking tone," for example.

- *Any limitations:* Most likely, you will sell the same product outside your hosting agreement using your own promotion efforts, affiliates, or other joint ventures. Your agreement needs to claim your right to ownership of your product and the right to continue to sell it in any way you choose. And it should state that your host will not be receiving commissions for sales generated from alternate promotions.

- *Commission payments and returns:* What date of the month will you be reconciling orders and making a payment to your host? And, how will you account for returns? Make your payment at the end of each month following the date a sale is made. This gives you enough time to process any returns and deduct those orders from the amount of commission due your host. This procedure should be included in your agreement.

- *Disputes:* Decide how a formal dispute will be handled.

- *Intellectual property rights:* Remember that this is your product you're offering to your host's followers. Be sure to include in your agreement that you still own all rights to your products.

- *Confidentiality:* During the course of a joint-venture project, you will likely be exposed to insider information as to how your host conducts business, such as access to the host's online shopping cart to set up your product promotion on his website. Now that's trust. You will wind up revealing some secrets of your own as well. It will be comforting to your host that you hold his practices in high regard and will not share any of his personal or business information with others.

Explain your value

Joint-venture hosts have a substantial public following. They got to where they are because they (more often than not) genuinely care about people. When you arrive at your meeting with your potential joint-venture host, be ready to promote a joint-venture opportunity with the host's audience in mind:

- ✦ How will his followers benefit from your product?

- ✦ What can they expect as a result of using what you produce?

- ✦ Why are you the best person to make this offer to his list?

A host is always pressed for time, so you need to present how easy your joint-venture process will be. Be prepared to do all the work and even bend over backward for your host. You must present that your host will

- ✦ **Make a ton of money without spending a boatload of time.**

- ✦ **Be at the top of your priority list.**

- ✦ **Get special treatment.** You might even decide to make a completely separate website just for your host to promote your product.

✦ **Benefit from your sales ability.** You will surely need to prepare customized sales copy for e-mails to be sent to your host's list, for example.

✦ **Be involved in the process.**

✦ **Have a new team player at his side.** You might well be invited as a guest speaker for a teleconference or even brought up on stage for a few minutes at an event in front of hundreds of people!

When it comes to joint ventures, think bigger than your normal day-to-day online sales strategies that trickle in from your search engine optimization (SEO) efforts and Google AdWords campaigns. Sure, those are all important. But they are most important to generate numbers that you will eventually use to present your offer to future joint-venture hosts. A huge growth opportunity awaits your company. Following the Internet marketing process from A to Z is what will get you there.

One last point: Dress well. Joint-venture hosts might wear jeans and a T-shirt to a meeting, but they appreciate it when you honor their stature by dressing professionally.

Chapter 3: Designing to Sell

In This Chapter

✓ Understanding the purpose of website design

✓ Preventing distraction from the sales process

✓ Using branding basics

✓ Keeping it legal

✓ Testing for usability

Do not be fooled by people you hear downplaying the importance of having a website for your business. Not only is it imperative to have a website, but the quality of its design is also more crucial than ever before. Even Google evaluates your website for quality design and even factors your branding into its algorithm. If Google thinks your design is important, you should too!

This chapter is devoted to using several design techniques to guide your website visitors through your online sales process without distracting them. You discover how to think about the effect of elements that appear on your site: branding, colors, fonts, and graphics. After making these key decisions, you're ready to consider how to pull these elements together on your site layout — and in particular, ways that make the best use of important areas on a web page. You also find tips along the way to help you design a site that's easy to use. The last section in this chapter explains easy ways to test your site's usability.

Branding Your Look

If you read any book on marketing or branding, you will see common examples of the ultimate goal of branding, such as Xerox "owns" the word *copiers*. McDonald's "owns" *hamburgers,* and Levi Strauss "owns" the word *jeans.* What word or phrase does your product or service own or aspire to own?

Branding is a simple concept to understand yet sometimes a painstaking process to implement. Big companies pay marketing firms thousands of dollars to have expert teams produce branding strategies over weeks and months of brainstorming. So, if you've been struggling with your branding for a while, you're not alone.

If you're new to this term, you will find many definitions for the word *branding.* Branding is simply getting prospects and repeat customers to see and remember your product as the only solution to their specific problem or need. Other alternative items might be similar, but nothing on the market is exactly like what you offer. Of course, branding is accomplished by all the things you hear about in formal definitions like creating a logo, establishing a corporate identity, packaging your product, advertising, bonding with your customers, and establishing loyalty.

Every word you write and every image you place on your website can help you build visitors' perception of you as a leader in your field. People buy from leaders and innovators, not from followers.

The following sections explain branding strategies that can help your visitors form a positive perception of you when visiting your website.

Creating taglines and slogans

Taglines and *slogans* are short phrases that convey important ideas to customers. During the branding process, your tagline should be created even before your logo design begins, because the meaning of your tagline will have an influence on that logo design. Create a branding tagline for your own website that will mirror your branding image but won't change over time. For example, Carpet Exchange (www.carpetexchange.com) has a great tagline — *Your floor store* — displayed online under its logo, as shown in Figure 3-1. It's short and meaningful, and it even rhymes!

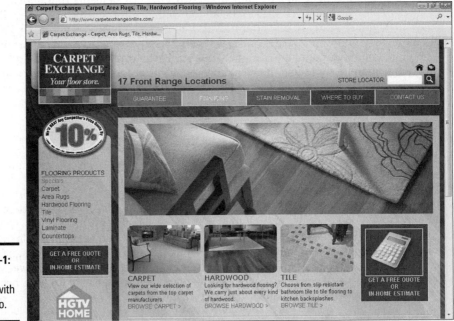

Figure 3-1: Pair a tagline with your logo.

TIP

Use www.rhymezone.com to come up with words that rhyme if you would like your tagline to rhyme, or use www.morewords.com to find words of a certain length, lettering, or number of syllables.

A branding slogan is a little different in that it changes depending on the type of promotion you're running. JELL-O is a good example. One of its slogans is *Every Diet Needs a Little Wiggle Room*. But, when winter comes around, it could change this tagline in promotions to *Every Vacation Needs a Little Wiggle Room*.

Developing a branded logo

Perhaps one of the most overlooked elements of doing business in general — let alone online — is the importance of having a meaningful logo. Many Internet marketing gurus will tell you not to waste your time or money producing a logo. But, if you are promoting a company on the web, a good logo is a vital ingredient: It helps you communicate a lot about your business to a website visitor in a fraction of a second. When people see your logo (or lack of one), they can immediately rate various elements of your business in their minds. This act of evaluation might even occur in their subconscious. Some of these include your

+ Level of professionalism

+ Ability to create or innovate

+ Enthusiasm for your product

+ Level of traditionalism

+ Attention to detail

WARNING!

Visitors will associate words with your business based on the appearance of your logo, such as funny, silly, exciting, desperate, growing, content, or curious. So, be careful what you ask your designer to create for you.

When it comes to your website, it's more important than ever to at least have a logo to identify your business, if not a logo for each of your products too! The following list invites you to take a look at some good logos that are memorable but also define the business and even the personality of the business:

+ www.ContractorsAccess.com: One look at this logo and you know exactly what this company produces: high-rise equipment that you see window washers standing on, among other things. So, a logo alone can sometimes bring it all together to tell a visitor what your business does.

+ www.monkeybizness.com: On the other end of the spectrum, you find Monkey Bizness, with the tagline *where kids monkey around*. Everything about this logo is playful and not too serious, from the font type used to the coloring and the slight animation of the monkey jumping up and down.

These two logos paints a memorable picture in your mind. And that's what branding is all about: creating something that remains in people's minds for days, weeks, or months to come.

Professional designers are your best resource for creating a logo that matches how you want your business to be perceived. Keep in mind that logos take time to conceptualize and create. So, be prepared that by the time you approve a logo, you might see several iterations, costing several hundreds of dollars. The best scenario from a time standpoint is when your website designer is also the creator of your logo. That way, you don't have to worry about the logo designer getting the right formats to your web designer and waiting for that communication to take place. But, many web designers do not work with logos and require a logo to be submitted before beginning work on your website. See Chapter 7 of this minibook for resources.

Creating a consistent look with CSS

If you're working with a web designer, you need to know whether your designer is formatting your fonts, as well as the rest of your site, with Cascading Style Sheets (CSS). This is important because a website can be designed on one computer yet appear totally different on the next. This is a browser and operating system issue as well as a display issue. The most dramatic differences can be seen if you look at a website on a PC versus a Mac, use Internet Explorer version 6 versus 9, use Firefox versus Chrome, or view on different monitors. Consistency, though, must be a key element when branding your site, and CSS is the common thread that allows that consistency to be maintained.

Among other things, using CSS helps ensure that

✦ Larger fonts don't appear too large

✦ Smaller letters don't come across as unreadable

✦ Text and other elements have a consistent look on every web page

✦ Rows and columns appear the same width and height

✦ Spacing between images and text is the same

✦ Border colors and thickness are identical

CSS styles can get pretty involved, and the details of crafting them are beyond the scope of this book. If you're interested in finding out more, see *CSS Web Design For Dummies,* by Richard Mansfield. If you're designing your own site, *Web Sites Do-It-Yourself For Dummies,* by Janine Warner, can walk you through the nuts and bolts of creating your site, including styling web page elements with CSS. And *Building Web Sites All-in-One For Dummies* by Doug

Sahlin, can help you use CSS in web design. (All books published by John Wiley & Sons, Inc.)

If you're not interested in designing your website, that's fine. Just share this information with your designer so that, together, you can plan for the appropriate CSS components to help every page of your site appear visually consistent, no matter what type of computer, monitor, or browser people use to view it.

Many designers do not have the programming expertise to migrate their own web designs into proper CSS styles. Expect the possibility that you may need to pay an additional helper who's more specialized in programming and CSS coding to finish the job when your design is complete. As the web gets more complex, the use of multiple specialists on the same project is becoming more common.

Styling Text on the Web (Droid Sans)

Website visitors rarely read text word for word on a website; instead, they scan information and wait for something to catch their interest. One important element of a website that captures people's interest and attention is font size and font type.

✦ **Font size:** Some designers like to push the limits by using huge fonts or really tiny text.

The Internet is a great place to test different methods, but don't get too carried away or your sales can suffer quickly.

✦ **Font type:** Use one of these fonts listed in order by popularity: Arial, Comic Sans, Verdana, Trebuchet, or Georgia. These are by far the most widely used and readable fonts on computer screens and browser types. Specifically, here are the strengths of each font

- *Arial* is great for headlines and subheadings.

- *Comic Sans* gives a site an informal look and is a good font type to use if your business has a more casual audience.

- *Georgia* is a good all-around font for screens with easy-to-read text for primary content and italics.

- *Trebuchet* is another good all-around font but only in standard 10, 11, or 12 point — or larger sizes like 18, 20, and 24.

- *Verdana* is the most readable font overall among web-based text fonts, but Trebuchet is becoming increasingly popular.

Be careful not to use more than two or three font types or colors for your website text. Also, don't capitalize everything in a sentence. In all capitals, it's like you're yelling at your visitors.

Using the Right Colors for Your Website

Website visitors react to color more than you might realize. That reaction can mean the difference between a visitor buying a product online with confidence versus a person being blinded by ghastly color combinations and hitting the Back button in less than three seconds. Talk to your designer about the potential uses of color. If you don't have a web designer chosen yet, make color options a point of discussion before hiring that helper. We all make decisions daily based on the colors we see, so color should be an important component of your website's design.

The following sections invite you to consider how color sets the tone for your website as well as how technical aspects affect color on the web.

Considering what colors convey

Here is a summary of how most people interpret and react to colors:

✦ **Blue** (the most popular) suggests honesty, trustworthiness, calming, and loyalty.

✦ **Black** displays authority, sophistication, power, elegance, and technical prowess.

✦ **White** symbolizes purity, peace, and youth: neutral and clean.

✦ **Red** excites with passion, energy, and excitement.

✦ **Pink** suggests innocence, softness, and sweetness.

✦ **Green** invites feelings of nature, growth, and regeneration.

✦ **Dark green** however, implies wealth and conservatism.

✦ **Yellow** is optimistic and cheery, yet can come across as too dominating if overused.

✦ **Purple** is associated with wealth, sophistication, and mystical, spiritual tones.

✦ **Brown** is genuine, although it often emotes sadness.

✦ **Orange** conveys happiness, freedom, creativity, playfulness, and confidence.

✦ **Gold** as you would expect, suggests expensive taste as well as prestige.

✦ **Silver** also emotes prestige but is cold and more scientific.

✦ **Gray** has a more corporate, somber, and practical appeal.

A good example of a website that uses colors in an interesting way is www.SecureFinancialGroup.com. The website features a trustworthy black-and-gold outline mixture, with gold and silver coins featured, of course. But, a subtle palette of grays is used for the navigation bar, which gives a calming effect to the visitor and yet a sort of scientific feeling that's appealing to people who want to invest. Clearly, this is a website trying to differentiate itself in the precious metals investing industry from the gold buyers that you see advertising on every city street corner.

If you have an existing website, study the colors. Do the colors work together to convey a meaning that is consistent with your business? If you do not yet have a website or are working on a redesign, this is a great opportunity for you to make a list of two or three colors to include in your design, plus a few that you want to stay away from.

Using web-safe colors

Even modern screens display colors differently. You may intend to have red text, but it could end up looking purple on some monitors. So you need to test your colors on multiple screen types to know what your visitors really see.

Years ago, when CRT monitors were only capable of displaying 256 colors, 216 colors were considered "safe" in that they displayed appropriately on monitors of the time. These web-safe colors became the standard recommended for use on the Internet. Today, all LCD monitors can view the whole spectrum of 16 million colors. But, when it comes to text, you should still use the same web-safe colors, because people are used to seeing those colors. Blue underline links and red headlines are two examples of web-safe colors because those are certain colors that people have come to expect.

Here is a great resource to see the most widely used web-safe colors in the color spectrum, along with their Pantone Matching System (PMS) color associations:

www.visibone.com/colorlab

PMS is a way for printers, paint manufacturers, graphic designers, and others to communicate exact colors to each other. Because all colors can be matched by using a mixture of varying levels of red, green, and blue, their properties can be documented and shared using what are called *hue values*.

Accounting for color-blindness in a design

Did you know that more than 1 in 12 visitors to your website might be color-blind? Did you also know that 90 percent of all color-blind people have the most problem seeing red and green? Here are some facts that you might not have known about people with a color weakness. They can

🖙 Distinguish between black and white

🖙 See all shades of yellow and blue

🖙 See dimmer shades of yellow, such as gold

🖙 Have trouble seeing greens and reds

🖙 Distinguish bright colors when contrasted with dark

Keep these points in mind as you choose colors for your site. A site with lots of reds and greens might be hard to read for people who are color-blind. To make your site more accessible, try yellows and blues, or use colors with a high-light and dark contrast.

Combining colors for your website

If your website uses a blue header for the top of your pages with an orange left column, what third color could you use that would match the other two? If you had to think about the answer, chances are you'll appreciate the free Color Calculator tool, offered by Sessions Online by School of Design at

```
www.sessions.edu/for-students/career-center/tools-quizzes/
    color-calculator
```

The tool helps you choose three colors based on the color wheel.

Adding High-Impact Photos

What do people look like when they're using your product or service? What lifestyle do they lead now that they finally took your advice? Good design means using photos well to describe more than just your company image, for example, the outcome of using your product or service. Here are some real-world examples:

✦ **Product shots**

- If you have a dude ranch vacation destination, show a group on horseback, all smiling because they're having a wonderful time in the beautiful country surroundings. Figure 3-2 shows a website promoting the Bitterroot Ranch in Wyoming (`www.bitterrootranch.com`). The purpose of the dude ranch is evident, and if you were to take a trip to the same place, that's the look you would expect to receive.

- If you sell jewelry, have a photo of a woman looking at her new diamond ring as her husband-to-be peers over her shoulder. Showing interaction of a buyer with a product, rather than showing just a picture of the item itself, sells the product better.

✦ **Concept shots**

- If you sell perfume, show a couple getting close.

- If you're a personal success coach, show a photo of parents spending more time with their children.

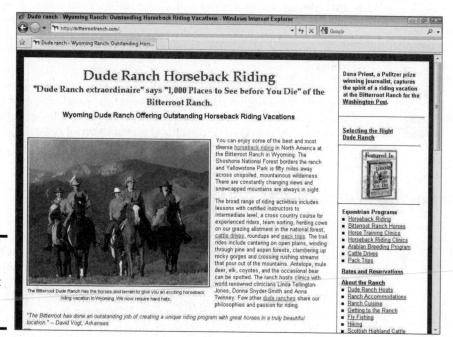

Figure 3-2:
Choose
photos that
sell the
outcome.

Create a vision in your mind of the positive outcome people will enjoy by using your product or service. That's the image to create using photos throughout your website.

To get these photos, you can either create your own or purchase them:

✦ **Create your own photos:** To create your own photos, you can hire a photographer in your area or try shooting and editing your own photos. Your best bet is to take high-resolution photos, crop and correct them if needed, and then size them for the web. Details about digital photography are beyond the scope of this book, but *Digital Photography For Dummies* by Julie Adair King (published by John Wiley & Sons, Inc.) explains how to compose, edit, and size photos.

Whether you create your own photos or buy them, use photo-editing software to make sure that they're optimized to display quickly when someone visits your website. Images that take too long to load will cause you to lose customers. Adobe Photoshop Elements is a popular choice for editing photos. You might also have editing software that came with your digital camera. Gimp software is a free option that you can download from www.Gimp.org.

When you get to the editing stage, you want to change the resolution setting to 72 ppi (pixels per inch) and save or export the file in .jpg format.

✦ **Buy photos:** An alternative to hiring a photographer is to purchase photos from an online gallery or a stock photo house. iStockphoto (http://istockphoto.com), Bigstock (www.bigstockphoto.com), and Clipart.com (www.clipart.com) are a few resources to get you started.

Downloading photographs or images from a website to use on yours is a potential copyright infringement and can be punishable by fines. If you must use existing photos and images, use a reputable company for your purchases and keep a printed copy showing proof of purchase for every image you use from its gallery.

Laying Out Content on Your Web Pages

Good web design is more than adding fancy colors and a visually exploding, movie trailer–like *splash page;* the layout needs to complement your branding while also inspiring visitors to take action. The "action" is that your visitor either clicks one of the links provided in the layout or progresses through the content on the page. Google is a good example. It uses a minimalist design, but its layout is very strategically created to provide only the information you want in a quick and easy way. When people think of visiting Google, they know to expect simple results — fast.

One of the easiest ways to get a simple, clean design is to use a template. If you use WordPress for your website, you can find predesigned WordPress themes such as WooThemes (www.woothemes.com), Template Monster (www.templatemonster.com), and Website Templates (www.website templates.com). You'll see hundreds of website designs that you can purchase for as little as $20, or you can simply get design ideas and have your designer create a more unique look for you that uses ideas from the templates. Chapter 4 of this minibook has more details on working with templates for WordPress.

In the sections that follow, you discover how to evaluate visitors' experiences on your current site layout (or the layout of your competitors). You also find tips for making the most of key areas on a page. Every page of any website should feature multiple opportunities for a visitor to take action of some kind. Those opportunities might include

✦ Buying a product for sale on your website

✦ Calling you for more information

✦ Signing up to receive a free report

✦ Connecting with you on Facebook, LinkedIn, or other social media

✦ Visiting another page of your website

In addition to the images, text, colors, and words displayed on your site, the placement of these key components is the most significant decision you make on your entire website.

Evaluating layouts with a heat map application

Designing a website is very similar to designing a store. In fact, your website really is a store — a virtual store on the Internet. Grocery store chains have spent millions of dollars in market research watching and documenting how shoppers enter the store, turn right or left, and then graze their aisles. You need to know how a visitor enters your website and what his eyes look at. For example, if you decide to have a sale this month, you might want to add a special sale image, say, at the top of your right column. Wouldn't you want to know if the majority of your visitors are seeing that special notice?

Fortunately, you don't have to pay thousands or even hundreds of dollars to know what your visitors look at first, when they enter your website, and where their eyes go next. You can use the free heat map tool at Feng-GUI online (`www.feng-gui.com`) to upload an image of your web page. Feng-GUI then displays how most people might be looking at that particular page when they see it for the first time. In Figure 3-3, notice how Feng-GUI displays the upper-right corner and the right column as viewed most often by the different weighting. Then the attention shifts to the middle of the page.

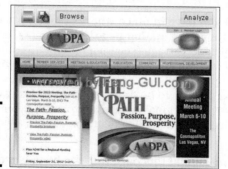

Figure 3-3: A heat map simulation.

The following steps explain how to create a similar map of your own site:

1. **Open your browser and visit the homepage of your website (or any subpage).**

   If you don't have a website yet, you could use a heat map analysis of a competitor's website to see what its visitors are interested in.

2. **Take a screen shot of your homepage (press the Print Screen button on your keyboard).**

3. **Open Microsoft Paint or your favorite graphics editor and paste your screen shot into a new document.**

   Paint is available on most Windows machines; choose Start⇨All Programs⇨Accessories⇨Paint. When a new document opens, simply right-click and then choose Paste from the contextual menu that appears. Your homepage should now appear in Paint.

4. **Save your screen shot by choosing File⇨Save As. Give your image a name and then choose .jpg from the Save as Type drop-down list.**

5. **Point your browser to** www.feng-gui.com **and scroll to the bottom of the homepage, where the free demo heat map utility is located. Click the Browse button to find and upload the JPEG file that you just created.**

6. **Click the Analyze button.**

   You see the most important areas of the page that your visitors' eyes gravitate toward.

Ask yourself the following questions after running a heat map simulation, whether you use your competitor's website or your own as the example:

✦ **Are these areas of the page where the attention of your visitors *should* go first?** For example, is your logo so dominating in the upper-left corner that your visitors see it first and immediately start scanning down the left navigation of your page, bypassing the fact that you have a special for the month appearing in your upper-right corner?

✦ **What feature should you have in place where the majority of your visitors look first when they land on that page?** For example, if you want to create an educational content page (see Chapter 5 of this minibook), the first thing you would want visitors to see is a captivating headline centered at the top of the page. But, on a professional speaker's website, you would want a meeting planner to be drawn to your speaking topics and one-sheet (a printable promotional brochure promoting your speaking availability) or a strong and convincing testimonial from a well-known company CEO.

✦ **Is there anything visual about this page that is a huge turnoff and a reason why so many people might leave the site prematurely?** See Table 3-1 for common possible reasons why people leave websites.

Table 3-1		**Why Visitors Leave Websites**	
Category	*Examples*	*How Long after Problem Noticed Do They Leave?*	*Reason for Leaving*
Visual	Graphics don't line up. Graphics aren't consistent with content. Too many graphics with not enough content. Too many animated images.	Less than 5 seconds	Visitor believes content or product will be of lesser quality and looks for something better.
Textual	Headline isn't related to search results. Text is too hard to read. Poor grammar and spelling. All text, no video.	Up to 10 seconds	Visitor becomes skeptical that solution is genuine.
Functional	Page loads too slowly. Links don't work. Searches don't display results. Too many animated images.	Up to 30 seconds	Visitor leaves for fear of pop-ups, viruses, and loss of time.
Social	Lack of social media icons pointing to LinkedIn, Facebook, Twitter, Google+, RSS, YouTube channel.	Up to 1 minute	Visitor sees your website as out of date and notes that you're not wanting to progress with new ways to communicate with your customers.

The visual component of your website is the first thing visitors see and is the most common reason why visitors leave in less than five seconds.

You can use Google Analytics to monitor the path that your visitors take when they arrive on your website.

Using the upper-right quadrant (URQ)

The upper-right quadrant (URQ) of a page on your website is one of the most critical areas because it's the first place people see when they arrive. In Figure 3-4, practically anything you would want to do on this website is featured in the URQ, including requesting a quote, contacting staff, viewing samples, calling for a quote, and making a request online.

Important info is
in upper-right quadrant

Figure 3-4:
Upper-right
quadrant
(URQ)
actions.

Another use of the URQ would be to eliminate a buying objection before the question even arises. In the site shown in Figure 3-5, the URQ is used for the sole purpose of showing visitors that the company has been in this online business for quite a while — since 1995!

There are no rules as to exactly what should be placed in the URQ, but this is an important area to test and modify often to see whether leads and sales increase or decrease. Yes, even a simple change to the upper-right quadrant of your website can impact your results. Here are some additional things to test in the URQ of your website:

✦ Your phone number (most popular addition to the URQ)

✦ A special promotion that you've never offered

✦ Important company news, like a finalized merger or new product release

Figure 3-5:
Use the URO
to eliminate
objections.

+ A testimonial or celebrity endorsement

+ A photo with a recognized authority figure in your industry

+ An award image

+ Better Business Bureau badge

+ Image of your new book cover

+ Search box so that visitors can search for a topic or specific product

Inspiring action with the horizontal navigation bar

Have you ever visited a website to look up movie start times, register for an
event, or get directions to a store? If so, you know how annoying it can be
when you can't find the information you need that should be featured in an
obvious place.

Proper use of the top horizontal navigation bar (the links or buttons you see
going across the top of a web page) is critical for increasing leads and sales
for your business. The top navigation area serves one purpose — to get a
visitor to go to another page. Part of the trick is knowing what obvious utilities or content should be featured. The other is how to graphically produce

the links to lead your visitors to those important sections. Determining what people expect can be discovered by

✦ **Reviewing competing websites:** Visit some of the websites you are in competition with. Run a heat map test on them to see where their visitors are looking. See the section "Evaluating layouts with a heat map application," earlier in this chapter, for details.

✦ **Participating in forums:** Search for a forum (otherwise known as a discussion board) focused on discussions with people in your industry. Pay attention to the forum categories and topics that participants are talking about. These could become specific titles for your main navigation.

✦ **Knowing your target audience:** Find people in your own network who fit your target audience and ask them what they would expect to see when arriving at your website.

Many visitors know exactly what they're looking for, and you want to provide that information immediately. Your challenge is to decide what actions your website visitors will want to take and feature them prominently in the top navigation area.

Here are a few additional rules you'll find useful when creating a horizontal navigation bar for a website:

✦ **Location:** Websites usually have a banner at the top of the page featuring a logo on the left and then some other graphics in the middle and right. Place horizontal navigation directly under the banner. That way, a visitor can first focus on the upper-right quadrant of the page and then scan across the graphics to give him confidence that he's at a website worth investigating further. Then allow him to naturally move down to where the horizontal navigation bar catches his eye.

✦ **Type:** Navigation bars include either buttons or text links. Sometimes when you roll your mouse over a navigation link, a menu of options unfolds. These are called *menu trees,* which contain either text links or buttons. Which is better, text links or buttons? That is more of a personal preference on your part. What is important is that your text or buttons are easy to view and identify. Do that much and you'll get the click. And, again, that's the only goal of your navigation bar — to get the click.

✦ **Number:** People like odd numbers. If we see anything on the web that is in even numbers, we're wondering where the next item is. So, keep three, five, or seven items on your horizontal navigation bar. In fact, limit the number to seven to avoid a cluttered navigation bar.

✦ **Order:** When you have a strong URQ that draws the eye of your visitor to the upper-right part of your page first, the next natural place the visitor will look is from right to left across your top navigation buttons.

What feature would you like your visitors to see first on that nav bar? Here are some options for your navigation bar:

- *Home:* Give your visitors an easy way of navigating back to your homepage.

- *Contact info:* If you want your visitors to contact you, include a Contact button.

- *About Me:* Most visitors are going to want to know more about you before buying something from you.

- *Blog:* Blogs have become expected. Turn to Chapter 5 in this minibook to find out how to integrate your blog into your website. Book VI is also devoted to blogging.

✦ What else goes into your navigation bar depends on your business. Here is an example of a typical top navigation bar for some different types of businesses:

Car sales: Home | About | Buy a Car | Sell a Car | Service | Blog | Contact

Speakers: Home | About | Speaking | Meeting Planners | Reviews | Blog | Contact

Membership: Home | About | Join | Calendar | Testimonials | Blog | Contact

✦ **Words:** The top navigation bar should be designed to get people to actually *do* something. People like to *do* things online. They like to search, view, register, find, review, subscribe, add, get, contact, evaluate, demo, download, play, go to, and discover things, for example. Use the words in your top nav bar to get people engaged with your website — to get them to do something. Consider using the following navigation bar:

Search Products | View Events Schedule | Subscribe Now

instead of this one:

Products | Events | Newsletter

Choosing scrolling over clicking

Some people believe that no one wants to scroll down a web page — that people would rather click for more information. But, if you think about it, the only reason we click through links instead of scrolling is to get to a page where the correct information is featured. When we get to the right page, we expect to find enough information to satisfy our curiosity, and we're happy to scroll when we are on a web page that provides us with the information we are looking for.

Valuable content (as described in Chapter 5 of this minibook) is what inspires people to want to scroll to read more and to consider all the details they need to make an informed decision. Good design is what allows the content to keep you engaged as a reader to scroll down the page, whereas forcing you to click to more pages would just be cumbersome and annoying.

A good example of this is on CoachClemens.com (`http://coachclemens.com/2012/01/08/overuse-leads-to-pitching-injury`), where the author introduces an important subject and just at the time when you have to scroll, you're riveted and willing to scroll (see Figure 3-6). See how you have to scroll to read the entire article? But the subject is captivating enough that it's worth it to us, the readers, to do so.

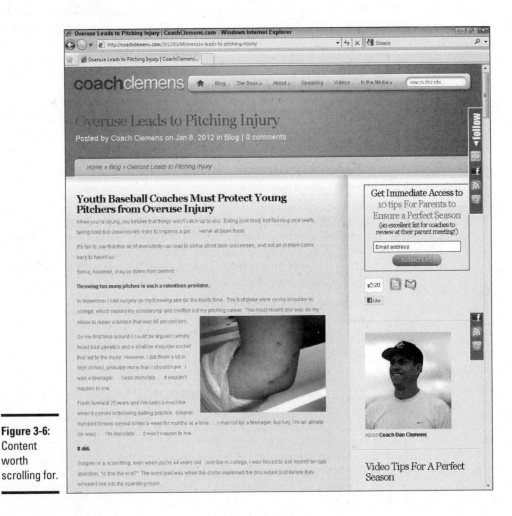

Figure 3-6: Content worth scrolling for.

Attracting attention with arrows, buttons, and more

Specific elements on a web page also encourage visitors to take action. Here are some next-action design elements to try:

✦ **Red arrows:** One of the most commonly used graphics online is a big red arrow pointing to something important. Why are they so popular? Because red arrows instruct people what to do, and people want to be directed. Think of using arrows as a courtesy to your visitors by guiding them to where they should be interested in going.

✦ **Guarantee sections:** Guarantees might be written in text, but it's the graphic piece that brings attention to it. After people are made aware that a guarantee is offered, they're often more willing to take the next step.

✦ **Outlined text boxes:** A page full of content needs to be divided into sections, or it will just look long-winded without purpose. But an outlined text box draws attention.

✦ **Inline text links:** Throughout the content of a page, consider featuring links to other pages where more topic-specific content can be found. These *inline links* should always be underlined and blue in appearance. Designers will try to be creative and convince you to use other colors. Programmers will use CSS styles to remove the underline from all text links because they believe the page looks less cluttered without a bunch of links all over it. But let's face the facts. Blue, underlined text links have been around since the word *hyperlink* was invented. When we see it, we know it's a link. Here are other colors as potential links:

  • Red is probably not a good color for links because red means "stop" in our society. We have red stop signs, red stop lights, and even red Corvettes make us stop and look.

  • Green is not a horrible choice for a link. After all, we look at green as meaning "go" whenever we're sitting at a stop light. The problem with green is that it doesn't stand out very well on a white background unless you use a larger font or bold the text. And, bolding every text link really drives designers crazy!

  • Yellow, orange, and even white links could be used when reverse text is concerned. Reverse text is when you have a very dark design forcing you to use very light colors for the text. In that case, try a lighter shade of blue for your links so that they stand out.

Yes, the color blue will be your best fit for a text link color. That's not just because of tradition or because it's what the pros do, but because blue works and we're conditioned to look for blue when we want more information on a topic. People look for blue, underlined links. And you don't want to let them down.

Completing the Website Preflight Checklist

Just as you would want to crunch numbers and run what-if scenarios before launching a new company, you want to put your plan to paper for your website design as well. Collect information on these 25 top items when submitting your project scope to a website designer for a price quote:

✦ Company information, including name, address, phone, and e-mail

✦ How long you have been in business

✦ The primary goal of your business (what you sell)

✦ A description of your business in 25 words or less

✦ A list of three groups of people who might benefit from your product or service

✦ Your branding slogan

✦ The main domain name for your website (search www.uownitdomains.com for available domain names and then register them)

✦ A list of at least three websites that you like and what you like about them

✦ A list of at least three websites that you dislike and what you dislike about them

✦ A list of at least three competing websites

✦ A description of your potential customers' demographic profile, which you can find by searching www.quantcast.com for a high-traffic website related to your target industry

✦ Whether your potential customers are Internet savvy or technically challenged. (You find this out by attending seminars or networking events where your target audience is present and talking with them.)

✦ What you would expect if you were one of your potential customers

✦ The goals of your website (sell product online, generate leads, and so on)

✦ Whether visitors ever need to print pages from your site

✦ What the top navigation buttons will be

✦ What the left navigation buttons will be

✦ What special features will be displayed in the right navigation area

✦ What should be included in the footer of every page of the site

✦ Whether you will supply photos, or whether the designer should include photos in the quote

✦ Whether you will supply content, or whether the designer should include copywriting in the quote

✦ Whether you will supply a logo, or whether the designer should quote a price for logo creation

✦ Whether the website will require an online shopping cart

✦ Whether you already have an Internet-capable merchant account

✦ Whether you will offer an online newsletter sign-up form on the website

If you need help with any of these points, check out the related sections earlier in this chapter.

Designing for Optimum Usability

Assuring that your website is usable by your audience is partly the responsibility of the designer and partly the responsibility of the programmer. If something as simple as a link to another page isn't functional, for example, a visitor will quickly become frustrated and leave the site searching for a better solution. The following sections introduce you to usability standards, many of which might be familiar to you if you've read earlier sections of this chapter. You also discover how to test your site to ensure that it meets usability standards.

Incorporating usability standards

Follow this ten-step checklist to evaluate the usability of your new website before its launch:

✦ Have all links on the site been tested to be functional?

✦ Does a CSS file contain all font sizes, colors, and table border details?

✦ Is alt text (alternative text) used for all images that have a possible description?

✦ Are links descriptive of what the user will see on the landing page?

✦ Does the site operate similarly on multiple browsers, versions, monitors, and operating systems?

✦ Can the navigation be easily followed and understood?

✦ Are text links underlined and blue?

✦ Does individualized metadata exist on each page of the website?

✦ Do you have a link to the homepage on every subpage?

✦ Are the URLs descriptive of what will be found on each page?

After you're sure that your website has passed the usability basics test, now it's time for the ultimate test — a live test for usability.

Testing live for usability

Usability testing is one of the most neglected aspects of creating and launching a website. Maybe you have had your friends or family take a look at the new design but have never brought in a *focus group* (folks who've never seen your website). After all, who has time for that?

If your website is a hobby for you, usability testing might be put on the back burner. However, if you're in business and you plan for your website to be a major contributor to your annual revenue, usability testing is essential.

You should always test your own website for usability by viewing it with multiple browsers, multiple versions of those browsers if possible, multiple screen sizes, and multiple computer platforms (PC versus Mac). But the ultimate test to see how truly usable your website has become is to invite people to your location and have a focus group with a live review session. That way, you can be present in the room to see visitors' first reactions. Here are some things to consider when testing for usability with a live group:

✦ Test each person on the same computer.

✦ Give each reviewer a checklist of things to try to find on your website.

✦ Write their comments as each navigates the site.

✦ Don't say a word.

Offer no assistance. That's what a usability study is!

✦ Share the results with the group at the end and allow open discussion.

✦ Be grateful for all feedback that you receive. Remember, if one person has a problem with your website's usability, another thousand future visitors will experience the same issue. So, don't be offended or angry; just fix the issue.

"Hot seats" are becoming more popular at seminars and workshops. In essence, a member of the audience volunteers to have her website brought up on-screen for all in the room to critique. If you ever have the opportunity to be in the hot seat, jump at the chance! Having several first-time visitors provide unbiased, immediate feedback about your website is worth the entire price of your registration.

The best news is that the work you do on the design, layout, branding, and usability of your website will serve as a tremendous training ground for when you begin to promote your core business through multiple websites.

Chapter 4: Creating and Connecting Multiple Websites

In This Chapter

✔ Establishing your core company website as the very heart of everything you do on the Internet

✔ Launching and connecting multiple websites to broaden your reach *Empower!!* and web presence

✔ Monetizing your core website with paying members

*F*ew would argue that our hearts are the most important organ in our bodies. Our brains are a close second. Arms and legs are important too. But, we're nothing without a strong heart. Your main company website is the heart of everything you do to market yourself and your business using the Internet. It should not be taken lightly.

This chapter presents the essential components for your core business website. You find out the appropriate sets of content your visitors expect to see when they arrive at your website and the variety of supplemental websites you can use to drive traffic to your core website.

Creating and connecting multiple sites with your core site help you to become more than just competitive, and position you to dominate your industry.

REMEMBER

You need to have control of any launched website, including graphics, usernames and passwords, backup files, and content. This chapter isn't just about website types and connecting them; it's about keeping you in the driver's seat.

REMEMBER

And as you build your network of websites, remember that good design and good content apply to each page of each site. More about specific design elements can be found in Chapter 3 of this minibook. After your design is approved, it's time to add content. This is the message you want to convey to your visitors, so take your time when crafting your message and use the components of Chapter 5 of this minibook to write effective copy to get your visitors to take action with you by buying online, calling you on the phone, or requesting more information by e-mail.

Planning Your Core Company Website

In addition to the website preflight planning instructions in Chapter 3 of this minibook, the most important question you can ask at the website planning stage is what amount of money have you budgeted for its production and support. You can conceivably pay nothing and have a live website. But, is spending as little as possible *always* the best answer?

Your core company website is the very heart of everything you do online for your business. Treat your business like the real business it is and invest as much as you can for a unique, high-quality website backed by top-notch designers, programmers, and support staff.

You also need to budget a number of designs. A lower-end or free themed website will usually have the same look and feel for every page of the website. A unique, custom-designed website will often showcase a homepage design, a secondary design for all the subpages, and then a third design for the blog area. Installing a theme that has three different designs will definitely require more implementation effort than a single theme to be used on all pages of the site.

Choosing WordPress

WordPress, a premier blogging tool, has evolved over the years to become a good choice for websites. Many large companies with thousands of website visitors per month use WordPress for their entire website, not just the blog area. Some companies, like the one shown in Figure 4-1, use WordPress for websites that don't even include a blog!

Traditional websites of yesteryear were like a baseball catcher's glove. The only thing you could do was to make the pages of your website and sit and wait for traffic to come your way. With WordPress, you are now able to push content from your website as well as to receive it from traffic sources.

The most important reasons to use WordPress for your entire website and not just the blog area include

✦ **Google loves WordPress.** When WordPress is set up properly, no website software will transport your content to Google's search results faster.

✦ **It's easy to customize.** WordPress is *open source* software, which means that you can modify and enhance its functionality, with some PHP programming and the addition of preprogrammed plugins to extend features.

✦ **It's easy to learn.** If you can write a letter in Microsoft Word, you can add, change, or delete content in a WordPress website. Figure 4-2 shows how similar the WordPress system looks to Word, where you see an icon to click B for bolding text, an icon I for italics, and additional buttons for left, right, and center justification.

Figure 4-1:
A website
powered by
WordPress.

Figure 4-2:
Writing a
blog post is
easy to do.

✦ **It's easy to support.** You'll find a vast sea of WordPress experts who are available to easily jump in to fix a problem.

✦ **It's mobile ready.** Install WordPress and then view the website on any mobile device. Enhance mobile user experience by installing the WPtouch plugin.

✦ **It's popular and free.** Because of its popularity and free open-source nature, WordPress can be quickly activated at no charge, other than the price of a standard Linux hosting account, at most major hosting companies. That way, you have full ownership of your website, which is vital to your success.

The developers of WordPress software offer "free" website hosting at WordPress.com, but that's not a good option for your core company website. WordPress can shut down your website without warning if you violate its terms. The most common websites that get shut down are those that make a significant amount of money in some way either through product sales, affiliate marketing, or lead generation. WordPress.com also restricts you from adding plugins and limits the amount you can customize the look and feel of your website. So, if you're starting a website to support a hobby or a nonprofit cause, WordPress.com is a potential free solution. But, if you want to make money and grow your business, always host with a commercial-level hosting company where you own the website and have full access to its contents.

Setting up a WordPress website

The following steps offer an overview of the steps for installing a WordPress website and then getting it up and running:

1. **Register a domain name with keywords related to your industry, or use your company name.**

   For example, your core domain name should reflect your business name (www.herenextyear.com), but your ancillary website can focus on industry-related keywords (www.motivationalspeakersworldwide.com).

2. **Buy a commercial website hosting account.**

   Be sure to subscribe to a Linux server website hosting account because WordPress will not function to its full potential on a Windows server.

3. **Install the WordPress software.**

   Contact your preferred website hosting company and have its support department install and configure WordPress to work with your domain name. Most hosting companies will initialize WordPress for you — look for an installation area within your hosting account to start the WordPress installation on your own, as shown in Figure 4-3. Or, you can download the WordPress blog software script from WordPress.org and connect it yourself to a MySQL database.

   If you need help, go to wordPress.org/support.

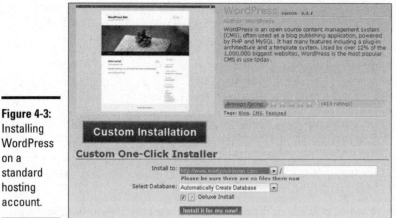

Figure 4-3:
Installing
WordPress
on a
standard
hosting
account.

4. **Log in through admin and adjust the settings and preferences as you desire.**

   For example, under Settings, you can give your website a title, set your discussion preferences, set your privacy so that your blog is visible to search engines, and much more.

5. **Install plug-ins, which you can search for by clicking the Add New link on the Plug-ins page.**

   Plug-ins are typically small software programs that are usually free. They are offered on standard websites for download and are also available through a directory of plug-ins as supplied by WordPress. Search for available plug-ins directly from within your WordPress admin area, as shown in Figure 4-4.

Figure 4-4:
Install plug-
ins on your
WordPress
site.

Here's a list of some important plug-ins that maximize your search engine optimization capability and ability to promote your website:

- *WP Super Cache:* Reduces server load

- *All-in-One SEO Pack:* Optimizes every post for search engines

- *Google XML Sitemaps:* Notifies Google that you've made changes (such as a new post if you're blogging)

- *Google Analyticator:* Links your site to your Google Analytics account so that you can monitor your website traffic whenever you log in to the WordPress administration area

- *WP-Email:* Adds a link with a form that allows readers to tell others about your website

- *WordPress Backups:* Keeps a current backup of your database files in case your website ever crashes

- *WPtouch:* Displays your website on mobile devices

6. **Add a FeedBurner account (**www.feedburner.com**), which helps auto-mate the promotion of every post.**

   Turn to Book VI, Chapter 2 to find out how to use FeedBurner to add syndication to your website.

7. **Apply your website design:**

   - *For a predesigned theme:* Click Themes, located under the Appearance menu on the left column of the dashboard area. Click Activate for the theme you want to install.

   - *For a custom-designed theme:* You have to slice the main design into smaller images and then add code to pull those images into the layout using Cascading Style Sheets (CSS), as shown in Figure 4-5.

Figure 4-5:
A small portion of CSS with sliced images.

```
#main {
    clear: both;
    overflow: hidden;
    padding: 0;
    margin: 11px 0 0;
    background: #cdcdcd url('images/main-bg.png') repeat-y top left;
}

.socialwidget a {
    width: 37px;
    height: 37px;
    display: block-inline;
    float: left;
    margin-right: 5px;
    background: url('images/social-sprite.png') no-repeat;
}
```

Chapter 3 of this minibook shows you how to use horizontal navigation bars. Your top navigation is produced by adding pages to your website through the WordPress administration area. You might need a custom menu; click Menus on the Appearance tab.

Create two or more secondary style sheets to handle programming bugs in some of the older website browsers, including Internet Explorer versions 8, 7, and 6.*x* and Firefox. Be sure to test your styles on both PCs and Macs.

Now you can begin to see how paying a bit more to have someone perform a thorough installation can be worth the investment.

8. **Include extra WordPress features on your website.**

   • *Search box:* Always offer a search box on your website so that visitors can find what they're looking for.

   • *Widgets:* You can add these add-on features to your website's left or right sidebars. The most common examples of widgets are newsletter opt-in boxes, calendars, lists of topic categories, most recent blog post titles, or just plain text. Figure 4-6 shows a text widget.

   • *Plugins:* More than a million plugins are developed by people all over the world who want to help enhance the power and functionality of WordPress. Activate your desired plugins prior to official launch so that you have full functionality.

   • *Footer:* Include a copyright notice, company name, phone number, address, and links to main sections of the website, as shown in Figure 4-7.

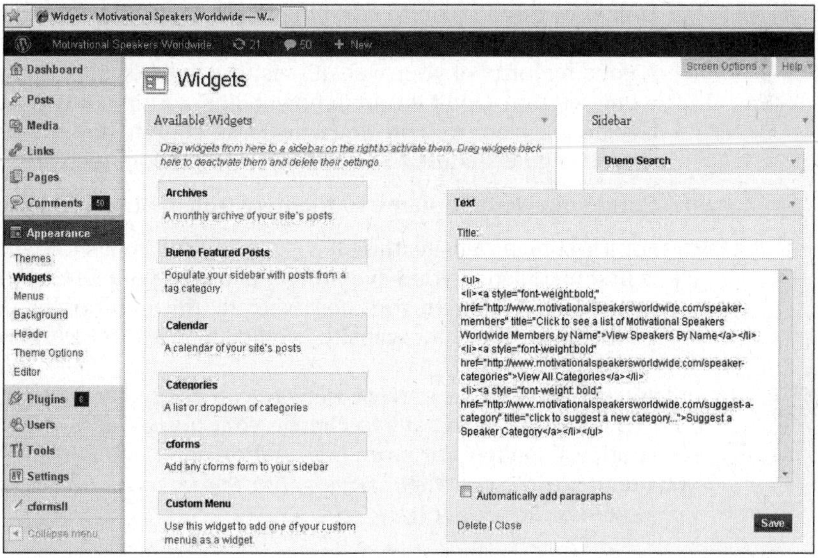

Figure 4-6:
Install a
sidebar
widget.

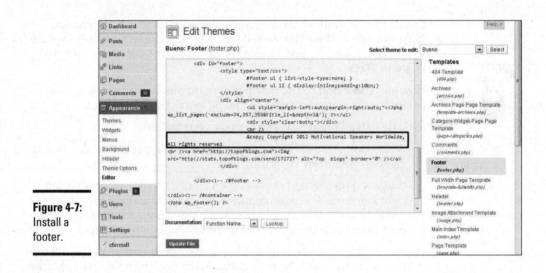

Figure 4-7:
Install a
footer.

9. **Add pages of content.**

   Refer to Chapter 2 of this minibook for ideas on creating top navigation and SEO optimized pages and Chapter 5 of this minibook for creating copy that sells.

10. **Include a blog section of the website.**

    Even if you don't plan to add blog posts daily, you should still activate a blog section of your website and plan to create a few posts per month. A good majority of your website visitors will be expecting you to have a blog section. Don't let them down! Plus, routine blog posts display to Google that your website contains fresh content and is worth sending its search engine spiders to see what's new on your website.

11. **Point your domain name to the new website hosting location.**

    For a first-time website, this step is usually accomplished when WordPress is first installed. If you have not yet changed your DNS settings to direct your domain name to your new website, this point of the process would be the time. Your new website is officially live after DNS propagates.

Did you know that your current website can be converted to WordPress? It's true! You may not even have to change your design, and your visitors won't even notice a change. For more information about converting your existing website to WordPress, visit `http://herenextyear.com/transfer-web site-to-wordpress.php`.

Pushing your website content

After you have the main components of your WordPress website set up, you can automatically push content to the world using a free tool like dlvr.it (`http://dlvr.it`).

Dlvr.it is a free web-based tool that allows you to post messages to multiple social networks at the same time. dlvr.it lets you schedule messages to post on future dates and times and enable real-time updates from your blog to the main social networks. When you make a blog post, a blurb is automatically distributed to your social networks with a link back to the blog post.

1. **Go to** `http://dlvr.it`.

2. **Sign up for a free account by entering your e-mail address and a password, and click the Sign Up button.**

3. **On the Deliveries tab, click the + Add Route button to begin the setup process.**

4. **From the Choose Your Source pop-up window, Choose New.**

5. **Right-click your website's RSS icon and select Copy Link Address.**

   You can get your RSS feed icon by subscribing to RSS creators like Feedity.com (`http://feedity.com`). You can copy and paste its HTML code.

6. **Paste your RSS URL into the Feed URL text field and make sure the Feed Active box is checked.**

7. **Click Save Source.**

8. **Choose the social networks you would like your website changes to be delivered to.**

   These include Twitter, Facebook, Tumblr, LinkedIn, and StatusNet.

9. **Once all your destinations are set up, click the Post tab in the top navigation bar and send a test post to your networks.**

10. **Manually add content and assign the post to be sent to any or all of the destinations you've just set up in the system.**

    Consider not autoposting to Facebook because Facebook gives higher weight to manual posts. If you manually post to Facebook, more people will see your content.

Now when you publish your blog posts, they are automatically sent to the networks you chose to connect with in dlvr.it.

Securing your WordPress website

Any web-based application that sports a URL to visit and an administration username and password to enter is inviting to potential hackers and thieves. WordPress is no exception. Fortunately, multiple levels exist for which you can secure your WordPress website. The process of securing your website from the outside world is called *hardening* WordPress. Here's what you can do to harden your website:

✦ **Change your username from Admin.** After you've logged in to your WordPress account, on the Users tab, change the default of Admin to something else. Most hackers know the Admin username and can easily break in to your website.

✦ **Use a strong password.** Use at least one uppercase letter, lowercase letters, and a symbol or two.

Use free password-management software, such as KeePass (`www.KeePass.com`), to keep track of all your passwords.

✦ **Install these security plug-ins:**

- *Login LockDown:* Restricts the number of times a person (or automated script) can attempt to log in to your admin page within a certain time period.

- *WordPress Firewall 2:* Blocks suspicious requests being made to your server, website files, or plug-ins.

- *WP Security Scan:* Scans your entire WordPress installation, looking for bugs, worm holes, or other opportunities for the bad boys to get in.

Using Free Blog Platforms to Supplement Your Website

WordPress.com and its nearest competitor, Blogger (owned by Google and hosted at blogger.com), are probably not the best choices for your core company website, because you don't have full ownership of the accounts and content. In other words, Blogger.com and WordPress.com can terminate your free accounts at any time they feel you have violated their terms of use. But, they are tremendous additions to your overall web presence. Here are some reasons to supplement your core website with hosted sites:

✦ **Drive more traffic to your business.** Both are attached to two of the largest networks of websites on the Internet. Blogger is owned by Google, and WordPress.com houses more than 35 *million* websites overall. Your free Blogger websites will get traffic simply from being included in the respective networks because other Blogger account holders can search for topics and blogs once inside their Blogger account. All you have to do is routinely add content to either your Blogger blog or WordPress.com blog and you have potential for getting at least some traffic.

✦ **Add links to your core company website.** When you make a blog post on your core site, make another post on your Blogger blog and WordPress.com blog with links back to your core site. Figure 4-8 displays a link from a blog at Speakerseeker.blogspot.com that points visitors to another website.

✦ **A great way to learn.** If you have an existing core company website that is managed by someone other than you, Blogger.com and WordPress.com offer a simple way for you to learn how websites work without needing to pay your designer or webmaster for help. You can contribute more toward the planning for your company website if you have some experience building your own.

✦ **Improves company website search presence.** Because Blogger.com is owned by Google, new blog posts you add to your company site will display on Google's search results faster when you add a blog post on Blogger.com.

Link to other
websites.

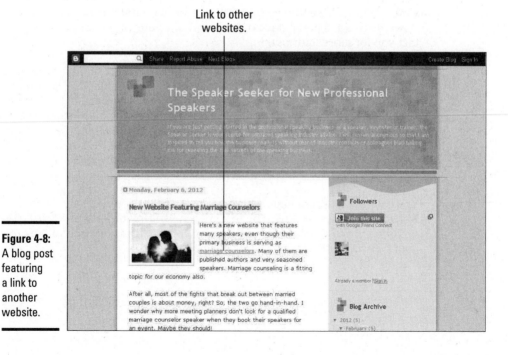

Figure 4-8:
A blog post featuring a link to another website.

✦ **Gain search results share.** When someone searches for your personal name on Google how many search results do they see? Hopefully, they will see your main company website, your Facebook page, your Twitter account, your LinkedIn profile, and links to some articles you've written and a few YouTube videos. Done correctly, and you can own the whole first page of search results on Google. But maybe you're not in the public eye and it's more important for you to gain search results share for product names and other keyword phrases. You can use Blogger.com and WordPress.com to create blog post content to appear on Google search results too, thereby adding to the overall search results share.

Reaching for Traffic with Content Sites

A *content site* is designed to feature dozens — if not hundreds, or even thousands — of pages surrounding a specific topic. These content pages are each optimized for organic search engine positioning, often using an automated process.

A content site is typically used to simply drive traffic to pages that feature Google AdSense ads, in hopes of monetizing the pages. However, the greater purpose is to cast a wide net: Your content site can introduce you to a wide variety of people searching for multiple topics related to your industry. Down the road, a percentage of them will buy your product or at least contact you for more information.

For example, one content site, Music Mates (www.musicmates.com), contains an automated voting script so that folks can vote for their favorite local musician or band, anywhere in the country. More than 6,000 of these pages are indexed on Google. When you search specifically for those voting sections (such as *best Denver rock band* or *best Miami country guitar player*), the individual voting page results for that phrase are usually in the top three results on Google. Each page includes a link to the core company site, as shown in Figure 4-9.

You can hire a programmer to create such a utility for your own content website. Or, you can subscribe to a system like Unique Article Wizard (www. uniquearticlewizard.com) to select content that you want to post to your website automatically when it's made available.

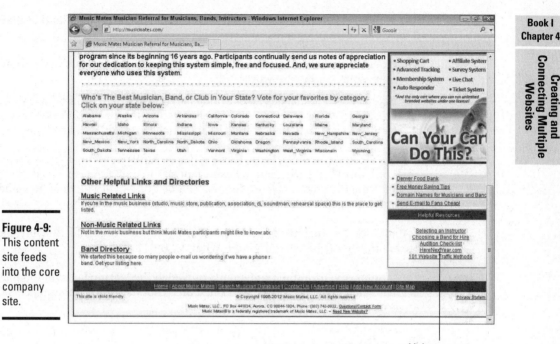

Figure 4-9:
This content
site feeds
into the core
company
site.

Link to a core
website.

Using Joomla! and Drupal

Business owners have always wanted to manage their own website content
instead of calling a designer every time even a minor change is needed.
Unfortunately, too many shy away from the opportunity even if it's made
available to them for fear of the process taking too long or just being too
technical.

Modern developments have made managing website content easier and less
technical than ever before. One way you can manage your website is with
WordPress. The following sections discuss two of the other major players in
web-based content management systems (CMS): Joomla! and Drupal.

Justifying Joomla!

Joomla! is free CMS software that allows you to make changes to the pages
of your website from your browser. After the design of the site is completed,
you can add as many new pages as you want so that your designer doesn't

have to. Using Joomla! (www.joomla.org) has two huge benefits that make it very desirable to business owners:

✦ **Open source:** Similar to WordPress, a programmer can customize how open source software works.

✦ **Extensions:** Joomla! has an enormous following where programmers have created modules — *extensions* (similar to plug-ins for WordPress) — with tremendous functionality, such as shopping carts and classified ads.

One drawback to Joomla! is its learning curve. And, you almost always need someone with PHP programming experience to install it. As easy as it might appear from the admin screen, Joomla! can be quite overwhelming to someone with no website-management experience.

For additional help, check out *Joomla! For Dummies* by Seamus Bellamy and Steven Holzner (published by John Wiley & Sons, Inc.).

For a larger organization, the benefits outweigh the learning curve. Joomla! is great when multiple people on a team are responsible for updating certain areas of websites.

Deciding on Drupal

Drupal (http://drupal.org) is the main competitor to Joomla! in that it is also free CMS software for updating, adding, and managing pages. But Drupal has two additional benefits. Its front-end look is entirely customizable, and the HTML code it produces is much cleaner than that of Joomla!. Better code has a positive impact on search-engine positioning.

Drupal also has a large following of developers and users, but they are definitely weighted on the programmer side. Whereas Joomla! has a visual approach to appeal to day-to-day administrative-level users, Drupal requires at least basic HTML knowledge to maintain.

Clearly Joomla! and Drupal serve one similar need, that is, enabling you to manage content. However, they differ in many important factors as well. Table 4-1 lists how designers, programmers, and administrative helpers have rated Joomla! versus Drupal. If you choose to use either, your choice can be made based on what's most important to you and your team from this list.

If you decide that Drupal is the system for you, *Drupal For Dummies,* by Lynn Beighley and Seamus Bellamy (published by John Wiley & Sons, Inc.), helps you use Drupal components to pull your site together.

Table 4-1	Comparing Joomla! and Drupal	
	Joomla!	*Drupal*
Popularity	👍	👎
Ease of learning	👍	👎
Number of design templates available	👍	👎
Ease of adding a custom theme	👎	👍
Search engine–friendliness	👎	👍
Number of add-ons available	👍	👎
Quality of add-ons available	👎	👍
Favored by programmers	👎	👍
Favored by designers	👎	👍
The CMS more people move to	👎	👍
User management	👎	👍
Ease of making global changes	👎	👍
Best process for organizing articles	👎	👍
CSS (Cascading Style Sheet) efficiency	👍	👎
E-commerce/shopping cart solution	👍	👎

Considering an alternative CMS

Choosing the CMS that's right for you is a very important challenge, to say the least. If you choose the wrong one, you might find yourself wanting to switch to the other after just a few months.

Implementing a Joomla! or Drupal CMS isn't as easy as you might hear. Each business is different, as is each web server. Configurations, setups, customizations, usage, and implementation speed all need to be considered when evaluating which CMS is truly right for your purpose.

Having someone at your side who has proven skills in PHP and MySQL programming will be absolutely essential to the success of your CMS. And, you will want modifications and additions along the way. Plan to spend at least $4,000 to $6,000 or more for implementation of either, whereas WordPress installations will be typically less in expense.

Consider using WordPress instead of Joomla! or Drupal for your main company website and blog, unless some user functionality is required that WordPress does not supply. It probably is your most logical choice for your entire website and CMS as well.

Managing a Membership Website

The hottest topic among Internet marketers for the past couple of years has been membership websites because of the lure of a term that's near and dear to every entrepreneurial heart: *recurring revenue.*

We all dream of having thousands of dollars added to our bank accounts each month without requiring additional effort on our part. Member-based websites can produce such a financial effect, although you should be aware that they are hardly an escape from continued effort.

Fortunately, membership sites have been around for many years, and they attract new members and retain current ones. The following sections explore these topics, as well as provide some initial steps to take.

Defining a true membership website

A membership website is one that allows and inspires website visitors to acquire a username and password to view protected content through the web. A member-based website doesn't always have to cost money to join.

Consider Yahoo! Groups. When you join a group, you become a member. You receive announcements whenever new content is added, and you're invited to share in resources provided to the group. The same principle applies to a true membership website, just on a larger scale.

Evaluating membership site types

The term *membership website* is often scary to some people and underestimated by others. Creating and maintaining a membership website can be the most complex or simplest process of your entire Internet marketing strategy, depending on what you want to feature and how you want the content to be accessed. Here are some types of membership websites to help you choose which one might be right for you:

+ **Adding a simple password-protected directory:** If you have a website of any kind right now, chances are you could have your webmaster or hosting company simply add a directory that's password protected to your account. Then, you could add new content to that directory and offer access to your customers or website visitors. In this event, every member would have the same username and password to access the password-protected area.

+ **Using a third-party–hosted membership system:** Premium Web Cart, — see Chapter 2 of this minibook — has its own self-contained members area system that is already integrated with its own shopping cart. Using an integrated system such as PWC is the fastest and least labor intensive method to starting a simple member-based website. Notice how simple and straightforward the look and feel are within PWC's members area, as shown in Figure 4-10. Take a test drive at www.premiumwebcart.com.

Figure 4-10:
The Premium Web Cart membership admin screen.

✦ **Using a self-hosted membership plug-in for WordPress:** The two primary competing plug-ins for WordPress-based membership websites are Digital Access Pass (DAP), at www.digitalaccesspass.com, and WishList, at www.wishlistproducts.com, but DAP seems to have pulled ahead in the features and functionality area as well as the quality of support and training.

✦ **Implementing aMember for custom membership functionality:** If your member site requires custom features beyond the normal supplying of content that can be provided by DAP or WishList, you need aMember software (www.amember.com). Such custom features might include setting up checklists where members can add information to their own account that tasks were completed on a certain date by a certain person. Maybe you want to add a forum that allows access to one level free of charge but then has a fee for a second level. Integrating systems is best accomplished with aMember.

No matter what route you take with a member-based website, you need to connect your shopping cart or other payment process with a payment gateway. That way, payments are authorized and deposited into your bank account. A good option is Authorize.Net (www.authorize.net), which has a monthly fee of $20 plus a small per-transaction fee of $0.10.

The secret to attracting members for a membership website and keeping them is to have an *anchor*. An anchor might be a monthly or weekly telecoaching program that's for members only. Maybe it's a set of tools that business owners use on a daily basis to implement and track their Internet marketing processes instead of trying to keep everything on Excel spreadsheets. Figure 4-11 shows an example from a membership area where clients can keep track of what steps they've taken with a variety of web-marketing tasks.

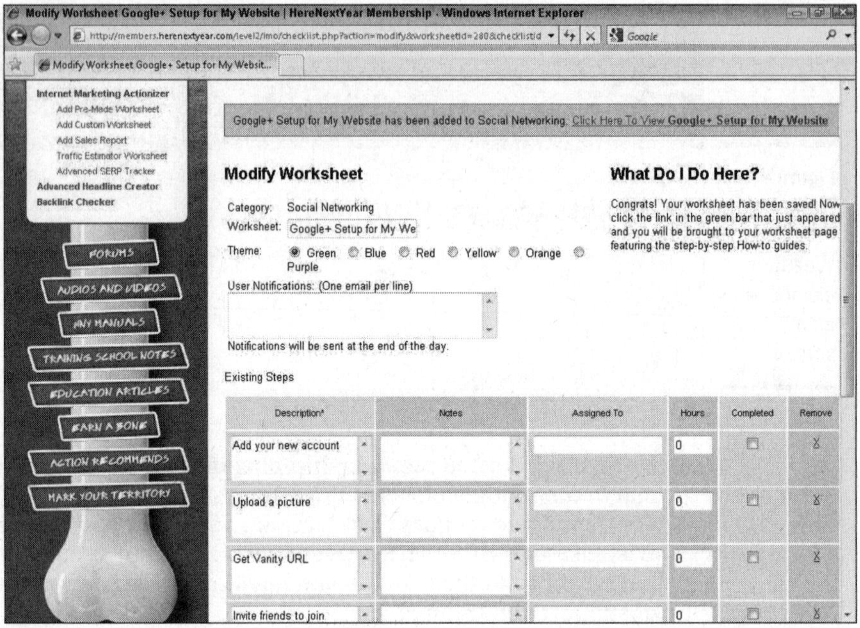

Figure 4-11: Attract members with an anchor.

Think of an anchor as being similar to website hosting. After you find a web-hosting company that works and doesn't go down all the time, you will keep your site hosted there until the end of time, right? That's an anchor. It doesn't matter what else is offered in the website membership area if you have an anchor that's valuable enough to your members. They'll keep using your system and paying you for years to come.

Calculating your revenue potential

Membership websites are cumulative. If you can keep your member retention high, your income will double or triple or grow by even more over time. Member sites that are promoted correctly have little problem getting 100 paying members within a month or two.

A few things need to be ironed out before you go live with your new member website, however. These include

✦ **Price:** How much will you charge for your member access? Most member websites have a free level and then two to five paid levels. Whatever price you offer for a member level per month should equate to more than 20 times the value over the course of a year. So, if you decide to charge $27 per month for your Level 2 membership, that would be $324 per year. Your value needs to be at least $6,000 over the course of the year for people to feel they're truly getting a good deal.

✦ **Involvement:** How involved do you want to be when it comes to adding new content and new features to your membership area? The average, moderately successful website will have new content added at least once weekly. That way, you can send an e-mail blast to your members telling them to log in to the membership area to access the new content.

You must stay in frequent contact with your members lest they forget about your membership program. Releasing new content that they don't have to pay for is a great reason to contact them. And, they'll appreciate that you're keeping them up to date.

✦ **Cost:** The average membership website takes about one quarter of one person's time to manage per week. If that person is just you, be careful to calculate how much revenue you must earn to make it worth your while. It won't be long before you'll want to bring in some help after you get some members.

Here's an example of how to calculate your revenue potential. Say that your membership fee is $27 for a low-cost member site (and it's very unusual to offer only a $27 member level). You have a high 30 percent churn rate of lost members and a very pessimistic projection for addition of new members. Still, with all those negatives, you could earn more than $34,000 per year. If you change the monthly fee from $27 to $79, you could earn over $100,000.

Most successful member programs have a lower level of pricing at anywhere between $5 and $30, a midrange price of $50 to $100, and a third level of pricing between $300 and $1,500 per month. Now you should be getting a feel for why membership sites are so tempting to business owners today.

Chapter 5: Creating Exceptional Copy That Sells

In This Chapter

✔ Writing clear, effective, and compelling copy for your website

✔ Using landing pages to drive sales

✔ Motivating customers to buy from you

*E*ven the prettiest website won't convert a single visitor to a customer unless you use well-written content to entice and inspire taking immediate action. Regrettably, lesser-quality content isn't typically the first thing on the chopping block when one tries to figure out why a website hasn't been earning its keep — but after you read this chapter, you'll understand why content should be one of the first things you examine closely for any improvement possible.

Fortunately, the Internet has been around for a while, so you can learn from others' experiences. You can follow proven strategies when it comes to writing content for your website. And, of course, you should avoid several taboos.

Understanding the Elements of Effective Website Copy

Everyone is a skeptic on the web. You've probably heard about — or maybe even experienced firsthand — some type of online credit card fraud. Or, maybe you know someone who bought a birthday present online, only to receive the package three weeks after the birthday (if at all).

As a website owner and producer of content, your responsibility is to prove to your visitors that you're worthy of earning their business. The following sections offer tips to help you evaluate current copy or write fresh copy that reassures visitors and helps turn them into customers.

Writing headlines with a hook

You have five seconds or less before a visitor to your website decides to take further action with you or your company. The first line of copy on your page needs to prove to your visitors that they arrived at the informational page they were looking for. A headline is the easiest way to accomplish this task.

A conversion rate is the percentage of website visitors that take some kind of action with you as opposed to leaving your website. This action can be a phone call, completing a contact form, walking into your retail store, or buying online through your shopping cart. Conversion rates can vary dramatically by making even a single change to the headline of a page.

A headline has one purpose: to get people to read more. To accomplish that, your headlines must

✦ Be intriguing and inviting

✦ Prove to your visitors that they're at the right place

Sometimes, accomplishing both of the preceding objectives in just a few words can be like two repelling magnets. People spend weeks and even months testing new headlines to get them just right.

Writing headlines can be the most challenging part of the copywriting process. Follow these steps to use a headline-writing tool to aid the process:

1. **Point your web browser to**

```
www.actionheadlinecreator.com
```

2. **To generate possible headlines, answer the four questions on the form and then click the Generate Headlines Now! button.**

The headlines generated appear in alphabetical order, as shown in Figure 5-1.

3. **Save the generated headlines for editing and future use by exporting them to a spreadsheet.**

Use a spreadsheet so you can keep track of when you test your headlines and the results.

Click the Download as CSV button, and then send the headlines to yourself or someone else by e-mail.

If you don't like any of the suggestions, you can always click the Clear! button, change the answers to the four questions, and rerun the report.

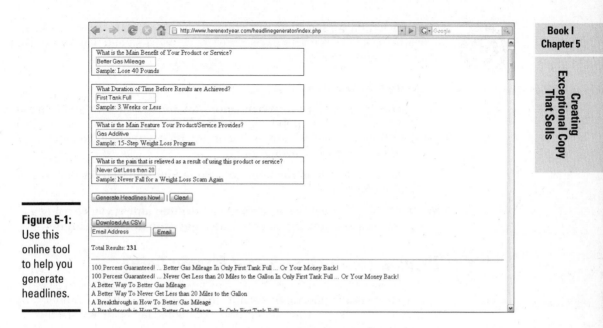

Figure 5-1:
Use this
online tool
to help you
generate
headlines.

4. **In your spreadsheet, tweak the words to fit.**

   One of the headlines the tool produced is *A Breakthrough in How to Save Gas . . . In Only in First Tank Full!* This suggestion is a good example of when you need to massage a headline that doesn't initially seem to be a good fit into something that works. You could change this headline to fit a possible promotion on a sales page in the following ways:

   - The first part of the headline, "A Breakthrough in How to Save Gas," isn't bad. But "A Breakthrough in Saving Gas" has a more fluid sound to it.

   - The second part needs more work. "In Only in" is not grammatically correct. So, that would have to go.

   - "In Only First Tank Full" doesn't sound right either. So, how about "See Results in the First Tank Full"?

   Your final headline might be, "A Breakthrough in Saving Gas . . . See Results in the First Tank Full!"

5. **To save your revised headlines for future use, choose File⇨Save, give your file a name, and then click OK.**

After you write your headline, remember to give it prominence and make it fit aesthetically on your web page. Here's how to format and place your main heading for maximize impact:

+ **Center the headline.**

+ **Put the headline in a different color than the rest of your text to make it stand out.** Red is a good color for headlines because it stops people in their tracks to read what is so important. Blue is another good color for headlines because of its authority.

+ **Make the font size of the headline two to four times larger than the rest of your text.**

+ **Don't use punctuation to conclude a headline unless you're using a question mark (um, if you're asking a question in your headline).**

Proving that you're a real human being

We buy things from people we know, like, and trust . . . and often even envy. Your website is an opportunity to start that relationship and then build upon it. Here are some ways to increase the human factor of any specific web page, or the website overall:

+ **Write from your heart, not from the dictionary.** For example, a CPA firm can take a dry sentence like this:

    We prepare individual, joint, and unincorporated small business tax returns.

    And personalize it, as follows:

    So many new clients would tell us their business and individual tax return horror stories with other CPA firms. We just knew we were really on to something special when they would thank us for making the process so easy.

+ **Add a good photo to your web page.** Adding a genuine and original photograph of yourself or your team to any website header or landing page turns a dry, faceless pile of words into a personal endorsement from you and can increase your opt-in and sales rates. Have a professional, studio-produced photo taken and get feedback from all your friends and family — you don't want to look too scary. If your picture captures the true essence of who you are, they'll tell you so. And, that's the picture to use for your website. Figure 5-2 shows a great example of an effective photo.

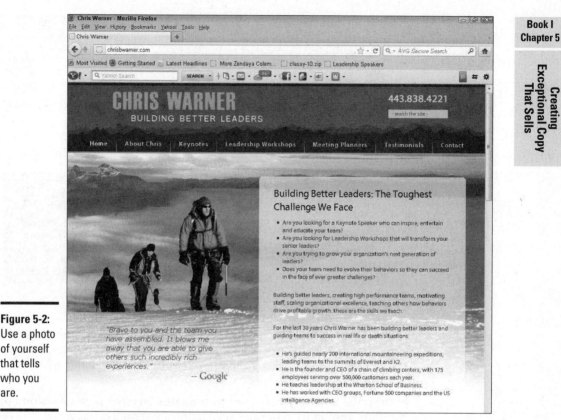

Figure 5-2:
Use a photo
of yourself
that tells
who you
are.

Courtesy of Chris Warner

TIP

✦ **Introduce yourself and your product with video or audio.** Video and audio are the highest forms of introduction available for placement on a website (see Figure 5-3). With today's tools, almost anyone can learn to create his or her own professional-looking videos from home for less than $1,000. At www.animalbehaviorassociates.com, you can find an example of a homemade video for a business that would've cost between $2,000 and $5,000 to produce in a studio with professional editors.

One of the most popular questions about audio and video is whether to begin the playback immediately when visitors land on the page or to give them the option to click a Play button. The answer, as you might have guessed, is to test your own results. (You test by using web analytics, the focus of Book III.) Try both ways by having your video start immediately for a couple of weeks and then having your video editor change the setting to force a playback button. If you have to pick one or the other and stick with it, have the automated playback begin immediately when visitors land on the page, but then offer a Stop button as well so that they can turn off the player if desired.

Figure 5-3:
Use video
to introduce
yourself on
a website.

✦ **Encourage contact by phone, e-mail, or live chat.** Welcoming communication builds visitor confidence and sets you apart from the rest of the many companies that use the web to avoid communicating with their customers.

✦ **Describe how you were once in the same position as your visitors by telling your story.** Consider this fictional example of a divorce attorney attempting to sell her services:

> *22 years ago, my high school marriage grew apart, only to land in divorce court with an attorney who had never been married and just didn't understand. I lost everything — including my dignity — and I vowed I would learn to fight for others to never let an experience like that happen to them. Now, with 18 years of experience in divorce law, I have a reputation for always . . .*

Good copy is all about getting people engaged so that they want to find out more about you.

✦ **Display your longevity and commitment to an industry.** Take a look at Isla Animals (www.islaanimals.org), a nonprofit animal rescue shelter. By looking at the pictures and exploring the site, it doesn't take long for you to realize that there is a real building with real people. With "Since December 1999" in the header (see Figure 5-4), you become convinced of its longevity as well. Everything about the website exudes a dedication to animal rescue.

Figure 5-4:
Earn trust by
displaying
dedication
to an
industry.

Proving your solution does what you say it will do

When it comes to writing promotional copy, there comes a point where you need to stop presenting more features and benefits and start proving that your offer solves the problem. Here are several methods for proving to your visitors that your product or service solves their problem:

✦ **Use testimonials in your website copy.** The best testimonial you can have on a website is a video of a customer telling the world how your product or service helped his specific situation. A recorded audio file is an adequate substitute. Printed testimonials are acceptable but are believable only if you can print the first and last names of the testimony provider, along with the city and state he or she lives in.

You must be given written authorization to use someone's full name and city and state residence for a testimonial!

When asking for a video or audio testimonial, you can help your customers decide what to say by giving them a checklist. You can use the following list for virtually any video or audio testimonial occasion and even try it yourself the next time you attend a seminar where testimonials are being taken onsite:

- Your name and website address

- Why you attended (or purchased a product)

- Your result or at least some bit of information you learned

- A strong recommendation for others in a similar position to attend the next time (or to buy now)

- Repeat your name and your website address

✦ **Provide links to letters of recommendation.** A three- or four-line testimonial is adequate, but getting a formally written letter of recommendation printed on your customer's letterhead with a signature of the person at the bottom is exceptional. When you receive such a letter, you will need to have it scanned. Save the scanned copy as a PDF or JPG image, upload it to your website, and add a link from within a page on your website to the document.

✦ **Share the fact that you've tried similar products.** You should always know your competition and the quality of product or service they are delivering. Buy as much as you can afford of your competitors' products so that you can speak wisely about how your offer fills gaps that the other products do not address. Most importantly, you must mention on your page that you're familiar with similar products but that certain elements of your product are what really set you apart from the rest. Here's an example:

> *Now, I've personally spent more than $20,000 out of my own pocket buying products that claimed I would learn how to speak 2nd-year college-level Spanish in 30 days. None of them worked because none of them offered V.R.I., my patent-pending, one-of-a-kind Voice Recognition Interpreter tool, where the automated attendant automatically tells you how to correct a sentence before you've even completed one! I can tell you for certain that nowhere else can you find this product anywhere on the market today, and soon it will change the way people learn languages forever!*

✦ **Show that no competing product is as easy to use.** The last thing people want is to learn something difficult or to implement something that takes time to figure out. We want speed of implementation and speed of results. Convince your prospective customer that your solution is simple. And, if it's not simple, you need to work on its methodology so that it *is* simple.

Continuing with the Spanish training example, you could use verbiage like this to describe the ease of use:

> *Learning a foreign language is known as one of the most difficult things to do, especially as an adult. I discovered why this was true after trying every Spanish CD and book I could find. When I created this product,*

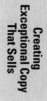

it was really for myself first. I needed a Spanish-learning process that was so easy that my mother at age 73 could figure it out! And, you know what? My mother and I have complete conversations today . . . in Spanish! She just loaded the CD into her computer and pressed the Play button. That was it. No manuals. No complex reading or study. It was all right there on her computer.

Don't invite your visitors to "check out the competition" — because they will! In the automotive sales business, salespeople will do anything they can to get you to buy their car while you're on the lot, because they know that after you leave, there is a slim chance you will return to buy their car.

✦ **Describe the product's popularity.** We all like to be part of something that's popular, and we shy away from being the first to experience something new.

Include a paragraph in your website copy that suggests to readers that they're really missing out on something and that your product is used by either a large number or a wide variety of people. For example:

Last month alone, more than 350 people made the choice to learn Spanish in 30 days or less using my system.

The objective of conveying your popularity is not to lie! Never lie to your audience. You don't need to fabricate numbers to be seen as popular, even if your business is in the start-up phase. Simply identify something about your business that really is popular and talk about it. Here are some examples — just add your own number and change the topic to be more descriptive of your business:

Of the more than 100 people I talked to last month who had attempted to learn Spanish through some other means, only 2 reported that the system they tried had worked.

100 people who started learning Spanish using my product last month can't be wrong.

Of the last 100 people who used my learning Spanish system, the success rate has been a whopping 94%!

Providing clear and easy calls to action

How many websites have you visited where you find yourself pulling out your credit card ready to buy, but the sales page never gives you a link or an Add to Cart button to click? Make it easy for your visitors to take the next step with you:

✦ **Display a phone number in plain view on every page of your website.**

✦ **Use different sizes of both links and buttons throughout your copy to take customers to order forms.**

✦ **Test different text on buttons and links, and then monitor which brings the best conversion rate.**

You have two ways to test the effectiveness of links and buttons on a sales page. First, you can use Google Analytics, as further described in Book III, to track the exact path a website visitor takes through your website from the page he enters through the entire ordering system. The other way is by split testing (or A/B testing) during a Google AdWords campaign, as described in Book IV, Chapter 4.

✦ **Keep your text links blue and underlined.** People are used to clicking links that are traditionally formatted as blue and underlined. Use a variety of graphic images to direct your visitors what to do next. See Chapter 3 of this minibook for more information on design.

✦ **Try providing a form at the end of your copy instead of links to other pages.** The less you force people to click things to get to the next step, the more chance you have of them taking that next step.

✦ **Reduce the number of distractions.** For other pages of your site, it's natural to offer navigation buttons, special offers on a variety of products, and other news items. When it comes to a sales page, though, reduce the distractions so that a visitor isn't tempted to deviate from the buying process.

For an effective result, add a red border around your Buy Now buttons. Then add an effect where the red border turns green when you mouse over the button. Your conversion rates will increase. That just goes to show that the most minute changes to your sales page can make a difference in your sales outcome.

Driving Sales with Landing Pages

Whether your visitors find you through search engines or banner ads, or by typing your website address into their web browser, the first page of your site that people see is known as the *landing page*. If your landing page copy isn't exactly what your visitors are looking for, they will leave your site and search for someone else's landing page that offers more relevant results.

The following sections introduce you to three of the most popular types of landing pages used to cast a large net, capture a wide range of visitors, and/ or receive targeted traffic — educational content pages, squeeze pages, and sales pages.

Create topic-specific pages throughout your website and drive traffic to those subsequent pages instead of trying to bring in all your traffic through the homepage. When a visitor lands on your homepage, too many choices are usually available. The visitor doesn't typically see what he was looking for within a few seconds and just clicks the Back button.

Creating educational content pages

Because most people search the Internet for answers to specific problems, create pages on your website to educate people on those issues. These *educational content pages* can develop into dozens, or even hundreds or thousands, in number for any website. Figure 5-5 shows an example of an educational content page.

Figure 5-5: Educational content pages drive more traffic to your website.

Educational content pages are

+ Fast and easy to create because they are short.

+ Enjoyable to read because they focus on one, specific topic.

+ Attractive to search engines because they are heavily optimized for specific keywords related to the problems people are searching to solve.

+ An opportunity to tell visitors that more is involved with the solution and that you have just the product or service to suggest.

+ One of the least-expensive ways to cast a large net to attract a wide variety of visitors in a short amount of time.

The following steps outline key tasks for a successful educational content page. When you create your pages, make sure to follow all the steps:

1. **Research where the traffic is.**

Before you write an educational content page, or plan to revise an existing one, find out what exact phrases people are searching for related to the topic you want to write about. Google includes a keyword search tool as part of its AdWords software (see Figure 5-6).

Your time is much better used by writing content pages for what people are searching for already rather than coming up with your own topics and hoping people somehow find them. See Book III for more details on keyword research.

Be sure to include the search phrases you find, as follows:

• *Create a headline that begins with the keywords people are searching for.*

• *Use the exact keyword phrase people are searching for when you give your content page a title and filename for basic search engine optimization standards.*

In Book II, you can find more detailed help with search engine optimization.

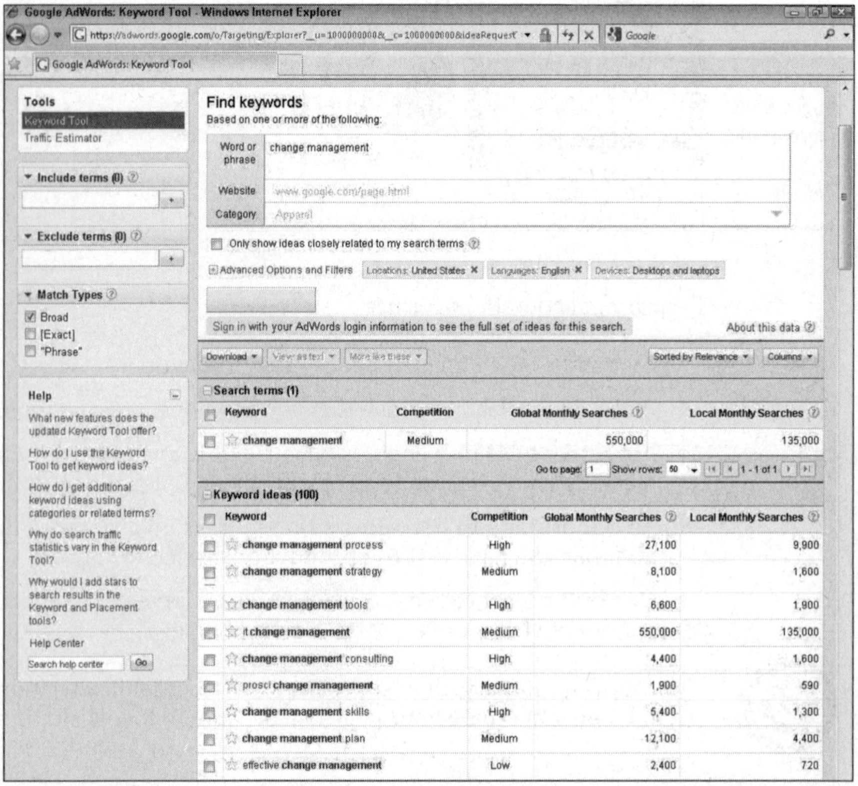

Figure 5-6:
Google's
keyword
search tool.

2. **Introduce the problem.**

   A paragraph that's three to ten sentences long usually works well.

3. **Suggest what the reader can do right now on his own to work toward a solution.**

   Add three to five bullet points or numbered steps. Never use only one suggestion, or two or four suggestions (people respond better to odd numbers).

4. **Add a summary paragraph after you have completed the bullet point section of your content page.**

   Use no more than four or five sentences.

5. **Explain how you can help with the problem.**

   This goes beyond what the reader can do and involves either a product you offer or a service you provide.

6. **Introduce yourself.**

   Write a three- to five-sentence signature line that introduces you to the reader more formally.

7. **Link to your content pages on other pages of your website.**

   You want visitors and search engine spiders to find the page. When you're creating these links, be sure to include a link to the content page on both your traditional site map and Google Sitemap areas. (See the following sidebar for details on site maps versus Google Sitemaps.)

TECHNICAL STUFF

The benefits of site maps

A "traditional" site map is a page of your website that was created only for the purpose of displaying links to all main sections of your website. You may have stumbled onto a site map page in the past; usually links to a site map appear at the bottom of the page. The idea with a site map used to be to allow a simple way for visitors to find anything on the website if they could not find the topic through the standard navigation buttons and links. But, the site map has another purpose, which is to be an easy way for search engines to find all your important pages and get them added to their search engine index. Site map pages almost never have fancy graphics for the links, but have text-only links, thereby making it easy for the search engines to crawl through the site.

A Google Sitemap is a little different: It's Google's way of keeping in direct contact with your site so that it knows immediately of any changes to your website. When you add a new page or change an existing page, adding a Google Sitemap helps to alert Google so that indexing of those new or changed pages can update its list more quickly. More on traditional site maps and Google Sitemaps is provided in Book II, which covers search engine optimization.

Don't confuse educational content pages with article pages. An *article* is something you usually write to be displayed on someone else's website. Article pages are typically longer than 400–600 words and often reference other websites or sources. Content pages are very raw and to the point, and are designed to be showcased only on your website.

Search engines have been working on reducing the amount of duplicate content on the Internet. Resist the temptation to duplicate your content pages and change only a few words on each page in the hopes of getting more search engine visitors just because you have more pages online.

Building your opt-in e-mail list with squeeze pages

Squeeze pages are short and simple pages that introduce additional content available to readers — but only if they're willing to register by providing an e-mail address. Figure 5-7 displays a squeeze page.

A squeeze page is a great way to accept targeted traffic for a very specific topic of interest and inspire visitors to register to be on your mailing list. Commonly, more than 20 percent of your first-time visitors to a squeeze page will complete and submit the opt-in form. Some points to keep in mind while creating a squeeze page include the following:

✦ **Great headlines are critical.** Going without a headline on a squeeze page or having one displayed that's not relevant to the topic is a traffic killer. See the section "Writing headlines with a hook," earlier in this chapter.

✦ **Show a good photo of yourself.** Conversion rates for a squeeze page always increase when you have a good photo of yourself (or whoever is writing to the visitor). See the section "Proving that you're a real human being," earlier in this chapter, for tips on including a photo.

✦ **Write as if you're talking to someone one on one.** Squeeze pages are very personal. Take away all the corporate flair, and just talk to your visitors as if they're right in front of you.

✦ **List the benefits of why your visitors should opt in to your list.** What will they get exactly, and why is it worth giving up their e-mail address to receive?

✦ **Promise to give away something after they do sign up.** This could be a free report, e-course, or consult sound files; or a coupon. Be creative. When you provide something of true value for free, an impressed subscriber will consider more strongly that your for-pay offer must have exceptional value as well.

✦ **Keep your subscription form to two fields — Name and E-mail Address:** Every additional field beyond those two will reduce your number of opt-ins substantially.

Figure 5-7:
Squeeze
pages
convert
more visitors
to opt-in
subscribers
than the
homepage
does.

The term *opt in* is a rather one-sided agreement. The website visitor agrees to give you an e-mail address so that he can get exactly what you were offering for free. It does not give you the permission to mercilessly barrage the subscriber with e-mails day and night until the end of time. In fact, think of every e-mail you send to your list to be like a fresh batch of chocolate cookies. If it doesn't taste great every time, the subscriber can unsubscribe anytime.

Book V, Chapter 3 offers more tips for building your e-mail list.

Providing all the facts through sales pages

A *sales page* serves three purposes:

+ To educate the visitor with the facts about a specific product, service, or event

+ To give the reader enough facts to make an informed buying decision

+ To provide the mechanism to actually take the next step in the buying process

Whereas educational content pages teach and squeeze pages build your list, sales pages are designed to convert readers into paying customers. Figure 5-8 shows a popular online training workshop sales page.

Sales pages come in a variety of shapes and sizes, and no general rule exists for how long or short a page should be for your particular product. The most important rule is to give just enough information to allow someone to make an educated decision. One word more is too much, and one word less is not enough.

Provide more information about your product as the price rises. Don't expect to sell a $100,000 diamond with three bullet points of text and a price. Conversely, you probably don't need a 20,000-word sales page to sell a $17 e-book. Also consider adding more details when you expect more time from your customer. If you expect a customer to be away from his family for a few days for a conference, that requires more information than a one-hour online seminar.

Figure 5-8: Product sales pages need to offer answers to all the questions people ask before making an informed decision.

Whether long or short, all good Internet sales pages have the following components:

✦ A main headline

✦ A description of the problem and why it's important to have the problem solved or alleviated

✦ Accurate and descriptive content to describe exactly how your product or service will solve the problem

✦ Proof that the item does what you claim or is what it appears to be

✦ A way to take immediate action, whether by buying online or by picking up the phone to call

The trickiest thing about a sales page is the order in which to display those five elements. To make things easier, you can follow the C.O.N.V.E.R.T. M.E. formula, the topic of the next section.

Writing Copy That Sells, Using the C.O.N.V.E.R.T. M.E. Formula

When someone buys something online, it's known as a *conversion* because the purchaser *converted* from a visitor to a paying customer. Only after you have proven yourself to your visitors can you focus on converting visitors to paying customers.

The following sections outline a step-by-step process that you can work through to create website copy that converts visitors to customers. The first letter of each step (and subsequent section) works as a mnemonic device to spell *c-o-n-v-e-r-t m-e* to help you remember the steps in the process. The following steps summarize the nine steps in the C.O.N.V.E.R.T. M.E. formula:

1. **Captivate visitors.**

    Write a headline with a hook.

2. **Offer just one testimonial.**

    Place one testimonial under the headline.

3. **Now address your visitors.**

    Use typical, letter-style formatting.

4. **Validate some facts.**

    Show industry percentages to reinforce the problem.

5. **E**xpose your solution.

   Clearly define your problem solver and describe how it works.

6. **R**ecapture attention.

   Don't let visitors leave just because you unveiled the secret.

7. **T**est for action.

   Determine whether they're ready to buy right now.

8. **M**otivate with value and urgency.

   "But wait!" It's for real!

9. **E**nergize visitors to buy.

   Give assurance that your offer really is a good deal.

Captivate visitors with a headline that hooks

Whoever wrote the suggestion that headlines should be short is probably broke. The secret to a good or bad headline is testing, not the number of words. You must test headlines for every page of your website where a product is sold or where someone is encouraged to take action of some kind, be it by phone, e-mail, chat, or completing a contact form. Even test headlines for educational content pages!

To test headlines, you need to watch your bounce rates. [A *bounce rate* is the percentage of overall visitors who visit the page on your website and immediately leave.] You can tell what your bounce rate is by looking at your visitation statistics logs within Google Analytics, which display the overall percentage of visitors who have left your site immediately, or under just a few seconds, on any particular page of your website. When you make a single change to your headline and then see your bounce rate percentage drop after a few days, you know you've made a better headline. Google Analytics is further described in Book III.

See the section "Writing headlines with a hook," earlier in this chapter, for tips on writing headlines.

Offer reinforcement of your headline

Not too many things will generate interest and hope that a solution is possible better than a well-planned testimonial. Pick one of your best and add the testimonial right under the headline that you added to your site in the preceding section. You can also use a subheadline or an interesting statistic to reinforce your headline.

TIP

Even better than just choosing what you feel is your best testimonial would be an endorsement from a celebrity or a recognized authority in your field. You can begin the process of getting a celebrity endorsement by contacting his or her agent or management company and offering to send your product for free evaluation.

Now address your visitors personally

A personalized letter allows you to have a conversation with a reader as if you're on the phone with each other. For example, Figure 5-9 shows how you can quickly engage a reader by addressing her personally with a letter on your website. Notice how right after the Dear Fellow Mom salutation, you see a bullet point list of issues that moms face daily. This list builds rapport with the reader and gets her to the next stage, where you are to validate some facts.

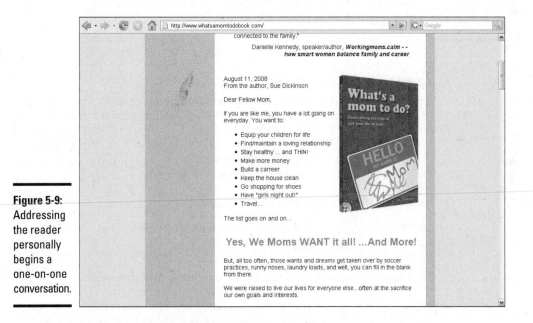

Figure 5-9: Addressing the reader personally begins a one-on-one conversation.

Validate some facts

Before you go deeper into the components of the actual solution, attempt to make a bond with a wide variety of people who might be experiencing the issue you can resolve for them. This is accomplished by adding some factual statistics that address those groups. Whenever possible, those facts and figures should be based on what people want most:

- More money
- More time
- Something fast
- Something easy

Another way to accomplish the same task is to ask questions (see Figure 5-10). The three questions should keep the reader reading for a solution to his problem.

Figure 5-10: Asking questions makes readers stop and think.

> Are you a business owner who is...
>
> › About to miss payroll because you **don't have enough money** in your bank account?
> › Putting expansion of your business on hold due to **lack of funding** for growth?
> › Missing out on what could be the transaction of a lifetime because you **couldn't get your hands on funding** to close the deal?

Expose your solution

Now it's time to rope in the visitors after they read the facts and figures by exposing exactly what your solution is. What kind of product or service are you offering? Use solution phrases to suggest an answer that is going to be unveiled shortly. Then, let your visitors know precisely what it is you're going to provide to them and what problems you will help them solve. For example, you can start your sentences with these:

- *That's Exactly Why I Decided to Create . . .*
- *And, Just When You Thought There Was No Solution . . .*
- *This New Opportunity Will . . .*

These are just a few examples of how solution sentences begin.

Be prepared to spend just as much time (if not more) creating and testing the wording of these solution statements as you will spend creating a captivating headline. The extra effort is worth it!

List your benefits clearly with bullet points and highlighting to make them easy to scan because most people won't read them word for word. Start each benefit statement with action verbs that at have energy and enthusiasm and that encourage people to keep reading. For a list of more than 360 action verbs, visit http://www.websitewaves.com/362-verbs-that-sell-when-writing-copy-for-your-website.html

Recapture visitors' attention

Solution sentences and benefits lists can get pretty long sometimes. The fact that some people scan through sales pages differently than others comes into play here. Maybe your reader skipped over the facts and figures area but started to read some of the benefits. Or, maybe the bullet points were skipped all together.

After you expose your solutions, it's time to recapture the attention of your visitors, as shown in Figure 5-11. This can be done in several ways, but a good strategy is to build more rapport with your visitor.

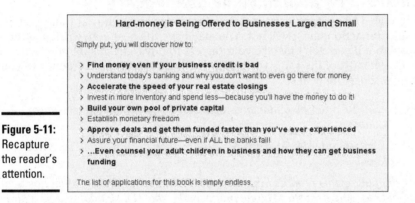

Figure 5-11: Recapture the reader's attention.

> **Hard-money is Being Offered to Businesses Large and Small**
>
> Simply put, you will discover how to:
>
> > **Find money even if your business credit is bad**
> > Understand today's banking and why you don't want to even go there for money
> > **Accelerate the speed of your real estate closings**
> > Invest in more inventory and spend less—because you'll have the money to do it!
> > **Build your own pool of private capital**
> > Establish monetary freedom
> > **Approve deals and get them funded faster than you've ever experienced**
> > Assure your financial future—even if ALL the banks fail!
> > **...Even counsel your adult children in business and how they can get business funding**
>
> The list of applications for this book is simply endless.

The phrase *Hard Money Is Being Offered to Businesses Large and Small* brings the reader back. The next few sentences start to recapture the attention of the reader. By showing part of the table of contents for the book and turning them into benefit statements, you build additional interest.

Test for action

At this point, you will have some readers who are convinced they should give your product or service a try. They just need one last nudge.

One of the best ways to get people over the hump of making a decision to take action with you, whether by calling you on the phone, submitting a contact form, or making an online purchase, is to offer more testimonials. Hopefully, one of the testimonials will resonate with the reader as someone else having been in a similar situation where his problem was solved, and a purchase may result from that single testimonial. Then, use a subheadline format to give a strong suggestion to buy right now.

- ✦ If you want a visitor to click a link to buy, suggest it like this:

    Buy Now or *Order Now*

- ✦ If you want the visitor to visit another page to learn more about dog food, tell her to click a link as follows:

    Learn more about dog food.

- ✦ If you want the visitor to call you right now, tell her specifically to

    Pick up the phone right now and call 800-555-1212 for your special . . .

Motivate by adding value and urgency

Although a few potential customers might be willing to buy at that point of testing for action, most will not. You may have the best copywriting in the world, but if you don't inspire your buyers to buy right this minute, you won't get most of the sales you should've closed. Add some urgency to your copy to close the deal.

- ✦ *You MUST order by midnight tonight because this item will no longer be available.*

- ✦ *You MUST order by Saturday because by then the event will surely be sold out.*

- ✦ *I'm pulling this product from the website tomorrow, and it will not be available for sale as a stand-alone product after that. I'll be adding it as a part of a bigger package, which will be available at a higher price next month.*

- ✦ *I can only provide technical support for this software for the next 25 people who order right away.*

- ✦ *Only 14 of these are left in stock. You must order now or risk never seeing an offer like this again!*

- ✦ *Rest assured there is a 90-day money-back guarantee.*

Energize visitors to buy

At this point, you have tested for action and provided all the motivation possible by adding value to the sale. Wrap things up and encourage your visitors to buy.

- ✦ Suggest a specific action again, such as *Click Here to Buy Online Now* or *Call This Number Now.*

- ✦ Sign your name or use your initials.

    For your own security, use a different signature than you would on a personal check.

✦ Add three postscript (P.S.) statements.

People respond better when things are presented in threes.

Some visitors will completely bypass everything you write in a sales letter only to look at the P.S. statements at the end. Use this format to capitalize on this fact:

✦ **P.S.:** Your statement No. 1

✦ **P.P.S.:** Your statement No. 2

Make this one a powerful reminder of the most important benefits.

✦ **P.P.P.S.:** Your statement No. 3

Then provide one final action statement or the order link.

If you sell a product online, your merchant account provider will probably require that you have a Terms of Use page and also a privacy statement. Go the extra step and provide a Disclaimer page, especially if your product or service has the potential of improving one's financial or health status.

Fear of being too wordy is very common. Not every sales page needs to have every component. Your conversion rates may increase if you do not have your signature or P.S. statements. Maybe you need two lists of benefit statements to make more sales. Continuous monitoring and testing are required to maximize your sales potential on the Internet.

Chapter 6: Lead-Generation for Business Growth

In This Chapter

✔ Setting up ways prospects can contact you through the web

✔ Capturing visitors even if they visit your website and don't buy

✔ Using multiple social networks to fuel your sales pipeline

*Y*our website is the dominant online tool for generating business leads. All your online marketing efforts should be with the intent to draw targeted leads to your website. After he arrives there, you want the visitor to buy what you're selling online or pick up the phone and call you with questions. Roughly 96 percent of those visitors will do neither!

This chapter is devoted to weeding out the chaff and capturing targeted leads. First you go through a series of steps to set up lead-capturing components on your website. Then you find specific traffic- building tips for acquiring those leads.

Perfecting Your Form

If you've ever added your name and e-mail address to a page on a website, you have experienced using a form. You probably also know how frustrating it can be to complete a form and submit it only to be met with an error page, realizing that your form submission didn't work! Web forms have been an integral part of website functionality since even before the first company website went live — for good reason, too. Forms allow visitors to do things, such as make contact with the website owner, opt in to a newsletter, comment on a blog post, or tell friends about a website they should become familiar with. The following sections cover all these functions in more detail.

Choosing the right contact form

Having a contact form on your website is quite possibly the most important utility your website will ever have. Positioned correctly, a contact form can save a sale from being lost or perhaps inspire someone to make contact with you for a vital question. Plus, if your e-mail goes down, a form can be set up to write the contents to a backup file. Figure 6-1 shows a typical contact form.

Figure 6-1:
A contact
form.

Every good contact form has five key components:

+ **Form field headings:** Be very descriptive with your form field headings. Rather than just using *E-mail* to identify that you want the visitor to add her e-mail address in a particular form field, be specific. For example, *Add Your Primary E-Mail Address Here.*

+ **Form fields:** The actual form fields can be made easily within most any content management system (CMS) that allows you to edit HTML, such as WordPress, Joomla!, or Drupal. They should be either to the right of each form heading or directly below it.

Keep the number of fields very limited for a contact form. If you try to get your visitors' life history in a single form submission, they will almost surely not complete the form. Most newsletter opt-in forms display only a first name and an e-mail address on a website so that the sign-up process is fast. Think of a contact form as being similar to a newsletter opt-in form, but do provide a larger text box for comments or a question in addition to the fields for name and e-mail address.

+ **Submit button:** Using the word *Submit* on a submit button isn't very inviting or engaging to a potential lead. But, submit buttons are easy to change. So, test some different wording, such as

   • *Please Respond Quickly*

   • *Tell Me More!*

   • *Yes! I Want to Know*

✦ **Backup file:** E-mail is getting increasingly unreliable. Never trust precious leads to only arrive in your inbox by e-mail. Your form contents can be set up to write to a data file that you can access daily.

✦ **Form-processing program:** This piece of the puzzle makes the form do what you want it to do when a visitor clicks that all-important Submit button.

A form-processing program can come in different shapes:

✦ **WordPress plug-in:** Clearly the simplest, cheapest, and probably the most popular method today of including a form on your website is with a free open source plug-in for WordPress. You can find many free WordPress plug-ins for forms processing.

✦ **Custom form-processing program:** Most web programmers (and many designers) can quickly create a simple custom form program for you in less than an hour.

Before contracting a programmer to create a custom program for you, find out from your website-hosting company whether your web server is using Linux or Windows. This will be the first question a programmer will ask to help determine which programming language to use when creating your form processor (typically PHP or ASP).

✦ **Freeware:** These small programs are written by programmers looking for exposure by offering various programs for the web, including form processing. Be aware that you will often need to customize the programs on your own to match your website. PHP JunkYard (www.phpjunkyard.com) is a good resource for such programs.

✦ **Third-party forms processors:** If you're not a programmer and don't have access to one, consider employing a company that allows you to produce and manage your own forms. Wufoo (www.wufoo.com) offers such a service with which you specify how your form looks and operates within its web-based system. Simply copy the code that Wufoo provides and then paste it into any page of your website where a form is desired. Wufoo can be used for a variety of forms, not only contact forms.

Creating an opt-in offer form

When you opt in through a form on a site, you choose (of your own free will) to receive more information about something. An opt-in form is a bit different than a contact form: A contact form is meant to initiate one-on-one conversation, whereas an opt-in form promises content of value. Here are some examples of opt-in forms:

✦ **Newsletter subscription form:** Probably the most common of all the opt-in forms on the web is the subscription to a free newsletter, such as the one shown in Figure 6-2.

Figure 6-2:
A newsletter
opt-in form.

An opt-in offer

TIP

Including an opt-in form in a prominent place on every page of your web-site is entirely acceptable and encouraged. After all, it's a safe bet that more than 95 percent of your visitors will *not* buy your product or call you on the phone for more details, no matter how good of a copywriter you are. But, they might just have enough interest to opt in to get to know you first.

✦ **Free white paper:** Newsletters are good. But, they must showcase extreme value like Author U's "The Resource" (refer to Figure 6-2) if you ever want to achieve high opt-in rates. Simply displaying "Sign up for my newsletter" doesn't cut it anymore. For most website owners, it's easier and more profitable to create a high-impact white paper to entice visitors to opt in.

For every 100 people who visit 101TrafficMethods.com, 10–20 of those visitors opt in to receive the white paper "101 Realistic Ways to Get More Web Site Traffic." Why is it in such high demand? Because it appeals to a wide audience. After all, who doesn't want to get more traffic to his website? The other reason is the staggering number 101. Most people can't come up with more than 10 or 15 ways to get traffic to a website. But 101? That's just crazy! People sign up for it just to see whether 101 methods are really available.

Each traffic method is also ranked by cost, ease of implementation, speed of setup and expected ROI, so the white paper goes above and beyond most people's expectations.

What white paper can you come up with that appeals to a wide audience, has the component of being staggering or alarming, and surprises new subscribers with unexpected high quality? This simple addition to your website could increase your lead generation from the Internet by 5–25 percent! Don't overlook this powerful tool.

✦ **Free e-course registration:** Use sequential autoresponder software, like what AWeber Communications (www.aweber.com) or Premium Web Cart (www.premiumwebcart.com) offers. With this kind of software, you can assemble a series of e-mails once, in a course format, to be delivered every day, every other day, once weekly, or virtually in any combination, in the same order, for each person who signs up.

✦ **Squeeze pages:** When you land on a website where the only action you can take is to add your name and e-mail address, you are being "squeezed" into opting in to receive more information. *Squeeze pages* — commonly used to promote conferences and higher-ticket items — are where you must opt in to gain access to a large amount of detail. Online, visit www.startawebsitedesignbusiness.com to see how this site "squeezes" you into applying for a free, five-day recorded e-course. You find more about squeeze pages in Chapter 5 of this minibook.

Considering Online Chat

When people want support, they generally don't like to wait for e-mail. The answer is online chat, which is increasing in popularity every year. Figure 6-3 shows an online chat option offered on a website.

If you're looking to add online chat to your site, here are the general steps to follow:

1. **Find an online chat provider.**

   Try Provide Support (www.providesupport.com), which offers easy customizability and supports its product through online chat, of course. Or search online for *free online chat software* for other options.

2. **Set up your account.**

   Including the following items as you set up your account can make your online chat feature truly helpful as a lead generator and customer service tool:

   • *Craft a description page* that details exactly what online chat is (because most people haven't used the feature yet and might mistake the phrase *online chat* as being something more of an "adult" chat room!).

- *Customize your graphic header* to look like the rest of your website.

- *Develop a custom exit survey* for instant feedback and gaining list subscribers.

- *Create a mechanism for chatters* to have the entire conversation e-mailed to them for reference.

Figure 6-3:
This website offers an online chat.

Chat online with customers.

3. **Add the code to your website.**

   For every page of your website, adding an online chat image is a simple copy-and-paste process. You can also easily copy the provided HTML code produced by the chat software and e-mail it to your designer or assistant to add to your pages for you.

4. **Monitor your computer.**

   When a website visitor lands on your website and chooses to chat with you using Provide Support's chat software, the sound of a phone ringing will emanate from your computer speakers. Click the Accept Call button, and you're ready to answer your visitor's question! You can see a how a chat begins in Figure 6-4.

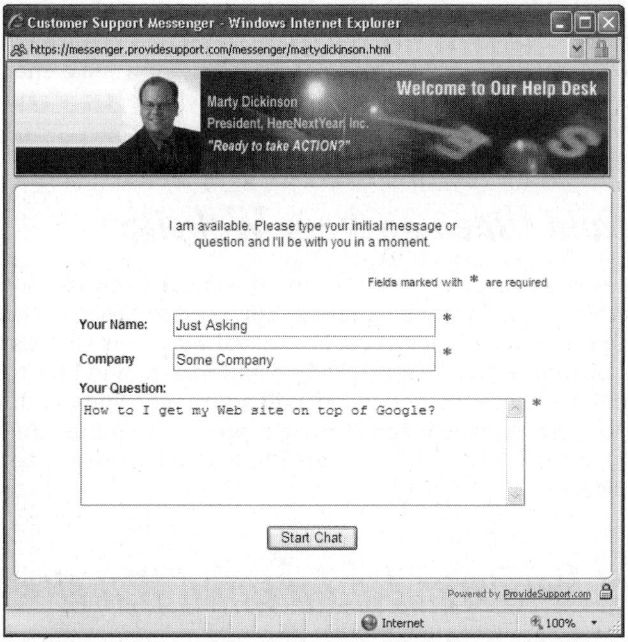

Figure 6-4:
Chat online
with a
visitor.

You can be chatting with five, ten, or potentially more prospects or customers all at the same time! How's *that* for efficiency?

5. Gain valuable user behavior information about your visitors.

Sure, Google Analytics can track the path of a website visitor through your website, but only an online chat system can allow you to actually watch a visitor migrate through your pages in real time.

One of the most important benefits of watching your visitors travel through your website in real time is to discover possible reasons why they're leaving without taking further action with you. For example, if someone spends, say, 20 seconds on the first page he sees on your website, then a full minute on the second page after he clicks a link, then only a few seconds on the third page before exiting your website, it's nothing to be alarmed about. But, if the next 30 visitors do the same thing, you'd better make a quick change to the third page because you're losing visitors!

If you're bold, you can even call out to your visitors and ask whether they have any questions about the page they're reading at that particular time!

You must be very careful about calling out to a website visitor before he chooses to chat with you! People are so used to being anonymous in their web travels that it easily freaks them out when a chat window interrupts their reading. Use this feature with extreme caution and social grace, or you will lose that visitor forever.

Using Audio and Video on Your Website

Today's Internet is too competitive to rely on written words alone to earn the trust of prospects and customers. You need to take the next step and differentiate yourself by being vocal and visual with your visitors through the use of audio and video. You can and should understand how to buy the right equipment, record audio and video, edit your recordings, and post the files to your website. All you need is the right process to follow, and a willingness to get involved. See Book VI, Chapter 7 to find out how to shoot, edit, and upload video.

Mining Social Networks for Targeted Website Traffic

Five years ago, visitors would come to your website and buy something or attempt to contact you. Now, they visit your website and then visit your social networks. If they like what they see in your social participation, they'll "Like" your Facebook Page, "follow" you on Twitter, or connect with you on LinkedIn or Google+. Then, they'll return to your website to take further action with you.

If your website does not feature links or buttons to the popular social networks, you are simply leaving money on the table!

But your website is only the beginning. You can use the social networks to mine for leads.

✦ **Twitter:** Search people's bios for your targeted keywords on Twellow. com (see Figure 6-5), and then create a Twitter list for easy monitoring. Make it a daily practice to add a few new potential lead sources to your Twitter list and then monitor your lists. When someone on your list makes a tweet that interests you, simply reply to the tweet and begin the conversation.

✦ **LinkedIn:** Join at least ten groups and participate in at least one discussion per day. Consider what groups your target audience might be a part of, search for those groups by keyword phrase as shown in Figure 6-6, and then join the groups.

Figure 6-5:
Searching
Twitter
bios using
Twellow.

Figure 6-6:
Finding
groups on
LinkedIn.

LinkedIn Answers is a great way for people to ask a question to a large number of people without formally joining a group. Your objective is to show your expertise by answering people's questions.

Be careful to not be too salesy in the LinkedIn discussion areas, as you could be reported as an abuser of the system. If enough people make the same claim, you could get locked out of your LinkedIn account. Of course, your main objective is to get your website in front of all those perusing eyes. Just be selective with how often and in what situations you suggest that people visit your website.

The web is a great place to become known as an industry expert in a very short amount of time. People want to follow industry leaders by joining their list, following them on social networks, and buying products they're selling. Participating in discussion centers like LinkedIn's Answers area is a great way to showcase your knowledge and display your willingness to help.

✦ **Facebook:** This is where you have the highest potential of establishing a meaningful, one-on-one dialogue with a new contact. But, the real key is using the messages and online chat features to take your connection to the next level.

✦ **Google+:** Google+ (also known as Google Plus or simply G+) is directly tied to Google search results. Use Google+ properly, and you could see each and every page or post to your website appearing on Google's organic search in as little as 5 seconds!

Book VII talks more about how to use the various social networks for marketing potential.

Chapter 7: Getting Help with Your Web Presence

In This Chapter

✔ Identifying Internet tasks worth paying for

✔ Finding the right people to help

✔ Assuring that you get what you pay for

✔ Staying in control of it all

*I*f you are feeling a bit overwhelmed with all the steps to follow and tricks and tactics to try while reading this book, try to relax. This is the chapter that will bring you hope and direction in finding help without spending too much too soon. One of the greatest truths of the Internet is that you can start very small, spend just a little, and allow your business to grow steadily and pay for its own growth over time. You get to choose which pieces of the process you want to accomplish on your own versus those functions that are better left to a hired hand (or two).

The struggling economy has forced virtually all Internet marketing services to be commoditized. Tasks that used to be sold for $1,000 or more are now available, for yes, as little as $5! See Fiverr a bit later in this chapter. The key is to understand that no one has ever become a millionaire on the Internet alone. You must build a team of your own or hire one that's already existing and proven.

Business owners near and far turn to out-tasking and outsourcing their Internet-related agenda. But how? In this chapter, you are introduced to the many types of helpers available to you — broadly called *Internet service providers* — and you see how to find them and engage with them properly to help with your projects.

Recognizing the Skills You Need Help With

What are you really good at? How do you enjoy spending your days? Do you like sitting in front of your computer screen for hours? Or are you more of a people person? Is your time better spent on the phone talking with prospects or in an online forum giving free advice? Do you jump out of bed in the morning to race to your computer at 5 a.m. to check your Google AdWords click-through rates, or would you rather meet your colleagues on the golf course for a morning of networking?

To maximize the Internet for your business, you have several main positions to fill: an Internet marketing team, if you will. For most business owners, accomplishing all roles solo — successfully, that is — is impossible.

+ **Vice President Internet Marketing (VPIM):** Keeps everything together; creates, directs, and monitors the plan and results; adheres to the budget; holds helpers accountable to their performance and deadlines.

+ **Marketing expert:** Creates the brand, logos, taglines, and *stickiness* (the ability of a brand or product to remain in someone's mind over time); promotes consistency among all promotions and packaging.

+ **Website design expert:** Works with the marketing expert to create the website's look and feel that combines brand consistency with proven sales strategy.

+ **Internet marketing expert:** Researches the competition; works with the sales expert to optimize the website and content for maximum sales conversion; builds the opt-in list and prepares e-mail campaigns and newsletters; conducts organic SEO (see Book II); manages CPC ad campaigns; implements inbound link campaigns, article creation, and syndication; manages blog setup and training; monitors shopping cart setup and testing; oversees audio and video production; provides progress reports to VPIM.

+ **Social networking manager:** Conducts all interaction on multiple social sites including, at least, Facebook, Google+, LinkedIn, and Twitter; adds business news daily; receives requests from followers; replies to comments; organizes contests; works closely with the Internet marketing expert to produce blog posts that build traffic; monitors content quality standards and adherence to company guidelines.

+ **Sales expert:** Writes effective and compelling sales copy; creates auto-responder sequences; trains affiliates; finds and attracts joint venture hosts; conducts teleseminars, webinars, and workshops to build product awareness; identifies customer needs.

+ **Publicity expert:** Writes and distributes press releases; finds opportunities for the VPIM to participate in talk radio shows and television programs.

+ **Programming and database expert:** Works with the Internet marketing expert to alter or customize tools that help increase sales, such as WordPress (or other content-management software), shopping carts, lead forms, and online registration scripts; manages online databases and assures that PCI Compliance standards are being met with online transactions.

✦ **Content manager:** Changes website content routinely and quickly upon request; edits video and audio and posts to website with appropriate players and codecs.

✦ **Coach or mentor:** Provides cutting-edge techniques; recognizes mistakes you might make; helps the team improve its skills.

✦ **Business owner:** Stays involved; relays customer approval to the rest of the team.

Attempting to understand and do all these functions on your own is a recipe for loss of sanity over time. So, consider which of these skills you have no interest in performing yourself, and make plans now to find resources to help.

Choosing an Internet Service Provider

You can't possibly do all the work yourself that the Internet requires for maximizing leads and sales to their fullest potential. You need to build a team or hire a team that's already established. By having such a team at your side, you'll be amazed how many more hours of the day are available to you. And, if the right team members are chosen, your sales and leads will likely increase dramatically within only a few weeks of hiring.

To that end, consider hiring an Internet service provider (ISP). Not an ISP like Comcast or AT&T, but people who provide services to help increase your leads and sales on the Internet. Same words, but different meaning.

Ten years ago, the term *Internet service provider* defined a company that would host your website or provide you with a connection to the Internet. Today, an ISP is anyone or any entity that offers any type of service that directly or indirectly helps you conduct business online: a broad definition to be sure.

You can probably find thousands of ISPs in your area: folks with full-time, non-Internet–related jobs by day who moonlight or even volunteer their time as self-proclaimed experts by night. On the other end of the spectrum, established companies with departments full of employees are ready to dedicate an entire team of experts and a combined 100 hours or more per week to your project. And as you might expect, several levels of ISPs fall between these two extremes. Which level of help is right for you? Table 7-1 can help you with that decision.

Table 7-1		ISP Types	
ISP Type	*Benefits*	*Challenges to Expect*	*Typical Budget*
Hobbyist	Lowest cost possible Easy to barter with Highest percentage of time allocated to your project because it's usually the person's only project	Lowest probability for fast results because every request requires experimentation and a learning curve Loss of interest Loss of time-sensitive opportunities	Free to $15/hour
Semipro	Easy to negotiate price Only 1 to 3 projects going at a time, which means you still get priority attention Work with the same person although he may have contracted helpers	Hard to contact during the day because he's still at the day job or has family obligations on weekends High rate of burnout Quality of performance reduces over time	$15–$30/hour
Full-time soloist	Same person works on your project over time Accessible on weekends if emergency arises Knows business very well because he makes his living online Always on the cutting edge of new strategies	These one-man shows do it all but get sidetracked by such administrative time-drainers as driving deposits to the bank and bookkeeping Longer lead-times for completed work	$30–$100/hour
Small-company team	You benefit from the cumulative range of knowledge among the team Team is paid based on results, so they're motivated to excel Extensive tracking systems are in place Low turnover	Often, the highest priced option You could become confused as to who you should be talking to on the team Possible lag time in accomplishing tasks if team members don't agree with each other	$100–$200/hour Monthly programs from $500 to $10K Possible revenue sharing

ISP Type	Benefits	Challenges to Expect	Typical Budget
Large ISP	Best chance of the ISP being around in a year or two Best chance of offering 24/7 support Best chance of having entire team under one roof	High turnover Rarely talk to same person twice Best chance for a buyout or merger and therefore package offering changes and price changes Services are likely "canned" instead of customized	Wide range of prices

Which ISP should you choose to help with your project? It largely depends on your budget, your commitment to running a business versus feeding a hobby, and your desired speed to market. For example, if you're working a full-time job and want to start a business on the side and get a website to get things rolling and test the waters, a hobbyist or semipro ISP is a perfect fit. Conversely, if you're part of a large company, you might want to hire a high-end agency. Small to midsized businesses enjoy long-term rewards and individual attention by dealing with the same people over time with the small company team.

Countless website designers have started by designing a free website for their church or for a friend and decided to leave their corporate job to make their millions as a web designer. A month or two later, they're starving for work, lacking the necessary skills on many fronts.

Others new to the world of self-employment accept any project that comes their way just to make a few bucks. They spend three times as long as they were compensated for just to figure out how to accomplish the task. After a few long nights, hours of trial and error, and an unhealthy dose of uncertainty, the ISPs of this caliber often just disappear without notice.

Finding good ISP candidates

The best ISP referrals typically come through other business owners and colleagues or mentors in your network. By asking for referrals from people you know, you can hear about their experiences firsthand.

If you get no referrals to a good ISP from other business professionals in your network, don't worry. The old saying, "Good help is hard to find," rarely applies when looking for a good ISP on the Internet, thanks to freelance websites such as Fiverr, 99designs, Elance, vWorker, and Craigslist. The challenge becomes selecting the right person or team from a sea of talented designers, programmers, and marketers while weeding out those who lack experience or longevity.

The following sections offer tips for finding good referrals as well as introductions to popular freelance resources.

Personal referrals

Begin your search for good personal referrals by reviewing websites owned by friends or business acquaintances. Search the search engines for related keyword phrases to their industry and see whether their websites appear on the first page of Google. When you visit those websites and evaluate them, look for components of proofing and copywriting that sell. If both are present, chances are good that the website was produced by a knowledgeable and reliable team that produces results! Ask for a referral to the site owner's ISP.

Fiverr

If you have not yet been introduced to the magic and creativity source of Fiverr (`www.fiverr.com`), prepare to be amazed with what some people are willing to do for just $5! Need a new logo? How about a trifold brochure? Maybe you want someone to create a video for your website saying your company name 100 times in 20 seconds while eating a sandwich. . . upside down! Get creative — it'll still only cost $5. Just post your project on the site (see Figure 7-1), review the replies from respondents to your posting, and choose the helper whom you feel is the most capable to complete the task. The Fiverr system takes your payment up front, but the helper is not paid until you authorize that the task is complete.

Figure 7-1:
A Fiverr project posting.

99designs

On a higher level of freelancing than Fiverr is 99designs (www.99designs. com). There you can post a sort of contest for a wide variety of design projects. Submit your requirements and how much you're willing to pay for the task. Designers will see your posting and compete with each other for your business by producing a better design than the next guy, as shown in Figure 7-2. You choose the winner and keep the design for your use, and the designer gets his payment.

TIP

With 99designs, be prepared to bid a large enough payment for the task to inspire several designers to start submitting their design ideas. Most logos are in the range of $300–$400.

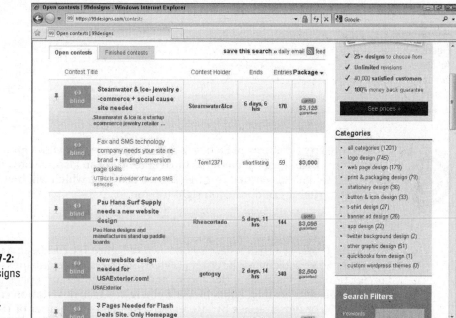

Figure 7-2:
A 99designs project posting.

Elance

Elance (www.elance.com) has for years been one of the more popular freelance systems for posting design, programming, and Internet marketing projects. After a project is posted, it's often only a few hours before a dozen or more available helpers respond to bid on your project. Today, Elance has categories for writing, administration, sales, finance, engineering, and legal, in addition to Internet development. Figure 7-3 displays an Elance posting.

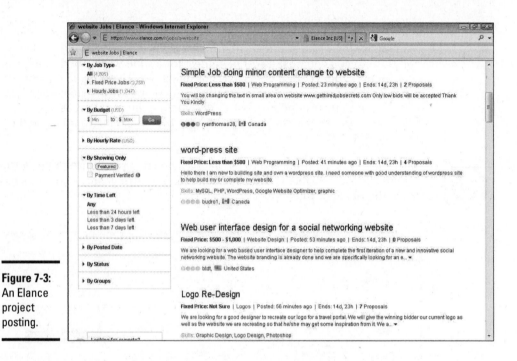

Figure 7-3:
An Elance project posting.

One of the great features of Elance is the ability to read reviews for an ISP's work over just the past six months or overall. You can also see how much revenue that ISP has earned through Elance projects, which will build your confidence that it can do the job right for you.

Craigslist

Craigslist (www.craigslist.org), shown in Figure 7-4, has been a favorite for years when looking for Internet service providers. Some business owners prefer Craigslist because of the speed, and sheer number, of replies to a services-needed posting. Launching a well-crafted task description can often generate 50 or more replies by interested helpers — in a matter of 15–30 minutes! Others enjoy the cost savings (real or perceived) by finding someone to work one on one locally instead of using a higher-end agency.

Posting help wanted ads on Craigslist can be a time-drain! Be prepared to evaluate a great deal of people in response to your ads. Talk to them on the phone and meet with them in person, if possible. Offer to pay each of your potential recruits a very small fee to perform a very small task. If the communication isn't there or something goes wrong with a small assignment, you've just avoided a big headache on a larger project.

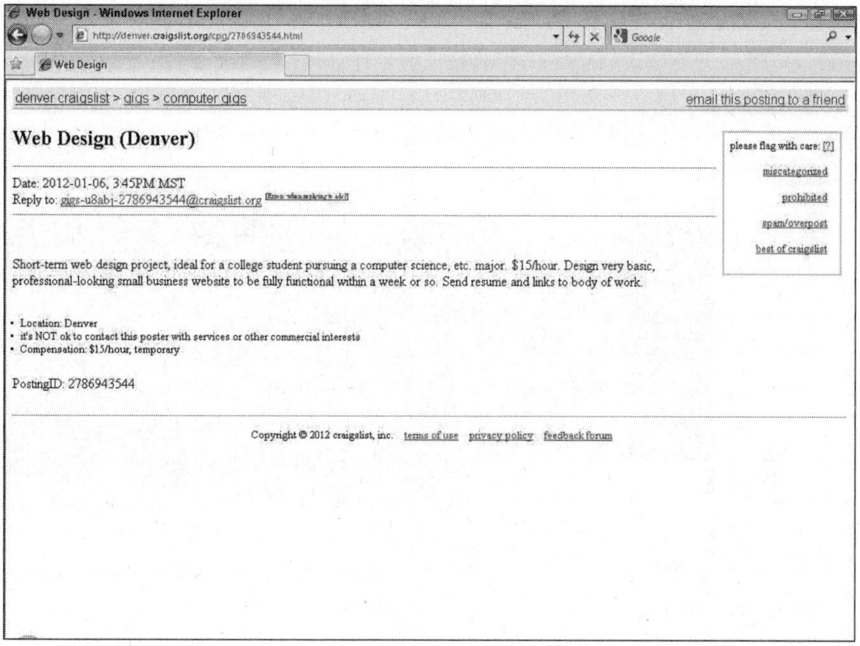

Figure 7-4:
A Craigslist
help-wanted
posting.

ISPs like Craigslist because it's completely free to review posts and reply to them. Because payment for projects occurs between the business owner and the ISP, Craigslist receives no additional compensation for the job. Another advantage to ISP's with Craigslist is that all the communication is behind the scenes, whereas VWorker and Elance publicly post project quotes.

Best of all, the Craigslist website is sorted by city, so you're more likely to get responses from local helpers than with Elance or vWorker.

Internet marketing agency

Internet marketing agencies will typically display their specialties so that you can quickly determine whether what they offer is a good fit for you and your business (see Figure 7-5). Rest assured that agencies want to save their time as much as yours. So, the good ones are willing to offer a free consult to see whether a good match exists.

Freelancers come and go. But, a good agency will be around to work with you over the next 5 or even 10 years or more. And, if they treat their helpers right, you'll appreciate talking to the same people year after year. Expect agencies to charge higher rates than designers competing for your cash at 99designs or Craigslist. But, having that technical backbone and established team available only through reputable agencies is value beyond compare.

Figure 7-5:
An Internet marketing agency.

Interviewing and selecting the right ISPs

Finding a person or team of people to help you promote your business on the Internet is much more than the equivalent of contracting a carpenter to reface your kitchen cabinets or a plumber to fix your sink. It's more similar to hiring an ER doctor to shock what could be your dying business back to life! You cannot afford to make wrong choices. After you review the ISP types to choose from (refer to Table 7-1) and gather a pool of potential candidates through referrals or middlemen (see the preceding section), follow these steps to choose the ISPs that are right for you:

1. **Contact the potential ISP by e-mail, phone, or social network with some questions ready, such as "How long have you been in business?"**

   However long it takes the folks to respond to your contact attempt is how long you can expect a response to take when you're a client. Be ready for the possibility that even your first contact attempt could turn into a free consultation to see whether your project is a good fit with the ISP's focus. Listen for the element of enthusiasm for your project. The last thing you want is a service provider that is not interested in what you plan to offer the world through your business.

2. **Find out how the ISP charges (by block of time, by project, or by both), not what they charge for.**

   This demonstrates to the ISP that you know the business — if only a little. Determine whether the ISP requires prepayment, partial down payment with the rest due upon completion, or simply net invoice amount due in 30 or 60 days (often called net-30 or net-60). All these options have benefits; you just need to be aware of what to expect.

3. **Ask what the ISP's typical turnaround time has been for similar projects it has worked with and whether there would be additional charges for rush orders.**

4. **Find out whether the ISP offers additional services related to the project.**

   For example, a website design company might recommend a preferred hosting company.

5. **Find out how long the ISP has been doing this work.**

   An ISP with five or more years in the business has a pretty good chance of still being in business the next time you need something added to your website. Few feelings are worse than being in need of immediate help from your ISP and hearing "This phone has been disconnected . . ." when you call.

   Plus, an ISP that has been around for a while probably has experience working with a number of clients in a variety of industries. So, you gain the benefit of having strategies applied for your project that produced results for another company in a related industry. Someone who has not had that industry experience will probably need to exercise some additional trial and error to get it right.

   On the other hand, if you're looking for someone to go totally against the grain for your project, you may want to seek someone who doesn't have much experience and can come up with ideas you wouldn't necessarily consider. The most important thing is that you want the truth. If a service provider lies about the number of years in business, he's bound to lie about other elements of your project, too.

   You can quickly find out the ISP's claim to length of service by asking for some website projects that he worked on in the early years and asking how he believes things have changed since he began in the business.

6. **Try to determine how you can be assured that the ISP will be around in six months or more.**

   Listen closely when you ask this question because you can usually hear nervousness in someone's voice if he's on the brink of going bankrupt. Be wary of hiring a person or team desperate for a sale.

Attracting the best ISP

Most ISPs prefer to do business with people who have some experience working with helpers to complete Internet tasks and projects. If you sound like a first-timer, chances are you might be ignored. So don't ask general questions, claim to have the world's next greatest idea, or use exclamation marks and triple question marks when e-mailing ISPs. Have your project well defined before you call, offer to e-mail your wish list during the call, and communicate with upbeat language throughout the e-mail.

Here are a few more do's and don'ts for attracting an ISP to work on your project.

Do: Say, Say, Say

"My website visitors would benefit if . . ."

"What safe font types do you recommend that would be consistent with my market?"

"I like some of the components of this other website. Can you produce something similar?"

"Are you taking on any new SEO projects?"

"How do you monitor accomplishments and benchmarks on a project?"

"What are your payment options?"

"I'm taking my involvement with the Internet to a higher level."

Don't: Don't Ask, Don't Tell

"How much do you charge for a website?"

"I know exactly what I want."

"Can we use some font other than boring Arial or Verdana?"

"Can you just make my website *pop* a little more?"

"I'd like you to just go to this other website and make the same design for me."

"Can you get my site on top of Google?"

"Do you have a money-back guarantee?"

"Can I pay you when the project is complete?"

"I'm brand new to the Internet."

Finally, don't settle for your helpers owning any part of your website or withholding usernames and passwords. Demand to have all original graphics and program files sent to you before final payment, and require that all accounts, usernames, and passwords for hosting, databases, domain names, or third-party applications be in your name. Website designers in particular have an issue with giving away their original artwork. Set them at ease that you will always go to them for changes to graphics but that you should have originals on hand in the event that they become unavailable for a long period of time or in case the relationship terminates.

You find some exceptions to the rule of ownership. For example, if you hire someone to manage your Google AdWords campaign, it is common practice for an ISP to not allow clients direct access to the AdWords account. For one, it would be easy for a novice to delete months of work and testing within seconds inside an AdWord campaign. Second, one learns proprietary techniques with experience, and an ISP would not want the client to cut and run without continuing to pay for those benefits received. You read about many of those techniques in Book IV.

One way to assure who owns what and to identify specific tasks to be performed for the proposed amount of money transacted is to have a written contract. Some ISPs go overboard with contracts. Sometimes clients overlegalize as well. The important thing is to at least have a simple checklist of one-liner descriptions showing what task will be completed, by when, and for how much. Hours of lawyer fees and time delays waiting for approvals are better spent making you money online! Be sure to ask what, if any, the contractual process is for any ISP you begin working with.

The "Do's" help to establish a rapport with the ISPs you interview about your project. When an ISP has a greater comfort level that you know what you're doing, you often get a better-quoted price. If not, at least your ISP will take more interest in your project when you express a certain level of professionalism and courtesy.

Deciding whether to outsource

If you decide to outsource your project to another country in a different time zone, be prepared for some challenges to occur in the areas of communication and time lag. Typically, your main contact will speak your native language, but only on a basic level. So, communicate on a basic level. Expect turnaround times for all requests to take at least 12 hours . . . even if an emergency arises.

And, prices are increasing. You used to be able to get a development project bid at $5,000 in the United States for a few hundred dollars overseas. Now, pricing isn't nearly as competitive.

Outsourcing does certainly have its opportunities, especially when you can guarantee ongoing work hours, month after month. For example, you can fairly easily find overseas ghostwriters to produce blog posts and articles for you on a weekly or even daily basis for just a few hundred dollars a month.

Setting ISP expectations and measuring results

Whether your ISP is helping with the production of a mere banner ad or rolling out your next millionth-visitor-in-a-week traffic campaign, you and your helper must be very clear on what the goal is for the project. How will your expectation be met? Do you require a certain number of new sales or more traffic? Maybe the completion of the project has nothing to do with traffic or sales, but is merely a convenience to you. Whatever the goal, write it down and have a mutual agreement on the outcome. Here are some specific steps you can take to assure that your goals are met:

✦ **Request frequent communication.** When you're working on a time-sensitive deadline, an update per day by e-mail is not too much to ask and keeps you confident that your project is being worked on. Give instant messaging a try to keep your telephone lines open and inbox less cluttered. Search Google for AOL Instant Messenger or use Skype's instant messaging system. Both are free and stable and contain chat logs so you can keep track of your conversations later.

✦ **Become aware of potential roadblocks.** Ask whether anything might prevent the deadline from being met. If you have an absolute deadline for the project to be completed, you might require up front that a fee reduction should be granted for every day after the deadline that the project is not launched. For example, if you hire an ISP to produce an online registration form for an upcoming conference, you might require that the form is live two weeks prior to the last day of the "early bird" special pricing offer. If the registration form is not complete until two or three days before the early bird date, you would lose significant registrations. If it is truly the ISP's fault for not getting the form live in time, a reduction in fee would certainly be warranted. But, if that ISP was waiting for content from you and could not go live without the approved information, the standard fee would be in play.

✦ **Use repetition.** Announce the goal on every phone call and decide together whether you're closer to or farther away from reaching that goal since your last conversation.

✦ **Give encouragement.** ISPs like to know when they're on the right track. Even though a project might not be complete, you can make complimentary comments on the job done so far. ISPs like to work for people they like. So, a little ego stroking pulls some weight when working with helpers.

✦ **Ask for activity reports.** With the help of an online project tracker, you can request progress reports at any time. If you pay your helpers in blocks of time or by the hour, keep a close watch on what has been accomplished for the time spent. Some software to try:

- *Basecamp* (www.basecamp.com) is a good system to use, especially when multiple people are on the same project team and need to coordinate who is in charge of completing which tasks by a certain date. Basecamp has a monthly fee starting at $20 and requires a bit of a learning curve.

- *Premium Web Cart* (www.PremiumWebCart.com) seems to be where people are going who are looking for an alternative to Basecamp. PWC has the added advantage of being completely integrated with a shopping cart, affiliate program, membership system, and CRM. See Chapter 2 in this minibook for more information on Premium Web Cart.

- *Google Docs* (http://docs.google.com) is the opposite of Basecamp because it's simply a web-based word processing and spreadsheet system instead of a true project tracker. Oh yeah, and it's free! You find very little learning curve with Google Docs because it's very similar to Microsoft Word and Excel. Google Docs is a great application for multiple people to contribute to the same document or allow some people to edit where others only receive viewing access.

- *Internet Marketing Actionizer* (http://members.HereNextYear.com): Launch pre-made web-marketing checklists of tasks or create your own. Then you can produce simple reports within seconds that display the dates of tasks performed, a description of the tasks, who performed them, and the total amount of time that each task required; see Figure 7-6.

When it comes to tracking billable time, it doesn't matter whether your ISP uses complex customized software or a simple e-mail once a week, as long as some mechanism is in place to provide you with that information when you need it.

Google+ for Joe Sabah has been added to Social Networking. Click Here To View Google+ for Joe Sabah

Modify Worksheet

Category: Social Networking
Worksheet: Google+ for Joe Sabah
Theme: ◉ Green ◉ Blue ◉ Red ◉ Yellow ◉ Orange ◉
            Purple
User Notifications: (One email per line)

Notifications will be sent at the end of the day.

What Do I Do Here?

Congrats! Your worksheet has been saved! Now click the link in the green bar that just appeared and you will be brought to your worksheet page featuring the step-by-step How-to guides.

Existing Steps

Description*	Notes	Assigned To	Hours	Completed	Remove
Add your new account	This is your main account so use your personal name.	Marty	.25	☑	X
Upload a picture	300 pixels wide X 300 pixels high	Amber	.5	☑	X
Assign URL redirect in HTDOCS	Create both JoeSabah.com/+ and JoeSabah.com/G+	Jeff	.25	☑	X
Add bio and profile	Add bio and profile	Marty	.5	☑	X

Figure 7-6:
Internet
Marketing
Actionizer.

✦ **Request sales and cost reports.** If you have a company managing a promotional campaign, demand reports at least once per week. Even with
   the most complex Google AdWords campaigns, running a sales report
   takes less than ten minutes. It's your money: Know where it's being
   spent.

✦ **Offer to check off a completed project.** When your project is close to
   completion, offer to sign off on the project. ISPs love clients who want
   things to be finalized. Extend the courtesy of acknowledging when a
   project is complete.

If you request a report and notice an abrupt change in communication by
your ISP, be on alert that something might have gone wrong. Helpers tend
to disappear into their caves when things don't go as planned or aren't
completed within the time they thought the project would go live. Be sympathetic at first. Unforeseen factors can creep into any project at any time even
for the most experienced firms. But, don't let it go too long. Be patient, yet
persistent, when needed.

Not every client/ISP relationship is going to work like a charm. If things are
not going how you planned, be the proactive business owner and confront
your helper to either get your money back or get the project fixed. This is
where trial and error, starting off with small projects when working with
a new helper, can pay off. If a helper can't finish a small task, he probably
won't finish a larger task.

Nurturing a good ISP partnership

When you find an ISP that you like and trust over a period of months, offer a little more incentive than a project fee or hourly rate to keep you and your project at the forefront of his mind. Devise a plan that offers a small compensation per month based on sales. This invitation is best made when the ISP is not expecting it. Offering such an incentive accomplishes several objectives:

✦ **Builds confidence:** The ISP is certain that you approve of his work.

✦ **Strengthens the team:** People like to be part of teams that accomplish things. Monetary incentives help your ISP understand that he really is a valued part of the team.

✦ **Sparks creativity:** Most ISPs start to get creative when they know they're going to get a piece of the pie. You will get occasional e-mails from them that read, "You didn't ask me to do this, but the idea just struck me and I had to try it out. What do you think about it?"

Book II

Search Engine Optimization

Contents at a Glance

Chapter 1: Getting Ready for SEO

In This Chapter

- Understanding why search engines exist
- Discovering what matters to a search engine
- Staying away from tricks and penalties
- Setting up your toolbox
- Making an SEO worksheet

Search engine optimization (SEO) is a long-term effort. It requires a lot of work and patience and a consistent strategy. It's like a Galapagos Tortoise — it bumps along, slow and steady. But it lives a long time.

This chapter helps you prepare for a lengthy campaign by explaining why search engines exist. You find out what works and what doesn't in the SEO world. This chapter also covers how to set up your SEO toolbox and helps you put your SEO worksheet together.

Understanding Why Search Engines Exist

Search engines drive the Internet. If you're going to grow your business online, you're probably going to depend on such search engines as Google and Bing to deliver a huge chunk of your customers and clients. A high placement in the search engine ranking pages (*SERPs*, if you want to feel all geeky) can drive tremendous growth.

You can leave those rankings to chance and hope for the best. Or you can use *SEO,* the practice of providing the best possible target for search engines.

SEO is a huge field, with thousands of little details that come together to make a successful campaign. If you're looking to dig deeply into this topic, get *Search Engine Optimization All-in-One For Dummies* by Bruce Clay and Susan Esparza (published by John Wiley & Sons, Inc.). If you want to improve your search rankings, this book is for you.

Search engine terms to remember

Crawl refers to what a search engine does when it reads and indexes a website.

Organic or natural search results are unpaid listings on a search result page.

Search engine ranking pages (SERPs) are the result pages you see when you complete a search on a major search engine.

Spiders or robots (bots) are software that the search engine uses to crawl your site.

Black hat SEO uses tactics specifically designed to improve search rankings and fool the search engines into providing a higher ranking than a website should actually receive according to a search engine's algorithms.

White hat SEO uses tactics to make a website as acceptable as possible to both visitors and search engines, without attempting to manipulate the search engines.

When you're finding out about SEO, it's hard to separate tricks from solid strategies. To understand how search engines work, you need to know why they exist.

Search engines deliver relevance. *Relevance* means that visitors click on search results and are happy with what the search engine found for them. When that happens, visitors come back, traffic to the search engine rises, and the search engine company's stock goes up.

For example, if you go to Google and type **pastrami**, you expect to find sites about pastrami. If you find a website about bread, you might not use Google again. Google wants to deliver the most useful websites relating to pastrami because it's good for its business. Same for every other search engine on the Internet. So, if you want to rank high, make it easy for search engines to figure out when and where your site should appear in the rankings.

Don't be fooled by hucksters who offer to help you move up in the rankings. They tell you they can trick the search engines into giving you a high ranking, even if you don't deserve it.

These tricks might include adding thousands of links on hundreds of websites, duplicating pages on your site, buying or stealing content from other sites and using it on yours, or connecting you to *link networks,* where hundreds of sites exchange links. Or, when asked how they will improve your rankings, the con artist might just say, "It's a secret."

Using tricks like these may get you some initial success, but they cost money, and you risk getting penalized by the search engines. Penalties cause you to disappear from the rankings or move down to four or five pages of the listings without warning. That can get expensive. For more information, see the "Avoiding Penalties" section, later in the chapter.

Search engines don't like to be fooled. If you're selling salami and engage in some trickery to gain a high ranking for pastrami, the search engine's programming team will remove you from the rankings.

Knowing What Helps a Site Rank

Key phrases

Search engines want to know which website offers the best value for users when they search for a particular concept. These concepts are represented by *key phrases*. *New York hotels, chocolate candy, bicycles,* and *wedding dresses* are all examples of key phrases.

Search engines are hierarchical thinkers. After reading billions of pages of content by using little software programs called *spiders,* search engines determine the relevance of each of those pages for a key phrase based on a complex series of rules.

When you go to a search engine and type a key phrase (*wedding dresses,* for example), the search engine picks the best matches by assessing the following:

links who referred them the most

✦ **A site's authority on the subject:** The search engine looks for links from other sites about wedding dresses to gauge the site's authority on wedding dresses.

Every link from other, relevant sites is a vote for the target site's authority.

Social Media

✦ **A site's social media reach:** The search engine looks at social media citations and "likes" for that site from other relevant social media users.

focus

✦ **The main focus of the site:** The search engine looks at the site structure, so find what its main focus is.

Pages dedicated

✦ **Which pages on those sites are most dedicated to the subject.**

✦ **Whether those pages are more relevant than all the other pages in the search engine's index.**

✦ **The overall "quality" of each site as defined by writing quality, site performance, and visitor response to that site's search listing.**

All you have to do is get yourself to the top of each of those pyramids, and you're rich!

Well, maybe it's not *that* simple. Thousands or even millions of other sites are all vying for that same top spot. To really compete, you're going to need to know how web pages are built and how search engines read them. If you know how search engines read sites, and you know how to build them, you can provide what search engines want: a structure that indicates what a page is really about.

Table 1-1 describes the factors that help a website rank, as well as the factors that have little or no impact on a site's rankings.

Check list. (handwritten)

Table 1-1			What Matters in SEO
Factors	*Matters*	*Doesn't Matter*	*Why*
Title tags	X		Title tags are at the very top of the hierarchy for each page. They're the first thing search engines look at. If the key phrase shows up in the title tag, search engines flag the page as relevant to that phrase.
Keywords meta tag		X	The keywords meta tag was so horribly abused by SEOs that search engines completely ignore it.
Description meta tag	X		The description meta tag actually does not affect your rankings, but is usually shown as the page "snippet" in the search engine results.
Headings (H1, H2, and so on)	X		Headings provide a content outline to the search engines when they crawl your pages. If the target key phrase shows up in a heading, that demonstrates relevance.
Paragraph copy	X		The more copy you have on your site, the easier it is to rank well. Don't just stuff copy with key-words, though. Read more on this in Chapter 6 of this minibook.
ALT attributes	X		Image ALT attributes definitely influence rank-ings.
Hidden text		X	Hiding text on your page and stuffing it with key phrases may seem like a neat trick. But search engines root this stuff out, and if you're caught, they'll penalize your site. Some sites have been banned a few hours after accidental addition of hidden text.
Site age	X		Older sites have higher rankings. You can safely assume that a two-year-old site will have more leverage than a two-week-old one.
Trust factors	X		Having a physical address on every page can definitely help make you look more trustworthy.
Image captions	X		Text captions near images help with image search results.
Bullets and lists	X		Bullets are more easily scanned, which makes for better linking opportunities. But they don't directly impact rankings. With Google's empha-sis on "site quality," you can bet this affects rankings.

new *Company* (handwritten note near "Site age")

Factors	Matters	Doesn't Matter	Why
Links	X		Links equal authority. Authority equals greater relevance. Don't just buy junk links, though. You need relevant links from relevant sites.
Link text	X		If the link to your site reads `Click Here`, that tells the search engines that your site is relevant to click here. If the link reads `Wedding Dresses`, it tells the search engine your site is relevant to wedding dresses. See how that works? This is less influential than it used to be, but it still matters.
Social media	X		Mentions and links on major social media sites, like Facebook and Twitter, have a huge effect on rankings.
Site speed	X		Slow sites definitely don't perform as well in the rankings as fast ones.
Writing quality	X		Yep. The search engines are learning to read, so lousy writing may hurt you in the rankings.
Filenames	X		Keyword-rich filenames on images and individual pages insert keywords into the site hierarchy.
URL	X		Keyword-rich web addresses can be a huge help, because every link to your site that uses the URL as the link text creates a keyword-rich link. This only works within reason, though. An exact match web address (pastrami.com for the word *pastrami*, for example) can definitely help with rankings. But that's the only time you'll really get a boost.
Submitting a website		X	You can certainly submit your website to Google and Bing, but it's better for these search engines to find you through links on other sites.
Number of clicks on your search listing		X	Click your listing as much as you want. The search engines still won't move you up.
PageRank		X	In testing, Google's Toolbar PageRank is slightly less accurate than guessing.

URL (handwritten note in margin)

Avoiding Penalties

Website owners often make the mistake of looking for the Miraculous Path to Search Engine Greatness. One does not exist. SEO is a long process. You need to write, optimize, build links, and slowly work your way up.

If you *do* find a short-term fix that works, it won't last. The road to a No. 1 ranking is littered with the shells of websites that tried all sorts of trickery and shortcuts.

At some point, you, your boss, your spouse, or your business partner is going to ask, "Why does this other site rank higher than ours?" You might discover that the other site bought 4,000 links, or that it has 1,000 near-duplicate pages. Then you'll ask yourself, "Why shouldn't I do that, too?"

Search engines aren't the keeper of ethics or laws. Strictly speaking, there's no ethical reason not to play games with them in an attempt to get a higher ranking. However, this is a lousy business plan. Only one or two cases exist where someone got away with trickiness for more than a few months. Assuming that your business plan allows growth over a period of years, it pays to practice *white hat* SEO tactics — relying on content and natural link growth, with a little help here and there — rather than tricks.

Black hat SEO professionals try to find loopholes and clever ways to fool search engines into providing a higher ranking than a site might actually deserve within that search engine's ranking system. They're not breaking any laws or doing anything unethical. They're just balancing risk versus benefit: Black hat SEO is very risky, but it can provide a huge benefit. However, it also nearly guarantees you'll get caught at some point. Any good black hat SEO pro will tell you that.

Search engines demand relevance, not tricks, and assuming that you want your rankings to have a life span beyond a couple months, you should give the search engines what they want. Although it takes longer, following the rules gives you a more resilient online business.

Anyone guaranteeing you a No.1 ranking, offering to submit you to 3,000 search engines, or contacting you out of the blue is probably going to rip you off. Also beware of tools that promise instant SEO ranking improvement with little or no effort. If it sounds too good to be true, it probably is.

An SEO tale of woe

A business owner named Jake received a call from a company promising him great search rankings. He worked with a white hat search engine optimization company and slowly began moving up in the rankings. Unfortunately, he became impatient.

He decided to find a new SEO company. This company's experts explained that they would modify his website to include dozens of hidden links that search engines would see, but visitors would not. In exchange, they'd add Jake's site to all of their other clients' websites. Best of all, the results were guaranteed: Top 10 rankings on Google and Yahoo! within two months.

Jake hired the new company, and within a few weeks, his site ranked in the top 10 for nearly every key phrase. He was ecstatic.

Then, a week later, traffic to his site plunged. He checked the rankings: He'd vanished from the search engines. Why? Google and Yahoo! had both found the hidden links, detected that they were indeed hidden, and removed his site from their indexes.

It took six months for Jake to get back into the search engines. In the long run, his business lost far more than it gained.

Setting Up Your Toolbox

Some fantastic tools are available to help you see how a search engine will evaluate your website. Use the tools mentioned in the following sections to set up your SEO toolbox.

Add-ons from Firefox

Firefox, Mozilla's web browser, allows developers to create their own add-ons. If you're not already using Firefox, you can download it at www.mozilla.org/firefox. You can find a huge collection of add-ons at http://addons.mozilla.org. The ones you want for SEO include the following:

+ **SeoQuake,** which collects and displays a few dozen relevant search engine statistics, including pages in the Google index, keyword density on the page, site age, and page rank.

+ **Live HTTP Headers** shows what your website is telling a search engine about each page.

+ The **Web Developer toolbar by Chris Pederick** lets you change how Firefox displays a web page. It's great for testing how your site looks without images or styles (how a search engine sees it).

✦ The **Yellowpipe Lynx Viewer Tool** enables you to see a web page in a text-only web browser — another good way to preview how a search engine will see your site.

These tools are really just the beginning. Dozens of other Firefox add-ons are available, including Rank Checker and SEOBook's SEO for Firefox.

SeoQuake

With SeoQuake, you can find information, such as page rank and Google index, about any site. You can look at search engine page results for Google and Bing. You can see the handy SeoBar, where all this information is stored at the upper-left corner of your browser. Click the arrow to expand the toolbar, as shown in Figure 1-1.

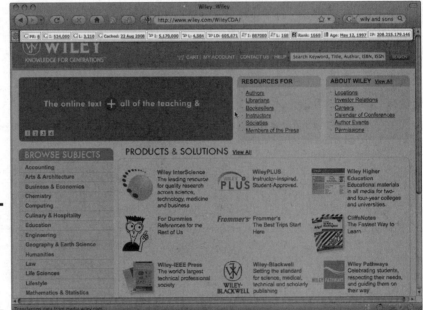

Figure 1-1: The SeoBar provides SEO information goodness.

Do not leave SeoQuake on all the time! SeoQuake *scrapes* the search engines for information. If you leave it on, you're basically pestering Google and Bing. They don't like that.

Hover over any of the items to see what they are, and then click any item to get more detail. Clicking the SEMRush Links item, for example, shows you a listing of all incoming links that one industry toolset, SEMRush, sees for the page.

Check the following items for your site as well as for your competitors' sites:

✦ **SEMRush links,** which shows the number of links to the site as seen by SEMRush, an industry SEO data- mining tool.

✦ **Google and Bing indexes** give the number of pages indexed by each search engine.

✦ **Site age.**

✦ **Density** is a critical feature. You can check a site to see which phrases are most popular or common on that page. This is a great insight into how optimized a page is for a specific phrase.

✦ **Twitter tweets** shows you the number of times this page has been shared via Twitter.

✦ **Facebook likes** shows the number of times people liked the page on Facebook.

✦ **Google PlusOne** counts the number of people who have given the page a +1 via Google's +1 feature.

✦ **WHOIS** shows you the owner, purchase date, and other information about this page's domain, if available.

If you want to geek out, you can also get specific data about links from within the site to one page, the page's `robots.txt` file, and the IP address of that website.

No search engine ever tells you the full story regarding links and indexed pages. Because SeoQuake pulls its data in large part from the search engines, take the results with a grain of salt. However, it's a great way to compare websites and measure progress.

You can have SeoQuake show up in your toolbar, too. Choose View⇨ Toolbars, and then choose SeoQuake Toolbar.

Live HTTP Headers

With Live HTTP Headers, you can find out if your website is working the way you expect it to. To use Live HTTP Headers, choose Tools⇨Live HTTP Headers. Browse to the web page you want to check. A lot of gobbledygook streams by in the Live HTTP Headers window, as shown in Figure 1-2.

Book II
Chapter 1

Getting Ready for SEO

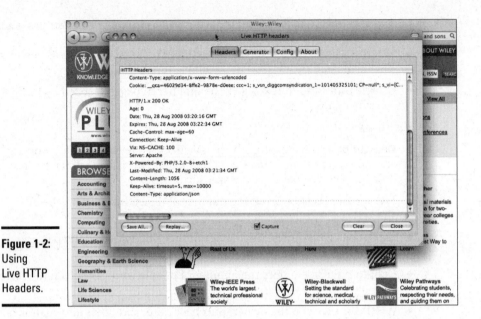

Figure 1-2:
Using
Live HTTP
Headers.

For now, you care about only one thing: the first HTTP note. If it reads 200 OK, as shown in Figure 1-2, your web server is telling all visiting browsers — including search engine spiders — that everything is fine and that they should index this page normally.

Test your site's Page Not Found error page, too. Go to www.yoursite address.com/asdfasdf and replace yoursiteaddress but keep the asdfasdf. Chances are that page doesn't exist. The HTTP note should read 404 (which means *Page Not Found*). If it reads 200, tell your webmaster that he needs to fix that. Find out more about other messages you may encounter in Chapter 3 of this minibook.

Web Developer toolbar

Web Developer is the most complex of the Firefox add-on tools. It lets you view your website without images or styles, which is exactly how a search engine sees it. If you're scared of terms such as *CSS* and *JavaScript,* skip ahead to the next section. You'll still be successful in your SEO efforts without this tool.

After the tool is installed, choose View⇨Toolbars⇨Web Developer Toolbar. Make sure that selected check box appears next to Web Developer Toolbar. The Web Developer toolbar, as shown in Figure 1-3, appears in Firefox.

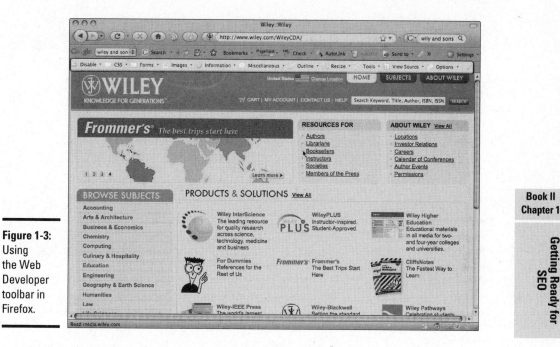

Figure 1-3:
Using
the Web
Developer
toolbar in
Firefox.

One good feature of the Web Developer toolbar is that you can disable
JavaScript and styles to get a more accurate picture of what the average
search engine sees when it crawls your website. Choose Disable⇨JavaScript
and CSS⇨Disable All Styles to do so.

Take some time, play around, and see how it all works. Just be sure that
you look up from the monitor once in a while. The Web Developer toolbar is
highly addictive.

Using Google Page Speed

Google Page Speed lets you evaluate site performance. It then provides you
with specific guidelines for giving your site a speed boost.

You don't have to install anything — Page Speed is available as a web tool. Go
to `http://developers.google.com/pagespeed` and enter your website
URL. What you get back will look something like what is shown in Figure 1-4.

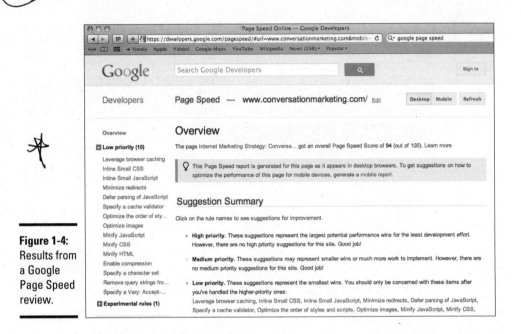

Figure 1-4:
Results from
a Google
Page Speed
review.

The resulting report prioritizes changes into high, medium, and low priority. Click any of those and you'll get a specific list of changes you can make to speed up your site. If you see Optimize Images under medium or high priority, handle that first. It's often the fastest and easiest way to give your page a speed boost.

Using webmaster tools

The major search engines provide insight into your site's SEO, too. Bing and Google both have webmaster toolsets that can ensure you create the best-possible search presence. These tools use the data search engines collect when they crawl your site to assemble detailed reports and

✦ Notify you if they find problems, such as duplicate content

✦ Show you who is linking to your site

✦ Report the most common queries used to find your site

✦ Tell you the last time the search engine crawled your site

✦ Allow you to modify (in a few cases) how your listings appear

The webmaster tools sites for the various search engines are as follows:

✦ **Google:** www.google.com/webmasters/tools

✦ **Bing:** http://webmaster.live.combing.com/webmaster

Book II
Chapter 1

Getting Ready for
SEO

What happened to Yahoo!?

Yahoo! is no longer an independent search engine. Bing bought the company in 2010. Since then, Bing has shut down Yahoo! Site Explorer and folded Yahoo!'s data into its own webmaster tools. Alas, poor Yahoo!, we knew you well.

To use webmaster tools, follow these steps:

1. **Set up an account with each search engine, as directed.**

2. **Verify site ownership by either uploading an authentication file or adding a meta tag to your site, as directed by the search engine.**

   If you have no idea what this step means, talk to your webmaster to get it set up.

Using Google webmaster tools

The Google webmaster toolset includes more than 20 gadgets. You want to explore them all, but you can't do without these:

✦ **Diagnostics➪HTML Suggestions** tells you, at a glance, whether any pages on your site duplicate title or description meta tags, or whether they're missing those tags.

✦ **Diagnostics➪Fetch as Googlebot** gives you a peek at how Google sees individual pages on your site.

✦ **Your site on the web➪Links to your site** tells you which pages on your site have links from other sites. And you can drill down to find out where those links come from.

✦ **Your site on the web➪Search queries** allows you to peek at the key phrases (and your rankings for those phrases) that drive traffic.

You can export these reports to TSV (Tabbed Separated Values) format if you're a real datahead, too.

Google webmaster tools are a *must have*. Don't leave them out of your toolbox! ✳

Using Bing webmaster tools

Microsoft's Bing webmaster tools are a treasure trove. Some of the service's reports overlap with Google webmaster tools, but you should check out the following:

- ✦ **Crawl** shows pages with crawl issues, redirection statistics, and total pages crawled/indexed by Bing and Yahoo!.

- ✦ **Traffic** shows you which terms drive visits to your site, how you ranked for them, and your click-through rate.

- ✦ **Index Explorer** is just dang nifty. With it, you can click through Bing's actual index of your site. It's a huge help for diagnosing crawl issues.

And, yes, you can export all these reports to TSV (Tabbed Separated Values) format.

Installing Xenu Link Sleuth

Xenu Link Sleuth is a great little program that crawls any website, giving you a list of broken and working links. It's also free, by the way. To use it, follow these steps:

1. **Go to** `http://home.snafu.de/tilman/xenulink.html`.

2. **Double-click the program, type the web address you want to check, and then click OK.**

   You can change the other settings to crawl a site faster or slower.

Use Xenu to find broken links. When Xenu detects a broken link, it also shows you the page on which it found the link, so it's relatively easy to find problems.

Xenu is available only for Microsoft Windows. Luckily, Peacock Media has a tool called Scrutiny that comes awfully close to Xenu's features. It costs money, but it's worth it. Download it at `http://peacockmedia.co.uk/scrutiny`.

Creating Your SEO Worksheet

SEO can take a long time. Plus, changes you make today might impact your rankings months from now, so it's important that you keep a record of relevant data and changes you make over time. That way, you can refer to those changes and better understand what worked and what didn't.

If you're serious about SEO, you're going to need to track a number of different statistics over time, including the following:

- ✦ **Traffic from organic search:** Your web analytics package (see Book III for in-depth web analytics information) should show you clicks from unpaid search rankings.

✦ **Keyword diversity:** The number of key phrases driving traffic to your website. Again, your web analytics package will give you this.

✦ **Incoming links, by search engine:** The number of links reported by Bing and Google.

✦ **Indexed pages, by search engine.**

✦ **Sales/leads/other results from organic search:** If your site has a goal, and your analytics package allows it, record the results you get. Traffic is great. Sales are better.

✦ **Keyword rankings:** Notice how this is last? That's because *keyword rankings don't matter.*

REMEMBER

Keyword rankings don't matter. Traffic and results do. Although ranking No. 1 for a phrase or two is one way to get those extra visitors, getting 500 top-10 listings for less prominent phrases may get you far more visitors and sales, leads, or whatever else you need. Don't obsess about keyword rankings. Obsess about traffic, keyword diversity, and success.

Record these numbers by month. You can record them by week if you're really obsessive. Whatever you do, don't check them every day — you may lose your mind.

See Chapter 8 in this minibook for information on search engine analytics and analyzing your results.

Focus on traffic not Keywords

1.) unpaid Searches
2.) Keyword diversity
3.) Incoming Links
4.) Indexed Pages
5.) Sales
6.) Keyword Rankings (Dont matter)

Chapter 2: Choosing the Right Keywords

In This Chapter

✔ Picking keywords that your visitors (not you) want

✔ Discovering keyword tools

✔ Using the right selection criteria

✔ Researching your competitors

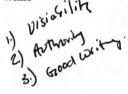

1.) Visibility
2.) Authority
3.) Good writing

At some point, not talking about keywords in regards to SEO is the dream. The truth is, keywords aren't the focus of a good SEO strategy — visibility, authority, and good writing are.

But you still want to focus on keywords. Search engines haven't gotten good enough at semantics to make us all forget about keywords. Someday search engines may be able to index and rank sites based on *concepts* — by knowing that cars and autos are the same thing — but until then, you have to make some pretty specific choices.

In this chapter, you find out how to pick the right keywords to bring traffic to your business website. Don't drive yourself crazy with keyword research. Your time is better spent on writing great stuff, working in social media, and improving your site. But some basic research always helps.

Thinking Like Your Visitors

Before you start thinking about tools, you must understand that you are not optimizing for the keywords *you* like or think should be associated with your product or service. You are optimizing for the keywords that *potential customers* associate with your product or service.

For example, say that you sell salad through the Internet. You've found a miraculous way to keep vegetables crisp and prevent lettuce from wilting, and you ship salad to suburban dwellers everywhere.

You research keywords and find that no one searches for *salad*. They search for *mixed greens* instead. You have a choice to make. You can insist on optimizing for *salad*, because that is what you sell. Or, you can optimize for *mixed greens*, get visitors, and then educate them as to why *salad* is better.

Don't try to shove your own beliefs about your product or service down the throats of your customers by picking the keywords *you* think they should use to find you. That never works in marketing, and it really doesn't work in search engine optimization. Understand what your visitors will use to find you. You can educate them as to why you're different, and why they should care, after they arrive on your website.

If a customer searches for *bicycles* and clicks a link to your site, she'll expect to see information about bicycles. If you sell cars, don't optimize for *bicycles* and then try to tell folks why cars are better. That just frustrates them. Go with your strengths: Optimize for *cars*.

Understanding the Long Tail

You never optimize for a single word; you optimize for a keyword and the hundreds or thousands of permutations on that word. So, if you're targeting *broccoli,* you're probably also targeting *cream of broccoli soup, broccoli recipes,* and *broccoli coleslaw.* These *long-tail* phrases — longer niche phrases that don't get as many searches — are the real beauty of search engine optimization. By optimizing for one word or phrase, you get the benefit of improved rankings for many more.

Go back to the *salad* example from the preceding section. You decide to optimize for *mixed greens.* After six months of hard work, you're still stuck on the fourth rankings page for that phrase. But your traffic from organic searches has gone up 300 percent. For these reasons, you're not sure whether you should fire yourself or give yourself a raise.

Taking a look at your traffic report, though, you notice something interesting. Traffic from longer phrases that include the words *mixed greens* has gone up. Phrases such as the following are now major traffic generators:

> *mixed spring greens*
> *mixed greens online*
> *buy mixed greens*
> *mixed greens salads*
> *really great mixed greens*
> *where can I buy mixed greens*

All these phrases are driving traffic to your site. Together, the six phrases drive more traffic than *mixed greens* would have.

Behold, the long tail! By optimizing for one phrase, you really optimized for six longer ones. Even though you didn't move up in the rankings for the target phrase, you did move up for these others, and they brought you traffic.

Long-tail phrases work for two reasons:

✦ You can optimize for many of them at once by focusing on one shorter phrase.

✦ Searchers that visit your website from long-tail phrases are generally better targeted and better customers. If folks comes to your website from a long-tail search result and you have what they want, they're likely to buy.

So the next time you're sweating bullets, staring at your rankings report and wondering why you haven't moved up, check your traffic report, too. The long tail might pay off big.

Finding the Right Tools

Luckily, you don't have to guess to find keywords. You can use some of the great tools available to help you with your initial brainstorming.

Using keyword services

Several companies have launched keyword services designed just for search engine optimization pros looking for the right targets. These services include the following:

✦ **SEMRush:** `www.semrush.com`

✦ **Keyword Discovery:** `http://keyworddiscovery.com`

✦ **Wordtracker:** `www.wordtracker.com`

All services cost a small monthly fee, but they are a good investment. They provide at-a-glance reports showing keyword demand, competition, and quality, as shown in Figure 2-1.

Be sure to know where these tools get their data! For example, none have access to Google organic search numbers (Google doesn't release that data). They're good at extrapolating, but you want to supplement your research with the tools described in the following sections.

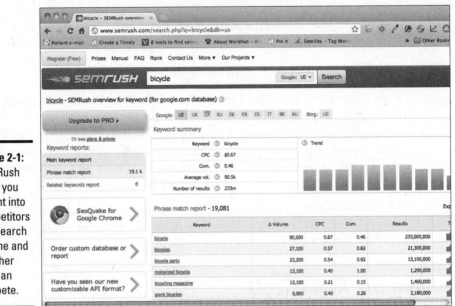

Figure 2-1:
SEMRush
gives you
insight into
competitors
and search
volume and
whether
you can
compete.

Working with the Google AdWords keyword research tool

The Google AdWords keyword tool is the only source for Google keyword search data. It's not perfect, but it's what you have.

You have to log into your AdWords account to use the AdWords keyword research tool. If you don't yet have an AdWords account, sign up! The account is free.

To show search volumes, follow these steps:

1. **Go to** `http://adwords.google.com/select/KeywordToolExternal`.

2. **Type a phrase in the text box, and click the Get Keyword Ideas button.**

   The report you receive, shown in Figure 2-2, shows searches performed in the previous month, average monthly search volume over the past 12 months, and advertiser competition in Google AdWords.

3. **Click the Columns option list and then choose Local Search Trends, as shown in Figure 2-3.**

   Doing this adds an additional column to the report. You see trended search data by month.

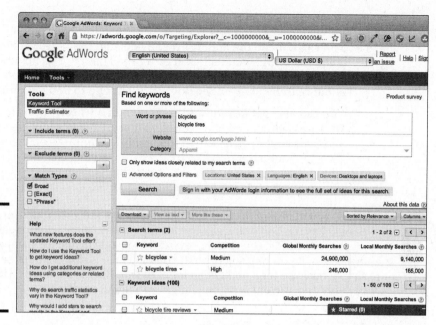

Figure 2-2:
Using the
Google
AdWords
keyword
tool.

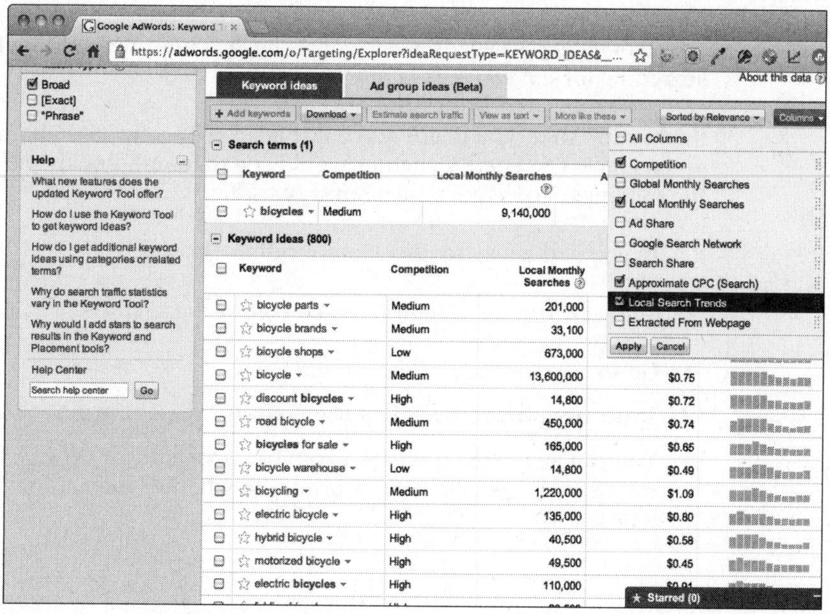

Figure 2-3:
Viewing
the search
trends data.

Be sure to try these other options:

✦ **You can change the Match Type.** By default, the Adwords keyword tool gives you search counts based on a Broad match. You might want to set the Match Type to Exact, to make sure that you don't get too excited about search volumes. See Book IV, Chapter 3 to find out more.

✦ **You can also get keyword ideas based on a website's content.** Click Website Content and enter a web address. Google's tool checks the page and pulls keywords based on the words and phrases on that page. The Website Content option is a great way to get ideas for keywords you hadn't thought of. You can also verify that your page is optimized for the right phrases and check competitors' pages.

At this point, you're probably thinking why use any other keyword tools? Google has the lion's share of the traffic anyway. Although Google does get most of the traffic, the Google keyword tool is designed for pay-per-click marketers. If you rely solely on it, you may miss some great niche phrases simply because they don't get a lot of bids in Google AdWords. Use the other keyword tools to ensure that you get an accurate picture.

Using Google Trends

All major search engines favor content that focuses on hot key phrases. For example, say that a famous movie star loses 45 pounds on a diet solely composed of mixed greens. The story hits newsstands, and suddenly everyone is searching for *mixed greens diet.*

If you knew that, you could add a few articles to your site about the mixed greens diet. The search engines would see that and quickly move you up in the rankings. You'd get a nice burst of traffic.

If only you had a way to check on trending phrases. . . .

Oh, but wait, you do! Google Trends. Follow these steps:

1. **Go to** www.google.com/trends.

2. **Type any phrase and click the Search Trends button.**

   You can see whether search volumes are rising or falling. The report even shows specific news stories and whether they affected search volumes.

The top section is the *search volume index,* the rise or fall in searches for that phrase. The bottom section is the *news reference volume,* which tells you online media mentions of the phrase.

You can get more advanced reporting at `www.google.com/insights/ search`, including seasonality, geography, and categories.

You can see a list of the top 100 hot phrases by clicking the More Hot Searches link, as shown in Figure 2-4.

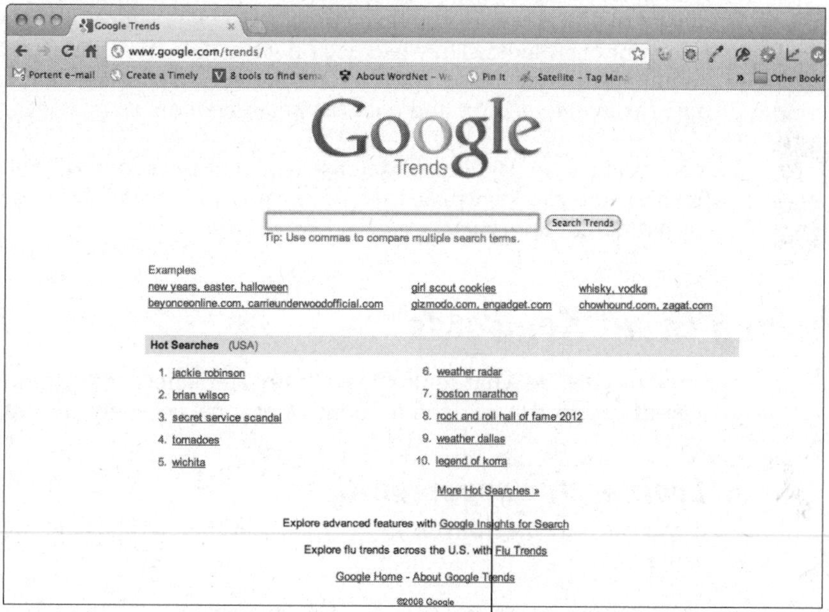

Figure 2-4: Clicking the More Hot Searches link produces the top 100 phrases.

Find what people are searching for.

Watching the news

We are media driven. It pays to keep current on TV, radio, and print news. If a relevant story seems to be gaining a lot of ground, work it into your website.

Going back to the (now somewhat silly) mixed greens example earlier in this chapter: If you see on the news that Mark Starguy is the movie star who lost 45 pounds on the mixed greens diet, you might want to mention his name here and there. Chances are that other folks watching the news will remember the star's name and *diet,* but not *mixed greens.* If you show up for *Mark Starguy diet,* you're set.

Using your brain

All the computers in the world can't match your brain for its ability to manipulate language. Don't rely on keyword tools alone. They will eventually lie to you (or at least tell a small fib): Keyword tools lack your insight into your customers. They can use only the data they have, and that means sometimes they'll miss important subtleties, such as the difference between *auto* (as in *automobile*) and *auto* (as in *automatic*).

Your brain is the last line of defense against keyword paralysis. If the tools are showing you keywords that simply make no sense, go with your gut and try a different approach.

Picking Great Keywords

After you decide what tools to use, it helps to know the criteria for choosing a great keyword. You need to judge relevance, competition, and value.

Looking for opportunity

If you use only one rule for keyword research, it's this: Find the opportunity gaps.

Look at your own traffic reports. Do any phrases drive quality traffic right now, but could still drive more? Start there. It's easier to go from #10 to #8 than it is to go from #100 to #1. But so many business owners try to rank for the toughest terms first.

If you want to rank #1 for *diamond rings,* more power to you. You might manage it someday. But find the terms that might generate more sales and traffic for you in the meantime.

Judging keyword relevance

Question whether the keyword you found is really relevant to your business. For example, *mixed greens* could mean mixed greens for salad. It could also mean mixed green paint.

After you choose a keyword, test it by using all the tools listed in the "Finding the Right Tools" section, earlier in this chapter. Make sure that you don't see any equally correct but totally irrelevant meanings creeping into the search results.

No keyword is 100 percent relevant. If more than half of the long-tail phrases using that word are relevant to your business, though, you probably have a winner.

Comparing competition and search volume

If you're facing 200 million other websites that are all vying for the No. 1 spot, you might want to choose a different keyword.

Go to Google and Bing and search for the phrase you've chosen. Look at three competitive factors:

1.3 billion

✦ **The number of competing sites:** If you find more than 10 million competing pages in the search results, you might be facing an uphill battle.

✦ **Where you rank:** If you're already on the second page of the results, you might not care how many sites are competing with you.

✦ **Your ability to compete:** If you have a daily newsletter on your site about mixed greens, you might be super competitive, even if a mob of other sites are trying to beat you. You're adding new, highly relevant content every day, and search engines love that. That steady content growth gives you an advantage.

Always balance competition against search volume. Some terms might be so relevant and offer so many potential visitors that any level of competition is worth it. For example, the phrase *wedding dresses* gets over one million searches per month. It's also one of the most competitive phrases on the entire Internet. But one million searches make *wedding dresses* so potentially valuable that if you have any chance of gaining a front-page ranking for it, you have to try. Other keywords might offer only a tiny trickle of traffic — and thus, very little competition.

Your best strategy is to mix your keyword list and optimize for both of the following:

✦ **High-volume, high-competition keywords** that require a long effort on your part before you gain any rankings

✦ **Low-volume, low-competition keywords** that can produce results sooner

This strategy lets you build traffic sooner while still aiming for the home run phrases later.

Checking your industry with Google Insights

You can also make sure that the keyword you chose fits your industry. (Are you offering *mixed greens* or *mixed green paint?*) You can use Google Insights to double-check your assumptions about your keyword's relevancy by following these steps:

1. **Go to** www.google.com/insights/search **and type your keyword in the text box.**

2. **Click the All Categories drop-down list and choose a category your keyword fits in, and then click the Search button.**

   Pshew. Looks like *mixed greens* really *is* about leafy stuff.

3. **If you're still worried, select a category you don't expect your keyword to fall into.**

   If you get a result of "Not enough search volume to show graphs," you know that you're in good shape.

Testing with pay per click

Because a search engine optimization campaign can take months to really affect your business, you may want to test your keywords by using a faster method — pay-per-click (PPC) marketing.

Because you can start and end a PPC campaign in a matter of minutes, doing so is a great way to get a rough idea of keyword viability.

Variables including budget, ad wording, competition, and landing pages can skew your results. Make sure that you use your head when you review the results. Read Book IV to find out how PPC works.

Building Your Keyword List

As you select keywords, keep track of them using a spreadsheet like the one shown in Figure 2-5.

games	875,296	1,120,000,000
free games	211,779	1,110,000,000
game	171,060	1,730,000,000
free online games	159,422	795,000,000
online games	128,390	1,080,000,000
chess	97,995	59,900,000
dress up games	79,615	46,800,000
video games	76,415	1,060,000,000
addicting games	69,728	1,710,000
play game	53,098	602,000,000
pc games	49,519	548,000,000
flash games	48,930	221,000,000
mahjong	47,968	21,400,000
free game downloads	40,693	261,000,000
play games	39,220	599,000,000
funny games	37,906	187,000,000
online game	32,993	997,000,000
computer games	32,044	475,000,000
board games	29,432	220,000,000
kids games	28,973	218,000,000
arcade games	27,791	80,000,000
free games online	26,613	726,000,000
fun games	25,955	553,000,000
bejeweled	24,598	7,380,000
free game	23,190	948,000,000
car games	22,840	536,000,000
video game	21,401	944,000,000
download games	20,883	938,000,000
card games	19,827	354,000,000
shooting games	19,624	54,800,000
family feud	19,622	2,790,000
diner dash	19,056	3,050,000
games online	17,749	1,110,000,000
free online game	17,617	845,000,000
bookworm	17,254	9,120,000
cake mania	17,211	4,870,000
racing games	16,859	123,000,000
math games	15,988	45,900,000
computer game	15,978	437,000,000

Figure 2-5: Keep a keyword spreadsheet to help you remember selections.

Keeping a spreadsheet can help you remember which keywords you selected, which ones you ignored, and why.

Your keyword list shouldn't be static. As you come up with new ideas, add them to the list. If you're a hard-core SEO geek, you might keep a small pad of paper with you at all times so that you can scribble down new phrases when they occur to you. If you're a more sane person (or have better ways to use your time), just keep your spreadsheet up to date.

Sizing Up the Competition

Always keep your eyes on the competition. If they're smart, they're keeping their eyes on you, too. Watch how your competitors rank for particular keywords, watch what they're doing to try to beat you in the rankings, and always look for places where you have an advantage. SEO is a zero-sum game: Only one No. 1 spot exists. So make sure that you're always tracking competitors.

Finding your keyword competitors

Hopefully, who your competitors are isn't a mystery. Go to Google and Bing and search for your target keywords. Consider the top-ten sites to be your primary competitors.

Use some of the tools covered in Chapter 1 of this minibook to find out about your competitors. Use the following:

✦ **SeoQuake** tells you how many links your competitors have, shows you their keyword density, and shows how many pages they have in the respective search engine indexes.

✦ **SEOMOZ's opensiteexplorer.org and Majestic's majesticseo.com** can both provide priceless intelligence regarding links and site authority.

Discovering your competitors' weaknesses

Several of the top-ten sites for a specific phrase probably aren't doing a very good job of optimizing their websites. They're in the top ten by luck or because no one else has done much SEO either.

You need to find those sites' weaknesses. If you can optimize your site better than they can, you have a good shot at replacing them in the rankings.

Use SeoQuake to see whether you can increase the keyword density — the percentage of total page text occupied by your key phrase — for target phrases on your site. Going above 5 to 7 percent keyword density isn't necessary. But if your competitors have 200 words on a page and 10 instances of a phrase, you can certainly put 250 words on a page and have 15 instances of the same phrase.

Use the Web Developer toolbar to see whether your competitors have built a good relevance hierarchy on their sites. If they don't have the target key phrase or a related phrase in their title tags or headings, you can get a huge advantage by putting the phrase in those elements.

Use the Web Developer toolbar to check for image ALT tags and other elements, too. ALT tags don't do much, but every little bit helps!

Figure out where your competitors have fallen down on the job. It's not magic. The vast majority of websites do a horrible job of SEO. Research the basics, and you can probably find lots of ways to outrank them.

Ignoring your competition

The vast majority of sites do a horrible job of SEO. If a keyword you selected looks just fantastic, but none of your competitors are using it, it might be their problem, not yours. What if all your competitors insist on optimizing for *salad,* even though no one searches for it?

You know your business and your customers. If your competition seems to be optimizing for key phrases that make no sense *and* if you can't find any evidence that customers are searching using those phrases, trust your judgment — ignore your competition.

The success of your business, not a top spot for a specific phrase, is what really matters.

Book II
Chapter 2

Choosing the Right Keywords

Biz
Competitors

Per
Competitors
Barbar J Oleary
Dominion Financial Ser

AD 1.) North Western Mutual
AD 2.) Morgan Stanley
    3.) First Command
    4.) Edelman
AD 5.) Chase
AD 6.) Edward Jones
AD 7.) Lockheed Advisory Services
AD 8.) Fair fax Financial Planners

Chapter 3: Eliminating Search Engine Roadblocks

In This Chapter

✔ Ensuring search engine visibility

✔ Avoiding problems

✔ Finding and fixing broken links

✔ Minimizing code bloat

*O*ne way or another, business owners often block search engines from reading their content. And by doing so, they're cutting off a huge segment of their audience. If a search engine can't find your content, it can't index it, which means that it can't determine relevance. When this happens, you don't get ranked.

This chapter covers a range of ways to ensure visibility, find and fix problems, and avoid problems that create search engine roadblocks. If you use a little common sense, though, you can easily test your website for problems: Use the Web Developer toolbar to check your entire site with CSS and JavaScript turned off, fix broken links, and write good, clean, fast-loading code.

Ensuring Search Engine Visibility

Websites are always disappearing from the Google rankings because a developer put a tagline on every page of the site that read

```
meta name="robots" content="noindex,nofollow"
```

Chances are that the developer put that tag there to prevent search engines from reading the site while she was building it. It's like covering a painting until it's unveiled. Leave that tag in place, though, and search engines ignore not only that page but also every single link on that page — which is like forgetting to remove the cover from the painting before the big show.

In the following sections, you find out how to make sure that you're not actively blocking search engines from crawling pages on your website.

Checking your robots.txt file

Go to www.*yoursiteaddress*.com/robots.txt. You might get a Page Not Found error. That's okay for your purposes: A no robots.txt file means you're not placing any broad limits on what search engines can and can't index on your site. You might also see a file that looks like this:

```
User-agent: *
Disallow: /blog.htm
```

This file is called the robots.txt file. It tells search engine crawlers, also known as *robots,* what to do when they visit your website. In this example, it's telling all search engines to ignore the blog.htm page. All other pages are searchable.

If you want to become a robots.txt geek, visit www.robotstxt.org. You can find out everything you ever wanted to know about guiding robots around your site.

What you *don't* want to see in your robots.txt file is this:

```
Disallow: /
```

This line tells a visiting search engine crawler to ignore *every page* on your website. A developer may add this line when he is building the site to prevent search engines from crawling it while it's under construction. If it is left there by accident, your site is invisible to search engines.

If your robots.txt file has any Disallow commands in it, check with your webmaster or developer to make sure that a reason exists. Disallow can be used to hide pages that change a lot, hide duplicate content, or keep search engines out of stuff you just don't want them crawling. Just make sure that you're not accidentally hiding content they *should* see.

Checking for meta robots tags

Using the meta robots tag is another way to hide pages from search engines. Go to any page on your website and view the source code. You don't want to see

```
<meta name="robots" content="noindex,nofollow">
```

If the meta robots tag is there, and it contains noindex, nofollow, or both, remove it. You have valid reasons to use this tag: You might want a search engine to ignore this page because it's a duplicate of another; you might feel that the information on the page is inappropriate for search results; or the developer might have hidden the page during development. But you should know those reasons. If you don't, delete the tag.

Do not trust your developer to remove the meta `robots` tag. When he builds your site, he's working hard, writing code so fast that his fingers smoke. Forgetting to remove that one little line of code is easy when you're facing a tough deadline and still have 4,000 lines of code to write. Remind your developer!

Eliminating registration forms

Don't put registration forms in front of great content! Visitors often have to complete these forms before they can download some kind of premium content, such as a white paper, or before they can read some articles on a site. Companies put them in place because they want leads — they want contact information for interested potential customers.

Book II
Chapter 3

**Eliminating Search
Engine Roadblocks**

If you have any registration forms hiding white papers, newsletters, or other information, remove the forms.

Your salespeople might howl. Your head of marketing might yell. Your CEO might stamp her feet. Remain calm and ask your staff for a one-month test — and here's why:

You spent two months writing a white paper. You put it up on your website, and you want to get something in return. So you add a little form that forces visitors to give you their e-mail address and name before they can read the paper.

That form hurts you in two ways:

✦ It greatly reduces the number of people who will read the content. You wrote that content to spread the word about your company, so you want people to read it.

✦ Search engines can't fill out forms, so they'll never see that great information. Which means, if you wrote a white paper on making a perfect carrot cake, folks searching for *perfect carrot cake* will never see your information. Never mind whether they call. They won't even know you're there.

Here are the arguments you may get in favor of keeping the forms, and the reply to each of them:

✦ **"We won't get any leads. People will just read the pages without contacting us."** Actually, by eliminating the form, you expand the number of people reading this information by a factor of ten or more. Because they're already looking for information, they're good prospects. Make sure the phone number and other contact information is in the paper, and they'll be in touch. Great content gets folks in the top of your sales funnel, so more openness is almost always better.

✦ **"Someone will steal our content."** Welcome to the Internet. That's going to happen regardless. Place a link to your site on every page of the article or paper. That way, any would-be plagiarists create a link back to your site.

✦ **"We need to see a return from this."** You will. Search engines generate the lion's share of traffic online. By removing the registration form, you gain far more leads and customers than you lose.

✦ **"I won't be able to reach people who read the article, because I won't have their contact information."** Actually, you can reach them by posting another great article. And another. You can build your reputation as an authority, reach more readers, and have far more marketing opportunities.

Dump the registration forms.

Eliminating login forms

You've probably already guessed that login forms are bad, too. If you haven't, well, they're bad.

Website owners might include login forms for the following reasons:

✦ They feel that they need to add value for registered members.

✦ They want to force registration.

✦ They don't want company secrets getting out.

Remove the forms anyway. If you remove your registration forms, you'll remove the need to add value for registered members. Also, hiding a few white papers behind a login doesn't give perceived value to members.

If you really have top-quality training content, tools, or products for sale for which you're offering a preview, keep the login. Otherwise, you don't need that form.

When it comes to company secrets, you need to think carefully. Is this information really a secret? Or is it just information you'd rather people didn't know? In both cases, a login form won't help you.

If you don't want people to find it, don't put it on the Internet. Someone will find the information, somehow, someday, and republish it to their heart's content.

Dump the login forms.

Providing a Way to Browse

Search engines move from page to page on your website by following links. They can't fill out forms, which means that they can't use that search box you have on your site (ironic, huh?). They also can't use a quick navigation box, such as the one shown in Figure 3-1.

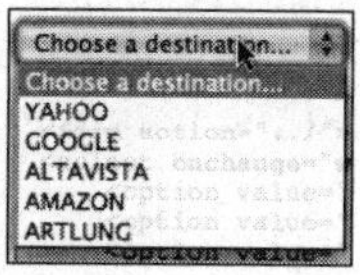

Figure 3-1:
Search engines can't follow form-based navigation.

So, if you have any of the following, make sure that a way exists to click through and browse the entire database by using regular HTML links:

✦ A location database that shows a list of local stores or other addresses

✦ A searchable directory of products

✦ An address book for your company's staff

✦ Any other data stored in a database and searched using a form

Say your site sells salads. On your homepage, you have a form that lets folks pick what ingredients they'd like in their salad and then see which premade salads they can order that fit their requirements.

If that form is the only way to find product information, and you don't have any regular links, you're blocking search engines from finding your products. *Remember:* Search engines can't use forms.

To fix the problem, add a Browse All Products link. Then let visitors drill down from there by ingredients, categories, or both.

Another example: You have a searchable database of stores offering your products. Visitors type their address or postal code, and the site displays nearby stores. Great for visitors, but not good for search engines, because they can't use a search form (ironic, isn't it?).

Add a link that lets visitors click instead of search, by choosing their state and then their city.

Search engines can follow that link, find all those pages, and add more content to their index of your site. Make sure that all your content is browseable.

Using Ajax and DHTML

Ajax allows you to build web applications. It allows a web page to load new information without requiring a new page load. That delivers faster, smoother web interaction and generally makes visitors happy. *DHTML* is a method used to create things like drop-down menus, simple animations, and special effects. You don't need to understand the technologies to understand the risk they pose in SEO.

Ajax loads content by using JavaScript. Search engines can't read JavaScript, so any content you load using Ajax is effectively hidden from the search engine. If you have content you really want a search engine to find, don't deliver it using Ajax.

Google does crawl Ajax-driven content but results are mixed, and it's hard to say whether this will really help with rankings. Play it safe and avoid the use of Ajax for major content.

Ajax is a nifty way to build great web applications, including shopping carts and search tools. Just be sure that you don't hide text content behind an Ajax application.

DHTML also loads content by using JavaScript. Same problem. You can make DHTML menus like the one shown in Figure 3-2 in such a way that a search engine can still find the links.

Figure 3-2:
Using DHTML to create a drop-down menu.

Ask your designer to make sure that he builds the menus to *degrade gracefully*. A web page that degrades gracefully provides basic navigation and all content in a sensible way, even if the browser visiting it doesn't support JavaScript or DHTML.

Take what your designers promise with a grain of salt, too. They're totally focused on designing something great. You can verify whether your page's DHTML navigation degrades gracefully. Open the page in Firefox. Using the Web Developer toolbar, disable CSS and JavaScript. If you can still see the links that are in the drop-down menus, your page is perfect. If you can't, go ask the designer to redo them. Ask nicely. He is probably tired at this point.

Avoiding All-Flash Pages

Adobe Flash is a great way to create beautiful, interactive animations for your website. Unfortunately, search engines can't read Flash animations, for the following reasons:

✦ **Search engines don't have the Flash plug-in.** Remember, search engines visit your website as a super-simple web browser. Flash is a plug-in that viewers have to add to their web browsers — without it, they can't see any of your Flash content. Search engines don't have that plug-in built into their software, so they typically can't read any of the content.

 ✦ **Flash compiles links, fonts, and structural information differently than a typical HTML page.** So even if a search engine *does* manage to read the content, it may read it as gibberish.

✦ **Flash is often used to load multiple pages of text, videos, and other motion graphics onto a single HTML web page.** That creates the same problems as Ajax, by hiding all but the very first snippet of information from visiting search engines.

✦ **Flash doesn't work on any of Apple's iOS devices, including iPads.** Do you really want to cut yourself off from all those users?

You can still use Flash animations. The old Portent Interactive homepage, shown in Figure 3-3, is a good example.

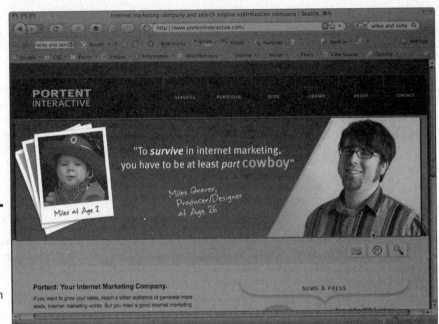

Figure 3-3:
The old
Portent
Interactive
homepage
used a Flash
animation.

You might be using Flash in a way that could hurt your SEO efforts. Pay attention to the following warning signs:

✦ Visitors click from page to page on your website from within Flash, without actually going to a new page.

✦ When you view the page using Yellowpipe Lynx Viewer, you see a blank page, or your page doesn't show large amounts of text.

✦ Your designer can't look you in the eye when you ask whether the website is SEO ready.

Designers often use Flash because it's the only way they know to get just the right fonts on the web. However, Cascading Style Sheets (CSS) are advanced enough to let designers get almost the same look and feel with a regular HTML page. See *CSS Web Design For Dummies,* by Richard Mansfield (published by John Wiley & Sons, Inc.), for more information.

Avoiding Client-Side Redirects

When search engines first appeared, many web developers looked for ways to show them super-relevant content. Sometimes, that super-relevant content was just lists of keywords on an otherwise blank page. Developers knew that they didn't want visitors to see that gibberish, so they used something called a *client-side redirect* to forward human visitors to a more friendly, comprehensible page.

These redirects used either JavaScript, to reroute a visiting browser, or a meta `refresh` tag, to do the same thing. Because search engines don't support JavaScript, and didn't understand meta `refresh` tags at the time, they stopped dead, while visiting web browsers redirected human visitors, who didn't even notice the redirect.

Search engines would see the super-relevant gibberish and give the website a high ranking. A nice trick, but one that search engines really didn't appreciate.

Search engines want to rank your site based on the same content that human beings see. The redirection tactic, known as *cloaking,* became an anathema.

Because of that history, search engines don't like to see any kind of *client-side redirect.* It's still one of the cardinal sins of search engine optimization. Make sure that your web team members know that they shouldn't use either method to reroute people around your website.

If you must redirect visitors from one page to another (say, because you have deleted the old page and now have a new one, or you've moved to a new web address), use a server-side or 301 redirect. Your web developer will know how to set this up. If he doesn't, find one who does.

Checking Your Site Using the Web Developer Toolbar

You can ferret out any problems with search engines by using the Web Developer toolbar. If you don't know what this is, turn to Chapter 1 in this minibook.

Using the Web Developer toolbar, disable JavaScript, meta redirects, and CSS. Click around your site. If you can get to every page without clicking on Flash, you're in good shape. Write down the pages you couldn't reach.

Hopefully, you can fix the problem. But if you can't fix it, you can provide an alternate way for search engines to get to those pages, such as a link in the footer of your website.

Avoiding Duplicate Content

Nothing hurts a search engine's quest for relevant content as much as finding the exact same words on two different pages. Duplication is bad for these reasons:

✦ **Duplication used to be another tactic used to fool the search engines.** Webmasters would take one website and replicate it across many different domains, linking them all together. That would fool early search engines into seeing many relevant sites interlinked, and therefore cause the engines to artificially inflate rankings. You don't want to risk being associated with this tactic — penalties are rare but severe.

✦ **Duplicate content creates confusion.** If a search engine finds the same content on two pages of one site, or two pages on two different sites, it has to basically guess which page should be ranked. Having duplicate words also makes it hard for a search engine to decide *which* page should be ranked.

✦ **Other webmasters who link to your content might link to either version.** All links to your site are votes. If half of all webmasters link to one page on your site and the other half link to the duplicate, you've split your vote and lose authority.

Most of the time, duplication is an accident. It's created by inconsistent linking, bad pagination scripts, or other sloppy website-building practices.

Google says that it can handle duplicate content for you. It's true — Google will often remove duplicates from its index, and it doesn't penalize you for it. The problem is, though, that Google still has to spend time crawling all of that duplicate stuff. That wastes what's known as *crawl budget,* and that hurts your SEO.

In the following sections, you find out how to detect duplicate content so that you can avoid it.

Finding duplicate content using Google

You can find duplicate content on and off your website by using search engines. To do so, follow these steps:

1. **Go to Google and type** site:www.*yoursiteaddress*.com.

(Type your actual website address.) Doing this shows all pages from your site that are currently in the Google index.

2. **Click through all the result pages.**

If you get to a message that reads `In order to show you the most relevant results, we have omitted some entries very similar. . .`, you have pages that Google considers duplicates.

3. **Click Repeat the Search with the Omitted Results Included.**

   The additional pages are your duplicates.

You can also find duplicate content with a more basic search. Copy one sentence from somewhere on your website. Make sure that it's not a sentence that others are likely to use. On Google, search for that sentence, in quotations marks. An example is shown in Figure 3-4.

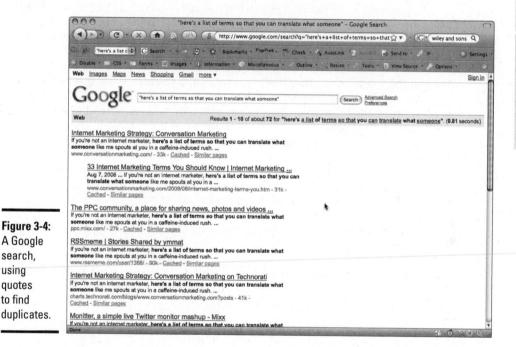

Figure 3-4:
A Google search, using quotes to find duplicates.

Google returns all pages in its index that include those words, in that order. This lets you find other sites that have copied your writing as well as pages on your own website that are duplicates of each other.

No matter how hard you try, you can never create a site that is 100 percent duplication free — it's impossible. The important thing is to make sure that you don't duplicate entire pages or sets of pages from one page to the next or, even worse, one website to another.

Linking to your homepage the right way

To a search engine, all three of the following URLs are unique pages on the Internet:

```
www.mydomainname.com
mydomainname.com
www.mydomainname.com/index.html
```

Although they're all pointing to the same page, search engines see each URL as unique. This is the most common form of duplication on the web.

If you have your homepage in a file called `index.html` and you link to it three different ways, search engines will find it at those three locations, with the exact same content. The search engine then has to figure out which page is the *real* page and ignore the rest.

In the worst case, other folks randomly link to each of the three addresses. You do the same on your own website. Search engines find all three links, splitting the relevance votes those links can deliver. Instead of getting three votes to one page, you get one vote each on three different pages that all compete with each other for authority in the search engines.

You can use a simple fix. Always link to your homepage exactly like this:

```
http://www.yoursiteaddress.com
```

Exactly like that, except replace *yoursiteaddress* with your actual website address.

Then, set up a 301 redirect from *yoursiteaddress*.com to www.*your siteaddress*.com. (See the "Using a 301 redirect" section, later in this chapter, for instructions on how to do this.)

That will reduce link confusion and prevent homepage duplication.

Using consistent URLs

Database-driven sites can often use very complicated page addresses (URLs), such as:

```
http://www.mysite.com?pageid=1&content=234&category=the
category
```

That's because database-driven sites use variables like `pageid` and `content` to determine what to display on each page of the site.

These page addresses don't present a search engine roadblock — search engines can handle dynamic addresses. However, if you link to this page like this:

```
http://www.mysite.com?pageid=1&content=234&category=the
category
```

and also like this:

```
http://www.mysite.com?pageid=1&content=234
```

and both links work, guess what? You have duplicate content. Dynamic, database-driven sites can create thousands upon thousands of duplicate pages, because they're generating these links the moment a browser visits the site. They automatically create the page addresses on request. So potentially *any* link format that works could end up being read by a search engine.

Incorrect homepage linking may create two or three duplicate pages. Incorrect database-driven site links can create copies of every single page on your site.

Make sure that you link to each page the same way.

Dealing with Broken Links

Broken links stop search engines in their tracks. If a search engine reaches a broken link, it can't find the page you intended (obviously) — but it might also give up on your website or reduce the relevance of your site. So you need to find those busted links and fix 'em.

Finding broken links

You can find broken links by using Xenu (on the PC) or Integrity (on the Mac).

After you run the tools, put your results in a list. Then, using your list as a guide, find all the broken links that you can fix and correct errors so that each link is once again functional.

Using a 301 redirect

Sometimes, though, a link is broken because it points to a page that is no longer there. In that case, you can use a *301 redirect*.

301 — the code the server sends to visiting browsers and search engine crawlers — means "This page isn't here any more — go to this other page, instead." When a search engine sees that, it follows the redirect, applies all the link relevance of the old page to the new page, and replaces the old page with the new one.

It's *very* important that you use a 301 — *not* a 302 — redirect. A 302 redirect says, "This page isn't here, but it'll be back soon." If a search engine sees that, it doesn't pass any link relevance and doesn't replace the old page with the new one.

You can set up a 301 redirect on either of the most popular web servers out there — Internet Information Server (IIS; Microsoft) or Apache. If you don't know how to do this, talk to your webmaster for instructions. This isn't something you can do yourself if you aren't familiar with these web servers.

Removing Code Bloat

Search engines like to see a high ratio of content to code: as few lines of code as possible per line of content. You have a few simple ways to remove code bloat and maximize the ratio of code to content.

Coding using standards

If you code using XHTML and CSS standards, you can automatically minimize code bloat. These standards keep the code that controls how things look in a single, separate CSS file, and put all the content in the XHTML page. This setup maximizes that ratio of content to code.

One critical benefit of coding with standards is that you can stop using HTML tables for layout purposes. Tables are meant to display data, not graphics.

If you want to become more familiar with XHTML, take a look at *HTML, XHTML & CSS For Dummies*, by Ed Tittel and Jeff Noble (published by John Wiley & Sons, Inc.).

Removing inline JavaScript and CSS

Another code-bloat culprit is JavaScript that's inserted right into the page, as shown in Figure 3-5.

That JavaScript code doesn't have to be there. Instead, you can move it into a separate `.js` file and include it by using JavaScript, such as

```
<script language="javascript" type="text/javascript" src="thescript.js">
```

You just removed 20 lines of bloat from your page.

You can do the same thing with blocks of CSS information, as shown in Figure 3-6.

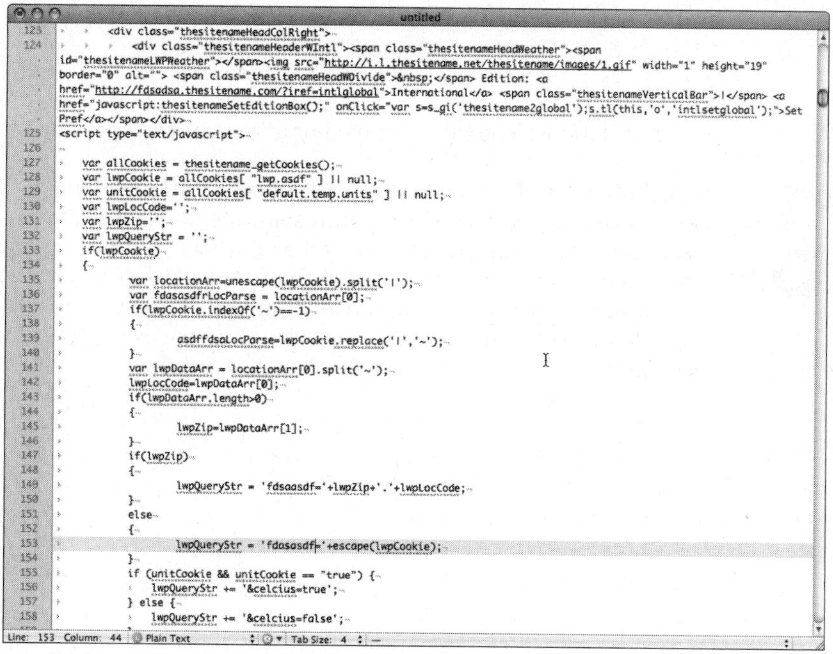

Figure 3-5:
Inline
JavaScript
in the
source of a
page.

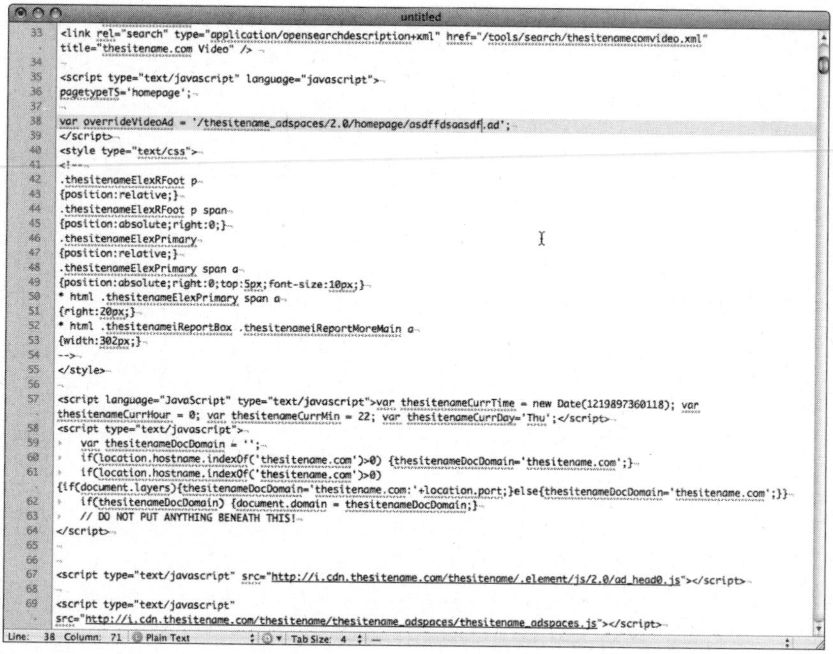

Figure 3-6:
Remove
inline CSS.
Naughty
developer!

Move that CSS code to a separate `.css` file by using this code:

```
<LINK REL="StyleSheet" HREF="style.css" TYPE="text/css">
```

Congratulations! You just removed another ten lines of code bloat.

Removing inline JavaScript and CSS has an additional benefit. When you put JavaScript and CSS information into separate files, visiting web browsers will *cache* the information on the users' hard drives. They download the scripts and CSS once and then load it from their own hard drives from then on. That speeds site performance and means that you use less bandwidth. Also, by putting these files in one place, you can more easily make site-wide changes and additions.

Chapter 4: Making Search Engines Love Your Site

In This Chapter

✔ **Creating and maintaining a great site structure**

✔ **Building great on-page structure**

✔ **Optimizing for trust**

Search engines want relevance. In this chapter, you find out how you can make your website more attractive to search engines by creating content clusters and using deep links. You also find out how to maintain your website after you optimize it.

After you understand how to structure your website, you can use a semantic outline to create an appealing structure for each page. You can also optimize your website for trustworthiness.

Structuring Your Site for Search Engines and People

Think of your website as a pyramid. At the top, you have the homepage. One click away from the homepage, you have the second layer of content. Two clicks away, you have the third layer. Each additional click moves you another layer down in the hierarchy until you can't click any farther away from the homepage. That's the bottom layer. Search engines award more relevance more readily to content that is closer to the top of the site pyramid.

You can bring content to the top of the pyramid by

✦ Creating content clusters so that you create individual, high-relevance *hub pages* within the site structure. You can then link to these high-relevance pages from your homepage and move the entire cluster up the hierarchy.

✦ Deep linking to extremely important pages directly from the homepage, which moves this content up the hierarchy.

Creating content clusters

You can use *content clusters,* groupings of related content, to help build relevance. When you link two or more related pages to each other and to a central *hub* or index page from which a visitor can find all those related pages, you create a cluster of relevant content.

These links lend authority, just as links from other sites lend authority. If you can link ten pages to and from a single hub page, you create more relevance than if you had a single relevant page all alone. So, you have strength in numbers — the more related pages you can link in clusters, the greater authority you can generate for your site.

Always link like with like. Keeping your content clumped together has two benefits:

✦ **Customers are happier.** Visitors to your site want to find all related content grouped together, like in a library. Content clusters and the hub pages that drive them make it far, far easier for visitors to see those groupings and find what they need.

✦ **Hub pages and clusters make search engines consider your site more relevant.** You concentrate authority from many relevant pages in a single hub page. And, you can link to that hub page from your homepage, which moves the entire cluster of content up in the site hierarchy.

Figure 4-1 shows a structure of a pretty good bicycle shop website with average navigation. Visitors can browse the usual sections — Products, About Us, and so on.

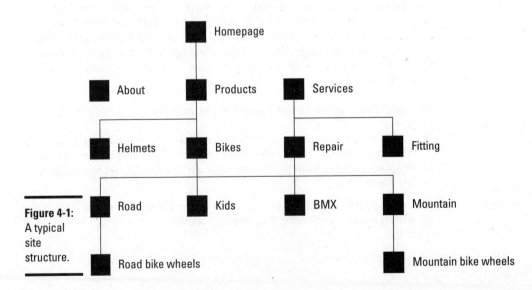

Figure 4-1:
A typical
site
structure.

The problem is that people don't look for *products*; they search for *bicycle repair* or *custom built wheels* or *kids bikes*. The bike shop website shown in Figure 4-2 might offer exactly what's needed, but the information is scattered around the site structure.

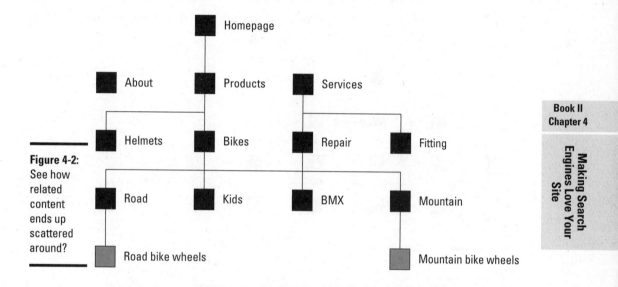

Figure 4-2:
See how related content ends up scattered around?

For example, if you come to this site looking for a set of mountain bike wheels, in the current site structure, you have to click at least two times just to begin your search. Plus, search engines come to the site and find the only bicycle wheel–related content four clicks from the homepage. That's four levels down the pyramid. To a search engine, that means wheels aren't very important on this website. So, the site's going to have a harder time gaining a decent ranking for wheel-related key phrases. Figure 4-2 illustrates the problem.

To fix the problem, you need to create a wheel-related content cluster around a single hub page that lists the links to all those wheel-related pages. Then, all those wheel-related pages need to link back to the hub page, as well. You don't have to reorganize your existing site, or make any massive changes. Instead, follow these steps:

1. **Find all the related pages on your website.**

   In the bicycle wheels example, the owner will find all wheel-related content.

2. **Create a single hub page that references all these other pages.**

   In this case, the owner creates a single page about wheels.

3. **Link to that hub page from each of those other pages.**

   To see how the bicycle shop owner would do it, see Figure 4-3.

4. **Link to the hub page from the homepage of your website, or from another web page that is no more than two clicks from the homepage.**

   In this case, the owner creates a link from the homepage to the Wheels page.

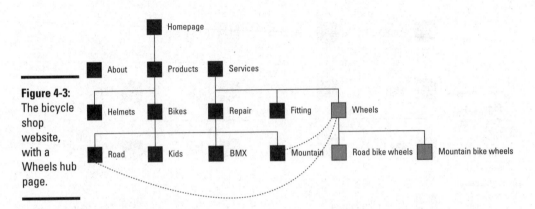

Figure 4-3: The bicycle shop website, with a Wheels hub page.

What did the bike shop owner just accomplish? Three things:

✦ He made it far easier for customers to find information about the wheels he sells. Visitors can now click the Wheels link on the homepage and immediately find what they need, rather than wandering three or more clicks from the homepage to try to find it.

✦ Search engines now see lots of wheel-related content one click from the homepage. The wheel-related content has been moved up in the site hierarchy.

✦ Search engines now see a single Wheels hub page with at least two other relevant pages linking to it. Remember, the links from the other two pages are votes. The new hub page is therefore more relevant to *wheels* and related phrases than the other two pages were when they were separated in the site hierarchy.

A hub page can't just be a list of links. It must have real utility for people as well as search engines.

Here's another example: Groomstand.com competes in a very difficult search engine optimization area — groomsmen gifts. It had hundreds of pages of content about groomsmen gifts, but these pages were spread throughout the site hierarchy. The revamped site now has a single grooms-men gifts shopping page, with product images and descriptions (shown in Figure 4-4). That page is linked from the homepage of the site, and from every groomsmen gift–related page. Visitors now have a single page to browse when shopping for these types of gifts. It also gives search engines a single page that has tremendous authority for the phrase *groomsmen gifts* because hundreds of relevant pages on the site link to it. Finally, it places that authoritative page one click from the homepage, thereby moving the entire content cluster within just one click of the homepage.

Figure 4-4: The Groomstand Groomsmen Gifts hub page.

You don't need to modify your website. You simply link to the same pages in a different way. The original structure can remain in place.

This kind of cluster consolidates related content, which funnels link relevance to a single page — the hub page. It lets you take the *votes* those pages have and point them at that single page, making it a super-relevant centerpiece for your website.

Don't create a cluster of fewer than 15 web pages. Unless you're working on a very noncompetitive key phrase, you can end up too diluted to move up in the rankings because you aren't sending enough votes from other pages on your site to that page.

Creating content clusters around hub pages builds a site structure that's better for search engines and people. It'll help you get higher rankings *and* improve your site's appeal to visitors.

Deep linking for special cases

A *deep link* is a hyperlink that goes directly to a page that's more than one click from the top of the site pyramid (the homepage). If another website links directly to a single product in your store, bypassing the homepage and any category pages, that's a deep link. You can also create deep links within your own site, by linking from your home or top-level pages to individual pages deep within your site's structure.

You'll most often do this to get a little extra boost for a page that's already on its way up in the rankings. Occasionally, a single page on your website suddenly shows up on Page 2 of the search engine result pages. Search engines consider it relevant for your target phrase.

If that page is a hub page, pat yourself on the back! If it's not, try this: Add a link to the page that's suddenly on Page 2 from the homepage of your website. By doing that, you move that page to the second level of your site's hierarchy, no matter how many clicks from the homepage it originally was.

Search engines attach more importance to content that's closer to the top of your website. If you link to this page from the homepage of your site, you move it to the top of the site hierarchy. You get more structural relevance.

Deep linking will rarely take you from no ranking to Page 1, but it can give you a boost, and it can place compelling content where visitors will find it.

Keeping the Structure Clean and Clear

After you do the work to create and improve a search engine–optimized site structure, you'll want to maintain it.

That means never moving content around, reinforcing that structure with great link text, using keyword-rich URLs (if possible), and avoiding some common site map issues. The following sections provide tips for accomplishing all four goals.

Keeping content in one place

Many large sites (particularly publications) create an archive section. After a few months, old content is moved to this section. So a page that used to be `www.`*`mynewspapersite.com`*`/june/2007/sports`

becomes

`www.`*`mynewspapersite.com`*`/archive/sports`

Search engines lose track of the content. And when they find it again, it's likely buried in the site hierarchy, five to ten links from the homepage.

The fix is simple: *Don't move your content. Ever.*

Make sure that your website is set up to accommodate a lot of content without an archive. Pages that stay where they were originally placed get you far more SEO leverage. If you archive content, you're effectively playing now-you-see-it, now-you-don't with the search engines.

Of course, you can still use archives. Just don't move your content to create them. Here's an example: If your business is a newspaper, your site might have thousands of pages of content per year. Your sports section probably has hundreds of pages, too. You can't keep all that content linked from the sports section homepage. The page will get larger and larger, making it impossible for visitors to find anything.

So, you create an archive hub page and one subhub page for each month of each year. On August 1 (as an example), you remove all links to July content from the sports section page and place them on the July archive subpage. You didn't actually move the July pages. If they were at `www.`*`mynewspaper site.com`*`/2012/07` before, they're still there now. Search engines and visitors can still find those pages at the same address, and you made room for new content and maintained links to the old.

Sub Hub

Writing great link text

The text contained in a link provides a hint to both search engines and visitors. A link tells them what they're going to see when they follow the link.

While link text doesn't carry quite the same rankings oomph it once did, it still matters. So read on, intrepid SEO-ers:

Search engines look at link text to gain insight into the target page's content. If you have a page that talks about bike wheels and a link that reads `Click Here`, for example, search engines have no idea. Although Click Here is accurate, using something like Click Here for More about Custom Wheels — or even just Custom Wheels — is far better.

Take a link's text and write it on a blank sheet of paper. Read it. Does it identify the page at which it points?

If your website has any of the classic links shown in the left column in Table 4-1, consider your options. Use the examples as a guide to come up with something more relevant.

Menu links

Table 4-1	Link Text Ideas
Original Link	*Better Link Examples*
Products	Business Gifts Computer Software Bicycles
About Us	Best Bicycle Shop Our Software Geeks 5 Years of Dentistry
Services	Internet Marketing Services Dental Services Bicycle Repair

Your website designer might say that your site design doesn't have room for long links. However, tweaking the design to allow a few extra characters is better than having your online store sit, unused, because no one can find it. If you can't change the design, create enhanced links elsewhere on the homepage.

Use great link text and you reinforce your site structure, and the meaning of the content within that structure, to both search engines and people. So, you boost your chances of a high ranking.

Using keyword-rich URLs

Even if you can't get a keyword-rich domain name, you still have control over page addresses. For example, maybe you really want `Seattle-bicycles.com`, but it's not available. So, you have to go with a less-perfect domain name, `brityup.com`. Hmmm.

Times have changed. There's no evidence that partial-match domain names, like, say, `bicyclesinseattle.com`, will help when someone searches for *seattle bicycles*. Nor will adding key terms to the rest of the URL. Those wonderful days of yore are long gone. But a strong argument still exists for easy-to-read, descriptive page URLs: Folks are more likely to click a search result with a URL that makes sense. So you should still try to make your URLs easy to read.

You need to use some common sense when doing this. If you create a stretched page or folder name, such as `bicycle-repairs-in-seattle`, you're trying too hard, and search engines are likely to ignore it. The page and folder names need to make logical sense, be brief, and not read like you're trying to shoehorn in every key phrase you're targeting.

Stepping away from the site map

You probably have a page on your website that lists every section and page — the site map. Search engines tend to ignore pages with more than ten links in the body of the page itself. That prevents website owners from creating related links pages with thousands of sites and then using those pages to build links for the sole purpose of improving rankings. Search engines want you to build your site for visitors, not around them. Long link pages are a sure sign you're doing the latter, not the former, so search engines typically ignore pages that have lots of links and no other content.

Step away from the traditional site map! If you must have one, put fewer links and include some descriptive text, too, so you get more of a directory than a site-map page. Create a nested structure of pages that lets visitors browse through an outline of your site, instead of a single page with dozens or hundreds of links. There's nothing wrong with a site map — it just won't help much with your SEO efforts.

Building a Semantic Outline

After you get a handle on the basics of structuring your website for search engines and people, you can create a structure for each individual page. Every page has a *semantic* outline — an outline that explains the meaning and structure of content on the page.

Search engines look for a semantic outline that conforms to XHTML and HTML conventions, starting with the title tag at the top.

The following is a good example:

> Title tag
>
> H1 (level 1 heading)
>
> H2, H3, and so on (lower-level headings)
>
> Paragraph text
>
> Links, captions, and other stuff

Don't underestimate the importance of the other stuff. But any SEO effort must optimize your title tags, heading tags, and paragraph text on every page. If you don't have your target key phrase in the title tag, level 1 heading, and somewhere in your body text, your other efforts won't get you anywhere.

A lot of SEO-ers argue that heading tags don't matter. But really, if you have a heading, you should use a heading tag to define it, anyway, right? Do the right thing. It's good for your web karma.

Begin your title tag with your key phrase, like this:

```
<title>Bicycle Repair and Sales - Ian's Bike Shop</title>
```

If you must put your brand name in the title tag, put it last. Ideally, though, leave it out entirely.

Also, make your title tag unique and relevant to each page. Repeating the same title tag throughout your website hurts your efforts to build keyword diversity and may get you penalized by the search engines.

Your heading elements should be enclosed in proper heading tags:

```
<h1>Bicycle Repair Services</h1>
```

You can get the same appearance by simply bolding the text and increasing the font size, like this:

```
<span style="font-weight:bold;font-size:18pt;">Bicycle Repair Services</span>
```

But that doesn't help as much. The heading is no longer defined as a heading within the page's semantic outline, so search engines won't accord it the same importance.

Use only one h1 element on a page. If you have additional headings, they should be level 2 and level 3 headings, nested appropriately. Think of your page as a traditional outline. Each outline has one item that states what the entire outline is about — your title and h1 elements. Under that top-level item, you have your first major topic. That's an h2 element. Under that, you might have more subtopics, which would be h3, h4, and deeper elements. Then under each of those, you might have descriptive text. Those are your paragraph elements.

Make sure that the ideas put forth in the title tag and heading tags support the paragraph copy, too. For example, loading up the title tags with keywords such as *repair* won't help if the page you're titling talks about buying new bikes. The semantic outline should fit together, just like the outlines you created in elementary school.

A great semantic outline makes sense to people and search engines alike. If you feel like you're twisting your writing to create the outline, reconsider what you're doing.

Optimizing for Trust

Not many people know this, but search engines are including trust in their ranking algorithms. This concept, called TrustRank, is how search engines separate legitimate web pages from spam. The search engines analyze pages and links for factors that make the pages seem more or less trustworthy, such as

**Book II
Chapter 4**

**Making Search
Engines Love Your
Site**

✦ Is the site a known distributor of illicit software or viruses?

✦ Is the site supported by a legitimate business enterprise?

✦ How long has the site been in operation?

Luckily, optimizing for trust is fairly simple. Do the following:

✦ **Use an old domain name.** After you establish a web address, keep it. If you must move, use 301 redirects to pass as much of the trust along as possible. (Read about 301 redirects in Chapter 3 of this minibook.)

✦ **Get your site evaluated by one of the security services, such as ScanAlert.** Then put the service's *sticker* on your site. Search engines actually do look for this. SEO geeks have spent hours going over patent applications, notes from search engineers, and all sorts of obscure tests. After a lot of debate, it's now consensus that security stickers help, if they're legitimate. You can also join the U.S. National Better Business Bureau and apply for accreditation. After you receive it, you can place the official BBB Accredited Business seal on your site, too.

✦ **Put your physical address and phone number on every page of your site.**

✦ **Take all reasonable security precautions.** If your site is ever attacked and exploited to distribute a virus or steal data, search engines may flag it and move you down in the rankings, or show a dire warning, such as the one shown in Figure 4-5.

✦ **Don't link to sites you know to be borderline scams or that may have a low TrustRank.** You can check sites' TrustRank at www.trust rank.org. Also, have a look at the SEOMOZ nifty Trifecta Tool at www. seomoz.org/trifecta.

> The site you are trying to visit has been identified as a forgery, intended to trick you into disclosing financial, personal or other sensitive information.
>
> **Suggestions:**
>
> - Return to the previous page and pick another result.
> - Try another search to find what you're looking for.
>
> Or you can continue to http://adwords.google.com.selectlogin.cn at your own risk.
>
> If you are the owner of this web site, you can request a review of your site using Google's Webmasters Tools.
>
> Advisory provided by Google

Figure 4-5: Danger! This page may be bad for you.

TrustRank is even harder to measure and quantify than PageRank. It's newer, the search engines have kept their measurement methods far more secret, and the definition of trust is far harder to define, anyway — but it's also easier to maintain. Behave yourself, don't cheat (by buying or otherwise spamming links), and don't link to other folks who might be cheating.

Measuring Your Website with Panda

In early 2011, Google began an ongoing rollout of its biggest ranking algorithm change ever: Panda. Panda adds overall page and site "quality" as a ranking factor. Quality still matters, but Panda changes the way Google evaluates it:

✦ **Sites, not pages:** Until now, Google has always looked at the Internet as a huge collection of pages, rather than a collection of websites. So, if you had 99 awful pages on your website, and one fantastic one, that fantastic one could rank well. The other 99 didn't do any harm. Now, Google looks at complete sites. So, those 99 pages could become an anchor, dragging down the rest of your site.

✦ **Language evaluation:** There are strong indications that Google is now evaluating writing quality. The Panda algorithm looks for spelling, grammar, and possibly even reader-friendly layouts and takes all that into account.

✦ **Overall site quality:** Panda also ups the importance of site speed, usability, and creating something folks use. If visitors "bounce" right back to Google the moment they see your homepage, that could hurt you in the rankings.

Trivia: Where Panda comes from

Google didn't name the algorithm after large, deceptively cuddly, black-and-white bears from China. It's actually named after Navneet Panda, a Google engineer who was instrumental in creating the new algorithm.

With all these changes, you can do three things to improve your rankings:

✦ **Avoid duplication.** More than ever, avoid duplication. Avoid even rewritten content — Google will catch anything remotely resembling a duplicate. Make sure that every page of your site has unique value.

✦ **Avoid "thin" pages.** Lots of sites have massive collections of user profile pages, "e-mail to a friend" forms, and other pages with 10–20 words and nothing else. These pages get flagged as low quality. Because low-quality pages can drag down the entire site's ability to rank, remove thin pages from your site, or exclude them from search engine crawls using `robots.txt` and the meta `robots` tag. Check out Chapter 3 of this minibook for information on `robots.txt` and meta `robots`.

✦ **Use Webmaster Tools.** Google provides direct feedback regarding your site in Webmaster Tools. Install it. Use it. Live by it.

Chapter 5: Understanding Blended Search

In This Chapter

- ✔ **Knowing what gets blended**
- ✔ **Optimizing products**
- ✔ **Optimizing news**
- ✔ **Optimizing images**
- ✔ **Optimizing video**
- ✔ **Optimizing for local search**

*I*n May 2007, Google released a new version of its search results dubbed *universal search*. Other search engines followed suit. The SEO industry calls it *blended search*.

Blended search mixes relevant news, images, video, and other content right into the traditional web search results on a search result page.

If a search engine decides that some other type of content (a photograph, for example) is more relevant than the top-ten web search results, the search engine replaces one of those web search results with the image.

Blended search presents more opportunities for you to grab real estate on the first page of search engine results. Every image, video, and press release you do, as well as your physical location, give you a shot at a top-ten ranking.

In this chapter, you find out the factors that search engines appear to use to rank blended content, and you see why they really aren't that different from the normal web content ranking factors.

As with many SEO topics, blended search optimization could take an entire book. This chapter is intended to just give you the basics. If you want to get more elaborate, talk to a professional search marketer.

Optimizing Products

Product pages on your website end up in the regular search rankings. But you have a second way to get them into the search engines — the product feed. A *product feed* is basically a spreadsheet of all the products in your store. You give that spreadsheet to the search engines, and they use it to create an index of your products. Products submitted through a feed show up in the blended search results, as shown in Figure 5-1.

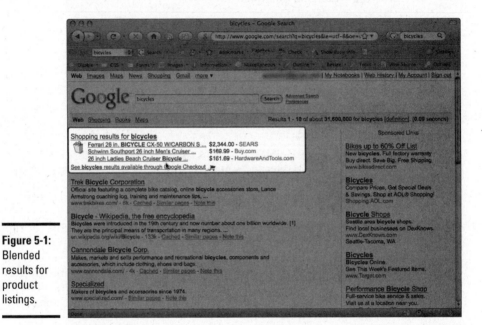

Figure 5-1: Blended results for product listings.

Google and Bing both provide ways for you to submit a list of products and prices. You can submit products to Google for free using its Merchant Center site at `www.google.com/merchants`, and you can get information regarding Bing product feeds at `http://advertising.microsoft.com/small-business/new-bing-shopping`.

Make the items in your product feed *more relevant* than the regular web search items that a major search engine would show on its first page. That's the only way your product will show up.

Here are six ways to optimize your product feed:

✦ **Submit a complete feed.** Although it might be tempting to submit a product name and price and be done with it, you should carefully fill in all the details. That way, if someone searches for *700c bicycle tire,* he'll find you because you completed the Size field.

✦ **Use existing categories.** Each search engine provides a list of categories that it typically uses in its product search directories. Use those categories, even if they're different from the ones on your site. It will help a great deal.

✦ **Submit individual products manually.** You can actually submit products one at a time, using a web form instead of a spreadsheet. This sounds horrible, but if you manually edit your feed, you can optimize product descriptions and other fields for best impact.

✦ **Include images.** A listing with an image draws far more clicks than a listing without.

✦ **Update your feed.** If you're selling products, update your feed to match your inventory cycle. You don't want out-of-date pricing, products you no longer sell, or incorrect information on the Internet.

✦ **Use custom fields.** For GoogleBase, add custom fields that make sense. For example, if you're selling shoes, you might add a custom field called Stars and list the stars who are currently wearing those shoes. If folks search for *shoes that Suzy Starlet wore* and your site shows up, they'll buy.

Optimizing News

Google and Bing also blend news headlines into their search results. Figure 5-2 shows news results blended right into a search result.

If you send a press release, try the following tips to get into the blended search results:

✦ **Optimize your press release.** Do all the stuff in this book! Making your press release relevant by including your target phrase in the headline, paragraphs, and other elements will definitely help.

✦ **Avoid using sales language, such as *best deal* or *fastest service*.** Press releases should be informative, not salesy. Don't write a marketing piece.

✦ **Use a newswire.** Unless you want to go through the pain of getting your website's press area accepted into the news sections of the two major search engines, you want to submit your press release by using one of the web-savvy newswires, such as PRWeb (`www.prweb.com`).

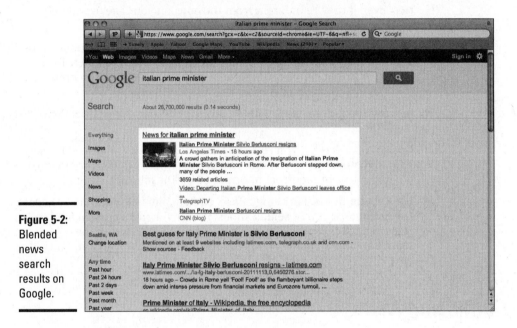

Figure 5-2:
Blended news search results on Google.

Optimizing Images

Getting an image included in a search result can generate a lot of traffic. You can increase traffic by as much as 200 percent in a single day because an image from your website landed on the front page of Google or Bing.

Images typically show up at the top of the search result, as shown in Figure 5-3.

The image rankings aren't as competitive as the traditional web rankings for most key phrases, so they might offer you an opportunity to grab a good position for phrases that are otherwise out of reach.

Book II
Chapter 5

Understanding
Blended Search

Figure 5-3:
Images
blended into
a normal
search
result.

However, search engines can't actually *see* images. So they use a number of cues to determine image relevance. Use the following tips to optimize images:

✦ **Use original images.** If you lift an image from another website, a newspaper, or something else, you have little chance of getting ranked. You may, however, get sued.

✦ **Use high-quality images.** You want images that are sharp and easy to interpret.

✦ **Optimize the content around the image.** If you have a picture of a carrot on a page, make sure that the page is well optimized for *carrot*. Put a text caption under the image that has the word *carrot* in it, too.

✦ **Use the correct formats.** Photographs should be in JPG, not GIF, format. GIF allows only 256 colors. JPG allows millions of colors and is a more logical choice for a photograph.

✦ **Make images accessible.** Put photographs in a separate images folder from the graphics that comprise your website layout. Make sure that the folder isn't disallowed in your `robots.txt` file.

✦ **Consider hosting your image on a third-party service, such as Picasa or Flickr.** If your image gets a lot of views and/or comments, you get an additional rankings boost. You'll sacrifice direct traffic and links to your site, though, so you need to weigh the benefit of a huge audience on a site such as Flickr against link building.

✦ **Give the image a keyword-rich name.** If you name an image `dpc12312432.jpg`, it's hard for a search engine to determine relevance. If, on the other hand, you name the image `carrot.jpg`, a search engine can immediately determine what it's crawling.

Optimizing Video

Video and images in blended search are similar in the following ways:

✦ Filenames must contain relevant terms. If the filename explains the meaning of the video — `bicycle-wheels-sale.mov`, for example — you'll get a good ranking.

✦ Overall page relevance helps determine video relevance.

✦ Originality, quality, and format can all make a difference.

A video search result can be just as compelling. See Figure 5-4 for an example.

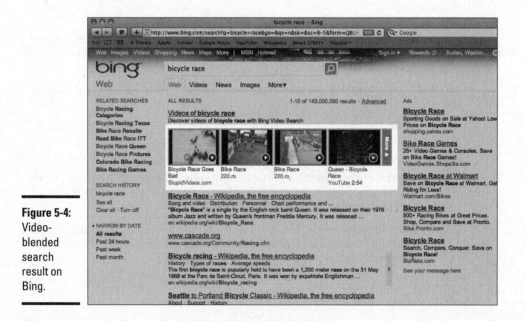

Figure 5-4:
Video-
blended
search
result on
Bing.

In addition to these factors, to optimize video, you need to

✦ **Make sure that you place the video on your website, and that you let your current customers or readers know it's there.** The number of views and *velocity* (how many views you get in how short a time) can boost you in the rankings, particularly if your video is hosted on a service, such as YouTube.

✦ **Consider putting all your videos in an RSS feed.** If you aren't sure what an RSS feed is, have a look at *Syndicating Sites with RSS Feeds For Dummies,* by Ellen Finklestein (published by John Wiley & Sons, Inc.). The RSS feed can give a search engine *hooks* to find all your videos.

✦ **Be organized.** And even more so with video than with images because videos typically show on pages with little or no text. Thus, organization might be the only clue a search engine has as to the meaning of the video. Put all your videos in a single directory. Create a set of pages, one video per page, that lets search engines find all the content.

✦ **Weigh the benefit of putting a video on a site such as YouTube, and potentially getting a lot of views in a short time, against getting the links and direct traffic from having that video on your website.**

✦ **Give your videos a relevant filename and surround them with relevant content.**

If you upload a video using a service such as YouTube, be sure to have lots of friends in your network first. Read Book VII for more information. More friends equals more views in less time, and this can mean a front-page ranking.

Optimizing for Local Search

If you're a local business, a top local search listing can drive customers faster than any other online marketing technique. Google and Bing are always experimenting with new ways to mix local search data into search results. In Figure 5-5, note how Google has added local information and reviews, and inserted several bicycle shops into the top 10 for *seattle bicycles.*

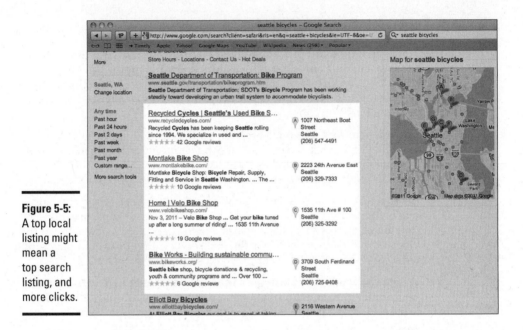

Figure 5-5:
A top local listing might mean a top search listing, and more clicks.

Local search optimization isn't difficult. But it *does* require a very sustained effort, around three different factors:

✦ Listings, on the local search engines and the directory sites they reference

✦ Reviews and bookmarks on those same sites

✦ Local data on your website

Optimizing your local search listings

The first step in local search optimization is making sure that your business is in each major search engine's local search directory. To do so, follow these steps:

1. **Search for your business on Google Places and Bing.**

2. **Make sure you fill out all fields requested by the search engine, including the description and hours.**

3. **Submit your website to InfoUSA.com** (www.infousa.com), **Yelp.com** (www.yelp.com), **Superpages.com** (www.superpages.com), **Yellowpages.com** (www.yellowpages.com), **and CitySearch.com** (www.citysearch.com).

The major search engines crawl these sites to determine relevance and location. Note that other sites are available, too. These basics will get you started.

4. **Make sure that your business is assigned to the correct category in the local listings.**

Getting citations

Now that you have the listings, it's time to get some attention. This requires the most sustained effort on your part, because you have to get past customers to review your business. Search engines look at the quantity of citations — bookmarks, reviews, and other mentions from people in your geographic area — as one indicator of relevance.

✦ **Send a polite note to all your customers or provide them with a coupon or other incentive, inviting them to review your business at Google or Bing.** The more reviews you get (even if they're not all good), the more easily you'll move up in the local rankings.

✦ **Provide an easy way for folks to bookmark your location on the mapping service of their choice.** More bookmarks or saved locations on Google or Bing mean a higher ranking, too (see Figure 5-6). Note how every listed local business in the *seattle bicycles* result has five or more reviews.

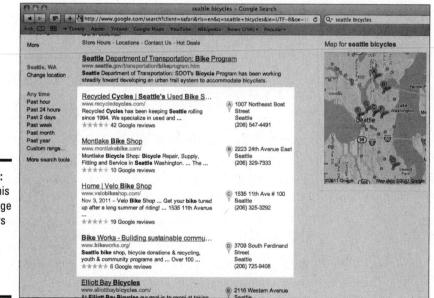

Figure 5-6:
A link to this Google page lets visitors easily bookmark your location.

Optimizing your site for local search

With all these steps, it's easy to forget that you can optimize your own site, too. Use the following tips to optimize your website for local search:

+ **Make sure that your physical address is on every page of your website.**

+ **Put your metro-area location in a few title tags on your website.**

+ **Have a very good contact page, with directions.**

+ **Consider geotagging your website.** No direct evidence exists that this impacts rankings yet, but it probably will soon. You'll need to read up on the geotagging of meta tags, which at the time of this writing still isn't a finalized standard.

+ **Use social media.** The more you can get folks in your area talking about you, the better. Search engines use this data to determine your importance.

+ **Get links from other local sites.** Join your local chamber of commerce, for example, and get a link from its website.

Chapter 6: Writing Great Copy for Search Engines (And Readers!)

In This Chapter

✔ Writing online copy that attracts customers, boosts sales, and helps grow your business

✔ Writing title tags and headings (that people will click)

✔ Setting a writing routine

*L*ike it or not, search engines care about words, so you're going to have to put your hands on a keyboard and write some stuff about your company or hire someone else to do it.

Keep the following in mind:

✦ Writing great copy takes time and practice, not necessarily natural talent.

✦ Hiring someone else to write is an option, but it's going to cost you. If you pay $5 for a page of copy, it will read like you paid $5 for it — lousy.

✦ Setting a routine makes writing easier.

In this chapter, you find some tips for writing great copy that both search engines and your visitors will like.

Writing Online Copy

You haven't even started writing yet, but two thoughts are probably going through your mind:

"I don't have anything to write about!"

and

"How many times should I repeat a key phrase on a page?"

Brainstorming tips

Can't think of anything to write? Try these five tips:

✔ Think about what your customers most often ask and write detailed answers to each of those questions. One well-written page can reduce calls and questions and make your customers happier. Plus, if that's the question they're asking, chances are they're typing it into the search engines, too.

✔ Write down the most ridiculous claim your competitors make. Then answer it, professionally and succinctly, but allow just a little of your passion to creep in. Those "Rank #1 on Google for $99!" e-mails can provide you with endless fodder.

✔ Go to your favorite search engine. Search for the latest news about your industry or product. If something in there gets you riled up, seems really clever, or otherwise grabs your interest, write down your thoughts.

✔ Look at every product or service you offer. If you can break them up into smaller subproducts or services, do it, and write about each of those. For example, bicycle repair can be broken up into tune-ups, wheel truing, frame repair, and painting. Accounting can be divided into tax, bookkeeping, and cash flow.

✔ Don't worry about writing for the web the right way. Get your thoughts written down first. Then you can tweak the copy for best impact. If you try to put together the perfect sentence before you write down that great idea, you might forget the idea before you hit the first key. Plus, the first way you write something is often the best.

After it's all written down, it's time to start editing. Start by removing so-called "stop" or "filter" words. (See the nearby section "Avoiding stop and filter words.")

You spend every day immersed in your business, so it might feel routine to you, but for your customers, it's a whole new world. You have a wealth of knowledge and information they've never seen or have forgotten. If you can clearly communicate that to them, you'll attract loyal customers. Even better, you'll demonstrate relevance and move up in the search rankings, too.

As for the second question: The maddening answer, borrowed a bit from Mozart, is "Precisely as many times as necessary. No more, no less." Search engines won't tell you "make sure that you use 2 percent keyword density!" Remember that they want relevance — not keyword density.

Avoiding stop and filter words

Stop words are words that search engines typically ignore in your search, including those shown in the following list.

a	in	where
about	is	who
an	it	will
are	la	with
as	of	www
at	on	
be	or	
by	that	
com	the	
de	this	
en	to	
for	und	
from	was	
how	what	
I	when	

Although stop words don't directly hurt your attempts to get a high ranking, they don't help either.

> "Our bicycles are really great, and anyone who comes here will wonder why they didn't before."

becomes:

> "Our bicycles really great anyone comes here wonder why they didn't before."

So, loading up on stop words can have unexpected results. Try to minimize stop words. It's good technique, too. Stop words tend to slow a reader's progress as he tries to learn what you're telling him. Fewer stop words mean clearer writing.

Filter words are those that may actually cause a search engine to ignore other content on the page. No one's proven that search engines actually penalize sites for using specific terms, but you can safely assume that words commonly associated with some industries, such as adult entertainment, may hurt your rankings.

But what are the odds you'd end up writing naughty language on your website?

It's easier than you think. Take this sentence for example:

"John was an adult who had a date with destiny."

Adult and date, in close proximity, might just trigger some search filters.

And try this example:

"The bushtit is a small bird."

The word — a real animal — likely got websites dinged. The problem went away as search engines matured and got better at determining the true meaning of words, but it's a great example of accidental filter words.

Stop *characters* can also confuse a search engine while it crawls your website. Be sure to replace any special characters — such as an ampersand (&), copyright notice, or bullet symbol — with an *entity*. An entity is a computer-friendly definition of a special character. The entity for &, for example, is *&*. Check with your developer and make sure that he takes care of that. He'll know what an entity is. If he doesn't, you should find another developer.

Keeping it simple

Online, more than anywhere else, simple writing is best. People still have a tough time reading text on a screen. Most Internet users tend to scan for answers and keywords before they read.

So always look at how you can shorten what you've written. Here are a few tips and examples:

✦ **Pare down the number of words whenever possible.** "Then things went from bad to worse" can just as easily be "Things got a lot worse."

✦ **Avoid slang and colloquialisms.** "They couldn't see the forest for the trees" might also be "They were stuck on the details."

✦ **More syllables won't make you sound smarter — folks will just skip the sentence altogether.** "Our expertise is unrivaled in our industry" could read "We're the best."

Using active voice

Many of us were taught to write in the passive voice, like this.

It's better to say, "Many of us learned to use passive voice."

See the difference? Instead of some mysterious third party out there who taught us, the latter gets straight to the point. Active voice is always clearer, easier to read, and often far easier to optimize for a search engine.

Here are a few examples:

✦ **Okay:** "Bicycles are repaired by our mechanics" is fine, but it's slow, wordy, and doesn't include *bicycle repair,* which is the real target phrase.

✦ **Better:** Instead, try "Our mechanics perform top-notch bicycle repair." It's not actually a shorter sentence, but it reads better *and* it includes your target phrase.

✦ **Okay:** "Mixed-green salads are good for you!" That reads pretty well, but it misses a few opportunities to deliver more marketing punch, and if your target phrase is *mixed-greens health benefits,* you miss that opportunity, too.

✦ **Better:** You can use active voice and write, "You already know about mixed-greens' health benefits."

✦ **Okay:** "We are Frank's favorite CPA firm."

✦ **Better:** "Frank says, 'I love this CPA firm!'" No big difference, SEO-wise, but it's a shorter sentence and makes Frank the speaker — the words are coming directly from him because active voice is used.

Getting to the point

Standard college and primary school writing style tells you to write according to an outline, as shown in Figure 6-1.

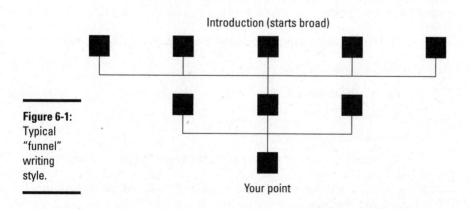

Introduction (starts broad)

Figure 6-1: Typical "funnel" writing style.

Your point

However, search engines lend more weight to text at the top of the page, not at the bottom. If your point is all the way at the bottom of the page, two things happen:

+ **Search engines accord it less relevance.** If your point includes your target phrase, you want to move it up.

+ **Readers are likely to give up before they get all the way down the page.** Your point is often your value proposition. You want to say that first.

So, make your point and state your value proposition at the very top of the page, not at the bottom. Compare these two brief product descriptions:

> *Our bicycle tires are made by hand. They also feature a Kevlar belt. They use our patented long-wear formula. And they are rigorously tested by our laboratory. So they'll remain flat-proof for years.*

They're flat-proof? Why didn't you say that in the first place! Try this instead:

> *Our flat-proof bicycle tires feature a Kevlar belt. They're handmade and rigorously tested by our manufacturing team. With our patented long-wear formula, they'll remain flat-proof for years!*

Much better. Not only does this version tell readers that these are flat-proof bicycle tires, but it also worked the value proposition right into the first sentence, so search engines will give this page high relevance for the phrase *flat-proof bicycle tires.*

Writing scannable copy

The description of the flat-proof bicycle tires from the previous section can be better though: You can make it more scannable. Remember, online readers tend to scan, not read. So, breaking your most important points into separate bullets and short, punchy paragraphs can help your readers. Using this format also provides a structure that search engines can more easily filter for the most important points.

You can revise the last example from the preceding section this way:

> *Our flat-proof bicycle tires*
>
> - *Feature a Kevlar belt*
> - *Are handmade*
> - *Are rigorously tested*
> - *Will remain flat-proof for years, thanks to our long-wear formula*

You can see how much easier it is for a reader to pull out the important features of this product.

Finding the right keyword density

So how many times should you use a keyword?

There's no solid answer, but these steps should give you a feel for what the right density is for you:

1. **Write your copy *first*, without considering your key phrase.**

2. **Look at your competitors' pages.**

   How many words do they have on a page? How many times do they repeat their target phrases?

3. **Review what you wrote.**

   Try to include 10 percent more copy than your competitor did.

4. **Use the same keyword density that your competitor did, with a maximum density of 3 to 4 percent.**

   Any more than that sounds ridiculous. Look for places where you used synonyms that you can easily replace with your target phrase.

Writing a Great Title Tag

Writing a title tag involves more than putting your keywords first. Search engines display the keyword tag at the top of each item in the search engine result pages (SERPs). Figure 6-2 shows an example.

Figure 6-2:
The title tag in a SERPs listing.

A well-written title tag might increase the odds that a searching customer will click your listing. If you balance the need for SEO with the need for an impactful title tag, you generally get more clicks *and* a higher ranking.

Getting past your brand

First, *don't put your brand first.* Your brand will be front and center when customers land on your website. In the meantime, focus on getting a high ranking and a click.

Here's an example:

```
<title>Harrison's Bikes: Seattle Bicycle Repair</title>
```

The brand went first. That placement reduces the relevance of the tag for *Seattle bicycle repair* because search engines more heavily weight the first words. Plus, readers won't see the benefit in clicking unless they read the whole title tag. Why make them work for it? Instead, use this:

```
<title>Seattle Bicycle Repair: Harrison's Bikes</title>
```

The key phrase is first. Even better:

```
<title>Seattle Bicycle Repair and Sales</title>
```

It leaves out the brand in favor of another keyword.

You can make a title tag as long as you want, but keep in mind that search engines ignore anything longer than 65 characters. The phrase at the end won't affect relevance as much as the one at the beginning.

Avoiding keyword stuffing

Try not to put a given keyword into a title tag more than once — twice if absolutely necessary. Search engines have long hated title tags like this:

```
<title>Bicycles and Bicycle Repair with Bicycle Sales at
   Harrison's Bicycles</title>
```

Plus, doing so is a terrible way to introduce customers to your company — the writing is poor and is hard to read.

Telling your story

Your title tag may well be the very first thing your customers see. It should say something important about you. If something sets you or your business apart — an award, a unique service, or something else — try to work it into the tag:

```
<title>Bicycle Repair and Sales - Rated Seattle's Number 1
    Bike Shop: Harrison's Bicycles</title>
```

Note that this `title` tag doesn't repeat any keywords. To a search engine, *bicycle* and *bicycles* are different words.

This `title` tag maximizes the chances that a customer will click. Rated No. 1? Sign me up!

Making it readable

After all this work, it pays to reread the `title` tag and make sure that it makes sense.

Like link text, a `title` tag should make sense all on its own. It needs to be totally self-contained. So,

```
<title>Bicycle Repair and Sales</title>
```

is okay, but it's missing important information, such as the location. The tag

```
<title>Seattle Bicycle Repair and Sales</title>
```

is far better. Now customers know it's in Seattle. Plus, search engines award greater relevance in local searches because *Seattle* is in the title tag.

 If you have a database-driven site and are editing your title tag using a maintenance or administrator control panel, you probably won't have to enter the `<title>` and `</title>` tags. The content management system will do that for you. But make sure that you can edit your `title` tags. If you can't, have a developer change it. It's worth the effort. Without editable `title` tags, your site doesn't have a prayer in the rankings.

Make sure that your `title` tag can stand on its own. It'll probably have to at some point. If folks create a link to your site, they might use the `title` tag as the link text. If your `title` tag clearly defines the page it titles, the link will clearly describe the page to which it points.

Writing a Great Description Tag

Meta description tags don't directly affect ranking. But a well-written description tag *can* cause more searchers to click through to your website. Search engines often use the description tag as the *snippet* in a search listing, as shown in Figure 6-3.

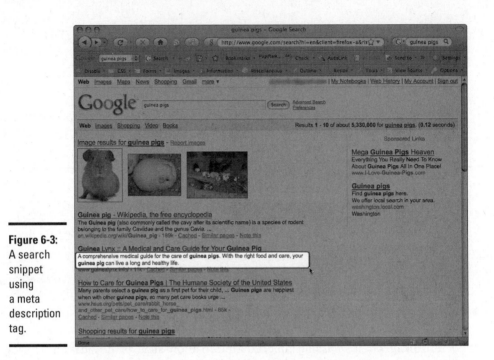

Figure 6-3:
A search snippet using a meta description tag.

So, you can edit the description tag and optimize it for your customers.

If you don't have a description tag, search engines will grab other text from your web page. You can't easily predict what search engines will grab either, and it can lead to meaningless search listing snippets. Use a description tag whenever possible.

Here's an example, which also shows the code for a description tag:

```
<meta name="description" content="Harrison's Bike Shop
    is located in Seattle's Alki neighborhood. Our award-
    winning bicycle repair mechanics can fix any problem!
    In business since 1902. Open 7 days a week. Call us at
    222.333.4444."/>
```

Why bother inserting `bicycle repair` in front of `mechanics`? It seems wordy, but search engines boldface the words you search for in the snippet, as shown in Figure 6-4. That will increase the chances of a click.

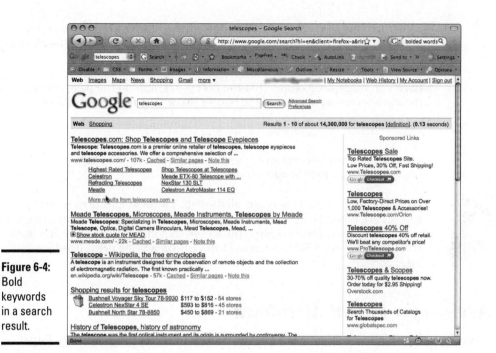

Book II
Chapter 6

Writing Great Copy
for Search Engines
(And Readers!)

Figure 6-4:
Bold
keywords
in a search
result.

Put a call to action — `Call us` — and the phone number at the end of the description. Sometimes, customers call you without even visiting your website. That's even better.

If your call to action is `Order online` or `Call for more information`, put that in your description tag, too. If your competitors' websites *don't* say "order online" and you do, you've just gained an advantage.

If you have a database-driven site, such as an online store or a site powered by a content management system, make sure that you can edit your description tags, too! Modify them as you find out what attracts more clicks.

Connecting Headlines to Copy

The heading is the first text your customers see. Like your `title` tag, it needs to stand on its own and contain your key phrase.

Unlike your `title` tag, though, it should directly support the paragraph beneath it. The `title` tag can be relevant to the entire page without referring to the first paragraph on that page. But even a level 1 heading needs to have some connection with the first paragraph of copy.

If your writing gets to the point (see the section "Getting to the point," earlier in this chapter), this shouldn't be a problem. Your point should be clear in the paragraph immediately following the headline.

Here's an example: Assume that the first paragraph on the page discusses the award-winning service of Harrison's Bikes. The heading could be

```
<h1>Award-Winning Seattle Bicycle Repair</h1>
```

That ties into the paragraph copy, connects to the `title` tag, and includes the target key phrase *Seattle bicycle repair*.

Writing a great heading is an art all its own. The best authorities on the subject are David Ogilvy and Brian Clark of Copyblogger. You can get *Ogilvy on Advertising,* by David Ogilvy (published by Vintage Books), at any bookstore. You can read Brian's helpful tutorials on writing great headlines at `www.copyblogger.com`.

Avoiding a Verbal Meltdown

Title tags, headings, descriptions, keyword density . . . it's easy to forget about the writing.

Avoid a verbal meltdown like this:

> "Bicycle repair at our Seattle bicycle shop is award-winning. Our bicycle repair experts will repair your bicycle 7 days a week. . . ."

Ultimately, you're writing for your customers. Yes, keywords matter. Yes, you want that top ranking. However, that's meaningless if your customers click the Back button after ten seconds on your web page.

Setting a Writing Routine

One other way to avoid a verbal meltdown is to set a routine. Maybe you can write about your company three times a week for 30 minutes. You don't worry too much about *what* you're writing. Just spend 30 minutes writing down what comes to mind.

You might come up with copy that you can use (with some editing, of course) or a nice list of ideas you can use later.

Follow these steps to set your writing routine:

1. **Find at least 30 minutes a week and put it into your calendar.**

   This time is absolutely sacred. Don't surrender it to meetings, television, or anything else.

2. **Get an egg timer or some other way to keep time.**

3. **Go someplace quiet, if you can, or put on headphones to block out distractions.**

4. **Set the timer.**

5. **Write for 30 minutes straight.**

   Do not stop to ponder sentences or decide whether you should use *toward* or *towards*. Just write, write, write. The idea is to get a complete brain dump.

6. **Stop at the end of the 30 minutes.**

7. **Later that day or the next, review what you wrote.**

It might be ready to post to your website or blog. If it is, pass it to a friend for a quick read. He might catch typos you missed. (Typos matter — search for *philsophy* online, and you'll see all the sites that misspelled *philosophy*. Those sites can't gain a high ranking for the correct spelling.)

If it's not ready to post, keep it anyway. Fiddle with it. See whether you can build on one or two paragraphs to create a complete page.

Brainstorming before you write each week is helpful. See the "Brainstorming tips" sidebar, earlier in this chapter.

Hiring writing help

Business owners rank the fear of writing slightly below the fear of public speaking. And they fear both more than death.

If you just can't bear the thought of having to write your own website copy, do the brainstorming that's described at the beginning of this chapter. Then go to a site such as Elance (www.elance.com) and hire a writer to create your content. Book I, Chapter 7 covers Elance and other ways to find help in more detail.

Just realize that you'll need to have someone — preferably an SEO pro — to optimize that copy and create the title and description meta tags.

Or, you can hire an SEO copywriter. Doing so might cost more, but you get a more polished product.

Chapter 7: Building Link Love

In This Chapter

✔ **Discovering why links matter**

✔ **Encouraging links**

✔ **Getting the easy links**

✔ **Staying out of trouble**

✔ **Creating link bait**

*L*ink building — getting other sites to link to yours — is critical to your search engine optimization efforts. However, many people ignore the rest of SEO and focus entirely on acquiring links. Link building is not the only component, and ignoring great copy, great code, and a well-structured site in favor of link building is a mistake.

This chapter explains why links matter, how search engines weigh links, the factors for quality links, and several tactics for building links to your site.

This chapter is very technical and detailed, so keep some perspective. You don't need to spend the next two years writing link bait. But you should do everything up to and including the suggestions in the "Leveraging Your Partners for Links" section. For everything after that section, you can read and learn. If you have time and a big budget, go for it. If you don't, take it as advice in case you're ever bedridden for a month with nothing to do but putter with your website.

Understanding Link Votes

To a search engine, every page on the Internet has a certain number of votes it can hand out to other pages through links. The exact number of votes each page has differs, depending on the site's overall SEO strength.

This voting concept first hit the search world in 1998, when Google launched the beta version of its now-dominant search engine. Google called the voting system PageRank.

To make things even more complicated, every vote can be worth more or less to your SEO efforts, depending on the relevance of the linking website, the text in the link, and dozens of other factors that search engines won't divulge (but users can try to guess).

Link *velocity* — the rate at which your site acquires new links — matters, too. If you get 2,000 links overnight and then nothing, that likely won't help as much as getting 10 new links per day for 200 days.

So, every link you get is a vote. Each vote is weighed by search engines according to relevance and other factors.

A lot of links is better. And links, like everything else, start with content.

Links that don't count as much

A link helps you only if it links directly to your website. If a link first goes to some type of ad-tracking server and then to your site, the search engines won't consider it a vote.

To check whether a link is direct, follow these steps:

1. **Navigate to the linking page and roll your cursor over the link.**

2. **Look in your browser status bar and see where the link points.**

   If it shows your page address, as in Figure 7-1, it's a vote. If it shows a redirection address or simply Done, as in Figure 7-2, it's not a vote.

Figure 7-1:
This link is a vote.

Figure 7-2:
This link is not a vote.

Some webmasters get tricky and use JavaScript to make it *look* like a link is a vote. Don't worry about it — they're in the minority, and the effort to find those fake votes probably isn't worth it.

Understanding nofollow

Another form of links that are less valuable are nofollow links. The major search engines now recognize a special command that webmasters can add to any link on their website:

```
<a href=http://www.harrisonsbikes.com rel="nofollow">
```

That `rel="nofollow"` command tells a visiting search engine to treat that link differently, by passing little or no authority through that link to the target page. SEO geeks refer to that link as *nofollowed*. Nofollowed links are less of a vote than followed links.

Us SEO nerds don't know as much about the value of `nofollow` links as we thought. They pass some value, but they clearly don't pass as much value as a normal link, and they appear to only pass value in specific circumstances. The best rule is to get a normal, followed link first. Don't ignore `nofollow` links, but don't stake your campaign on them, either.

You can easily detect `nofollow` links by using SeoQuake. In SeoQuake, `nofollowed` links have a line through them, as shown in Figure 7-3. Turn to Chapter 1 of this minibook if you need to install SeoQuake.

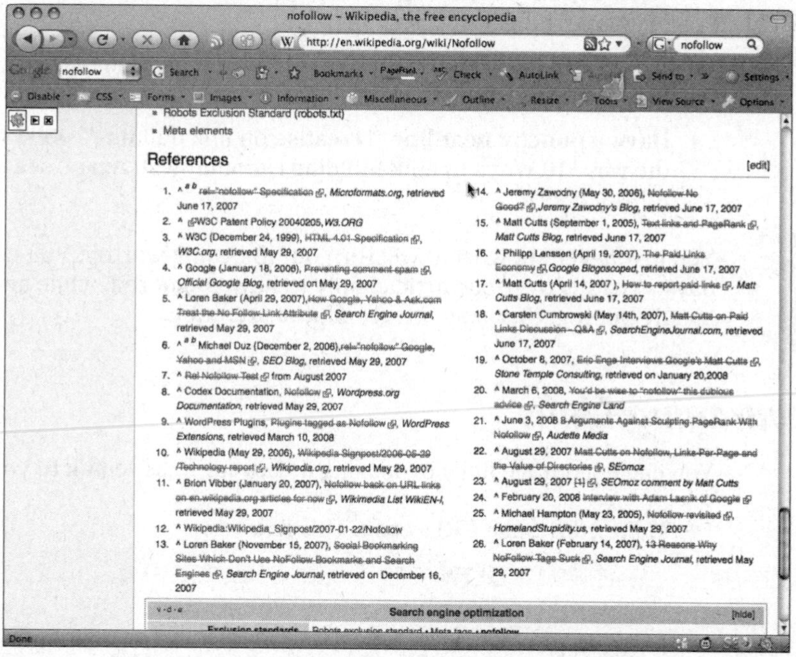

**Book II
Chapter 7**

Building Link Love

Figure 7-3:
Nofollowed links in SeoQuake.

 Using `nofollow` as some form of SEO tool will probably hurt you. If you use `nofollow` on a link on your site, it doesn't redistribute that link vote to another page. Instead, it burns the vote. Poof. Also, using a `nofollow` command might not prevent a search engine from crawling content. It's not a security tool. It's not a way to hide content. And it's not a way to improve your rankings.

Writing Link-Worthy Content

The best way to acquire links is to attract them naturally, with interesting, useful information. The importance of writing great content appears in almost every blog post on the subject of link building. Try these tips:

✦ **Be original.** Copying or rewriting someone else's content might get you noticed in court, but it's not going to help you build links.

✦ **Write quality stuff.** Publishing polished content should go without saying. Have others help you edit before you go live.

✦ **Avoid the sales pitch.** No one will link to your services page if it just includes a sales pitch. You need to write something that has general value.

✦ **Write for easy scanning.** See Chapter 6 of this minibook for information on copywriting.

✦ **Include images.** Even if they're just silly, images make folks more likely to link to your site.

✦ **Have a punchy headline.** "Treatise on link building" won't get attention the way "10 Ways to Link Building Nirvana" will. Again, see Chapter 6 in this minibook.

You just never know what will turn out to be link-worthy. You can spend days sweating over one article, only to have it ignored, while another page hastily put together may attract a lot of attention.

Encouraging Links

You can encourage links by making it easy for folks to link to your site, too.

✦ **Make your page URLs easy.** This link

```
www.harrisonsbikes.com
```

is better than

```
www.harrisonsbikes.com/index.aspx?category=1&products=2&special=
    no&catid=234&productid=12312
```

✦ **Consider providing an easy way to bookmark each page on your site.** See Book VII for more information.

✦ **Provide an easy way for customers to forward links to friends.** You never know when a tool such as the one shown in Figure 7-4 will prompt a visitor to forward your page to her friend, the top-100 blogger.

Figure 7-4:
Encourage
forwards.

Using absolute URLs

When you link to one page of your site from another, use an *absolute* URL:

```
www.harrisonsbikes.com/products.html
```

instead of a *relative* URL:

```
/products.html
```

An *absolute* URL contains within it all information necessary to find that web page, no matter where you are on the Internet. A *relative* URL contains only enough information to help you find that web page from within the same website.

Although the latter is easier from a development standpoint, the former means that if someone steals your copy (it happens), he will inadvertently link back to you, too.

These links won't be worth much, but they can help, and you might as well get the benefit.

Saying thanks

A simple thank you can go a long way. If folks link to you, send them a note to say you appreciate it. Remember, they just voted for you. They might vote again, too.

Getting Easy Links

Some links are no-brainers. Although they're not the highest-value votes on the Internet, your competitors have them. Go get them because they're easy and because they level the playing field.

Submitting to directories

Thousands of directories are out there. Search engines track a sizable chunk of them and count links to you from those sites as votes.

**Book II
Chapter 7**

Building Link Love

Many of these directories are free. Start with the following:

✦ **DMOZ.org:** It'll take a long time to get into this directory, but submit your site, check back every few months, and if you haven't showed up, try again. A link from DMOZ is worth it.

✦ **Any and all local business directories in your area:** The Chamber of Commerce, the Better Business Bureau, and neighborhood associations are all a good start.

✦ **Industry associations:** If you belong to any industry associations, be sure that you're in their directories, too.

Some pay directories that are worth the investment include the following:

✦ Best of the Web at `botw.org`

✦ The Yahoo! Directory at `http://dir.yahoo.com`

✦ `joeant.com`

As a rule, only submit to directories that fit your business. They should be industry-specific to you. Or they should be general-purpose directories designed to help folks find different kinds of resources.

Never submit to a directory that requires you to link back!

Submitting to design galleries

If you have a site that's 100 percent XHTML-compliant, you can submit it to one of the many galleries that feature standards-compliant sites.

You can also submit to galleries that feature particularly striking designs. Clearly, though, your website must be particularly striking.

Be honest in both cases! If you spam every directory site hoping they won't check for standards compliance or design quality, you'll be disappointed.

Commenting on blogs

When you leave a comment on a blog, the blog author usually asks for your web address, as shown Figure 7-5. Enter your web address, and the blog typically adds a link back to your website from the post.

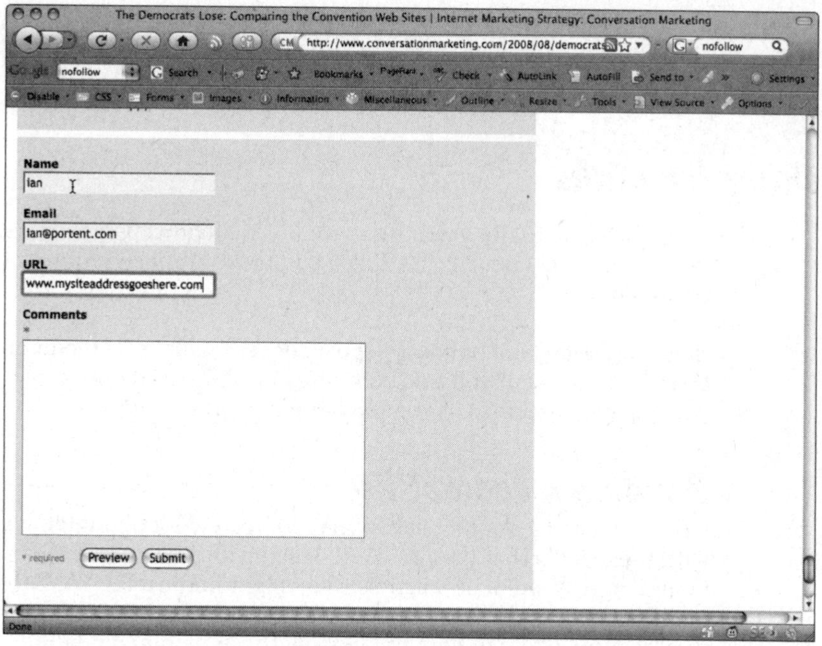

Figure 7-5:
Add your
web
address
in a blog
comment.

Before you go to every blog on the web and start entering comments (such as "Interesting!") just to get a link, understand that the search engines long ago closed this loophole: Most blogs include `nofollow` links from comments (see the section "Understanding nofollow," earlier in this chapter). Some, however, have stopped doing this because blog software has gotten better at filtering out short, useless messages entered strictly to create links. Remember: `nofollow` does pass some value — just not as much as a regular link. Comment because you want to, not to grub for links.

Comment when it makes sense and when you really have a comment. You might get the additional benefit of a link.

Leveraging Your Partners for Links

If you own a large company and you have distribution partners or local retailers, ask them to link to you. You might want to provide an incentive, such as a discount on merchandise or additional training. Regardless, links from partners are often an untapped resource.

If your company sells or distributes products from another, larger company, ask the company to include a link to you in its distributor directory (assuming that it has one).

Asking for Links

You'll rarely actually need to ask for links. Most webmasters receive at least ten e-mails a day begging for links, and most of those requests end up in the trash bin.

However, some link builders report success using this technique. The math *does* make sense: If you ask 1,000 sites for links, and only 1 percent listen, you still gain ten links. If you have the time, it can work.

Building a contact list

First, you need a contact list so that you can work on building a relationship with these folks that goes beyond begging for links. Send them an occasional helpful note about a new article they might find useful. Wish them a happy holiday. Remember their birthday. If you ask people who know you for a link, they're more likely to help out. Follow these recommendations to help you get started:

✦ **Start with folks you know.** If you have a relationship with other website owners, start by contacting them. You have a far better chance.

✦ **Find sites related to your industry, and see whether they allow you to contact the webmaster.** If they do, add them to your list, too.

✦ **Find blogs related to your industry.** Add them to a separate list, because you want to market to them via social media, not by sending e-mail. See Book VII for more information.

✦ **Pick up the phone.** Don't just call and say, "Gimme a link." Instead, research the site owner a bit, figure out what they may need, and offer to help with some phone advice or a little development time. Then ask for a link at the end of the work.

Don't spam. If the site doesn't have a webmaster contact address on it, don't contact the site. You're already interrupting people who likely don't know you.

Being polite

Send an e-mail to each webmaster. Send it once. If you don't hear back, cross the webmaster off your list. You tried. Maybe you ended up in his spam folder, or maybe he just ignored you. In either case, contacting him repeatedly will, at best, annoy him.

Make your e-mail very brief — no more than four or five sentences. Get right to the point, with a message like this:

> *I'm the owner of Harrisonsbikes.com. You wrote a fantastic review of our RoadBike2000. We have it hanging in our store! If possible, could you link to our site from your review? Thank you!*

That's it. You've taken but a few seconds of the webmaster's time. She'll appreciate your brevity.

Building a Widget

You can also build links by giving people a tool to put on their own websites. Widgets are fairly commonplace now and can serve a wide variety of purposes. Widgets can

✦ Provide the latest headlines from another website

✦ Show weather information for your area

✦ Show information about the site on which the widget is placed

✦ Play video

  YouTube and other services use widget-style code if you embed their video in your site.

If you include a link back to your own website as part of the widget, as shown in Figure 7-6, every person who uses your widget gives you a link.

Follow these rules for widget link building:

✦ **Don't overdo it.** Google, in particular, is sensitive to *widgetbait* link-building tactics. If this is your sole link-building strategy, you're headed for trouble.

✦ **Make it original.** Avoid using weather-prediction widgets, fortune-telling widgets, and random photo widgets that are available. Make yours very relevant to your business. Harrison's Bikes, for example, might have a widget showing results from local bike races.

✦ **Make it simple.** Provide a single chunk of code that webmasters can cut and paste into their own websites. It must be a one-step process. If it isn't, they won't use it.

✦ **Make it fast.** If your widget grabs information from your website before loading, make sure that it's fast. Nothing drives webmasters crazier than a widget that slows the load time of their own website.

✦ **Include a link.** Make sure that the widget includes a link back to your website, and make sure that it's a direct link.

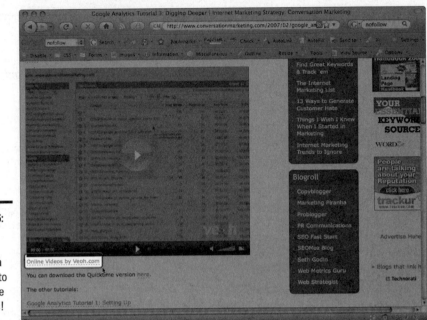

Figure 7-6:
A widget that includes a link back to the source site. Links!

Some companies do nothing but develop widgets. Get in touch with them if you have an idea you'd like to see come to life. Elance.com is a good place to start.

Creating Quality Links

If you have control over links made back to your website, you can do a few things to maximize the quality of the votes they provide. The following sections cover how to get quality links.

Including keywords

A link with relevant keywords in it provides a much better boost to your SEO efforts around that key phrase. For example:

```
<a href="http://www.harrisonsbikes.com">Seattle Bicycle Repair</a>
```

is far better than:

```
<a href="http://www.harrisonsbikes.com">Harrison's Bikes</a>
```

When search engines see a link with `Seattle Bicycle Repair` as the link text, they will assume that the website to which it points is about Seattle bicycle repair and count that link vote toward relevance for that phrase.

Don't turn down a branded link — they're still helpful. Even an image link with no text can help. But a keyword-rich link is pure gold.

If all the `a href` stuff made your head swim, don't worry. It's just HTML. Pay attention to the bolded text — that's what matters for this section.

Varying link text

Here's the flip side of keyword-rich links: You don't want dozens of identically worded links. Ideally, you want some variation in link text.

The main time to worry about this is if you're reaching out to a partner network or using a widget to get a lot of links using one strategy. If you do that, try to use at least five different versions of link text. Variety gets you more votes.

Getting relevant links

A link from a relevant site is far more useful than a link from a site that has nothing to do with your business.

If you happen to get links from irrelevant sites, don't worry about it, but do focus your efforts on relevant sites.

Staying Out of Trouble

You can get into trouble when link building because for years, link building has been abused as an SEO strategy. So, search engines have put automatic filters and whole teams of engineers and editors in place to check for

✦ Sudden, unexplained link growth

✦ Links from *bad neighborhoods*

That's SEO shorthand for a group of sites known to be sleazy. If you go out and acquire 100 links from sites selling suspicious pharmaceuticals or get-rich-quick schemes, you might end up associated with them in the search engines. That will hurt your ability to get a high ranking.

✦ Signs that you're selling links

✦ Any other sign that you're getting links purely to improve your ranking

Yes, they know we're out there doing just that. They just don't want us to go too far in the process. And no, they won't tell us what too far is. Fun, huh?

You can get yourself into trouble in a few classic ways, though. Steer clear of the topics in the next few sections.

Link buying and selling

At one point, anyone with a budget could go out and buy dozens of links from quality websites, thereby helping his or her rankings. Ah, the good old days.

Alas, it wasn't to be. In 2007, Google cracked down hard on websites that were selling links. As a result, those sites either dropped out of the Google index or fell so low in the rankings that they might as well have.

If you sell links, you risk severe penalties from search engines. They *really* don't like that. Yes, you'll find all sorts of ridiculous double standards. It doesn't matter. Shaking your fist because you got dumped from the rankings but another site didn't won't help you after you're penalized.

Don't sell links. And, if you buy links, you risk

✦ Acquiring a lot of links suddenly and tripping the search engines' spam alarms

That can result in a temporary but automatic drop in the rankings — that's no fun at all.

✦ Getting caught up in the mess if a link broker is discovered and his websites are banned

✦ Spending a lot of money on links that end up worthless

Don't buy links.

Link exchanges

Exchanging links with another website probably won't hurt you, but it won't help, either. Search engines figured out this trick years ago and ignore any reciprocal links.

Link trading *can* hurt if you end up in a bad neighborhood. If you're linking to those sites and they link back to you, they may take you down with them if they get penalized.

Link networks

Never, *ever,* join a link network. Most of these networks ask you to provide link text and a URL. Then they seed your URL among many other sites, in exchange for you posting a few links from their network.

It sounds good, but it makes inclusion in a bad neighborhood even more likely than a link trade. Plus, you give up all control over who links to you and how. And, these networks are known as the worst offenders when it comes to SEO cheating.

Don't use link networks, link "wheels," or whatever folks name them to try to get you to buy. Ever.

Creating Great Link Bait

Link bait is currently the most misunderstood, worst-employed link-building strategy. Few people are good at using it.

By definition, *link bait* is any piece of content written or created in such a way that it's going to attract a lot of links. You need to understand the following about link baiting:

✦ The most common link bait is in the form of a list.

"Top 10 ways to . . ." is a formula that just seems to work.

✦ Great link bait typically includes images.

✦ Great link bait is easy to scan.

Brainstorming link bait

This kind of link building starts with a really compelling idea. You can use a few strategies. The following sections discuss the more popular strategies.

Cracking up the readers

If you take a look at Digg.com — Digg often shows some of the most successful link bait pieces — note that at least half the front-page pieces at any one time are funny, or at least ironic.

Humor can work very well. Just be sure you don't cross the boundary between funny and tasteless, unless you really mean to.

The Guinea Pig Olympics, shown in Figure 7-7, collected links faster than guinea pigs make baby guinea pigs.

Figure 7-7:
A humorous site that collected a lot of links.

Making the reader angry

Making readers angry is risky. If you can make a controversial statement that generates discussion on other websites, you can attract a lot of links from blogs, discussion forums, and online groups. That's great link building. Go too far, though, and you could end up alienating your audience.

Controversial link bait works only after you have a few other successes, and you have a dedicated audience. They're more likely to forgive and more likely to defend you — which, of course, generates more discussion and more links.

Puzzling your readers

If you're a top-notch writer, you can write something to get your readers buzzing about what you meant. For this to work, though, you need a large audience (for the buzz) that is pretty patient with you. Most folks go online for answers, not questions.

Examples include famous bloggers saying they're quitting blogging (they never do), pundits apparently reversing their opinion (they're actually not), and really bizarre April Fools' Day announcements (see the section "Cracking up the readers," earlier in this chapter).

Offering great content

Obviously, if you can offer great information, you can attract links in short order. Examples of informative link bait include the following:

The 30-second T-shirt fold

Step-by-step instructions on using Photoshop to do any number of things

Instructions for fixing a common problem in a popular car

The best way to enjoy a popular theme park

Ten bizarre facts about an animal, invention, country, or famous person

Some of these might seem silly. But if you think about it, they'd be a lot of fun to write.

And that might be the single most important item to keep in mind: Great link bait should be fun to write. If you don't enjoy writing it, most folks won't enjoy reading it — and you won't make much progress.

Using images in link bait

Images are the core of just about any successful link bait piece. Sometimes the images are directly involved, as in the Guinea Pig Olympics in Figure 7-7. Sometimes they're just supporting material, as shown in Figure 7-8.

Book II
Chapter 7

Building Link Love

Figure 7-8:
This site uses images as link bait.

Note how these images have all been modified in somewhat silly ways. Both of these examples are humorous link bait posts — in this type of article, it makes sense to use images as props for the joke.

Host these images on your website, not by using a service such as Flickr. It's possible that an image will become stand-alone link bait. If it does, you want the links pointing at your web address, not at Flickr.

Using video in link bait

Video might *seem* like the perfect link bait, and using video can be very effective. However, it typically requires a lot of work, or a lucky break — say, you're the first person to capture a particular event on video, or you happen to film something very funny happening in everyday life.

The more likely route is that you carefully prepare and produce a fantastic video. That's not easy: A high-quality, 30-second YouTube video can take ten hours to create.

Videos you might want to prepare include the following:

+ A how-to piece around one of your products or services

+ An interview with a leader in your industry

+ Ten ridiculous things you can do with your products

Other possibilities exist. For example, an ad agency in San Francisco did a video of its entire team lip-syncing a popular song.

Embed the video on your website. It's fine to use a hosting service like YouTube or Vimeo, but be sure folks can find the video on your site. Otherwise, you end up helping YouTube build links, which won't really do much for your website.

Managing expectations

Link bait is not magic! It takes a lot of work and a long time. Manage your expectations for success by knowing that

+ **If you create ten top-notch link-bait pieces, you can expect one to succeed.** If you're expecting 100 percent success, you're being very unrealistic.

+ **Link bait, by definition, needs to be attention-getting.** Writing something about how wonderful your product or company is does not work.

+ **Link bait is a long-term investment.** Sometimes it can be months, even a year or two, before a piece of link bait really starts attracting links.

Researching Your Competitors' Links

One easy way to find good links is to see who links to your competitors. You can simply search for links to a competitor's website by typing **link:www.competitorsite.com** into Google. Google will then show you a portion of the site's links. But the operative word here is *portion*. Google shows what Google wants. So, you can't get a great competitive link list using the `link:` operator.

Use the following strategies to research competitors' links:

✦ **Use OpenSiteExplorer.org, by SEOMOZ.** SEOMOZ's toolset uses a huge links database that it builds and updates every month. It's a great resource. OpenSiteExplorer has a free version that offers limited data and a paid version that provides more data than you can shake a stick at.

✦ **Do a blog search on Google or Bing for your competitors' brand names.** The results might show blogs that reviewed their products. Those blogs might be willing to review yours, too — in which case, you might get a link.

✦ **Use MajesticSEO.** MajesticSEO offers another links database. Combine it with OpenSiteExplorer, because they each provide different crawl results and because they offer slightly different ways to slice the data. Like OpenSiteExplorer, Majestic has a free version that you can test drive.

✦ **Do a Google News search to find out which newswires your competitors use.**

After you build a list, check each link. Politely contact the bloggers, buy space in the same website directories, and figure out how you can attract links from the other websites. Something made those sites decide to link to your competitor. Read what the competitor wrote on the page that attracted the link and look at what the linking site said about it. That should give you a clue as to what will attract similar links in the future.

Understanding the New Value of Links

Links have evolved from the single dominant authority-passer to one part of a far more complex formula.

Google and Bing treat links very differently than they have in the past. Some major differences are as follows:

✦ **Link position matters more.** Google now applies a "rational surfer" model to links. The more likely it is that a normal person would click a link, given its location and style, the more value it passes. So, those tiny links at the bottom of the page aren't going to do much for you.

✦ **Link text matters less.** It used to be that if you wanted to rank for *running shoes,* a link with the text *running shoes* was the most valuable. That's not necessarily true anymore. Exact link text doesn't help as much as it used to. In fact, too many links with the same text may trigger penalties. Don't obsess about link text as much.

✦ **Artificial change is bad.** Search engines are far better at detecting "fake" link acquisition. If you go out and buy 1,000 links in a week and that triples your link count and authority, you'll likely end up with worthless links. You'll get a nice, temporary jump in the rankings. Then you'll plunge.

Links are now one form of citation. All forms of citation matter: brand mentions that don't link to you, nofollowed links, social media votes and "likes," and whatever else the web gurus come up with.

Links are still a big, big deal. Ignore them and you have very little chance of improving your rankings. Just be aware that social media and smart overall marketing can help, too. Be sure to read Book VII, and make that part of your SEO campaign, too.

Chapter 8: Analyzing Your Results

In This Chapter

✔ **Using your tracking worksheet**

✔ **Knowing what you should track**

✔ **Detecting plagiarism**

Chapter 1 of this minibook discusses how to set up an SEO worksheet. In this chapter, you put it to good use so that you can keep track of how your campaign is performing over time.

SEO is a long-term process. Changes you make now may take months to actually impact your traffic, so you need your worksheet to provide a long-term look at what worked and what didn't.

Using Your Tracking Worksheet

You should now have a worksheet that looks something like Figure 8-1. If you haven't set up your worksheet yet, get going!

Figure 8-1:
Basic SEO
tracking
worksheet.

SEO Worksheet: Harrison's Bikes

	Organic Search Traffic	Keyword Diversity	Yahoo! Links	Google Links	Live Links	Yahoo! Pages	Google Pages	Live Pages	Signups
Jul-08	2341	500	1000	968	450	1000	200	241	44
Aug-08	2334	1200	1010	1175	1096	1134	1099	1124	52
Sep-08	1500	1301	1111	1227	1135	1185	1140	1141	33
Oct-08	3123	1512	1240	1307	1264	1299	1279	1283	62
Nov-08	4121	1622	1232	1528	1380	1521	1476	1485	70

The tracking worksheet helps you do the following:

✦ **Boost morale:** Search engine optimization is a long-term game. Progress may happen in months . . . or years. You can look back six months and see that you really have gotten a lot more traffic and conversions.

✦ **Match changes in search with changes in sales:** If your offline or phone-driven sales jump 90 percent and your search traffic jumped 90 percent the same month, but nothing else changed, chances are that your SEO efforts helped create that burst.

✦ **Obtain a big-picture look at what helped search engine optimization:** If you added ten new pages in March and your keyword diversity jumped 50 percent in April and May, that's valuable intelligence that you can use to guide your next steps.

If you're getting fewer than 10,000 visits per month, you can update the worksheet monthly. If you get more than that, you might want to consider weekly updates, but you must consider how much time you have to devote to updating your worksheet. If you're reading this book, you probably have other responsibilities, such as paying bills and running your business. Prioritize accordingly.

The following list explains each of the basic statistics on your worksheet and describes where to find this data in Google Analytics or on the search engines themselves. See Book III for more about web analytics in general.

✦ **Traffic from organic search:** In Google Analytics, choose Google Analytics➪Traffic Sources➪Sources➪Search➪Organic. The report that appears shows you all of the keywords generating traffic to your site and the amount and quality of traffic generated, as shown in Figure 8-2.

✦ **Keyword diversity:** In Google Analytics, choose Google Analytics➪ Traffic Sources➪Sources➪Search➪Organic. Keyword diversity tells you the number of unique phrases generating traffic to your site, as shown in Figure 8-3. It's a fantastic measure of campaign health. More phrases means folks are finding you more ways, which makes for a more stable flow of traffic. Dropping out of the rankings for one or two phrases isn't a big deal if you have 1,000 traffic-generating phrases.

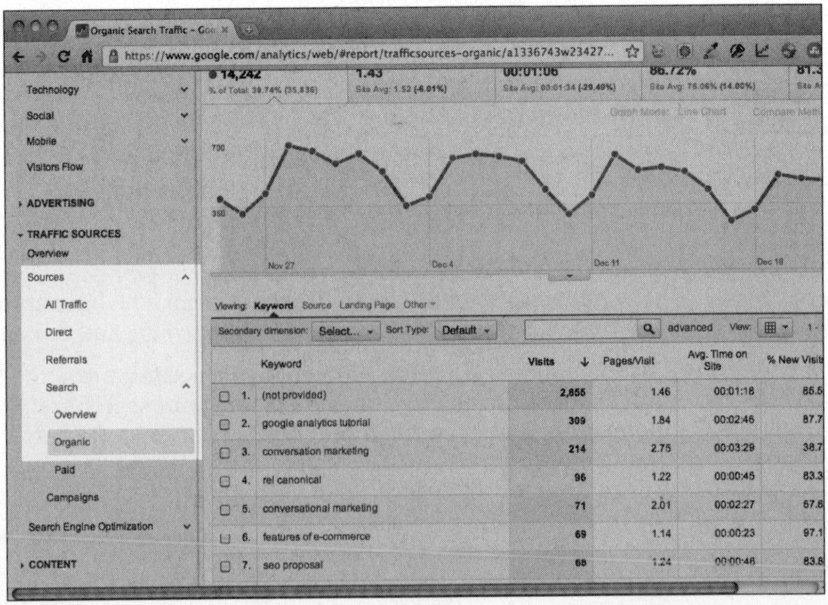

Figure 8-2:
Viewing organic traffic in Google Analytics.

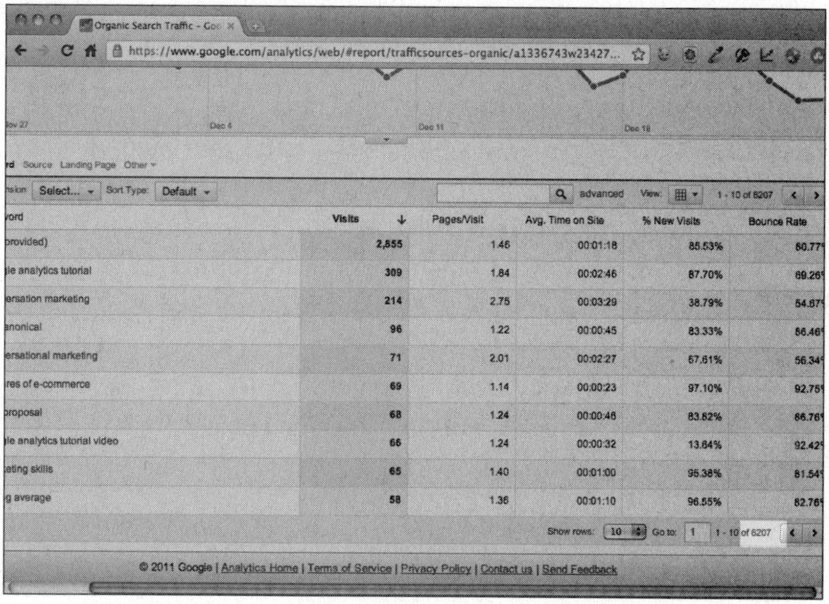

Figure 8-3:
The keyword diversity metric.

✦ **Incoming links, by search engine:** Links are votes. So you want to keep track of progress as you build links. These two reports help:

• *Blekko:* Search for your site's web address. Then, next to the first result, choose SEO⇨Links.

• *Google:* Choose Google Webmaster Tools⇨Your site on the web⇨Links to your site⇨Total links.

✦ **Indexed pages, by search engine:** You need to know if search engines are seeing all of the pages on your site. Luckily, you can do that via Google Webmaster Tools: Choose Google Webmaster Tools⇨Diagnostics⇨Crawl Stats.

✦ **Conversions from organic search:** SEO is marketing. Marketing works if it drives business. You can measure that by looking at conversions from organic search. Choose Google Analytics⇨Traffic Sources⇨Sources⇨Search⇨Organic. Then select the relevant goal set. Goals must be set up to use this metric. See Book III for instructions.

Setting up the links page

You want to track which links you have and which ones you want, too. Add a tab to your worksheet. On that page, have columns for the following:

✦ The competitor and other links you want to get

See Chapter 7 of this minibook for more about researching competitors' links.

✦ The date you requested the link

✦ The date you got the link

Having these columns helps you keep track of your link campaign and ensures that you don't pester webmasters with multiple e-mails.

Entering your keyword list

See Chapter 2 of this minibook for more information on keyword research.

Add a tab to your worksheet. On that page, have columns for the following:

✦ The keywords you're targeting

✦ Your current ranking on Google and Bing

✦ Changes from the previous report

This information is the *least* important data you'll collect — traffic and conversions matter far more. See Book II, Chapter 2 to understand why. Don't go nuts updating the keyword list every day. Checking once per month is more than enough.

Watching for Plagiarism

Strictly speaking, watching for plagiarism isn't part of analyzing your campaign results. But plagiarism can hurt your brand and your SEO campaign. Because search engines don't like duplication, an unauthorized copy of writing on your website can really hurt you. So you should check for folks who are copying your website at least as often as you check these statistics.

Keep another tab on your spreadsheet to record copycats and indicate when you contacted them.

You can find copies by using search engines or you can use a handy tool — Copyscape.

To use the search engine method, follow these steps:

1. **Copy one unique phrase from your website.**

2. **Paste it into the search field on your favorite search engine.**

3. **Surround the phrase with quotes.**

   On the search page that appears, if you see websites in addition to your own, they're copying you!

To find copies automatically, follow these steps to use Copyscape:

1. **Go to** www.copyscape.com.
2. **Paste the address (URL) of one page on your website.**
3. **Run the report.**

Copyscape doesn't crawl your entire site, though, unless you pay for the service.

If you catch someone copying content on your website, do the following:

1. **Find the Contact Us page on the website.**
2. **Send the webmaster a polite note asking him to remove the content.**
3. **If the webmaster doesn't reply, use a WHOIS tool, such as the one at** www.whois.net, **to find the domain owner's address and send him the same polite note.**
4. **If that doesn't work, contact the web hosting company and let them know, too.**

You might end up needing a lawyer. Generally, website owners back down quickly if they know they've been caught copying.

Finding "Dead" Pages

Your site may have pages search engines never seem to find. Those pages may be buried deep in your site navigation, or you may have search roadblocks that shut out the search robots.

Whatever the case, dead pages are missed opportunities. Ideally, every page on your site has value, and every page on your site gets indexed.

Finding dead pages is the first step to getting dead pages back into the index. Here's a quick way to do it:

1. **In Google Analytics, choose Content⇨Site Content⇨Pages.**

    The site content report appears, as shown in Figure 8-4. It's a good start, but you need to take a few more steps.

2. **Choose View⇨Pivot.**

3. **Select Medium from the Pivot By drop-down menu, as shown in Figure 8-5.**

    Medium refers to your type of traffic source, such as organic, pay per click, or e-mail.

4. **Sort the entire report by the organic column, in ascending order.**

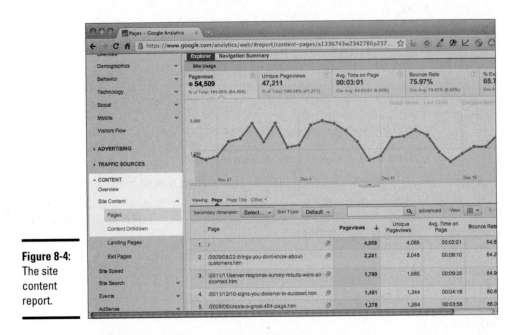

Figure 8-4:
The site content report.

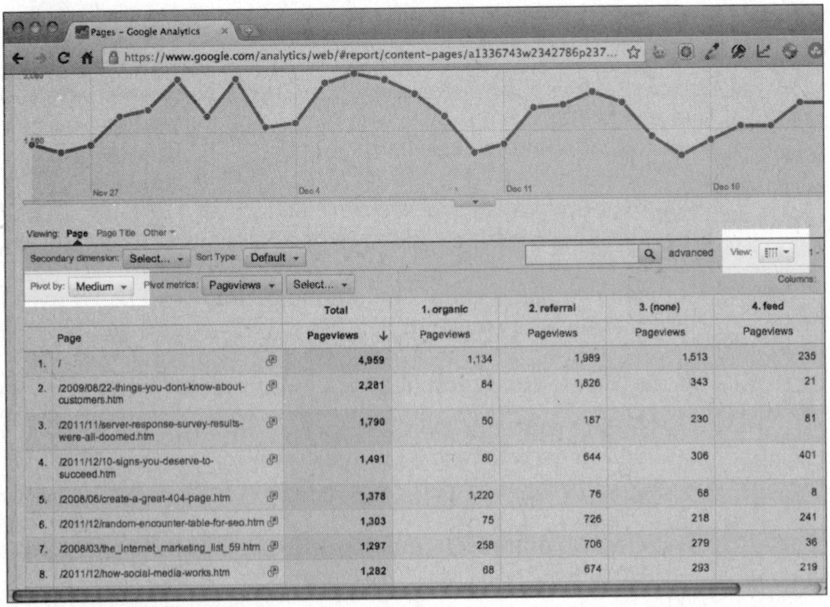

Figure 8-5:
The pivot report.

You now see the pages that got zero clicks from organic results, as shown in Figure 8-6. Many of those may be weird pages that don't make sense. Ignore them. You want to find instances of pages that you know are legitimate, but get no clicks from organic search.

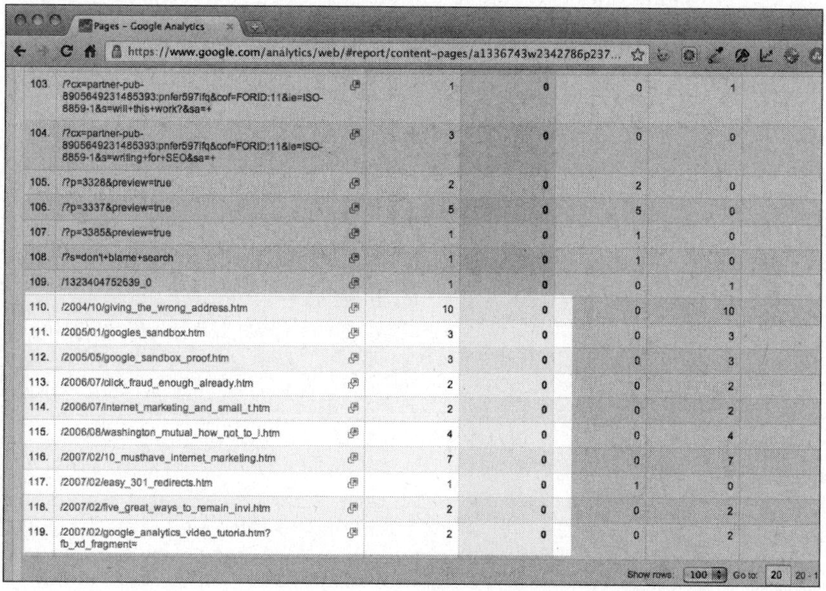

Figure 8-6: A list of legitimate dead pages.

Check to see whether those pages show up in search results. If they don't, you just found a dead page. Take a look at Chapter 3 of this minibook and make sure that you don't have any roadblocks.

Measuring the Long Tail

In Chapter 2 of this minibook, you find out about the long tail — the many less-searched but super-relevant phrases that form the bulk of your search traffic.

You can get a good look at your long-tail search terms using Google Analytics or another analytics toolset. Go back to your organic report, and you'll see a list of keywords. Export that report to Microsoft Excel or the spreadsheet program of your choice.

Look at the top traffic-generating term. How many visits does it get? Then find all the terms that get 10 percent or less of those visits.

This is not exactly scientific. But it'll give you a quick, at-a-glance look at your long-tail search traffic.

Google has started hiding search-term data for logged-in Google users. Instead of showing the key phrase for those users, Google put all those results under the oh-so-unhelpful "(not provided)" keyword. You can see that as much as 25 percent of search data end up as "not provided," as shown in Figure 8-7.

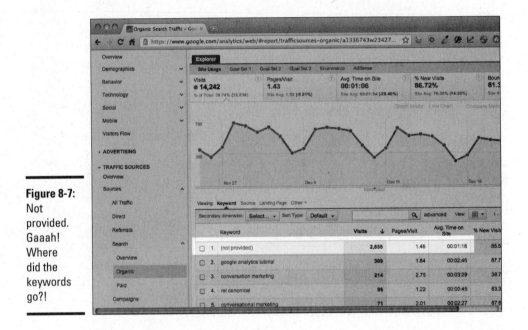

Figure 8-7:
Not provided. Gaaah! Where did the keywords go?!

Because your site probably gets most of its traffic from your long-tail search terms, Google's change is a major headache for tracking that traffic: You no longer have complete search-phrase data.

No great solution for this problem exists. Google Webmaster Tools provides search-phrase data, but it's very inaccurate. So analytics data remains your most reliable source. Here's what you can do:

✦ **Take Google's "not provided" result into account when you're measuring the long tail.** Remember that you're still getting 75 percent of the search-phrase data, and try to work with that.

✦ **Look at historical data.** Find terms for which you still rank but no longer see traffic data. Chances are that these terms have ended up in the "not provided" section.

Knowing What to Do If Your Numbers Fall

Relax! Okay, that may be impossible. But, if you see your organic search traffic and rankings start to plunge, consider these possible causes:

+ **The search engines might be updating their algorithms.** If you're playing above board, your old rankings will likely return.

+ **You might be seeing a temporary *dance* as the search engines update their indexes.**

+ **Your developer or designer might have made a change that removed a page from your website or confused the search engines.**

If your problem is one of the former two issues, you can't do much but keep doing what you're doing and grit your teeth.

Still, it pays to check whether some change you didn't know about — or perhaps a change you made — had unintended consequences. Do the following:

+ **Check with your developer and designer.** Ask them whether they made any changes to the website.

+ **Check your webmaster account on each major search engine.** The search engines might alert you if they detected many errors or something suspicious.

+ **Look for "thin" pages.** See Chapter 4 of this minibook. If you've added user profiles or some form of automatically generated content, you may have generated a lot of "thin" pages and torpedoed your site's rankings.

+ **Check your links.** Did you suddenly lose some?

+ **Check for seasonal changes.** If you've been recording SEO data for over a year, you can see whether seasonal trends moved you up or down in the rankings.

What you should *not* do is suddenly change your strategy. If you're sticking to organic SEO — not buying links or engaging in attempts to trick the search engines — you're not doing anything intentional that's hurting your rankings.

Chapter 9: Hiring an SEO Professional

In This Chapter

- ✔ Figuring out how to find candidates
- ✔ Checking qualifications
- ✔ Asking the right questions
- ✔ Knowing what to expect

After reading this minibook, you might decide that you need to hire an SEO consultant instead of trying to improve your search rankings yourself. And hiring a consultant might be a wise decision. Search engine optimization is a time-consuming and demanding Internet marketing task.

Finding an SEO Professional

A good SEO professional is someone you work with for months or years. She can advise you and help you make long-term improvements to your website. And she is also aware of your business objectives beyond higher rankings or more traffic. Try the following places to start your search:

✦ **Talk to other business owners.** Find out whether they've worked with anyone, and if so, how they liked that person. Referrals are still your best information source.

✦ **Check industry associations and analyst websites,** such as SEMPO, at www.sempo.org, or SEOMOZ, at www.seomoz.org. Both have market-places where you can request bids, and both provide lists of members or recommended vendors.

✦ **If you're looking for someone local,** search for *(your city/town name) search engine optimization.* If an SEO consultant can't get a top-10 rank-ing for that search, you might want to consider using another consultant.

Avoid looking in the following places:

✦ **In your inbox:** Never talk to an SEO professional who e-mails you out of the blue.

✦ **Any website or professional who guarantees you a ranking:** No honest SEO professional does this.

✦ **Any website or professional who asks you to put links to his other clients on your website:** That's a link exchange network, as described in Chapter 7 of this minibook.

✦ **Any website or professional who emphasizes optimizing your meta tags:** You've probably read enough now to understand why optimizing meta tags is only 5 percent of the battle.

Checking Qualifications

After you have your list of firms, you can narrow your search by checking a few qualifications. It's very important to perform an initial check because it helps you focus your search on the consultants who best fit your needs. Take these steps:

1. **Search Google Blog Search for the company name.**

   Make sure that you don't find dozens of angry posts about horrible things the company has done. You are bound to find a few — everyone gets a few folks angry occasionally. But if you see a long history of complaints, think twice.

2. **Visit a firm's website in Firefox, with the Google Toolbar installed.**

   What is its PageRank? Don't worry if it's low. But if it's 0, the company might have been penalized by Google. If it has been, do you want those folks working for you?

3. **Type the first key phrase in the company's title tag into the two major search engines (Google and Bing).**

   How does the company rank?

4. **Read the firm's blog (and it had better have one).**

   What's the company's philosophy? Does it "play it very safe" and "white hat"? Or, does it push the limits of what the search engines will tolerate? Make sure to find a firm you're comfortable with.

5. **Call the firm.**

   Talk to representatives on the phone or in person, and make sure that you're comfortable working with them. You're going to be spending a lot of time with them.

You want a firm that has demonstrated competency, that has folks you can work with, and that will stick around if you decide to work with them for a few years.

Ask for references. However, only a moron would give you *bad* references. It's comforting to hear how wonderful the agency you're about to hire really is, but realize that you're probably not going to get a clear picture this way.

One qualification you don't need to worry about is experience in a similar industry. It's just not that critical to SEO success. Whatever your industry, the challenges of gaining a good ranking remain largely the same.

Knowing What to Ask an SEO Professional

Before you start working with an SEO consultant, you must either meet him or talk to him on the phone. Get the answers to the following questions:

✦ **What is the consultant's SEO process?** What can you expect to see happen in the first month? The process should make sense to you. If he can't explain it, don't hire him.

✦ **What is the first thing he would do on your site?** The SEO professional should look at your website before speaking with you. Or, he should ask whether he can look later. Either way, don't demand a lot of information — this is what you pay him for, and he shouldn't have to give information away for free. Instead, look for a sensible recommendation that demonstrates he gave your site some thought.

✦ **How are results reported?** If he mentions ranking reports, don't hire him. Traffic matters more than rankings. Any good SEO pro will know that.

✦ **How long has he been an SEO professional?** There's no specific right answer here, but a response like "six months" should give you pause.

✦ **If you're unhappy with the service, can you end your contract before the scheduled end date?** Many unethical agencies bind you to a contract and charge your credit card month after month.

✦ **How often will he speak with you?** Your SEO professional needs to periodically review results and strategy with you.

✦ **Does any service cost extra?** Many SEO firms charge extra for copywriting and other work. That's fine — just make sure that you know before you start.

Don't worry about specific answers to these questions, except where noted. The main thing you're trying to get is an impression of the person or company you'll be working with. SEO is marketing, and it requires a lot of communication between you and your consultant.

Knowing What to Expect

More SEO campaigns have fallen to incorrect expectations than any other form of marketing. Here's what you should know before you start:

✦ **SEO takes a long time.** Expect at least a minimum six-month contract; one or two years is better. If you try to sign an SEO professional to a shorter contract, you'll likely either rush her (so she won't do solid long-term planning) or you'll chase off the best practitioners.

✦ **Don't expect fast results.** See the preceding bullet.

✦ **Do expect regular reports.** These should include all the data from Chapter 8 of this minibook. A screen capture of your Google Analytics output doesn't count! A true report should include analysis: what's worked, what hasn't, and what's coming next.

✦ **Expect that your SEO professional wants a certain amount of work from you.** He is going to give you lots of recommendations and requests for changes to your site. He'll ask for content, and he'll want information about your competitors. That's a good thing.

Costs vary widely from one SEO professional to the next. Some charge as little as $99.95 per month. Others charge $10,000 or more per month. The difference? The level of service. For $99.95 per month, expect very little. The SEO firm may or may not answer the phone when you call, probably won't do any work outside of a few automated directory submissions, and might not get you results. At the top end of the pay scale, an SEO professional writes SEO-optimized articles for your website, regularly analyzes your site for potential problems, researches keywords, and generally does whatever it takes to move you up in the rankings.

Most SEO pros charge based on a monthly fee. They might also offer one-time reviews where they check your website, write a report recommending changes, and then ride off into the sunset. If you have your own development team, this second option is a good one. If you don't, though, the monthly engagement works better.

Good SEO professionals often negotiate their fees depending on how challenging they think your campaign will be, how much work they're expected to do, and how long you plan to work with them. If you have a site that's already well optimized but needs a little help and you're hiring someone for a year, expect your monthly fees to be lower. If you have a site that's an SEO disaster, and you're in a very competitive industry, *and* you want everything done in three months, you're going to pay more per month.

When it comes to cost, the real question is what makes sense to you and your budget. Don't hire a *bargain* you don't trust. Your money will be wasted.

Book III

Web Analytics

The 5th Wave   By Rich Tennant

"Sales on the website are down. I figure the
server's chi is blocked, so we're fudgin' around
the feng shui in the computer room, and if that
doesn't work, Ronnie's got a chant that should do it."

Contents at a Glance

Chapter 1: Getting Started with Analytics

In This Chapter

↙ **Seeing the differences between reports and analytics**

↙ **Setting expectations**

↙ **Discovering how analytics software works**

↙ **Setting up Google Analytics**

You build your site, launch it, and wait. And wait. And wait some more. Is it working? Are you getting visitors? Are they doing what you want them to do? How will you know?

Enter the traffic report. A *traffic report* is a list of numbers and information about how folks are using your site, as shown in Figure 1-1. It is also the foundation for web analytics.

Figure 1-1: A traffic report.

Web analytics comprises using a traffic report to draw conclusions and adjust your marketing strategy. So, if a traffic report is the pencil and paper, web analytics is the process of putting pencil to paper and creating a blueprint for your next steps.

The distinction between traffic reports and web analytics is critical: Many traffic-reporting packages — including the popular Google Analytics — refer to themselves as *web analytics packages.* They are not, however. Only one web analytics tool exists: your brain. Don't forget it.

In this chapter, you find an introduction to web analytics and traffic reports. You discover what's possible with analytics but also what's beyond its reach. You find out how traffic-reporting tools work and receive guidance on choosing one from the options available as this book goes to press. The chapter wraps up with a step-by-step explanation of getting set up with Google Analytics.

This entire minibook takes a very high-level look at analytics. It gives you the bare essentials to monitor and improve your site. It does *not* teach statistics. If you want to read about statistical analysis, rolling averages, and so on, take a look at *Statistics For Dummies* or *Statistics Workbook For Dummies,* both by Deborah Rumsey (published by John Wiley & Sons, Inc.).

If you want to get a more in-depth look at web analytics, check out *Web Analytics For Dummies,* by Pedro Sostre and Jennifer LeClaire (published by John Wiley & Sons, Inc.).

Knowing What's Possible (Or Not)

Traffic reports are useful tools, but a reality check is helpful as you begin venturing into the world of web analytics. Specifically, you need to understand what you can and can't do when determining your key performance indicators (KPIs) — sales, leads, or other statistics that directly affect your business — and that's the first step in any web analytics plan.

The following sections offer an overview of what data traffic reports can collect and what you can glean from that data. You discover the limits of that data and what effect your data collection has on your visitors' privacy. (*Hint:* Not much, unless they agree to it.) Read on for details.

Ultimately, the purpose of analytics is to establish a narrative so that you can tell which changes have a positive or negative effect on your site and on your business over time. That helps you figure out what works and what doesn't, which leads to improved results.

Collecting data and what it can tell you

Traffic reports, at a minimum, show you

✦ How many times people visit your website

✦ Which pages are most popular

✦ What sites send you visitors

✦ How much time visitors spend on your site

Those are the basics. Additionally, most traffic-reporting tools now provide more powerful features, including

✦ E-commerce sales tracking

✦ Conversion goal tracking (more on this later)

✦ Search-keywords reports that show which keywords folks use to find you

✦ Campaign performance measurements so that you know which e-mail marketing pieces, banners, and other ads generate traffic

✦ "Attribution," showing how different traffic sources work together to generate conversions

With most traffic-reporting tools, you can

✦ **Find out your best sources of traffic and business** — such as search engines, a specific website, the e-mail you just sent, or something else that you didn't expect — so that you know where to focus your advertising dollars and effort.

✦ **See which pages on your site get the most or least attention** so that you understand what your site visitors like — and give them more of it.

✦ **Figure out which parts of your *shopping cart*** (that one login form, for example, or an intimidating billing information page) **drive away visitors** so that you can tweak it to improve checkout rates.

✦ **Discover which pay-per-click (PPC) advertising campaign generates the best return on investment (ROI)** so that you can spend more on the keywords and ads that deliver the best results.

Understanding the limits of reporting

Traffic reporting isn't black magic. You can't peek at your visitors through their monitors and discover every detail of their lives. Nor should you.

However, most traffic-reporting tools cannot

+ **Tell you someone's identity:** Virtually all (99 percent) traffic reporting is anonymous. Although most reporting tools know that person A visited your site at 12 noon on Thursday, looked at four pages, signed up for the e-mail newsletter, and then left, they don't know who person A actually *is.* That's a good thing. Paranoia about traffic reporting is bad enough without that kind of intrusion.

+ **Accurately determine where someone lives:** They can sometimes do this, but not consistently.

+ **Deliver 100 percent accuracy:** And this is okay. See the section "Choosing Your Reporting Tool," later in this chapter.

Minding visitors' privacy

You'll find a lot of hysteria about traffic reporting, analytics, and privacy. Folks are horrified that websites might be tracking where they came from, which pages they clicked on, and how long they stayed on a particular site.

Humbug.

The data that web servers collect is anonymous and aggregated. That is, if you visit an online store, the store owner knows *someone* came and looked around. The owner doesn't know it was you unless you already created an account on the site, logged in, and gave him permission to watch you.

Compare this with the many security cameras, credit card reports, and phone records kept by every retail company on the planet, and you can see that web statistics tracking is just not much of an intrusion.

As a website owner, though, you must act responsibly:

+ Have a clear privacy policy on your site explaining what, if anything, you do with the data you collect.

+ Never collect and store personal information unless you're capable of protecting it — and then, only if necessary.

+ If you're using a traffic-reporting service, stick with a reputable provider, such as Google Analytics or Adobe SiteCatalyst. Research all of them, and make sure that if a security breach has ever occurred, the provider properly handled it.

+ *Never,* ever, ever provide your analytics data to a third party unless you were granted permission by your audience.

Knowing How Reporting Tools Work

When you know a little bit about how reporting tools work, it's easier to understand what a specific reporting tool can or can't do for you. Reporting tools have two ways of collecting data:

✦ Processing log files

✦ Receiving data from JavaScript-based web bug reporters

Geekery ahead! But it's helpful to understand the basics of reporting technology, so don't skip this section. Although you'll come across techy-sounding words like *JavaScript,* you don't need to actually understand log files or JavaScript code. You just need to know what's going on behind the scenes in your traffic reports.

Log file reporting

When someone visits your website, your web server records basic information in a file called a *log.* Exactly what your server records might vary, but it usually includes

✦ When the visitor arrived

✦ What pages the visitor looked at

✦ Where the visitor came from

✦ Possibly, a unique identifier so that the server knows when that visit ended

Log file–reporting tools crunch through the thousands (or millions!) of lines of the server log file and create understandable reports based on the data. Tools range from simple, free packages such as Analog (www.analog.cx) to sophisticated packages such as Splunk (www.splunk.com), a super-customizable log file analyzer.

This approach has some drawbacks:

✦ If you don't control your server, you might not control what the server logs store. That can lead to poor reporting.

✦ Log files can get big — fast! — occupying a lot of space on a server.

✦ Web servers can have a lot of trouble distinguishing between different *sessions:* a single visit to a site by a single person. This can lead to inaccurate data.

Still, log files are simple, and if your web server is properly configured, the data is available when you need it. You don't need to modify your site, either. If you don't have much control over your site's code, but you can easily install/enable new software on your server, using a log file analyzer may be your best bet.

Web bugs and JavaScript

Other tools require that you actually place either a web bug or special JavaScript snippet on each page of your site. See Figure 1-2 for an example. The JavaScript "fires" when someone visits your web page. It then sends back data to the analytics service about the visitor, the page the visitor is viewing, and where the visitor came from.

This approach allows greater precision: Reporting tools can use sophisticated JavaScript to more accurately measure when a session starts and ends. They can also interpret all sorts of additional campaign data, thereby giving you greater ability to track campaign performance.

However, web bugs require that you add code to every page of your site. And, because they use JavaScript, they can slow page performance or fail completely if the visitor's browser doesn't process JavaScript. This means that JavaScript-driven reporting tools typically don't log search engine crawler traffic, and may miss some user visits as well.

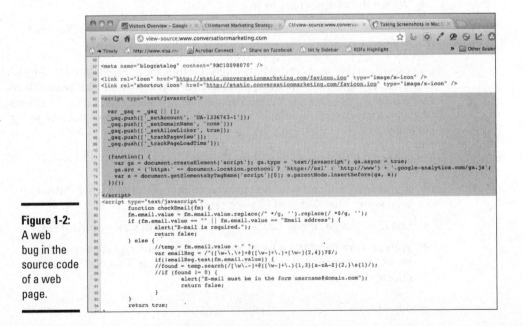

Figure 1-2:
A web bug in the source code of a web page.

While JavaScript solutions can give you sophisticated reporting with minimal work, log file solutions can give you basic reporting or the most complex, complete dataset, but very little in between. Keep that in mind when choosing: If you have a lot of control over your site's code, but cannot install new software on your server, you'll want the JavaScript solution.

Choosing Your Reporting Tool

You want to choose the right reporting tool from the start. Although switching to another tool is indeed possible, it's not easy because all reporting tools deliver slightly different data. So, choose one and stick with it.

The following sections give you a few options, explain the pluses and minuses of different solutions, and help you prepare for your installation.

Deciding what you need

No web traffic–reporting tool is totally accurate. Different web browsers might generate different results for JavaScript web bugs, and log files might fall victim to server errors or privacy-blocking software. Thus, all traffic-reporting tools will overcount some items but undercount others.

The best you can hope for is consistent inaccuracy: By using the same tool, in the same manner, over time, you can ensure that your margin of error stays consistent, and that you have consistent metrics for proportional comparison, even if they're not precise.

Here's the main lesson of consistent inaccuracy: Choose your traffic-reporting tool carefully so that you don't have to change tools again later on. Data reported by different tools can vary by as much as 30 to 40 percent. It's no fun trying to explain to your boss why page views suddenly fell by 30 percent. Stick with one reporting tool. If you *do* have to switch, run both tools side by side for a while so that you can figure out the differences and allow for them when you finally disable the old software.

The following tips can help you choose a reporting tool that you can hopefully stick with:

✦ **A balanced approach is best.** Use a JavaScript-based tool for quick, sophisticated tracking; use a log file–based tool for very basic tracking or ultra-sophisticated troubleshooting. If you can have tools in place that use both, even better.

✦ **Consider what kind of data you'll be collecting.** See the earlier section "Collecting data and what it can tell you" for a list of possible data you'll want.

✦ **Convenience matters.** Make sure that your reporting tool can do things such as e-mail you reports automatically so that you don't have to constantly log in to review data. That takes time. The e-mailed report also acts as a reminder and ensures that you will regularly check your data.

✦ **Clarity matters, too.** When you look at the reports, do they make your head spin? If the answer is yes, either this isn't the right tool for you or you need some training before you dive into the data.

✦ **Flexibility is key.** Look at the tool's custom reporting capabilities. Can you export data to Excel? Generate your own reports? If you can't, this tool will probably outlive its usefulness for you pretty quickly.

Surveying your options

As of this writing, at least a dozen very good web traffic–reporting tools are available. Some are free; some aren't. Table 1-1 outlines examples of what you can find on the market as this book goes to press.

Table 1-1	Web Traffic–Reporting Tools		
Tool	*Description*	*Cost*	*Web Address*
Adobe SiteCatalyst	A premium web analytics tool, Adobe's system allows you to track conversions, segment your audience, and watch click behavior.	At least $500 per month. It's not an impulse buy.	www.omniture.com
Google Analytics	This tool offers a wide feature set, including conversion tracking and segmentation. It also integrates with Google AdWords (of course), is easy to set up, and includes more advanced features (such as click behavior).	Free	www.google.com/ analytics

Tool	Description	Cost	Web Address
Mint	Mint is a great, simple web-based analytics tool with everything from basic traffic reporting to screen real estate data.	A flat $30 per site.	`http://haveamint.com`
Splunk	Splunk is designed for all sorts of log file analysis, including weblogs. It's amazingly powerful but takes a long time to learn. If you're not a serious networking geek, steer clear, but if you are, you won't find a better toolset.	Free for starter setup. $2000+ per year for very large sites.	`www.splunk.com`
Analog	This log-based reporting solution is popular on many web hosts.	Free	`www.analog.cx`
Sawmill	Sawmill is an old analytics favorite. It's a powerful, configurable, log file–processing tool.	Lite: $99 Pro: $199 Enterprise: $699	`www.sawmill.net`

You can, of course, build your own tool. But with as many options as are available, you'd need a really good reason. Start with one of these solutions or another out-of-the-box solution. You can add your own analytics tools later if you really need to. Chances are that you won't.

The rest of this chapter uses Google Analytics for most of the examples. It offers a great feature set and is free. Plus, most of the procedures for using Google Analytics will work just as well in other packages.

Making Sure Your Server Is Set Up

If you're using a log file–based solution, you need to make sure that your server will log the data you need. Even if you aren't going to use a log file–based solution, you should ensure that your server is logging a complete dataset for emergencies. That includes

✦ Session time

✦ Referring cookie data

✦ IP address data

✦ HTTP status code

You don't need to know what this is. If you record it, your reporting tool will do the rest.

The details of how these work is outside the scope of this book. Contact your webmaster to make sure that your server is configured to track all visit data, and you'll be all set. If you don't, though, and your server isn't tracking everything, you can't go back and get it later.

If you're using a JavaScript web bug–based system, you don't need to worry about this. But you still should. Your log files are your backup: If the JavaScript system fails or gets disabled, you can use the log files to collect data and fill the gaps.

Setting Up Google Analytics

After you choose your reporting tool, you have a setup process to follow. In the following sections, you set up Google Analytics. Google Analytics offers JavaScript-based reporting, so you then need to add that script to each page in your site. Tracking search terms your visitors type also takes a little up-front work. And of course, you don't want people in your office skewing your results, so you find out how to exclude them from your traffic reports.

Google Analytics also offers goal and e-commerce tracking. *Goal tracking* reports the completed lead forms, purchases (but not dollar amounts), or views of any page on your site that, if viewed by a visitor, indicate you achieved one of your KPIs. *E-commerce tracking* is goal tracking plus specifics regarding items sold and dollars collected. For details on these, see Chapter 5 of this minibook.

Google is updating Google Analytics on a daily basis. Features and navigation change every month or two. This is great, because the toolset continues to expand and improve. However, it may mean that some of the screens and instructions in this minibook are out of date. Fear not! The basic structure of screens and features should remain the same. If you get lost, look around and find the relevant feature, or try the Google Analytics help documentation.

Create your account

To create your account, follow these steps:

1. **Go to** www.google.com/analytics.

2. **Log in to your Google account or sign up for one.**

If you don't already have a Google account, you need to create one.

When you're logged in, you see the Google Analytics setup screen.

3. **Click the Sign Up button.**

The next page lets you set up your account and create your first profile (see Figure 1-3).

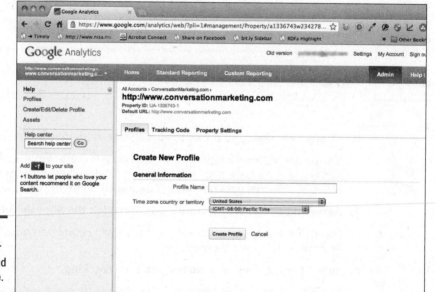

Figure 1-3:
Set up your account and your profile.

4. **Enter a profile name you'll remember and the domain you want to track and click the Create Profile button.**

Google Analytics divides each account into profiles. A *profile* is a grouping of reports for a particular domain or subdomain. Think of it as a folder: It's just an easy way to keep things organized.

5. **Select the web protocol for your site.**

If your web address begins with http:// select http:// as your web protocol, as shown in Figure 1-4. If your web address begins with https://, select https://.

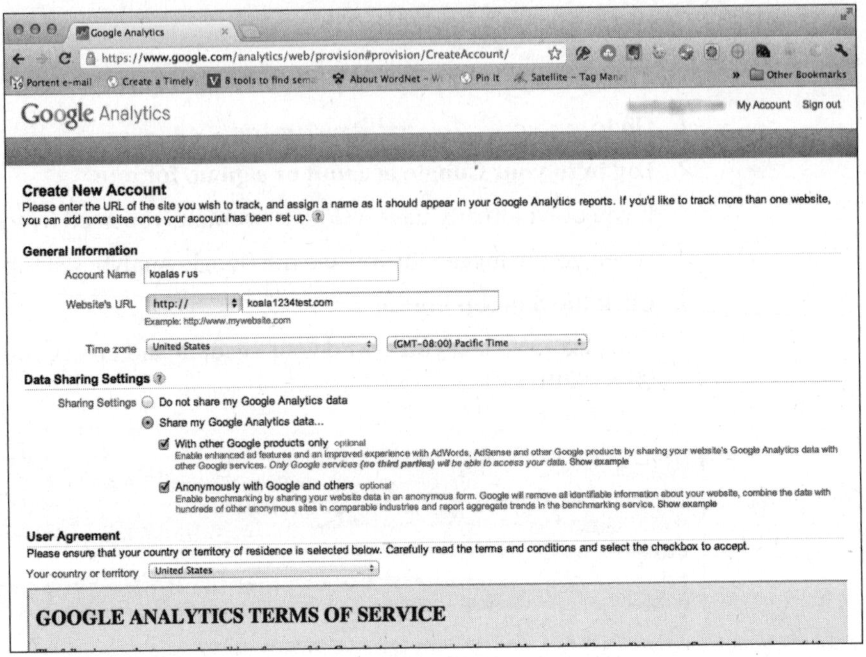

Figure 1-4:
Set up
your web
protocol.

6. **Choose whether you'd like to share your analytics data.**

   If you choose yes, Google will use this data for anonymous benchmarking. Unless you have a strong objection, choose yes. It helps you and other businesses get comparison data without giving away any secrets.

7. **Agree to the terms and conditions and click the Sign Up button.**

   On the next page, you can set up the tracking code you need to add to your website to enable tracking.

8. **Select the number of domains you'll be tracking.**

   Scroll down the page, and you'll see options for the number of domains to track (see Figure 1-5).

   - *Single domain*: Choose this if you're tracking one domain.

   - *One domain with multiple subdomains:* If you want to track multiple subdomains (for example, mine.site.com and your.site.com) with the same Google Analytics report, select this option.

   - *Multiple top-level domains:* If you want to track multiple, unique top-domains with the same Google Analytics report (for example, www.mysite.com and www.yoursite.com), select this option.

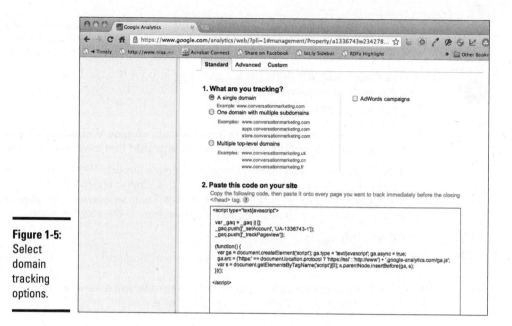

Figure 1-5:
Select
domain
tracking
options.

9. **If you're going to track AdWords campaigns, check that box.**

10. **Copy the code and paste it into a text editor so that you have it available for installation on your site.**

11. **Click Save.**

It may look like nothing happened. You'll see a small success callout at the top of the page (see Figure 1-6).

Figure 1-6:
Success,
oh-so-subtle.

You can set options around dynamic content, and custom tagging/tracking using the Advanced tab. That's beyond the scope of this book. Take a look at *Web Analytics For Dummies* if you want to set up advanced options.

The code is slightly different for each site in your profile. Don't reuse the same code among multiple sites.

12. **Click Property Settings.**

13. **If you have Google Webmaster Tools set up, choose Webmaster Tools Settings⇨Edit. Select the Webmaster Tools profile that matches your site.**

    This is strictly a convenience: Google Analytics imports Webmaster Tools search query data so that you can view it in a single report. This saves you from having to open Google Webmaster Tools whenever you want to view this data. See Book II for more information on Webmaster Tools.

14. **Click Apply again.**

    Your account is added, and you have the tracking code.

If you look at the accounts list, you'll see the profile you added, as shown in Figure 1-7. Click that, and you'll see your website.

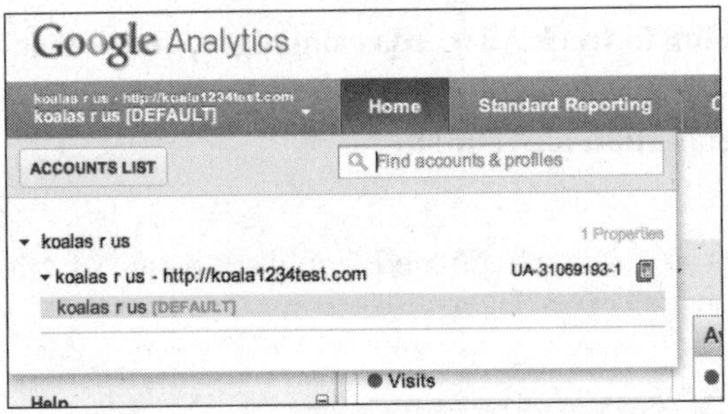

Figure 1-7:
Your website listed in the accounts list.

Installing the tracking code

Remember that tracking code you copied in the last step? You need to install it on your website so that it can start sending data to Google Analytics.

This procedure varies depending on whether you have a blog site, a traditional site, or a CMS-driven site. (*CMS* stands for content management system.)

1. **Access your site with whatever editing tool you're using.**

    If you have a blog, you'll want to look at the Templates or Design tool. If you have a traditional site, you'll probably use a File Transfer Protocol (FTP) tool. If you're using a CMS, you'll want to edit your site template.

2. **Copy the Google Analytics tracking code to your Clipboard by first selecting all the code and then choosing Edit⇨Copy in the text editor where you pasted it.**

3. **In your editing tool, paste the tracking code right before the closing `</head>` tag on each page of your site:**

   - *If you're using a blogging tool or a CMS,* you might have to paste the code only once.

   - *If you're using a traditional website,* you might need to paste the code into each page. It's worth the effort, though.

4. **Save the edited code to your website.**

5. **If necessary, republish the site to update your code.**

   See Figure 1-8 for properly installed Google Analytics code.

6. **Wait a half hour or so. Log back in to Google Analytics and look for the profile you added.**

   It should now read `Receiving data`. It may be 3-4 hours before you see any actual data, but your code is properly installed.

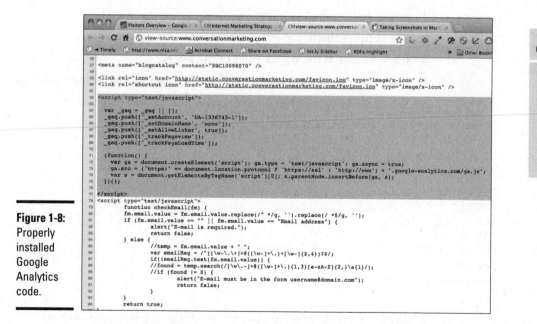

Figure 1-8: Properly installed Google Analytics code.

Finding the tracking code again

If you didn't copy the tracking code when you set up your account, here's how you can find it again:

1. **Log in to Google Analytics.**

2. **Click the website profile for which you want to see the code.**

3. **Click Admin at the upper-right corner of the screen.**

4. **Click the Tracking Code tab.**

   The code is at the bottom of the page.

Tracking site search

If you have a search box on your website, it makes sense to track what folks type into it. You can find out a lot about your audience. Chapter 4 of this minibook talks about analyzing site searches.

To set up a site search, follow these steps:

1. **Log in to Google Analytics.**

2. **Select the website for which you want to track site search.**

3. **Click Admin at the upper-right of the page.**

4. **Click the Profile Settings tab and scroll down to Site Search Settings.**

5. **Select the Do Track Site Search radio button (see Figure 1-9).**

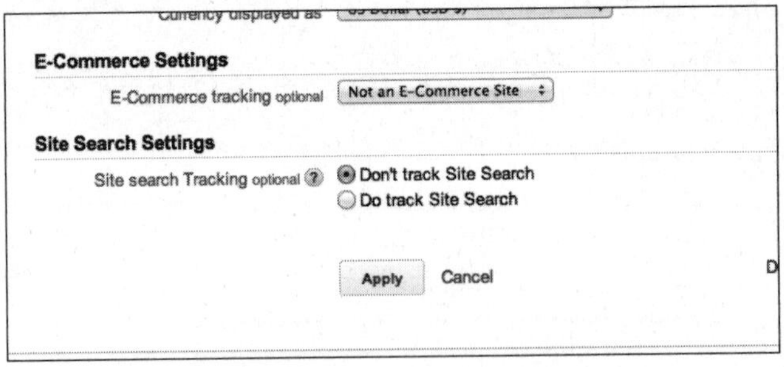

Figure 1-9: Search tracking, set up in Google Analytics.

6. **Leave this page open in your browser. Open a separate browser window for the next few steps.**

7. **In the new browser window, go to your website.**

8. Search for *buggy bumpers,* using your site's search tool.

9. Look at the address of the search result page.

   You should find the words `buggy bumpers` in the address, as shown in Figure 1-10, as well as a query attribute (such as `q=` or `search=`).

10. Enter the query attribute into the **Query Parameter** field in Google Analytics.

11. Click **Apply.**

   You're done. Within a few hours, you'll start seeing the phrases people search for on your site.

Figure 1-10:
The search query attribute.

Excluding your office

Your analytics package won't distinguish between customers and folks at your company unless you tell it to. Because you want the most accurate numbers, set up a filter to exclude everyone who works at your organization.

That kind of filter depends on the IP addresses used by your office. If you don't know what that means, it's best not to fiddle with it. Instead, contact your webmaster or your Internet Service Provider for help in finding the IP address.

Then you set up the filter, as follows:

1. Log in to Google Analytics.

2. Select the website for which you want to set up a filter.

3. Click **Admin** at the upper-right of the page.

4. Click the **Filters** tab.

5. Select **+ New Filter.**

6. **Give the filter a name you'll remember, such as *Exclude IPs*.**

7. **Under Filter Type, choose Exclude Traffic from an IP Address.**

8. **Type your IP address.**

See Figure 1-11 for a completed filter.

9. **Click Save.**

You might need to exclude multiple addresses. You can create a separate filter for each one, or you can use regular expressions (also called *regex*). regex is beyond the scope of this book and involves very high-level development expertise.

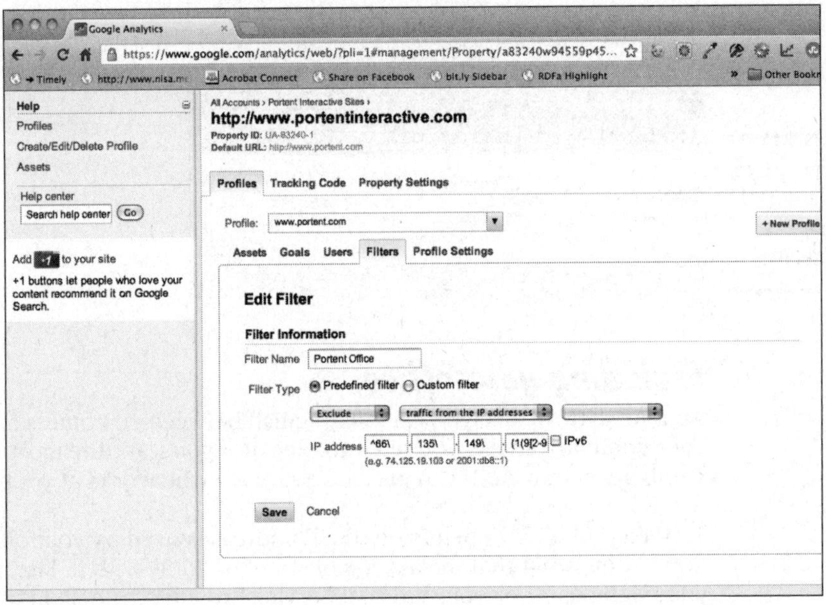

Figure 1-11:
A completed
IP filter.

Chapter 2: Tracking Traffic Volumes

In This Chapter

✔ Avoiding hits

✔ The five basic metrics

✔ How to interpret basic data

*A*ll the fancier metrics for tracking traffic and user behavior that you can read about later in this book are built on the five basic ones covered in this chapter. You need to understand these five metrics — and how to interpret them — if you're going to do more advanced analysis and know how to use that data to improve your site.

This chapter uses Google Analytics. The reports are much the same from one reporting package to another, though. Follow along with these examples, and you'll be able to apply what you glean here to any reporting toolset.

Seeing Why Hits Are a Lousy Metric

First off, though, you need to avoid one metric when tracking traffic and user behavior: hits.

You probably hear a lot of folks talk about hits. "I got a million hits last month!!" is a claim you hear a lot.

That's great, but hits are almost meaningless when it comes to measuring audience or marketing performance. Simply defined, a *hit* is any one *file* downloaded from your website, any one time. Every image, script, and stylesheet linked to a page counts as one file — and thus, one hit. Seeing as how one page can contain 1 file or 1,000 files, hits don't tell you much from a marketing viewpoint.

Look at Figure 2-1, which shows a single web page. That page, though, holds dozens of images. Do the math, and you can see that a single view of that page generates about 80 hits. Take it a step further: If ten people visit the page, that's 800 hits. Wow!

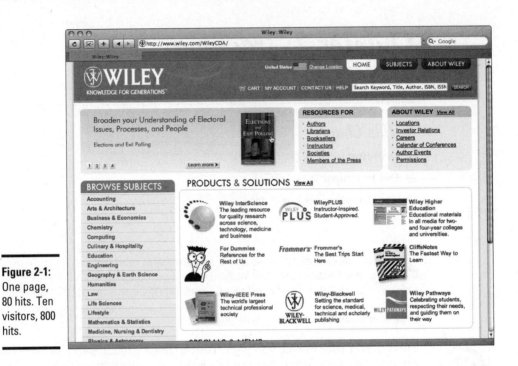

Figure 2-1:
One page,
80 hits. Ten
visitors, 800
hits.

On the other hand, a simpler page — such as the Google homepage — contains only a few files. Do the math again to see why these base numbers are important: A view of one of your simpler pages might be just as important to your business as a view of a more complex page — *but the simpler page generates fewer hits.*

Having laid out the preceding argument to why hits aren't necessarily the end-all–be-all metric that people assume, hits are indeed a valuable measure. They're great for measuring server load and also a good way to figure out how to speed page load times. But because they're a lousy marketing metric, avoid relying on them.

Understanding the Five Basic Traffic Metrics

Traffic, in terms of web visitors, actually comprises five different ingredients:

✦ **Sessions (also called *visits*):** A *session* is any one person visiting your website any one time. If someone visits your site ten times in a week, those visits count as ten sessions, whether she stayed on the site for 5 minutes or 50.

✦ **Unique visitors (called *uniques* if you want to sound terribly professional):** A *unique visitor* is any one person visiting your website any number of times during a defined period. If someone visits your site ten times in a week, she still counts as only one unique visitor.

✦ **Page views:** A *page view* is any one visitor viewing one page of your site, one time. A page must have a unique address, or *URL*. If someone visits your homepage but then clicks a link to your Contact page, those are two page views.

✦ **Time on site:** This is the total amount of time one visitor spends on your site in the course of a single session. Average time on site is an invaluable measure of visit quality and visitor interest.

✦ **Referrers:** If someone clicks a search result link at Google and lands on your site, Google is known as the *referrer*.

Any traffic-reporting toolset — even the most basic — must provide these five metrics. If yours doesn't, replace it. These five metrics typically show up right on the first page — the *dashboard* — of your traffic-reporting package, as shown in Figure 2-2.

Figure 2-2:
The five
metrics
in Google
Analytics.

Tracking sessions (visits)

Because a session is defined as any one visit to your site, sessions are a good general measure of site use and load (more on this in a moment). Think of sessions as foot traffic in a traditional retail store: The same people might go in and out of the store, but that doesn't matter. If the store's full, it's full.

In your traffic-reporting tool, you'll find sessions either under a section called Sessions (surprise!) or Visits, as shown in Figure 2-3.

Don't use sessions to measure the following:

✦ **Audience size:** If someone visits, leaves, and then returns to your site many times, one person can generate multiple sessions in any time period. So, sessions can be far higher than unique visits (a more accurate measure of audience).

✦ **Ad performance:** Advertising — whether pay-per-click ads, e-mail, banners, or other creative elements — is created to bring you new customers. Because sessions don't differentiate between new and repeat visitors, they're not a good measure of ad performance. Counting unique visitors (see the next section) is far better.

Figure 2-3:
The Visits report in Google Analytics.

Do use sessions to see

✦ **Site activity in the broadest possible terms:** More sessions mean more traffic, which may also mean a higher load on your web server. Sessions are a good way to judge how much strain your site is under.

✦ **Conversion rate based on foot traffic to your site:** If you want to know how many visits it takes to get a sale or lead, you need to know how many sessions you get in a given time period.

✦ **General interest in your site:** Even though one person can generate many sessions, sessions are still a great way to see how much interest you're generating. At a high level, whether five or ten people generated those 100 sessions isn't critical. The average level of interest remains the same.

✦ **Peak times of the day, month, or year:** Many businesses are cyclical by day or season. Peaks or lows in sessions might fit a pattern that tells you your customers are more active at a specific time of day or year. In Figure 2-4, the session graph of one day shows a common cycle.

Figure 2-4:
A typical
daily traffic
curve.

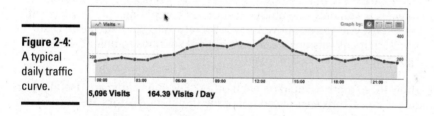

Among analytics experts, sessions can sometimes get a bad reputation. Folks will skip them and move on to unique visitors, which appear to provide better data. However, sessions do provide valuable information.

Tracking unique visitors

Unique Visitors reports are a good measure of audience size, ad performance, and the effect of blog mentions or other *noise* — news reports about you or a competitor, for example — on your site.

Don't use unique visitors to measure the following:

✦ **Per-visitor interest:** Unique visitor data can tell you how many people come to your site. On its own, though, it tells you nothing about how much they liked the site. Combine this data with page views and time on the site to make that kind of analysis. (You can read about page views and time on the site earlier in this chapter.)

✦ **Overall site activity:** If 100 unique visitors come to your site in a week, that might seem like a small group. However, if they each come to the site 100 times, that's 10,000 sessions. Use sessions to track site activity, not unique visitors.

Do use unique visitors to measure

✦ **Audience size:** Unique visitors are a great absolute measure of your audience in a given time period. After all, 10,000 sessions are great. If this represents only 100 unique visitors, though, your audience isn't that big.

✦ **Overall ad performance:** If you just purchased an ad — say, on a blog — and your unique visitor count increases, that could mean the ad's working for you. You want to dig deeper with page views and referrers, but unique visitor count is a good initial clue.

✦ **Changes over time:** Watch unique visitors over time. If your audience (unique visitor count) suddenly doubles in size after that local news coverage, you know that story had an impact.

✦ **Comparison with sessions:** A single visitor generating ten sessions in a week is still only one unique visitor. By comparing unique visits with sessions, you can see how many folks return to your site more than once. In many businesses, a high ratio of sessions to unique visits is good: It indicates visitor loyalty.

See how these metrics build on each other? Sessions alone are useful, as are unique visitors, but sessions compared with unique visitors are even better.

Any traffic-reporting package can deliver a Unique Visitors report much like the one shown in Figure 2-5. However, log file analysis tools (such as older versions of Urchin or WebTrends) require additional setup to report unique visitors. Otherwise, they'll report sessions only. Check your traffic reports to make sure that you're measuring unique visitors. They're a must-have metric.

Tracking page views

If unique visitors are the people, page views are their footprints. Page views are the measure of interest in specific areas of your site. Most traffic-reporting tools will give you a few different ways to look at page views, as shown in Figure 2-6:

✦ **Overall page-view count for your entire site:** Look for a Pageviews report to see the aggregate view.

✦ **A page-by-page look at which pages get the most attention:** Look for a report called Top Content or Top Pages to see a comparison of popular pages.

Figure 2-5:
A Unique
Visitors
report.

Figure 2-5:
A Unique
Visitors
report.

Figure 2-6:
Aggregate
and page-
by-page
reports.

Don't use page views to measure audience size. One visitor may view 100 pages, while another may only look at 1. Having one customer who walks through your store and looks at every product isn't as good as having ten who look at a few products each. The same holds true on the web. Page views are an awful measure of audience size.

Do use page views to measure

✦ **Visitor interest:** Combined with visitor data, page views are a great reflection of visitor interest. Page views per visit, as shown in Figure 2-7, are one indicator of just how interested your audience is in what you're showing them. If someone stays on your website and looks at ten pages, chances are that visitor is more interested than someone who stays on your website and looks at only one page.

✦ **Content performance:** Pages that get more page views are better performers. They also tell you what your audience wants to hear. A page that gets 4,000 views in a month is probably drawing more interest than a page that gets 1,000.

✦ **Ad performance:** Most traffic-reporting tools show page views per visit generated by specific referrers. (See the section "Tracking Referrers," later in this chapter.) Ads that generate more page views per visit are usually better performers.

Figure 2-7:
Page views
per visit
in Google
Analytics.

Page Depth	Visits	Pageviews	Percentage of total
<1	24	0	0.05% Visits / 0.00% Pageviews
1	39,069	38,069	78.30% / 53.04%
2	6,268	12,536	12.89% / 17.47%
3	1,933	5,799	3.98% / 8.08%
4	940	3,760	1.93% / 5.24%
5	437	2,185	0.90% / 3.04%
6	298	1,788	0.61% / 2.49%
7	175	1,225	0.36% / 1.71%
8	124	992	0.26% / 1.38%

Visits: **48,618** — % of Total: 100.00% (48,618)

Pageviews: **71,776** — % of Total: 100.00% (71,776)

Again, see how the different metrics can be combined? Page views are a great measure of raw site usage. Page views per visit (per session) give you an added dimension: visitor interest.

Tracking time on site

Time on site is a useful metric when combined with page views, visits, sessions, and average time. Together, they give a more complete view of site performance and user interest. Consider the examples in the following sections.

Balancing page views with time on site

Time on site is the perfect balance for page views. Page views can be inaccurate. If someone comes to your site, looks at ten pages for five seconds each, hates what she sees, and then leaves, you might *think* you just got a quality visitor because she looked at ten whole pages. That's a lot of page views for a single visitor.

But — and here's the rub — she was on the site for only 50 seconds. Yikes.

If you track time on site, you can compare time on site with page views to make sure that you're getting an accurate measure of visitor interest. Most web-traffic tools now show time on site and time on page right alongside page views and sessions.

Weighing sessions and unique visitors with time on site

You can use time on site to balance session or unique visitor counts, too. If your unique visitor count spikes suddenly because of a surge of traffic from a site like StumbleUpon (see Book VII on social media marketing), that's great. However, also checking average time on site helps you assess how valuable that traffic surge really was.

✦ **If average time on site plunged,** you might have gotten a lot of new visitors, but they were far less interested and probably won't give you much long-term benefit. Figure 2-8 shows one instance where that happened: The average time on site plunged, which isn't the direction you want to go in.

✦ **If, on the other hand, your average time on site stayed consistent or improved, even when your number of visitors jumped,** those additional visitors spent at least as much time on your site as the rest. That's good: You added more quality members to your audience. Figure 2-9 shows one burst of traffic from StumbleUpon: Much better!

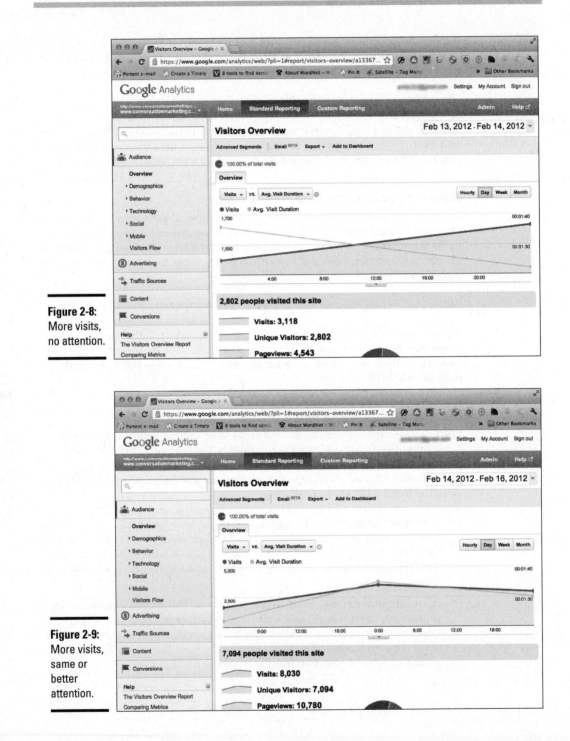

Figure 2-8:
More visits, no attention.

Figure 2-9:
More visits, same or better attention.

Tracking Referrers

Referrers complete the basic traffic-reporting toolset. A *referrer* is a web page that points to your website. When someone clicks a link, that web page becomes a referrer. Referrers come in many flavors:

✦ A traditional web page that might have a link to your site

✦ A link in an e-mail that someone reads in a web-based e-mail reader, such as Hotmail or Gmail

✦ A search result on a search engine

So, a referrer tells you where visitors came from when they reached your site.

Think about it: If you ran a vegetable stand and every single person who walked up had a sign on their forehead that read, "I saw your ad in the newspaper" or "John at the corner store told me about you," you'd immediately know which advertising worked and which marketing didn't.

Referrers are like that kind of sign. Combine them with the other metrics in this chapter, and you can see which referrers generate quality traffic, as shown in Figure 2-10.

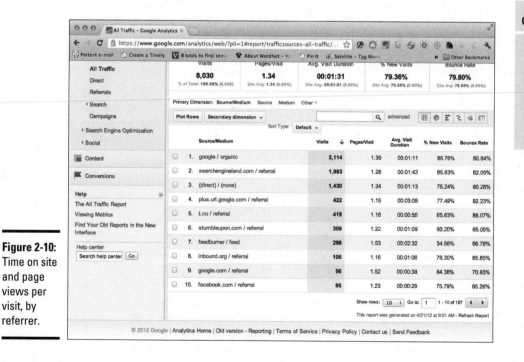

Figure 2-10: Time on site and page views per visit, by referrer.

Combine them with sales and conversion data (more on this later in this minibook), and you can actually measure return on investment (ROI) from many of your online marketing efforts.

That makes referrers a must-have in your analytics toolset. If your reporting tool doesn't show referrers, get a new tool.

The following chapter is dedicated solely to referrers. They're that important!

Chapter 3: Measuring Your Best Referrers

In This Chapter

✔ **Defining a referrer**

✔ **Analyzing referrers**

No Internet marketing campaign can survive — let alone succeed — without *referrers,* the web pages that point to your website. (You can find the basics of referrers in the previous chapter.)

But the business intelligence you can gain from this seemingly simple stat goes far, far deeper. It pays to have a really solid understanding of this metric, which is why measuring referrers is the sole subject of this chapter.

If you're using a log file–based tracking solution, make sure that your server is set up. Otherwise, you could miss a lot of valuable referrer data. (Flip to Chapter 1 of this minibook for details on tracking solutions that use log files versus JavaScript.)

You can apply referrer data to improve your online business in so many ways. This chapter barely scrapes the surface of referrer tracking. Here, you find out where referrer information comes from, basics about stats you find in your referrer data, and examples for analyzing referring site data. In the next few chapters, you discover how to start combining other metrics — such as conversion rates and visit quality — to help you get even more value from this data.

Understanding Referrers

Geekinese alert! This section has to get a little technical so you'll understand exactly how referrers are tracked and what the tracking data means. Don't let it scare you off. You're a smart person. You bought this book, after all.

Here's how referrer tracking works in the background as you (or your visitors) use the Internet:

1. You use a search engine, visit a website, or receive an e-mail message.

2. You click a link on the page.

3. That link directs you to another website.

4. When you land on that other website, the web server that powers that site asks your web browser where you came from.

5. Unless you turned off this feature, your web browser delivers that information — the *referrer* — to the web server.

6. The web server logs the data.

7. If you're using a JavaScript web bug–based traffic-reporting tool (see Chapter 1 of this minibook), your reporting tool logs it, too.

That referrer data typically includes

+ The referring site address, such as `www.google.com`

+ The complete referring URL

    For example, if you came from a search for *buggy bumpers* on Google, the URL might be `google.com?q=buggy+bumpers`. If you came from the `contactus.htm` page on a company site, the URL might be `www.thesite.com/contactus.htm`.

With that data, any good traffic-reporting tool can determine

+ Where a visitor came from

+ If the visitor came from a search engine, what keywords that person used to find your site

+ The specific page on the referring site from which the visitor came

+ Sometimes, whether the visitor clicked a specific ad or link on that page

Augh! My privacy!

A lot of folks get the heebie-jeebies when they find out that every web server knows the site that referred them. But it's really not that bad. You *can* turn off your browser's ability to deliver this data if you want. But 99 percent of the time, web servers just know that some nameless person came from site A or B. They don't know who that person is. The only time they'll specifically know that you are who you are is if you create an account on that site and give them permission to track that data. Hopefully, you trust them at that point.

You can see why referrer data is so valuable. With it, you can figure out which websites, keywords, and ads generate sales, leads, or other quality visits to your site.

Without referrer data, you're driving with your eyes closed. But enough negativity. Time to talk about driving with your eyes open.

Checking Out the Referring Site Data in a Traffic Report

Most reporting tools don't show referrer data front and center on the main dashboard. You need to drill down to find it. Using Google Analytics as an example, this section walks you through the steps of finding your referring sites and introduces the common metrics you see along with those sites.

Although the following steps focus on Google Analytics, you can use these basic steps to work with most reporting tools. To find your referrals, follow these steps:

1. Go to www.google.com/analytics **to get to Google Analytics.**

Chapter 1 of this minibook explains how to get started with Google Analytics.

2. Click Traffic Sources in the sidebar on the left.

If you're using a different traffic-reporting tool, Traffic Sources might be called Referring Sources, Referrals, or Links. Be sure to click around if you don't see the referrer reports right away.

If you can't find a traffic sources tool, your traffic-reporting tool might not be properly configured. If that's the case, it's time to have a chat with your webmaster.

3. Check out the overview page to see which websites send you traffic.

The graph shows the flow of traffic from referring sites. The list below the graph shows all the sites that sent you traffic.

In Figure 3-1, the graph at the top shows overall traffic from other sites. The rest of the page gives you a quick at-a-glance view of search traffic, and the breakdown between search, nonsearch, direct, and campaign-related traffic.

Figure 3-1:
The Traffic
Sources
dashboard
in Google
Analytics.

4. Click the Sources and then Referrals on the left side of the screen.

This will show you all nonsearch referring sites, as shown in Figure 3-2.

Figure 3-2:
Referring
sites in
Google
Analytics.

You'll see six different categories of information. Here's what each category means:

+ The **Source** is where the visitors came from: the site.

+ **Visits** tells you how many clicks you got from that referring site. Note that these are visits, and not *unique visitors*. Some reporting tools use one, and some use the other. See Chapter 2 of this minibook for the difference.

+ **Pages/Visit** shows the average number of pages visitors looked at on the site after coming from this referrer.

+ **Avg. Visit Duration** shows the average time that visitors spent on the site after coming from this referrer.

+ **% New Visits** tells how many visitors came to the site from this referrer who hadn't previously visited the site in this time period. This data can help you see whether the referrer is sending you new visitors, or just referring the same visitors to you again. Both might be valuable: A new visitor is a potential new customer.

+ **Bounce Rate** shows how many people came from this referrer, looked at one page on the site, and then left without looking at any others. A high bounce rate isn't necessarily bad, but it bears investigation.

Some referrer reports include an item called *Direct* or *Not Set:*

+ **Direct:** Someone came to your site by typing your web address directly into his web browser. Because this visitor didn't click a link to get to your site, you have no referrer.

+ **Not Set:** This might mean the same thing. Or, it might mean that for whatever reason, the reporting tool couldn't interpret the referrer.

Analytics isn't an exact science.

In the next section, you drill a little deeper into the referring sites data and check out examples of what you can glean by investigating your referring sites.

Analyzing the Referring Sites Data

You can turn a Referring Sites report into real business intelligence by asking yourself three questions (using Figure 3-2):

Book III
Chapter 3

Measuring Your
Best Referrers

✦ **Which sites sent you the most traffic?**

In Figure 3-2

- StumbleUpon is far and away the biggest referrer.

- Twitter is second. Any click from `t.co` is a click from Twitter.

- Then comes Facebook.

If any of your top referrers come as a surprise, you'll want to do some research.

✦ **Which sites sent you the most attention?**

In Figure 3-2

- StumbleUpon generates a healthy two pages per visit (not bad for a blog), but less than 1:07 time on the site. If your goal is to balance time on site and pages per visit, StumbleUpon isn't the best site to be getting the most attention.

- Facebook generates fewer visitors, but they spend over twice as much time on the site.

- Google+ also sends quality visitors who pay attention.

✦ **What insights can you gain?**

The answers to this question are a bit more open ended than the preceding ones, but here are a couple of thoughts to glean from Figure 3-2 to give you an idea of what you might do with your referral data:

- StumbleUpon sends a lot of traffic, but those visitors don't stick around very long. Can you improve the *stickiness* (the length of time they stay on the site) for StumbleUpon users? This might prove difficult, but that site is a huge traffic generator, so it's good to take better care of that audience.

- Google referrals only show a time on site of about 44 seconds. That's very low compared with the site average (1:38). Is the site broken for folks coming from whatever Google property they're using?

The following steps outline an example of how you might dig a little deeper into your referral data by using Google Analytics, using that Google Image Search referral as an example:

1. **From the Referring Sites overview page, click Google in the Sources column on the Site Usage tab.**

   What appears on the screen is shown in Figure 3-3.

   Ah-HAH! It's mostly Google Image search (imgres).

Figure 3-3:
This
information
is not very
helpful.

2. **Click the link (imgres in Figure 3-3) to dig a little deeper.**

   This information isn't very helpful because what you want to know is which keywords generated those referrals.

3. **To see the keywords, choose Traffic Sources: Keyword from the Secondary Dimension drop-down list.**

   The result is another dead end (although keywords aren't always a dead end, as the next section explains).

   You'll get used to dead ends like these if you do web analytics long enough. Luckily, you have other options.

4. **Choose Landing Page from the Secondary Dimension: Traffic Sources drop-down list.**

   The Landing Page option shows which pages on the site generated these referrals, as shown in Figure 3-4.

   Interesting. The results show that the number-one landing page was a post that contains an image of Snidely Whiplash (a cartoon character from the Rocky and Bullwinkle series).

   That information is pure gold: At least some of the Google Image referrals are relatively worthless. They're folks looking for Snidely Whiplash, but that's not the main focus of the blog (which is Internet marketing).

**Book III
Chapter 3**

**Measuring Your
Best Referrers**

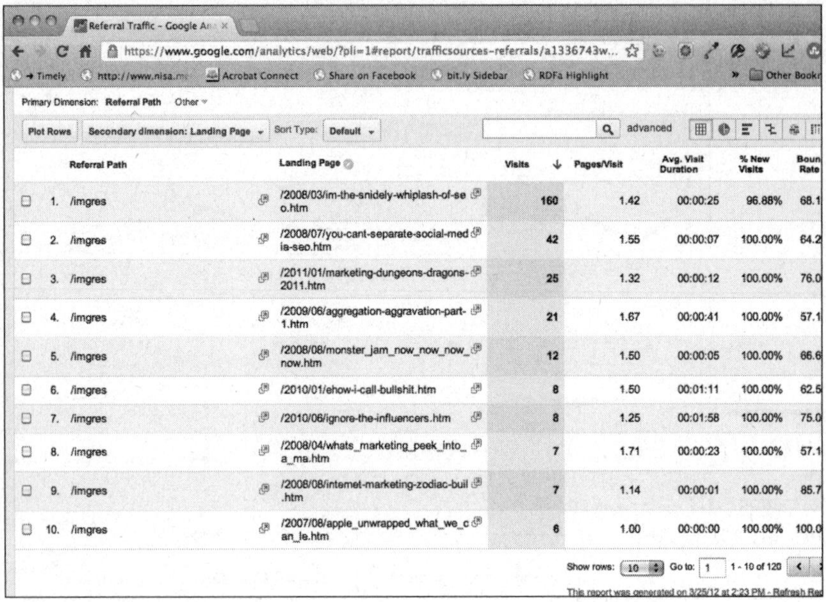

	Referral Path	Landing Page	Visits	Pages/Visit	Avg. Visit Duration	% New Visits	Boun Rate
1.	/imgres	/2008/03/im-the-snidely-whiplash-of-seo.htm	160	1.42	00:00:25	96.88%	68.1
2.	/imgres	/2008/07/you-cant-separate-social-media-seo.htm	42	1.55	00:00:07	100.00%	64.2
3.	/imgres	/2011/01/marketing-dungeons-dragons-2011.htm	25	1.32	00:00:12	100.00%	76.0
4.	/imgres	/2009/06/aggregation-aggravation-part-1.htm	21	1.67	00:00:41	100.00%	57.1
5.	/imgres	/2008/08/monster_jam_now_now_now_now.htm	12	1.50	00:00:05	100.00%	66.6
6.	/imgres	/2010/01/ehow-i-call-bullshit.htm	8	1.50	00:01:11	100.00%	62.5
7.	/imgres	/2010/06/ignore-the-influencers.htm	8	1.25	00:01:58	100.00%	75.0
8.	/imgres	/2008/04/whats_marketing_peek_into_a_ma.htm	7	1.71	00:00:23	100.00%	57.1
9.	/imgres	/2008/08/internet-marketing-zodiac-buil.htm	7	1.14	00:00:01	100.00%	85.7
10.	/imgres	/2007/08/apple_unwrapped_what_we_can_le.htm	6	1.00	00:00:00	100.00%	100.0

Figure 3-4: See which landing pages generate referrals.

No hard-and-fast rules exist for what's "good" or "bad" traffic. That's why no one should tell you, "More than one minute is a good time on site stat." You have to see what's average for your site and go from there.

See how powerful referrer data is? In just a few minutes, you can diagnose a possible problem, find the source, and eliminate it. But wait, there's more!

Tracking Referring Keywords

If you're getting traffic from search engines (and you'd better be), folks are finding you by searching on keywords. Knowing which keywords they're using to find you gives you a hint as to the questions they might need to have answered when they first land on your site.

This section holds true for both paid and unpaid keywords.

The following steps walk you through an analysis of referring keywords, using Google Analytics and blog results:

1. **Go to** `www.google.com/analytics` **and log in. Then click the site profile for which you want to see the report.**

2. **Click Traffic Sources in the sidebar on the left and then click Search. Then click Organic or Paid.**

   The Referring Keyword report that appears will usually look a lot like the referring site report. See Figure 3-5 for keyword traffic.

3. **Review your keyword report for results that are consistent — and check for anything new or unusual.**

   Looking at this report, it's easy to see that *Google Analytics Tutorial* is a top traffic generator. That's from a series of posts a long time ago, and it still generates traffic. A quick look at search results on Google shows that the blog is No. 1 and No. 2 for the phrase.

   The next few keywords aren't surprising, except for *marketing skills*. That's a tough keyword, and it's hard to get a respectable ranking for it on any search engine.

4. **To find out the referring sites for a keyword, click it in the results list. On the page that appears, choose Source from the Dimension drop-down list.**

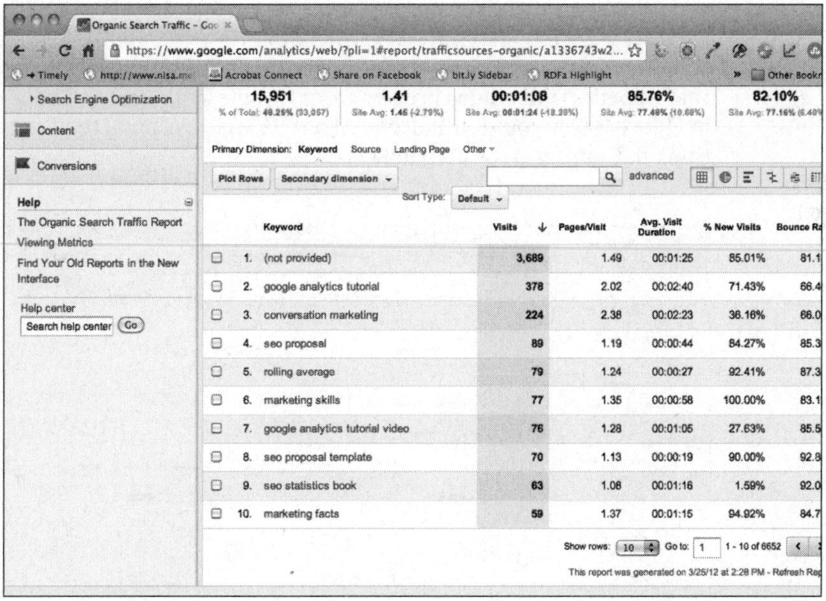

Figure 3-5:
The
Referring
Keyword
report.

The conclusions you can draw from this sleuthing are as follows:

✦ According to a Google search, the blog is near the top of page 1 for that phrase. That explains it.

The page views/visit and time on site aren't bad, and this is a really tough keyword to keep a top-3 ranking. The task is to write more on the subject to aim at staying on page 1.

✦ One other keyword leaps out: *SEO proposal template*. It gets 1.28 page views per visit but a meager 19 seconds onsite. That's awful.

The web page that keyword sends people to shows a fake proposal template, and folks are probably expecting a real proposal template. Instead, they're getting a bit of sarcasm. The task is to write a serious proposal template that gets people to stay longer on the site.

You may have noticed that Google shows `not provided` for many referring organic keywords. Google claims this is privacy related. It doesn't matter. The result is that you can't see a huge chunk of your keyword data. If you look back at Figure 3-5, almost a third of the organic keywords end up in `(not provided)`! Yikes!

Luckily, you get a separate keyword query report. On the left side of the screen, click Search Engine Optimization and then click Queries. The report that appears pulls data directly from Google Webmaster Tools, as shown in Figure 3-6. If you don't already have Google Webmaster Tools set up, see Book II, Chapter 3 for instructions.

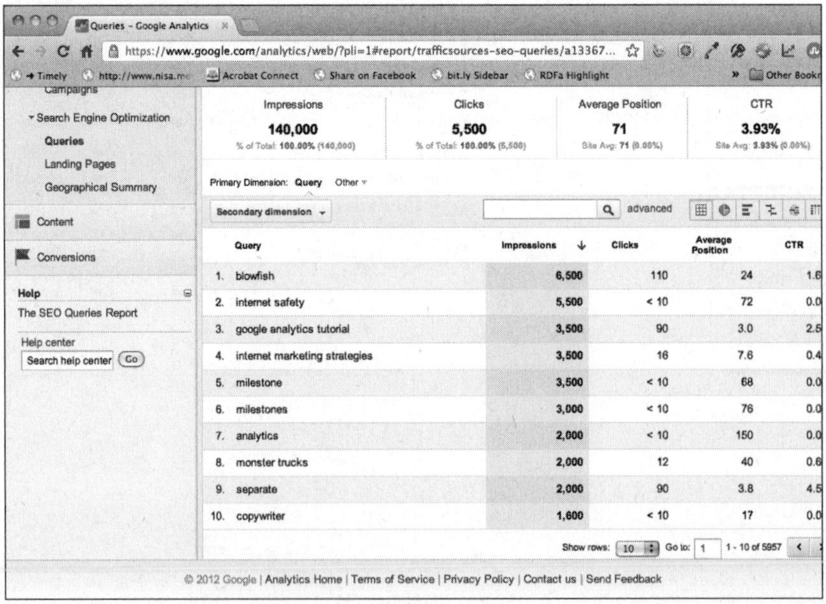

Figure 3-6: The Queries report showing all the keyword referrers.

Getting fancy

Digging into referring site data can be exciting. If you find that the basics outlined in this minibook just aren't enough, you might be interested in more advanced topics, such as

✔ **Custom tagging and campaign management:** Use these tools to track every banner, keyword ad, blog post, and anything else that sends traffic to your site on a very individual, targeted basis. Check out *Web Analytics For Dummies,* by Pedro Sostre and Jennifer LeClaire (published by

John Wiley & Sons, Inc.), or read the documentation for your traffic-reporting toolset for more information.

✔ **Referrer-based page customization:** You can actually grab this referrer data on the fly to customize pages so that they provide the best user experience. Amazon.com uses this data as part of its product recommendations on the homepage. If that makes your brain hurt, you're not alone. But it is a powerful feature on many sites.

It's not perfect, but it at least gives you a clear idea of what's driving traffic. And it's all you have.

Chapter 4: Measuring Visit Quality

Measuring visit quality involves tracking what's typical for your site and using what you know to set benchmarks. You might notice that doesn't include absolute measures of quality visits.

Measuring visit quality is not a science. What you find in this chapter is simply a process for setting some benchmarks that you can try to improve upon. Your mission, should you choose to accept it, is to

✦ Build traffic, but not at the expense of these benchmarks

✦ Increase time on site and page views per visit

✦ Keep these benchmarks in mind as you look at other statistics

Note that this chapter assumes that you're familiar with the basic measures discussed in Chapters 2 and 3 of this minibook. If you're looking for information on tracking some form of conversion like a sale or a lead, you won't find that here; flip to Chapter 5 in this minibook, instead.

Setting Quality Targets

Take a look at Figure 4-1. How can you tell which referrers are generating good or bad visits? Argh: It's nothing but a bunch of numbers — but, it's not as hard to decipher as it might look.

Figure 4-1:
A whole lot
of numbers.

	Source	Visits ↓	Pages/Visit	Avg. Time on Site	% New Visits	Bounce Rate
1.	stumbleupon.com	8,815	1.90	00:01:18	93.56%	38.83%
2.	google.com	542	1.79	00:01:51	49.82%	65.88%
3.	images.google.com	327	1.35	00:00:29	97.55%	72.48%
4.	twitter.com	284	1.42	00:00:47	79.58%	82.39%
5.	45n5.com	149	2.09	00:01:56	83.89%	61.74%
6.	conversationmarketing.com	129	1.40	00:00:36	86.82%	68.22%
7.	mixx.com	114	1.22	00:00:52	87.72%	91.23%
8.	onlinebusiness.about.com	106	1.74	00:02:17	91.51%	70.75%
9.	cseglobe.com	102	1.36	00:01:17	46.08%	84.31%
10.	sphinn.com	91	1.33	00:00:53	73.63%	83.52%
11.	reddit.com	84	1.05	00:00:14	100.00%	96.43%
12.	delicious.com	75	1.83	00:01:59	52.00%	70.67%
13.	facebook.com	64	1.52	00:01:26	76.56%	79.69%
14.	trumpuniversity.com	59	3.41	00:05:03	89.83%	62.71%
15.	bloglines.com	56	1.50	00:02:11	46.43%	76.79%
16.	netvibes.com	56	1.61	00:00:38	33.93%	60.71%
17.	westseattleblog.com	55	1.82	00:01:11	85.45%	74.55%
18.	marketing.alltop.com	49	1.80	00:01:09	46.94%	36.73%
19.	affiliatedragon.com	47	1.04	00:00:34	8.51%	95.74%
20.	digg.com	47	1.36	00:00:59	89.36%	85.11%
21.	seokratie.de	47	1.32	00:00:52	91.49%	78.72%
22.	onetakemedia.net	41	2.54	00:02:07	41.46%	53.66%
23.	plurk.com	40	1.80	00:03:08	12.50%	70.00%
24.	elance.com	39	3.18	00:05:23	62.05%	46.15%

To make these numbers mean something, you have to set parameters for *good* and *bad*. If you're looking for hard-and-fast ways to do this, you're in the wrong place. Because every website is different, every business has a different profile of a "quality" visit.

You need to set target numbers for the kinds of visitors you want. Even if you have a goal on the site — such as a sale, lead, or white paper download — you still need these separate measures of visit quality. The key is to figure out what your benchmarks are so that you can focus on improvement rather than producing a perfect set of numbers.

So why not just focus on sales or whatever your ultimate goal is? Well, because even if visitors don't make a purchase, they might still show enough interest to return later, tell a friend, or do something else you want them to do. You can't just rule out visitors who don't buy anything. Rather, think of their potential: They might still have a lot to offer your business.

The following sections walk you through setting these benchmarks for your business.

Setting benchmarks for page views per visit and time on site

To set benchmarks for these numbers, you need to have been running your traffic-reporting tool for at least two to three months. That gives you enough data to set your benchmark, which you do by following these steps (which use Google Analytics as an example):

1. **In Google Analytics, from the Audience menu, click Overview in the sidebar on the left.**

2. **Note the pages/visit number, as shown in Figure 4-2.**

    For details on accessing this data in a different tool, you need to check your documentation, but know that this is the data that you want.

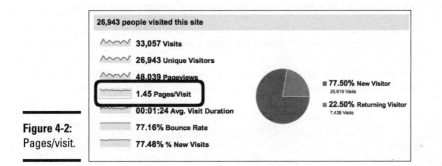

26,943 people visited this site

~~~~ **33,057** Visits

~~~~ **26,943** Unique Visitors

~~~~ **48,039** Pageviews

       1.45 Pages/Visit

       00:01:24 Avg. Visit Duration

       77.16% Bounce Rate

       77.48% % New Visits

■ **77.50%** New Visitor
25,619 Visits

■ **22.50%** Returning Visitor
7,438 Visits

Figure 4-2:
Pages/visit.

3. **Look at the average for the past two to three months.**

    In Google Analytics, set the date range to the last two to three months by clicking the dates at the top-right of the page and then selecting the start and end dates. The Pages/Visit number just below the chart now shows you the average.

    That average is your target. You want to improve upon that. Visits that exceed this average are good. Visits that don't aren't necessarily bad, but they're not as desirable. See the section "Applying Those Targets," later in this chapter, for the details.

    Note the average time on site for the last two to three months, which will be your target.

Calculating your loyalty benchmark

This section explains how to find out how many returning visitors you have and how to use this as a benchmark for increasing the percentage of returning visitors, which reflects visitor loyalty. The following steps help you set the target, again using Google Analytics:

1. **Open the report that calculates your percentage of repeat visitors.**

   In Google Analytics, the best place to start is the New vs. Returning report, shown in Figure 4-3. To access this report, click Audience and then click Behavior in the sidebar on the left. Then click the New vs. Returning option. For this benchmark, the time frame isn't that important, so you can set it for as little as a month. Just be sure that you use a sufficiently long time period to account for weekly rises and falls in traffic, as well as any seasonal changes.

   In other reporting tools, you can look for the Returning Visitors or Visitor Loyalty report. The data will be the same: a comparison of one-time and returning visitors.

2. **Take a look at the percentage of returning versus new visitors.**

   In Google Analytics, you find this info on the Site Usage tab (toward the bottom of the screen). Figure 4-3 shows a returning visitor percentage of 22.50%, so that's the loyalty target (which is something you always want to increase). But you can't forget about adding new visitors, either. Figure 4-3 shows 25,619, so that's the new visitors target to improve upon.

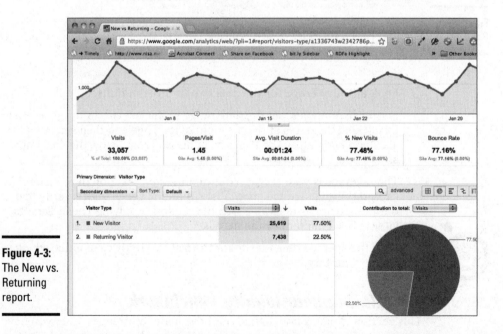

Figure 4-3:
The New vs.
Returning
report.

Applying Those Targets

After you have your targets defined, it's time to apply them. In analytics, *applying your targets* means that you're using your benchmarks and seeing whether you improve upon them. If you improve upon them, your site is improving. If you don't improve, you need to continue tweaking your site to improve.

You can apply your targets across every statistic, turning those reports into true analytics. In the following sections, you take a look at a couple of examples.

Checking your top content against your targets

Look at the Pages report shown in Figure 4-4.

You can use the time on page data to decide which page is your best as far as visitor attention. If time on page for one page is above the average for the rest of the site, you know that page is beating the *benchmark* — target — that you set. That means that the page is doing its job. It also means you should review that page to figure out why folks like it and spend more time there. Then apply what you found to the rest of your site.

Figure 4-4:
A top Pages
report.

For example, in the Pages report in Figure 4-4, one page has visitors spending 7:46 on the page. That's the highest time on page for any of the top pages! Review the top pages to see what exactly is so interesting to visitors, and whether you can apply the same ideas to the rest of the site. If you can, you might be able to improve the entire site.

Don't get too myopic. If you focus on the time on page data and ignore the pages themselves, you might miss something important: If visitors spend twice as much time on one page, perhaps that page has twice as much information. Always look at this data in context.

Drawing conclusions based on multiple targets

In this section, you see an example of how you can bring the different statistics together. Take a look at the referrer report (All Traffic) in Figure 4-5. (Choose Traffic Sources⟹Sources⟹All Traffic.) Look at pages/visit, average time on site, and percentage of new visits. If a single referrer brings you above-average counts of new visitors, pages/visit, *and* time on site, you know the referrer's a winner.

However, if the numbers start to mix, drawing conclusions gets harder. What if you have a page that brings a lot of new visitors, but lousy pages/visit and time on site numbers? Table 4-1 outlines the rules for referrers of all types.

	Visits	Pages/Visit	Avg. Visit Duration	% New Visits	Bounce Rate
	33,057	**1.45**	**00:01:24**	**77.48%**	**77.16%**
	% of Total: 100.00% (33,057)	Site Avg: 1.45 (0.00%)	Site Avg: 00:01:24 (0.00%)	Site Avg: 77.48% (0.00%)	Site Avg: 77.16% (0.00%)

Primary Dimension: **Source/Medium**   Source   Medium   Other▾

Plot Rows   Secondary dimension ▾   Sort Type: Default ▾   advanced

	Source/Medium	Visits ↓	Pages/Visit	Avg. Visit Duration	% New Visits	Bounce Rate
1.	google / organic	15,324	1.42	00:01:10	85.51%	82.0
2.	(direct) / (none)	5,856	1.50	00:01:28	71.88%	75.7
3.	stumbleupon.com / referral	2,523	1.20	00:01:21	93.42%	57.4
4.	feedburner / feed	2,021	1.56	00:01:29	45.18%	73.2
5.	t.co / referral	1,241	1.35	00:01:05	59.63%	82.8
6.	seomoz.org / referral	385	1.94	00:02:21	54.81%	64.6
7.	facebook.com / referral	347	1.45	00:01:40	71.47%	76.9
8.	plus.url.google.com / referral	321	1.37	00:01:06	57.63%	79.7
9.	google.com / referral	275	1.49	00:00:56	85.45%	69.0
10.	feedburner / email	241	1.63	00:10:05	39.42%	68.4

Show rows: 10 ▾   Go to: 1   1 - 10 of 619 ◄

This report was generated on 3/25/12 at 2:42 PM - Refresh Re

© 2012 Google | Analytics Home | Terms of Service | Privacy Policy | Contact us | Send Feedback

Figure 4-5:
A referrer report.

Table 4-1			Drawing Conclusions from Multiple Targets
Pages/ Visit	*Time on Site*	*New Visitors*	*Conclusion*
Above Average	Below Average	Below Average	Might be good or bad. You're getting some interest, but the first page folks land on isn't working for them, so they're moving on to other pages on your site pretty quickly. On the bright side, maybe that page is very easy to figure out, and visitors are responding. Test different page configurations to find out more.
Below Average	Below Average	Above Average	Not good. You're getting new visitors, but they don't like what they're seeing. Look at revamping that first page, and make sure that you're reaching the right audience. This referrer might be so perfect that visitors find what they need very quickly. Check conversion rates.
Below Average	Above Average	Above Average	Probably good. This referrer is sending folks who take their time and read everything on the page. Make sure that you have a good, clear call to action, though. The low page-view count might indicate that visitors don't know what to do. Check the bounce rate (see the next section).
Above Average	Above Average	Above Average	Clearly a winner. Check conversion and bounce rates to make sure, but this referrer is sending you lots of new, high-quality traffic.

Learning More with Bounce Rate

You can further measure visit quality with *bounce rate*. A bounce occurs if someone visits one page of your website and then leaves without clicking to any other pages.

Bounce rate data, like the Bounce Rate column in Figure 4-6, tells you the percentage of visitors who bounce from a particular page. You can find bounce rate data in most of the content reports. Choose Content➪Site Content as a starting point.

Which bounce rate?

In Internet marketing, *bounce rate* can refer to two different things. As used in this chapter, *bounce rate* means the number of people who visit your site, view one page, and then leave without clicking to any other page. In Book V, though, *bounce rate* means the rate at which e-mails sent to a list never reach the recipient. Both are correct uses of the term. Anytime you see bounce rate in a traffic report, though, it's referring to the bounce rate regarding web analytics.

	Page		Pageviews ↓	Unique Pageviews	Avg. Time on Page	Bounce Rate	% Exit
1.	/		4,936	4,237	00:01:46	63.41%	57.46%
2.	/2009/08/22-things-you-dont-know-about-customers.htm		2,137	1,884	00:07:46	59.74%	83.90%
3.	/2008/06/create-a-great-404-page.htm		1,813	1,673	00:04:10	86.25%	83.56%
4.	/2007/02/google_analytics_video_tutoria_1.htm		1,449	1,271	00:02:57	73.45%	69.98%
5.	/2009/07/10-questions-for-social-media-experts.htm		1,375	1,224	00:04:00	84.23%	79.64%
6.	/2012/01/making-cats-into-turnips-using-google-webmaster-tools-query-data.htm		1,354	1,245	00:04:40	85.83%	78.14%
7.	/2008/03/the_internet_marketing_list_59.htm		1,092	970	00:04:22	72.08%	69.51%
8.	/2007/09/streaming_video_creating_a_pro.htm		948	892	00:04:59	93.13%	91.35%
9.	/2012/01/5-signs-you-should-shut-up.htm		804	750	00:04:38	82.97%	80.85%
10.	/2012/01/in-internet-marketing-be-significant-or-be-roadkill.htm		795	641	00:03:21	74.94%	62.52%

Show rows: 10 | Go to: 1 | 1 - 10 of 1434

Figure 4-6: Bounce rate data.

Bounce rate is another way to judge visit quality. It shows you

✦ Pages that just drive people away

✦ Pages that draw visitors further into your site

✦ Most importantly, problems with landing pages

Analyzing your homepage

Bounce rate is a great statistic to analyze for your homepage. Unless you have a one-page website, chances are you want as low of a bounce rate as possible. The report in Figure 4-7 shows how small changes in homepage content and layout can affect bounce rate.

As you add interesting items on your homepage, you can see the effect those stories have on bounce rate. That, in turn, tells you what your audience likes or doesn't like and can learn from that.

Figure 4-7:
The bounce rate for a homepage.

![REMEMBER icon]

Don't use bounce rate in a vacuum. Look at time on site, and think about what your site does. Sometimes, a high bounce rate is okay. If you have a blog, for instance, a lot of readers will drop in from an RSS feed or a link on another site, read something, and then leave. The more article-focused your site is, the less bounce rate might matter.

Spotting bottlenecks and missed opportunities

One of the best things you can do with visit quality measurement is to find bottlenecks or missed opportunities in your site: namely, places where a lot of visitors who might have otherwise become customers end up leaving or going off course.

Look at the content report in Figure 4-8, which shows a list of pages with time spent on each page and bounce rate.

See item 8? It has a 93.73 percent bounce rate. That's not always a bad sign. If many readers are finding their way to this page from other blogs, they might simply read and then move on.

However, any top-ten page on your site that's shedding over 90 percent of visitors is probably costing you some valuable opportunities. Yeah, you might have a bad bounce rate, but if you know about it, you can do something about it. You could add more links to other articles, for example, or look at whether something in the page is driving visitors away.

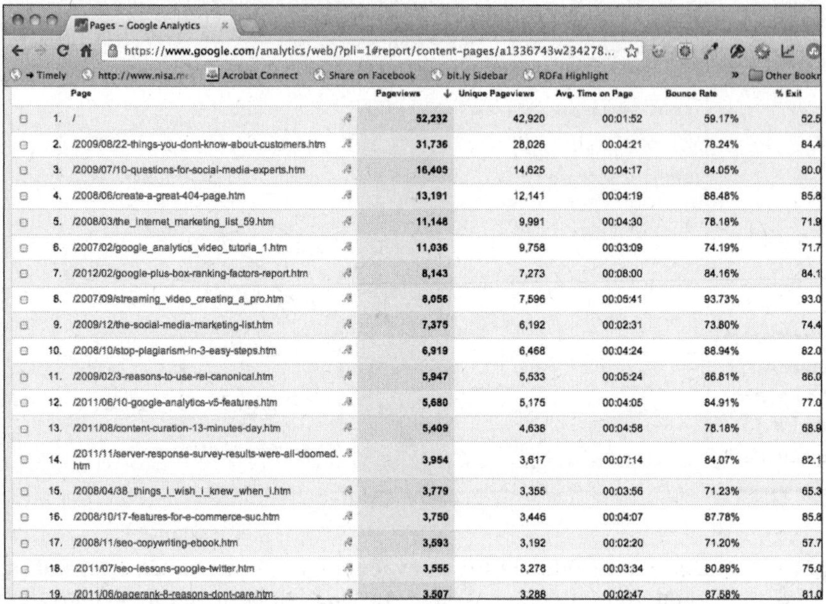

Figure 4-8:
A content report.

	Page	Pageviews	Unique Pageviews	Avg. Time on Page	Bounce Rate	% Exit
1.	/	52,232	42,920	00:01:52	59.17%	52.5
2.	/2009/08/22-things-you-dont-know-about-customers.htm	31,736	28,026	00:04:21	78.24%	84.4
3.	/2009/07/10-questions-for-social-media-experts.htm	16,405	14,625	00:04:17	84.05%	80.0
4.	/2008/06/create-a-great-404-page.htm	13,191	12,141	00:04:19	88.48%	85.8
5.	/2008/03/the_internet_marketing_list_59.htm	11,148	9,991	00:04:30	78.18%	71.9
6.	/2007/02/google_analytics_video_tutoria_1.htm	11,036	9,758	00:03:09	74.19%	71.7
7.	/2012/02/google-plus-box-ranking-factors-report.htm	8,143	7,273	00:08:00	84.16%	84.1
8.	/2007/09/streaming_video_creating_a_pro.htm	8,056	7,596	00:05:41	93.73%	93.0
9.	/2009/12/the-social-media-marketing-list.htm	7,375	6,192	00:02:31	73.80%	74.4
10.	/2008/10/stop-plagiarism-in-3-easy-steps.htm	6,919	6,468	00:04:24	88.94%	82.0
11.	/2009/02/3-reasons-to-use-rel-canonical.htm	5,947	5,533	00:05:24	86.81%	86.0
12.	/2011/06/10-google-analytics-v5-features.htm	5,680	5,175	00:04:05	84.91%	77.0
13.	/2011/08/content-curation-13-minutes-day.htm	5,409	4,638	00:04:58	78.18%	68.9
14.	/2011/11/server-response-survey-results-were-all-doomed.htm	3,954	3,617	00:07:14	84.07%	82.1
15.	/2008/04/38_things_i_wish_i_knew_when_I.htm	3,779	3,355	00:03:56	71.23%	65.3
16.	/2008/10/17-features-for-e-commerce-suc.htm	3,750	3,446	00:04:07	87.78%	85.8
17.	/2008/11/seo-copywriting-ebook.htm	3,593	3,192	00:02:20	71.20%	57.7
18.	/2011/07/seo-lessons-google-twitter.htm	3,555	3,278	00:03:34	80.89%	75.0
19.	/2011/05/pagerank-8-reasons-dont-care.htm	3,507	3,288	00:02:47	87.58%	81.0

Chapter 5: Using Conversion Goals

In This Chapter

✔ Setting conversion goals

✔ Analyzing goal conversions

✔ Handling technical issues with goal tracking

✔ Interpreting conversion data

A major step in moving from reporting to analytics is knowing what you want to measure in terms of your business goals. This goes beyond visits or traffic, and usually moves to leads or sales or something similar.

In the biz, we call those *conversions.* A conversion occurs any time a visitor changes from a visitor to a customer (a sale) or a potential customer (a lead). Conversions can also occur when a visitor somehow takes a significant step toward offering value to your business. Regardless, a visitor converts into something more valuable than a passerby. Get it?

Although tracking page views, time on site, and traffic quality is helpful, you need to know how your site is helping you achieve those goals. This is where web analytics really shines. Virtually all major web analytics packages — including free ones, such as Yahoo! Analytics and Google Analytics — support sophisticated goal tracking.

This chapter talks about selecting, tracking, and analyzing conversions using Google Analytics. If you use a different analytics program, you can still follow along. Most work similarly to Google Analytics.

Determining Key Performance Indicators

Goals are based on specific metrics that drive your business and website. These metrics — what make or break success — are *key performance indicators,* or KPIs. KPIs track the health of your online marketing efforts, for the good (success KPIs) or for the not-so-good (warning KPIs).

A KPI is *not* the same as a conversion goal! A KPI is a general measure of success for your business. It can be applied to your business's online efforts, offline work, brick-and-mortar store, website, or anything else. A conversion goal, on the other hand, is a specific event: an online sale or an in-store sale. You measure KPIs in terms of conversion goals. Don't confuse the two.

Before you go any further, write down your KPIs.

The ideal KPI will

✦ **Give you at-a-glance insight:** This gives you information as to how your website is performing.

✦ **Stand on its own as a measure of success or failure:** You shouldn't need to look at other data to get a basic idea of site performance.

✦ **Make business sense:** Interpreting a typical KPI won't require an expert web analyst.

✦ **Be long-lived:** KPIs can change, but not often. You want to be able to compare KPI data day by day, month by month, and year by year. (See the section "Maintaining consistent goals," later in this chapter, for more on the importance of consistency.)

Success KPIs are those that, if they increase, indicate you're doing well. They might include

✦ Number of sales

✦ Number of leads

✦ Conversion rate for leads or sales

✦ Number of E-Mail a Friend submissions

✦ Number of e-mail newsletter sign-ups

✦ Number of white paper (or other) downloads

Warning KPIs are those that, if they increase, mean something could be wrong. They might include

✦ Cost per sale

✦ Cost per lead

✦ Form abandonment rate

✦ Complaint frequency

✦ Bounce rate

No two businesses are exactly alike, so chances are you'll have some unique KPIs. The most common KPIs are

✦ Cost per sale

✦ Cost per lead

✦ Revenue

✦ Return on investment

For a very detailed look at all things web analytic, check out *Web Analytics For Dummies,* by Pedro Sostre and Jennifer LeClaire (published by John Wiley & Sons, Inc.).

Write down at least two (and preferably more) KPIs for your website. After you have your KPIs, you're ready to move on to the next step — setting your conversion goals.

Defining Conversion Goals

Goals? KPIs? What's the difference? It might seem like they're the same, but they're not. KPIs measure performance. Goals measure *success* and only success. All goals are KPIs. Not all KPIs are goals. Dizzy yet?

KPIs are signs of a response to your message and site. Goals are what happen when the visitor does what you want him to. Goals are always narrowly defined success KPIs, such as

+ A sale

+ A lead

+ An e-mail newsletter sign-up

+ A download of a specific article

+ A view of a specific page

Maintaining consistent goals

You *must* select goals you'll have around for the duration of any campaign. Consistency is critical.

For example, say that you're doing a new product launch campaign. As part of that campaign, you're offering to send visitors a free product in exchange for an e-mail sign-up. You need to track those e-mail sign-ups throughout the launch campaign! If you switch from tracking e-mail sign-ups to, say, tracking product purchases halfway through, you'll have no way to compare the performance of different advertising strategies.

Many goals will exist for the entire life of your business: Sales and leads are great examples. In those cases, it's important that you track those goals the same way over time.

For example: You're tracking the sales conversion goal based on views of the final checkout page. Then you decide to track the final order confirmation page, instead. That will throw off your numbers and make it impossible to track performance over time.

So you need to change your goals?

Always maintain consistent goals. If you do have to change, do the following:

1. **Measure the old and new goals side by side for a full business cycle (a week, a month, or longer).**

2. **Compute the average difference.**

3. **Apply that formula to future calculations.**

   Be very careful when you use this kind of percentage conversion because you're not going to get even 75 percent accuracy. But, it's better than nothing.

Checking out conversion goal pages

Here's one hallmark of a great conversion goal: a specific, unique *goal page* that indicates conversion. Consider these examples of a conversion:

✦ **If a customer buys something from your online store,** the last page he should see is the one that reads "Thank you for your business!" and has your order information on it. You know, for certain, that anyone reaching that page bought something and therefore did something you wanted him to do.

✦ **If a visitor subscribes to an e-mail newsletter,** he should land on a Thank You for Your Subscription page. That page is the goal page for e-mail sign-up. See Figure 5-1 for an example.

✦ **If a customer completes a Contact Us form** on your website, the resultant Thank You page for that form is a goal page, too.

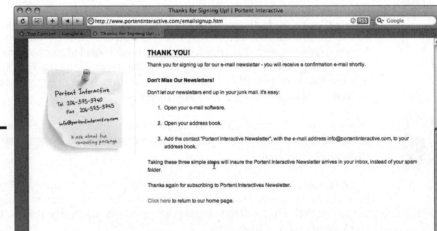

Figure 5-1:
The goal page for an e-mail newsletter sign-up.

A goal page almost always marks the *end* of the goal process. In other words, it marks a *conversion*. The visitor has become a customer, lead, or subscriber. The visitor has converted from being a generic audience member to a participant in your business.

Figuring out your conversion goals

Now, it's time to define the goals and goal pages for your site. Review your KPIs. Do any of them map easily to a specific goal on your site? For example, a KPI of *revenue* would map to the Thank You for Your Order page in your shopping cart.

✦ **If your KPIs are some of your goals,** find the goal page for a completed conversion for each goal. Then visit that goal page and copy and paste that page's address (as shown in Figure 5-2) next to the KPI (as shown in Figure 5-3).

✦ **If none of your KPIs are goals,** look at your site again. If you still can't find anything, read the next section to find out a bit about finding those hidden goals.

Finding hidden goals

Your site might not have any clear, well-defined goals if it

✦ Doesn't have e-commerce

✦ Lacks an e-mail newsletter (shame on you!)

✦ Doesn't collect leads

Regardless, all sorts of measurable goals reside on your site. They might be hiding, but they're there. You just have to coax them out.

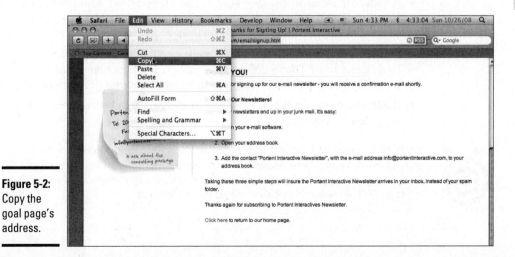

Figure 5-2:
Copy the goal page's address.

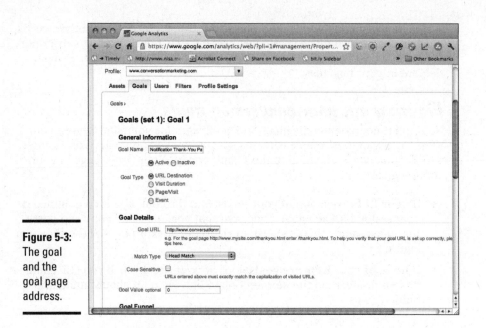

Figure 5-3:
The goal
and the
goal page
address.

Hidden goals might include

✦ **A download:** If you have a white paper, brochure, or other information on your site in PDF format, folks might download it. If they download it, chances are they're more interested than the average passersby. With a little work, you can track those downloads as a goal.

✦ **A page view:** If folks view one particular page on your site, does that tell you they're going to call? Think about those folks who view the Contact Us page. You can easily track that as a goal.

✦ **A video:** If a visitor watches your entire video about your corporate philosophy, that's definitely a win. Someone with a bit of technical expertise can help you track completed views as goals, too.

✦ **A Forward to a Friend link:** Does your site have a Forward This Page to a Friend tool? That's definitely a goal. Track how many folks forward pages to friends; those people are interested enough to recommend you.

✦ **A ZIP code search:** If you have lots of stores and a visitor tries to find one, that's a conversion.

You can have even fancier hidden goals: You can track all visitors who look at more than seven pages on your site as a conversion, for example. Tracking these types of goals generally requires a fair amount of expertise, though, so this topic is not discussed in this chapter.

Hidden goals are rarely worth as much as a sale, but they're still conversions because visitors who complete them have taken a step toward working with you. Track those visitors, and you get a peek at how your site is performing in terms of your business.

Attaching Monetary Value to Goals

Goals don't mean much if you can't attach some real value to them. All goals have some worth to your organization. It's important to track that worth because you need to see whether you profited in landing that conversion.

For example, say you sell a widget in your online store for $100. Yay! Unfortunately, when you look at your ad spending, you spent an average of $120 per sale. Hmm. That conversion actually cost you.

Attaching and tracking value keep you focused on growth and keep you from spending two dollars to earn one.

Valuing e-commerce conversions

Easy, right? An e-commerce conversion is worth the sale amount, minus any costs:

```
ECOM Value = Sale Amount - (Shipping + Handling + Other)
```

You'll want to figure out the average value of an e-commerce conversion, too, if possible.

But you need to figure out another critical metric: namely, the *lifetime* value of that conversion. How much will that new customer earn for you over time? You must know this! It could be perfectly reasonable to spend $120 to get a $100 sale if the lifetime value of that customer is $500.

Here's how you can figure it out, where *Customer Lifetime* is the average length of time a customer buys from you with no additional outside influence:

```
Lifetime Value = (Total Sales/Year ÷ Number of Customers) ÷ Customer Lifetime
```

By knowing the lifetime value, you put your sales in context and make sure that you don't shut down an ad buy that's actually paying off for you in the long run.

Valuing leads

Attaching a value to a lead is a bit more difficult. Someone fills out a Lead Request form, which is one of those really common Please Send Me More

Information forms you find on many websites. That doesn't directly translate into value for your company.

So, you need to figure out the value of a lead, using averages:

```
Lead Value = (Lead to Customer Conversion Rate) x (Avg. Customer Value)
```

Here's an example. Say you run a business where your website generates 100 leads per year; of those leads, 10 percent become customers. The average customer pays $10,000 per year for a consulting contract. So

```
10% x $10,000 = $1,000
```

Your average lead value is $1,000.

You *do* need to be able to compute the value of a customer and the conversion rate of leads to customers. That's important to your business regardless of Internet marketing, though. If you don't already know customer value, divide total sales over at least one year by the number of customers in that year. It's not perfect, but it'll do.

Valuing soft goals

Soft goals, like a white paper download, are even harder to track. The connection between that conversion and an ultimate conversion to a customer is distant. So take any numbers you compute here with a grain of salt.

To figure out the value of a soft goal, you must know the following:

✦ **Total goals:** The number of downloads, page views, or anything else.

✦ **Estimated conversion rate:** This is the hard part. You might not get enough information to track conversion rates directly, so you have to estimate based on three different statistics:

- Total *unique visitors* (each visitor returning to your site any number of times) to your site

- Percentage of those visitors who complete the goal (% Goal)

- Percentage of unique visitors who become customers (% Conversions)

✦ **Average value of those customers** (Avg. Value)

Then calculate the conversion rate, as follows:

```
Soft Goal Value = % Goal x % Conversions x Avg. Value
```

Here's an example of a soft goal–value calculation: Say you have a white paper on your site. You know the following:

✦ Your site receives 10,000 total unique visitors per year.

✦ Ten percent of those visitors (1,000 people) download the white paper (% Goal).

✦ If you keep track of their names, you know that 10 percent of the white paper readers become customers (% Conversions).

✦ You can then expect that in one year, you'll get $250,000 in sales from 25 customers, or an average value of $10,000/customer (Avg. Value).

So, the value of one white paper download to your business is:

```
10% x 10% x $10,000 = $100
```

So one white paper download is worth $100 to your business.

Valuing the immeasurable

Some goals can't be easily valued. A voter doesn't carry a monetary value (hopefully). Neither does a potential parishioner in a church.

You don't have a great way to attach a consistent value to these goals. But you *can* assign point values to them.

You can assign an arbitrary value: one point per new person who visits a political website, for example. Then, compute the cost of each point over the longest possible time period and use that cost as your measure. Work to improve on that cost, and you have a cost instead of a value, but it's still a baseline metric.

Setting Up Goal Tracking

Setting up goal tracking is straightforward — if you know the goal page.

Broken or badly configured shopping carts where the last checkout page was viewed aren't so easy to track. Be sure to test and verify that your goal page really is unique within your site, and that multiple goals don't share a single page.

In a program like Google Analytics, you identify the goal page to the program, and it does the rest. Here's how:

1. **Log in to Google Analytics.**

2. **Select the website for which you want to track the goal.**

3. **At the upper-right of the screen, click Admin.**

4. **Click Goals.**

5. **Click +Goal under any goal set.**

6. **Open a new browser window and go to your website.**

7. **Complete the form, checkout, or other process you want to track.**

8. **Copy the address of the final page in the process.**

    It'll usually be a Thank You–style page. See the section "Checking out conversion goal pages," earlier in this chapter, for an introduction to goal pages.

9. **Paste that address into the Goal URL field.**

10. **Name the goal, leave the other settings alone (you find out more about those in Google Analytics Help, later), and then click Finish.**

    After your goal is configured (refer to Figure 5-3), Google Analytics reports all goal completions.

You can then compare paid search keywords, organic search keywords, advertising, e-mail campaigns, and most other aspects of site traffic in the context of goal conversion.

You can also use Google Analytics to set a minimum time on site, page views/visit, or a specific JavaScript-fired event. Read *Web Analytics For Dummies* for more information.

Setting up e-commerce tracking

If your site includes a store, you'll probably want to know how much money you're earning from each traffic driver — a search engine result, a review on another website, or a link from a blog — or ad on the site.

To set up this tracking in Google Analytics and in most other reporting tools, you need to alter the final page of your checkout process to send the sales data to the tool. The code will typically resemble what is shown in Figure 5-4.

If that looks like gibberish, don't try to set up e-commerce tracking on your own. Instead, talk to your developer or webmaster about getting set up.

Even if you have to pay someone to get e-commerce tracking working, though, it's worth it. Figure 5-5 shows you just how much detail you can get with e-commerce data built into your analytics report. Figure 5-5 shows the value of a page view on a single page, based on how many customers made a purchase after seeing that page. That kind of insight can help you steer customers to the pages that will best answer their questions and likely get them to buy.

Figure 5-4:
Tracking
code for an
e-commerce
site.

```
script type="text/javascript">
var pageTracker = _gat._getTracker("UA-XXXXX-1");
pageTracker._trackPageview();
pageTracker._addTrans(
    "1234",               // Order ID
    "Mountain View",      // Affiliation
    "11.99",              // Total
    "1.29",               // Tax
    "5",                  // Shipping
    "San Jose",           // City
    "California",         // State
    "USA"                 // Country
);

pageTracker._addItem(
    "5678",               // Item Number
    "DD44",               // SKU
    "T-Shirt",            // Product Name
    "Green Medium",       // Category
    "11.99",              // Price
    "1"                   // Quantity
);
pageTracker._trackTrans();
</script>
```

Figure 5-5:
Dig deep
with
e-commerce
tracking.

**Book III
Chapter 5**

**Using Conversion
Goals**

Tracking goals manually

If for some reason you can't set up goal tracking in your traffic-reporting tool, all is not lost.

Remember that your goals have goal pages. You can still track those pages by page view. You can see goal conversions by looking at the top pages report. Follow these steps:

1. **In Google Analytics, go to the Top Content report.**

2. **Look for the page that is your Thank You page at the end of the checkout process or that appears after the reader completes the information request, or whatever else represents a completed conversion goal.**

   Figure 5-6 shows one conversion for one unique page view on an e-mail sign-up confirmation page.

You can check what's driving traffic to that goal page, too, by clicking the `/emailsignup.htm` link in the Page column of the report. See Chapter 3 of this minibook for a refresher on tracking referrers.

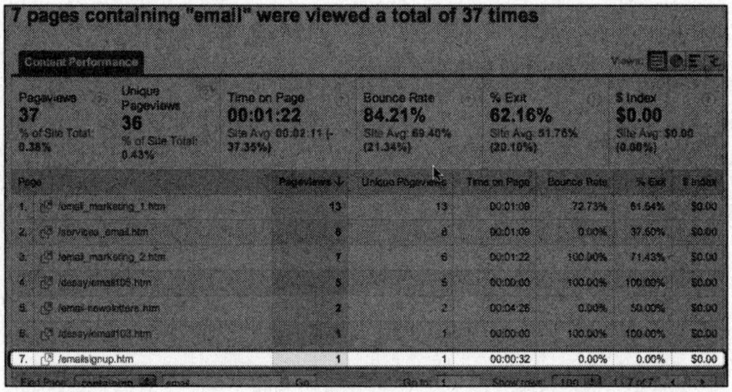

Figure 5-6: Top pages showing conversions.

Interpreting Conversion Data

After tracking is set up, the reporting tool shows you conversion data for your goals in a separate report. That data requires some interpretation. The following sections offer a few examples of typical problems and opportunities you might find.

The costly keywords

The first thing to look at is your list of keywords generating traffic to the site. Some of them are pulling their weight; others aren't.

Figure 5-7 shows that one such keyword isn't generating any revenue. If you're spending money on a keyword, consider whether those are dollars well spent. You might want to let go of any keywords that aren't generating revenue.

Almost any paid search campaign, no matter how well managed, can benefit from an occasional review of actual conversion performance. See Book IV for more about paid search.

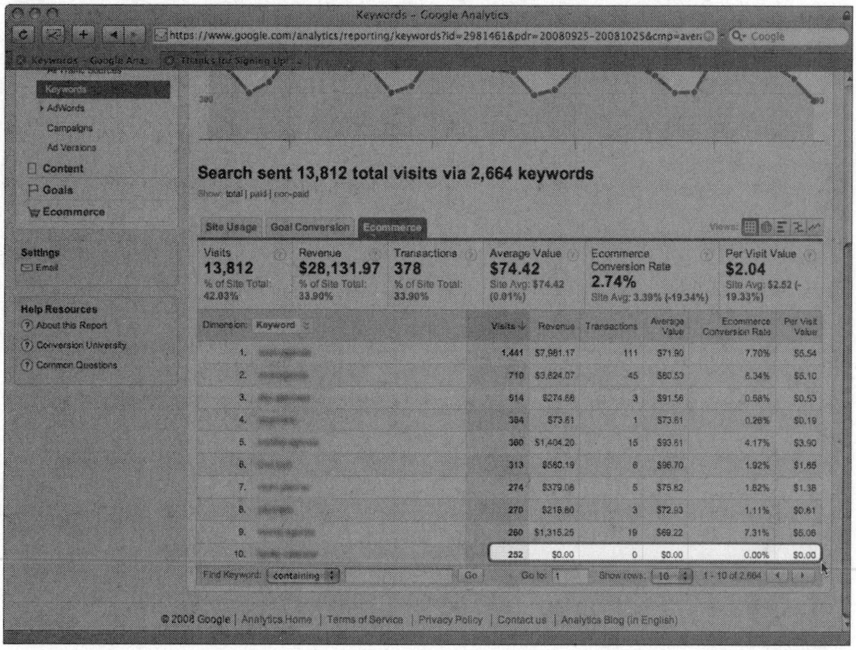

Figure 5-7:
The keywords report.

Book III
Chapter 5

Using Conversion Goals

The hidden gold mine

Sometimes, one page or product on your site generates a far higher conversion rate than the others. A report like the content report with dollar index in Figure 5-8 can reveal them.

In that report, it's clear that one page is generating incredibly high value because it has a very high $ index. It might be a fluke; but then again, it might not. But it certainly pays to check.

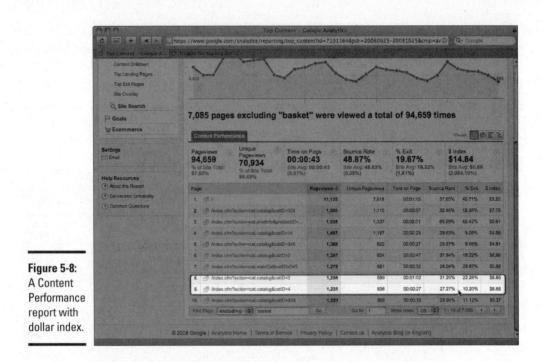

Figure 5-8:
A Content Performance report with dollar index.

The great landing page

Along the same lines as the Hidden Gold Mine, conversion data can show you the one page on your site that drives the best or worst conversion rate when it acts as a landing page.

A *landing page* is any page from your site at which visitors from other sites arrive. They *land* there.

Because search engines and other websites link to whatever page on your site they choose, every page of your site could be a lander. So you need to spot which pages are becoming landing pages, and adjust them to best answer visitors' questions.

Look at the report shown in Figure 5-9. It shows a few pages that have become major landing points for visitors coming from other sites.

You can use that data to find the landing pages that get the most traffic, and then make sure that they're also driving proportional conversions. If they are, great! You've confirmed that things are working. If they aren't, you can tweak them to do a better job.

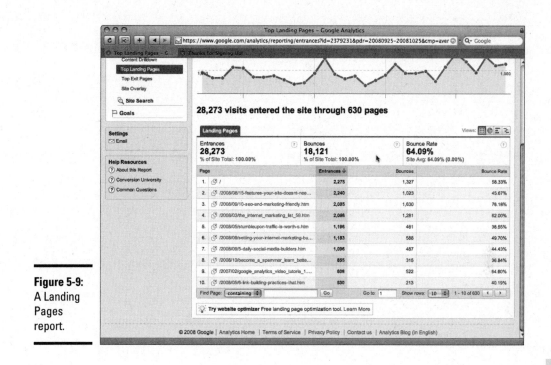

Figure 5-9:
A Landing
Pages
report.

Chapter 6: Using Goal Funnels

In This Chapter

✔ **Finding funnels**

✔ **Setting up funnel tracking**

✔ **Analyzing funnel data**

Some goals have multiple steps from beginning to end: A shopping cart checkout process, a multiple-page form, and a survey are all good examples. Such multiple-step processes are called *funnels.*

Funnels consist of many small conversions in succession. If visitors complete only the first few pages, they don't complete the ultimate goal. Remember that the goal is a conversion that ties directly to a KPI, like a completed sale or someone requesting more information from your sales force. See Chapter 5 in this minibook for a refresher. Conversions are what drive your KPIs: They're what help you succeed.

For example, in a shopping cart, each page of the checkout process is a small goal. The visitor must first enter a billing address and click Next Step. That's one goal. Then the shopper must select Shipping and click Next Step again. That's another goal, and so on, until the shopper clicks Place Order, which is the goal you care about. When someone clicks Place Order, he pays you money. That money goes to revenue, which is a KPI.

If a visitor completes the first goal — entering billing information — and then abandons the order, you need to know about it. Something might have happened. For example, a usability issue might have become obvious, a link might be broken, or a 25-field form might have intimidated the user into leaving.

Find out where these bailout points are, and you can greatly improve your goal-conversion rate.

But more goal funnels exist than just checkout. Figuring out how to find them is a good first step.

Finding a Funnel

Anytime you have multiple steps in a conversion process, you have a funnel. Some funnels occupy multiple pages but only a single endpoint and goal, such as the checkout process shown in Figure 6-1. A multiple-page, lead-generation form, such as the one shown in Figure 6-2, works the same way. These point-to-point processes are linear. The visitor starts at one end of the funnel and concludes on the final goal-conversion page. They're the easiest funnels to track.

Figure 6-1:
A typical checkout process.

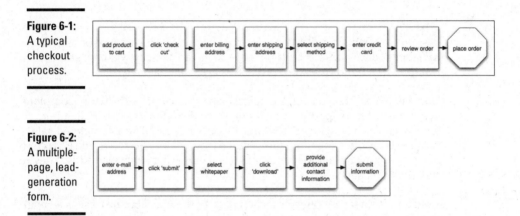

Figure 6-2:
A multiple-page, lead-generation form.

Finding the right funnel and tracking it can get more complicated if you have a funnel with one starting point and multiple endpoints. For example, the process shown in Figure 6-3 has three valid goals to track: an e-mail sign-up form, a download, and a purchase.

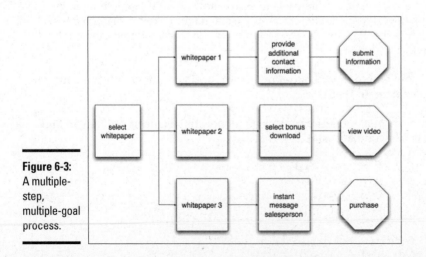

Figure 6-3:
A multiple-step, multiple-goal process.

AJAX: Friend or foe?

AJAX — Asynchronous JavaScript and XML — is a nifty technology that allows developers to change what's displayed on a web page without actually reloading the page. It's a great way to create beautiful websites and interfaces (such as Flickr). However, it's an analytics nightmare. Until recently, analytics was built around tracking page views. AJAX, however, reduces page views. So, a multiple-step process that's handled by AJAX, instead of taking you from one page to the next, can be tricky to track.

The single entry point and multiple exit points comprise a funnel, but any endpoint is a conversion. Deeper conversions are better, but they all generate value to the business. Don't rule out this type of funnel. It still matters! By tracking depth and results, you can find ways to improve conversion rates at all levels.

Other goal funnels on your site might include the following:

✦ **Forward to a Friend:** This one has two steps. Click to start the process, and then enter a friend's e-mail address and forward the page.

✦ **A dealer search:** The visitor first enters a ZIP code, and then clicks a result and clicks Contact This Dealer. This funnel is another one that's worth tracking.

✦ **AJAX-driven process:** This funnel folds numerous pages into a single page. It's still a funnel, however. Tracking it requires a little JavaScript expertise, but if you made the investment in the process, it's worth the extra work.

Regardless of your final goal, look at any conversion process on your site that requires more than one button or link to complete, and you have a funnel.

Setting Up Goal Funnel Tracking

Some reporting packages, such as Adobe Site Catalyst (`www.omniture.com/en/products/web_analytics/sitecatalyst`), allow you to track a basic goal funnel by using the conversion funnel tracking or the fallout report builder. For other packages, such as Google Analytics, you need to know the unique address of each page in the checkout process and then add those addresses to a goal funnel report.

Book III
Chapter 6

Using Goal Funnels

The following steps use Google Analytics and a shopping cart. This procedure works in just about every reporting tool that includes funnel tracking. Follow these steps:

TIP

1. **Step through the checkout process and record the URL of each page in the process.**

   Cut and paste each page's URL into a spreadsheet as a temporary notepad, as shown in Figure 6-4.

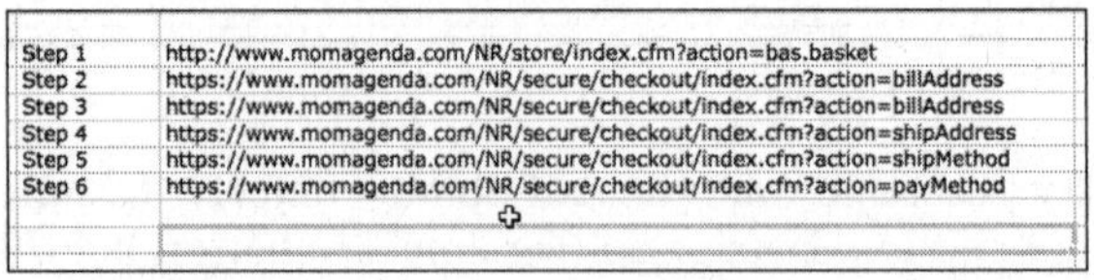

Figure 6-4:
The
checkout
process,
page by
page.

Step 1	http://www.momagenda.com/NR/store/index.cfm?action=bas.basket
Step 2	https://www.momagenda.com/NR/secure/checkout/index.cfm?action=billAddress
Step 3	https://www.momagenda.com/NR/secure/checkout/index.cfm?action=billAddress
Step 4	https://www.momagenda.com/NR/secure/checkout/index.cfm?action=shipAddress
Step 5	https://www.momagenda.com/NR/secure/checkout/index.cfm?action=shipMethod
Step 6	https://www.momagenda.com/NR/secure/checkout/index.cfm?action=payMethod

2. **In Google Analytics, click the website profile for which you want to add a funnel.**

3. **Click the Goals tab.**

4. **Click + Goal or click the goal to which you want to add the funnel.**

   Chapter 5 of this minibook explains how to set up goals in Google Analytics.

5. **On the Goal Settings page that appears, set up your goal.**

6. **In your new or existing goal, add the funnel for tracking by entering the unique address of each page in the checkout process under the URL.**

7. **Give each page a name you'll understand.**

   Figure 6-5 shows you an example.

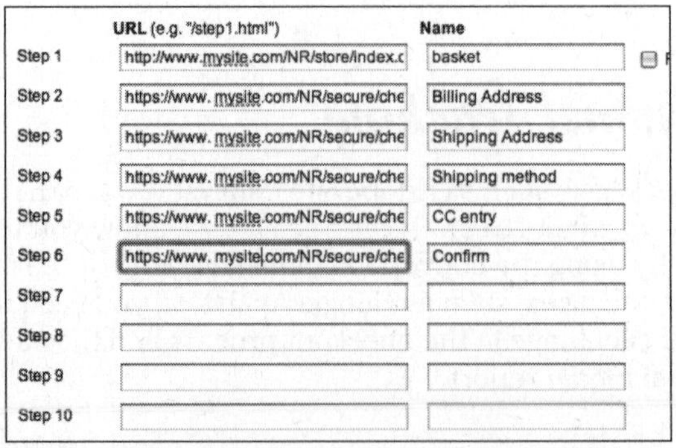

Figure 6-5:
Setting
up a goal
funnel for
checkout.

	URL (e.g. "/step1.html")	Name	
Step 1	http://www.mysite.com/NR/store/index.c	basket	
Step 2	https://www.mysite.com/NR/secure/che	Billing Address	
Step 3	https://www.mysite.com/NR/secure/che	Shipping Address	
Step 4	https://www.mysite.com/NR/secure/che	Shipping method	
Step 5	https://www.mysite.com/NR/secure/che	CC entry	
Step 6	https://www.mysite.com/NR/secure/che	Confirm	
Step 7			
Step 8			
Step 9			
Step 10			

8. **Save your new funnel.**

   Within a few hours, you'll have goal funnel data.

Some carts use the same page throughout so that even as customers move from billing to shipping to payment information to place an order, the page keeps the same URL. Don't despair: You can work around this situation in several ways. For example, go to Google Analytics (www.google.com/analytics) and type **goal funnel** in the Search box at the top of the page to see its solution. Or, talk to your developer.

Interpreting Goal Funnel Data

After you have the data, you need to use it. The typical reporting tool shows you a report resembling the one shown in Figure 6-6.

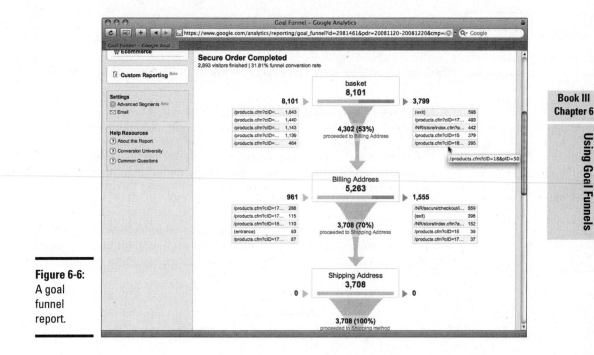

Figure 6-6: A goal funnel report.

Book III
Chapter 6

Using Goal Funnels

This report shows you, step by step, how many folks move through the process. Check your funnel reports for these items:

✦ **The biggest abandonment point:** Figure 6-7 shows that only 53 percent of visitors proceed from their shopping baskets to the page where they enter their billing addresses. That's a loss of customers in the checkout process. If you can reduce that abandonment at that point, you can greatly improve the overall conversion rate.

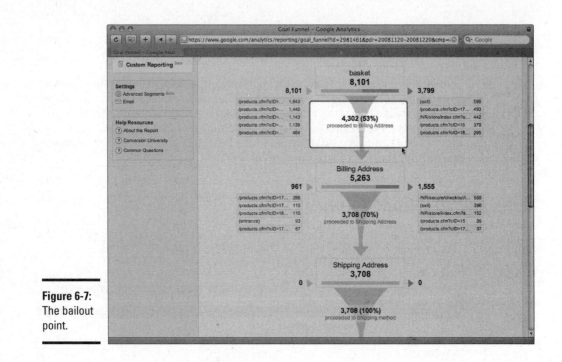

Figure 6-7:
The bailout
point.

✦ **Unexpected entry points:** Figure 6-8 shows where site visitors are entering
   the checkout process at the Billing Address page. The checkout process
   starts at the Cart page, and that's what should be the entry point. But if
   you think about it, that must mean that people are adding products to
   their carts, looking around a bit more, and then moving to the Checkout
   page. It might make sense, therefore, to add a Proceed Directly to
   Checkout step.

Put the two together, and you can make one immediate improvement to this
cart: Let customers go directly to the Checkout page without first approving
their shopping baskets. That would probably reduce instances of bailout.

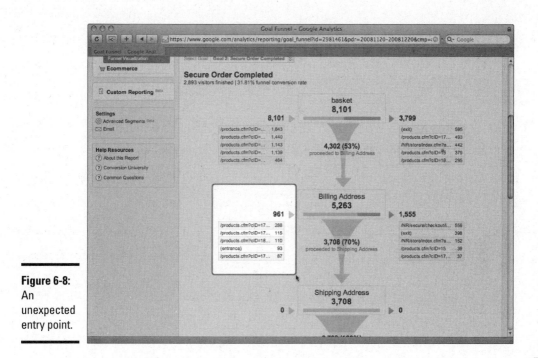

Figure 6-8:
An
unexpected
entry point.

Book IV

Online Advertising and Pay Per Click

The 5th Wave   By Rich Tennant

"We have no problem funding your website, Frank. Of all the chicken farmers operating websites, yours has the most impressive cluck-through rates."

Contents at a Glance

Chapter 1: Grasping PPC Methods

In This Chapter

✔ **Getting to know pay per click**

✔ **Understanding search engines and relevancy**

✔ **Deciding whether PPC is right for you**

*P*ay per click (PPC) — also known as *cost per click (CPC)* — is a type of paid advertising, such as a paid search, sponsored listings, sponsored links, and partner ads. In a PPC model, the advertiser pays the site that hosts the ad space only if a user clicks its ads and goes through to the *destination URL* or *landing page* — the location on the Internet where the person who clicked the ad ends up.

In this chapter, you discover how pay per click works and find tips to help you decide whether you need to add PPC to your web-marketing strategy.

Seeing How Pay Per Click Works

PPC ads are often used in search engines like Google, Yahoo!, and Bing, generally along the top and right sides of the pages that contain search results. These ads don't appear unless someone performs a search in that engine, and the ads that *do* appear are those that the engine deems most relevant to the user's search results (see the next section in this chapter). This way, someone who searches for a baseball glove (see Figure 1-1) isn't shown ads for shoes.

To get your ads to show up alongside relevant searches in a search engine, the search engine walks you through the PPC account creation.

Each search engine's process is a little different, but here are the most basic steps you should be prepared to complete:

1. **Create a PPC account with the search engine.**

   See Chapter 2 in this minibook for details on creating an account with each of the major search engines.

Figure 1-1:
A Google
search
result page,
with PPC
ads related
to that
search.

2. **Create campaigns and ad groups around the products or services to be advertised.**

   A *campaign* is where you set many of your options, such as budget and geography. *Ad groups* are tightly targeted groups that make up the campaign and that house your ads and keyword lists. For more information on both topics, see Chapter 2 in this minibook.

3. **Determine a list of keywords.**

   Keywords are words and phrases that describe, or are features of, the products or services to be advertised.

4. **From the list of keywords, create ads that use those keywords to better explain to potential customers what benefits, features (such as styles and colors), or sizes are available.**

So when a user searches for, say, women's red high-heel pumps, she sees ads that are specifically tailored to people who are searching for that product. The search engine determines how well the advertiser's campaigns and keywords match the search; if they match well, the search engine displays the advertiser's ad on the result page.

Knowing How Search Engines Determine Relevancy

How do search engines determine what ads to show when? And to what degree can they really calculate which advertiser is more relevant than another? Each engine has an algorithm developed in-house that sorts out which ad to show, when to show it, where on the result page to show it, and how much to charge the advertiser.

Depending on the search engine, many known factors determine relevancy, along with several unknown factors. Most search engines use the following known factors to determine relevancy:

+ **Keyword list:** Do the keywords in the keyword list match what the person typed?

+ **Ad copy:** Does the ad mention what the person is looking for?

+ **Landing page:** Does the ad go to a page that has what the person is looking for?

+ **Bid:** How much are you willing to pay to get that visitor?

  The amount of your bid in conjunction with these other factors determines where on the page your ad will display and how much you'll actually pay. (For more information on bidding, see Chapter 5 in this minibook.)

For a complete list of known factors for a specific search engine, consult the search engine's help center.

Search engines keep some relevancy criteria unknown to the public to keep the playing field level for all advertisers and to preserve a good user experience. This system cuts down on false advertising and misleading, spam-type ads; it also rewards advertisers who are adhering to the rules and editorial guidelines of the search engine.

Figuring Out Whether You Need PPC

PPC advertising has evolved as a way for companies, people, and sites to purchase a spot on the first page of search results. Often, the first results page has room for only about ten results, and few people click to see what's on page 2, 3, or beyond. So if your site has low *natural search rankings* (where your website appears in the search results), PPC is a way to buy a spot in front of the most people.

Suppose that your law firm practices landlord–tenant law, but your website is pretty outdated, and you haven't had a chance to do any search engine optimization updates (see Book II for more on SEO). When a user searches for, say, *landlord tenant lawyer* or *landlord law firm,* your firm's website is on page 10 of the search results.

That page is buried pretty far back, so the chances of getting noticed by people who are specifically searching for your type of law firm are low. Often, instead of going through the search results page by page, searchers change their search terms and try again. In this case, your firm stays buried. So how do you find new clients?

Certainly, you want to work on your SEO, but that project takes time — not only to research what to do but also to implement and wait for the results. In the meantime, you can buy yourself a spot on that first page of results and be seen by people who are looking for the service you provide. For this example, your law firm can even create geotargeted campaigns (see Chapter 7 in this minibook for help on geotargeting) that show your ads only to people in the geographic region that your law firm serves. Whether that region is a metropolitan area or an entire state, PPC gets your firm's name directly in front of people who are already interested in what you do.

The lists of benefits and drawbacks in the following sections might help you determine whether PPC is right for you or your company. The size and complexity of the campaigns you're considering might be too large, for example, and you should outsource the management or initial setup. You might be able to find a firm that will set the program up for you and even include lessons or continuing support as needed. Also, several companies have created PPC management software to help automate the process. These programs tend to be best for large accounts across several engines with budgets to match. If this situation fits your case, you'll need to do a lot more research, starting with a basic search for *pay per click management software.* The search engines themselves don't recommend one software program over another; in most cases, in-house teams manage accounts for their biggest clients and search-marketing agencies.

At the very least, start small and build up. As you work with a search engine's program and get a better feel for it and for PPC management, you'll be much more efficient, and then you'll be able to create keyword lists and campaigns easily and bid with the best of them.

Benefits of using PPC

Trying out PPC advertising has several benefits:

+ It's a form of advertising that anyone can do.

+ It gives advertisers a lot of control of their budgets and audiences.

+ It has a great amount of accountability in terms of where the sale occurred, how much it cost, and which keyword and ad triggered the sale.

If PPC advertising is done correctly, the results can be measured very accurately to give you an idea of where you can put your advertising next.

Getting measurable results

PPC not only allows you to purchase a spot in front of potential clients, but it also allows you to test things quickly. If you're redesigning an outdated site but aren't sure which version of the Contact Us page you want to use, for example, you could set your campaign to send half of your visitors to one page and the other half to another page. Then you can measure the response in easily interpretable results, such as these:

+ What keywords did people use to find your site?

+ How many people filled out the form on a landing page?

+ How many people called the firm directly?

+ How many people left the site after visiting the landing page?

With PPC, you can drive visitors to your pages quickly and often, rather than wait for visitors to appear naturally.

Spending your money wisely

PPC enables you to set daily budgets for an account or campaign and edit bids on a per-keyword basis. If you're trying to determine which keywords to target for SEO purposes, you can use PPC to measure the success and popularity of those keywords for yourself and, at the same time, limit the amount spent on that experiment. You can also set your budget to spend by time of day or geographic region and even turn your ads off when necessary, either automatically or manually. PPC gives you a lot of flexibility for managing both the amount spent and the frequency of your ads.

Finding niches

Particularly if your company is in a highly competitive market, you can use PPC to find a niche that isn't as competitive as others or that you can specialize in. Searchers give you a lot of information when they come to your site: what keywords brought them there, what pages they visited, how quickly they left, and what they bought or downloaded. If your law firm is receiving conversions from the keyword phrase *lawyers for landlords,* you can build a specific ad group and ad around that keyword to target searches better — and at a better cost to you. (See Chapter 5 in this minibook for more on budgeting and spending.)

Possible drawbacks of PPC

So far in this chapter, you've had a brief introduction to PPC and discovered some of the benefits of creating and running a PPC campaign. But beware — PPC isn't for everyone or every company. Fortunately, you'll know quickly whether your PPC campaign is working out. If not, consider whether you should seek a professional consultation or call the experiment quits.

**Book IV
Chapter 1**

**Grasping PPC
Methods**

Here are some situations that could limit the success of your PPC campaigns:

✦ **Not enough budget to spend for your industry:** If you're trying to generate leads for a machine that retails for $80,000 and are spending only $500 a month for PPC, you're not spending enough. If your product is expensive, and the average cost per lead for the industry is expensive, don't expect to bid $1 and get 500 leads.

✦ **Poorly designed website:** You can bring all the visitors to your site that you want, but if your site is hard to navigate, the shopping cart is difficult to understand, or you don't provide information about things like shipping time and charges, people are going to be far less likely to buy. You may have what they want, but if they can't find it or the cart fails, they can't buy.

✦ **Slow page loads:** If it takes longer than a couple of seconds for the pages on your site to load, chances are that the visitor is going to leave and search for another site. Slow load time creates a poor user experience — and now it's also a factor for Google AdWords in determining relevancy (see the section "Knowing How Search Engines Determine Relevancy," earlier in this chapter). The slower your site is, the lower it is in the list of search results.

✦ **Not enough volume:** Sometimes, the problem simply is that not enough people are searching for the keywords you're bidding on. If your niche is too targeted, you won't be able to bring new traffic to your site. In this case, you should expand your keyword list before calling it quits. (For tips on working with keywords, see Chapter 3 in this minibook.)

✦ **No analytics:** If you're not using an analytics program of some kind to track the results, how can you honestly tell what's working and what isn't? Guessing is never the way to go, especially because PPC is such a measurable form of advertising. See Book II, Chapter 8 for information on choosing an analytics package that suits your needs.

✦ **Setting it and forgetting it:** PPC campaigns need to be managed actively. Simply setting things up and logging in only once a month is a recipe for disaster. Particularly at the beginning, you need to log in daily — if not more than once per day — to tweak your keyword lists, budgets, and bids. When you have a better understanding of what's working and what isn't, you can cut back on the amount of management. Still, you should never just leave the campaign running unchecked.

Chapter 2: Combining PPC and Search Engines

In This Chapter

✔ **Choosing which search engines to use**

✔ **Setting up a Google AdWords account**

✔ **Setting up an Bing Ads account**

*N*ot all search engines have a pay-per-click (PPC) platform to display ads with their search results. Some search engines have partnerships with larger search engines such as Google and Bing — both of which have their own PPC services — to show their ads on those engines, thereby generating revenue for the partners to split.

Before you start investigating smaller search engines, be sure that you've evaluated Google and Bing to see whether those search engines alone can meet your advertising needs. This chapter shows you how to set up an account in each of those search engines, expand that account, and adjust its settings to suit your preferences.

Selecting a PPC Search Engine

Before you bring out the credit card and keyword list, you want to make sure that you've done your homework when it comes to selecting a search engine's PPC platform. Although the search engines may seem to be pretty similar, they differ on some big points. Also, depending on the industry or field that you're advertising for, one engine could be much more beneficial than another in terms of return on investment (ROI), audience reach for volume and targeting, costs, and time spent managing your campaigns. The following sections give you some research pointers.

Researching search engines

Before you set up a new account on a search engine for PPC advertising, be sure to research the engine to see whether it meets your needs and those of your industry. Some PPC platforms are geared to business-to-consumer sales, for example; others target business-to-business sales. Some engines have considerably more traffic than others and are on the rise; others are falling off.

The best way to check out a search engine is to use it yourself. Perform some searches for items in your keyword list (see Chapter 3 in this mini-book) to see how much competition you have, how much search volume the engine has, and what the results page looks like overall. If the engine's user interface is clunky and the ads are hard to find on the results page, those results are indicative of the performance of the ads. If you can't find what you're looking for, how would you expect anyone else to find it? If the ads aren't in prominent places on the results page (such as across the top or down the right side), users aren't going to look at them; they'll go straight for the prominent results or move their search to another engine.

Comparing the top three search engines

The top three search engines, in order of search volume, are Google, Yahoo!, and Bing. They're tops in terms of volume of traffic (searches performed), quality of results, quality of the ads that appear with the results (*relevancy*), and the average cost per click (CPC) compared with ROI. Here's how the top three compare:

✦ **Google:** This engine is by far the most sophisticated PPC search-engine platform overall, and it delivers the best bang for your buck. It has the most traffic and the best management tools, and it garners you results faster than any other search engine. Through Google, you should be able to find out what works and what doesn't work within a short period.

The audience that uses Google is greatly varied; therefore, a large, diverse audience will be searching for your product or service.

✦ **Yahoo!:** This engine teamed up with Bing in 2010, and ads served on Yahoo.com and Bing.com now come from Bing Ads. You cannot segment whether your ads are shown on Yahoo.com or Bing.com; all search traffic is aggregated and shown as one source. If you want to show ads on Yahoo.com, you'll need an Bing Ads account.

✦ **Bing:** This engine has less search volume than Google does, even with the addition of Yahoo.com search traffic. While it is lower in volume, Bing Ads can be lower in costs and simpler to manage overall. It has the advantage of being the default search engine for many Windows and PC machines. If you're targeting a less technically savvy audience, this could be an advantage for you.

In the following sections, you find out how to establish a PPC account with Google AdWords and Bing Ads.

Managing multiple PPC accounts

If you plan to have an account that encompasses more than one PPC account, you'll want to look into setting up a main account so that you have to log in to each engine only once to access all the accounts.

✔ Google provides a My Client Center account for this purpose. `http://www.google.com/intl/en/adwords/myclientcenter`

✔ Bing's comparable multiple account service doesn't have a special name. You need a

customer service representative to help you set up this account. If you don't want to do that, you could also use its Agency Management option instead to handle multiple logins and access. See `http://adcenterhelp.microsoft.com/help.aspx?project=adcenter_live_std&market=en-us&querytype=keyword&query=682yek&tmt=&domain=adcenter.microsoft.com&format=b1` for more information.

Using Google AdWords

If you've decided to give Google AdWords a try, the following sections walk you through the process, from setting up your account to getting it activated and getting your ads running. If you need help during setup, Google AdWords provides a toll-free number with live operator assistance during weekdays. See the sign-up page for hours of operation and contact numbers.

Creating an account

Follow these steps to sign up for AdWords:

1. **Go to the sign-in page for Google AdWords at** `http://adwords.google.com/select/Login` **and click the Start Now button.**

   You need a Google account to sign up for AdWords.

2. **Sign up for a brand-new account or sign in to an existing account:**

   - *If you don't have an account:* Select the I Do Not Use These Other Services radio button, and follow the prompts to set up your account.

   - *If you have an account you'd like to add AdWords to:* Select the I Have an Email Address and Password option and then the I'd Like to Use My Existing Google Account for AdWords option.

Book IV
Chapter 2

Combining PPC and Search Engines

If the e-mail address you choose is associated with another AdWords account, you'll have to choose a different address or create a new e-mail address to use with AdWords. You can only have one AdWords account associated with an e-mail address. However, you can have as many different e-mail addresses associated with a single AdWords account as you want.

3. **Use your Google account username and password to sign in to AdWords at** www.adwords.google.com.

4. **Select the country, time zone, and currency you'll be paying in (USD$ is the default), and click Continue. See Figure 2-1.**

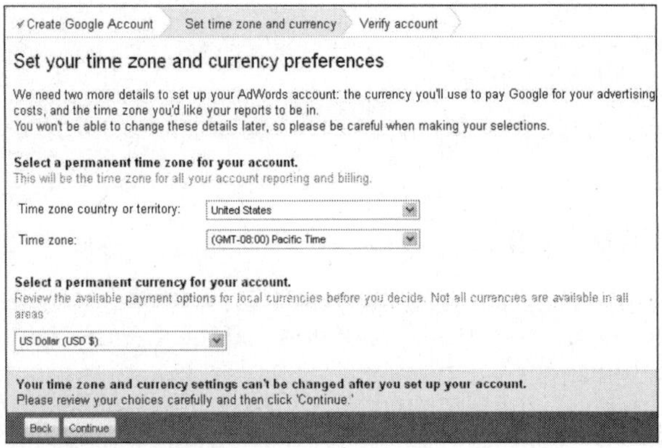

Figure 2-1:
Selecting currency, time zone, and country settings.

The settings on this page cannot be changed after you click Continue.

Google sends an e-mail message to your Google account e-mail address to verify the account creation.

5. **When you receive the e-mail, click the link in it to go to the AdWords verification page.**

Setting up your first campaign

After you create your AdWords account, you're ready to set up your first campaign. Follow these steps:

1. **Sign in to AdWords.**

2. **Click the Create Your First Campaign button.**

3. **Click the Campaign Type button and select the Search Only radio button for your first campaign.**

See Chapter 7 in this minibook for more on the additional campaign types.

4. **Name your new campaign something descriptive in the Campaign Name text box.**

This name is for your purposes only; come up with something you'll remember.

5. **Select where you want the ads in this campaign to display.**

The United States and Canada option is selected by default. If you want to change that setting, click the radio button for the country that you want to target or select the Let Me Choose option to enter an address or more specific area like a state or metro area.

As you type in the location field, a list will pop up, allowing you to edit your preference (see Figure 2-2) and to see the traffic estimates for that area. For more on geotargeting, see Chapter 7 in this minibook.

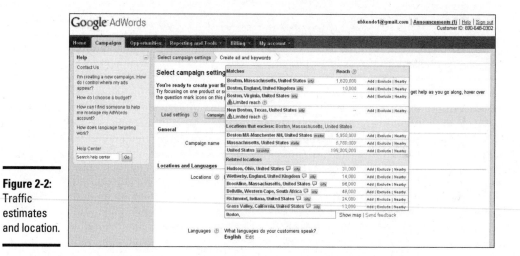

Figure 2-2:
Traffic
estimates
and location.

6. **Leave the Location options (advanced) set to the defaults:**

- *Target:* People in, searching for, or viewing pages about your targeted location (recommended)
- *Exclude:* People in, searching for, or viewing people about your excluded location (recommended)

These options will enable those within your chosen locations to see your ads the most effectively and efficiently for your budget.

7. **Select the language in which you want your ads to display.**

The default is English. If you need to change it, click the Edit button.

8. In the Network and Devices area, select whether you would like to target different devices like mobile phones or tablets with full browsers.

If you're unsure at this time, leave the default of all devices enabled, as shown in Figure 2-3.

9. In the Networks section, select the Let Me Choose radio button and leave the Search options enabled. Click the Display Network option to disable it at this time.

For more on using the display network as a new advertiser, see Chapter 7 of this minibook.

Figure 2-3: Bidding, budget, delivery, and advanced settings selections.

Networks and devices

Networks ⑦	⦿ All available sites (Recommended for new advertisers)
	○ Let me choose...
Devices ⑦	⦿ All available devices (Recommended for new advertisers)
	○ Let me choose...

Bidding and budget

Bidding option ⑦ Basic options | Advanced options
⦿ I'll manually set my bids for clicks

　　🔍 You'll set your maximum CPC bids in the next step.

○ AdWords will set my bids to help maximize clicks within my target budget

Default bid ⑦ $ ▢
This bid applies to the first ad group in this campaign, which you'll create in the next step.

Budget ⑦ $ ▢ per day
Actual daily spend may vary. ⑦

⊞ Delivery method (advanced)

Ad extensions

You can use this optional feature to include relevant business information with your ads. Take a tour.

Location ⑦ ☐ Extend my ads with location information
Product ⑦ ☐ Extend my ads with relevant product details from Google Merchant Center
Sitelinks ⑦ ☐ Extend my ads with links to sections of my site
Call ⑦ ☐ Extend my ads with a phone number
Social ⑦ ☐ Increase the social relevance of my ads by associating them with my Google+ Page

Advanced settings

⊞ Schedule: Start date, end date, ad scheduling
⊞ Ad delivery: Ad rotation, frequency capping
⊞ Demographic
⊞ Social settings
⊞ Keyword matching options
⊞ Automatic campaign optimization (Display Network only)

[Save and continue] [Cancel new campaign]

10. **In the Bidding and Budget area, choose a Basic option to start with:**

    The Basic options are best to start with because they give you the most control and allow you to see the progression of the account without any of the fancier options enabled until you're ready to experiment with them.

    - *I'll manually set my bids for clicks:* Choose a cost-per-click amount and enter a default bid in the default bid box.

    - *AdWords will set my bids to help maximize clicks within my target budget:* Choose this if you have a specific amount of clicks that you would like to reach and are less concerned about your cost per click, but rather your overall daily budget.

11. **Choose your daily budget and type it into the box.**

    See the next section in this chapter for more details.

12. **Choose a delivery method:**

    - *Standard:* Shows ads evenly throughout the course of the day. This option is enabled by default. Until you know the volume of traffic and conversions your campaign is going to receive, you'll want to wait to experiment with other options.

    - *Accelerated:* Shows your ads as often as possible until your budget runs out.

13. **(Optional) Choose an ad extension.**

    Ad extensions are enhancements to text ads like sitelinks, locations, or phone numbers.

    You can skip this part for now and come back when you are more comfortable with the basics of PPC. You can find out more about extension ads in Chapter 7 in this minibook.

14. **(Optional) Set a definite start or end date for your campaign, or adjust your ads so that they rotate evenly.**

15. **Click the Save and Continue button to move on to the Create ad group, Ad and Keywords section.**

16. **Name your ad group something descriptive that will help you know what the contents are.**

17. **Choose the text ad option radio button and fill in the Headline, Description (Line 1 and Line 2), Display URL, and Destination URL text boxes, as shown in Figure 2-4.**

    For details on writing your ads and for definitions of the different parts of the ads, see Chapter 4 of this minibook.

Figure 2-4:
Enter your
ad text,
display
URL, and
destination
URL on this
page.

18. **In the text box, type the keywords that you want to add to your campaign and click the Estimate Search Traffic button to see amount of searches performed on those keywords.**

    Google shows you how many impressions you can expect for that CPC amount, ad position, and clicks and how much you might spend in a day. This tool is great to use to adjust your budget. If you make any changes, click the Re-Estimate search traffic button to see what effect your changes have on Google's estimates (see Figure 2-5).

    This option is for traffic-driving, ad-impression purposes only; it doesn't take into account conversions or other goals of that nature. Google is just estimating how much it would cost to get the most visitors possible to your site.

Figure 2-5:
Google
results
for the
keywords
*internet
marketing.*

    For details on creating a keyword list, see Chapter 3 of this minibook.

19. **Scroll down to the Ad Group Bids section and enter the default bid that will apply to your first ad group.**

20. **Click the Save and Continue to Billing button or the Set Up Billing Later button.**

See the "Setting up billing in AdWords" section, later in this chapter, for your options.

If choose to set up billing later, you will be shown your completed campaign setup of ads, keywords, and settings.

You can click the Back link at any time to edit information. Also, Google allows you to change many settings, even after you set up and launch a campaign — add or remove keywords, use the keyword-generation tools, and edit match types, for example. For more information on these features, see Chapter 3 of this minibook.

Setting daily budgets and bids

Now that your account and first campaign is configured and running, you might want to revisit your daily budgets and bids after gathering some statistics. You can change your daily budgets and max CPC bids at any time. From the campaigns tab after signing in to your AdWords account, follow these steps to set some of those options:

1. **Click the blue Edit link next to the Budget setting you made during the initial setup.**

2. **Change the amount by typing your amount in the box.**

Click the plus sign next to View Recommended Budget to find what Google recommends your daily budget to be based on your keyword list (see Figure 2-6). For more information on setting budgets and bidding, see Chapter 5 of this minibook.

Figure 2-6:
The daily recommended budget tool.

> **Bidding and budget**
>
> Bidding option ⑦ **Focus on clicks, manual maximum CPC bidding** Edit
>
> Budget ⑦ $ 20.00 per day
>
> ⊟ View recommended budget | Learn how budget affects ad performance
> Your budget is OK. We do not recommend changes at this time.
> To make the most of your budget, try optimizing your campaign.
> Actual daily spend may vary. ⑦
>
> Save   Cancel

3. **Click the Save button to save your new budget amount.**

4. **To change the bidding option of a campaign, click the blue Edit link in the Bidding and Budget section on the Settings tab:**

- *I'll manually set my bids for clicks:* Choose this option to specify the maximum amount that you're willing to spend per click.

- *AdWords will set my bids to help maximize clicks within my target budget:* In this option, you tell Google what you want your average CPC to be for the entire campaign, and Google does its best to hit that target, getting as many clicks as it can for that price. Choosing this option means that Google decides when, how often, and for which keywords to show your ads to meet that average price. Be sure to click the CPC Bid Limit radio button to be able to enter the maximum CPC you want to target.

- *Enhanced CPC:* This option requires that conversion tracking be enabled in the account. To enable this option, place a piece of code on the final page in the conversion process on your website to trigger a conversion to be counted in AdWords. This option works best on campaigns with steady conversion data, ten or more a day, every day, in order to work.

- *Focus on conversions or CPA Bidding:* This option also requires conversion tracking to be enabled. In this option, you tell Google what you like the average cost per action (or conversion) to be for that campaign. Google will then adjust the CPC and how often the ads are served to try and meet that goal.

The best practice is to start with the manual CPC bidding option. Manual CPC is the easiest type of bidding to edit and keep an eye on, because what you see is what you get. If you choose the Automatic CPC bidding option instead, although you set a preferred price, the actual CPCs can vary a lot from that figure and can be confusing if you're just starting with PPC. (For more information on automatic bidding and other options, see Chapter 5 in this minibook.)

5. **Click the Save Changes button.**

Setting up billing in AdWords

After you set up your account, you'll need to set up billing to get your ads running if you didn't do it before:

1. **Click the Billing tab and choose Billing Preferences to open the Billing Options page.**

   When you're ready to enter your billing information, you see the page shown in Figure 2-7 only once.

2. **Set your country location and currency.**

   You can't change this information later so be sure it's correct before moving on.

To change other pieces of billing information at any time after setup, simply click the My Account tab and the Billing Preferences link. The Billing Preferences page is where you can change your billing address, form of payment, and credit card information.

3. Click Continue.

Figure 2-7:
Choose the time zone and currency for your billing address.

4. Fill in the billing profile information with your name, billing address, and phone number. When finished, click Continue.

You're taken to the Choose Your Settings page (see Figure 2-8), which contains a lot of options.

Figure 2-8:
Set your payment option.

5. **Choose to make your payments automatically or manually.**

   Automatic payments means that you pay Google after your account has accumulated clicks and costs. You have the option of paying by credit card or direct debit from a bank account:

   - *Bank account:* If you choose the bank account, your AdWords account is tied to a bank account that Google can debit after clicks have accrued.

   - *Credit Card:* If you choose this option, Google charges your credit card for clicks in the same manner that it withdraws money from a bank account.

   Manual payments means that you deposit a set amount of money from which Google will debit clicks and costs. Your only option is to use a credit card. You set an amount for Google to charge you, and Google credits your AdWords account for that amount. Every so often, as the clicks add up, Google debits that amount from your account, and you have to refill the account as the balance lowers. You can elect to have the account refill automatically or do it yourself manually each time.

   Google's billing cycle is 30 days. Your card is charged after 30 days or as you reach each of the following thresholds, whichever comes first:

   - First billing threshold: $50

   - Second billing threshold: $200

   - Third billing threshold: $350

   - Fourth (and final) billing threshold: $500

   After you hit all these thresholds, $500 becomes your regular billing rate. If you are a large enterprise, however, you can request to go on invoicing and have your threshold increased. You will need help from an AdWords employee to enable invoicing as well as to meet several spending requirements.

6. **Click Continue.**

   After you select your billing option, Google presents its Terms of Service page.

7. **Review and agree to the terms of service; then click Continue.**

   If you don't agree to the terms of service, you can't be an AdWords advertiser.

8. **On the Billing Preferences page, input your billing information and credit card number.**

9. **Click the Save and Activate button.**

   Google charges your card a one-time, nonrefundable $5 activation fee. Your account is live, and your first campaign is showing ads!

Expanding Google AdWords

When your account is active, you can add campaigns, ad groups, and keywords through the AdWords dashboard. In the following sections, you explore all these expansion options.

When you expand a PPC account, always think beyond just keywords — think of the account as a whole or, at the very least, by campaigns. See Chapters 3 and 4 in this minibook for help with keyword lists and ad copy, respectively; see Chapter 5 in this minibook for help with budgeting and bidding.

Adding a new campaign

When adding your second campaign, the process is identical to the first campaign you set up, with all the options as before with one addition: You can copy the settings from the first campaign by selecting the Existing Campaign option in the Load Settings section, as shown in Figure 2-9.

If you want to keep the same location targeting, search network, daily budget, bidding, and device settings, it's a great timesaver.

Figure 2-9:
Copying the settings from your first campaign.

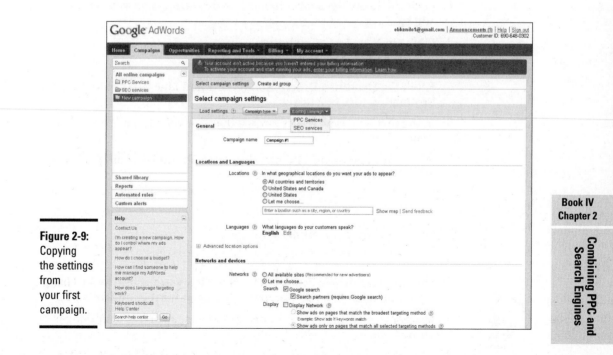

AdWords Express

AdWords Express (formally known as Google Boost) was specifically designed for local businesses targeting local customers who want to perform minimal maintenance with a simplified paid search program. You do not have to have a website as you do for the standard AdWords program; you can direct clicks to your Google Place page instead.

This feature does not utilize keyword and bidding features. Instead, you choose a category, write the headline and ad description, and choose a monthly budget. Your ads will appear on search results pages as well as in Google Maps results.

You can sign up at `www.google.com/adwords/express`.

Adding an ad group to an existing campaign

If you'd like to add ad groups to existing campaigns, you can go back at any time and add as many ad groups as you need. To add an ad group, follow these steps:

1. **From the Campaigns tab, click the desired campaign you want to add to.**

2. **Click the New Ad Group button.**

3. **Type the name of your ad group.**

4. **Fill in the Headline, Description (Line 1 and Line 2), Display URL, and Destination URL text boxes.**

5. **In the text box, type the keywords that you want to add to your ad group.**

6. **Enter your maximum CPC bid in the default bid box, and click the Save Ad Group button.**

   For help on setting bids, see Chapter 5 in this minibook.

Adding an ad to an existing ad group

To add an ad to an existing ad group, follow these steps:

1. **On the Campaigns tab, select the campaign you want to make changes to and then click the ad group to which you want to add an ad.**

   Make sure that the screen is open to the Ads tab and is displaying your current ads.

2. **Click the +New Ad button and select the type of ad from the drop-down menu. Select Text Ad to create a new text-only ad.**

A template appears, providing blank fields where you can create your new ad:

- *Text ads:* The most common ad is all text, with 25 characters for the headline, 70 characters for the body (35 characters for each line), a display URL, and a destination URL. These ads appear on search engine results pages. This is the default choice.

- *Image ads:* These are the Google Display Network. Also called *banner ads,* these ads appear on sites that have opted in to showing AdWords ads. Image ads can be uploaded into ad groups, or you can use one of Google's many templates to build one. You'll find myriad technical requirements for Flash ads, editorial content, size of ad, size of file, and images being used. See the AdWords Help Center for the list of requirements.

- *Display ad builder:* This tool is where you would access the many templates to build your own image ads.

- *WAP mobile ad:* This ad format is for mobile devices, specifically for sites that have a mobile version to drive clicks to. WAP ads are shorter and allow an image variation as well. See Figure 2-10.

3. **Enter your ad copy.**

   For information on ad testing and ad copy, see Chapter 4 in this minibook.

4. **Click Save Ad.**

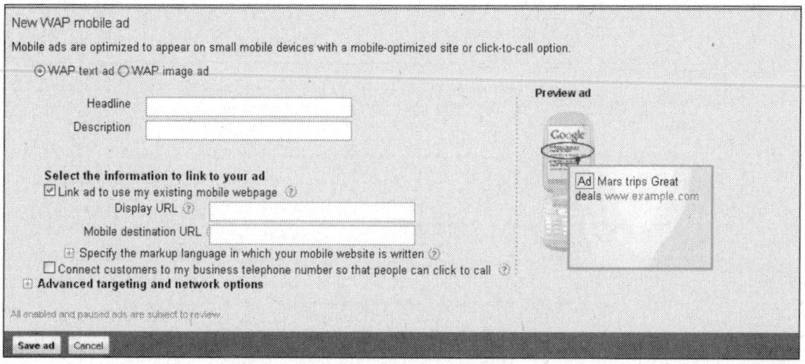

Figure 2-10: WAP mobile ad options.

Additional AdWords settings

Google AdWords makes many tools available for free to users. This book touches on most of them, but Google is continually adding and improving tools. To find the latest tools and changes, visit the Help Center by clicking its link in the upper-right corner of any AdWords page.

Using Bing Ads

Microsoft's search engine is called Bing, and the PPC ads served alongside those search results are provided through Bing Ads.

Microsoft has been making strides to improve its PPC service's interface, tools, search quality, and volume, by adding programs such as Bing Travel, Bing Ads Desktop (an offline PPC ads editor), product search, and expanded reporting options. For more information on offline editors and analytics programs, see Chapter 7 in this minibook.

If you use Microsoft Excel 2007 to help you keep track of your campaigns, you can enable an add-in for Bing Ads. For more on the Excel add-in, see the Bing Ads Help Center.

Creating an account and a campaign

To create an Bing Ads account, follow these steps:

1. **Go to Bing sign-up page at** `https://secure.bingads.microsoft.com/signup`.

2. **Fill in the User Information, Company Information, Market Setting, and Marketing Preferences fields.**

   You're taken to the Signup Is Complete page with several options (see Figure 2-11).

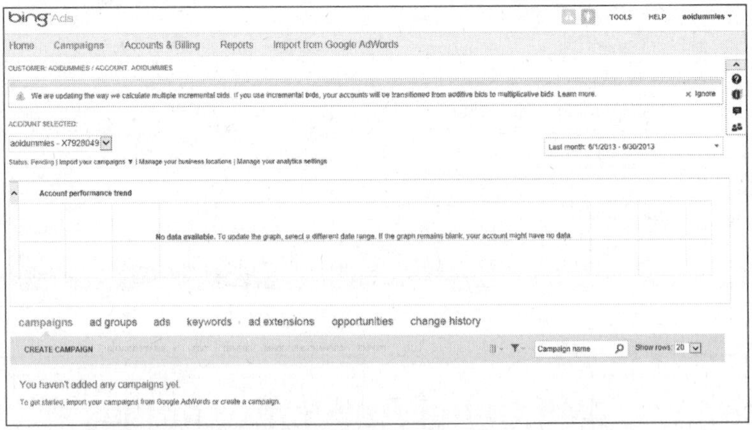

Figure 2-11: The Bing Ads account options page.

3. **Click the Create a New Campaign link.**

   The General Settings page appears, as shown in Figure 2-12.

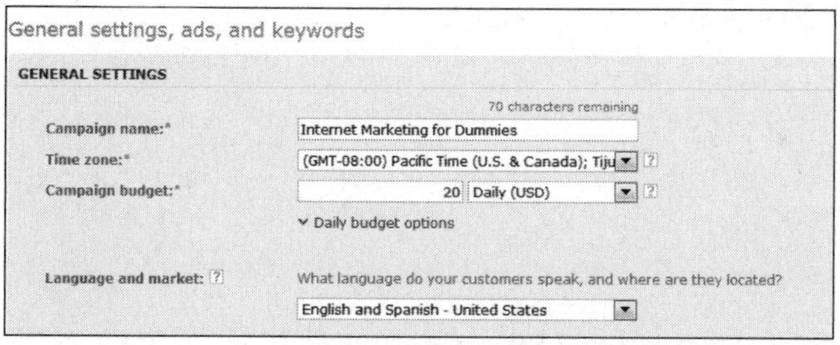

Figure 2-12:
Bing Ads
account
general
options.

4. **Enter the name of your campaign in the Campaign Name text box.**

   Name your campaign something descriptive that you can remember.

5. **Choose the time zone you are in or that you want to use as the default for your campaign from the Time Zone drop-down menu.**

   For example, if you live in Seattle but are creating a campaign to show ads to customers in New York, choose the Eastern Time option instead of Pacific Time.

6. **Enter the amount of budget you want to spend per day or the amount you want to spend per month in the Campaign Budget text box.**

   Choose Monthly from the drop-down menu if this is your monthly budget.

7. **(Optional) Choose the default language for your campaign from the Language and Market drop-down menu.**

   The default language setting is English and Spanish – United States. If you're targeting a different type of English or language, change that here.

8. **Click the blue Locations link and choose the location where your ads will be shown:**

   • *All locations worldwide:* This is the default and means that every country that shows Bing Ads is enabled. You'll want to change this to the countries you'd like to show ads in.

   • *Selected cities, metro areas, states/provinces, and countries/regions*: Choose this option if you want to target a specific region — the United States, for example, as shown in Figure 2-13. You can then click the drop-down arrow to narrow your locations to states, cities, and metro areas.

   • *Near a business or other location:* This option allows you to target a specific address or location of your choosing.

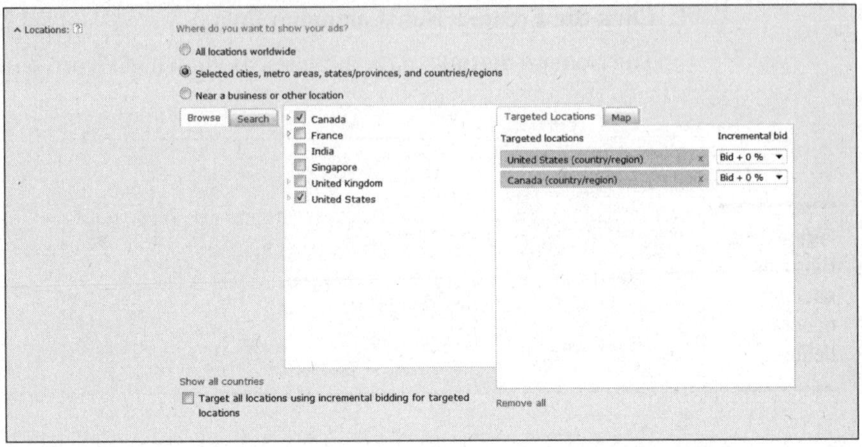

Figure 2-13:
A campaign location targeting options in Bing Ads.

At this time, you can set an incremental bid for each targeted location. If you are new to PPC, leave this setting at +0% for now. For more on incremental bidding, see the section "Setting incremental bidding," later in this chapter.

9. **Choose the ad type.**

Text ad is the default choice. Choose it unless doing a mobile ad.

10. **Enter your title, text, display URL, and destination URL.**

As you enter the destination URL for your ad, Bing Ads begins generating a suggested keyword list with traffic estimates based on that site.

For more on writing ad copy, see Chapter 4 in this minibook.

11. **Select Keywords from the Bid Type drop-down list and enter the keywords you want to bid on into the Keyword box.**

If you're familiar with the different match types, you can identify which ones you would like to use. If you are unfamiliar with match types, type the keywords in by themselves. For more on keyword match types, see Chapter 3 in this minibook.

12. **(Optional) To add any of Google's suggested keywords, click the Add button next to the keyword.**

You can add as many or as few of the suggestions as you feel are right for your new campaign, as shown in Figure 2-14.

13. **Click Save.**

The Bids, Targeting and Advanced Settings page appears, as shown in Figure 2-15.

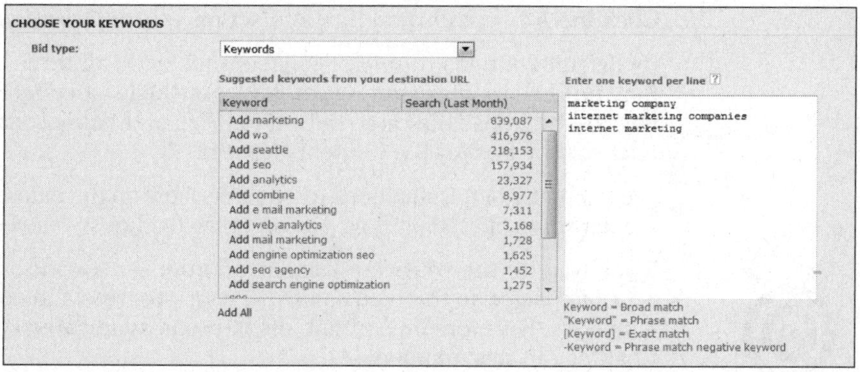

Figure 2-14:
Suggested
keyword list
in Bing Ads.

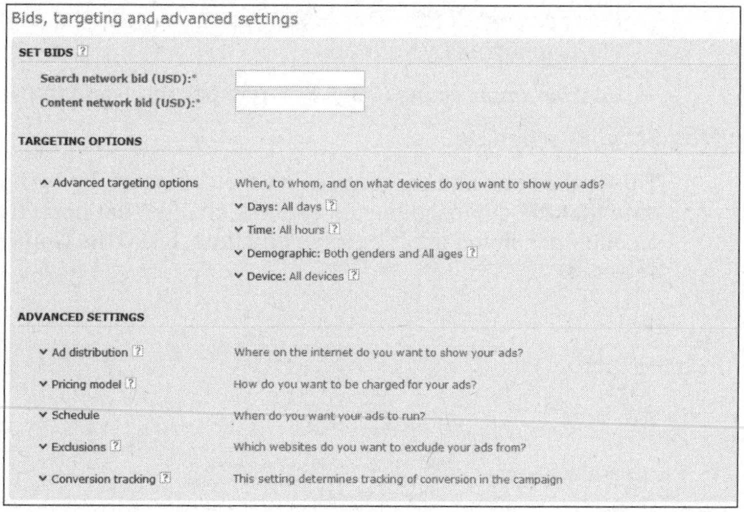

Figure 2-15:
Bids and
targeting for
Bing Ads.

14. **Set the maximum bid for both the search and content networks in the Set Bids section.**

These bids apply to the Search and Content networks and can be different amounts. Take this step regardless of which network you plan on running. You can always edit this later.

15. **(Optional) Specify any targeting and demographic options in the Advanced Targeting Options section.**

You can target traffic by a specific time of day, day of the week, or device (mobile devices or desktops). By default, all devices are enabled.

You can also target by demographic in incremental bids. Leave this section disabled for now until you're more versed in PPC.

16. **Click the Ad Distribution link and set up your distribution.**

    By default your ad group/campaign is enabled to all three networks that Bing Ads has to offer (see Figure 2-16). For the least complicated and best start, choose the radio button for Bing and Yahoo! Search. And uncheck the box for the Content Network.

    See Chapter 7 of this minibook for greater detail on the differences between the networks offered on Bing Ads and how to choose between them.

    If you want to run your campaign on additional networks, set up separate campaigns so that you can track your progress and costs more efficiently. For more on content, display, and syndicated search, see Chapter 7 in this minibook.

17. **Set the pricing model:**

    - *Cost per Click (CPC):* This is the default option; you pay only for clicks incurred by your ads.

    - *Cost per Impression (CPM):* You pay per thousand impressions.

18. **Set your schedule.**

    This is the start and end dates for your campaign. If you have a specific date that the campaign needs to start, change that here; the same with an end date. If you don't have an end date, leave the None radio button selected.

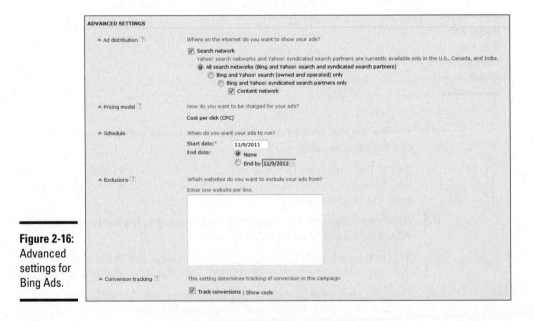

Figure 2-16: Advanced settings for Bing Ads.

19. **(Optional) Enter your exclusions.**

Fill in this section if you're running a content or syndicated search targeted campaign and know of some websites that you would like to exclude from your advertising. If you don't have any specific sites, leave this section blank.

20. **(Optional) Enable conversion tracking in your campaign by selecting this check box.**

Bing Ads displays the code needed for the conversion goal page on your site. For more on how to install conversion tracking on your site, see the Bing Ads Help Center. It will require a snippet of code to be added to your website.

21. **Click Save.**

Adding billing information

Your account isn't quite ready to run yet; you have to add payment information. Follow these steps:

1. **Click the Accounts & Billing tab and then click the Payment Methods tab.**

2. **Click the Add a Payment Method button and choose to add a card or add PayPal account.**

3. **Fill in all information fields for credit card information or PayPal login, including the billing address and click the Add button.**

You should now see your just added payment method to the Payment Methods screen. The nonrefundable $5 setup and activation fee will be charged. That's it!

Editing settings

You might need to tweak your account or campaign settings after your ads have started running. To do so, follow these steps:

1. **Sign in to your account.**

You should see everything from your initial setup in the dashboard.

2. **Select the campaign you just created and then click the Edit Campaign Settings link.**

The Campaign Settings page opens (see Figure 2-17).

**Book IV
Chapter 2**

Combining PPC and Search Engines

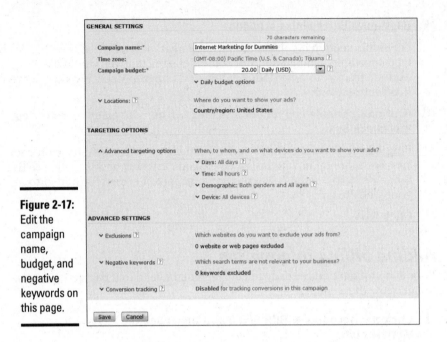

Figure 2-17:
Edit the
campaign
name,
budget, and
negative
keywords on
this page.

3. **Change the settings as desired.**

You can change the name of the campaign and edit the budget settings. You can also adjust the days of the week, times of the day, and other targeting options here that you entered during the initial setup. You can also add negative keywords for the campaign. For more on negative keywords, turn to Chapter 3 of this minibook.

4. **Click Save.**

5. **Click the ad group you created during the initial setup.**

The Manage Selected Ad Group page opens.

6. **Click the Edit Ad Group Settings link.**

7. **Change the settings as desired.**

You can edit the name of the ad group, add negative keywords at the ad-group level, and enable or disable the content network, which is all the Bing partners as well as the syndicated search partner network. You want to retain the search network for Bing and Yahoo! only so that your ads show on those search results pages. This can be found under the Ad Distribution setting. For more help with the content network, see Chapter 7 of this minibook.

For any ad group settings that are different from the campaign level, the ad group settings take precedence and override any campaign level settings.

Setting ad schedules

Ad scheduling allows you to tell Bing what times of day and days of the week you do or don't want to show your ads. Bing Ads offers all seven days of the week, and doesn't allow for specific hours, but rather blocks of time.

The default settings show your ads on all days at all times. If you know that you have peak hours or days of the week, however, choosing different settings (as shown in Figure 2-18) is a great idea. For best practices on ad scheduling, check out Chapter 5 of this minibook.

To set your ad scheduling options, click the blue link for the option you'd like to edit. Click the check box next to the times/days you want to target and click Save when you finish.

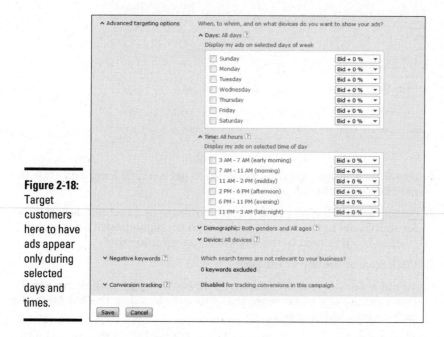

Figure 2-18:
Target customers here to have ads appear only during selected days and times.

Adjusting keyword lists

If you accepted the default options when you entered your initial keyword list, the match type was broad and the maximum CPC was applied to all keywords in that ad group. You can always go back and set separate bids for specific keywords or change the overall maximum CPC.

You can enable incremental bidding and target users by gender or age by increasing your bid when Bing detects a user in your desired demographic (age, gender, or time of day).

To adjust your keyword list or use the incremental bidding tool, follow these steps:

1. **If you want to edit the match types, click the ad group for which you want to edit the keywords; then click the Keywords tab.**

Your selected keyword list appears (see Figure 2-19). If you need more information on the different match types, see Chapter 3 of this minibook.

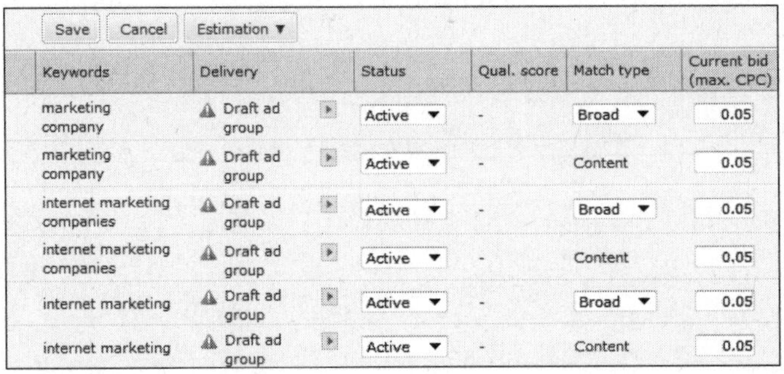

Figure 2-19:
Editing a keyword list.

Keywords	Delivery	Status	Qual. score	Match type	Current bid (max. CPC)
marketing company	⚠ Draft ad group ▸	Active ▼	-	Broad ▼	0.05
marketing company	⚠ Draft ad group ▸	Active ▼	-	Content	0.05
internet marketing companies	⚠ Draft ad group ▸	Active ▼	-	Broad ▼	0.05
internet marketing companies	⚠ Draft ad group ▸	Active ▼	-	Content	0.05
internet marketing	⚠ Draft ad group ▸	Active ▼	-	Broad ▼	0.05
internet marketing	⚠ Draft ad group ▸	Active ▼	-	Content	0.05

2. **Hover your mouse over the keyword to get a pencil icon, and click the pencil to open the drop-down menu.**

3. **Select the match type per keyword to Phrase or Exact and adjust bids for individual keywords as desired with the same pencil icon in the current bid box next to the keyword you want to edit.**

4. **Click Save at the top of the page.**

5. **To bid separately for ads displayed on content pages, click the pencil icon next the site or keyword that you want to adjust the bid for in the current max bid column.**

This option allows you to set a separate bid for ads on the content network. By default, Bing selects your maximum CPC bid for all networks. You want to be able to bid separately. Chapter 7 in this minibook goes over content network bidding practices in more detail.

6. **Edit negative keywords, {param} options, and destination URLs on a per-keyword basis:**

 a. Click the Columns button and select the check boxes next to the options you want to display.

b. *Select the check boxes for the individual keywords you want to make changes to, and click the Edit link.* The columns to adjust these settings are then displayed. See Figure 2-20.

7. **Click the Save button at the top of the page.**

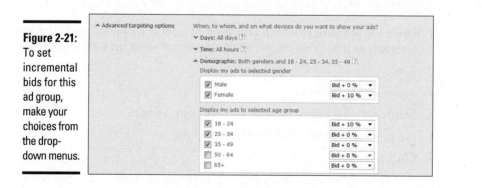

Figure 2-20: Editing a keyword list with all columns enabled.

Setting incremental bidding

Incremental bidding increases the amount of your bid when Bing detects a user in the chosen demographic, time of day, or day of the week. You can set this at the ad group or campaign level in the settings area of a campaign or ad group under targeting options.

Suppose that you want to capture more female customers. To set up your incremental bidding, you'd specify 10 percent for Female in the gender section. Bing then increases your maximum CPC when females see your ad, so you gain a better position more often. See Figure 2-21.

Figure 2-21: To set incremental bids for this ad group, make your choices from the drop-down menus.

**Book IV
Chapter 2**

Combining PPC and Search Engines

1. **Open the ad group that you want to apply incremental bids to and click Edit Your Ad Group Settings.**

If you want to apply incremental bids to all ad groups in a campaign, click the Edit Your Campaign Settings link from the campaign page.

2. **In the Advanced Targeting Options area, click the down arrows to open the different sections to set your selected hours of the day, location, and days of the week for incremental bidding.**

Bing increases your bids by 10 percent during those times and at those locations. Incremental bids must be set in increments of 10 percent.

3. **Set incremental bidding amounts based on males and/or females in the gender section and based on age in the age groups section.**

4. **Click Save.**

Incremental bids add up quickly. You pay the increased price only if the user clicks your ad, but if you enabled a 10 percent boost for females and a 20 percent boost for ages 18–24, and if a 20-year-old female runs a search, your ad receives a 30 percent incremental bid boost. Technically, this user is in the key demographic that you're targeting, but incremental bids can get expensive fast, so consider your maximum CPC when you choose your incremental bids.

Expanding Bing Ads

After you create your initial campaign and ad group, you'll want to expand them at some point. In the following sections, you add campaigns and ad groups, as well as find out how to increase the number of keywords in your keyword lists.

Adding a campaign

To add a campaign to your Bing Ads account, follow these steps:

1. **Open the account to which you want to add a campaign, and click the Campaigns tab. Click the Create Campaign button on your dashboard.**

The Create a Campaign page opens.

2. **Name your campaign.**

3. **Select your targeting options and set your budget.**

4. **Fill in your first ad's text and keyword list.**

5. **Click Save.**

When you create a new campaign, you're not given the opportunity to name the ad group that must be created to go with it. Bing Ads creates a placeholder name of Ad Group #1. To change this name to one that describes your ad group, click Edit Ad Group Settings.

Adding an ad group to an existing campaign

To add an ad group to an existing campaign, follow these steps:

1. **Click the campaign from the Campaigns tab to which you want to add the ad group.**

2. **Click the Create Ad Group button.**

3. **Name your ad group and determine whether you want to use the campaign level settings for targeting and negative keywords.**

   If not, click the Define Ad Group Level Settings for Targeting and Exclusions radio button and adjust.

4. **Fill in the ad copy and keyword lists, and click Save.**

Adding an ad to an existing ad group

To add an ad to an existing ad group, follow these steps:

1. **Click the ad group to which you want to add an ad.**

2. **Click the Ads tab.**

3. **Click the Create an Ad button.**

4. **Add your headline, body, and URLs.**

5. **Click Save.**

Chapter 3: Making Keyword Lists That Sell

In This Chapter

✔ Selecting and organizing keywords

✔ Selecting match types

✔ Working with keyword destination URLs

✔ Understanding advanced keyword-targeting techniques

✔ Expanding and contracting keyword lists

The *keyword list* is the foundation on which your campaigns are built. A good, well-organized keyword list can make a lot of difference in how your account performs — or doesn't perform.

This chapter shows you how to build, expand, and organize your keyword lists for the most effective return on your investment. It also shows you how to segment individual keywords further to give your site's visitors the best user experience possible.

Choosing Keywords

Generate keywords that describe the product or service being offered, such as colors, styles, sizes, or brands. Depending on how popular these terms are, they might have to be sectioned into separate ad groups or campaigns.

Also, if you sell a variety of products, you should have a separate ad group for each product you promote.

Suppose that you sell two different types of pens: ballpoint and gel. Also suppose that you want to promote six kinds of ballpoint pens but only one type of gel pen. Putting the keywords for the gel pen in with those for the ballpoint pens may save you a little time, because you don't have to create a separate ad group for the gel pen, but overall, combining these keywords won't produce your desired pay-per-click (PPC) result or return on investment (ROI). (See Chapter 1 in this minibook for details on PPC.)

For the same reason, you wouldn't bid on the keyword *pen* in either ad group. The term is too general and *high traffic* (a very popular term likely to generate a lot of impressions and clicks), and it isn't as targeted as *ballpoint pen* or *gel pen.* A high-traffic keyword like *pen* may need to be in its own campaign because it's so broad that it will generate a lot of traffic, much of which could have nothing to do with your pen. Your ad could show up for inquiries having to do with *pig pen, pen pal, pent up,* and *penny,* for example.

The best practice is to decide on the subject of your campaign before you start selecting keywords. Sketch out your subject and keep it in mind while you're building your ad groups and keyword lists.

Organizing Keywords in Ad Groups

Organizing your keywords in ad groups makes the overall management of your campaigns easier and cleaner, and it shows much more clearly which keywords are successful and which ones aren't. The following sections include several examples of just how granular you need to be when you organize your keywords in ad groups.

Suppose that you sell floral wedding invitations. You want to promote the type/brand Floral Wedding Invitations, and you know that rose, lily, and daisy invitations are very popular. To plan your campaign, you might create a table like Table 3-1.

Table 3-1   Ad Groups and Keywords for a Sample Campaign

Ad Group	Keywords
General Floral Wedding Invitations	*flower wedding invitations, floral wedding invitations, flower wedding invites, floral wedding invites*
Rose Wedding Invitations	*rose wedding invitations, rose wedding invites, pink rose wedding invitations, pink rose wedding invites, red rose wedding invitations, red rose wedding invites*
Lily Wedding Invitations	*lily wedding invitations, lily wedding invites, calla lily wedding invitations, calla lily wedding invites*
Daisy Wedding Invitations	*daisy wedding invitations, daisy wedding invites, yellow daisy wedding invitations, yellow daisy invites, gerber daisy wedding invitations, gerber daisy wedding invites*
Floral Wedding Invitation Branded	*floral wedding invitations, floral wedding invites, floral company wedding invitations, wedding invitations floral*

Make your keyword lists as segmented and relevant as possible from the start. Although it may seem like a lot less work to cram everything into a few ad groups, that practice will actually create more work and headaches for you down the line as the account matures.

The example in Table 3-1 is a highly segmented campaign of several ad groups and keywords. Even though the ad groups are highly targeted, they're within the same campaign, which will give you greater control of cost and allow you to add negative keywords easily. (For more information about negative keywords, see the section "Knowing the match types," later in this chapter.)

The fewer keywords you use in an ad group, the better. A good rule is to have no more than 30 keywords in an ad group. A keyword list of several hundred terms is hard to manage and affects both the ad group and the campaign in many negative ways, including relevancy, quality score, ease of ad-text creation, and bidding. The more targeted and more specific your ad group is, the more benefits you reap from search engines in terms of PPC, relevancy (see Chapter 1 of this minibook), and ad position.

Working with Match Types

Match types are what you use to tell the search engine the context in which you want your ads to be shown. A broad match type, for example, tells the search engine that you want the ad to appear more often and in conjunction with keywords that are similar to your keyword, even if they're not exactly the same. A phrase match type is more targeted, allowing other words to appear before and after your keyword, whereas an exact match tells the search engine to display your ad only if the user types the exact keyword. The following sections describe these types in detail.

Knowing the match types

Most search engines use at least four basic match types: *broad, phrase, exact,* and *negative.* Google AdWords has an additional match type called *modified broad.* The modified broad type is in between broad and phrase matches and uses an anchor (signified with a + sign) on words within the keyword that are required to appear in the user's search term. You can choose to anchor one word in the keyword, two words (dual anchor), or all the words (full anchor).

If you find yourself leaning toward a full anchor option, consider phrase match instead to start with.

Table 3-2 describes all five match types and gives specific examples of keywords used with those match types.

Table 3-2	Match Types	
Match Type	*Ad Display*	*Example*
Broad	Ads are displayed for keywords in singular, plural, and synonym forms. This option is the most inclusive one and triggers ads more often than the others.	The keywords *bicycle parts* trigger ads for *bike parts, bicycle part, parts for bikes,* and *bicycles.*
Phrase	Ads are displayed for keywords in plural form, and the keywords must be in the same word order as the search term.	The keywords *green tea cups* trigger ads for *green tea* and *cheap green tea cups* but not for *tea green cups.*
Exact	Ads are displayed only if what the user searched on matches a keyword in your list.	The keywords *health care plans* trigger ads only for *health care plans* (plural), not for *health care plan* (singular).
Negative	Ads are not displayed in conjunction with these keywords.	The keywords *glass vases* would have negative keywords to exclude other media, such as *ceramic, porcelain, china,* and *plastic.*
Modified Broad	Ads are displayed for keywords in singular and plural forms, provided that one of the anchor words appears in the search term.	The keywords *bicycle +parts* would trigger ads for *bike parts, used bicycle parts,* and *parts for bicycles,* but not for *used bikes, bicycles for sale,* or *bicycle tires.*

Choosing the right match type

When you know what the match types are, your next decisions are what match types to use for your situation. The following list outlines the best-case scenarios for the different match types. If you find that your situation falls between two categories, you can use both match types in the same ad group and test them against each other. A phrase match might convert better for you than an exact match, or a broad match might bring you more of what you want than a phrase match.

✦ **Broad:** This match type is best for *long-tail* keywords (three words or more), misspellings, and URLs, and for maximizing the number of times your ad appears.

✦ **Phrase:** This match type is a good place to start if you're not sure what the keyword will do and if you're very budget conscious. It's also a good choice for keywords that are popular enough that you need to filter out some searches (for items you don't carry, for example). Also, a phrase match often turns up great keywords that you'll want to add or block out as the campaign progresses.

✦ **Exact:** This match type is best for keywords that are popular and short (one to two words) and that might rack up several thousand *impressions* (how many times your ad appears to users) very quickly. Exact match is a good way to control costs and targeting, because it cuts down on impressions for broader search inquiries; the typical user is searching for something specific.

✦ **Negative:** This match type is best for keywords that you don't want your ads to appear in conjunction with. Popular negative keywords include *discount, cheap, free,* and *used.*

✦ **Modified Broad:** This match type is best for when a broad match has too much traffic and has too many variation possibilities but you don't want to cut off too much search volume with a phrase match. It works well with three or more word phrases.

Implicit and explicit bidding by match type in Bing Ads

Bing Ads allows you to more tightly monitor and bid on the same keyword but with different match types. You can bid on every match type of the same keyword and each engine will show you that keyword's performance for that match type, but Bing Ads allows you to take that one step further and offers up a strategy of bidding a different amount for match types that are more or less important to your campaign performance.

Implicit bidding is where you set the bid at the ad-group level, and it applies to all the keywords within that ad group, regardless of match type. This maximum CPC (cost per click) works for all match types of the same keyword in that ad group as well. If you're new to PPC, stick with this method until you're comfortable with PPC before testing explicit bidding. This method requires no additional action on your part and is enabled by default.

Explicit bidding is where you do one of two things:

✦ **Include broad, phrase, and exact match types to your ad group for the same keyword.** You pay the same for all three types.

✦ **Qualify the most important keyword for all the possible auctions.** Choose which of the three types is most relevant for your ad group and leave that match type's bid at the maximum CPC for the ad group. Then, for the other two match types, change their bids to the minimum bid. You won't overpay for less relevant match types, and you force the system to prioritize your chosen match type over the others.

The second method gives each match type a bid on a scale, with the exact match being the highest (because it will be the most relevant and have the fewest impressions), then the broad match, and then the phrase match. You want to scale it so that the broad match is 85 percent of the amount of the exact match and the phrase match is 75 percent of the amount of the exact match. The phrase match in Bing Ads is less effective overall when doing complex bidding strategies, which is why you should make it lower than the broad match.

To keep explicit bidding simple, create three ad groups in one campaign, one for each match type; add the same keyword lists to each group; and set the maximum bid at the ad-group level utilizing the same bidding ratios.

Segmenting Keyword Lists by Destination URLs

When you have a complete keyword list organized by ad groups and match types, you can segment the list even further. This situation applies if you want to drive visitors to a specific product or place, but starting a separate ad group doesn't make sense.

In the example shown in Table 3-1 earlier in this chapter, some of the keywords indicate specific colors for rose wedding invitations: red and pink. Rather than drop visitors off the product page for rose wedding invitations, you can take them one click further by using a keyword destination URL for each color. Select the URL for the product page of the pink rose wedding invitation, for example, and direct visitors there specifically for the keywords *pink rose wedding invitation* and *pink rose wedding invites.* This strategy works especially well if you have only one type of product but still want to have the keyword so that when someone does search on it, your ad appears.

Both Google and Bing offer keyword destination URL targeting:

✦ **Google:** You have to use the offline AdWords Desktop Editor or go through an export and import of an Excel spreadsheet using the AdWords template.

The desktop editor is a free download from Google AdWords and is the easier choice. See Chapter 7 in this minibook for more on the AdWords Editor.

✦ **Bing:** Follow these steps:

1. *Log in to your Bing Ads account and click the ad group's name to open the ad group.*

2. *Click the Keywords tab to open the entire keyword list for that ad group.*

3. *Click the Columns button in the navigation area and select the Dest. URL check box, as shown in Figure 3-1. Then click OK.*

   The Destination URL field now is visible.

4. *Click the keyword(s) that you want to add a keyword-level destination URL to.*

5. *Enter the URL and click the Save button.*

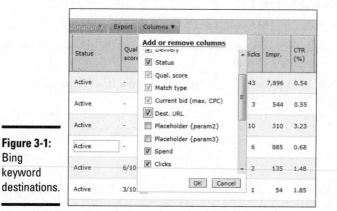

Figure 3-1: Bing keyword destinations.

Using Advanced Keyword Targeting in Bing Ads

Bing Ads offers a deeper keyword destination URL targeting if you really want to get into all the nooks and crannies of keyword-targeting tools. This level of keyword URL targeting is optional and won't have a major effect on your account. If you've organized and deployed your ad groups and keyword lists as efficiently as you can, with maximum relevancy, you don't need these tools. In fact, using them is overkill unless you have generic ad groups and campaigns, and you need to make your ads as dynamic as possible.

Bing offers a {param} or dynamic text option for ads that contains place-holder text. If the ad copy contains a dynamic keyword or {param} and your keyword list contains keywords that are too long to fit within the {param} parameter of the ad text, you can specify something else to display instead. Suppose that the ad copy reads Save on {param2}, but the keyword that the user searched on is *cheapest Hawaiian vacation packages,* which is too long to display. If you configure {param2} as *Hawaiian vacations,* the ad will display *Hawaiian vacations* instead. Follow these steps to set the text in the keyword list for dynamic insertion:

1. **Click the ad group's name to open the ad group.**

2. **Click the Keywords tab to open the entire keyword list for that ad group.**

3. **Click the Columns button in the navigation area, select the Placeholder {param2} check box, and click OK.**

   The Placeholder {param2} column now appears in the main navigation area, as shown in Figure 3-2.

4. **Click the keyword(s) that you want to add alternate text to.**

5. **Enter the alternate text and click the Save button in the top-left corner above the Keywords column.**

   How you enter the text in this field is exactly how it will appear in your ad, including capitalization.

Figure 3-2: A Bing Ads ad with {param2} set.

Keywords	Ad group	Delivery	Status	Qual. score	Match type	Current bid (max. CPC)	Placeholder {param2}	Spend ▾	Clicks	Impr.	CTR (%)	Avg. position	Avg. CPC
floor door stop	Door Stops	Eligible	Active	9/10	Broad	2.00		3.99	4	56	7.14	1.89	1.00
door stop	Door Stops	Eligible	Active	9/10	Exact	2.00	Door Stop	1.72	1	53	1.89	1.13	1.72
door stops	Door Stops	Eligible	Active	9/10	Exact	2.00		1.60	2	83	2.41	1.06	0.80

You also need to set up your ad copy to use dynamic insertion. See Chapter 4 in this minibook to do so.

Expanding Keyword Lists

As any PPC campaign progresses, it becomes more and more apparent which keywords are generating the quality of traffic you want and which ones are not. The best way to determine how your keywords are performing is to use an analytics or conversion tracking package (see Chapter 7 in this minibook) that can tell you the amount of revenue a keyword has generated, the number of page views, the amount of time visitors spend on the site, and how quickly they leave. Depending on your PPC goals (see Chapter 1 of this minibook), these stats determine whether a keyword is a keeper.

If you started your campaign with only a few keywords as a test or simply want to increase impressions for your ads, you're ready to expand your initial keyword list to grab additional traffic. The best way to start is to use the search engine's free keyword-generation tool. Often, this tool also estimates the impressions and clicks that those keywords might generate. The tool gives you a few options for generating additional keywords:

✦ Selecting keywords in your current list

✦ Entering the URL of the site

✦ Selecting categories

When you use keyword-generation tools, review the keyword suggestions carefully before adding any of them. Never add all keywords suggested. The search engines reach far and wide to come up with keyword suggestions, and accepting all of them will result in a large ad group that's difficult to manage. In addition, you might add keywords that aren't relevant to your ad group.

Adding keywords in Google

Google AdWords offers a free keyword-generation tool to expand your current keyword lists. To use it, follow these steps:

1. **Open the ad group to which you want to add keywords.**

2. **Click the Keywords tab and then the + Add Keywords button.**

The Add Keywords page opens.

3. **Choose your keywords with one of these methods:**

• *If you know what keywords you want to add:* Type them into the empty box. Skip to Step 7.

• *If you want to use keywords generated by Google:* Scroll through the list of suggested keywords provided by Google on the right side and click the blue Add link for any that you want to add. Then skip to Step 7.

• *If you want to generate your own keywords:* Click the Keyword Tool link. The Find Keywords Tool page opens, as shown in Figure 3-3. Continue with Step 4.

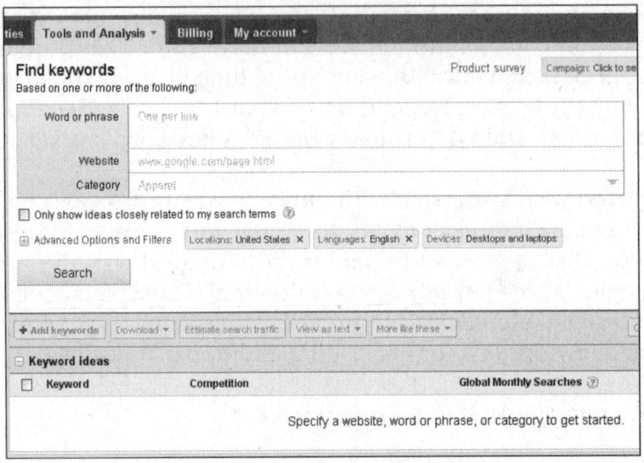

Figure 3-3:
The Google
AdWords
keyword
tool.

4. **Choose one of the following options for your keyword research:**

   - *Descriptive Words or Phrases:* In the text box, type words or phrases that describe the product or service that the ad group targets.

   - *Website Content:* In the text box, enter the destination URL and let Google make suggestions based on the content of this page.

   - *Category:* Click this box and a drop-down menu of categories to choose from appears for you to choose from.

5. **Click the Search button.**

   You see a long list of suggestions with estimated search volume both locally (USA) and globally, as well as advertiser competition.

6. **Select the check box for each keyword that you want to add to your ad group.**

7. **Click the Add Keywords button.**

8. **Click Save.**

   You stay on the Keyword Tool page.

Adding keywords in Bing

To add a keyword to an existing ad group in Bing Ads, follow these steps:

1. **Open the ad group to which you want to add a keyword.**

2. **Click the Keywords tab, if it isn't already open.**

3. **Click the Add Keywords button.**

   The Add Keywords page opens, as shown in Figure 3-4.

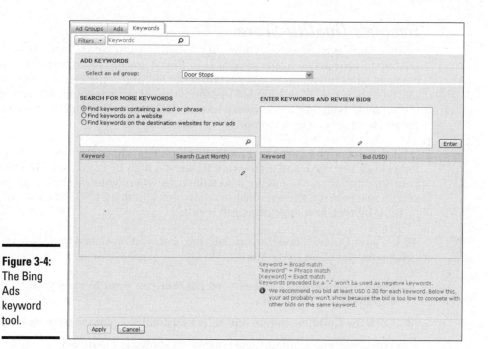

Figure 3-4:
The Bing
Ads
keyword
tool.

4. **Enter your desired keywords in the Enter Keywords and Review Bids box and click Enter or search for a keyword with one of these methods:**

   • *Find Keywords Containing a Word or Phrase:* In the Enter Keywords and Review Bids text box, type words or phrases that describe the product or service that the ad group targets.

   • *Find Keywords on a Website:* In the text box, enter the destination URL and let Bing make suggestions based on the content of this page.

   • *Find Keywords on the Destination Websites for Your Ads:* Enter a destination URL for a content network site that you'd like the ads to appear on. (This option applies only to ad groups enabled into the content and search partner display networks. For more on this, see Chapter 7 in this minibook.)

5. **Click the Apply button.**

   Your new keywords are added to the existing keyword list.

Understanding Quality Score

Both Google AdWords and Bing Ads have a *quality score* metric — an internal scale to help you see how you're doing at the keyword level according to the search engines. It's a scale of 1 to 10, with 1 being the worst and 10 being the best.

**Book IV
Chapter 3**

**Making Keyword
Lists That Sell**

Google's Quality Score

Quality Score is a secret algorithm that Google uses to "score" each keyword relative to your account, the keywords in the ad group, the ad text, the landing page, your bid amount, and several other factors, some known and some not. Quality Score is also applied to other areas of your account, like ads and the account itself, but the keyword level is the most visible and the easiest for you to make changes to in order to help yourself.

Quality Score is one of the factors that determines what your CPC will be for a single keyword, and if you want to lower a high CPC, you need to raise your Quality Score. Your score also influences where your ad shows up on a search results page and establishes what your minimum CPC bid has to be to show up on a first page of search results.

To see your Quality Score in your keyword list, you first need to add a column for it. Follow these steps to do so:

1. **Open the ad group and keyword list that you want to view your scores on.**

2. **Click the Columns button and select Customize Columns from its menu.**

The Customize Columns page opens, as shown in Figure 3-5.

3. **Click Add next to Qual. Score in the Attributes section.**

4. **Click the Save button.**

Now, when you look at your keyword list, you find a column devoted to the Quality Score (look ahead to Figure 3-6).

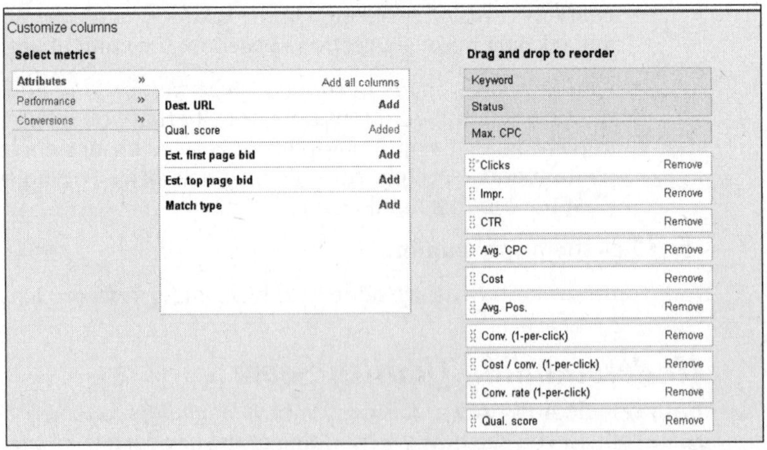

Figure 3-5: Adding the Quality Score column to Google AdWords.

You're looking at your Quality Score and you're probably wondering what that number means. If you see a 7, you're above average and at a good place to be. If you're in the 2–5 range, you want to work on increasing your score to help with your overall CPC and relevancy to searchers clicking on your ads.

A Quality Score of 2 or lower will often garner a `Rarely shown due to low quality score` warning in the Status column of your keyword list, as shown in Figure 3-6. This means that Google is finding that this particular keyword isn't relevant to the ad group, the other keywords, the ad, the landing page, or even the behavior of the users utilizing this term for search.

Figure 3-6:
AdWords
Quality
Score.

	Keyword	Status	Max. CPC	Clicks	Impr.	CTR	Avg. CPC	Cost	Avg. Pos.	Qual. score
	emergency room	Rarely shown due to low quality score	$3.00	3	1,692	0.18%	$0.79	$2.37	1.3	2/10
	24 hour urgent care	Eligible	$3.00	2	110	1.82%	$2.90	$5.80	4.5	4/10
	urgent care	Eligible	$3.00	1	984	0.10%	$2.01	$2.01	5.7	3/10
	er	Rarely shown due to low quality score	$3.00	0	0	0.00%	$0.00	$0.00	0	2/10
	emergency department	Rarely shown due to low quality score	$3.00	0	70	0.00%	$0.00	$0.00	2.6	2/10

For example, someone who searches on a broadly generic term like *doctor* may not be looking to book an appointment, but instead the definition of one, how to become one, or the name of a location or a school that certifies doctors. When terms like this come up, Google often discourages advertisers from blindly bidding on them and instead suggests refining their keyword lists and targeting an action or behavior — depending on what searchers have done in the past.

When considering your Quality Score, you need to focus on its relevancy. If your ad group has keywords that are closely related to one another, your ad copy matches (see Chapter 4 in this minibook for more on this), and when you take visitors to a related page on your site, you will see better Quality Scores. As it pertains to your keyword list, the best you can do to increase your Quality Scores is to delete poor-performing keywords and keywords with Quality Scores of less than 5 that aren't as important to you.

Quality Score isn't everything. Google won't stop showing your ads altogether if you have a poor Quality Score. You just won't show as often as you'd probably like.

Bing's Quality Score

Bing Ads's Quality Score focuses on your keyword's competitiveness with other advertisers and places much heavier emphasis on the landing page. The three major influencers of Quality Score in Bing Ads are as follows:

✦ **Keyword relevance:** The specific keyword itself and its relevance to other advertisers and ad copy in the Bing Ads marketplace.

✦ **Landing page relevance:** The relevance of your ad and landing page to the searcher's query.

✦ **Landing page user experience:** An aggregate score assigned based on the quality of all the pages on your site. This is subject to your site's compliance with the Microsoft Advertising Bing Ads Editorial Guidelines.

To see your Quality Scores in Bing Ads, follow these steps:

1. **Open an ad group and click the Keywords tab.**

2. **Click the Columns button.**

3. **Select Qual. Score from the drop-down list and click OK.**

4. **In your keyword list, hover your cursor over the tiny arrow underneath the 1-10/10 and click it.**

Your Quality Scores for all three elements display, as shown in Figure 3-7.

Bing Ads's Quality Score is more of an indicator of competitiveness in the market and for landing pages. It doesn't affect ad position or CPC cost.

Status	Qual. score	Match type	Current bid (max. CPC)	Spend ▾	Clicks	Impr.	CTR (%)	Avg. position
Active	10/10 ▸	Broad	1.00	14.79	17	313	5.43	1.65
Active	10 ▸						13.04	1.26
Active	10 ▸						18.60	1.02
Active	10 ▸						16.67	1.28
Active	10/10 ▸	Broad	1.25	6.39	6	43	13.95	3.37
Active	10/10 ▸	Broad	1.50	6.06	6	24	25.00	1.33
Active	9/10 ▸	Broad	0.90	5.88	7	185	3.78	5.05

Quality Score: 10 out of 10 ✕
Keyword relevance: **Good**
Landing page relevance: **No problem**
Landing page user experience: **No problem**
Click here to learn how to improve your quality score.

Figure 3-7:
Bing Ads
Quality
Score
examples.

Contracting Keyword Lists

Just as any keyword list might need expansion, it might need contraction at some point in its career, which is what you find out about in the following sections.

Analyzing underperforming keywords

Using the statistics from conversion tracking or analytics tools, determine which keywords aren't meeting your goals and delete any terms that are driving lots of impressions and costs but aren't performing to your expectations.

If you're not sure about a keyword, pause it and watch what happens. (For help with pausing, see Chapter 2 in this minibook.) See whether your impressions or traffic decrease while your conversions or other statistics improve. Often, a keyword can eat up your budget, leaving little funds for the rest of your keyword list, which could generate more conversions. By removing the budget-eating keyword, you might get your ads to appear more often on better-quality terms, and your money will be better spent.

Deciding when a keyword should be deleted

Deciding when to delete a keyword depends on your industry and goals, but the best approach is the commonsense approach: If a keyword is generating thousands of impressions but no click-throughs, sales, conversions, or good time on site or page view results, something's wrong.

Check your ad copy first. Is the keyword relevant to the ad and vice versa? A poor ad click-through rate (CTR) means that people are searching and seeing the ad but not finding what they're looking for. If the keyword and the ad are relevant to each other — particularly if the keyword in question is in the ad copy or headline — the problem is with the keyword.

If you feel that the keyword should still be in your list, try adjusting the match type. You may be going too broad, and irrelevant searches are driving up your impressions. (For details on match types, read the section "Choosing the right match type," earlier in this chapter.)

In Google AdWords, you can see a Search Query report, which gives you a good idea of what search terms your ad is appearing for. This report is also a good way to find additional negative keywords (refer to Table 3-1, earlier in this chapter) to use in your ad groups and campaigns. This option is located at the ad-group level on the Keywords tab. Click the See Search Terms button and select All to see all the queries that triggered an impression of your ads.

An alternative solution is to turn the term into a *long-tail keyword* (a longer, more specific keyword, usually three words or more) to increase relevancy by adding more qualifying words around it, such as colors, model names, or brands. For example, instead of a short generic term such as *dog collars,* you bid on specific types of dog collars such as *leather dog collars* or *green leather dog collars.*

At this point, if the keyword still isn't performing, it's time to cut it, despite how much you may want to bid on it. Part of good PPC management is accepting that sometimes a keyword or ad isn't relevant to the search engine or the searchers.

Chapter 4: Writing Ads That Earn Clicks and Pay You Back

In This Chapter

✔ **Understanding the structure of ads**

✔ **Writing compelling ads**

✔ **Testing ads**

✔ **Determining which ads are successful**

Ad copy is a two-second chance to catch a searcher's attention, so clearly, your ads need to grab and keep a reader's attention.

In this chapter, you find out how to create pay-per-click (PPC) ads that are not only catchy and retain attention, but also catch the attention of the kinds of users you want to bring to your site and cause desired behaviors, such as purchases, downloads, or page views. (For more information on PPC in general, refer to Chapter 1 in this minibook.)

Working with PPC Ads

A PPC ad is made up of the following elements:

✦ Headline

✦ Body

✦ Display URL

✦ Destination URL

Each component should be constructed carefully and separately, yet all the parts should flow together as a whole. In the following sections, you find tips for writing each part. (For more details, see the section "Writing PPC Ad Copy," later in this chapter.)

Creating the headline

Your headline is the most important part of your ad. Most often, searchers don't read whole ads; they scan the headlines to narrow their choices. Keeping this fact in mind, the best practice for any PPC ad is to use a high-traffic keyword (your most revenue-generating one, if possible) in the headline.

A *revenue-generating keyword* is one that you know brings in results, whether those results are sales, downloads, or sign-ups. A *high-traffic keyword* is one that drives a lot of impressions and clicks but doesn't necessarily result in sales. Some campaigns have a keyword that meets both those criteria. Check your analytics package, if you have one (and if you don't, you should!), or check the past performance of that keyword in the PPC interface to determine what your high-traffic and revenue-generating keywords are. (For details on analytics, see Book III.)

If the keyword you want to use is a longer, more targeted word, simply using the keyword alone as the headline (depending on length) is all you need to do to capture a searcher's attention. Typically, search engines limit a headline to 35 characters.

Also, break up your ad groups so that high-traffic keywords are broken up appropriately, making it easier to write new ads and maintain the ad group (see Chapter 2 in this minibook).

Figure 4-1 shows an example of an ad with a high-traffic keyword as the headline.

Figure 4-1:
Increase
revenue
potential
with a
high-traffic
keyword.

Crafting the body

The body of the ad can be two separate phrases, two separate sentences, or one longer sentence that wraps around from the first line of the ad to the second line. The important thing is to get your message in the body of your ad within the normal 70-character limit.

The search engine you use determines the character limits. Typically, the body must be no more than 70 characters long, including spaces and punctuation marks. Be sure to consult the search engine's editorial guide for its character limits. You don't have a lot of space, so make every word count! For more on writing body copy, see the section "Writing PPC Ad Copy," later in this chapter.

Planning the display URL

Often thought of as the place where you plug in your web address, the display URL can be useful in ad optimization as well. Consider the following points as you write your ads:

✦ Starting the URL with `http://` and starting it with `www.` can often yield very different results. (See the section "Testing for Successful Ads," later in this chapter.)

✦ The same goes for beginning the URL with no prefix at all (`leather dogcollars.com`, for example).

✦ It may be worthwhile to test adding a keyword to the display URL. The URL `www.leatherdogcollars.com/studded`, for example, could drive more traffic than `www.leatherdogcollars.com`.

Choosing the best destination URL

The destination URL is the location where the user arrives after clicking your ad. This URL could be the homepage, a product page, or a specially crafted landing page. The choice of a destination URL can affect your visitor's experience, so keep the following guidelines in mind:

✦ **Deliver on the promise of the display URL.** Most search engines require the destination URL to match the site that's advertised in the display URL. This requirement makes for a much better user experience and prevents advertisers from spamming users. Suppose that you click an ad for women's sandals (`www.womenssandals.com`) but arrive on a site that sells diet pills. Clearly, this site isn't what you were looking for. This practice causes users to distrust PPC ads. (For more on search engines' policies on destination URLs, see Chapter 6 in this minibook.)

✦ **Keep in mind your keyword list and ads.** If the ad is promoting leather dog collars — a very specific product — you should direct the user to a product page offering different types of leather dog collars or a product page for a specific leather dog collar.

A highly targeted group of keywords can perform even better with a combination of the two. An ad group targeting the keywords *studded leather dog collars,* for example, would attract more searchers without selection or color features listed, because the features *(studded* and *leather)* are built into the keyword itself.

✦ **Don't drop users off on the homepage without considering their user experience.** You should direct users to a homepage via a PPC ad only for branded or very general terms. If your keywords are *dog collars,* and dog collars are the only products you sell, the homepage is an acceptable place to send visitors. If you also sell cat and ferret collars, however, you want to select the dog category or product page as your destination URL.

The more that users have to click around and search on your site for what they're looking for, the more likely they are to click the Back button and look elsewhere. You want to direct people to the item or service they're looking for in the fewest clicks possible.

Writing PPC Ad Copy

You have only a few characters to get your point across, so you have to make every word count! Use the keywords in your ad group, use attention-getting language, and follow the editorial guidelines of the search engine for spelling and grammar, and you'll find that writing ads comes naturally. The following sections give you a few methods that make the process even easier.

Follow the benefits/features model

Try following the benefits/features model to start with. The *benefits/features model* is a standard PPC ad practice dictating that within the ad, you state both a benefit to the searcher and a feature of the product or service you're promoting. The first line of the ad states a benefit or feature (on sale, free shipping, in stock), and the second line of the ad states the remaining benefit or feature (colors, sizes, quality).

Traditionally, ads that mention benefits tend to perform better than ads that focus on features. Customers are more drawn to offers of free shipping, in-stock availability, and cash-back offers than they are to ads that focus on selection, styles, and sizes.

Craft the call to action

You also need a clear call to action, where you tell the potential customer what you want him or her to do. Figure 4-2 shows two clear calls to action using the *leather dog collars* keywords. The ad on the left shows the feature of selection, the benefit of price, and the call to action *Shop Dog Collars Online Now.* The ad on the right shows the features of style and color, the benefit of a sale, and the call to action *Shop Now!*.

Figure 4-2:
These ads have different calls to action.

> Leather Dog Collars
> Huge Selection, Great Prices!
> Shop Dog Collars Online Now.
> www.exampledogcollars.com

> Leather Dog Collars
> Sale on Leather Dog Collars.
> Shop Lots of Styles & Colors Now!
> www.exampledogcollars.com

As you write your ads, also keep these points in mind:

✦ If you're writing to attract buyers, drive traffic, or promote a time-sensitive offer, aggressive copy with a clear call to action is your best bet. An exclamation point adds a sense of urgency (*Buy now!* or *On sale!*).

✦ If you're trying to get people to download a white paper or simply to visit your site, you need to be less aggressive and more informative. Give people a reason to visit in your call to action, such as *free download* or *thousands of articles*.

A more aggressive call to action targets an immediate response, such as purchasing a sale item. A more informative call to action is intended for those who are researching or browsing around.

Focus on goals, grammar, and guidelines

You should have a clear picture of what you want your ads to do before you start writing them. For more information on setting PPC goals, refer to Chapter 1 in this minibook.

Be sure to use proper grammar, as the search engines' guidelines dictate. Acceptable uses of punctuation, spelling, and abbreviations vary from search engine to engine, but all search engines require a more formal approach.

Keep these points in mind:

✦ **Spelling counts.** Search engines reject misspellings, which are also unprofessional and spammy-looking.

✦ **Editorial guidelines count.** Often, search engines immediately reject ads that don't follow their guidelines, such as using all capitals (*FREE*) or using numbers or letters in place of words (*2* instead of *to*). An ampersand (&) is okay to use in place of *and,* however. Turn to Chapter 6 in this minibook for more editorial guidelines.

Avoid common mistakes

Avoid making these common mistakes in writing PPC ad copy:

✦ **Neglecting to use your keywords, which are the words and phrases that you're bidding on:** Any search terms from your keyword list that the user types will be boldface in the ad, so make sure to use keywords that will make your ad stand out.

✦ **Using too many keywords:** The body of the ad should be populated with keywords but not stuffed to the point where the entire ad would appear in boldface. This situation could cause *ad blindness* — a condition in which the searcher doesn't even see the ad due to its overly zealous approach. Also, ads crammed with keywords look like spam and are less likely to attract the kind of traffic that you seek.

✦ **Using poor grammar or spelling:** Not only does poor grammar or spelling make your ad look unprofessional (or like it could be some sort of scam), but also, the search engines have editorial guidelines in place that reject ads with gross misspellings. Poor grammar is harder for search engines to catch, but grammatical errors make life much more difficult for users if they have to decipher your ad before clicking it.

✦ **Using too much fragmented text:** Use complete sentences or phrases whenever you can because this kind of language lends authority and authenticity to your offer.

Testing for Successful Ads

Testing ads is extremely important to any PPC campaign. Different industries have very different keyword lists, and users themselves behave in very different ways when conducting searches and completing actions, such as sales or downloads. The ads and keywords you would use for the wedding industry, for example, attract a certain kind of user who displays specific behavior on a website; you'd need to use different ads and keywords for the different type of user in the heavy-machinery industry. To determine which ad will generate the most successful actions for your industry, you need to conduct tests to find your most successful combinations.

Conducting A/B tests

The most basic test and best practice is *A/B split testing,* in which you create two slightly different ads and run them both at the same time, with the same destination URL, splitting the traffic between them.

A/B tests range from simple to complex. The best practice is to start simple and work your way up in terms of complexity. The more *variables* (differences) you have in your ads, the harder it will be to track down the most successful variable. If you run two different ads against each other, one will inevitably outperform the other, but you'll have to do some guesswork about the determining variable.

Viewing example tests

Following are examples of tests you can run, starting with a simple A/B test and working up to more complex variations:

Headline
Ads have different headlines but identical body copy:

Women's Shoes on Sale
Save on Hundreds of Styles!
Shop Women's Shoes Online.
www.womensshoes.com

Sale: Women's Shoes
Save on Hundreds of Styles!
Shop Women's Shoes Online.
www.womensshoes.com

Capitalization of body copy
Ads are identical except for capitalization schemes:

Rebuilt Garbage Disposals
Save on Garbage Disposals Rebuilt
By Experts! Don't Pay Full Price.
www.garbagerebuild.com

Rebuilt Garbage Disposals
Save on garbage disposals rebuilt
by experts! Don't pay full price.
www.garbagerebuild.com

Capitalization of display URL
Ads are identical except for the capitalization of the display URL:

Office Supplies
Shop Pens, Paper, Clips & More!
Ships Same Day, Guaranteed.
www.OfficeSuppliesOnline.com

Office Supplies
Shop Pens, Paper, Clips & More!
Ships Same Day, Guaranteed.
`www.officesuppliesonline.com`

Extended display URL
Ads are identical except that one ad has a longer display URL:

Great Comic Books
Thousands of Back Issues Online!
Shop All Our Comic Books.
`www.joescomicdungeon.com/marvel`

Great Comic Books
Thousands of Back Issues Online!
Shop All Our Comic Books.
`www.joescomicdungeon.com`

Dynamic headline
Ads are identical except that one ad uses a dynamic headline:

`{Keyword: Plant Seeds}`
Hundreds of Flowers, Vegetables &
More! Shop Our Seed Catalog Now.
`www.seedpackets.com`

Plant Seeds
Hundreds of Flowers, Vegetables &
More! Shop Our Seed Catalog Now.
`www.seedpackets.com`

Dynamic ad copy
Ads are identical except that one ad uses dynamic copy:

Organic Makeup
Shop `{Keyword: Organic Lipstick}`
100% Organic & Cruelty Free!
`www.organicmakeups.com`

Organic Makeup
Shop Organic Lipstick.
100% Organic & Cruelty Free!
`www.organicmakeups.com`

Destination URL
Ads are identical except that the URLs go to different locations. One
goes to the homepage and the other to a product page, or one goes to a
landing page and the other to a product page.

In the following sections, you find out how to set up an A/B test in the top two search engines' PPC programs: Google AdWords and Bing Ads. (For more information on these programs, refer to Chapter 2 in this minibook.)

Setting up an A/B test in Google AdWords

By default, Google AdWords is set to *optimize,* so it determines which of your ads is best and shows that ad most often. To do an A/B test, you need to set it to *rotate.*

To set up an A/B test in Google AdWords, follow these steps:

1. **Open the desired campaign, and click the Settings tab.**

2. **Scroll down to Advanced Settings, click Ad Delivery, and then click Edit for Ad Rotation.**

3. **Select the Rotate radio button and click Save.**

Setting up an A/B test in Bing Ads

Bing automatically rotates ads when an ad group contains multiple ads, eventually selecting the ad to show most frequently (based on impressions, clicks, and age of ads). You have no way to change this setting. Every time you change an ad, however, Bing resets the ads to rotate. For more information about changing ads, see the section "Determining When to Change an Ad," later in this chapter.

Using dynamic keyword insertion

Dynamic keyword insertion (DKI) is a great way to write highly targeted ads with minimal effort. This technique inserts the keyword that the searcher used directly into your ad. The trick is composing your ad so that the text makes sense — grammatically and logically — to the searcher when the keyword pops in.

You can use DKI in both headlines and ad copy as long as the searched term is short enough to fit within the character limits.

Be sure to use a keyword from the ad group as placeholder text. Don't leave *Keyword* in as the default, as shown in the following example. Use a keyword from that ad group's list. If the search term doesn't quite match a keyword in your list, the search engine might show your ad with the placeholder keywords instead.

The following two examples illustrate what to do and what not to do. The good example shows *Mother's Day Gifts* as the placeholder keyword, whereas the bad example doesn't have anything after {Keyword: }. As a result, the word *Keyword* could appear to users as a headline.

Good example:

```
{Keyword:Mother's Day Gifts}
```
Mother's Day Gift Sale.
Huge Selection, Free Shipping!
`www.gifthouse.com`

Bad example:

```
{Keyword}
```
Mother's Day Gift Sale.
Huge Selection, Free Shipping!
`www.gifthouse.com`

Format the placeholder keyword as you want the keyword to appear in the ad:

✦ If you use `{keyword}`, the term appears in lowercase.

✦ If you use `{Keyword}`, the first letter of the word is capitalized.

✦ If you use `{KeyWord}`, all initial letters of the search term are capitalized.

Determining When to Change an Ad

Ad testing is a continual process of trying to find the best combination to bring you the most quality traffic. Because your offers might change, and because product availability, seasonality, and prices might fluctuate, you need to change underperforming ads as often as you can.

Measuring success in 100 clicks

A good rule in determining when to delete, pause, or edit an ad is *100 clicks*. Depending on the industry and search volume, it could take a day to reach that number, or it could take a month. If you have low search volume and won't reach 100 clicks in a month, you have a different kind of problem (see Chapter 3 in this minibook).

After you reach the 100-clicks mark, assess your success so far. Is the ad doing what you need it to? Are users clicking through to your site? If not, it's time to change the ad. Add a keyword to the headline or body, change the headline completely, or add a feature or benefit that you didn't use before. (See the section "Conducting A/B tests," earlier in this chapter, for specific examples to test.)

At best, a week is a good minimum test if you want to go by time and not by volume (100 clicks or more), and one month is the longest period you should let a test run. At that point, a clear winner should emerge, and you should edit one of the other ads to begin a new test.

Using goals to make changes

The winning ad can be determined by your goals:

✦ If your goal is revenue, the winner is the ad that generated the most revenue.

✦ If your goal is traffic, the winner is the ad that generated the most clicks.

✦ If your goal is downloads . . . well, you get the idea.

For more information on PPC and goals, see Chapter 1 in this minibook.

Using click-through rate to make changes

Suppose that you're not sure which ad is doing what, and the only statistics you have to go on are clicks, click-through rate (CTR), and cost per click (CPC). In this case, the ad with the better CTR for the lowest CPC is your winner.

Be sure to compare the *ad-serving percentages* — the amount of time that an ad was shown in comparison with the other ads — to ensure that both ads had a fair amount of time. If one ad runs for a week and another ad runs for two weeks, however, the numbers of times the ads were shown will be different. Take that difference into consideration when making your decision.

Don't make the mistake of not checking on your campaigns at least once per week. An editorial issue, bidding issue, or billing issue could knock your campaigns offline and leave you without any ads! To prevent such issues from going unnoticed, set up notifications in your account so that when something does occur that turns your ads off, you receive an e-mail alerting you to that fact. Look in the account settings section of your search engine for e-mail notification preferences.

Using conversion tracking to make changes

One of the best tools to have in your PPC ad-management toolbox is conversion tracking within the PPC search engine's interface. This tool shows you at a glance which ad caused conversions — the goal of your PPC efforts. A *conversion* is completed when the user goes to a specific URL that you determine. A sales conversion, for example, would be a Thank You or receipt page; a download conversion would be a download-complete page. Knowing how much each conversion costs you, and which keywords and ads contributed to those conversions, greatly reduces the time that you spend digging around in analytics programs.

Both Google AdWords and Bing Ads offer this kind of visibility through their PPC interface if you install all the tracking codes on the needed pages. Each set of codes is different, but all sets are supposed to be able to coexist on one page without breaking or interfering with the others.

You must set up conversion tracking separately in each search engine for the process to work properly. (Each search engine offers implementation guides in its help center if you need additional support.)

Follow these tips to set up your conversion tracking in Google AdWords and Bing Ads:

✦ **Google AdWords:** Conversion tracking is a tool on the Tools and Analysis tab under Conversions. Create a new action (such as a sale or purchase), obtain the snippet of code, and place it on the page where completed conversions take place (such a Thank You page). The code must be inserted between the `<card>` and `</card>` tags. See the Google Help Center for a tutorial video and live support via phone and chat.

✦ **Bing Ads:** To use conversion tracking in the Bing Ads interface, open the Tools tab and select Campaign Analytics. Create a goal, name it, and select the options that fit what you want to track. Bing Ads offers the ability to add different steps in the conversion process as well as to set a conversion period. Save and generate the code to be pasted onto the final page of your conversion process. Check out the Bing Ads Help Center for more information by clicking any of the ? icons next to each step in the process. See Figure 4-3.

Figure 4-3:
Bing Ads
Campaign
Analytics
Help &
Options.

Create goal
To define your goal, create each step in the goal, and then click **Save and generate code.**

Goal settings

Goal name: ? Goal #2

Step 1 name: Step 1 Type: Prospect ✕

Conversion step name: ?

Conversion step name ✕

A conversion step tracks a transaction on your website, such as someone making a purchase, signing up for a newsletter, providing account information, and so on.

Revenue and cost track

Track conversion revenues s   h as sales taxes.

Revenue to track: ?

⊙ None
○ Constant
   Value:
○ Variable

Cost to track: ?
☐ Non-advertising costs
☐ Tax
☐ Shipping

A conversion step is one type of step that can be in a goal. Each goal can have up to six steps, but only one of them can be a conversion step. If a goal has other steps, then the conversion step must be the last step.

After you have saved your goal, copy and paste the conversion step code into the page on your website that you want to track. For example, if you want to track when someone makes a purchase, you would paste the conversion step code into your purchase confirmation page.

▸ **Wait, there's more…**

▸ **Support**

Conversion period ?

The conversion period is the   lt in a completed goal.

Number of days: 7

Chapter 5: Budgeting and Bidding on Keywords

In This Chapter

✔ **Setting your PPC budget**

✔ **Deciding what to spend per keyword**

✔ **Managing the bidding process**

✔ **Targeting your spending by industry and niche**

This chapter talks about the most important aspect of your pay-per-click (PPC) account: money. The amount you spend and how you spend it determine the overall outcome of your campaigns — unless, of course, you have an unlimited budget and don't need to see a positive return on your investment. Very few marketers fall within that category, though.

The very first question you should ask yourself is, "How much can I spend?" After you establish how much you can spend, you can really expand and optimize your account.

In this chapter, you decide where to set your daily budgets and how much to bid on a per-keyword basis. Depending on your industry, these costs can vary greatly, but if you follow the general rules of thumb in this chapter, you'll be managing your campaign costs like a pro.

Determining Your PPC Budget

Establish your PPC marketing budget with the assumption that you might not make it all back. Any get-rich-quick promises or pitches that guarantee that you'll quadruple your return on investment are just as fishy as they sound. Not all industries, products, or services flourish in PPC. Industries that sell equipment retailing for thousands of dollars might have a much harder time than a site that sells shoes, for example. Those types of industries should consider PPC to be a tool for gathering leads for sales and increasing brand awareness. Building your campaigns smartly and capping the amount you spend per day with careful budgeting, however, ensures that you get the most bang for your buck.

Researching your assets

To determine your PPC marketing budget, you need to do some research on your assets. Decide exactly how much you want to dedicate to PPC marketing, and stick to that budget to start with. If the campaigns are going very successfully for you, reevaluate your budgets and reinvest some of that success, if necessary. If you aren't doing well, consider making edits to your campaigns (such as pausing underperforming ad groups or keywords) before you turn everything off and call it quits. Whichever path you choose, make sure that your business has the money to spend and won't be in dire need if the investment isn't returned.

Deciding the reach of your budget

You need to determine how much you want to spend per day and per campaign. The best practice is to set budgets at the campaign level per day rather than rely on a monthly budget. If you rely on a monthly budget, the search engine is stretching — and at some points, even stopping — the display of your ads to stay within that monthly budget limit. A daily budget does the same thing, but on a much more granular and flexible level. By budgeting one day at a time, you ensure that your campaign starts each day with the same amount of funds. By contrast, if you're on a monthly budget, depending on how fast clicks accumulate, you could be out of money before the end of the month and have no ads showing.

Google AdWords and Bing Ads have both monthly and daily spending limits; you can tell the search engine the absolute most you want to spend per day or per month. If you choose a monthly account budget, the search engine simply takes the amount you enter and divides it among the days of the month, evenly distributing funds to your campaigns or ad groups. If you choose to do daily budgeting instead, the search engines add up all the campaign budgets and show the total cost of all your campaign budgets combined per day within the dashboard interface.

Plan on setting an overall monthly amount to spend because a month gives you enough time to gather the data you need and buy the necessary ad impressions, but use daily budget features on the campaign level.

Whichever style of budget you choose, stick to it across all your campaigns. Setting one campaign to daily and another to monthly is a recipe for confusion, making it very easy for you to overspend.

Considering ad schedules

You want to make sure that your ads are showing on the necessary days and at the necessary times. Your industry might have more actual sales at the end of the month, when potential customers get paid, for example. But earlier in the month, those potential customers were shopping around, saw your ad, and visited your site. They could return to your site later to make a purchase, arriving via a bookmark or a copied link, or they might enter another similar search term and look for the ad, particularly if you're often in the first or second ad spot. For this reason, you want to make sure that your budget fits your ad-serving needs so that when people search for your products or services, your ads are showing for those searches. See the section "Bidding by Day and Time," later in this chapter, for more on this.

Setting and sticking to your budget

After you figure out how much you can spend, stick to that number. PPC is a little like gambling; you shouldn't assume that you're going to "win" big every time. Determine what you can spend, assume that you won't make your investment back — and never go back into your savings for more money if you don't! If what you tried didn't work and you want to try again, change your account through optimization techniques (discussed throughout this minibook, such as ad copyedits in Chapter 4) before spending more money.

For further help with determining what your marketing budget should be, consult *AdWords For Dummies,* by Howie Jacobson (published by John Wiley & Sons).

Entering Your Budget in the Top Two Search Engines

If you already have an account with Google AdWords or Bing Ads, the search engine should have required you to enter a campaign budget during account setup. (For help with the setup process, see Chapter 2 in this minibook.) Just follow the steps in the following sections to set or adjust your budget.

Setting a budget in Google AdWords

To set your budget in Google AdWords, follow these steps:

1. **Log in to your AdWords account.**

2. **On the Campaigns tab, click the dollar/day number under the budget column.**

3. **Enter the new budget amount and click Save (see Figure 5-1).**

   You can also edit the amount of your daily budget for a campaign on the Settings tab.

Figure 5-1:
Set a
Google
AdWords
budget.

☐	⦿	Campaign #3	$100.00/day	Ended	0	0	0.00%
☐	⦿	Campaign #4	$ 10.00 per day Save Cancel				0%
☐	⦿	Campaign #6	Actual daily spend may vary. ⑦				0%
☐	⦿	Campaign #7	$2.00/day	Eligible	0	0	0.00%

4. **In the Delivery Method section on the Settings tab of a campaign, choose the speed at which you want your ads to appear by clicking the plus box:**

   • *Standard* delivery is selected by default, and means that Google will adjust impressions throughout the day to meet the budget that you just entered.

   • *Accelerated delivery* means Google will show your ad continuously until the budget you entered is spent, unless you're using Conversion Optimizer or enhanced CPC bidding.

Using the Accelerated delivery method can cause your budget to run out very quickly or not at all. If you choose this option, be sure to check in on your campaign regularly to monitor the speed of the spending.

Google also offers a Manager Defined Spend feature, which allows you to set and track a budget efficiently from a dashboard. To use this feature, you must be managing several accounts through a My Client Center and must be on invoicing terms with Google. For more information on this feature, see the AdWords Help Center (http://support.google.com/adwords/?hl=en).

Setting a budget in Bing Ads

To set your campaign budget in Bing Ads, follow these steps:

1. **Log in to your Bing Ads account, and click the Campaigns tab.**

2. **Select the campaign for which you want to edit the budget, and click in the box under the budget column next to the campaign that you want to edit.**

3. **Enter the new budget and click the Save button.**

You can also edit a campaign budget in the settings of the specific campaign or from the campaigns tab. Follow these steps:

1. **Open the campaign and click the Edit Your Campaign Settings link.**

2. **In the General Settings section of the page, enter the desired budget amount in the Campaign Budget (USD) text box and choose a duration (Daily or Monthly) from the drop-down menu.**

3. **Click Daily Budget Options to choose the type of daily budget from the drop-down menu.**

   If you choose Monthly, be advised that this will also change the delivery rate of your ads to accelerated. Here's the difference between standard and accelerated:

   - *Standard* (see Figure 5-2) spreads your budget over the entire day.

   - *Accelerated* shows your ads repeatedly until the ads have gotten enough clicks to eat through the entire budget. This setting means that you could be out of money in two hours or, on the flip side, generate a lot of impressions but never hit the budget cap, depending on the volume and popularity of your industry and keywords.

4. **Click Save.**

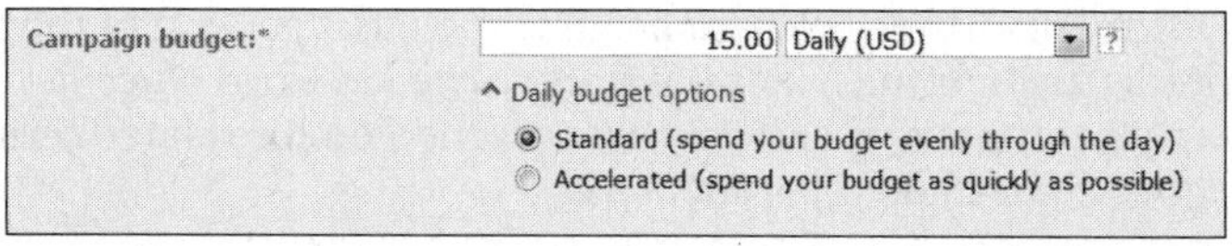

Figure 5-2:
Set a Bing
Ads budget.

| Campaign budget:* | | 15.00 | Daily (USD) | ▾ | ? |

⌃ Daily budget options

◉ Standard (spend your budget evenly through the day)
○ Accelerated (spend your budget as quickly as possible)

Budgeting by Campaign

Only you can tell a search engine how much per day you want to spend and where you want to spend it. If you have a budget of $3,000 per month, which works out to $100 per day, you need to divide that $100 among your campaigns.

All campaigns are unique, with different ad groups and different budget requirements. Some just have more expensive keywords, more traffic, or less traffic than others. You need to assess each campaign individually by those same measurements to determine how much to budget for each one.

Estimating traffic

Good old common sense plays a major part in predicting whether a campaign will be a high-traffic campaign. The more generic your keywords are, the more popular they'll be — and the more times your ads will show up. You can find some guidelines in the section "Deciding what to bid," later in this chapter.

When you're starting a new campaign, use the search engines' free traffic-estimation tools (see Chapter 7 in this minibook) to generate a predicted number of impressions and clicks for the keywords in your ad groups. If the search engine is predicting a lot of clicks for a campaign, you'll want to set a higher budget for it than you would for a campaign that isn't expected to receive a lot of clicks.

Also, run a search for some of your keywords in the search engine and see how many search results and competitor ads appear. If a keyword generates a full page of relevant ads, it's popular!

Setting an example campaign budget

Every single campaign has different factors that influence how much it spends and when — and even those factors vary from day to day. Unfortunately, only you can tell where to put your money. But to help you better understand how to set budgets by campaign, this section outlines an example account to guide you through the process.

In this example, you sell office-cubicle furniture through three campaigns:

✦ **Office Furniture:** This campaign is the most generic of the three and is predicted to bring in a lot of traffic. The keyword *office furniture* is also highly competitive and is often searched on for related terms such as *desks, chairs,* and *filing cabinets.*

✦ **Cubicles:** This campaign also generates a fair share of traffic, but the keyword is more targeted and very relevant to what you're selling.

✦ **Panel Systems:** This campaign is a much lower-traffic campaign than the others, but the keyword is very highly targeted. People who are searching for *panel systems* are familiar with the fact that this keyword is an industry term and, therefore, are knowledgeable about the product.

If you have $100 per day to spend, here's how much each campaign will receive:

✦ **Office Furniture: $15**

Why: The keyword *office furniture,* although relevant, isn't as relevant as it could be to what you're selling. Keywords related to this phrase will bring in a lot of searches but not a lot of conversions, as people looking for items other than cubicles will click the ads. This campaign is also more expensive than the others because you don't offer office furniture other than cubicles, and other, more-relevant vendors that also sell office furniture are bidding on these keywords, too.

✦ **Cubicles: $60**

> *Why:* The keyword *cubicles* is going to be your No. 1 source of conversions. It describes what you sell, it's highly relevant, and it's in a popular set of search terms. Your ads will show up often, and you'll receive a better cost-per-click (CPC) price because of the relevancy.

✦ **Panel Systems: $25**

> *Why: Panel systems* may be a low-volume keyword, but it's highly relevant to your campaign. By targeting searchers who are familiar with industry terms, you're targeting educated customers who already know what they want. You're simply getting your products out in front of them. The clicks you pay for in this campaign are going to be high-quality clicks that create a better return on your investment.

Bidding on Keywords

One of most complex aspects of PPC management is bid management. Most search engines require you to set your bids when you set up an ad group.

Bids are set at two levels:

✦ **Ad-group level:** At the ad-group level, you must set a maximum bid — the largest amount that you're willing to pay for a single click. You may not pay that actual amount, but be prepared to do so.

✦ **Keyword level:** A keyword-level bid is the maximum CPC you're willing to pay for that single keyword.

> By default, all keywords receive the ad group's maximum CPC. If you want to change the amount you're bidding on a single keyword, see Chapter 3 in this minibook to edit your keyword bids in the Big Three search engines.

Knowing how CPC is determined

Cost per click (CPC) is determined by the search engines based on their own algorithms. These algorithms calculate various factors to determine the minimum bid for a given keyword, the smallest amount that the search engine will charge for that keyword, and the rate you pay for it.

Search engines keep their algorithms as closely guarded secrets so that advertisers can't exploit or cheat the system. Google and Bing, however, use several known factors to calculate CPC:

Book IV
Chapter 5

Budgeting and Bidding on Keywords

✦ Relevancy of the keyword to your ad

✦ Relevancy of the search query to your keyword

✦ Destination URL (where the ad takes the searcher)

✦ Daily budget amount

✦ Keyword bid amount

✦ Amount of competition

✦ Relevancy of the competitors for that keyword compared with you

✦ Quality score, which is awarded by the search engine (see Chapter 3 of this minibook)

Deciding what to bid

When you select your keywords or use keyword tools to add new ones (see Chapter 3 in this minibook), most search engines show you an estimated number of searches, CPC, and cost per day for each keyword. Those estimates are valuable tools for determining your maximum CPC. For more information on predicting a keyword's CPC through traffic-estimation tools, see Chapter 7 in this minibook.

A best practice in setting a maximum bid for an ad group is to start high and lower that bid as necessary. This practice gives you a running start with the search engine. Your ad will appear quickly and often, giving you results much sooner than if you start low and try to work your way up. This technique also places your ads in good positions on the results page; a higher position on the page means increased visibility to searchers.

Bidding by Day and Time

Each industry is unique and has a unique web-traffic pattern. Some days of the week might be better in one business segment than in another, or some times of the day might be better — or a combination of both. For this reason, it might be in your best interest to set your campaigns up to run and spend more or less on specific days of the week or hours of the day.

Suppose that (as in most commercial-goods businesses) your company's traffic and sales are strongest during the week and decrease over the weekend. You want to set up your campaigns to reflect those traffic patterns so that when customers are online looking for you, they can find your ads quickly and easily, and you don't have to stretch your budget over gaps of time that bring you poorer-quality traffic.

The following sections discuss ad scheduling in Google AdWords and Bing Ads.

Automated bidding options

Google AdWords has a few automated options that set and adjust bids for you based on performance, click-through rate, budget, and impressions:

- ✔ **Maximum CPC Bidding:** This setting (the default) means that you're setting the maximum CPC manually, using the amount that you entered when you set up the ad group.

- ✔ **Automatic Bidding:** This setting (see the top figure) bases bidding on maximizing your budget to get as many clicks as possible. You enter your max CPC limit for that campaign, and Google manages your bids to target that amount as the ceiling while staying within the daily budget. The max CPC amount is optional: If you leave the check box deselected, AdWords uses the daily budget amount to bid for you throughout the day. This is a good option if you have little time to maintain your accounts and have a set budget that must be spent for traffic generation.

- ✔ **Enhanced CPC:** This setting dynamically adjusts your max CPC up and down for each impression using conversion data

working toward an overall CPA (cost-per-acquisition) goal. You need to have conversion tracking in AdWords enabled to use this feature. While it won't exceed your daily campaign budget, the average CPC could swing as much as 30 percent higher over the max CPC you set at the ad group level. This option is best if you have a flow of regular conversions, have specific CPA goals, and are focusing on overall return and not concerned as much with the CPC amount.

- ✔ **Conversion Optimizer:** When you choose this option (see the bottom figure), you specify the maximum amount that you want to pay for a conversion or your CPA amount. You must have conversion tracking in AdWords enabled to use this feature. Google AdWords will make a recommendation of what it thinks your CPA bid should be based on data already accumulated in the account. This option is best if you have a goal CPA already in mind and have a regular flow of conversions happening already in the campaign prior to activation.

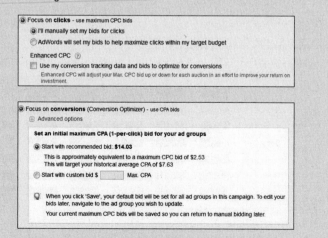

Scheduling options in Google AdWords

Google AdWords' Ad Scheduling option is the most complex system for adjusting your campaign costs to different traffic patterns. You'll find this tool on the campaign settings page of each of your campaigns. By default, all campaigns are set to show your ads every day, all day, until the budget is depleted.

Google allows you to choose whether your ads run every day of the week, or just on weekdays or weekends. You can also choose the times of day when those ads run.

Basic ad scheduling

To enable basic ad scheduling in Google, follow the steps in this section. If you're using an automatic bidding method, such as enhanced CPC, this feature is unavailable to you.

1. **Open the campaign for which you want to enable this feature, and click the Settings tab.**

2. **Scroll down to the Advanced Settings section.**

3. **In the Schedule section, click the blue Edit link next to "Show ads all days and hours."**

   You'll see a chart that shows when your ads are currently scheduled to run (see Figure 5-3) as well as the time zone that your account is in. Make sure to keep that in mind when choosing hours of the day to run ads. A start time of 8 a.m. EST would be 5 a.m. PST, and an end time of 5 p.m. EST would turn ads off on the West Coast at 2 p.m. PST.

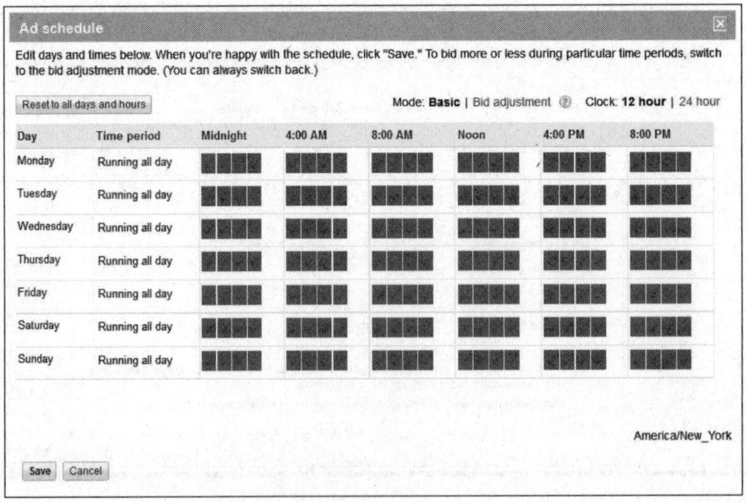

Figure 5-3: Check when your ads are scheduled to run.

4. **Next to the day you want to change the ad schedule for, click the times you want the ad to run.**

   To utilize this schedule for other days, click the Copy button at the bottom of the scheduling box and select either All Days or All Weekdays. If you're running ads on the weekend, you don't have the option to copy the schedule to weekdays; however you can copy your preferred schedule to the entire weekend.

5. **Click the Save button.**

   You return to the Edit Campaign Settings page.

Advanced ad scheduling

Advanced ad scheduling (see Figure 5-4) allows to you set hours of the day and incremental bids for those hours. Incremental bidding is set on a scale of 100 percent; you can raise or lower your bids during different hours of the day. Google AdWords allows you to bid both higher and lower than 100 percent, whereas Bing Ads only allows you to bid in excess of 100 percent in increments of 10 percent.

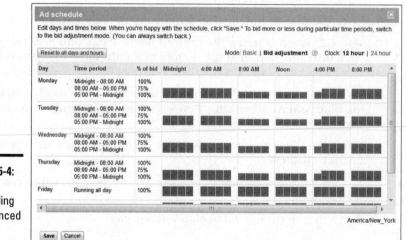

Figure 5-4: Ad scheduling in advanced mode.

Book IV Chapter 5

Budgeting and Bidding on Keywords

Suppose that you want your campaigns to run from 8 a.m. to 8 p.m., and you receive most of your traffic between 11 a.m. and 1 p.m. You can set your account so that Google or Bing automatically increases the amount that you're bidding between those hours to 110 percent, which means that Google or Bing takes all the set bids in that campaign and increases them by 10 percent between 11 a.m. and 1 p.m. You don't see the bids change physically; the amount that you specified as your maximum CPC still appears. The only place you see a difference is in the amount of clicks billed.

In addition, you can not only set your bids to increase from 11 a.m. to 1 p.m., but you can also determine the days of the week when incremental bidding takes place. If Mondays, Tuesdays, and Thursdays are your best revenue-generating days, you can apply that strategy to only those days, and leave the bid amount for Wednesdays and Fridays from 8 a.m. to 8 p.m. at 100 percent. Or on Google AdWords, you can decrease the bids for off days or off hours by choosing an amount less than 100 percent. Entering 90 percent, for example, tells Google that during those hours, you want to bid 10 percent less than your maximum CPC setting.

If you edit your maximum CPC setting later, take this feature into account if you have it enabled!

To set up advanced ad scheduling, follow these steps:

1. **Open the campaign for which you want to enable this feature, and click the Settings tab.**

2. **Scroll down to the Advanced Settings section.**

3. **In the Ad Scheduling section, click Edit.**

4. **Click the blue Bid Adjustment link.**

5. **Click the time period or % of bid next to the day that you want to edit.**

6. **When finished entering the desired times of day and percentages, click the Copy button at the bottom of the Running dialog box to copy these same days and times to other days of the week if desired.**

7. **(Optional) Add multiple blocks of time in the same day by clicking the blue Add Another Time Period link to enter another block of time and/or percentages.**

8. **When the times and percentages for each day are set up to your satisfaction, click OK.**

9. **Review your new ad schedule and click the Save button to commit the changes.**

    You return to the Edit Campaign Settings page.

These settings cannot be copied to other campaigns in the web interface; you must go into each existing campaign and edit the settings manually. You can copy them using the Google AdWords Editor, however. For more on this, see Chapter 7 in this minibook.

Know what schedule you want to implement before you get started; the operation may time out on you. Don't dilly-dally when setting up ad scheduling.

Scheduling options in Bing Ads

Bing allows you to target your customers by days of the week and by specific blocks of time but also at the campaign and ad group levels (see Figure 5-5). If you enable ad scheduling for an ad group that is also enabled at the campaign level, the ad group settings will take priority. Bing Ads also offers demographic bidding, which you can find out about in Chapter 7 of this minibook.

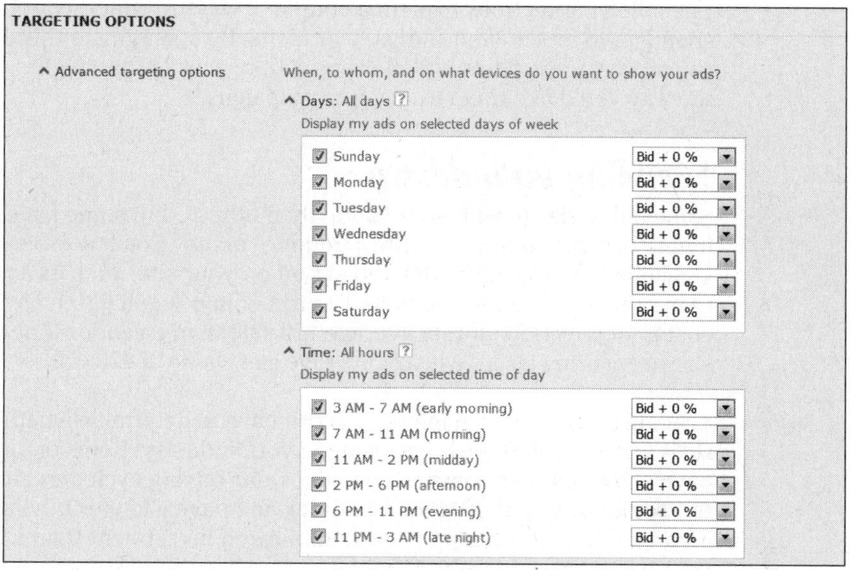

Figure 5-5: Bing Ads ad scheduling.

To set up ad scheduling in Bing, follow these steps:

1. **Open the campaign or ad group, and click the Edit Your Ad Group Settings link.**

2. **In the Targeting Options section, click the Days link to edit for specific days.**

3. **In the Available list, select the days of the week when you want your ads to appear using the check boxes, as shown in Figure 5-5.**

4. **Also in the Targeting Options section, click the Time link to edit for specific blocks of available times to show your ads using the check boxes.**

5. **Click the Save button.**

You can set incremental bids on Bing Ads for both time *and* day. Bing Ads aggregates these amounts, so if you do a 10 percent increase for Mondays and a 10 percent increase for the hours of 7 a.m.–11 a.m., your bids will be increased by 20 percent on Mondays during the hours of 7 a.m. to 11 a.m.!

Tailoring Your Spending

The following sections explain a couple of ways in which you can tailor your spending to match your industry or niche. By spending in these areas, you can avoid excess costs and overpopular keywords that might not perform the way you'd like them to in your campaigns.

Spending by industry

Some industries have higher traffic than others, and some have a much higher *cost per conversion* (the amount of money you have to spend to get someone to perform the desired action on your site, such as a purchase) than others. A vendor that sells T-shirts online is going to have a much lower cost per conversion for its average $20 sale than a vendor that sells particle size–measuring lasers with an average sale value of $20,000.

Keeping this example in mind, now you have to determine whether PPC is the right way for you to be advertising in your industry. Items or services that have a low cost per conversion and a short buying cycle tend to fare better than industries that are more complex and have a longer buying cycle. Clearly, a T-shirt is a much less complicated investment than a laser, and your budget should reflect that fact.

Spending by niche

You can find the proverbial PPC gold mine if you can carve out a nice niche for yourself. The niche needs to be highly relevant to your keywords, ads, and account structure, and must have low competition — and your site or landing page must exemplify the same niche.

Suppose that you sell Christmas ornaments, which are very popular items in general. Think about what kinds of ornaments you sell. Is a type or brand exclusive to your company? Do you sell a style that's unique or unusual?

Perhaps you have a collection of marine mammal Christmas ornaments — in particular, sea otter ornaments. That product is unusual, so related keywords will come up in search queries often, which makes them highly relevant to your product.

TIP

To maximize a niche like this, create a separate ad group for keywords associated with *sea otter ornaments* and *sea otter Christmas* in a broad match (refer to Chapter 3 in this minibook), create ads that use the same keywords (see Chapter 4 in this minibook), and set a modest daily budget — say, $10, with a maximum CPC of 50¢. This daily budget should exceed the amount of clicks that you would accumulate in a day — that is to say, you'll rarely reach the spending limit for this daily budget. The bids should be set high enough that your ads consistently show up in the first two ad positions.

Make your ad's landing page the product page for the sea otter ornaments, and if you don't have a dedicated page for that product, select a product page offering several items related to the niche. This scenario is a great example of creating and exploiting a niche.

For more information on using budget, bidding, and keyword tools, see Chapter 7 in this minibook.

Chapter 6: Legally Speaking: PPC and the Law

In This Chapter

✔ Sticking to editorial guidelines for ads and keywords

✔ Following trademark and copyright regulations

✔ Fighting click fraud

*O*ne of the most common pitfalls of pay-per-click (PPC) management to which new users fall victim is getting ads returned from search engines because of editorial guidelines. Sometimes, the problem is simply a matter of trying to use a shortcut such as an ampersand (&) instead of *and* or *2* instead of *to.* But in some cases, the problem is more serious, such as a copyright or trademark infringement.

This chapter walks you through the most common editorial issues you're likely to run into and shows you how to avoid copyright or trademark errors. At the end of the chapter, you discover about click fraud.

Understanding Editorial Guidelines

Editorial guidelines are always set forth by the search engine or the distributor of PPC ads, so many variations exist. The major search engines have similar rules and regulations that are fairly easy to follow, but if you run into issues or have questions, consult the help center for that particular engine.

Ad editorial guidelines

Most search engines are similar in their requirements for the format, language, and grammar of an ad. If you're using PPC honestly and writing ads that advertise what you're selling, you shouldn't have a problem.

Here are the most common rules to follow:

✦ **Watch your language.** Don't use sexually explicit or offensive language, such as swearing.

✦ **Don't make false claims.** One example of a false claim is offering a price or promotion in the ad but not making that same offer on the landing page. Another example is saying that you're "No. 1" or "the cheapest" without being able to prove your claim.

Proving your claim requires verification by a third party. See your search engine's help center for its specific policy on this issue. Google AdWords, for example, allows you to make such a statement as long as you can show — through a link to or a direct quote from an independent third party — that your claim is true. This information must be available within one or two clicks of the destination URL for the PPC ad.

✦ **Keep the ad copy clean.** Avoid using all capital letters for anything but acronyms (FREE, BUY NOW), excessive punctuation (Save Now!!!!), or repetition beyond two words (Buy, Buy, Buy!).

✦ **Mind your grammar.** Use proper grammar. Sentences and phrases must be logical and must make sense.

✦ **Use standard typography.** Things *not* to do include using inappropriate spacing (Buy S h o e s!) and using numbers or symbols as words (Deals 4 U here, Not 2 be 4gotten!).

✦ **Don't use generic *click* calls to action.** Examples include text such as *Click here* and *Click this ad*.

If you simply craft your ad to sell what you're selling without trying to be gimmicky or spammy, you'll be just fine. See Figure 6-1 for an example ad with three editorial violations: *4* instead of *for,* all caps (*ONLINE*), and an extra exclamation point.

Figure 6-1:
This ad contains three editorial violations.

All in One Reference
Internet Marketing Desk Reference!!
4 Dummies! Shop ONLINE Now.
aio.marketing.dummies.com

Most search engines will catch a big editorial issue; they display an error message telling you what the issue is and preventing you from saving the ad (see Figure 6-2). If the ad contains multiple or more subtle errors, the search engine allows you to save the ad but rejects it on further review. The engine stops running the ad and sends a notification e-mail to the address associated with the account.

If you receive an error message and feel that the ad doesn't contain an error or that the search engine is mistaken, you can request an exception, which allows you to enter a short explanation of the situation and run your ad for the time being. Even though the search engine will review the ad again, it may still reject the ad if it doesn't accept the reason you're requesting the exception. If the Request an Exception dialog box does not appear, you may not request an exception online. You will need the assistance of a search engine representative to get your ad copy through.

Figure 6-2:
A Google AdWords error message for an ad that violates editorial guidelines.

Headline:	All in One Reference	Max 25 characters
Description line 1:	Internet Marketing Desk Reference!!	Max 35 characters

❶ **Punctuation - nonstandard punctuation** ⓘ
Google policy does not permit excessive or unnecessary punctuation or symbols, or use of nonstandard punctuation, including tildes (~), asterisks (*),and vertical rules (|). Please see our full policy.
▸ Request an exception

❷ **Punctuation - nonstandard punctuation** ⓘ
Google policy does not permit excessive or unnecessary punctuation or symbols, or use of nonstandard punctuation, including tildes (~), asterisks (*),and vertical rules (|). Please see our full policy.
▸ Request an exception

Description line 2:	4 Dummies. Shop ONLINE Now.	Max 35 characters
Display URL: ⓘ	http:// aio.marketing.dummies.com	Max 35 characters
Destination URL: ⓘ	http:// ▾ aio.marketing.dummies.com	Max 1024 characters

Keyword list guidelines

Building your keyword list (refer to Chapter 3 of this minibook) can be a difficult task, especially because you have to be aware of editorial guidelines as well.

Most of the guidelines apply directly to the ads that you're building with your keywords, so if you follow those guidelines (see the preceding section), you should have minimal issues with your keyword lists.

In keyword lists, you can bid on trademarked and copyrighted terms (see the section "Trademark and copyright guidelines," later in this chapter) but with some caveats. If you're selling or promoting drugs (prescription or otherwise), pornography, counterfeited items, gambling, fireworks, fake documents, weapons, or scams, you won't be allowed to add those keywords to your keyword list. If you try, an error message should appear, pointing out the specific problem.

The best practice for keyword lists is to follow the general guidelines of the search engine. If you can't sell a product online, you won't be able to purchase keywords for it, either.

Display and destination URL guidelines

The display URL, which is listed inside the ad below your ad copy, usually is just long enough for the main URL of the website you're advertising. (See Chapter 4 of this minibook for information on optimizing your display URLs.) Although it's representative of your site's address, it may not be the same as the destination URL — the address of the page you're sending visitors to. The destination URL, which can be much longer than the display URL, leaves lots of room for you to send visitors deep within your site and even to append a tracking code, if necessary.

A *tracking code* is a piece of code that you can paste onto the end of the destination URL for a PPC ad. This code doesn't hurt or influence anything in the ad, but it helps tell your analytics package (if you have one) where the visitor came from, on what keyword, and on which ad. Depending on the analytics package you selected, this code may not be necessary; consult the software's help system or representative for information about tracking PPC ads in different search engines.

Display URLs

For your display URL to comply with search engine guidelines, it must have a domain extension (such as `.com`, `.net`, or `.edu`) and must be somewhere on the site you're advertising. If you use the display URL `www.shoesonline.com`, for example, users must be taken to that site when they click your ad — not to any other site (such as `www.fraudschemes.com`).

Destination URLs

A destination URL must work. When users click the ad, they should be taken to the listed URL, not to an error or Page Not Found page.

The destination can't be under construction; it must be a web page with content ready for people to view. It also must be a working website — not an image, a video, a document, or an additional URL that requires users to open another application or program to go any farther on your site.

Trademark and copyright guidelines

Before considering trademarks and copyrights, you should know the difference between the two:

+ **Trademarks:** A *trademark* can be a word, logo, phrase, or image that people or companies own to represent themselves or their businesses. Trademarks are owned at country level, so if you want to use a trademarked term to advertise in several countries, you have to get permission for each country. You can get this permission with the help of the search engine you're trying to advertise with. See each search engine's help center section on trademarks, which should outline that search engine's process for receiving permission to use trademarked terms.

+ **Copyrights:** A *copyright* applies to material (such as a book, musical composition, or artwork) that belongs to its creator (such as the author, musician, or artist).

You need to know how to work with trademark and copyright issues if you're a reseller of items (shoes, makeup, books, or CDs, for example), a parts or replacement parts seller, or an informative site (such as for product reviews). If you fall under any of those three categories, you may use trademarked terms in your ad copy, provided that you use keywords in a descriptive or generic way (this means that you cannot claim to be the original site or trademark owner) in your ad copy and the landing page that searchers are brought to clearly sells the goods or services corresponding to those keywords.

For replacements parts, you must also have a landing page that clearly sells (or facilitates) the goods or services for that trademark. Informational sites must have informative details about the specific goods or services on the landing page for the corresponding keywords.

If none of those situations applies to you, you can't use the names of the specific trademarks in your ads without permission. You can still bid on the trademarked terms as keywords, but the keyword can't appear in your ads. If it does, the search engine could disapprove your ad or someone could even file a complaint against you.

This restriction works both ways, however. If you find an advertiser using your trademark in an ad improperly, you can file a complaint with the search engine. Often, the search engine will tell you to contact the advertiser directly first; the search engine may not mediate or participate in disputes such as this without the filed complaint. If contacting the person or company that's using your trademark isn't successful, you should file the complaint online through the search engine's help center. Filing a complaint forces the search engine to look into the issue further and shut down the offending advertiser's ads.

If you have a copyright issue, the same procedure applies. Contact the advertiser directly and ask him or her to cease. Check the search engine's help center for specific details on filing a copyright or trademark complaint. When the complaint is on file with the search engine, someone there will look into the issue further and possibly stop the offending advertiser from using your copyright. The search engine will also add you to its ever-growing database of copyrights, and if any future violations occur, you'll already have a history on file.

If you do have permission to use a trademark as a reseller from the trademark owner, have the owner "white-list" you when possible. This means that you are on file with the search engine as someone who has permission to use that trademark. That is something that you will need to work out with the trademark owner independently of the search engine.

Dynamic keyword insertion with trademarks and copyrights

Dynamic keyword insertion is a great tool — a neat way to generate custom ads based on what the user is searching for. Dynamic insertion involves a placeholder phrase in the headline or ad copy that's populated by the search term that the user typed, provided that the search term matches a keyword in your keyword list. (See Chapter 4 of this minibook for more information on this tool.)

Warning: If you're using dynamic insertion and include copyrighted or trademarked terms in your keyword list, your ad could be populated with those keywords. Unless you fall under one of the three allowed situations, don't use dynamic insertion in conjunction with trademarked or copyrighted keywords. (Refer to the section "Trademark and copyright guidelines," earlier in this chapter.) You can still bid on them as keywords; you just can't have the terms show up within the ad.

Suppose that you're reselling Avon makeup products, and one of your keywords is *avon makeup.*

In this case, the headline would read Avon Makeup, which includes a trademarked term. Unless you are an authorized reseller, you have to refrain from using dynamic insertion with this particular keyword list. (For information on exceptions, refer to the section "Ad editorial guidelines," earlier in this chapter.)

Dealing with Click Fraud

All PPC search engines have some level of *click fraud,* which occurs when a person, computer, or automated program clicks an ad for malicious purposes. The actual amount that occurs on a day-to-day basis is an ongoing debate in the PPC industry. For the purposes of your campaigns, simply keep an eye out for potential fraud, and call or e-mail the search engine if you suspect that click fraud has occurred so that representatives can look into the situation further.

Recognizing click fraud

Some programs go out on the Internet and click ads repeatedly, eating up advertisers' budgets and driving up their clicks with no intention of being honest users who are searching for or researching something specific. Each search engine has ways of dealing with obvious and/or massive click-fraud issues. A search engine will credit your account for whatever funds it feels were spent on fraudulent clicks.

Detecting click fraud

The best way to detect click fraud is to check your server logs and study IP addresses and patterns in the clicks to your site. If you see several hundred visits coming from the same IP address within a few hours or minutes, you could be experiencing click fraud.

Another way to detect click fraud is to examine where in the world your clicks are coming from. If they're coming from a non-English–speaking country or from a country you don't advertise or sell to, and a lot of activity is going on, click fraud may be going on. If your campaigns are correctly geotargeted (set to display only in specific countries; see Chapter 7 of this minibook), this situation shouldn't be much of a problem. You can combat it further by implementing ad scheduling — not showing ads outside the time zones in which you want to advertise. For details on ad scheduling, refer to Chapter 5 of this minibook.

All sorts of programs have been developed to detect and prevent click fraud. If you decide to invest in one of these programs, be sure to do a lot of research and participate in live demonstrations before signing up. Click fraud–detection programs can be pricey, but they might be worth the investment if you're working with a large number of keywords and ads. If you're just starting out or dabbling in PPC, you're not likely to need these programs.

Each search engine that serves PPC ads also has some sort of click fraud–detection program in place. Check for lines in your billing details titled something like "Service Adjustment," "Free Clicks," or "Click Quality Adjustment." If you see a credit to your account for a couple of dollars or a few cents, the search engine determined that some of the clicks your ads received were not legitimate clicks and credited you the amount of clicks it found to be fraudulent.

Search engines are continually tightening and improving their methods for detecting these activities, even though they report a much lower percentage of fraudulent clicks than the companies that create click fraud–detecting programs do. Each side has a deeply vested interest, and any release of specific detection information would provide assistance to the perpetrators of click fraud.

Reporting click fraud

Don't hesitate to call the customer service department of the search engine in which you're experiencing the issue. Be prepared to show your server logs highlighting the activity if you can. If the activity is obviously suspicious, the search engine may simply credit your account the amount it charged you for the clicks.

Suppose that one of your campaigns sees an average of 2,000 impressions per month and gets about 200 clicks. But one day, you log in and find that your campaign generated 2,000 impressions and 85 clicks during a single day. If you haven't made any changes to your account that could generate more clicks, you could be experiencing click fraud. Bring those stats to the attention of your customer service representative. Make sure that the representative takes a close look, and be persistent.

Chapter 7: Using Tools, Tips, and Tricks of the Trade

In This Chapter

✔ **Working with offline editors**

✔ **Managing keyword traffic**

✔ **Placing demographic bids**

✔ **Using geographic targeting**

✔ **Structuring display/content network campaigns**

✔ **Displaying extension ads**

*E*very industry has insider tips and golden bits of information to make your job either easier or more efficient, and the world of pay per click (PPC) is no different. In fact, because PPC can be so granular and complicated, you can find a lot of tools (some of them free) to make managing a PPC account much easier on yourself.

This chapter introduces some of the most popular tools and practices used by experts in the PPC industry. Not every tool is required for every campaign, but based on your PPC goals, you should be able to determine which of these tools may work for you.

Using Offline Editors

Both Google AdWords and Bing Ads have offline editors that allow you to see your entire account and all your campaigns, ad groups, and keywords without having to wait for pages to load or multiple screens to click through.

The editors are organized a little differently, but they have the same purpose: to enable you to make PPC edits faster and more easily than you could with an online editor.

To use an offline editor, you load the program and the account you want to work on. (If you load the account without many of the stats and go for a basic download, the process is even faster.) Then you can go offline, sit at a bus stop or on an airplane, and make the edits you need to make. When you're ready, simply go back online and upload your changes. Offline editors also make sharing changes among team members easier, holding proposed changes and saving previous work should you want to revert back to what you had before you uploaded changes.

These two editors allow you to do the following things:

✦ Copy entire campaigns, ad groups, ads, and keywords.

✦ Add negative keywords and websites (display/content network only). *Negative websites* work like negative keywords; they're sites on which your ad will not appear. For more information, see the section "Managing a Display/Content Network Campaign," later in this chapter.

✦ Use keyword suggestion tools and upload the suggested keywords.

✦ Change budgets and bids.

✦ Use campaign-level settings like geography, language, bidding methods, devices, and start and end dates.

✦ Find and replace text.

✦ Export and import Excel spreadsheets in a template format.

The following sections dive into a little more detail about each offline editor.

Google AdWords Editor

Google AdWords Editor continually undergoes upgrades that make it work more smoothly and provide more bells and whistles. You can save a copy of your entire account to upload again later, for example. Suppose that you hire a company or contractor to make some changes in your PPC account, but things don't work out, and you want to go back to your original account. Simply download a copy of your account before granting the company or contractor access, and save the copy. Later, if you need to, upload the old account to replace the new one.

Google AdWords Editor is free. Just download it from www.google.com/ intl/en/adwordseditor and then import your AdWords accounts.

Each time you start your work in the editor, click the Get Recent Changes button to get the editor up to date with the most recent stats. A drop-down menu gives you a choice between the basic and minimum cost per click (CPC). If you choose the basic option, you'll be up to date in a jiffy. If you go with the full version, updating takes only a few seconds more (depending on the size of your account) and includes first-page bid estimates, which the basic version doesn't provide. Figure 7-1 shows the main dashboard.

Click different tabs to see different parts of your account, such as campaigns and keyword lists. You can also import statistics such as cost and performance; you just have to wait a couple of minutes for those stats to load. Click the View Statistics button in the top navigation bar, and select either the entire account or an ad group and the date range for which you want to download statistics.

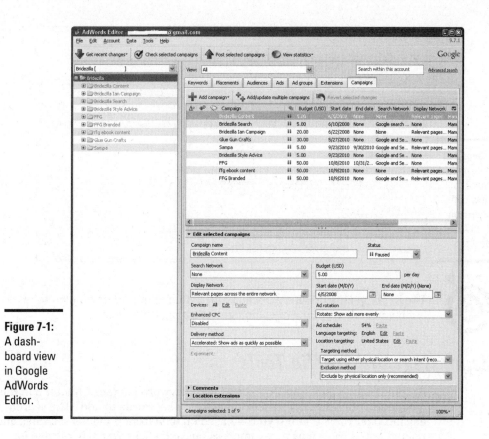

Figure 7-1:
A dash-
board view
in Google
AdWords
Editor.

For more information on using the AdWords Editor, click one of the help
links on the main page.

The Bing Ads editor

Bing Ads's editor is also constantly undergoing upgrades and feature additions and is a free tool. Download it at

```
http://advertising.microsoft.com/small-business/support-
    center/adcenter-downloads/adcenter-desktop
```

Figure 7-2 shows the Microsoft Bing Ads Desktop.

In many ways, the Desktop gives you the same capabilities as the Google
AdWords Editor. You can download and upload entire campaigns or
accounts for storage, change bids, edit ads, create new ad groups, and
import statistical information such as click-through rates (CTR) and impressions. Additional features allow you to add dynamic text, use the keyword
tool to generate and add keywords, and find and replace text.

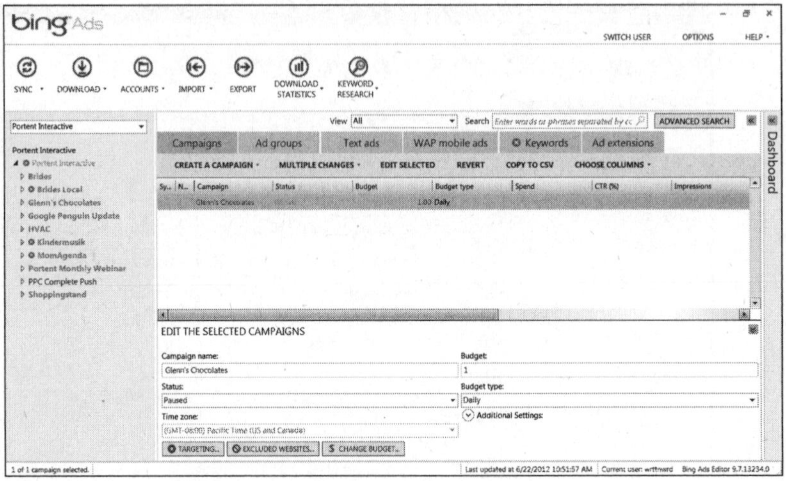

Figure 7-2:
A dash-
board
view of the
Microsoft
Bing Ads
Desktop.

TIP

The Desktop cuts down significantly on loading time, so if you plan to work in Bing beyond a couple of campaigns, it's a big timesaver.

Using Keyword Traffic Tools

At some point, you'll want to expand your keyword list (see Chapter 3 in this minibook). But how do you determine which keywords to add? The search engines offer tools that tell you — based on data from previous searches and related searches — how many impressions and clicks you may receive for your new list of keywords.

The following sections discuss the traffic-estimating keyword tools in Google and Bing.

Estimating traffic in Google

Google's free keyword tool predicts — based on the keywords, URLs, or categories you select — how many clicks and searches you'll record for that month. This tool can also show you the amount of competition and peak months of the year for searches on your selections.

To access the keyword tool, follow these steps:

1. **Log in to your AdWords account.**

2. **Select the ad group for which you want to do traffic estimates.**

3. **On the ad group's Keywords tab, click the + Add Keywords button.**

4. **Choose how you want to add keywords: Enter specific words and phrases, use suggested keywords by Google based on your website content, or click the link for the Keyword Tool.**

   For these steps, click the Keyword Tool link to use the full capabilities of keyword list expansion in Google.

   The keyword tool opens on the Tools and Analysis tab.

5. **Select the method (you have three options) you want to use to generate suggestions. Then click Search.**

   You can choose from these three methods to generate suggestions:

   - Type a "seed" word or phrase.

   - Paste the URL of a website or a category.

   - Choose a category from the drop-down list provided by Google.

   For these steps, type a seed word into the Word or Phrase box and then click Search.

   Google now shows you a list of keywords related to the term that you entered, with pertinent information like competition and estimated number of searches per month. (See Figure 7-3.)

   TIP

   You can filter your results further by changing the match type (see Chapter 3 in this minibook), adding words to exclude or include, or choosing one term and selecting More Like This from the drop-down list to see terms that are similar to your original keyword.

   TIP

   Google also has a free site that's dedicated to tracking trends on keywords over time. On the Google Insights for Search site (`www.google.com/insights/search`), you can enter a keyword and see how many searches were made on it over time as far back as 2004. You can filter searches by location worldwide and by time ranges, as well as compare keywords.

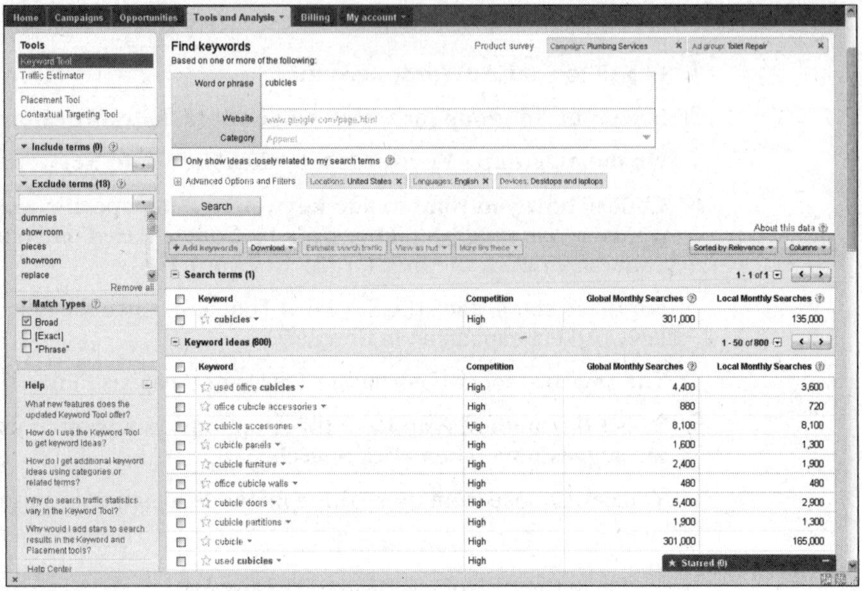

Figure 7-3:
Estimated
traffic for
keywords
related to
cubicles.

Estimating traffic in Bing

To use the free traffic-estimating tool for keywords in Bing Ads, follow these
steps:

1. **Log in to your account.**

2. **Open the ad group that you want to add keywords to.**

3. **Click the Keywords tab and then click the Add Keywords button.**

The Add Keywords Tool page opens, as shown in Figure 7-4.

4. **In the Search for More Keywords section, choose the method in which
you would like to search:**

• Use a "seed" keyword that you type

• Paste a URL of a website

The third option — find keywords on the destination websites for your
ads — applies to the content network only if you're searching for specific
sites in which to display your ads.

Bing displays a list of keywords and, next to them, the number of
searches from the previous month. (See Figure 7-5.)

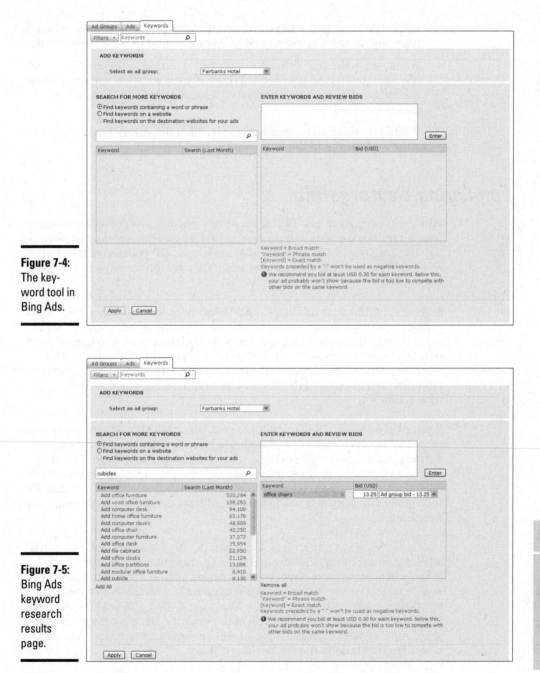

Figure 7-4:
The key-
word tool in
Bing Ads.

Figure 7-5:
Bing Ads
keyword
research
results
page.

5. **Click Add next to the keyword you want to use, and select the match type next to the keywords that you want to add to your keyword list.**

   When you make selections, the keyword is added to the new keyword box area and the ad group–level bid is displayed. Here you can change the bid for that specific keyword or leave it as is to apply to the ad group–level bid.

6. **When you finish selecting keywords, click the Apply button to save your work and add the keywords to the ad group.**

Employing Geotargeting

When you set up any new PPC account or campaign, you're asked to select your target market area — a process called *geographic targeting* or *geotargeting.* The countries, states, cities, metro areas, or ZIP codes you select are the ones where users will see your ads when they search for keywords in your keyword list.

Making sure that your ads are shown in locations appropriate for your business is important. For example, what if you want to target a specific state more closely, or run ads in just a few states because your company serves only those areas and doesn't have the licenses required to operate elsewhere? From a single dashboard, you can use geotargeting to optimize or filter out certain areas of the country or to run campaigns that serve multiple countries.

If you plan on advertising in multiple countries, you should set up a separate campaign for each country and then use ad scheduling to show those ads during peak hours in that country's time zones — especially in AdWords because your account is set to run ads based on the time zone you selected during setup. (For more information on ad scheduling, refer to Chapter 5 in this minibook.) Bing Ads will use the IP address of the user to determine his time zone.

Local businesses in particular can benefit greatly from this feature so that ads for a flower shop in Miami aren't being shown in Denver, for example. When a Miami business chooses to show ads only in the Miami area, the search engine will treat the ad a little differently, giving the ad a higher average position among searches in the Miami area. Also, the search volume for one city will be less than that of an entire country, because it's such a targeted area, so the average daily cost will be significantly lower than that of a campaign that targets the entire United States.

The major search engines' PPC platforms offer slightly different options for geographic targeting. For information on adjusting these settings, refer to Chapter 2 of this minibook.

Understanding Demographic Bidding

Demographic bidding is a great tool if you have a certain audience that you're trying to reach. If you know that your product is wildly popular among women 35 to 49 years old, for example, you can increase the amount that you're bidding to increase the chance that women in that age group will see and click your ad.

Bing Ads offers an option that allows you to increase your bid in percentage increments based on the predicted gender or age of the searcher. (Google AdWords, unfortunately, doesn't allow you to bid at a demographic level.) This option applies to both search and content networks on the ad group level.

To place a demographic bid in Bing Ads, follow these steps:

1. **Open the ad group or campaign you want to use.**

2. **Click the Edit Your Campaign Settings link.**

3. **Scroll down to the Advanced Targeting Option section and click Demographic (see Figure 7-6).**

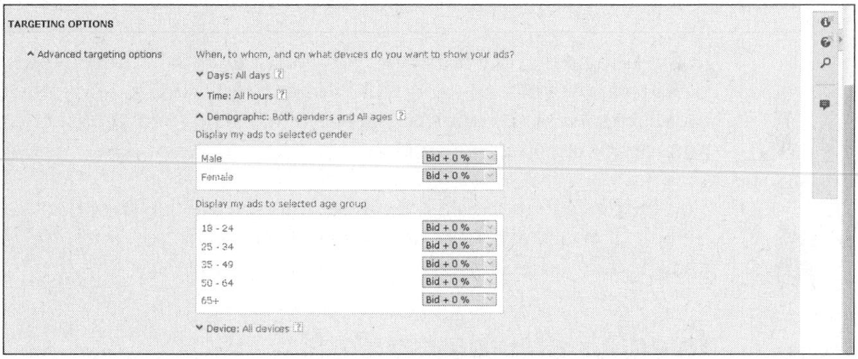

Figure 7-6:
Set bids that increase based on location, time, and demographics.

4. **Set the options you want to use in the Gender and Age Groups sections.**

   Options are set in increments of 10 percent and are cumulative. When you choose both Gender and Age Groups options, for example, your choices will be added together for a total percentage increase. If you set your bids at a 10 percent increase for women and a 10 percent increase for the 18–24 age group, for example, your bid is increased by 20 percent when a woman in the 18–24 age group is detected as the user.

5. **Click the Save button.**

**Book IV
Chapter 7**

Using Tools, Tips, and Tricks of the Trade

Managing a Display/Content Network Campaign

A display or *content network* (or *partner network,* as it's sometimes called) is a set of websites affiliated with the search engine that are authorized to show PPC data provided by that search engine. The ads appear on those websites alongside their content, not alongside search results. If you're on a website about chocolate (see Figure 7-7), and the person who owns the site is serving Google ads, you see ads related to chocolate alongside the article or even in the middle of the article.

Figure 7-7: Google AdWords display network ads, displayed in the upper-right corner.

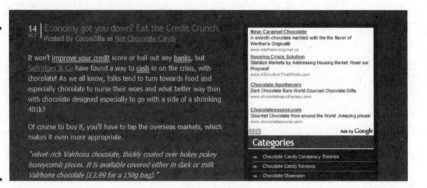

In the Google display network, you can specify which websites are authorized to show your ads and which ones aren't. In Bing Ads, the ads appear on Microsoft-owned sites or partner sites. The following sections go into the nuances of each engine's networks.

You participate in display, content, and partner distribution networks by default. If you don't want to participate in them, you must opt out at the campaign or ad group level.

Google's display network

Of the three main search engines, Google's display network gives you by far the most control of where your ads appear, when and to whom, as well as CPC and negative sites. Although total transparency isn't available yet, you can get a much better idea of which sites are working for you and which ones aren't. The Google display network is a busy one, and the best way to manage your account effectively is to separate your display and search campaigns at the start.

Tips for success in display and content networks

By following these examples, you can avoid costly mistakes and separate out your data (such as CTR, click through rate) to see more efficiently what is working in your campaigns and what isn't working:

✔ **Create separate campaigns for your search and display/content networks.** You can use some of the same keywords and ads. They won't overlap or compete, because the ads show on different networks.

✔ **Don't use exactly the same keywords and ads in all your search and display/content campaigns.** Chances are that you'll use some of the same keywords in both campaigns, but make the ad copy in the content campaign much more aggressive, gimmicky, or attention-getting. Remember, the ad appears amid web-page content, not in a targeted search result.

✔ **Choose a keyword list that describes the sites on which you want your ad to appear.** If you sell an energy-drink powder that's perfect for hikers, bikers, and people on the go, for example, create an ad group around one of those niches, such as hiking, and create a keyword list that will get the ad picked up by sites with similar content. Keywords might include *hiking drinks, hiking sites, places to hike, hiking equipment,* and *hiking supplies.*

✔ **Don't mix display, content, and partner networks.** Create separate campaigns for any networks you want to run ads on.

✔ **Limit keywords to three words (preferably two).** Long-tail keywords for more targeted searches, such as *pink daisy wedding invitations,* are good for search campaigns. Getting ads with a lot of long-tail terms on display/content networks is harder due to lower volume.

✔ **Bid lower on the display/content network than on the search network.** The average CPC is generally lower, and a high maximum CPC can rack up clicks fast. Whatever your search CPC is, slash it in half to start the content campaign and adjust as needed.

Remember: It's normal to see a lower CTR in a display/content network–only campaign than in a search campaign. A search results page means that someone was specifically looking for that item; a display/content ad is trying to persuade someone to leave the page he's looking at now and go to the advertiser's site.

✔ **Keep track of the network sites.** If your display/content campaign is racking up impressions but no clicks, check which sites your ads are appearing on. You may need to add some sites to your lists of excluded domains.

Google's display network allows you to choose between managed placements (website addresses that you choose) and automatic placements, where Google chooses which sites to show your ads on based on your keyword list. You also have the option of interest categories, where you can choose an "audience" from Google's list of available audiences such as Arts & Entertainment or Beauty & Fitness. From these top-level lists, you can drill down even farther to Hair Care or Fashion Modeling and see an estimated number of "members" in these audiences. These audiences are put together by Google through its analysis of Google display network sites' content, user cookies, and traffic thresholds to determine whether a site is a "fashion" site or a "cooking" site.

Click the Audiences tab in your Google AdWords account to view the available interest categories. (See Figure 7-8.) If you don't see the Audiences tab in your AdWords account, click the little down arrow at the end of the row of tabs and choose Audiences from the drop-down menu to enable it.

Save this option for when you are more comfortable with basic PPC and are running a display network campaign on managed or automatic placements.

Figure 7-8:
Google
AdWords
interest
categories.

Add audiences		
Select audiences to reach people based on their interests. Learn more		
Interest categories ⓘ Remarketing lists ⓘ Custom combinations ⓘ		
Add audiences from these lists	Selected audiences: 0	
Search by list name Search		
Categories	**Global users** ⓘ	
Arts & Entertainment	50M+	add
Autos & Vehicles	50M+	add
Beauty & Fitness	50M+	add
Beauty Pageants	1M-2M	add
Body Art	10M-20M	add
Cosmetology & Beauty Professionals	1M-2M	add
Face & Body Care	30M-50M	add
Fashion & Style	10M-20M	add
Fashion Designers & Collections	3M-5M	add
Fashion Modeling	3M-5M	add
Fitness	30M-50M	add
Hair Care	30M-50M	add
Spas & Beauty Services	3M-5M	add

Save   Cancel

Disabling other options

Before you create a Google display network campaign, make sure that all your other campaigns have the display network option turned off. You have to repeat this process for each campaign individually. Follow these steps:

1. **Open a campaign.**

2. **Click the Settings tab and scroll down to Networks and Devices. Click the Edit link in the Networks section.**

3. **Select the Let Me Choose radio button and deselect the Display Network check box (see Figure 7-9).**

4. **Click Save.**

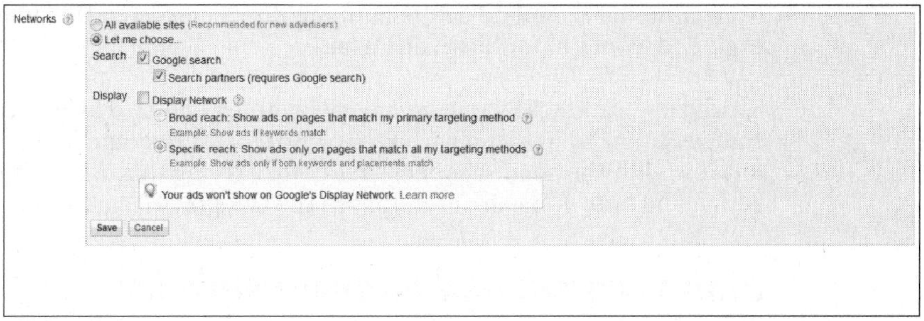

Figure 7-9:
Enable or
disable the
Google,
search,
and display
networks.

The search partner network is made up of sites that work directly with
Google to provide Google search results, such as Google Product Search,
AOL, and Ask.com. You can opt out of this network as well, but first check
your traffic volumes before opting out.

Enabling a display network campaign

To create a Google display network campaign, follow these steps:

1. **Create and save a new campaign as you normally would.**

   For details on setting up a campaign and expanding the keywords list in
   Google, refer to Chapter 3 in this minibook.

2. **Click the Settings tab to open the Campaign Settings page.**

3. **Deselect the Google Search and Search Partners check boxes, and
   select the Display Network check box.**

4. **Click the Save button.**

Remarketing on the Google display network

Google AdWords offers a remarketing tool through its display network that
allows you to set a cookie on a user's computer who visits your website
through a display network ad. Remarketing occurs after the person has left
your site and a specific amount of time (set by you) has passed in days.
Google will then show that person ads that you wrote or uploaded specifically to remarket with. You would not want to show them the exact same ad
as you did before, but rather something that speaks to the person's first visit
to your site.

For example, if someone were to click a display network ad, come to your
site, and place an item in the shopping cart but not check out, you could
remarket to her 7 days later (or however long you'd like), reminding her
of the unfinished transaction. At the same time, you can set it so that

users who did complete a checkout are not remarketed to and instead are excluded from being shown ads again.

Setting up remarketing can be a very complex and confusing process for someone new to working with PPC or AdWords. Become familiar and comfortable with the search aspect first before trying this. For more on remarketing and how you can set it up, see the Google AdWords Help Center.

Bing's content and partner networks

Bing opts all new ad groups into its search, content, and syndicated search networks by default. The search network is the search engines of Bing.com and Yahoo.com and is referred to as the *unified marketplace*. This means that ads shown in search results on Bing.com and Yahoo.com are serving ads from Bing Ads, and you can't tell which search engine an ad served on. It is all aggregated together.

The content network comprises all Microsoft properties, including Bing Money, Bing Autos, Jobs, and Windows Marketplace. Other participating partner websites like NBC.com and Online.wsj.com are included. The content network is only available to U.S., Canada, and India customers.

The concept remains the same as Google's display network: Ads appear alongside relevant content on web pages across these properties at a given CPC. You can set a different maximum CPC for the content network.

The syndicated search partner network is a collection of publishers (websites) that have partnered with Bing/Yahoo! search and show Bing Ads ads on their sites, alongside search results performed on their site. For example, if you were to go to the PCWorld website (a syndicated search partner) and search for *netbook laptop,* you would be shown a page of search results. Alongside those results on PCWorld would be ads from Bing Ads, as shown in Figure 7-10.

The syndicated search partner network contains some high-quality sites like PCWorld but also a lot of very low-quality sites, parked pages, and often irrelevant sites. Make sure that if you want to use this network, you set up a separate campaign. Do not combine it with Bing and Yahoo! search or the content network. Check often on which sites are showing your ads, and begin excluding sites that are irrelevant or performing poorly.

Figure 7-10:
A syndicated search partner network results page.

You can also disable this network at the ad group level until you're comfortable with PPC and Bing Ads. To opt out at the ad group level, follow these steps:

1. **Open the ad group.**

2. **Click the Edit Your Ad Group Settings link.**

3. **Click the Ad Distribution link under Advanced Settings, as shown in Figure 7-11.**

4. **Select the Bing and Yahoo! Search (Owned and Operated) Only radio button.**

   This step enables your ads to only show on Bing.com and Yahoo.com search results pages.

Figure 7-11:
Select or
deselect
search,
syndicated
search
partner,
and content
networks
here.

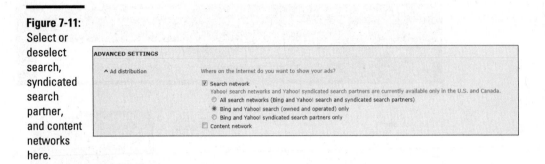

5. **Deselect the Content Network check box, and leave the Search Network box selected.**

   This step makes it so you are now opted out of the Content Network.

6. **Click Save.**

Using Extension Ads

Both AdWords and Bing Ads offer *extension* ads, ads that show more than just the 70 characters of body text, headline, and display URL, that you can also control. They are a nice way of calling extra attention or adding information to your ad for searchers. Extensions are enabled at the campaign level and affect all ad groups in that campaign. So make sure that all your ad groups make sense or match up to the type of extension you select for the entire campaign.

Extension ads don't show with impression. They show up to 30 percent at most and can't be controlled in terms of the amount of impressions (more or less).

Google AdWords offers these types of extension ads at this time:

✦ **Location:** These work with a manual address that you enter or the one associated with your Google Places account. If you have a brick-and-mortar business, these are especially useful. Log in to Google Places and follow the instructions to link accounts. See Figure 7-12 for a location extension ad.

✦ **Sitelinks:** You can add up to ten additional links and text to different pages on your site. The additional line of text can be up to 35 characters long, and AdWords will show anywhere from zero to six of your sitelinks depending on the searcher's query, the CTR (click-through rate), and the competition on the page. When you first enter the text and URLs of the pages you want to feature, Google will optimize them to show the most popular or relevant links first. See Figure 7-13 for an ad with sitelinks.

Figure 7-12:
A Google
AdWords
location
extension
ad.

At this time, you cannot see a breakdown of CTR or impressions per
sitelink. You only see how many times in total that sitelinks were shown
with an ad, clicks, conversions, and CTR.

Sitelink extension ads are useful for campaigns that cover a range of
options. For example, a campaign that focuses on specific types of wom-
en's shoes could have links for sneakers, pumps, boots, and clearance.
Or, a campaign that focuses on a restaurant location could have sitelinks
for menus, happy hour, reservations, directions, and special occasions.

Figure 7-13:
A Google
AdWords
sitelinks
extension
ad.

If you're using a third-party tracking/analytics package or bid management program, append the end of your ad destination URLs with a tracking code to add that to each of your sitelink URLs too.

✦ **Call:** This allows you to enter a phone number manually to show with
ads, as shown in Figure 7-14. Call extension ads also have *call metrics,*
where Google assigns a trackable phone number to your account to be
shown to searchers that forwards to the phone number you entered at
setup. When a person calls that number, Google can tell whether someone answered the phone, how long the call lasted, and how many people
called in total. The cost is $1 per call instead of a CPC (cost per click).

It cannot tell whether a sale is made, however. You still need to match your call logs with your AdWords account call metrics to determine which calls converted into sales or sign-ups.

Pacific Coast Feather Co. 1 (888) 708 0742
www.pacificcoast.com/ +1
Save Now & Through March: Free Shipping on Feather Beds!
+ Show products from Pacific Coast Feather Company

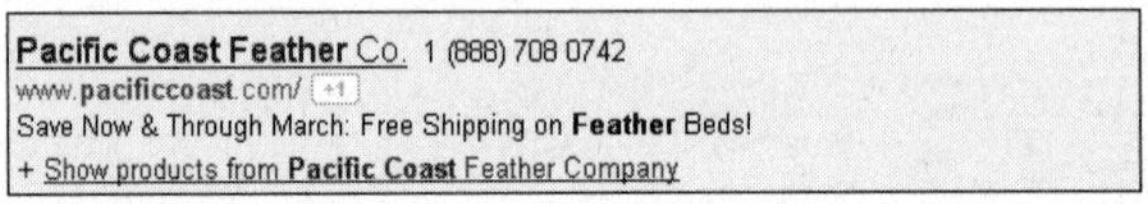

Figure 7-14: A call extension ad.

✦ **Product:** These are the most complicated of the extension ads offered by Google because they require a Google Base/Google Merchant account. If you have a product feed that you're using on Google Shopping for free, you can link this account to AdWords in Settings and begin to show products alongside your ads. AdWords shows up to four products underneath your ad text with little "plus" boxes; when clicked, these boxes expand to show a product from your feed. (See Figure 7-15.) If a searcher clicks the plus box, it does not count as an impression. It only counts if the searcher clicks the product and is taken to your website. The click also only counts in the AdWords and not in the Google Merchant center.

The products shown are chosen largely by Google to be the "most relevant" to the searcher's query. You can control which products show up with which campaigns and group them as you like by adding parameters to the shopping feed that you submit to Google Merchant. For more on this, see the Google Merchant Help Center.

Ads for feather beds
Why these ads?
Feather Beds 1 (888) 747 8816
www.pacificcoast.com/
Rest in a Comfortable Featherbed: Free Shipping - Save thru March!
– Hide products from Pacific Coast Feather Company for feather beds
Pacific Coast Baffle Box Feather ... $149.99
Pacific Coast Feather Bed Cover - ... $59.99
Pacific Coast SuperLoft Feather ... $199.99
Pacific Coast Lumbar Feather Bed - ... $199.99

Figure 7-15: A Google AdWords product extension ad.

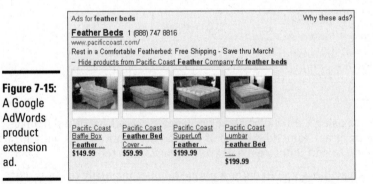

In addition to product extension ads, you find product listing ads, which you can control even further and show one product at a time with an image and an optional line of promotional text. Product listing ads can be controlled with attributes in the Google Merchant shopping feed and on the Auto Targets tab in the AdWords interface. For more on product listing ads, consult the AdWords Help Center.

Product extension and product listing ads are the most difficult of the available options to set up and run if you're new to PPC. Before diving into these, make sure to read through the Google Merchant Help Center, as you'll need to satisfy the requirements for a product feed before you can utilize these.

Bing Ads offers two types of extension ads: location extension ads, where you input the physical address of the location you want to display with your ad text, and image/product ads. The product ads extension is in beta at this time and requires the assistance of a customer service representative from Bing Ads or Yahoo!. This program is called RAIS, or Rich Ads in Search, and comes in several formats or image, videos, and text. You'll need to fill out an Excel template, supply product images and videos in very specific formats, and adhere to strict size limitations. After the spreadsheet of ads and images has been entered into the system, you can manage and run these ads from your Bing Ads account. For more on RAIS, contact an Bing Ads representative.

Location extension ads are enabled at the campaign level. They're great for brick-and-mortar businesses in particular and appear on Bing and Yahoo! search results pages. Simply click the Manage Your Business Locations link on the Campaigns tab, add your locations, and save. Then go to the Ad Extensions section of your campaign settings and select the Location Extensions check box.

Book V

E-Mail Marketing

Contents at a Glance

Chapter 1: Adding E-Mail to a Web Marketing Strategy

In This Chapter

✔ Discovering the benefits of e-mail marketing

✔ Combining e-mail with other media types

✔ Understanding E-Mail Marketing Providers (EMPs)

*W*alking into a business where the first dollar of profit is framed victoriously is always a great reminder of how important the first customer is to any small business. Your first customer represents validation of your business idea and proof that your products and services are valuable enough to cause someone to part with his money in order to obtain them.

The first dollar of profit is certainly cause for celebration. However, you need a plan to deliver ongoing communications to build a steady influx of customers — or your framed dollar of profit will start feeling lonely.

This chapter shows you the benefits of using e-mail in combination with other marketing media to communicate with customers and prospects, and then shows you how to take advantage of e-mail marketing services to help you manage your strategy.

Understanding the Benefits of E-Mail Marketing

E-mail might seem like a cost-effective way to deliver your marketing messages. For the most part, it is, because you can send personalized, targeted, and interest-specific messages to a large number of people. The value of e-mail marketing doesn't end with the cost, however. E-mail marketing has certain advantages over other forms of direct marketing for your business and for the people who request and receive your e-mails.

Asking for immediate action

You don't have to wait around too long to determine whether an e-mail message was successful.

According to a 2011 MailerMailer.com Email Marketing Metrics Report, more than 80 percent of the e-mail you send is opened in the first 48 hours after delivery.

After an e-mail is opened, it doesn't take long for your audience to take immediate action because people can take action on an e-mail with one click of the mouse. Immediate actions include

- ✦ Opening and reading the e-mail
- ✦ Clicking a link
- ✦ Clicking the Reply button
- ✦ Forwarding the e-mail
- ✦ Printing the e-mail
- ✦ Saving the e-mail

Chapter 5 of this minibook covers asking for immediate action in detail.

Gathering feedback

E-mail is a two-way form of communication, and even commercial e-mail can be used to gather feedback and responses from your audience. People can easily reply to e-mails, and many consumers love to share their opinions when it's easy for them to do so. Feedback from e-mails comes in two basic categories:

- ✦ **Stated feedback** happens when someone
  - Fills out an online form
  - Fills out an online survey
  - Sends a reply
- ✦ **Behavioral feedback** happens when you track
  - Link clicks
  - E-mail open rates
  - E-mails forwarded to friends

Generating awareness

When was the last time you mailed thousands of postcards, and your customers began crowding around copy machines trying to duplicate the postcard so that they can place stamps on them and forward the message to their friends? E-mail programs have a Forward button with which users can easily send a copy of your e-mail to one or more people in your recipient's address book. E-Mail Marketing Providers (EMPs) also provide a trackable Forward link that you can insert in your e-mails so that you can find out who is forwarding your e-mails. To find out more about EMPs, flip ahead to the section "Taking Advantage of E-Mail Marketing Providers," later in this chapter.

Staying top-of-mind

If you send periodic e-mails with valuable content, people who aren't ready to buy right away are more likely to remember you and your business when they become ready to buy. If your content is valuable enough to save, your prospects and customers might even create tags with your company name on it and start filing your e-mails in a special folder outside the regular inbox for future reference. When the e-mails are read again later, your message is communicated again. Here are some ways that e-mail can be used for top-of-mind awareness and future reference:

✦ Archive your e-mail newsletters on your website.

✦ Ask people to save your e-mails, as shown in Figure 1-1, to a folder in their e-mail program.

✦ Ask people to print your e-mails and post them.

✦ Print your e-mails and place them in a flip-open book on your retail store counter so that you can refer to recent offers and show samples of the value of your e-mail list.

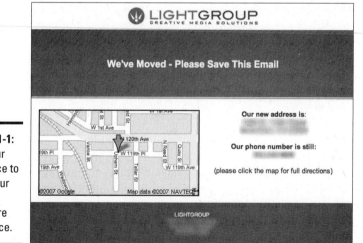

Figure 1-1:
Ask your
audience to
save your
e-mails
for future
reference.

Combining E-Mail with Other Media

In marketing, you're likely to employ several media and messages over a period of days, weeks, months, and years to communicate everything necessary to attract and retain enough customers.

Delivering your messages by combining different media is an effective way to market your business, but you'll probably find it more affordable to lean heavily on a few communication media where delivering your message results in the highest return. E-mail is one such medium because it's cost-effective and the returns are generally outstanding.

Keeping the design elements and personality of your e-mails and other messages similar or identical over time — *branding* — reinforces each of your messages and makes each successive message more memorable to your audience.

 Consumers are more likely to respond positively to your e-mail messages when they can identify your brand and when the content of each message feels familiar to them. Plan all your marketing messages as if they were one unit to ensure that each message contains design elements that become familiar to your audience when multiple messages are delivered.

Here are some branding ideas to help you give all your marketing messages a familiar look and feel:

✦ **Make your logo identifiable and readable in all types of print and digital formats, with color schemes that look good online and in print.**

In general, your logo and colors should look consistent on

- Signs
- Order forms
- E-mail sign-up forms
- Your website
- Receipts
- Business cards
- E-mails

✦ **Include your company name in all your marketing.**

Incorporate your name in

- E-mail From lines
- E-mail addresses
- Your e-mail signature

- Online directories
- Your blog

✦ **Format your messages consistently across media.**

When repeating messages in multiple media, make sure that the follow-ing elements are formatted consistently in your e-mails:

- Fonts
- Layouts
- Images
- Headlines
- Contact information
- Calls to action

   You can read about calls to action in Chapter 4 of this minibook.

Sending commercial e-mail to complete strangers is illegal. To keep on the right side of the law, combine at least one other medium with e-mail to initi-ate relationships with prospective customers. For more information about the legalities of sending commercial e-mail, see Chapter 2 of this minibook.

Taking Advantage of E-Mail Marketing Providers

The days when you could send a single e-mail and *blind-copy* hundreds of other people — by adding e-mail addresses to the BCC field in an e-mail — are over. Spam filters, firewalls, junk folders, and consumer distrust are all reasons to turn to professionals for help with your e-mail strategy. *E-Mail Marketing Providers (EMPs)* are companies that provide one or more of the following commercial e-mail services:

✦ Improved e-mail deliverability

✦ Database and list management

✦ E-mail template design

✦ E-mail message and content creation

✦ Social media integration

✦ Tracking reports

✦ E-mail automation

✦ Advice and consulting

To find an EMP and compare prices and product features, search for *e-mail marketing providers* in your favorite search engine.

Exploring provider benefits

EMPs allow you to accomplish much more with your e-mail marketing than you otherwise could on your own. Some EMPs even provide various levels of outsourcing for higher prices if you don't want to do your own e-mail marketing. Here are a few examples of the kinds of benefits that EMPs provide:

✦ **Give your business a professional look.** EMPs can help you create great-looking e-mail communications without programming knowledge. Most EMPs provide templates with consumer-friendly layouts to accommodate any type of message. Some EMPs provide template-creation wizards that allow you to control all your own design elements for a low cost, and some EMPs either include professional services to help you with semicustom designs or allow you to completely outsource and customize your template designs. Here are some of the templates that EMPs usually provide:

- Newsletters

- Promotions

- Announcements

- Press releases

- Event invitations

- Greeting cards

- Business letters

Figure 1-2 shows an e-mail template that an EMP provides.

✦ **Keep your marketing legal.** EMPs are required to incorporate current e-mail laws for customers to easily comply. Reputable EMPs take compliance a step further than the basic legal requirements and adhere to more professional standards that reflect consumer preferences. Examples of professional standards include the following:

- Safe one-click unsubscribe links

- Privacy statements

- Physical address added to e-mails

- Sending from a verified e-mail address

✦ **Help you with logistics and reporting.** EMPs can help you manage the data and feedback associated with executing your e-mail strategy. Here are some examples of ways that EMPs can help you manage your information:

- Storage and retrieval of subscriber information

- Reports on deliverability

- Automated handling of subscribe and unsubscribe requests

- Tracking information on blocked and bounced e-mails

Figure 1-2:
This e-mail
template is
ready for
content.

Courtesy of Constant Contact

✦ **Help with content:** EMPs want you to be successful because if your
e-mail messages are effective, you'll likely reward your EMP by being a
loyal customer. Many EMPs have resources available that can help you
develop your content and use best practices. Examples include

- Online communities

- Webinars

- Tutorials

- Classroom-style training

- Consultation

✦ **Teach you best practices.** EMPs can give you valuable information on
consumer preferences that would be too expensive or impossible for you
to obtain on your own. EMPs send a lot of e-mails on behalf of their customers, and they're good at staying up to date on consumer preferences and
professional standards. Some EMPs are willing to share their knowledge to
make your e-mails more effective. Some things you might find out include

- Best times and days to send

- How to improve your open rates

- How to avoid spam complaints

- What to do when e-mail is blocked or filtered

- How to design and lay out your content

Chapter 2: Becoming a Trusted Sender

In This Chapter

- ✔ Understanding spam laws
- ✔ Getting permission
- ✔ Familiarizing yourself with e-mail laws
- ✔ Minimizing spam complaints

Spam-blocking and -filtering technology has improved, but everyone who uses e-mail still deals with spam on one level or another. The main difference between the spam of today and the spam of the past is the fact that consumers increasingly apply the word to unwanted e-mails, whether or not those e-mails are technically spam.

Consumers are always skeptical of e-mails unless they know and trust the sender, and they're more than willing to report your e-mails as spam to their Internet service provider (ISP) if your e-mail is unwanted or doesn't appear trustworthy.

Every e-mail marketing strategy is subject to numerous legal and professional standards that apply to commercial e-mail. Consumers also expect marketing e-mails to come from a trusted source with just the right frequency and amount of relevant content. Here are the three authoritative benchmarks for determining whether your commercial e-mails are regarded as spam:

- ✦ Legal standards, as outlined in the CAN-SPAM Act of 2003 and the 2008 revisions to the Act
- ✦ Professional standards, as outlined by consumer advocates and the e-mail marketing industry
- ✦ Consumer preferences, as dictated by consumers themselves

Adhering to e-mail professionalism keeps your e-mails legally compliant and improves your relationships with the people who receive and open your e-mails. This chapter discusses how to become a trusted e-mail sender, minimizing consumer spam complaints while maximizing the trust between your business and your existing and future e-mail list subscribers.

Complying with Spam Laws

Spam is bothersome enough that lawmakers enacted the CAN-SPAM (Controlling the Assault of Non-Solicited Pornography and Marketing) Act of 2003 to help prosecute spammers. Names aside, the law makes certain e-mail marketing practices illegal and gives legal definitions to many best practices.

The following sections summarize the basic tenets of the CAN-SPAM Act of 2003 and the revisions made in 2008. You can read the CAN-SPAM Act at

```
http://business.ftc.gov/documents/bus61-can-spam-act-
    compliance-guide-business
```

and you can access the 2008 revisions at

```
www.ftc.gov/os/2008/05/R411008frn.pdf
```

to make sure that your own e-mails comply.

This section is intended to broaden your understanding of industry practices and shouldn't be used to make decisions regarding your own compliance to the law. Contact your attorney if you need more information.

Determining which e-mails have to comply

The CAN-SPAM Act of 2003 applies to commercial e-mail messages, which the law distinguishes from transactional or relationship messages. In general, the CAN-SPAM Act defines the two separate kinds of e-mail messages as follows:

✦ A **commercial e-mail** is basically an e-mail containing an advertisement, promotion, or content from a business's website.

✦ A **transactional or relationship e-mail** is basically anything other than a commercial e-mail.

Although understanding that some e-mail messages fall outside the definition of commercial e-mail is important, understanding that all e-mails sent in the name of your business can be construed by the recipient as commercial in nature is equally important. Best practice is to make sure that all your business-related e-mails are legally compliant.

The CAN-SPAM 2008 revisions specify that e-mails forwarded to others by a recipient may be subject to all the CAN-SPAM requirements. For example, if you send a coupon to a customer and your customer forwards that coupon to a friend, your customer's forwarded e-mail might be subject to CAN-SPAM rules. Talk to your E-Mail Marketing Provider (EMP) to make sure that your forwarded e-mails are CAN-SPAM–compliant.

Collecting e-mail addresses legally

The CAN-SPAM Act makes certain types of e-mail address collection illegal and requires permission from your e-mail list subscribers before you send certain types of content. (The CAN-SPAM Act uses the term *affirmative consent* instead of *permission*.)

Potentially illegal e-mail address collection methods aren't always easy to spot, so the best practice is to make sure that you have explicit permission from everyone on your list to send them e-mail. Here are some best practices for steering clear of potentially permissionless e-mail addresses:

✦ **Never purchase an e-mail list from a company that allows you to keep the e-mail addresses as a data file.** E-mail addresses kept in a data file are easily bought and sold, and e-mail addresses with explicit permission are too valuable to sell.

✦ **Never collect e-mail addresses from websites and other online directories.** This isn't a good practice because you don't have affirmative consent (or permission) from the owner.

✦ **Don't use an e-mail address collection service.** The exception is a service that collects confirmed permission from every subscriber that it obtains.

✦ **Don't borrow an e-mail list from another business and send e-mail to that business's e-mail list.** Those subscribers didn't explicitly opt in to receive your e-mails.

✦ **Don't rent an e-mail list unless you're certain that the list rental company's practices are legally compliant.** Most rental companies don't have permission-based lists. (You can read more about list rental in Chapter 3 of this minibook.)

Including required content in your e-mails

The CAN-SPAM Act requires you to include certain content in your e-mails. Include the following in your e-mails to stay CAN-SPAM–compliant:

✦ **Provide a way for your subscribers to opt out of receiving future e-mails.** You're required to remove anyone who unsubscribes from your e-mail list permanently within ten days of the unsubscribe request, and you can't add that person back without his explicit permission. When providing an opt-out mechanism, remember that it's illegal to charge someone to opt out or to ask for any information other than an e-mail address and opt-out preferences. Your opt-out process also has to be accomplishable by replying to a single e-mail or by visiting a single web page. Your EMP can provide you with an opt-out link that automatically unsubscribes in one click.

✦ **Make sure that your e-mail includes your physical address.** If your business has multiple locations, include your main address or the physical address associated with each e-mail you send, as shown in Figure 2-1.

Figure 2-1:
Adding a
physical
address to
your e-mail
is required
under the
CAN-SPAM
Act.

Courtesy of Wonderland Homes and Constant Contact

If you work from home and don't want your home address in every e-mail, the CAN-SPAM 2008 revisions confirm that you're allowed to include your post office box address as long as the post office or box rental company associates the box to your legitimate business address.

✦ **Make sure that your e-mail header information clearly identifies your business and doesn't mislead your audience in any way.** Your e-mail header includes your From line, Subject line, and e-mail address. Make sure that your e-mail's From line information clearly and honestly represents your business. The term *misleading* is open to legal interpretation. Speak to your attorney if you have questions.

✦ **Make sure that your e-mail's Subject line isn't misleading.** Don't use the Subject line to trick your audience into opening your e-mail or to misrepresent the offer contained in your e-mail.

✦ **Make sure that your e-mail clearly states that the e-mail is a solicitation.** The exception is when you have permission or affirmative consent from every individual on your list to send the solicitation. (Read more about permission later in this chapter.)

✦ **Make sure that your e-mail complies with any applicable guidelines for sexually oriented material.** If your e-mail contains such material, make sure that your e-mail's Subject line complies with the CAN-SPAM Act supplementary guidelines and also clearly states that the content of the e-mail is adult in nature without being explicit in the way you describe the content. You can access the supplementary guidelines on the Federal Trade Commission (FTC) website at `http://business.ftc.gov/documents/bus61-can-spam-act-compliance-guide-business`.

Asking for Permission

According to a recent study conducted by the Messaging Anti-Abuse Working Group (www.maawg.org), the majority of consumers consider unrequested e-mails to be spam. Collecting information without asking for permission can cause prospective subscribers to hesitate — or worse, they could perceive you as a spammer who abuses their privacy. Obtaining permission also ensures that your list starts out in compliance with the current CAN-SPAM laws.

Taking some time to formulate a professional permission strategy before embarking on e-mail collection tactics can reward your overall e-mail strategy with loyal subscribers who love to open, read, and take action on the e-mails you send.

Deciding on a permission level

When formulating your permission strategy, put yourself in the prospective subscriber's shoes so that you can assess the level of permission necessary to meet individual expectations.

Each type of permission is a two-way notion. You should be able to attest to each subscriber's level of consent, and your subscriber should feel that he did indeed authorize you to send him e-mail. This type of two-way permission comes in three basic levels, each with a higher level of demonstrated consensus: implied, explicit, and confirmed.

Level 1: Implied permission

Implied permission happens when someone shares her e-mail address with you in the course of normal business communications. The transaction implies that the purpose of giving you the e-mail address is to receive e-mails from you in reply. This level of permission isn't recommended as a best practice, even though it's sometimes suitable in the recipient's view. (Read on to find out why this isn't a best practice.)

An example of implied permission is a prospective customer who fills out an online form to obtain a quote for your services. The form includes an E-Mail Address field. The prospect shares her e-mail address within the form, expecting that you'll use that e-mail address to send the quote. If you send the quote and then begin sending weekly promotions without disclosing the fact that sharing an e-mail address on the quote form results in additional e-mails, however, you run the risk that your new subscriber will feel violated.

The main reason why implied permission isn't considered one of e-mail professionalism's best practices is that it doesn't take much extra effort to move from implicit permission to a higher standard. In the previous example, the business owner could easily add a link to his permission policy under the E-Mail Address field. Or, he could insert text that reads

> *By sharing your e-mail address, you'll receive your quote via e-mail along with concise weekly product updates to which you can safely unsubscribe at any time.*

Level 2: Explicit permission

Explicit permission happens when you include text or language disclosing how you plan to use the prospective subscriber's e-mail address. For example, an explicit subscriber might be a website visitor who clicks a Sign Up to Receive Our Weekly E-Newsletter link and then clicks another link on the following page to submit additional information that he types into an online form. Explicit permission also happens when prospective subscribers contact you and explicitly ask to be added to your e-mail list.

Explicit permission doesn't have to be a lengthy or complicated process, but the benefits of obtaining explicit permission are worth having a straightforward process. Here are some examples of explicit permission that you can adapt to your own subscriber situations:

- ✦ **Verbal:** When someone shares his e-mail address by handing you a business card or dictates an e-mail address to you during a phone conversation, you could query, *Is it alright if I send you my weekly event invitation e-mail?*

- ✦ **Written:** If a prospective subscriber sends a single e-mail to you and you want to add him to your e-mail list, you could reply to the e-mail and ask, *By the way, may I add your e-mail address to my list so that you can receive my monthly e-newsletter?*

- ✦ **Physical:** Some subscribers physically add their e-mail address to a guest book or sign up via a paper form. If you have such an arrangement, you could post a professional-looking plaque or sign next to the guest book or sign-up form that states, *Thank you for giving us permission to send you our weekly e-mail coupons by signing our guest book. We promise never to share your e-mail address with anyone outside the company without your permission.*

- ✦ **Incidental:** Sometimes, you can ask for explicit permission in the context of a transaction related to your e-mail information. For example, you might want to give online shoppers the ability to receive cross-promotions by selecting a check box during the checkout process. The text describing the check box could read, *Select this check box to receive periodic promotions that enhance the value of your purchase.* Just be sure that the default setting on the check box is deselected (cleared), or else it's no longer an example of explicit permission.

Don't mix your list messages

A restaurant owner, who also owned a travel agency, decided to place sign-up cards on each table in his restaurant so that his restaurant patrons could sign up for his travel newsletter. Lots of restaurant patrons filled out the cards, but they were confused when they began receiving a travel newsletter because they thought they were signing up to receive e-mails from the restaurant.

To ensure that permission is viewed as explicit on both sides of the information exchange, be as clear as possible in your messaging and context. For example, don't send coupons when your subscriber signs up to win a prize, unless you clearly state your intentions. When your context and messaging are as clear as possible and you still notice subscriber confusion, consider using an even higher level of permission.

Level 3: Confirmed permission

Confirmed permission happens when someone implicitly or explicitly subscribes to your e-mail list, and you respond to the subscriber with an e-mail requiring the subscriber to confirm his interest by reading your intended usage and then clicking a confirmation link. If the subscriber doesn't confirm, his e-mail address isn't added to your list, even if he explicitly filled out and submitted a form or physically signed your guest book. Figure 2-2 shows an example of a confirmation e-mail.

Figure 2-2:
A prospective subscriber must click an additional link for confirmed permission.

Courtesy of Constant Contact

Although confirmed permission is the most professional form of permission, it's also the most difficult for subscribers to understand. Therefore, confirmed permission isn't always suitable. Generally speaking, confirmed permission should be used when you want to be *absolutely sure* that your subscribers want your e-mail.

Confirmed permission is the appropriate level if

+ You send sensitive information.

+ Your subscribers tend to forget signing up.

+ You want to have a physical record of the subscriber's authorization to send e-mail.

Confirmation e-mails generally have low response rates, so if you're using explicit permission to build your list, you might lose subscribers who really want to be on the list but fail to read the confirmation e-mail and click the required link. The trade-off, however, is that your confirmed subscribers are more likely to receive and open your e-mails.

Inheriting a list: Getting permission after the fact

Sometimes, you might find yourself in possession of an e-mail list with questionable — or even no — permission. This often happens when you obtained your list in one of (or more of, but not limited to) the following scenarios:

+ You purchased an existing business and inherited an e-mail list without knowing the source of the e-mail addresses on the list.

+ Your list contains e-mail addresses collected over a long time period, and you can't identify each type of associated permission.

+ You purchased a list or built your list with low permission standards before you read this chapter — and now you're wondering whether your list is useless.

Sending e-mails to a permissionless list might violate the current CAN-SPAM laws and is likely to result in a high number of spam complaints from recipients.

Follow these steps to determine the permission status of an inherited list with questionable permission:

1. **Sort your list by source.**

If the source doesn't imply a two-way business relationship and the recipient likely won't recognize your e-mail address, discard the e-mail address or set aside the contact info to ask for permission.

Sources can include order forms, business cards, e-mail correspondence, guest books, or purchased lists. Inherited lists rarely detail the source as a field in a database or a note on the back of a business card, so determine the source by matching each record to other clues.

For example, if your list is contained in a customer relationship management system database, you might be able to export all the customers who made a purchase — and assume that names were obtained as the result of a business transaction.

Always discard purchased lists because purchased lists are almost never permission-based to begin with. (See the section on building a list with list brokers in Chapter 3 of this minibook for more information about purchased lists.)

2. Sort your list by date; discard any addresses belonging to customers who haven't made a purchase in over a year.

E-mail addresses belonging to customers who made purchases in years past and haven't returned shouldn't be used. Older e-mail addresses should be kept only if the person who owns the e-mail address is a recognizable current customer.

3. Check your list visually; discard any addresses that begin with ambiguous names or that are part of a distribution list.

Ambiguous names include `Webmaster@` or `Info@`. *Distribution lists* (single e-mail addresses that forward the e-mail to multiple addresses behind the scenes) make it impossible to tell whether the underlying e-mail addresses are permission based.

4. Sort the rest of your list by category.

At this point, consider using different messaging, depending on your relationship to the person who owns the e-mail address. If the e-mail address belongs to a prospect, you might want to proceed more cautiously than if the e-mail address belongs to a person who has purchased a product several times.

5. Confirm permission to send e-mail.

If, and only if, an e-mail list passes the preceding four steps and you're certain that the people who own the e-mail addresses on your list will recognize your business and your relationship to them personally, contact them to confirm permission.

- *If you have a small list:* Confirmation can be verified with a phone call or an e-mail containing a confirmation link.

- *If you can't contact people personally:* Send a professionally written confirmation e-mail.

Verifying permission for an old, outdated, or questionable list can prove frustrating even if you follow these steps because people change their e-mail addresses from time to time and because your database might not include the information you need to effectively sort through an inherited list.

If the aforementioned steps seem highly labor intensive or prove to be impossible — or if you can't make a determination because of the organizational state of your database — you should probably bite the bullet and discard the list or attempt to reestablish permission with the people on your inherited list without sending an e-mail.

If your list contains additional contact information other than the e-mail address, consider using direct mail, phone calls, and other advertising methods to drive the prospects through an explicit sign-up process on your website or at a physical location.

Minimizing Spam Complaints

Spam is also known as *unsolicited commercial e-mail.* Although numerous stories, analogies, and myths exist about the origin and meaning of *spam,* one thing is for sure — consumers don't like receiving it.

Even if your e-mail doesn't meet the legal definition of spam, consumers can easily report your e-mail as spam and thus impede your ability to send e-mail in the future. For example, Yahoo! customers can deem your e-mail as spam with a click of a button (see Figure 2-3). Most ISPs (including AOL, Yahoo!, Gmail, and Hotmail) give their customers Spam buttons to use to block suspected spammers.

Protecting your e-mail list

A quality list of permission-based e-mail subscribers segmented by interest and behavior is something to be proud of. Lists and data are assets and represent a significant competitive advantage to your business.

When it comes to e-mail data, protecting your asset is as important as building it in the first place. Don't violate the trust of your e-mail list subscribers by sharing their e-mail addresses with others who don't have permission to send to your list. Don't abuse your e-mail list subscribers by sending information they didn't ask for or by using their permission as a platform for selling lots of unrelenting banner ads in the body of your e-mail newsletters.

As a general rule, don't do anything with your e-mail list data that isn't explicitly agreed to and expected by your subscribers.

Report this e-mail as spam.

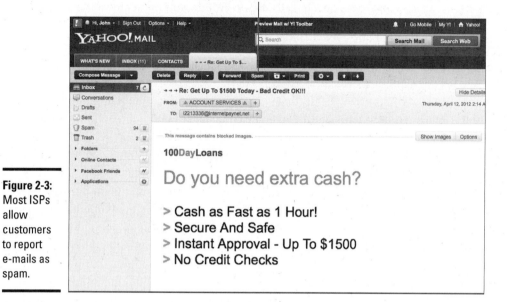

Figure 2-3:
Most ISPs
allow
customers
to report
e-mails as
spam.

If your e-mails are perceived as spam by your audience and you receive too many spam complaints, ISPs will block your e-mail server from sending e-mails to their customers. As few as two spam complaints per 1,000 e-mails can block your e-mail server temporarily, and higher percentages can result in your server being added to a permanent block list.

Because consumers have control over the Spam button, no e-mail marketing strategy is immune to complaints. Keeping your e-mails in line with the following guidelines is the best way to ensure that your spam complaints remain within industry tolerances.

Allowing your audience to unsubscribe from receiving e-mails

The CAN-SPAM Act requires that you include a way to let your audience unsubscribe from receiving future e-mails from you, but the law doesn't specify which mechanisms are appropriate for processing unsubscribe requests. You can ask your subscribers to reply to your e-mails with their unsubscribe request and manually keep track of your unsubscribed prospects and customers, but this process can be tedious with larger lists.

The most professional practice, and the most automated, for processing unsubscribe requests is to use an EMP to automatically and permanently remove anyone who unsubscribes from all e-mail lists in one click. Figure 2-4 shows a one-click unsubscribe link in the footer of an e-mail.

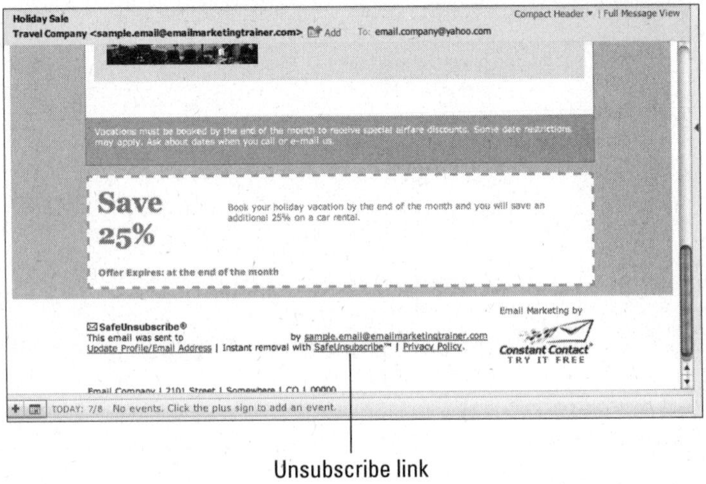

Figure 2-4: E-mail recipients can safely unsubscribe in one click with this link.

Unsubscribe link

Courtesy of Constant Contact

Most reputable EMPs automatically insert a one-click unsubscribe link into your e-mails. When a subscriber clicks the link, the EMP automatically removes the subscriber or changes the status of the subscriber in the EMP's database to Unsubscribed so that the subscriber stops receiving e-mails immediately.

Providing a one-click unsubscribe mechanism gives your potential e-mail list subscribers confidence when subscribing to your e-mail lists and encourages them to differentiate your e-mail from spammers who use dubious opt-out methods, if any.

Keeping your e-mails from looking like spam

To avoid having your e-mails reported as spam, understand how consumers evaluate e-mails. When you think about whether your audience is likely to perceive your e-mail as spam, remember that spam is in the *I* of the receiver:

✦ *I* **don't want it.** Unwanted marketing e-mails are perceived as spam by most consumers, especially if they feel that they didn't authorize the sender to send it. Sometimes, consumers even start to perceive e-mails as spam after they receive them for months just because they no longer want them.

✦ *I can't verify it.* If consumers can't tell whether an e-mail came from a legitimate source, they perceive it as spam. Most consumers look at the From line in an e-mail header to determine whether an e-mail is familiar.

✦ *I think it's too frequent.* Consumers tend to perceive frequent e-mails as spam when they feel that the content is irrelevant, repetitive, or too long.

Even when consumers don't perceive your e-mail as spam, they might be inclined to click the Spam button on your e-mail for one or more of the following reasons:

✦ They can't figure out how to unsubscribe from your e-mail.

✦ They don't trust the unsubscribe link in your e-mail.

✦ They accidentally click the Spam button while sorting through their e-mail inbox.

✦ They unintentionally include your e-mail while clicking the Spam button on a large group of other spam e-mails.

Keeping spam complaints to a minimum is a matter of adhering to professional practices and consumer preferences over the course of your entire e-mail marketing strategy.

Regardless of the method of accepting permission, always take your prospective subscriber's circumstances into account. Even explicit permission can result in spam complaints or negative emotions if your subscriber doesn't remember subscribing or doesn't recognize the e-mails you send after subscribing.

You can minimize your spam complaints over time by doing the following:

✦ **Say thanks.** Send a welcome e-mail immediately after the subscriber joins the list, as shown in Figure 2-5.

✦ **Send e-mail reminders.** Insert a paragraph of text at the top of every e-mail reminding the recipient how you obtained his e-mail address.

✦ **Keep your e-mail frequency in line with your e-mail content and your e-mail list subscribers' expectations.** You can read more about the relationship between frequency and content later in this list.

✦ **Reinforce branding.** Include your logo and colors on your sign-up form and make sure that future e-mails match your brand. (Read more about this in Chapter 4 of this minibook.)

✦ **Reinforce familiarity.** Make sure that every e-mail's From line is memorable and familiar. (Read more on this in Chapter 4 of this minibook.)

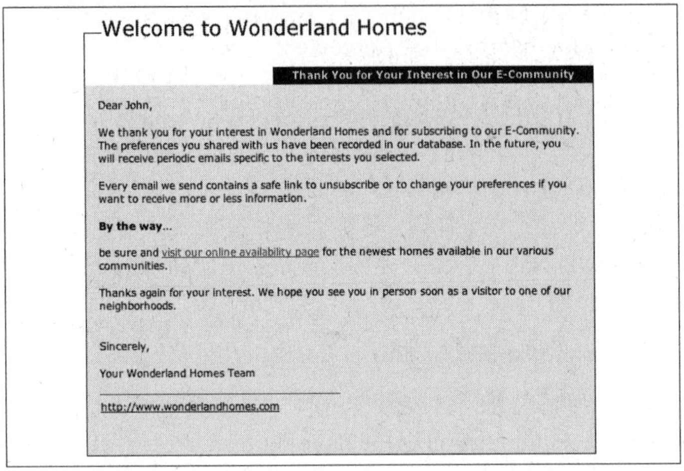
Welcome to Wonderland Homes

Thank You for Your Interest in Our E-Community

Dear John,

We thank you for your interest in Wonderland Homes and for subscribing to our E-Community. The preferences you shared with us have been recorded in our database. In the future, you will receive periodic emails specific to the interests you selected.

Every email we send contains a safe link to unsubscribe or to change your preferences if you want to receive more or less information.

By the way...

be sure and visit our online availability page for the newest homes available in our various communities.

Thanks again for your interest. We hope you see you in person soon as a visitor to one of our neighborhoods.

Sincerely,

Your Wonderland Homes Team

http://www.wonderlandhomes.com

Figure 2-5: This welcome e-mail reinforces permission and helps reduce spam complaints.

Courtesy of Wonderland Homes and Constant Contact

- **Send a reminder letter.** Send a permission reminder letter periodically that tells your subscribers exactly how you obtained their e-mail address and gives them links for updating their preferences and unsubscribing.
- **Make your e-mail content valuable so that your e-mail list subscribers continue to want your e-mails.** You can read more about creating value in your e-mails in Chapter 5 of this minibook.
- **Make your sign-up process memorable for your list subscribers and clearly identify your business in every e-mail's From line so that your audience can verify the source of your e-mails.** Ideas for optimizing your e-mail's From line appear in Chapter 4 of this minibook.
- **Ask everyone who unsubscribes from your e-mail list to tell you why he or she doesn't want your e-mail.** You can then adjust your strategy accordingly.
- **Use an EMP that authenticates your e-mails.** You can read more about e-mail authentication in Chapter 7 of this minibook.
- **Include a description of your e-mail content and your typical frequency in your sign-up process.** For example, if you send a monthly e-mail newsletter along with periodic promotions to your e-mail list, your e-mail list sign-up form might include a sentence that reads

  Signing up allows you to receive our monthly e-mail newsletter as well as periodic special offers related to our newest products.

✦ **Send only the content that your e-mail list subscribers expect you to send.** For example, if potential e-mail list subscribers share their e-mail address to receive a quote for your services, don't send them offers unless they gave you permission as part of requesting a quote.

✦ **Allow your e-mail list subscribers to choose their own interests.** If you send several distinct types of e-mail content — such as coupons and event invitations — give your e-mail list subscribers a list of categories to choose from when signing up. Make sure to give them a mechanism for changing their interests, such as a link to their profile, in every e-mail.

Chapter 3: Building a Quality E-Mail List

Collecting e-mail addresses isn't an easy task. Some people are so bothered by unsolicited e-mails that they're willing to share almost anything else with you before they will share their e-mail addresses. Others might give you their e-mail addresses, but when the e-mails they receive from you don't meet their expectations, they resort to unsubscribing or marking the e-mails as spam, even if they're loyal customers.

Fortunately, an e-mail list needn't be large to be effective. The best e-mail lists are those that contain the names of loyal repeat customers, referral sources who respect others' privacy, and interested prospects who know you and your business well enough to recognize your e-mails.

This chapter guides you through some of the best tactics for building a permission-based e-mail list with a high number of quality subscribers. The chapter summarizes how and where to collect information, what information to collect, and how to prepare your database. A quality list helps ensure that your e-mail messages are received by the people who are most likely to respond with repeat and referral business.

You need to collect permission in addition to collecting contact information to send successful e-mails. If you need to collect permission, see Chapter 2 of this minibook.

Preparing Your E-Mail Database

Sending e-mails to your list requires your list data to be stored in a useful electronic format, so take care to enter your data into a database while you collect. Building and maintaining an electronic database allows you to

+ **Organize and view your list data easily.**

+ **Sort your list data into categories to send targeted e-mails.** For example, you might use your database to sort your data by ZIP code so that you can send a more targeted event invitation to a list of people in a specific ZIP code.

+ **Process and keep track of unsubscribed contacts.**

+ **Query your list to extract useful information and reports.**

You don't need a highly sophisticated database for effective e-mail marketing, although additional database features can improve your ability to target your contacts with specific messages. Some E-Mail Marketing Providers (EMPs), such as Infusionsoft, have a robust built-in database or *customer relationship management* (CRM) system. Whether you use a well-known CRM database or a more basic solution, most databases can export data in one or more compatible formats. Ask your EMP for a list of supported formats, and then check the export feature on your database to see whether you have a match.

Keep in mind that databases with a lot of complex features are more expensive than simpler applications. Make sure that any fancy functionality in your database can return more than a dollar for every dollar you spend to gain that function. You can always upgrade later when your e-mail marketing strategy outgrows your initial functionality.

If you're not sure which database will give you the best results, start with a basic database application or with your EMP's built-in database utility. Figure 3-1 shows an example of a simple EMP database feature set.

If you use an external database, make sure that the database you choose can easily transfer data to or synchronize data with your EMP. Doing so allows you to send e-mails without having to maintain two databases.

Whether you use a well-known database application or a customized solution, most databases can export data in one or more compatible formats. Ask your EMP for a list of supported formats, and then check the export feature on your database to see whether you have a match. You can read more about what information to put in your database later in this chapter.

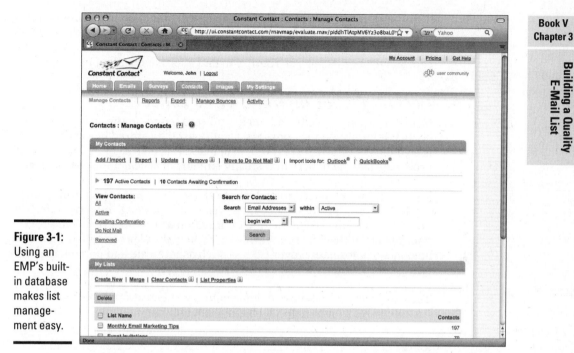

Figure 3-1:
Using an
EMP's built-
in database
makes list
manage-
ment easy.

Courtesy of Constant Contact

Don't store your data in an EMP database system alone unless the service allows you to access the data belonging to unsubscribed contacts. Just because someone unsubscribes from receiving future e-mails doesn't mean that she isn't a good customer or prospect. Phone numbers, mailing addresses, and behavioral information become even more useful when someone has unsubscribed from your e-mail list.

Collecting Contact Information

The quality of your e-mail list depends greatly on where and how you collect the information in the first place as well as where and how you store and manage the data. The best way to ensure that you collect quality information is to obtain information and permission directly from the person who owns the information in the first place — namely, your prospects and customers.

Your challenge is to provide multiple opportunities and incentives for prospects and customers to share their information as well as to manage the resulting data effectively and efficiently.

If you already have a database of prospective e-mail list subscribers or if you have a lot of contact information from various sources waiting to be entered into a single database, flip to Chapter 2 of this minibook before adding those contacts to your e-mail list. There, you find information about inheriting a list.

Deciding what information to collect

Many businesses have been bought and sold based on the strength of the contact information they possess. Quality list data stored in a useful format is a goldmine for targeting your e-mail marketing messages and converting prospects and customers into steady streams of repeat and referral sales.

The two things you need to collect are an e-mail address and permission to send someone a professional e-mail. Generally speaking, enlisting subscribers is easier if you ask for as little information as possible. You'll improve your results in the long run, however, if you make plans to gather increasing amounts of information over time — such as interests and personal information — as you interact with customers and prospects.

Table 3-1 lists several types of information you can ask prospective e-mail list subscribers for to help you build a valuable list.

Table 3-1	E-Mail List Information Collection		
Category	*Description*	*Use*	*Examples Include*
Essential Information	Information that your customers or prospects expect you to know	Use to personalize your e-mails	Preferred e-mail address First name ZIP code
Behavioral Information	Indicates how your audience is likely to act toward your e-mail content	Use privately to group your list subscribers into categories for targeted messages	Prospects Coupon users Repeat purchasers Advocates Very Important Customers (VICs)
Personal Information	Reveals important details about the person you're sending to	Use to send more relevant information	Gender Marital status Family info Preferences

You don't have to obtain all subscriber information upon the first contact with a prospect or customer. As long as you have a good permission-based e-mail address, you can ask for more information in future e-mails by

✦ Sending short, relevant e-mail surveys

✦ Asking for information in the context of your regular e-mails

✦ Using forms and links on your website to collect information from people who are browsing or making purchases

✦ Asking for more information through other marketing media as more trust develops in your relationship

Getting to know your list members better

Believe it or not, most of your prospects aren't interested in everything that you decide to send in the context of an e-mail strategy. When you collect contact information and permission, consider asking your prospective subscribers to share their interests. Using interest information allows you to sort your e-mail lists into categories and send information relevant to that category.

Instead of open-ended questions, come up with some basic list categories and ask your prospective subscribers to self-identify when signing up. Here's an example of an open-ended question and an example of a category-specific question:

✦ **Open-ended question:** "Why do you dine with us?"

✦ **Revised category-specific question:** "Which answer best describes why you dine with us?"

- Money-saving offers

- New menu items

- Wine recommendations

- Live music and special events

When is essential information essential?

How your prospects and customers view essential information is likely to depend upon how personally you interact with your prospects and customers at the beginning of a relationship. People are also more comfortable sharing information when they understand how you'll use the information.

For example, an online retailer could be viewed as intruding when asking a site visitor for a physical address before he's ready to make a purchase. After the site visitor decides to check out with an item in the shopping cart, collecting a physical address becomes necessary to ship the item.

Getting personal with demographic interests

Asking for *demographic information* — such as age or income — can prove difficult because people are concerned about privacy and they generally aren't as willing to share demographic information unless they know why you need it and how you use it. To get the information you need, though, try combining demographic and interest questions as one category so that you can make inferences without being too direct. Here's a sample of possible list titles for specific types of businesses:

- Spare-no-expense travel destinations
- Singles-only event invitations
- Golfing with kids younger than 12
- Entertaining with limited space
- Gardening on a budget

Some people will tell you what interests them only when they feel that they'll get preferential treatment as a result. Try positioning interest information so that the reward is receiving the information. List ideas include

✦ Priority, reserved event tickets

✦ Members-only discounts

✦ First-to-know product announcements

✦ Early-bird access to product-specific sales

Figure 3-2 shows a registration form that allows the reader to indicate a variety of interests.

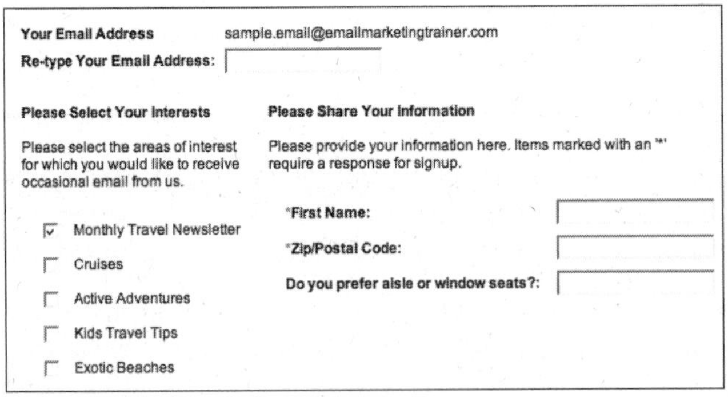

Figure 3-2:
Give your
subscribers
a selection
of interest
categories.

Your Email Address   sample.email@emailmarketingtrainer.com
Re-type Your Email Address:

Please Select Your Interests   **Please Share Your Information**

Please select the areas of interest for which you would like to receive occasional email from us.   Please provide your information here. Items marked with an "*" require a response for signup.

☑ Monthly Travel Newsletter
☐ Cruises
☐ Active Adventures
☐ Kids Travel Tips
☐ Exotic Beaches

*First Name:
*Zip/Postal Code:
Do you prefer aisle or window seats?:

Don't give your subscribers too many choices too early. Ask them to adjust their interests over time and collect information as you interact. You can also collect interest information without asking your subscribers by tracking their click behavior. For more about e-mail tracking, see Chapter 6 of this minibook.

Posting sign-up links online

Placing a sign-up link in every online presence possible is a great way to collect information with explicit permission. A *sign-up link* is a text box, button, or text that usually links to a sign-up form or a confirmation page that allows your subscriber to enter and submit additional information and preferences. Figure 3-3 shows three different types of sign-ups.

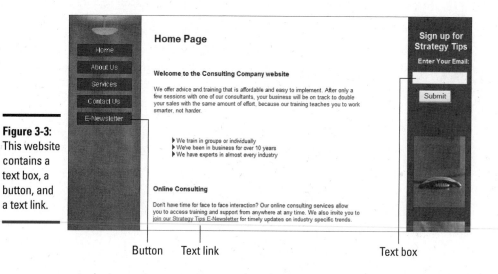

Figure 3-3:
This website contains a text box, a button, and a text link.

Button   Text link   Text box

Some means of putting sign-up requests on a site include

✦ **Text boxes:** These allow your subscribers to enter information without clicking through to an additional sign-up form. Text boxes can ask for an e-mail address, or they can contain several fields making up an entire form.

✦ **Buttons:** These are graphical representations of links that take the subscriber to a form to complete and submit. Buttons can be images with text, flashing boxes, icons, or other creative graphics.

A sign-up button should stand out, but don't draw too much attention away from the content of your website for visitors who are already subscribers.

✦ **Text links:** These are short headlines of plain text linked to a sign-up form. Text links are ideal if you want to add an option to subscribe within the context of other information or if you want to put a line of text in your e-mail signature.

✦ **Check boxes:** These are usually employed on multiuse forms to save additional steps. For example, someone who is making an online purchase already has to fill in her name and address, so adding a sign-up check box to the shipping form is a great way to gain permission to use the information for shipping the item and sending future e-mails.

If you use check boxes, leave the box deselected (cleared) as the default setting because you don't want people who overlook the box to become disgruntled when they receive future e-mails and feel that they were added to your list without their permission.

✦ **Social applications:** Social media sites such as Facebook allow applications to be added. You can build your own e-mail address collection applications, or you can use handy plug-ins built by your EMP, as shown in Figure 3-4.

Figure 3-4: Add a sign-up tab to your Facebook business Page using your EMP's application.

Courtesy of Casa Alvarez Mexican Restaurant

Creating a media mailing list

Most media entities accept press releases via e-mail and will post additional e-mail addresses for communicating newsworthy information person to person. If you're planning to send press releases, be sure to keep your media list separate from your customer list so that you can restrict media personnel to news-worthy press release e-mails only. Permission, privacy, and professionalism matter just as much to the media as they do to the consumer, so kindly contact your media professionals and ask them to be on your press release list before you start sending.

Whether you employ forms, buttons, text links, or any other element, experiment with different placement ideas. You can place a sign-up link almost anywhere that HTML (HyperText Markup Language) is possible. Try adding a sign-up link to the following locations:

✦ **On every page of your website**

✦ **On social media sites**

✦ **In your e-mail signature, as shown in Figure 3-5**

✦ **On your blog or personal website:** You can read more about blogs in Book VI.

✦ **In banner ads and online advertising:** You can read more about online advertising in Book IV.

✦ **On other websites (with permission)**

✦ **In e-mails that your noncompeting colleagues send to their customers (with permission)**

✦ **In online directories**

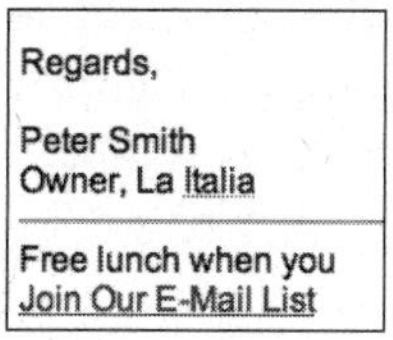

Figure 3-5:
Place a
sign-up
link in your
e-mail
signature.

Collecting information through mobile devices

Mobile devices such as tablets and smartphones represent an opportunity to easily collect e-mail addresses on location. All the following methods of mobile e-mail address collection are worth using in your business.

Texting an e-mail address

Use your advertising to ask customers and prospects to text their e-mail address. Here are two ways to ask for e-mail addresses by text message:

✦ **Ask people to text their e-mail addresses to your mobile phone number.** If you don't expect a lot of volume or can't afford a short code or text-messaging platform, this method allows you to accept e-mail addresses from people on your mobile phone and add them to your address book so that you can send people e-mails. It's highly manual, and you have to share or advertise your own mobile phone number, so use this method only if you can't afford better technology.

✦ **Ask people to text their e-mail addresses to your short code.** A *short code* is a short phone number, usually four to six digits long. To enable this for your business, you need to buy or rent a short code, and then you need to make sure that your text-messaging application is set up to populate your database with e-mail addresses sent by text. If you have a *dedicated short code* — one that you own — you can ask people to text their e-mail addresses directly to your short code. Your platform's database can automatically recognize the e-mail addresses and put that information in the proper database fields for you.

If you use a *shared short code* — one that you rent or share with other people — you need to ask people to include your keyword along with the e-mail address. For example, "text *KEYWORD emailaddress* to *12345*," where *KEYWORD* is your short code keyword, *e-mailaddress* is the sub-scriber's e-mail address, and *12345* is your shared short code. (You can read more about short codes and keywords in Book VIII.)

Providing forms in mobile websites and apps

Your mobile website should include a sign-up form so that people can join your e-mail list from their mobile phones, as shown in Figure 3-6. List the domain name of your sign-up form in all your ads (for example, www.your company.com/sign-up). Keep your sign-up form short.

Figure 3-6:
Make sure
sign-up
forms are
formatted
for mobile
devices.

Courtesy of Constant Contact

People signing up might be typing on a very small keyboard. Ask for an
e-mail address and a first name and allow them to select from an appropriate
list. You can collect additional information later.

You can use mobile websites and applications to collect e-mail addresses at

✦ **Networking events,** so that you don't need to take a business card and
type the info in later

✦ **Trade shows,** when you're walking the floor or working your booth

✦ **In your store,** if you have a physical location and you interact in person

✦ **In your office,** during an appointment

Collecting information in person

According to the Ten Foot Rule, whenever anyone is within ten feet of you,
ask for her contact information. A warm body or a verbal conversation can
equate to a captive audience for communicating the benefits of joining your
e-mail list.

Always ask for permission when you collect information in person. Here are some ways to connect and collect without being intrusive:

+ **Swap business cards.**

    Ask whether that person's preferred e-mail address is on the card.

+ **Place a guest book on the counter in your store or office.** Keep a tablet handy so that you can ask people anywhere to sign up on your website from anywhere.

+ **Place a basket for business cards on your table at trade shows and events.** Make sure to place a sign on the basket that states your intent to send e-mails.

+ **Train your employees to take down customer information.** Ask anyone who answers the phone at your business to ask for e-mail addresses and permission when customers and prospects call.

Collecting information through print

Adding sign-up information to direct mail and print advertising is a great way to help maximize your advertising dollars. You can use print to drive people to your website or store, you can ask them to fill out a paper form and return it, or you can ask them to send you an e-mail requesting to join the list.

Here are some ideas for using print to drive people to a sign-up process:

+ **Send a postcard offering an incentive (such as a free gift or an entry into a drawing) to return the card to the store with the recipient's e-mail address filled in to a space on the card.** Be sure to explain your intended usage and also ask permission in the text.

+ **Position your sign-up incentive to add value to your print offer.** For example, you could print

    Free child's haircut with subscription to our preferred customer e-mail list.

+ **Add your sign-up incentive to the back of your business cards.** For example, a discount store's business card could include

    Our e-mail list members save 10% more! Join online, in person, or by phone.

✦ **Purchase an intuitive domain name and place it in your print advertising to promote sign-ups.** In the preceding example, the discount store could purchase a domain such as www.JoinMyEmailList.com, and point it to the sign-up form on the company website.

Offering Incentives to Increase Sign-ups

Because your e-mail list is an asset — hopefully containing e-mail addresses belonging to loyal customers who spend more money as well as referral sources who love to tell others about you — offering an incentive in exchange for an e-mail subscription is really the least you can do to thank and reward your most valuable contacts.

Offering incentives for joining your e-mail list can reward your business in at least two ways:

✦ **Increased sign-ups:** The number of people willing to share their contact information with you is likely to increase if they feel that they're getting something of value in return.

✦ **Increased loyalty:** An incentive rewards your subscribers and can cause loyalty, repeat business, and referrals to increase.

Not all incentives are all liked

After you determine where and when to ask for e-mail addresses and permission, decide how to ask. For example, if you offer subscribers a link to Join the E-Mail Blast, people who don't want a blast or don't know exactly what they are likely to receive will pass on the opportunity to subscribe.

Find out what motivates your prospects and customers before determining an incentive. For example, some people will join an e-mail list in exchange for a discount on all future purchases. On the other hand, some people associate discounts with words like *cheap, discontinued, last year's model,* or *out of style.*

If your customers aren't motivated by discounts, consider using a more creative strategy, such as a Very Important Customer (VIC) club, where e-mail subscribers are the first to know about the latest high-tech products available at a reasonable price.

Giving subscribers immediate incentives

Some incentives, such as ongoing discounts, can be an inherent part of being on the list — and are, therefore, immediate upon the subscription. Immediate incentives abound and could include

✦ Discounts or reward points on every purchase

✦ VIP access to special events, front-row seats, and so on

✦ Access to members-only information

✦ Free trials, gifts, or additional services

Giving subscribers future incentives

Some incentives aren't immediate but are instead forthcoming for members of the list. For example, imagine a clothing store that has a 48-hour sale twice per year, and only e-mail list subscribers are invited to save 50 percent if they order within the 48-hour period.

If e-mail list subscribers are the only customers invited to the event, the invitation is the incentive, but it isn't immediate because the subscriber has to wait for an invitation to take advantage of the incentive.

Because the sale happens only twice per year, the store could send other e-mails between the sales with other offers and information. Imminent incentives are limited only by your own creativity and could include the following promotions:

✦ Early shopping hours during the holidays

✦ Invitations to periodic private events

✦ Random rewards, such as prize drawings

 If you can't think of an incentive to offer your e-mail list subscribers or if the intrinsic value of the content in your e-mails is the incentive, use your messaging to be as clear as possible about what subscribers can expect in place of an incentive.

For example, asking potential subscribers to Sign Up for Friday Quick Tips tells them what to expect. Comparatively, asking a subscriber simply to Sign Up for Our E-Mail List is too generic and might cause prospective subscribers to hesitate — or, worse, disappoint subscribers when their expectations are not met.

Permission and privacy as incentives

Adding a privacy and permission policy to your data collection forms as well as clearly stating your intended usage upfront helps put people more at ease when sharing information. Even if no one reads your privacy and permission policy, the fact that a link to privacy information appears is often reassuring.

Remember that people who share an e-mail address always do so with personal expectations

in mind, and sometimes those expectations are hard to determine. As a best practice, make sure that your privacy and permission policy benefits your subscriber more than your business. Keep your privacy and permission statements short, using information in accordance with people's expectations at the time of information exchange.

Building a List with List Brokers

List brokers are marketing companies that collect and sell contact information. If you decide to build a list with the help of a list broker, recognize the significant differences between obtaining a list of physical addresses or phone numbers and obtaining e-mail addresses.

When you contact a reputable list broker to obtain e-mail addresses, the process isn't as simple as selecting demographic information and paying to receive a data file because the e-mail addresses on a brokered list must, by law, be permission based.

The process of obtaining e-mail addresses from any list broker is full of potential pitfalls because consumers get annoyed by unsolicited mail. If the broker you choose doesn't understand or adhere to permission laws and trends in the consumer landscape, sending e-mail to the list you obtain can damage your image and your future ability to send e-mail.

Because the consumer ultimately decides what *unwanted* e-mail looks like, you can do everything right and end up with negative results. Furthermore, most EMPs discourage or disallow using rented lists and almost never allow using purchased lists.

As of this writing, obtain e-mail addresses by using the collect-where-you-connect methods discussed earlier in this chapter. If you still feel it's best to proceed with the services of a list broker, however, read on and proceed with caution.

Sticking to quality

Confirmed-permission lists are the only viable option for sending e-mails through list brokers. Confirmed-permission lists can be quite expensive because they are more difficult to obtain and because they contain e-mail addresses belonging to people who (at least for the moment) are interested in receiving specific types of information. You can expect to pay between 10 and 30 cents per e-mail address to send a single e-mail to a confirmed-permission list.

Confirmed-permission lists vary in quality, so remember to ask any broker some tough questions about the process used to obtain permission. The acid test of quality for a confirmed-permission list is whether the subscriber remembers opting in and also whether members of the list expect an e-mail from you as a result.

Make sure to clarify the following information, and use the responses to judge the likelihood of a memorable experience for the list subscriber:

+ **Where and how the e-mail addresses were obtained:** Make sure that any online forms used to obtain the e-mail addresses ask for explicit permission to share the e-mail address as opposed to stating usage in a separate permission policy.

+ **When permission was confirmed:** List subscribers might not remember opting in if permission was confirmed at the onset of the subscription and time has passed between the initial confirmation and the e-mail you intend to send. Ask the list broker to provide the opt-in date with any sample list or count.

+ **How interests were selected:** Some list brokers make assumptions about their subscribers' interests based on where the information is collected as opposed to brokers who actually ask subscribers to select or state their interests. For example, someone who fills out a survey and indicates that he loves live jazz music is a more valuable list subscriber than someone who purchases a jazz CD from a music website and fails to share whether he purchased it as a gift or was motivated by another interest. Make sure that interest information was supplied by the subscriber before paying an additional fee for an interest-based list.

Renting to own

Because quality confirmed-permission lists are so valuable, beware of supposed confirmed-permission lists for sale as a data file. Quality confirmed-permission lists are always rented out because the e-mail addresses are too valuable to sell.

As you might guess, *list rental* means that the list broker will never give you the e-mail addresses used to send your e-mail. Instead, you supply content to the list broker, and the list broker formats and sends your e-mail to the list.

Because list rental buys only one sending opportunity, include a sign-up link in your brokered e-mail. Simply asking the recipients to Buy It Now is asking for a small percentage of responses.

Including a sign-up link asking recipients to subscribe to your personal e-mail list can make it possible to own the information provided by people who are interested but who aren't ready to buy the moment they receive your brokered e-mail. If the list broker doesn't allow a subscription link in the e-mail, make sure that any links in your brokered e-mail lead to a *landing page* that includes your sign-up box, button, or link.

If you can capture sales and information by using a rented list, make sure that your e-mails continue to meet or exceed all possible professional standards to help keep subscribers interested and happy to be on the list after they've confirmed.

For more information about e-mail professionalism standards and best practices, visit the Email Experience Council website at www.email experience.org.

Chapter 4: Constructing an Effective Marketing E-Mail

In This Chapter

✔ Creating From and Subject lines

✔ Creating and laying out e-mail content

✔ Branding your e-mails

Deciding how to design and lay out your e-mail content is possibly the most important step in executing your e-mail marketing strategy. Designing your e-mail content entails choosing a format, such as a newsletter or event invitation, that matches your message and placing your content in visually appealing arrangements.

E-mail design is important because consumers tend to scan e-mails instead of reading them in their entirety. If your e-mails aren't easy to scan, no one will pay attention long enough to grasp your message or take action.

In addition to making your e-mails easy to scan, good e-mail designs enhance your business image by giving your e-mails a consistent and professional brand identity. Brand identity makes your e-mails more inviting and recognizable to your audience and tells your audience that your e-mail comes from a trustworthy and familiar source.

In this chapter, you find out how to organize and design your e-mail content so that your audience can easily scan and understand your message. You can also brand your e-mails to enhance your business image and identity.

Creating From and Subject Lines That Get Noticed

Creating an effective e-mail begins with placing familiar and motivating information into every e-mail header. The *header* is the portion of your e-mail that contains the following:

✦ A From line

✦ A From address

✦ A Subject line

✦ Messages and code inserted by e-mail programs

Individual e-mail programs display portions of your e-mail's header information so that users can sort and prioritize their e-mails and decide whether to view and open each e-mail. Figure 4-1 shows how Yahoo! Mail displays headers. You can look ahead to Figure 4-3 to see how Gmail handles headers on a smartphone.

An e-mail header

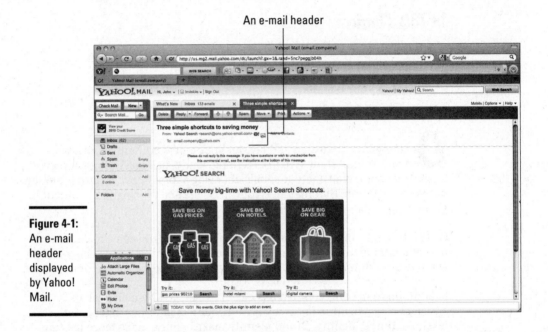

Figure 4-1: An e-mail header displayed by Yahoo! Mail.

When used appropriately, your header information helps your audience to identify you as a trustworthy sender and also helps to determine whether your e-mails are worthy of immediate attention.

Although you can't control all the information in your e-mail headers, you can control three important pieces of information that are most useful to your audience and to the deliverability of your e-mails:

✦ **From line:** Your *From line* is a line of text that tells the recipient of your e-mail who the e-mail is from. Most e-mail applications and EMPs allow you to add a line of text to the header of your e-mail to identify yourself.

✦ **From address:** Your *From address* is the e-mail address that is associated with you as the sender of the e-mail. Some e-mail programs display your From e-mail address along with your From line, but others display one or the other.

✦ **Your e-mail server's From address:** A *server address,* also known as an *Internet Protocol (IP) address,* is a unique number that identifies the server you use to send your e-mail. Most Internet service providers (ISPs) look at the e-mail server address in your header to see whether your server is recognized as a sender of legitimate commercial e-mail or whether your server has been reported as sending unsolicited e-mails. If you send e-mail from your own e-mail server or if your e-mail hosting company sends your e-mails from a server that is unfamiliar to the major ISPs, you can change the servers you send your e-mails from by switching to an EMP with a good reputation. (You can find out more about working with an EMP in Chapter 1 of this minibook.)

In the following sections, you create an e-mail header that makes your e-mails more familiar to your audience and prompts your audience to open your e-mails.

Filling out the From line

Altering your From line helps to ensure that most e-mail programs display enough information for your audience to identify and trust you as the source of your e-mails. Changing your From line is usually a matter of typing sender information in your e-mail application's account options, but EMPs allow you to create unique header information for each specific e-mail campaign during the campaign-creation process, as shown in Figure 4-2.

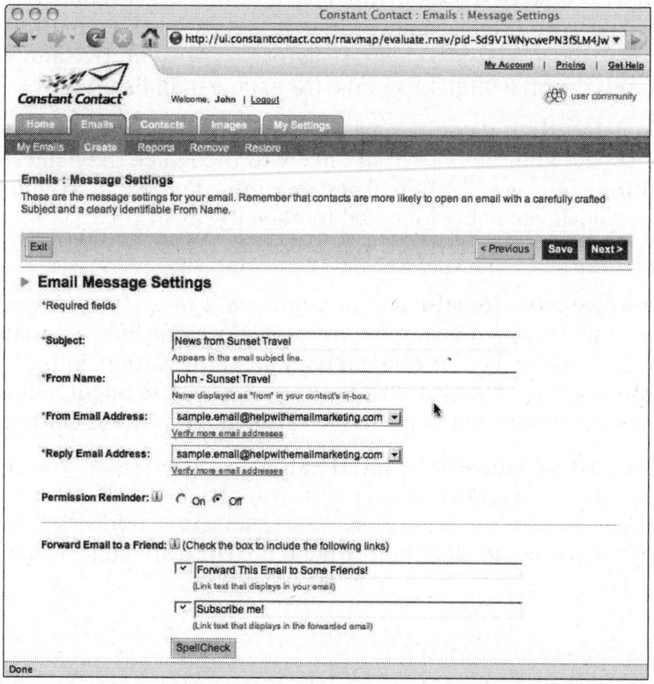

Figure 4-2: This EMP interface allows you to create header information.

Ask yourself how your audience is most likely to recognize you, and then craft your From line to include that information.

Including the following information in your headers keeps your e-mails familiar to your audience:

✦ **Your name:** If you're the only employee for your business or if your audience is most likely to identify with you personally rather than with your business name, use your name.

✦ **The name of your business:** If your audience is likely to recognize the name of your business but won't necessarily know you by name, use your business name. If your business commonly uses initials instead of spelling out the entire business name, make sure that your audience recognizes the abbreviation. For example, if your business is Acme Balloon Consultants, Inc., don't place ABCI in your From line unless you are sure that your audience can identify you by your company's initials.

✦ **Your name and your business name:** If you're a personal representative of a larger well-known business or franchise, use your name along with your business name. For example, you might use your first name followed by your business name, as in

    Steve - Sunset Travel

✦ **Representative name:** If you have multiple representatives in your business who your customers and prospects know by name, divide your e-mail addresses into separate lists by representative and use the most familiar representative's name for each e-mail list.

✦ **Your location:** If you're part of a large franchise or have multiple locations and your audience isn't likely to recognize the names of individuals within your organization, use geography. For example, you might use your business name followed by the city, as in

    Sunset Travel, Denver

✦ **Your website domain:** If your audience is more likely to recognize your website domain name over your name or your business name, use your domain name. If your domain uses an abbreviation, initials, or an alternate spelling of your entire business name, you might still want to use your business's full name in the From line for brand clarity.

✦ **Your e-mail address:** In addition to making sure that your From line identifies you and your business, you can create an e-mail address that serves as your From address. Create an e-mail address that identifies who you are and what you're sending. Here are some examples:

- *If you're sending a newsletter and your audience recognizes your personal name:* Send your e-mail newsletter by using

   newsletter@yourname.com

- *If you're sending coupons and your audience recognizes your business name:* Send your e-mail coupons by using

   coupons@yourbusinessname.com

- *If you're sending an event invitation and your audience recognizes a personal representative as well as your business name:* Send your e-mail invitation by using

   event_invitation@repname.businessname.com

- *If you're sending an announcement and your audience recognizes your website's domain name:* Send your e-mail announcement by using

   announcement@yourdomain.com

Current CAN-SPAM laws prohibit you from misrepresenting your From line and your From address. Make sure that the information in your From line honestly represents you and your business, and also make sure that you send your e-mails from a real, working e-mail address. For example, if you're a member of the local chamber of commerce, don't send the other chamber members e-mail using the name of the chamber in the From line. Reputable EMPs require you to send e-mails from a verified e-mail address to ensure that your e-mails are CAN-SPAM–compliant. For more information about professional standards and the CAN-SPAM laws, see Chapter 2 in this minibook.

Writing a Subject line

Your e-mail *Subject line* is a line of text that gives your audience a hint at the content in your e-mail. The most effective Subject lines are those that prompt your audience to open your e-mails to look for specific information.

Consistently coming up with good Subject lines is tough because most e-mail programs display only the first 30 to 50 characters, which gives you a limited amount of text to get your point across. In fact, most mobile devices only show the first 20–30 characters. Figure 4-3 shows how Gmail displays Subject lines on a mobile screen.

Save the information highlighting the benefits of your products or services for the body of your e-mail and use your Subject line to tell your audience why to open your e-mail immediately. Stating the immediate benefit of opening the e-mail creates a sense of urgency and tells your audience that your e-mail is important.

Figure 4-3:
E-mail
Subject
lines
displayed
by Gmail
on a mobile
screen.

Creating a sense of urgency with your text helps to increase viewer openings, but urgency can easily wear off if your Subject lines make urgent statements without hinting at the content in your e-mail. For example, Subject lines such as `Only 10 left` or `Sale ends soon` don't communicate the main subject of your e-mail — and are urgent only when they are used infrequently.

The following examples show how you can create urgency while still hinting at the main idea of the message. In each example pair, the first is a Subject line without urgency, and its mate is a revised Subject line with added urgency:

Not so good: What you need to know about Denver real estate

Better: What you need to know *now* about Denver real estate

Not so good: Flower sale

Better: Flower sale – early entry information

Not so good: Seminar invitation

Better: Last chance to register

Not so good: Tips for remodeling your kitchen

Better: Tomorrow's tips for remodeling your kitchen today

Test your Subject lines by sending the same e-mail with different Subject lines to a small sample of your list to determine which Subject line is going to result in the most openings. For example, if you have a list of 1,000 subscribers, send your e-mail to 100 list subscribers with one Subject line and to a different 100 list subscribers with another Subject line. Wait a day or two, and then send your e-mail to the remaining 800 with the Subject line that received the highest number of openings.

You might want to look at your junk folder occasionally to see what the spammers are up to so that you don't inadvertently copy some of their Subject line techniques. Here are some Subject line mistakes to avoid:

✦ Excessive punctuation, such as lots of exclamation points or question marks

✦ Symbols, such as dollar signs and asterisks

✦ Words with all capital letters (usually perceived as yelling)

✦ Your recipient's first name in the Subject line

✦ Using `RE:` unless the e-mail is really a response to a previous e-mail Subject line

✦ A blank Subject line

✦ Vague Subject lines that attempt to trick the reader into opening your e-mail. For example

  • `Hey you`

  • `Check this out`

  • `RE:`

  • `Personal information`

  • `Hi!`

The current CAN-SPAM laws prohibit Subject lines that are "likely to mislead a recipient, acting reasonably under the circumstances, about a material fact regarding the contents or subject matter of the message," so make sure that your Subject lines clearly and honestly represent the content in every e-mail. For more information about Subject line compliance, see Chapter 2 in this minibook.

Branding Your E-Mails to Enhance Your Image

Branding is the use of graphic design elements to give your business a consistent and unique identity while forming a mental image of your business's personality. Examples include

✦ Graphics and logos unique to your business

✦ Text and fonts that differentiate your business

✦ Colors used consistently to give your business an identity

Branding your e-mails helps your audience to immediately recognize and differentiate your e-mails from the unfamiliar e-mails they receive. Keeping your e-mail branding consistent over time allows your audience to become familiar with you and your e-mails as they receive multiple e-mails from you.

The following sections show how you can brand your e-mails to match your identity and the expectations of your audience.

Branding your e-mails with colors and design elements requires using HTML. If you don't know HTML, look to your EMP. Most EMPs allow you to customize your e-mail templates with your branding elements. If you aren't using an EMP to send your e-mails, a web designer can help you create a custom look and feel for your e-mail templates.

Matching your e-mails to your brand

All your business communications should contain consistent branding elements, and your e-mails are no exception. Matching every e-mail to your brand gives your audience confidence and makes your business more memorable every time your audience clicks to access your website or walks into your store and sees the same branding elements.

You can design your e-mails to match your brand in the following ways:

✦ **Include your logo in your e-mails, as shown in Figure 4-4.** Position your logo in the upper-left quadrant or top center of your e-mail, where readers are most likely to see it.

Using a company logo along with identifiable design elements brands your e-mail and reinforces your company's image.

Figure 4-4:
Use a
company
logo.

Courtesy of Avalon Photography

✦ **Use the colors from your logo in your e-mails.** If your logo has multiple colors, pull the colors from your logo and use them for the borders, backgrounds, and fonts in your e-mails. If your logo uses only one color, you can use a graphic design program to create a palette of colors that works well with the color in your logo. A lot of free and low-cost color-matching and color palette tools are online. Use your favorite search engine to find your favorite.

✦ **Use the colors from your website in your e-mails.** When readers click from your e-mail to your website, they might hesitate if your website looks different from your e-mail. When you design your e-mails, use the colors in your website in a similar fashion. For example, if your website uses a gray background with black text, use the same colors for those elements in your e-mails.

✦ **Match your website offers with your e-mail offers.** If your e-mail includes an offer with a specific design, make sure that your website uses the same design elements in the offer if you're directing people to your website to complete a purchase or to read more information about the offer in your e-mail.

✦ **Match your print communications to your e-mails.** If you're sending direct mail or printing ads to follow up or reinforce your e-mail messages, make sure that your print communications match your e-mails as well as the rest of your communications.

✦ **Use fonts that match your brand in your e-mails.** Consistent fonts add to the overall look and feel of your e-mails as well as add emotion behind the text. Keep your fonts consistent in all your communications, and use the same fonts for similar visual anchors. For example, if your e-mail contains three articles with three headlines in one column, use the same font for each headline in the column. The benefits of font consistency are negated if you use too many different kinds of fonts in one e-mail. Stick with two or three different fonts in each e-mail to avoid heaping visual distractions on your audience.

✦ **Make sure that your e-mails reflect your business's personality.** Just as you want design elements that match your brand, your writing should match your business's personality, too. Show your e-mails to a few trustworthy friends or advisors and ask them to tell you whether your writing style is a good match for your image. If you aren't a good writer, consider using a copywriter to help you maintain your image using the text of your articles and offers. Tell your copywriter whether you want the text in your e-mail to make your business seem

- Serious or humorous

- Professional or casual

- Formal or friendly

- Exclusive or universal

- Urgent or customary

- Insistent or politely persuasive

Maintaining brand consistency with multiple e-mail formats

If you use multiple formats and each format doesn't match your brand with enough consistency, your audience might not recognize every e-mail you send. At the same time, if your audience can't tell the difference between your formats, you lose your ability to effectively communicate the appropriate amount of urgency in each of your e-mail formats. For example, if your readers recognize your e-mail as a lengthy newsletter format, they might be inclined to read it later. If your audience recognizes your e-mail as an event invitation, they might be inclined to take immediate action by responding with a reservation.

The best way to brand multiple e-mail formats is to match your brand identity in each format while keeping your e-mails just different enough for people to know that each e-mail is unique. Figures 4-5 and 4-6 show two distinct e-mail formats with similar brand identity.

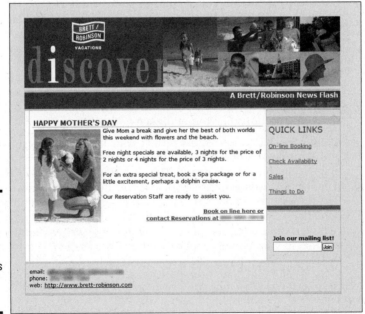

Figure 4-5: This e-mail is branded to identify the business and offer a news flash.

Courtesy of Brett/Robinson Vacations

Making the difference just noticeable

If you look at a 1950s Coca-Cola bottle and a Coca-Cola bottle produced today, you'll notice a significant difference. Big companies (such as Coca-Cola) continuously research their branding elements to keep them up to date with consumer preferences. Still, Coca-Cola wouldn't dare to change the branding on its cans and bottles too rapidly, or consumers might have a hard time identifying them on the store shelves. Marketing experts use a concept known as *the just-noticeable difference* to change brand identities over time. That is, you change the brand just enough to be noticeable but not enough to be unrecognizable. If you need to change your e-mail branding elements, such as when your website gets a new face-lift, make sure to change your branding elements slowly over time so that your audience still recognizes your e-mails while the changes are taking place.

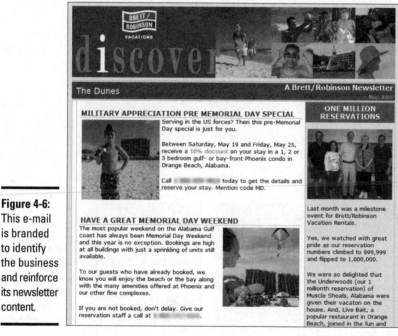

Figure 4-6:
This e-mail is branded to identify the business and reinforce its newsletter content.

Courtesy of Brett/Robinson Vacations

Here are some ways you can brand multiple e-mail formats with consistency while giving each format a unique identity:

✦ Use the same top-bar image with slightly different colors for each format.

✦ Change the colors in your logo slightly for each format.

✦ Use slightly different colors for backgrounds and borders in each format.

✦ Use graphical text to create a unique title for the top of each format.

The ABCs of E-Mail Layout

Consumers tend to focus their attention on your e-mail content by using the layout in the e-mail as a guide for their eyes. E-mail marketing experts often use e-mail heat maps to determine which areas of an e-mail are likely to draw the most attention. An e-mail *heat map* is an image generated by a special device that tracks eye movement when someone looks at an e-mail. You can see several examples of e-mail heat maps at www.eyetools.com.

Heat maps use different colors and shading to illustrate which parts of an e-mail draw the most attention. Data gathered by using heat maps and testing various e-mail designs helps to shed light on the e-mail designs and layouts that are most likely to get your content noticed.

A good way to visualize your content positioning is to mentally divide each of your e-mail templates into quadrants and then position your visual anchors and related content according to the order in which consumers tend to focus their attention on each quadrant.

Figure 4-7 shows how the majority of consumers scan e-mails. Most consumers begin reading in the upper-left quadrant and then continue in one of two directions, depending on the strength of the visual anchors in the adjacent quadrants: across the page (the figure on the left) or down the page (the figure on the right).

Figure 4-7: Most consumers focus their attention on the upper-left quadrant of an e-mail and then scan across the page (left) or down the page (right).

Courtesy of Constant Contact

Because the upper-left quadrant tends to get the most attention from consumers, position your most important content there in your e-mail.

And although you don't have to divide your content into quadrants visually, you should emphasize important content in the upper-left quadrant. Here are some examples of positioning e-mail content in the upper-left quadrant:

✦ **Display your brand.** Your audience is more likely to read your e-mail when they recognize the source of the e-mail. Make sure that your business name, logo, and other brand-identifying design elements appear somewhere in the upper-left quadrant.

✦ **Begin your e-mail message with a main headline.** A main headline doesn't have to reside completely within the upper-left quadrant, but main headlines get more attention if they begin there.

✦ **Include your e-mail's main call to action.** A *call to action* is a statement that asks your audience to do something specific, such as purchasing a specific item, clicking a link, or dialing a phone number. If your e-mail contains valuable offers, make sure that your main offer is contained — or at least referenced — in the upper-left quadrant. If your e-mail's main intent is to get your audience to read a specific section of your e-mail that contains your main call to action along with supporting information, make sure to use the upper-left quadrant to prompt your audience where to look.

✦ **Place the strongest visual anchors.** Visual anchors — such as images, links, headlines, icons, bullets, and graphics — can reinforce your audience's perception of your most important content. Strong visual anchors used in the upper-left quadrant help minimize how long your audience spends trying to figure out what content is important enough to read. Figure 4-8 shows an e-mail with visual anchors throughout the body of the e-mail.

✦ **Limit the size of images.** Images draw attention, but if you include an image in your e-mail that takes up most of the upper-left quadrant, your audience might miss the text associated with that image. If you decide to use an image in the upper-left quadrant, use one small enough to allow the inclusion of the first few words of a text headline. You can read more details about images later in this chapter.

✦ **Show your audience where to look next.** If your e-mail includes important content in different quadrants, use navigation links and directions in the upper-left quadrant to help your audience navigate the e-mail. For example, the e-mail's upper-left quadrant might contain a table of contents with navigation links. You can read more about navigation links later in this chapter.

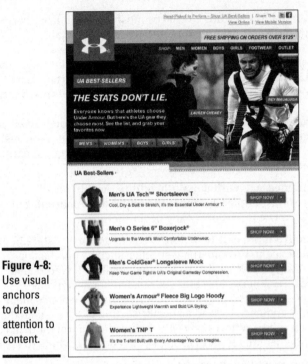

Figure 4-8:
Use visual
anchors
to draw
attention to
content.

Including Images in Your E-Mails

Images can enhance the look and feel of your e-mails and help to reinforce the messages contained in the body of your e-mails. Images are strong visual anchors that help to communicate your main message and divide your text into more easily scanned sections.

Proper image positioning makes your e-mail appear inviting and easy to read. Arbitrarily positioned images are cumbersome to scan and can cause your e-mail to appear cluttered.

Placing images in your e-mails requires more than an eye for design, however, because images and e-mail browsers don't always play well together. Embedding images into the body of your e-mail can cause deliverability issues and make your e-mail slow to download, so you need to take a few extra steps to ensure that your images are ready to include.

The next sections cover what kinds of images you can include in your e-mails and describe how to effectively place them in your e-mails.

Using columns to organize your content

Positioning visual anchors in quadrants is a fine way to attract attention to multiple groups of content, but unless you organize your visual anchors and related content into patterns, your audience won't be able to effectively prioritize the additional content that your visual anchors are trying to emphasize.

Using columns to organize your visual anchors and related content allows your audience to locate different groups of content as they scan your e-mail. Most EMPs provide e-mail templates with lots of column-based layouts, and web designers and some EMPs can assist you in creating more customized column-based layouts.

Choosing a file format for your images

Images are graphic files that graphics programs can read and display on a computer screen. Whether you obtain your images with a digital camera or buy them online from a provider of royalty-free stock photography, make sure that your images are formatted for use in e-mail:

✦ **Use a file format that e-mail browsers can read.** An *image file format* is the type of compression used on an image to limit the amount of data required to store the image on a computer. *Compression* changes the amount of space the image takes up when stored on a computer, and image compression causes the graphics to display differently (especially when you reduce or enlarge the dimensions of the image). The three best file formats to use in e-mail browsers are

   • *JPG or JPEG (Joint Photographic Experts Group):* This format is a standard for Internet and e-mail images and works well for most images.

   • *GIF (Graphic Interchange Format):* This format is best for images with only a few colors.

   • *PNG (Portable Network Graphics):* This format is similar to GIF compression but can display colors more effectively.

If your image isn't already in one of these three formats, use a graphic design application or image editor to save the image as a JPG file.

✦ **Check your file size.** The *file size* of your image refers to the amount of data your image contains measured in kilobytes (K). Images should be less than 50K to download quickly enough for most e-mail users. If an image you want to use in your e-mail is greater than 50K, you can change the file size in a graphic design or image-editing application:

   • *Reduce the dimensions of the image.* Smaller images contain less data.

   • *Reduce the image resolution to 72 dpi. Image resolution,* also known as dots per inch (dpi) or pixels per inch (ppi), refers to how many dots (or pixels) are in each inch of your image. The more dots per inch, the more detail your image is capable of displaying. More dots require more data, however, so images with higher resolutions download and display more slowly than images with lower resolutions.

72 dpi has enough resolution to appear properly on a computer screen, but images printed at 72 dpi are likely to appear fuzzy. If your audience is likely to print your e-mail and it's important that your images are printed with more definition, link your audience to a PDF version of your e-mail containing print-quality images that are 300 dpi or higher.

Don't embed: Referencing your images

Never embed images in your e-mail as a file or attached to your e-mail because embedded and attached images usually cause a higher percentage of your e-mails to be filtered into junk folders.

Instead of embedding or attaching images, use image references that point to images stored in a public folder on your website server. An *image reference* is a line of HTML that tells your computer to display an image that's located in a folder on a remote server. Here's an example:

```
<img src="http://www.yourwebsite.com/public/imagefolder/imagename.jpg">
```

If you aren't comfortable using HTML to create image references in your e-mails, you can use an EMP to help you reference images. If you can't store images on your website server or if you don't have a website, you can use an EMP with an image-hosting feature. That way, you can store your images on that server and automatically create image references to insert the images you upload to your e-mails. Figure 4-9 shows an EMP interface that allows you to reference images in a folder on your server or images that you upload to the EMP's server.

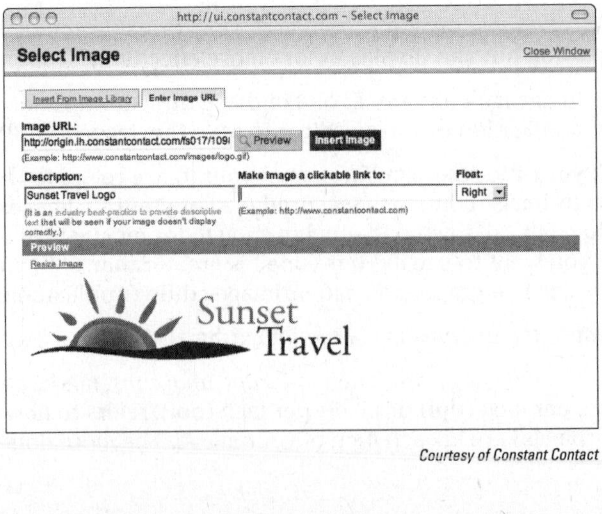

Figure 4-9:
Use an EMP to insert image tags in HTML to avoid attaching images to your e-mail.

Courtesy of Constant Contact

Whether you code your own image references or use an EMP, you need to know the URL of the image you're referencing.

To find the URL of an image that's on your website, follow these steps:

1. **Open your web browser.**

2. **Navigate to the page that contains the image you want to include in your e-mail.**

3. **View the image properties by right-clicking (Windows); or by Control-clicking (Mac) and choosing the appropriate option given by your Web browser to copy the URL or image location.**

Some browsers allow you to view the URL by selecting image properties, and other browsers require you to open the image in a new browser window to view the image URL.

With Internet Explorer, you can find the URL in the Address (URL) field of the Properties dialog box. With Firefox, you can copy the URL directly or view the image by itself and copy the URL that appears in your navigation bar.

If your image isn't already on your website, follow these steps to find the location of your image file:

1. **Upload the image file to a public folder on your server.**

2. **Go to your website server's file manager and find the folder that contains your image.**

The image URL is the folder location followed by the image filename. For example

```
http://www.yourdomain.com/public/site/image_files/filename.jpg
```

When you reference image locations, you must have permission to use the images if you don't own them, even if they're publicly accessible on a website. Also keep in mind that you can't determine the location of background images and images that appear in Flash websites by clicking the image. You have to find the image location by using the folder address on your server or by finding the reference in your website's HTML.

Including Text in Your E-Mails

Text is mandatory in e-mail marketing messages. Plain, text-only e-mails significantly underperform compared with e-mails that include HTML design elements along with the text in the message, so applying design elements to your text is a balance. Too much plain text can make your e-mails appear unapproachable and difficult to read. Comparatively, too many design elements can cause distractions and make your messages more difficult to understand.

When used correctly, different fonts and text styles can create moods in your e-mails and change the tone of the words that you use:

✦ *Headlines* can help to entice your audience to read longer sections of text or take action on your e-mail content.

✦ *Paragraphs of text* can give your audience important information, help them form opinions, and give them compelling reasons to purchase your products or services.

✦ *Links* in your e-mails let your audience click keywords and phrases to take action on the content of your e-mails without having to use another medium. (Check out the next section for more about using links effectively.)

It's important to choose fitting text elements for your e-mails to enrich your e-mail's meaning as well as to ensure that your text communicates the main idea of your e-mail quickly and effectively. To accomplish greater success with text, apply deliberate use of fonts and styles instead of opting for plain text.

Fonts are graphical representations of letters in the alphabet. Fonts are useful for

✦ Making your words more legible

✦ Giving your words more emphasis

✦ Suggesting moods and emotions to reinforce your words

✦ Branding your e-mails and making your e-mails look more professional

In addition to applying different fonts to your text, you can also alter your fonts by applying different style elements to the font. This section includes tips for choosing fonts and applying stylistic changes to them so that the appearance of your text matches your e-mail's theme and message.

Because most e-mail programs use HTML to display e-mails to their users, you need to apply fonts and styles to your e-mail text by using the HTML code that tells the e-mail program which fonts and styles to apply when it displays your text to the user. Here's an example of a line of HTML code that defines various font elements for a headline:

```
<font color="#FFFFFF" face="Arial, Verdana, Helvetica, sans-
    serif" size="5" style="FONT-FAMILY: Arial, Verdana,
    Helvetica, sans-serif;FONT-SIZE:18pt; FONT-WEIGHT:bold;
    COLOR:#FFFFFF;">
    Headline Here</font>
```

A good rule is to make your headlines 2 to 4 point (pt) sizes larger than your paragraph text. For example, if your paragraph text is 12pt, use 14pt or 16pt for your headline.

To avoid the HTML hassle, most EMPs allow you to specify fonts and apply style elements to your fonts by using font tools in a special user interface. Figure 4-10 shows a font and style toolbar in an EMP interface.

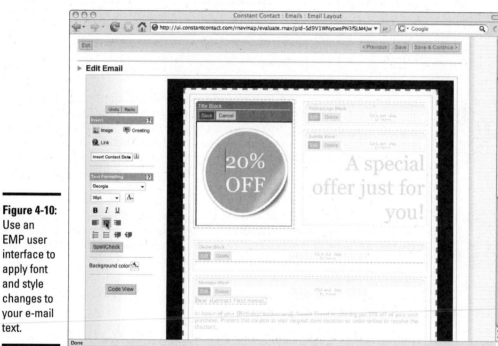

Figure 4-10: Use an EMP user interface to apply font and style changes to your e-mail text.

Courtesy of Constant Contact

Fonts specified in HTML tell the user's computer to display the applicable text, using the specified font. Any font specified in the HTML code has to be available on the user's computer to display properly.

Because most people don't go to the trouble of installing the latest fonts on their computers, formatting e-mail text by using fonts that are common to the majority of computers helps ensure that your text looks the same on your audience's computers as it does on yours. Figure 4-11 shows a list of fonts that are commonly available on default operating systems.

Figure 4-11:
Use commonly available fonts to ensure that text displays properly on your audience's computers.

Arial	Lucida Console
Arial Narrow	System
Comic Sans MS	Tahoma
Courier New	Times New Roman
Garamond	Trebuchet MS
Georgia	Verdana
Impact	

If you want to use text in a font or style that's not commonly available or one that's not possible with HTML, you can use graphic design software to create an image of the text you want to use. Use this option sparingly, however, because images take longer to download than text, and e-mail programs don't usually display the images in an e-mail until the recipient enables them. You can read more about image blocking in Chapter 6 of this minibook.

Including too many different fonts in a single e-mail can make your text look disorderly and cluttered, so make sure that you limit your e-mail's text to only two or three different fonts. Using one font for all headlines and another font for all body text is an acceptable standard.

Including Links in Your E-Mails

Your e-mail isn't going to sell anything to your audience if you don't make it easy for your audience to take action on your message. Placing links in the body of your e-mails gives your audience easy ways to

✦ Visit specific pages on your website

✦ Download files and additional information

✦ Order your products or services by clicking through from your e-mail to an online shopping cart

✦ Jump to specific sections of your e-mail by clicking instead of scrolling

The following sections show you how to include the most effective links in your e-mails so that you can drive your audience toward actions that benefit your business objectives.

E-mail links can be tracked back to the clicker when you use an EMP. You can read more about link tracking in Chapter 6 in this minibook.

Making your e-mails accessible

People with disabilities and physical challenges need to be able to read your e-mail content and respond accordingly. Some disabled and aging e-mail users can read and respond to your e-mails only if you design your e-mails with their challenges in mind. And some disabled people, such as those with visual impairments, have special tools that verbally read your e-mail or otherwise help them comprehend e-mail and other online content. Some e-mail designs make such tools cumbersome to use, so design your e-mails accordingly — or provide two versions of your e-mail.

Visual impairments aren't the only disabilities that might make your e-mail difficult to understand. Here are some tips for making your e-mails accessible to many types of disabled and aging subscribers:

✔ **Provide a link to a text-only version of your e-mail** to allow text-reading devices to easily read your content to people with visual impairments. Make sure that your e-mail begins with the link and a summary of your e-mail content so that visually impaired subscribers can tell whether your e-mail is worth listening to in its entirety. Also make sure that your text version adequately describes any video, images, charts, and graphics in your e-mail.

✔ **Use image descriptions,** also known as *alt text,* when including images in your e-mail. Reading devices read alt text so that a visually impaired person knows what images are in the e-mail. This is especially important when you use images that contain text.

✔ **Use fonts and point sizes that are easy to read** so that people with diminished vision can interpret them. Make sure that the text version of your e-mail avoids using absolute font sizes in your HTML; otherwise, your fonts can't be enlarged (not good).

✔ **Use text and background colors with sufficient contrast** so that words are easy to read.

✔ **Provide a link to a text-only transcript** of any audio used in your e-mail.

✔ **Make sure that any forms you ask your subscribers to fill in** can be tabbed through in a logical order. Along the same line, design your forms to minimize the number of keystrokes necessary to complete the form.

✔ **Keep your e-mail designs short, concise, and easy to scan.** Avoid distracting design elements — such as blinking text, flashing images, or audio and video streams — that can't easily be turned off.

If you use an EMP to design your e-mails, talk to those folks about accessibility requirements. You can read more about making all your Internet marketing efforts accessible at www.w3.org/WAI.

Using text links

Text links are clickable words or phrases that result in certain actions when clicked. Links use HTML to tell the computer what to do when someone clicks the link, so your e-mail links need to contain HTML to work in e-mail programs.

If you're using raw HTML to create links for your e-mails, a simple link to a website looks like this:

```
<a href="http://www.yourwebsite.com">Link Text Here</a>
```

Most e-mail programs and EMPs allow you to enter a URL into a user interface, and the program then takes care of adding the HTML behind the scenes to turn your text into a link that points to the URL you entered. Figure 4-12 shows an EMP interface that allows you to create text links in your e-mails.

To link to a landing page on your website (HTML websites only), follow these steps:

1. **Open your web browser and navigate to the page where you want your link to point.**

2. **Highlight all the text in your browser's address bar (including the** `http` **part).**

3. **Copy the text:**

   • *Windows:* Right-click the selected text and choose Copy.

   • *Mac:* Control-click the selected text and choose Copy.

4. **Paste the URL into your e-mail program's link-creation user interface.**

   • *Windows:* Right-click and choose Paste.

   • *Mac:* Control-click and choose Paste.

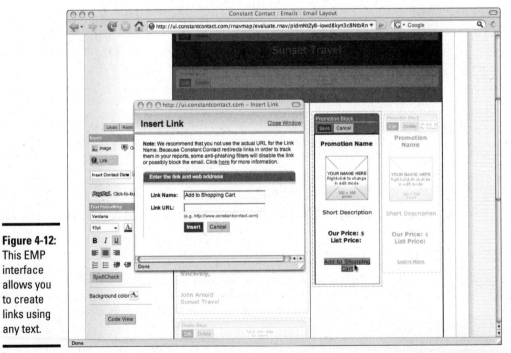

Figure 4-12:
This EMP interface allows you to create links using any text.

Linking to an e-mail address

Instead of linking text to another web page, you might want to link text to an e-mail address. This type of link opens a new message in your visitor's default e-mail program, often with the To text box filled with an e-mail address you designate in the link. To link to an e-mail address, type **mailto:** followed by the e-mail address you want to link to into your e-mail program's link-creation user interface. For example

```
mailto:email.company@test-
      email.com
```

If you want an e-mail link to prefill the Subject line or From line, or if you want to use an e-mail link to include several e-mail addresses, you can find a free e-mail link encoder that automatically generates the code you need at the following website:

```
http://email.about.com/
      library/misc/blmailto_
      encoder.htm
```

E-mail links tell the user's computer to open the default e-mail program on the user's computer. If the person clicking your link uses a web-based e-mail program (such as AOL or Yahoo!) instead of a desktop e-mail program (such as Outlook or Outlook Express), the link won't allow him to use his web-based application. To eliminate confusion for web-based e-mail users, spell out the e-mail address in your link so that folks can type it in their preferred e-mail program when necessary.

One of the most important things about text links is choosing the appropriate words to name the link. Although you can't use every tip for every link you name, you can apply these tips to links throughout your e-mails as appropriate:

✦ **Name your links intuitively.** A good rule for naming links is "what you click is what you get." In other words, name your links to tell your audience exactly what is going to happen when they click the link. Here are some examples:

- *If your link downloads a file:* Include the file type in parentheses. For example, a link that downloads a Portable Document Format file could read

```
              More Info on This Product(PDF)
```

- *If your link takes the reader to a website where he might have to search or scroll to view information:* Include the directions in your link. For example, if a link takes your audience to your blog, your link could read

```
              Details on my blog (scroll to article 5)
```

- *If your link requires additional clicks or actions after the initial click:* Name your link describing the first step in the process. For example, a link that reads `Donate Your Car` isn't as clear as a link that reads

```
              Read 3 steps to donating your car.
```

- *If you're linking to an e-mail address:* Include the e-mail address in the link because e-mail links open the resident e-mail program on the user's computer, and users who use a web-based e-mail program won't be able to use the link. (See the nearby sidebar for more on linking to an e-mail address.) For example, instead of using a link that reads `E-Mail Us`, your link should read

  `E-mail us at` *`company@yourdomain`*`.com.`

✦ **Name links using the text in your articles and headlines.** Avoid link names, such as `Click Here`, because links attract attention and your audience won't be able to identify interesting text links if you give them generic names. Figure 4-13 shows an example of text links within the body of a paragraph.

Figure 4-13: This e-mail uses text links in the body text.

> **Membership Renewal Offer - A $300 value!**
> **Free Networking for a Year!**
>
> Renew your chamber membership this month and you'll receive free admission to every networking event for an entire year.
>
> If your membership isn't up for renewal, you can still take advantage of this special offer with our new 3-year membership. Read More

✦ **Name links to give you information about the clicker.** Because e-mail links are trackable back to the clicker, naming your links in ways that give you insight into the motivations of the clicker makes your click reports more meaningful. For example, if your e-mail newsletter contains an article that includes three of the best places to golf with kids and you provide your readers with a link to view more information about family golf vacations, getting a group of people to click a `Read More` link isn't as valuable as getting a group of people to click a link that reads

  `Are your kids under 12? Read about the best places to golf for younger kids.`

✦ **Name links by describing the immediate benefits of clicking the link.** You're likely to get more clicks when you give your audience good reasons to click. Instead of naming links by highlighting the mechanics of the click — as in `Go to Our Website` — include the benefits in the link. For example, try

  `Shop on our website and receive an additional 10% off and free shipping.`

Text only, please

Text-only e-mails are a reality for people who check their e-mail on mobile devices. Some people also install e-mail filters and firewalls on their computers to convert HTML e-mails into text to protect their systems from malicious programs and files. When a device or filter converts an HTML e-mail into text, the e-mail can become garbled and confusing for the recipient. Some conversions result in displaying the entire HTML code; others show the text along with long lines of code for links, images, and other design elements.

Because sending text-only e-mails to everyone eliminates links and tracking altogether, you might want to use an EMP that allows your e-mail list subscribers to choose a preformatted, text-only version of your HTML e-mails. That way, your e-mail is converted before it's sent and formatted to look good to the recipient. Some services even allow you to create and edit text-only versions of your HTML e-mails so that you can control the content of the text version completely.

Making your images into links

Consumers like to click images, so making your images clickable gives your audience more opportunities to engage in your information. Making images into links requires using an image tag `<src>` combined with a URL link tag `<href>` in HTML. Here's an example:

```
<a href="http://www.yourwebsite.com">
    <img src="http://www.yourwebsite.com/filename/imagename.jpg/></a>
```

TIP

If you aren't familiar with coding your own image links, use an EMP with a user interface for creating image links. Figure 4-14 shows an EMP interface that allows you to insert a URL to add a link to an image.

Figure 4-14:
This EMP interface allows you to insert a URL to make an image into a link.

Courtesy of Constant Contact

Here are some tips for making your image links more effective when you include them in your e-mails:

✦ **Make your image links intuitive.** If your image doesn't make the destination of your link clear to your audience, you're probably better off with a text link or using text to tell your audience what will happen when they click the image.

✦ **Link logos to your website.** Most people expect your logo to link to your website's homepage, so including link functionality in every logo allows your audience to easily access your homepage information.

✦ **Link single images to more images or larger images.** When space allows only one image or smaller-size images, you can link your images to web pages that contain more images and images with higher resolutions. Remember to make sure that the content related to the image states or implies that the image links to more images.

Adding navigation links

Navigation links are HTML links that allow your audience to jump to visual anchors within the body of your e-mail. If your e-mails have one or more headlines or bodies of content that your audience has to scroll to for viewing, you can include navigation links in your e-mail to

✦ Highlight the content that your audience can't see immediately.

✦ Allow your audience to access the information by clicking a link instead of scrolling.

You can also include links to your website to allow your audience to jump from your e-mail to specific content on your website.

Navigation links are actually anchor links in HTML. *Anchor links* are HTML tags that reference a specific portion of content within an HTML document and automatically scroll the browser to the top of the referenced content when clicked. To create an anchor link, you have to create a name for the anchor using an anchor tag and place the anchor in your website code at the beginning of the content you want to link to. Then you add a link in your e-mail text that points to the anchor. Using your HTML or website editor of choice, follow these basic steps (the specifics depend on the editor you're using):

1. **Use an anchor tag to place your anchor, and include the** name **attribute to identify the anchor's name.**

Use the first word of the headline or section of content for the anchor name so that you can remember how to name your anchor link later.

- *To set the anchor in text,* include an `<a>` anchor tag with a name attribute within your paragraph tags:

  ```
  <p><a name="anchorname">headline or
  title</p>
  ```

- *To name an image as an anchor,* include the `name` attribute within the image tag:

  ```
  <img name="anchorname" src="http://www.emailtrainer.com/
  sample/image_file/imagename.jpg">
  ```

If you're new to HTML, note that you should replace `anchorname` in the preceding examples with whatever name you'd like to use. Also, `headline or title` stands in for the text that actually appears on your site, and the URL in the preceding image tag also stands in for the location and filename of the image you want to use.

2. **Create your anchor link by inserting the `<a>` anchor tag in your HTML e-mail text, with the `href` attribute pointing to the anchor name you specify in Step 1, and preceded by a `#` character.**

   - *To create a TOC link that scrolls to your anchor tag,* use the following:

     ```
     <a href="#anchorname">TOC link text</a>
     ```

     Details on TOC links appear in the next section.

   - *To create a navigation link that scrolls to an anchor link on your website,* use the following:

     ```
     <a href="http://www.yourwebsite.com/page.html#anchorname">
     navigation link text</a>
     ```

Most EMPs allow you to create navigation links in your e-mails, and many include navigation links in basic e-mail template designs.

Including a table of contents in your e-mails

An e-mail *table of contents (TOC)* is a special group of navigation links that lists headlines; each headline is linked to a different section of content within your e-mail. Figure 4-15 shows an e-mail that includes a TOC in the upper-left quadrant.

TOCs are necessary only when your e-mail has lots of content that your audience has to scroll to view. If you decide you need a TOC in your e-mail because of the amount of content in your e-mail, take a moment to think about whether you're sending too much information in a single e-mail. Cutting down on your content and increasing your frequency might be a better solution to making your e-mails easier to scan.

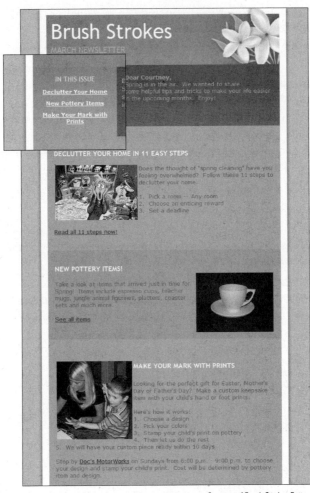

Figure 4-15:
This e-mail includes a TOC to help readers find information quickly.

Courtesy of Brush Strokes Pottery

If you can't reduce your content, using a TOC is a great way to summarize your content and allow your audience to find and access the content that interests them most. Here are some tips for including a TOC in your e-mails:

✦ **Include a heading above your table of contents.** Use wording, such as `Quick Links` or `Find It Fast`.

✦ **Keep your link headlines short.** You can use the first few words of the article headlines to which you're linking, or you can repeat short headlines as your main headlines and then use subheadings in your articles to expand on main headlines.

✦ **Make your link headlines clear.** Links should clearly communicate the content readers will see when they click. Clever links that intend to generate curiosity are generally harder to understand than clear link headlines and might cause disappointment if the linked message doesn't meet the clicker's expectations.

✦ **Keep your TOC above the scroll line.** The *scroll line* is the point at the bottom of your audience's screen where the e-mail content is no longer visible in the preview pane without scrolling. The whole point of a TOC is to keep people from scrolling. Thus, if your TOC is so long that it stretches beyond the preview pane, your e-mail probably has too much content.

Book V
Chapter 4

Constructing an
Effective Marketing
E-Mail

Linking to files in your e-mails

E-mail can deliver attached files of all sorts, but attaching files should be reserved for sending personal e-mails to a small number of people at a time. Most e-mail programs and e-mail servers have security settings that send e-mails with attached files to a junk folder when the program suspects that the e-mail is commercial in nature.

Even though file attachments are e-mail delivery killers, you can still use files by linking to them within the content of your e-mails.

To link to a downloadable file (if your file is already accessible with a link on your website), follow these steps:

1. **Open your web browser and navigate to the page that contains the link to your file.**

2. **Copy the link:**

- *Windows:* Right-click and choose Copy Shortcut.

- *Mac:* Control-click and choose Copy Link Location.

3. **Paste the shortcut into your e-mail program's link-creation user interface:**

- *Windows:* Right-click and choose Paste.

- *Mac:* Control-click and choose Paste.

If your file isn't already on your website, use the following steps instead:

1. **Upload the file to a public folder on your server.**

2. **Type the location of the file into your e-mail program's link-creation user interface.**

For example

```
http://www.yourdomain.com/public/site/public_files/filename.pdf
```

The next section describes some of the files that you might want to include in your e-mails along with tips on how to link to them.

Linking to video files

Video can be a powerful selling tool for some businesses, but deliverability is a challenge if you try to send an entire video file in an e-mail. Instead of delivering a video in its entirety — embedded in the content of an e-mail — insert a screenshot image of your video and include a link to play the video on your website, as shown in Figure 4-16.

Figure 4-16: Host videos on your website or YouTube and link them to your e-mail content by using a screen shot of the video.

Thanks for your interest in marketing with online video. I hope you enjoy the following video.

More John Arnold Videos on
You Tube

If your video has sound, warn people before they click in case they're reading your e-mail at the office or in a place where sound might cause a distraction.

Linking to sound files

Sound files can allow your audience to multitask by listening to information while they scan and click the links in your e-mail. Like other files, sound files should be hosted on your website and linked to text or images in your e-mail. Links to sound files that contain soothing music or other mood elements can distract your recipient from more important clicks, so make sure that sound helps to communicate your main message.

If the message itself is your sound file — say, you're announcing your latest podcast or an archived radio show appearance — link the user to your website to play the sound file so that he can surf all your valuable information while listening. Figure 4-17 shows an e-mail with a link to a sound file. For more on podcasting, see Book VI, Chapter 7.

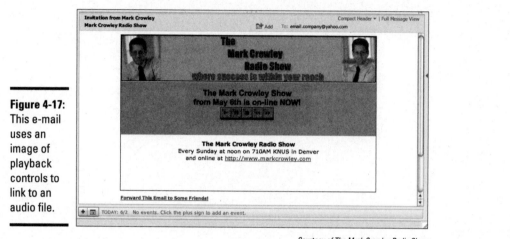

Figure 4-17:
This e-mail
uses an
image of
playback
controls to
link to an
audio file.

Courtesy of The Mark Crowley Radio Show

Linking to document files

Portable Document Format (PDF) files are the most popular files for e-mail delivery. As with other files, don't attach PDF files to your marketing e-mails. Instead, link to their location on your website. When linking to a file, make sure to tell your clickers that their click will result in a specific type of download.

For example, if a short, summarized article in your newsletter ends with a link to the entire article in PDF format, make sure that the link includes (PDF) in the text of the link or use an icon to indicate that clicking will result in a document download. If the document is long and the information the clicker wants to obtain isn't on one page, make sure to tell the clicker where to find the information. For example, your link might read

```
Read entire article (PDF page 3)
```

Chapter 5: Making Your E-Mail Content Valuable

In This Chapter

✔ Determining the value of your e-mail content

✔ Including valuable offers in your e-mails

✔ Coming up with a strong call to action

✔ Making your e-mails inherently valuable

✔ Giving your e-mails relevance over time

When people subscribe to your e-mail list, they share personal information with the expectation of receiving something valuable. Consumers aren't likely to value multiple e-mails that highlight only the distinguishing characteristics of your business. Repetitive e-mail content results in subscriber boredom. And boring your audience leads to low open rates, lost clicks, and unsubscribe requests.

Keeping your e-mail content valuable over time helps ensure that your list subscribers keep their attention and their subscription active while you attempt to capture purchases from them throughout the course of each buying cycle. The two basic types of value when it comes to e-mail content are

✦ An offer that is valuable when acted upon

✦ An *inherent* value, that is, content that's valuable in and of itself

Valuable content won't automatically make your audience rush to your business to part with their money. Your e-mail also needs to have a strong call to action to give your content a purpose and prompt your audience to help you meet your objectives.

This chapter covers some fundamental guidelines for including value in your e-mail strategy to deliver important information about your business while giving your audience continued reasons to open, read, and take action on your e-mails, no matter which stage of the buying cycle they're in.

Sending Valuable Offers

Offers are conditional statements that give your audience one or more reasons to make an immediate decision instead of postponing a decision.

Offers don't necessarily have to require a purchase decision to have value. Sometimes offers are necessary just to motivate your audience to consider all the information related to making a purchase decision. Whether your offers ask for an immediate purchase or just a visit to your website, your offers have to be valuable, or your audience won't take action on them.

Because the value in postponing a decision almost always has to do with the fact that people prefer to hold on to their money, offers usually take the form of discounts and savings. However, some people value other types of offers. The following sections describe money-saving offers as well as other types of offers.

Creating content to promote something

When the main idea of your e-mail is to promote your products or services, your e-mails need to include descriptions and images that support your promotion. Here are some ideas and sources for creating promotional content to include in your e-mails:

✦ **Ask manufacturers for content.** Companies that manufacture your products are great sources for product descriptions, images, and headlines.

✦ **Take digital photos.** Use a digital camera to create product photos and show your services in action.

✦ **Ask your customers for descriptions.** Sometimes your customers can describe your products or services in ways that speak to your audience better than you can.

✦ **Ask people to write testimonials.** Asking people to tell you about their experiences can be interesting and relevant to your audience as well as be powerful motivators. Testimonials don't have to come from your customers. Sometimes you can find examples of other people who have used products and services like yours and demonstrate how their testimonial applies to your business.

Make sure that you have permission to use testimonials.

✦ **Check your e-mail.** Keeping track of the types of e-mails your customers and prospects send to you can give you insight into the topics that interest your audience. When your customers and prospects ask questions and make inquiries about your business, use your answers to help you develop content that promotes how your products or services help solve their problems. For example, a business consultant who gets several e-mails asking about the impact of mobile marketing is wise to create an e-mail addressing the most common questions or concerns related to mobile marketing and the services provided by the consultant.

Cashing in on coupons

Coupons are traditionally printed on paper and redeemed in person, but e-mail coupons can take many forms, such as

✦ Printable HTML designs on a web page or in an e-mail for use in a brick-and-mortar store

✦ Codes that customers enter into a form field when making an online purchase

✦ Links that include special HTML code that applies a change to the price field of a product database when someone clicks to view the product or add it to an online shopping cart

Most E-Mail Marketing Providers (EMPs) allow you to create dotted-line borders to give your coupon content the appearance of being clippable. If you format your coupons to have a traditional cut-out look on-screen, make sure that your coupons include redemption directions because consumers need to know how to redeem your coupon. (After all, they can't just cut it out of the computer screen.) For example, if you intend for your consumers to print the coupon, cut it out, and come to your store for redemption, include those instructions in your e-mail. Figure 5-1 shows an e-mail that includes traditional-looking coupons as well as directions for using the coupons.

Coupons contained in the body of your e-mail can be forwarded to anyone, so make sure that you're ready to honor the unlimited use of your coupon by individuals who aren't on your e-mail list. If you want to make sure that your coupon is used only by a few selected individuals, you can ask your audience to request an official copy of the coupon. Or, give every coupon a unique code and tell your audience that you will allow only one use per coupon code. Some EMPs allow you to merge database fields into your e-mail so that you can assign unique numbers to each customer's printable coupon. If your coupon is redeemable online, you can use the same code on every coupon and require your audience to create an account or log in before using the coupon code so that you can keep track of unique redemptions.

You should also think through the financial implications that your coupon might create if someone tries to abuse your offer. Including an expiration date and limiting the number of redemptions per product or customer can help to limit any attempts to maliciously exploit your coupon's basic intentions.

Figure 5-1: Include redemption directions with coupons.

Courtesy of Fajita Grill

Including incentives

Incentives are limited-time offers that reward a specific action. Incentives differ from coupons in that no physical redemption process is involved to take advantage of an incentive. Incentives are highly flexible; they can take the form of financial savings or special privileges. For example, a low financing rate might be the initial incentive to purchase a particular car, but membership to an exclusive automobile club is an additional incentive for purchasing the same car.

Incentives are particularly useful when you can identify your audience's specific interests and then match your audience's interests with your incentive. For example, if you know that your audience likes baseball, you might include two free tickets to a baseball game as an incentive for making an immediate purchase.

Using giveaways

Giveaways are complimentary products or services that are awarded to a single winner or a limited number of participants who take a specific action. Giveaways allow you to offer your audience a chance at winning a valuable prize or special privileges without having to worry about meeting the demand for a high number of requests for freebies. In addition to rewarding purchases, using giveaways can motivate your audience to

✦ Share more of their interests and contact information

✦ Respond to surveys and polls

✦ Forward your e-mails to friends and colleagues

Figure 5-2 shows an e-mail that offers a giveaway to reward a visit to the store.

Figure 5-2: This e-mail offers a giveaway to a limited number of people who visit the store.

Courtesy of Abode

When your giveaway involves a prize drawing or contest, make sure that your giveaway complies with all applicable laws in your area. In the United States, you can usually find your local contest laws online at your state's Secretary of State website.

Making gains with loss leaders

A *loss leader* is an offer to purchase a product or service that results in a financial loss to your business to gain a new customer who represents more profitable revenue in the future. For example, a camera store might be willing to sell a specific type of camera for far less than all its competitors to obtain highly profitable printing and accessory sales from those customers.

Loss leaders are useful when some of the people on your e-mail list have to experience the quality of your products or services firsthand before they can understand the true value that's inherent in your regular prices. Because loss leaders represent a customer acquisition cost, reserve them for obtaining customers who have never purchased from you before.

Extending urgent offers

Sometimes, products or services are valuable enough to cause an immediate purchase decision all by themselves because they fulfill a need that your audience perceives as an emergency. For example, a landscaping company might offer to blow out sprinkler systems for their audience because a cold front is moving in that has the potential to freeze pipes and cause serious

water damage.

E-mail offers that highlight urgent needs are most effective when used sparingly.

Writing an Effective Call to Action

Even when your content is valuable, most consumers simply scan and delete your e-mails unless you prompt them with alternatives. If decreasing your deletion rate is one of your objectives, every e-mail you send needs to include a strong call to action. A *call to action* is a statement that prompts your audience to complete one or more specific tasks in favor of your objectives.

Calling your audience to action isn't as simple as including your phone number in the body of your e-mail or giving your audience lots of links to click. Consumers need directions and compelling reasons for taking specific actions, especially when their actions require spending time or money.

Anyone who reads e-mail is familiar with the stalwart phrase Click Here, but such generic phrases are not necessarily models for writing an effective call to action. An effective call to action acts like a little sign that allows your audience to visualize the steps involved to take advantage of your e-mail's content. Figure 5-3 shows an e-mail offer that includes the call to action Contact Us Today!.

Figure 5-3: This e-mail includes an offer and a call to action.

Courtesy of Impressions Marketing

Words are the building blocks of a strong call to action, and the quality and the number of words that you choose significantly affect how many responses your call to action receives. The most effective way to write a call to action is to begin with one or more *action* words: verbs that propose a specific task to your audience.

The following list offers calls to action, paired with strong verbs that you could choose to help motivate a reader to act:

✦ **Read your e-mail:** Read, look, consider, notice, scroll

✦ **Fill out a form:** Contact, respond, comment, advise

✦ **Save your e-mail:** Save, keep, store, file, move

✦ **Request information:** Download, request, learn, e-mail, compare

✦ **Print your e-mail:** Print, post, bring, hang

✦ **Visit a physical location:** Drive, come, park, attend

✦ **Forward your e-mail:** Forward, share, send, refer

✦ **Visit a web page:** Visit, view, go, navigate

✦ **Make a purchase:** Buy, add, purchase, own, order

✦ **Register for an event:** Register, reserve, sign up, R.S.V.P.

✦ **Phone your business:** Call, phone, dial

✦ **Make an appointment:** Schedule, arrange, meet, set up

Here's how you can build on action words to create a strong call to action. You can see the progression of the call to action as you make it stronger and stronger:

1. **Combine your action word with the subject of the action word.**

   Order *this item*.

2. **Include the place where the action happens.**

   Order this item *online*.

3. **Add the urgency of the action.**

   Order this item online *before Friday*.

4. **Finish with an adjective to underscore the value that's inherent in the action.**

   Order this *hilarious* item online before Friday.

The combination of one or more action words along with your supplementary words makes a complete call to action. Writing an effective call to action can become more of an art than a science, but becoming a good call-to-action writer is just a matter of practice.

Turning your action words into links is a great way to prompt your audience to click to take action. (You can read about creating links in Chapter 4 of this minibook.)

Giving Your E-Mail Content Inherent Value

E-mails containing valuable information based on your knowledge and experience are generally more effective over long periods of time than e-mails that repeatedly contain only offers. Even when your offers are compelling, people aren't always ready to take action right away.

The longer your sales cycle and average time between repeat purchases, the more you need to include inherently valuable content in your e-mails to keep your audience subscribed and interested. Figure 5-4 shows an e-mail that contains an offer with a "quick tip" section included as inherently valuable content to enhance the overall value of the e-mail.

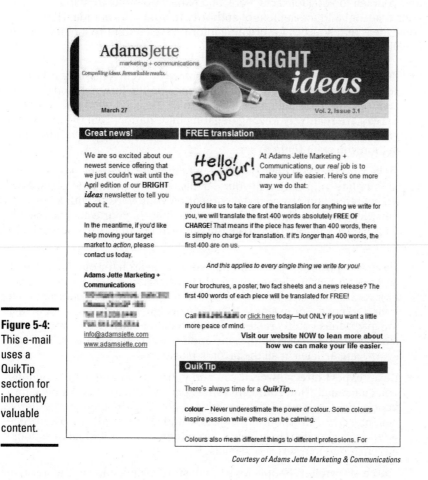

Figure 5-4: This e-mail uses a QuikTip section for inherently valuable content.

Courtesy of Adams Jette Marketing & Communications

Inherently valuable content is most valuable when your content is relevant to your audience's stage in the buying cycle and targeted to your audience's interests. To make sure that your content is appreciated, ask your customers what they're interested in before you start creating inherently valuable content.

The following sections detail how you can create inherently valuable content or combine it with various related offers.

Creating content to inform your audience

When the main objective of your e-mail is to deliver information, you might find yourself looking for facts, data, and expert opinions to help you make your case and add an element of authority to your information. Here are some ideas and sources for creating informative content to include in your e-mails:

+ **Be an aggregator.** Sometimes the best way to tell your story is to let someone else tell it. Information abounds on the Internet, and the chances that your audience is going to find exactly what you want them to read are relatively low. Aggregating information from the Internet is a great way to generate content and inform your audience with the information you want them to see.

Make sure that you have permission to include excerpts of other people's online information in your e-mails before you include them. Also, ask whether you can post the content on your website with a link to the outside source so that people who click links in your e-mail are sent to your website before they have the opportunity to link to someone else's website.

+ **Have an opinion.** If you don't have time to search for outside content and ask for permission to aggregate information, you can save yourself and your audience a lot of time by summarizing outside information for your audience. For example, a fashion designer who reads a lot of fashion magazines could create an e-mail that summarizes the two most stylish ways to tie a scarf so that the audience doesn't have to read all the scarf-tying articles in all the fashion magazines.

+ **Be an expert interviewer.** If you find yourself running out of opinions, you can usually find someone with expert information and advice for your audience. Instead of borrowing content, ask someone whether you can interview him about his expertise and share it with your audience. Interviews can also be broken up into themes or individual questions and included in a series of e-mails.

+ **Find a storyteller.** People love to tell stories, and some of them can help you to inform your audience. Start by asking your current customers to tell you stories about their experiences with your business and your products or services.

Adding tips and advice

If your products or services require special knowledge for customers to use them, or if your audience needs a trusted opinion to buy your products in the first place, including tips and advice in your e-mails can reinforce your expertise.

Here are some ideas for including tips and advice in your e-mails:

✦ **Start a tips and advice e-mail newsletter where the bulk of your content is informative.** For example, a gardening center might send an e-mail newsletter with tips for keeping gardens alive with less effort, or advice on plants that thrive with little or no attention. The gardening newsletter could include related offers for plants mentioned in the newsletter, or separate offers could be sent after the audience has enough information to engage in the buying cycle.

✦ **Include one tip in each promotional e-mail you send with a link to additional tips on your website.** For example, a shoe store could include the location of a secret hiking trail in every e-mail with a link to an archive of hiking trails featured in the past. If you include single tips in your e-mails, make sure that your website's Tips page includes related offers.

✦ **Share your opinion.** If you and your audience have the same beliefs, sharing your opinion can strengthen your customer relationships. For example, a store that sells recycled products might have a customer base that's more likely to be concerned about the environment. Such a customer base might be more loyal to a company that includes opinions concerning recycling issues along with offers to purchase recycled products.

✦ **Share another opinion.** If your audience doesn't perceive you as an expert in your field, find an expert who is willing to share an opinion. You can ask permission to include opinions in your e-mails or interview an opinionated expert and include the highlights of the interview in your e-mail.

✦ **Dedicate a section of your e-mail newsletter to answering customer questions.** For example, a website designer could answer a different customer question related to search engine optimization in every e-mail.

Providing instructions and directions

If your products or services require your customers to follow detailed instructions, include information that gives your audience timesaving shortcuts. For example, an e-mail promotion from an online auction might include steps for setting up account options. Here are some ways that you can include instructions and directions in your e-mails:

✦ **Ask your customers to submit creative shortcuts.** You can then feature the shortcuts in your e-mails.

✦ **If your directions involve several detailed steps, include one step with details in each e-mail.** For example, a hobby store could include instructions for building a great model airplane, beginning with choosing a model and ending with painting and displaying the model.

✦ **Include instructions that are valuable for reference, and ask your audience to save them in their e-mail inboxes.** For example, a promotion for a product that includes a one-year warranty could include return and refund instructions along with instructions for saving the information in case a problem occurs with a recent or future purchase.

Putting in entertaining content

Some audiences value e-mail content that gives them a good laugh or diverts their attention with an interesting story. If your products or services are related to entertaining content and your audience values diversion, the following examples of entertaining content might be appropriate:

✦ **Retell the stories you hear from your customers that relate to using your products and services.** For example, a business that sells boats might include interesting stories about customers who live on the ocean or use boats to help people in the community.

If you include such stories, make sure that you have permission from your customers before you send those stories to your list.

✦ **Include links to online videos that are related to your products or services.** For example, a guitar store might include a link to a video showing a different guitar hero who plays the guitars that the store sells.

As with any link to content you don't own, make sure that you have permission to include the link, and also make sure that the content you're linking to is legally obtained.

✦ **Write your own stories about your experiences or knowledge relating to your products or services.** For example, the owner of a restaurant might include stories about her trips to the French vineyards that inspire the wines featured in the restaurant.

Including facts and research

If you sell products or services that are enhanced by helpful facts and research, you can include them in your e-mails to add value to related offers. Here are a few possibilities:

✦ **Conduct your own research and publish your findings in your e-mails.** For example, a men's clothing store could conduct a poll and find out how many women think it's fashionable for men to wear pink shirts. The results of the poll could be included along with a pink shirt sale if the results support wearing pink shirts — or blue shirts if the results indicate that pink is out of favor.

✦ **Include facts and research through external sources.** Facts and research abound on the Internet, and the people who publish them are usually willing to share their findings with proper attribution to the source. If you locate facts and research that interest your audience, ask the source whether you can include them in your e-mails.

Finding Help with Content Creation

You can turn to many sources for help in creating interesting and relevant content for your e-mails. Marketing companies and content providers can help you when

✦ You don't have time to create e-mail content.

✦ Your content isn't giving you the results you want.

✦ You don't like creating your own content for your e-mails.

Marketing companies and content providers often have services that range from small amounts of copywriting to fully outsourced, turnkey solutions. Most companies that provide content creation for e-mail marketing provide one or more of the following services:

✦ Copywriting, using themes and ideas that you provide

✦ Formatting content that you provide into HTML for e-mail

✦ Custom e-mail template design

✦ Advice and consulting

✦ Image creation, design, and licensing

✦ Matching your website content to your e-mails

✦ Archiving e-mail campaigns to your website

For a list of marketing companies and content providers that can help you with e-mail content design and creation, ask for a list of business partners, education partners, or professional services at www.constantcontact.com.

Chapter 6: Tracking Your E-Mail Campaign Results

In This Chapter

✔ Navigating e-mail tracking reports

✔ Understanding e-mail statistics

✔ Tracking other responses

*O*ne of the most practical and valuable features of using e-mail to market your business is using e-mail tracking reports to find out what your audience is doing with your e-mails after you send them.

Most E-Mail Marketing Providers (EMPs) can track your e-mails and allow you to view the results in an e-mail tracking report. In this chapter, you find out how to make sense of the data in an e-mail tracking report as well as discover other creative ways to track responses not captured in a tracking report.

Understanding Basic E-Mail Tracking Data

You have to be an advanced HTML and database programmer to track e-mails on your own; using an EMP makes the task much easier. EMPs automatically add special tracking code to the links you include in your e-mails. The tracking code is unique to each individual on your e-mail list and is also tied to each e-mail campaign. EMPs also have programs that automatically read the code from other e-mail servers when they return undeliverable e-mail so that you don't have to do the hard work to determine why a particular e-mail wasn't delivered.

E-mail tracking reports are analytical summaries of the results of a given e-mail campaign that can tell you

✦ Which e-mails bounced

✦ Why they bounced

✦ Who opened your e-mails

✦ What links the person clicked

✦ Who unsubscribed from your e-mails

✦ Who forwarded your e-mails or shared them on social media

Figure 6-1 shows a summary e-mail tracking report, generated by an EMP, that allows access to the report details when the user clicks the summary statistics. Making sense of the data in an e-mail tracking report takes a little getting used to because the technology involved in the e-mail tracking process causes the data to take on a slightly different meaning than you might expect.

The following sections explain the origins of the data found in a typical e-mail tracking report so that you can interpret the true meaning of each number being reported. These sections also include references to current industry statistics so that you can decide whether your data warrants any action to refine your strategy.

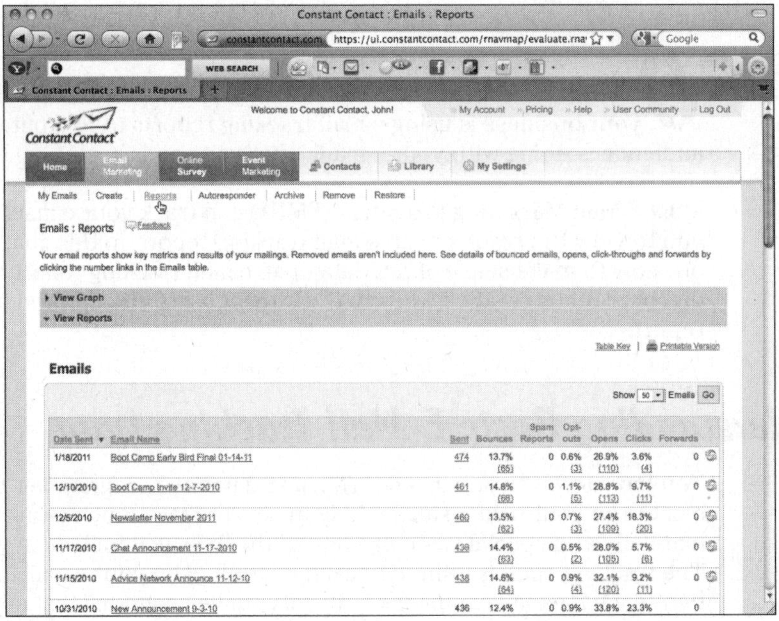

Figure 6-1: Use an e-mail tracking report to view summary statistics.

Courtesy of Constant Contact

Calculating your bounce rate

Bounce rate is the number of e-mails that were returned as undeliverable, expressed as a percentage of total e-mails sent. EMPs calculate bounce rate by taking the total number of bounced e-mails and dividing by the number of e-mails sent. You can calculate your own bounce rate as follows:

1. **Divide the total number of e-mails that bounced by the total number of e-mails sent to get the total number of bounces per e-mail.**

For example, if you send 100 e-mails and 20 of them bounce, you bounced 0.2 e-mails for every e-mail sent.

2. **Multiply your bounce per e-mail rate by 100 to get your bounce rate as a percentage.**

    For example, the bounce rate for 0.2 bounces per e-mail is 20 percent.

According to Epsilon's Email Trends and Benchmark guide (2010), the average bounce rate for commercial e-mails is anywhere between 2 and 15 percent, depending on the industry. If your bounce rate is higher than that, turn to Chapter 7 of this minibook to find out how to lower it.

Calculating your nonbounce total

Nonbounce total is the number of e-mails that were not bounced and therefore assumed delivered. EMPs calculate the nonbounce total by subtracting your total number of bounced e-mails from the total number of e-mails sent. You can calculate your own nonbounce total as follows:

Total e-mails sent
<u>–Total bounced e-mails</u>

Nonbounce total

For example, if you send 100 e-mails and 20 of them bounce, your nonbounce total is 80.

Nonbounce total is sometimes expressed as a percentage, but the nonbounce total is more useful as a real number because e-mail open rates are actually based on your nonbounce total instead of the total number of e-mails sent. (Find out about open rate in the next section of this chapter.)

Your nonbounce total isn't the same as the total number of e-mails delivered. Some e-mails aren't reported as bounced because software on the user's computer or a portable device — not an e-mail server — bounced it, and some e-mail servers falsely deliver your e-mail to a junk folder that users can't access. (For more information about e-mail filters and other nondelivery issues, read the next chapter in this minibook.)

Even though you can't be sure whether your nonbounced e-mails are being delivered, you can assume that your nonbounced e-mails are reaching your audience until you have good reasons to believe otherwise. Because nonbounce total is basically the converse of the bounce rate, the average nonbounce rate is between 85 and 98 percent, according to Return Path.

Calculating your open rate

Open rate is one of the e-mail marketing industry's most misleading terms. It actually measures the number of specific interactions with an e-mail server after the e-mail is sent, expressed as a percentage of nonbounce total. Your e-mail isn't counted as an open until one of the following interactions occurs:

✦ The recipient enables the images in your e-mail to display either in the preview pane or in a full view of the e-mail.

In Figure 6-2, images are not enabled and the e-mail is not tracked as being opened. In Figure 6-3, images are enabled and the e-mail shows up on the tracking report as being opened.

✦ The recipient clicks a link in the e-mail.

EMPs calculate open rate by taking the number of tracked opens and dividing it by your nonbounce total. Here are the steps involved in calculating open rate:

1. **Divide the total number of tracked opens by the nonbounce total to get opens per e-mail assumed delivered.**

For example, if 80 of 100 e-mails you send don't bounce and 20 of them are tracked as opened, you received 0.25 opens per e-mail.

2. **Multiply the number of opens per e-mail by 100 to get the open rate as a percentage.**

For example, the open rate for 0.25 opens per e-mail is 25 percent.

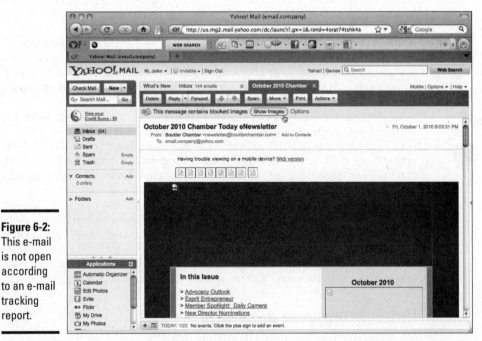

Figure 6-2:
This e-mail is not open according to an e-mail tracking report.

Courtesy of the Boulder Chamber of Commerce

Figure 6-3:
This e-mail
shows as
open on
an e-mail
tracking
report.

Courtesy of the Boulder Chamber of Commerce

You calculate your open rate by using your nonbounce rate instead of the total e-mails sent because your open rate indicates the strength of your e-mail's identity and content apart from the strength of your deliverability. Because e-mails that aren't delivered can't possibly be opened, they're excluded from your open-rate calculation.

According to Epsilon's Email Trends and Benchmark guide, the average open rate is roughly between 14 and 41 percent, depending on the industry.

Because the default setting on an increasing number of e-mail programs is to block images until the user clicks to enable them, some people scan through e-mails without enabling images at all. In such cases, the true number of e-mails that your audience views is probably higher than your e-mail tracking report's open rate indicates.

Plain, text-only e-mails without any links or images are not trackable unless your audience replies to them directly. Make sure that your EMP inserts a blank image in every e-mail to ensure that open tracking is possible.

The image-only open-rate approach

Ordinarily, sending an e-mail that contains only an image isn't recommended because your audience sees a big blank space instead of the image until the image display is enabled by clicking a link in the recipients' e-mail program. If, however, you're trying to get a true sense of your open rate, sending an image-only e-mail requires your recipients to enable the images to see any of your e-mail's message. With this method, you can ensure that an *open* reported on your e-mail tracking report actually represents someone who has looked at the content of your e-mail because open tracking works only when someone enables the images to display in your e-mail.

Calculating your click-through rate

Your *click-through rate* is the number of unique individuals who click one or more links in your e-mail expressed as a percentage of total tracked opens. Links could include

✦ Web links that point to web pages such as links to your website

✦ Social links that point to social media actions, such as when someone likes your e-mail content, as shown in Figure 6-4

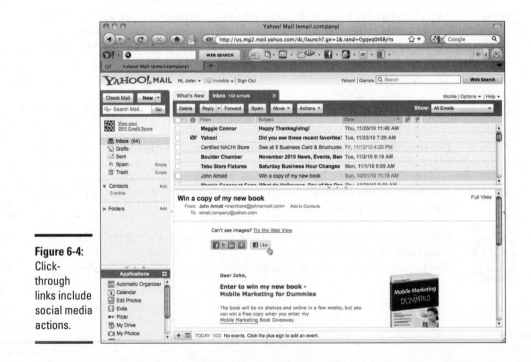

Figure 6-4: Click-through links include social media actions.

EMPs calculate the click-through rate by taking the total number of unique individuals who click a link in your e-mail and dividing by the total number of tracked opens. Here are the steps for calculating click-through rate:

1. **Subtract any multiple clicks attributed to a single subscriber from the total number of clicks on all links to get total unique clicks.**

   For example, if your e-mail contains one link and ten people clicked the link twice, subtract ten from the total number of clicks.

2. **Divide the total number of tracked opens by the total number of unique clicks to get clicks per open.**

   For example, if 30 of your e-mails track as opened and you receive 3 unique clicks, your e-mail received 0.1 clicks per open.

3. **Multiply clicks per open by 100 to get the click-through rate.**

   For example, the click-through rate for 0.1 clicks per open is 10 percent.

Because clicking a link in your e-mail causes the e-mail to track as an open, your click-through rate never exceeds the number of tracked opens. Your e-mail might receive more total clicks than tracked opens, however, because some people click a single link multiple times or click more than one link in your e-mail.

Even if your audience clicks multiple times, your click-through rate represents only the number of unique individuals who click one or more links. Most e-mail tracking reports also allow you to view the total number of clicks attributed to each unique individual as well as show you exactly which links are clicked.

Tracking Nonclick Responses

Some e-mail marketing objectives can't be accomplished through a click. For example, if your goal is to increase the number of phone calls to your sales representatives to increase appointments — and, ultimately, close sales — your e-mail requires an approach to tracking and evaluation apart from click-through reports and web analytics.

The following sections explain how you can track nonclick responses and calculate return on investment (ROI) so that you can measure your effectiveness in converting customers outside the realm of your website.

Tracking in-store purchases

If the goal of your e-mail is to generate purchases in a brick-and-mortar store, you need to find a way to track the foot traffic that results from your e-mails and also compare any increase in foot traffic against any increase in sales. Here are some ideas for tracking your in-store visitors and linking them to your e-mail marketing efforts:

✦ **Ask your e-mail audience to print the e-mail and bring it with them when they visit your store.** Count the number of e-mails you receive over a fair test of time (such as one month) or over the course of a series of e-mail campaigns.

✦ **Ask your e-mail audience to mention your e-mail when they visit your store.** Offer your audience a gift so that they have an incentive to mention your e-mail — even if they don't walk up to the counter to buy something. Count the number of gifts you give away to determine how many visitors result from your e-mails.

✦ **Have your sales staff ask all store visitors whether they received your e-mail.** Count the number of visitors who say that they remember receiving it.

✦ **Promote a specific product or service and a specific offer in your e-mail.** Count everyone who visits the store in search of the offer. Figure 6-5 shows an offer that only appears in the e-mail so that all inquiries can be attributed to the e-mail.

Figure 6-5:
Mentioning a special in your e-mail (and nowhere else) allows you to track inquiries.

Courtesy of McDonald Garden Center

Tracking phone calls

If the goal of your e-mail is to increase the number of inbound phone calls, your e-mail needs to include a method for tracking which phone calls result from your e-mail. Here are some ideas for tracking your phone calls and linking them to your e-mail marketing efforts:

TIP

Simple event registration

Asking people to tell you in advance whether they're coming to your event is a great way to make room arrangements and prepare enough materials. However, asking people to fill out a long online registration form or take multiple steps to preregister before making a commitment might create a barrier to preregistration, especially if your event is free. Because you can track e-mail links to the clicker, you can create two links for each event and ask your audience to click one of them to indicate their intentions. For example, your two links might read I'd like to attend and No, thanks.

After you create the links, you can point one link to a landing page that reads Thanks

for confirming your attendance, and you can point the other link to a landing page that reads Thanks for giving up your seat.

Make sure that your landing page also has additional links, such as maps, directions, and other important event information. After you count the number of unique clicks on each link, you can plan for the appropriate number of visitors and send a follow-up e-mail that delivers more event information and asks your preregistered guests to confirm their attendance or purchase their tickets.

✦ **Ask your e-mail audience to mention your e-mail when calling.** Count the number of callers who mention it.

✦ **Set up a special phone number to accept calls from your e-mails and publish that number in your e-mails.** Every time a call comes to that number, you can count the call as coming from one of your e-mails.

✦ **Promote a specific product or service in your e-mail.** Count each call related to that product or service.

✦ **Ask your e-mail audience to request a specific person in your organization when they call.** Count the increase in the number of calls that person receives.

✦ **Tell your sales staff to ask callers how they found your phone number.** Count every caller who references your e-mail.

Tracking event attendance

If the goal of your e-mail is to increase event attendance, your e-mail needs to include a method for tracking how many event attendees resulted from sending your e-mail. Here are some ideas for tracking your event attendance and linking attendance to your e-mail marketing efforts:

✦ **Ask your e-mail audience to bring your e-mail to the event.** Count the number of attendees who bring the e-mail.

✦ **Ask your e-mail audience to mention your e-mail or include a code in the e-mail that gets them into the event.** Count the number of attendees who mention the e-mail or code.

✦ **Ask your e-mail audience to preregister by calling or replying to your e-mail.** Count the number of attendees who preregistered or replied.

Tracking e-mail replies

Sometimes, asking people to reply to your e-mails is enough to meet your ultimate objectives. An EMP can't track a reply to your e-mail, but you receive an e-mail from your list subscriber with a Subject line that reveals the source of the reply. For example, say you send an e-mail with a Subject line that reads `Last chance to register`. When someone replies to your e-mail, the Subject line reads `RE: Last chance to register`.

Counting the number of replies you receive from your e-mails isn't particularly useful, but replies can be very useful when you track the qualitative information inherent in your replies. Here are two ideas for tracking replies and putting the information to good use:

✦ **Keep track of the nature of each reply.** Record whether your reply contained a complaint, suggestion, or inquiry and then track the reply to its source. For example, if you receive enough replies from people who want to know your hours of operation, you might include a link to your normal business hours in your future e-mails or make the information easier to find on your website.

✦ **Keep track of your response to each reply and the result.** For example, if your response to a complaint results in a resolution or an order fulfillment, make a note of the situation so that you can address anyone with a similar complaint using your website, Help files, or blog. You can also share the information with everyone on your sales team so that they can address future complaints successfully.

Evaluating E-Mail Click-Through Data

Every time someone clicks a link in your e-mail, you have the opportunity to track the click back to the individual and use the information to accomplish more meaningful objectives and increase the value of your e-mail list.

You have to be an advanced HTML and database programmer to write your own link-tracking code, so use an EMP that can generate link-tracking code automatically for you. An EMP also provides a click-through report for each e-mail campaign. Figure 6-6 shows a detailed click-through report, generated by an EMP, that shows each link in the tracked e-mail and allows the user to view the individuals behind each click.

Emails : Reports : Click-through Statistics
Click-through Statistics

Here you can compare the effectiveness of each link in this email by viewing the click-through statistic. For recent emails, you can click on the unique click-through number to see the contacts who clicked on a link.

You may save the contacts who clicked on this email as a new list - the new list will not be displayed on your Visitor Signup Form as a default. Contact click-through data is maintained for 90 days from the day of the email.

< Back   Printable Version

Email Name: New Workshop Calendar 3-06-07

Date Sent: 3/7/2007

Email Link	Unique Click-throughs	Click-through Distribution
http://colorado.constantcontact.com/	34	9.9%
http://colorado.constantcontact.com/learning-center/books/index.jsp	4	1.2%
http://colorado.constantcontact.com/regional/bio.jsp	8	2.3%
http://colorado.constantcontact.com/regional/bio.jsphttp://colorado.constantcontact.com/regional/bio.jsp	3	0.9%
http://colorado.constantcontact.com/regional/events.jsp?trumbaEmbed=view%3Devent%26eventid%3D59878132	52	15.2%
http://colorado.constantcontact.com/regional/events.jsp?trumbaEmbed=view%3Devent%26eventid%3D64116411	159	46.4%
http://colorado.constantcontact.com/services/index.jsp	4	1.2%
http://community.constantcontact.com/	2	0.6%
http://www.bouldersbdc.com/?site_id=167&id_sub=7726&page_id=4724&productgallery_id=1	77	22.4%
Total Click-throughs	343	100%

Save as List

Figure 6-6:
Click-
through
reports
show links
in tracked
e-mails.

Courtesy of Constant Contact

The next sections include tips and techniques for extracting practical meaning from your click-through data and for acting on your click-through data to make your e-mail marketing efforts more effective over time.

Using click-through data to target your e-mail offers

Someone clicking an e-mail link in response to an article or offer allows you to make assumptions about your clicker's interests. For example, a bookstore that receives 100 link clicks leading to information about a guitar book can assume that those 100 subscribers are interested in guitars.

Placing your clickers into different e-mail lists based on their interests allows you to send future e-mails with more-targeted offers. For example, if a bookstore compiles its 100 guitar book clickers in a guitar-interest list, the bookstore could include offers and information related to guitars in every e-mail sent to that specific list.

Here are some tips to help you determine your audience's interests and for dividing your e-mail list by using click-through interests:

✦ **Turn your links into data mines.** Clicks are much more meaningful when you write them in ways that affirm the clicker's personal information. For example, if a golf store sells kids' golf equipment as well as adult golf equipment, the store might include a link that points to kids' golfing tips:

```
Do you have kids under 12 who golf? Read our
        latest kids' golfing tips.
```

The golf store can save the names of those who click the kids' tips link as a list and then target their kids' equipment offers to those clickers because they are more likely to value them.

✦ **Rearrange your e-mails by interest.** You don't need to send a completely different e-mail to each subscriber with a different interest. Instead, you can make small changes to your e-mail content based on the interest list you're targeting. For example, you can send the same e-mail newsletter to all your lists while changing the Subject line or rearranging the order of your articles to highlight the most interesting content for each of your interest lists.

✦ **Change your offers by interest.** People often respond to calls to action in your e-mails based on the strength of your offers. When you send offers to different interest lists, keep your call to action the same but change your offer according to each interest. For example, if your e-mail contains a call to action asking your audience to take a survey, you might offer one interest list a discount for taking the survey while offering another interest list special privileges. (You can read more about creating valuable offers in Chapter 5 of this minibook.)

Using click-through data for intelligent follow-up

When someone clicks an e-mail link but doesn't follow through with a purchase or other commitment, you can use your click-through report to follow up with your clicker and find out what might have caused him or her to abandon the conversion process.

Following up with e-mail can be effective, but it's also a good idea to collect phone numbers and mailing addresses from your subscribers in case you need to follow up outside the inbox. For example, a consultant who sends an event invitation with a registration link could compare the list of subscribers who click the registration link with the number of completed registrations and then call each person who clicked *without* registering. Such follow-up can help you determine what might have prevented the registration from going through. The phone calls might reveal that those who didn't register had questions that your website didn't answer or felt uncomfortable typing a credit card number into the registration form.

Here are some tips for following up on the data in your click-through reports using e-mail as well as other forms of communication:

✦ **Send a second-chance offer** to those clickers who did not follow through by making a purchase or other commitment. You can use another e-mail or a postcard highlighting a more compelling second-chance offer.

✦ **Send a postcard thanking your clickers** for considering your offer and asking them to consider an alternative product or service.

✦ **Call your clickers** and ask them whether they have any questions.

✦ **Send a survey to your clickers** asking them about any interests that the link seems to have uncovered.

✦ **Thank your subscribers** who forward your e-mails.

✦ **Send a postcard to clickers who unsubscribe** from your e-mail list telling them that they are still valued and thanking them for considering your products and services.

Using click-through data for testing your offers and calls to action

A spike or a decline in your click-through rate usually means that your offers or calls to action aren't compelling. Sending your offers and calls to action to a small and random portion of your e-mail list and tracking your click-through rate allow you to test your offers and calls to action before sending them to your entire e-mail list. Here's how you can create and execute your own click-through test:

1. Randomly select 10 percent of your e-mail list subscribers from your database and copy them to a new database or category in your database.

2. Create two versions of your e-mail and send each one to half of your test list.

3. Wait 48 hours and compare each e-mail's click-through report to see which links received the most clicks.

4. Create a final version of your e-mail using the elements that produced the most clicks and send it to your entire e-mail list.

If your sample click-through rates are lower than you expect in both versions of your e-mail, you can adjust your offers or calls to action accordingly and test again using a different test list. You can improve a low click-through rate with these simple techniques:

✦ Rewriting your headlines to attract more attention to your offer

✦ Adjusting your offer to deliver more value

✦ Moving your call to action to a more visible location

✦ Rearranging your layout to make your offer easier to scan

Chapter 7: Maximizing E-Mail Deliverability

In This Chapter

✔ **Dealing with bounced and blocked e-mail**

✔ **Understanding e-mail content filters**

✔ **Maximizing delivery rates**

✔ **Working with emerging delivery technology**

Thinking about the early days of postal mail delivery conjures up images of Pony Express riders traveling long distances and risking their lives to get mail delivered, proudly in the name of the United States of America. Although sticking a stamp on a letter or postcard and dropping it off at a U.S. Postal Service office doesn't necessarily assure its delivery to someone's mailbox, mail carriers most often do succeed in delivering your mail to the mailbox of the intended addressee. Or, they return your mail to the mailbox specified in the return address, along with a clear reason for the failed delivery.

E-mail delivery, though, isn't quite as trustworthy as the U.S. Postal Service. Even e-mail sent to a correct e-mail address doesn't always reach the inbox, and returned e-mail doesn't always include unmistakable reasons for the failed delivery.

However, the good news is that the positives of e-mail marketing greatly outweigh the deliverability issues inherent to sending commercial e-mail. This chapter uncovers the various reasons why some e-mail fails to reach an inbox and then offers solutions for maximizing your e-mail delivery rates.

Managing Bounced and Blocked E-Mail

Sometimes, e-mail is simply returned to the sender either by the e-mail server or by a software application, such as an e-mail program or delivery control system. You hear the terms *bounced* and *blocked* applied to returned e-mail somewhat interchangeably, but the two have some slight differences:

✦ **Bounced:** A *bounced e-mail* happens on a per-e-mail basis when an e-mail is returned because of conditions that make a particular e-mail undeliverable, such as a full e-mail inbox or an e-mail address that is misspelled or doesn't exist. Bounces can be hard or soft, which you discover in a bit.

+ **Blocked:** A *blocked e-mail* happens on an all-inclusive basis when an e-mail is returned because of characteristics that make a particular type of e-mail unwanted, such as when a systems administrator decides to refuse all e-mails with attachments or all e-mails from a particular sender.

E-mail is usually returned with code that indicates the reason for the bounce or the block. Most of the time, the code is unintelligible to the average human. Figure 7-1 shows an example of an e-mail returned to the sender with a bounce code.

When you team with an E-Mail Marketing Provider (EMP), you don't have to spend time scanning through lines of HTML because most EMPs automatically file bounced and blocked e-mails into a bounce report. A *bounce report* shows how many of your e-mails bounced and were blocked as well as the plain-English reason for the bounce or block response.

Figure 7-2 shows a bounce report generated by an EMP. You can see the number of bounced e-mails by category as well as individual bounced e-mails and associated database records.

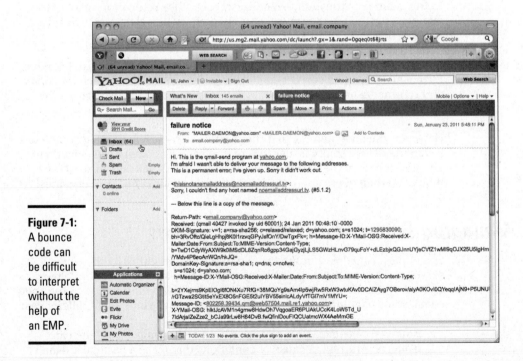

Figure 7-1: A bounce code can be difficult to interpret without the help of an EMP.

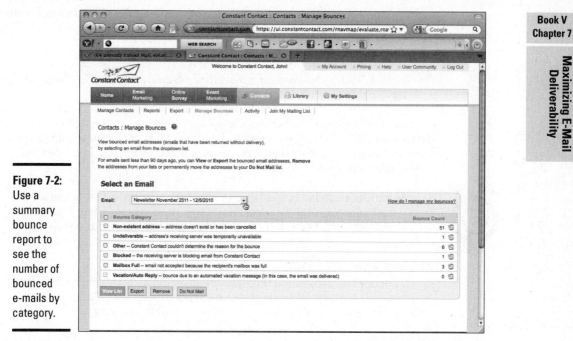

Courtesy Constant Contact

Figure 7-2:
Use a
summary
bounce
report to
see the
number of
bounced
e-mails by
category.

Although some bounced or blocked e-mails will never get delivered, some bounced and blocked e-mails are *temporary,* that is, the e-mails might be delivered if you try sending again later. The following sections explain how to take the appropriate action on each type of bounced and blocked e-mail so that you can refine your e-mail list — and get your e-mails delivered to more of your list subscribers.

Taking action on bounced e-mail

Bounced e-mails are generally unavoidable because the causes of bounced e-mail fall outside your direct control. However, you can take some reasonably effective steps to minimize bounced e-mail.

The following sections show you how to deal with bounces and when to take corrective action.

Dealing with hard bounces

A *hard bounce* is an e-mail that's returned because a permanent condition makes delivering the e-mail impossible. When your EMP's bounce report shows e-mails delivered to nonexistent addresses, your e-mail can't be delivered to that address no matter what action you take. *Nonexistent* e-mail addresses are either

✦ Misspelled (for example, `name@hotmai.lcom`)

✦ Invalid (such as when your subscriber's e-mail address is no longer in service due to a job change)

You can check your hard-bounce report for obviously misspelled e-mail addresses and correct them in your database. Most of the time, though, you can't tell whether an e-mail address is misspelled or invalid. In those cases, you need to obtain a new e-mail address.

If your hard-bounce list is too large to contact each individual to obtain a new e-mail address, or if you don't have any alternative contact information for the subscribers, remove those e-mail addresses from your e-mail list.

Dealing with soft bounces

A *soft bounce* happens when the delivery of an e-mail is delayed temporarily. Soft bounces happen because of technical conditions inherent in the technology that make e-mail delivery possible. Examples include

✦ A full mailbox

✦ A server that's temporarily down

✦ A software application that can't accept the e-mail

When an e-mail address bounces for a reason that's temporary in nature, try resending your e-mail later or simply wait until your next e-mail campaign to see whether the same address still bounces. If an e-mail address bounces repeatedly for temporary reasons, contact the subscriber for a more reliable e-mail address.

Reducing blocked e-mails

Blocked e-mails are sometimes temporary and sometimes permanent, depending on whether the server or software blocking the e-mail does so in response to the content of a single e-mail or the characteristics of a specific type of e-mail. The following sections show how you can keep from being blocked by someone on your e-mail list.

Responding to a challenge response system

A *challenge response system* is a software program that returns all unrecognized e-mail to the sender with instructions for getting the e-mail delivered that only a live person is capable of following, to verify that the sender is a real human being — not a computer generating e-mail addresses. Figure 7-3 shows an e-mail returned by a challenge response system that asks the sender to click a link and fill out a form.

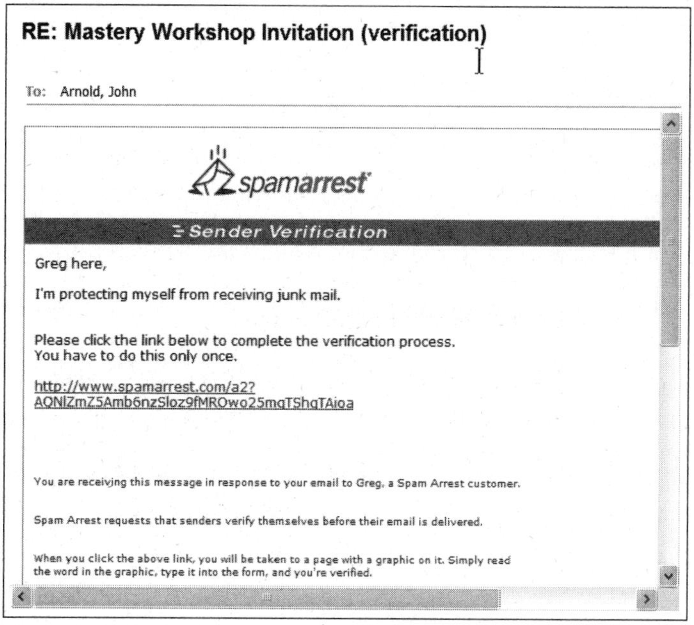

Figure 7-3:
This
challenge
response
e-mail asks
the sender
to verify its
legitimacy.

Courtesy of SpamArrest

Keeping up with e-mail address changes

According to a study conducted by Return Path, more than 30 percent of your e-mail list addressees are likely to change their e-mail address each year. Because losing your entire e-mail list every three to four years isn't going to help improve repeat business, periodically remind your list subscribers to update their e-mail addresses.

Because most people keep their old e-mail address active for a short period of time between changes, sending a subscription reminder every two to three months is a good way to ask your list subscribers to share their new e-mail address before their old e-mail address is deactivated. If you have a large e-mail list, make sure that your subscription reminder links your audience to a secure, online form where they can update their own information and save you from replacing your selling time with data entry. Here's an example of text you might use in your subscription reminder:

```
Subject Line: Subscription
    Reminder

Body: This e-mail is sent every
    other month to remind you
    that you are subscribed
    to the ABC Company e-mail
    list. If your contact
    information or interests
    should change at any time,
    please select your interests
    (link to interests form)
    or update your contact
    information (link to secure
    profile form) so that
    we can continue to send
    you valuable offers and
    information.
```

Challenge responses are generated by third-party applications that integrate into e-mail applications. For example, someone who wants to eliminate computer-generated spam might purchase a challenge response application to verify all e-mails sent to his AOL e-mail address. If you send e-mail to someone with a challenge response system, the returned e-mail might ask you to click a link and enter specific characters in a form field or reply to the e-mail with a specific subject line. Following the instructions in the returned e-mail adds your server address or e-mail address to the subscriber's friends list or address book so that future e-mails are delivered without a challenge. Spam-blocking technology is getting better all the time, so you probably won't run into challenge responses too much.

Keeping your e-mail address or server off a block list

A *block list* (also known as a *blacklist*) is a database that contains the domain names and server addresses of suspected spammers. Block lists are maintained by Internet service providers (ISPs) and other companies that monitor spam complaints across the Internet. Server addresses and domain names are added to block lists based on the number of spam complaints logged by consumers.

If you send an e-mail that gets too many spam complaints, the server you use to send your e-mail might be added to one or more block lists. To keep your server off of block lists, keep the number of spam complaints you receive under 1 in 1,000 e-mails and use a reputable E-Mail Marketing Provider. (You can read more about avoiding spam complaints in Chapter 2 of this minibook.)

Avoiding spam trap e-mail addresses

A *spam trap* is a false e-mail address placed on the Internet by a company with an interest in reducing spam. When spammers using web crawlers to capture e-mail addresses try to send an e-mail to the spam trap e-mail address, the sender's domain and server address are automatically added to the block list. (A *web crawler* is a computer program that searches the Internet for specific types of content, such as lines of text that look like an e-mail address.) Many companies share their spam trap block lists. If you happen to send e-mail to a spam trap address, your deliverability could be doomed.

Here are some ways to avoid spam trap e-mail addresses:

✦ **Don't surf the Internet to obtain e-mail addresses.** Besides risking your deliverability, this behavior is also illegal.

✦ **Don't send e-mail to a purchased list.** Purchased lists are often collected without permission and can contain spam trap addresses.

✦ **Send a welcome e-mail to every new list subscriber and immediately remove e-mail addresses that return your welcome e-mail.** That way, you can weed out anyone who tries to maliciously join your e-mail list by using a known spam trap address.

Getting past e-mail firewalls

An *e-mail firewall* is a piece of hardware or a software application programmed to identify and block e-mails that appear untrustworthy. Firewalls can be customized and configured to block almost any e-mail element. For example, a system administrator at one company might configure a firewall to block e-mails with certain types of content, and another system administrator might configure a firewall to block e-mails from certain senders while ignoring the content altogether.

Because firewalls have so many variables, telling whether your e-mail is being blocked by a firewall is usually impossible. If you use an EMP that provides blocked e-mail addresses in its bounced report, however, you can at least find out which e-mail addresses are being blocked and then take action to try to get the e-mail delivered.

Changing your tactics to get e-mail delivered to a blocked address is difficult, but the following remedies might prove effective:

✦ **Ask your audience to add your e-mail address to their address book or contacts list when they sign up for your e-mail list.** Some content-blocking systems allow e-mail to go through if the sender's e-mail address is in the recipient's address book.

In your welcome letter and subscription reminders, give your audience instructions for adding your e-mail address, as shown in Figure 7-4. This e-mail asks the reader to help ensure delivery by adding the sender's e-mail address to the reader's address book.

Figure 7-4:
Help ensure
delivery.

> You are receiving this email from Anderson-Shea Inc. because you purchased a product/service from us, subscribed on our website, or are a friend or family member. To ensure that you continue to receive emails from us, add char@andersonshea.com to your address book today. See how
>
> You may unsubscribe if you no longer wish to receive our emails.
>
> ### New from Lantern Moon
>
> Greetings!

Courtesy of Anderson-Shea, Inc.

✦ **Obtain an alternative e-mail address from each of your blocked subscribers.** Sometimes, half the battle with blocked e-mail is knowing that a particular e-mail address is being blocked. When your EMP's bounce report shows a particular blocked e-mail address, you can ask your subscriber to provide a different address.

✦ **If the blocked e-mail address is a work address, ask the IT expert at your subscriber's company to add your EMP's e-mail server address to the friends list on the company's e-mail server.** A *friends list* (also known as a *white list*) is a database containing e-mail addresses from welcome senders. Some firewalls ignore their blocking instructions when the sender's e-mail address exists in the friends list.

Reducing Filtered E-Mail

An *e-mail filter* is a program that scans the content of your e-mail to identify whether your e-mail contains unwanted content. If your e-mail contains content that's identified as potentially unwanted, the program places the e-mail into a holding place (such as a junk folder) or tags the e-mail with a message to identify it as potentially unwanted.

Filters are different from programs that block and bounce e-mails because filters don't return the e-mail to the sender.

Sometimes an e-mail is filtered even though the recipient wants the e-mail. Desirable e-mail content that still gets filtered is a *false positive.* False positives are all too common because of the enormous amount of spam e-mail content that's similar in nature to legitimate e-mail content. Some e-mail filters result in more false positives than others because the people behind the filters get to decide what kinds of content are considered unwanted. For example, an e-mail that contains the word *drug* might be filtered by a systems administrator who believes that certain prescription drug advertisements are spam, even if the word is being used by a bookstore to describe a book.

Unfortunately, you can't tell whether your e-mail is filtered unless the recipient notifies you that your e-mail landed in the junk folder or that your e-mail is being delivered with a filter tag. The following sections explain how you can get a higher percentage of your e-mail through the most common types of filters.

Establish your sender reputation

Getting more e-mail delivered starts with sending your e-mail from a reputable e-mail server. According to a recent study conducted by Return Path (www.returnpath.com), 77 percent of e-mail delivery issues occur because of the sender's reputation. Most companies that provide e-mail delivery for their customers consider the reputation of the sender when filtering e-mail.

Because your own e-mail server isn't likely to have a reputation, delivering your mail through an EMP with a respectable and well-known reputation is one of the most important steps you can take to maximize your e-mail deliverability. Make sure that you choose an EMP that can

✦ **Authenticate your e-mail:** *Authentication* allows e-mail servers to identify the sender of an e-mail. (Authentication is covered later in this chapter.)

✦ **Eliminate customers with high spam complaints:** EMPs send e-mails from their own servers on behalf of their customers even though the e-mails appear to come from their customers. Because too many spam complaints might cause the EMP's servers to become block listed, make sure that your EMP takes action when one of its customers receives too many spam complaints. Reputable EMPs keep their overall complaint rates low — and your sender reputation as clean as possible.

✦ **Affirm the quality of its customers' e-mail lists:** Although EMPs can't guarantee or predetermine the quality of their customers' e-mail lists, reputable EMPs require customers to adhere to strict permission policies to caution their customers when attempting to use e-mail addresses that could generate a high number of complaints.

✦ **Adopt a policy for spam tolerance:** Some businesses, such as those in the financial and medical industries, inherently receive a lot of spam complaints because their legitimate e-mail content looks similar to a lot of spam e-mails. Use an EMP that either has options for such businesses or has a policy to refer such businesses to another service that specializes in industries where spam complaints may be higher than average.

✦ **Keep customers from sending repeated e-mails to unknown users:** Spammers send billions of e-mails to every possible e-mail address hoping to uncover real addresses. Because ISPs (such as AOL, Yahoo!, and Hotmail) spend a lot of money bouncing e-mails sent by spammers, they aren't appreciative of e-mails sent to nonexistent addresses. As a result, your deliverability could suffer if your e-mail server is labeled as a nuisance. To help protect your sender reputation (as well as that of the EMP), most reputable EMPs stop sending your e-mail to nonexistent e-mail addresses after two or three attempts even if you don't remove the e-mail addresses yourself.

E-mail filters often rely on sender reputation before content filters, so make sure to put your EMP to the test. You can check your EMP's sender reputation against the competition by signing up for a free account at Sender Score (www. senderscore.org). Type the domain name of the company and then click each of its listed e-mail servers to see the sender score for each server used to send e-mail on behalf of the EMP's customers. A score of 0 on a particular e-mail server is the worst, and a score of 100 is the best. After you feel comfortable that you're sending e-mail via a reputable EMP, you can be sure that your efforts to optimize your e-mail content won't be wasted.

Understand automatic content filtering

A small percentage of e-mail content filters are controlled completely by e-mail system administrators to keep their users from administering their own filter settings. The e-mail system administrator (usually IT personnel at a company, or an ISP) sets up the automatic filter with specific global parameters that apply to all e-mail users in the same way.

Because automatic e-mail filtering is generally controlled by technically knowledgeable people with all kinds of backgrounds, the types of e-mail content that get filtered through automatic filtering vary widely. For example, one system administrator might decide to filter HTML e-mails, but another might decide to filter e-mails with attachments. If someone on your e-mail list wants your e-mail and his or her system administrator has strict filter settings, your e-mail has a greater chance of false positive identification. (You can read about false positives earlier in this chapter.)

Automatic filtering affects a relatively small percentage of your e-mails. You can't do much about it unless you happen to know the system administrator and you can coax him or her into relaxing a particular company's filtering standards.

Understand user-controlled content filtering

The majority of e-mail filters are included within e-mail programs and written with broad consumer preferences in mind to filter e-mail content that has spam-like characteristics. E-mail filters within e-mail programs almost always allow the user to access the default filter settings and alter them according to user preferences.

Filters often look for spam-like content, so avoid simulating spammer techniques. Recent examples include

✦ Generic Subject lines and anonymous From lines

✦ PDF attachments containing advertisements

✦ Images of entire advertisements without any plain text

✦ Excessive promotional phrases and words

Most consumers don't alter their default e-mail filter settings manually, so avoiding false positive filtering by the most common e-mail filters is partly a matter of building your e-mails to exclude the most commonly filtered content. Figure 7-5 shows a sample of the headers in a junk e-mail folder.

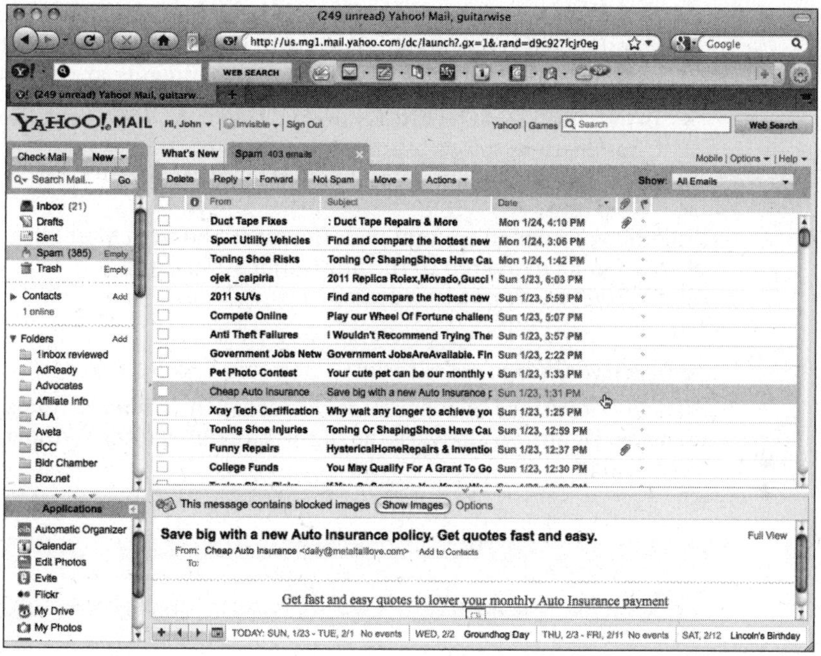

Figure 7-5:
Filters often
look for
spam-like
content.

Read some of the e-mails in your own junk folder to see examples of what to avoid: namely, the most common types of content that spammers include in their e-mails.

You can prevent your e-mails from looking like spam if you do the following:

✦ **Don't include your subscriber's first name in the Subject line of your e-mails.** The practice is common among spammers because most consumers can't understand how a complete stranger could know their first name. (Spammers use web crawler programs to pull the information out of your e-mail headers.) After being tricked a few times, most consumers associate this technique with spam.

✦ **Always include a From line in your e-mail header.** Excluding the From line is an attempt by spammers to trick people into opening e-mails in the hope that the consumers are curious to find out who the e-mail is from. Most filters automatically identify e-mails with no From line as untrustworthy.

✦ **Avoid excessive punctuation (such as strings of exclamation points!!!!!) and "crafty" symbols (such as ¢ents or dollar ign).** Spammers often use strings of punctuation to make their offers more eye-catching, and the practice is just as attention-catching to e-mail filters.

✦ **Don't send marketing e-mails with attachments.** Consumers are understandably nervous about e-mail with unfamiliar attachments, and e-mails sent to more than a few people with attachments are usually filtered.

✦ **DON'T WRITE SENTENCES IN ALL CAPITAL LETTERS.** Writing in all capital letters draws attention to e-mail headlines, and this tack is as annoying to consumers as it is noticeable to e-mail filters.

Building your e-mail content with the most common filter settings gets more of your e-mail delivered to the inbox, but several types of user-controlled filters aren't so simple to sidestep.

Individual filters

A small percentage of consumers do access their filter settings to make changes. Figure 7-6 shows some of the individual filter settings available in Yahoo! Mail.

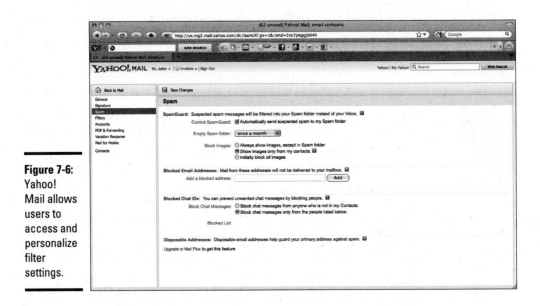

Figure 7-6: Yahoo! Mail allows users to access and personalize filter settings.

If someone on your e-mail list accesses his personal filter settings to set up a filter, your e-mail content is obviously subject to being filtered based on the personal settings for that user. Because you can't know every personal setting in an individual filter, you can do little to get your e-mail through. Accessing filter settings allows the user to personally filter one or more of the following e-mails:

✦ From specific senders

✦ Containing specific words or phrases

✦ With links or images (usually converted to plain text only)

✦ From senders not in the user's address book

✦ With certain domain extensions, such as .biz or .info

✦ With certain types of encoding, such as international languages

✦ With attachments

Trained content filters

Some filters begin with broad default settings and are automatically updated based on whether the user identifies certain e-mails as unwanted. The most common example is the Spam button (as you can read about in Chapter 2 of this minibook), which is a clickable link in an e-mail program that reports the e-mail as spam to the e-mail system administrator. Clicking a Spam button not only reports an e-mail as unwanted but also scans the content to identify content that recurs frequently in the reported e-mails.

When a user clicks a Spam button, a filter scans the e-mail to look for words, phrases, and other types of content to determine whether there is a pattern to the types of content being reported as spam by the user. For example, if a user continues to click the Spam button on multiple e-mails containing the phrase *discount meds,* the filter begins to learn that phrase and automatically filters any e-mails containing that phrase to a junk folder.

Trained content filters work fairly well, but a filter can't distinguish between wanted words and unwanted words in an e-mail that is marked as spam. Because spam e-mails share many common characteristics with legitimate e-mails — such as the phrase Click Here — some legitimate e-mails are identified as false positives.

Understanding E-Mail Authentication

Filtering and blocking technologies are constantly improving. Although it might seem as if spammers are always one step ahead of the game, several promising technologies are emerging to help reduce spam.

Keeping up with emerging technology is important so that your e-mails are optimized for current deliverability standards as well as poised to comply with emerging technology that might cause your e-mails to go undelivered.

Spammers forge the e-mail addresses they send e-mails from by using technical tricks to replace the legitimate header information in an e-mail with false information. Several major ISPs have developed technology to validate the From information in an e-mail. The following is a list of the most popular sender authentication methods. The list also represents the most likely technology to emerge as standards for your own deliverability.

✦ **Sender ID:** This technology, developed by Microsoft, uses an algorithm to select a header field containing the e-mail address responsible for sending the e-mail. The sending e-mail address is then checked against a list of authorized e-mail servers for that e-mail address.

✦ **DomainKeys:** This technology, developed by Yahoo!, uses cryptography to generate a set of unique public and private encryption keys. All outgoing messages are digitally signed by the sender using the *private key* (known only to authorized senders), and the public key is published with the sender's Domain Name Service (DNS) so that recipients can use the public key to validate that the correct private key was used by the sender.

✦ **Sender Policy Framework (SPF):** SPF is similar to Sender ID in that the technology validates the sender's From information by allowing the owner of a specific domain to specify his or her e-mail sending policy or SPF. When someone receives an e-mail that appears to originate from the specified domain, the e-mail server receiving the message can check the SPF record to see whether the e-mail complies with that domain's specific policy.

Self-publishing your own authentication information is beyond the scope of this book, but you can easily employ authentication technology in your e-mails by using a reputable EMP that complies with current authentication standards to send your e-mails.

Book VI

Blogging and Podcasting

The 5th Wave   By Rich Tennant

"I'm sorry. I'm answering e-mail right now. And since when does the Taco Bell Chihuahua have a blog anyway?"

Contents at a Glance

Chapter 1: Picking Your Blog Topic

In This Chapter

✔ Finding a blog topic you care about

✔ Creating goals for your blog

✔ Calculating the size of your audience

Folks seem to think that blogging is a magical concept. But blogs aren't mystical. A *blog* is simply a toolset with which you write and publish entries (*posts*), and then visitors can comment on those posts. It's all about the content, you see.

To have a blog — and use it for web marketing — you need a solid topic up front. Choose something about which you're passionate and knowledgeable. That way, you can build a base of followers, which in turn drives traffic to your site (or sites) — and ultimately, your endeavor.

Choosing a Blog Topic

If you're going to write a blog, you need a topic: a *focus*. Without one, you'll have a tough time attracting an audience. Your goal is to reach the point where your audience seeks you out because you consistently offer information that they find helpful in light of their interests.

No focus means no consistency, which means no audience.

Picking that topic can be tougher than you might think. Common questions and concerns that you may have include

> *I don't want to pick a narrow topic. I'll be stuck writing about it forever.*
>
> *No wants want to hear what I have to say.*
>
> *My topic is so boring. Why would anyone read it?*
>
> *I can't think of anything.*

All the preceding questions translate to one issue: fear. We're all trained to be terrified of writing. Starting in grade school, we're told that we'll lose two points for a missing comma or four points for an incomplete sentence, and we'll flunk the class if we use *than* when we should use *then*.

Well, you can let go of that fear now. Blogging is the best form of writing therapy on the planet. People read blogs for content, not for grammatical perfection. Of course, you should strive to write grammatically correct language lest your readers think that you're not well educated or that your work is sloppy in general. But one misplaced punctuation mark doesn't mean that you get an F.

And, if you hate writing, you can do a blog that's a series of videos. (More about that in the next few chapters.)

Before you read the rest of this chapter, just *relax.* Take a breath. Smile. You're among friends.

If you read nothing else in this chapter, remember these key tips:

✦ Write about something that excites you. ✔ *matter Financial Plany Exams*

✦ Write about something you know. – *Financial Plans.*

You're probably thinking, "But I'm doing this to grow my business!" If you're blogging for your business, you should be enthusiastic about it, too.

Think about it, and find the one or two or many things you care about in your career. For example, if you're a passionate collector of bottle tops, that's your blog topic. If you're an Internet marketer and truly care about the profession, write about it.

Don't select a topic simply because you think that a lot of people search for it, or because you think that it would have a big audience. Here's why:

✦ **Blogging requires a long-term commitment.** You can more easily write regularly on a topic in which you're interested. And, you can more easily write regularly if you know a lot about the subject material.

✦ **Your audience won't hesitate to point out subject matter mistakes.** That's not a big deal: Mistakes happen. But make sure that you're right more often than not. Knowing the topic is important.

✦ **Your audience knows if you're not passionate.** You won't attract as many dedicated readers.

✦ **It's no fun if you write about a topic with which you're unfamiliar.** Writing about a familiar topic is much more fun than struggling to write about an unfamiliar topic.

"What if no one is interested in my topic?" Many folks ask that question. Someone is always interested. If you have a business and you're selling products successfully, chances are good that you have an audience.

Narrow blog topics work

The blog Glue Gun Crafts (`www.gluegun` `crafts.com`) covers crafts made with glue guns. That's a narrow topic. Still, the blog receives a healthy number of visitors and even earns a little money.

Consider what you do, and then ask yourself these questions:

✦ How can I make this topic funny?

✦ How can I make this topic fascinating?

✦ What can I say about this topic that will prompt discussion?

✦ Which questions are asked repeatedly?

Here are a few examples:

✦ **If you sell cash registers,** you could blog about the coolest-looking cash registers.

✦ **If you're a management consultant,** write a blog about applying your favorite time-management technique to midsize companies.

✦ **If you're a roofer,** create a question-and-answer blog for homeowners.

✦ **If you're a real estate agent,** blog about your favorite staging techniques.

✦ **If you're a chef,** write about the best frozen foods with taste testing.

✦ **If you're a teacher,** come up with a daily list of homework tips.

You have dozens of possibilities. *Never* start by telling yourself, "What I do is boring." It's not!

Thinking about Your Blog Goals

After you decide on a topic, determine what you're trying to achieve by writing this blog. When you answer, keep the following concepts in mind:

✦ **Few blogs succeed in the first six months of life.** Whatever your goal is, give yourself at least 6 to 12 months to reach it.

◆ **For the first six months, you almost certainly will "speak to an empty room."**

◆ **Only a handful of blogs generate appreciable direct income through advertising or other cash generators.** Most are marketing tools with indirect benefits for your business.

If you're blogging for your business, your first priority should be the business, not your online ego.

Set your goals in six-month cycles. That time frame gives you enough time to work while giving you something to work toward.

Set a six-month goal for your blossoming blog. Consider the following goals as a starting point:

◆ Answer the top 20 questions asked by customers.

◆ Write 42 posts.

◆ Send 20 potential clients to read the blog.

◆ Find two potential clients on the web.

If you're feeling truly ambitious, strive for these results:

◆ Use your blog to write a book.

◆ Sign up at least 300 subscribers.

◆ Get at least half your traffic from search engines.

All these goals are attainable and provide a substantial boost for your business.

Bad goals include

◆ Earn a five-figure income.

◆ Rank No. 1 for a competitive phrase in the search engines.

These two goals, although attainable, are quite difficult to reach. Plus, they don't necessarily help your business. Earning $10,000 from your blog, for example, doesn't help if you spend the equivalent of $20,000 worth of your time to do it. And, ranking No. 1 for a relevant phrase *might* help, but you need to do a lot of research first. See Book II for more on search engine optimization (SEO).

Sizing Up Your Space

After you pick a blog topic and create goals for your blog, it's time to figure out who else is writing about your topic and how big your audience might be.

Using Technorati

Technorati.com is a blog search engine. When you visit it and search for your topic, you find a list of blogs written about your subject or a related topic. Even better, you see them ranked according to the number of other blogs linking to each of the listed blogs.

Be sure to click the Posts tab so that you see results only from blogs.

Figure 1-1 shows all the blogs that include *internet marketing*.

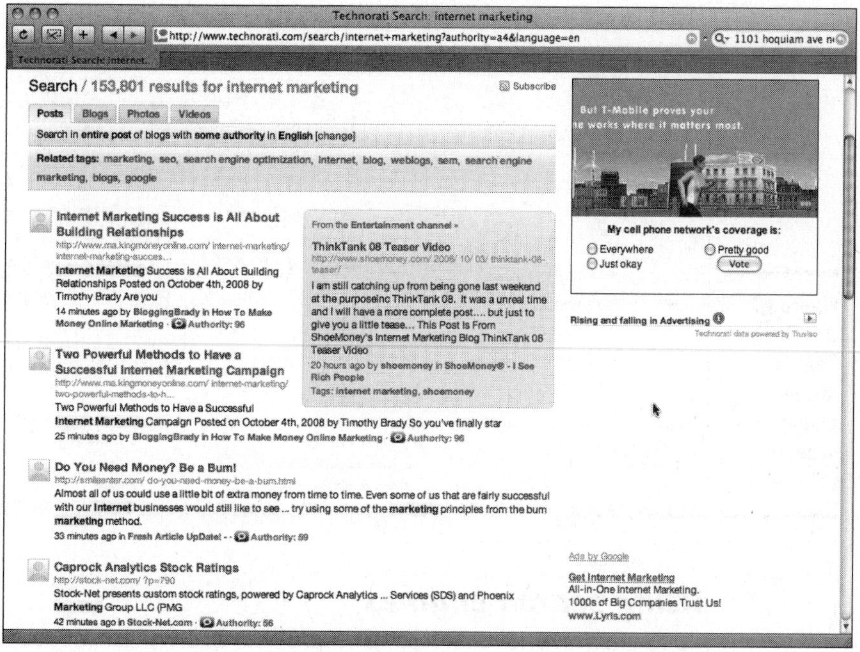

Figure 1-1:
A Technorati search result.

Using Google Trends

Google Trends shows you changes in search volume for different terms over time. Using this information is a good way to figure out whether your blog topic is on the upswing.

Visit `www.google.com/trends` and search for a key phrase. You see changes over time in both search volume and news references, as shown in Figure 1-2.

If you see the message `Not Enough Search Volume` as a result, it doesn't mean that your topic is never searched. It only means that people haven't searched for the phrase the number of times (potentially thousands) that are required to show up in Google Trends.

If a phrase *does* show up in Trends, though, you know it's very, very hot — and it's worth pursuing the topic.

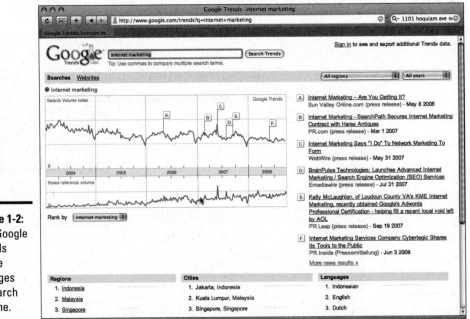

Figure 1-2:
Use Google Trends to see changes in search volume.

Using search engines

Go to your favorite search engine and search for your chosen topic. Use the Blog Search option, if your search engine has one. Google Blog Search is shown in Figure 1-3.

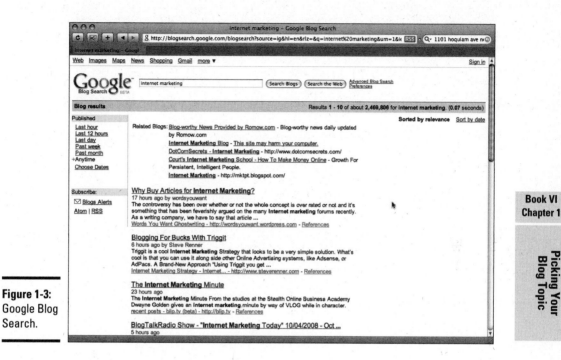

Figure 1-3:
Google Blog
Search.

Check for the following:

+ **How many other bloggers write about your topic?** If you find millions, you may have a hard time standing out.

+ **What do other bloggers say about your topic?** You might have a valuable counterpoint.

+ **Can you fill any gaps in their knowledge?**

+ **What kinds of comments do those bloggers get?** Comments can give you insight into unanswered questions that you can respond to.

The key here is to figure out where you can offer the most value to readers. That's your opportunity to turn your blog into a valuable marketing platform.

Chapter 2: Getting Yer Blog On

In This Chapter

✔ Choosing a blogging tool

✔ Setting up your blog

✔ Changing the look of your blog

✔ Putting your first post in print

Blogging is defined, in part, by the tools you use to publish the words you write. These tools tend to be extremely easy to set up, but you still have to do a little work.

This chapter helps you select the best tool for your purpose and then set up the tool and perhaps customize it. After you accomplish all those tasks, you write your first post.

Choosing Your Blog Platform

First things first: Choose your tool. All blogging tools have certain characteristics in common:

- ✦ They work in your web browser.

- ✦ They publish your written material on a website.

- ✦ They enable site visitors to then write comments in response to your entries (called *blog posts*).

- ✦ They include a way for visitors to subscribe to your blog by using the *RSS* feature. (For more about that, see the section "Creating your RSS feed," later in this chapter.)

Apart from those similarities, though, the various blogging platforms differ widely. The following sections describe four of the most popular ones in detail and then list a few others that you might want to investigate.

Blogger and WordPress.org: Easy and free

Blogger.com is a basic blogging service owned by Google. You can sign up in a few quick steps and start publishing your first posts in a few minutes. Figure 2-1 shows the Blogger authoring tools.

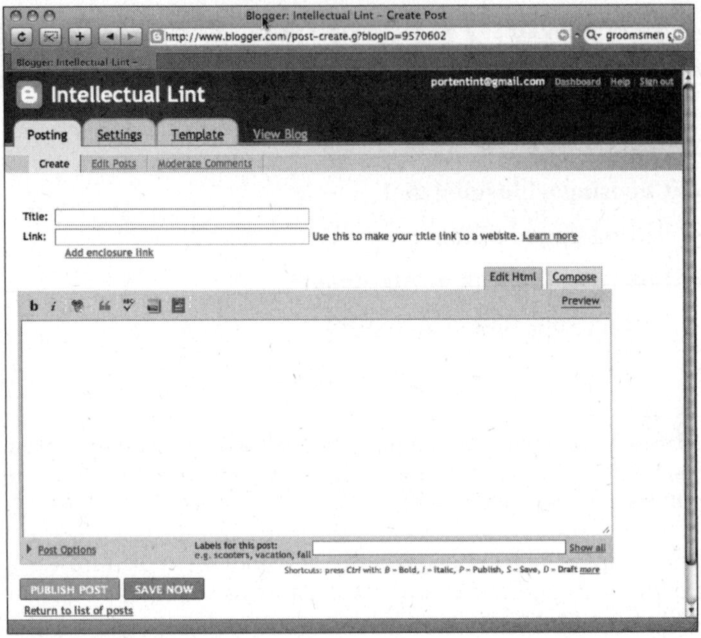

Figure 2-1:
Writing
a post in
Blogger.

WordPress.com is a hosted version of the now-ubiquitous WordPress blogging toolset. In this sense, *hosted* means that WordPress has its own web servers, with WordPress already set up, so you don't have to install anything. Like Blogger, it's easy to use and offers a helpful, prebuilt solution. You can see what a WordPress.com blog looks like in Figure 2-2.

WordPress.com and Blogger's strengths are listed here:

✦ They're easy to use. They're *really* easy to use. The moment you set up your blog, you have commenting and subscriptions and all the other basic features of a successful blog.

✦ You don't have to install any software.

✦ They're free.

✦ You can use lots of prebuilt designs.

✦ You're not responsible for maintaining the code that powers the site, because upgrades happen automatically.

Book VI
Chapter 2

Getting Yer Blog On

Figure 2-2:
A blog
hosted on
WordPress.
com.

However, both WordPress.com and Blogger have some drawbacks, too:

✦ **No customization:** If either of these blogging platforms were a car, the hood would be welded shut. You can't customize either one to any great degree. Even WordPress.com Premium, which allows you to modify the look and feel a bit, won't let you add plug-ins or make changes to the underlying blogging software.

✦ **SEO weakness:** Both systems have some drawbacks from a search engine optimization (SEO) standpoint. Because your blog isn't part of your website, it doesn't help you add useful content to your site. See Book II for more information about SEO.

✦ **No quick updates:** Someone else is responsible for maintaining the code. You get the idea: If something goes wrong, it may be a little while before it gets fixed.

Blogger and WordPress.com are helpful places to start. If you later decide to make blogging a part of your Internet marketing strategy, you'll probably move to a more customizable solution.

TypePad is another hosted blogging solution with features similar to WordPress.com and Blogger. Although TypePad isn't as popular as Blogger or WordPress.com, it's worth a careful look if you want to set up a blog quickly. You can use TypePad Micro for free, or pay a fee to have more control over your blog's design.

Most people start with a hosted system like Blogger and then move to a custom system. When you make that change, a little research pays off.

WordPress installed: A sports car

WordPress also offers its blogging platform in a software program that you can install on your own website. And that means you can run WordPress on your own server. Some businesses even use WordPress to drive their entire website (see Book I, Chapter 4). You can find it at www.wordpress.org.

The software is free. If you know your way around a web server, you can install it in about ten minutes. If not, many web hosts are willing to set up a WordPress blog for you.

WordPress installed looks and works like WordPress.com, with a few critical differences:

✦ **You can customize WordPress installed.** The entire blog is built on PHP, a common web programming language.

✦ **You can take advantage of how other folks have already customized WordPress installed.** Hundreds of *plug-ins* (extensions built to add new capabilities to WordPress) are all available on the WordPress.org website.

✦ **You can maximize SEO with WordPress installed.** By using a few plug-ins, you can make WordPress an SEO powerhouse. Don't worry about this concept yet; just understand that the option exists later on, if you want it.

✦ **You can make your WordPress installed blog part of your website.** If you install WordPress on the same server that hosts your website, your blog can live at www.*yoursite*.com/blog or a similar URL, as shown in Figure 2-3.

WordPress installed has some challenges, though:

✦ **You're totally responsible for your installation.** If you want an upgrade, you have to do it. If something goes wrong, you have to either fix it or pay someone else to fix it.

✦ **You need to know a bit about installing software on a server.** Or, you have to hire someone else who knows about it. Some hosting providers can set it up for free for you, but you'll still need to take the time to learn how to use it or pay your provider to put the finishing touches on the setup. The cost is low, but it's still a cost.

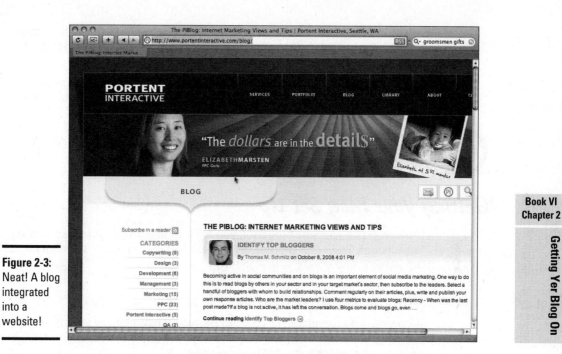

Figure 2-3:
Neat! A blog
integrated
into a
website!

WordPress is like a popular sports car: It is by far the most often-used
installed blogging platform on the planet. A huge community helps support
you if you decide to use it, but it's not intended for the web novice. You need
to either gain expertise or hire someone with that expertise. Otherwise, you
end up in a ditch.

For all the ins and outs on WordPress installed, check out *WordPress For
Dummies,* by Lisa Sabin-Wilson (published by John Wiley & Sons, Inc.).

Other blog options

You have many other options for blogs or blog-style sites. Here are a few:

✦ **Joomla!** (available at www.joomla.org) is a free, PHP-driven blogging
and content management system (CMS) that offers an amazing array of
tools in a single package.

✦ **ExpressionEngine** (www.expressionengine.com) is a CMS and blogging tool in one.

✦ **Textpattern** (www.textpattern.com) is a flexible, textile-based content manager that's PHP driven and open source.

✦ **LiveJournal** (www.livejournal.com) is a hosted blogging system that
you don't have to install, much like WordPress hosted and Blogger.

✦ **Tumblr** (www.tumblr.com) is another hosted blogging system that, at the time of this writing, is enormously popular. It's a fun system if you want to get started fast.

✦ **Drupal** (www.drupal.org) is a broader social "plumbing" system — a CMS plus comments, membership, accounts, and messaging — that includes blog features.

This list isn't exhaustive, by any means. For even more blogging choices, search for *blogging software*.

Getting Your Blog Set Up

After you choose your blog tool, you need to take the next steps: First set up an account. Then design your blog's look and feel, configure comments, set up pinging, and create your RSS feed.

Blog account setup

Depending on the platform you choose, you might need to simply set up an account, as shown in Figure 2-4. In that case, you just need to visit the blogging site and enter some basic information.

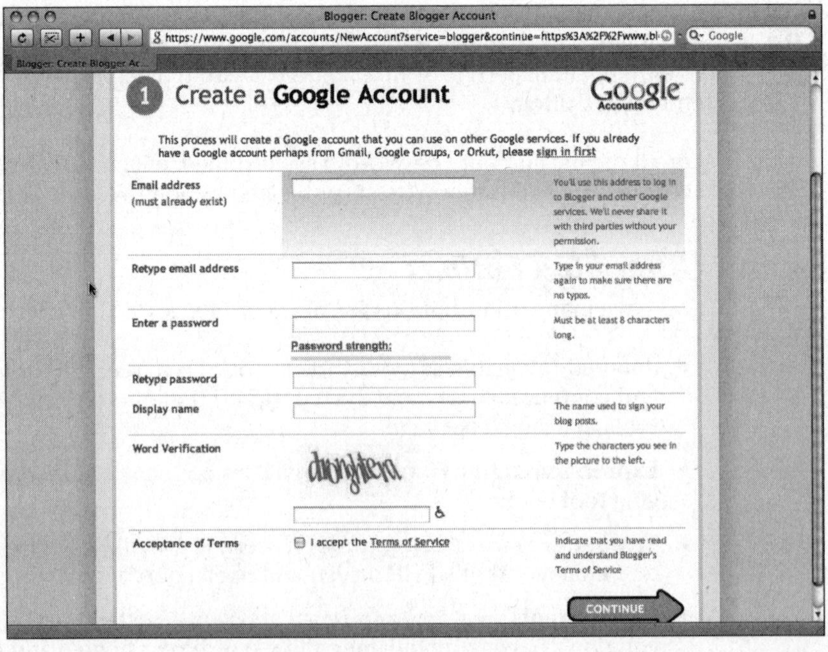

Figure 2-4: Setting up a blog on Blogger doesn't take much effort.

If you're using an installed blogging tool, you need to

1. Download the required software and install it (or pay someone else to do it for you).

2. Configure it for your server and website.

3. Set up your login and password.

4. Make a short post and comment to ensure that everything is working properly.

Picking your blog look

After the basic setup is complete, make your blog look just the way you want. You have a few options, from the easiest to the most difficult.

Easy: Use a preinstalled template

Most blogging systems come with a set of templates that you can easily select. If you're happy using one of these templates, changing the look of your blog is as easy as choosing from a group, as shown in Figure 2-5.

Installed platforms such as WordPress and Movable Type are supplied with a few templates, too.

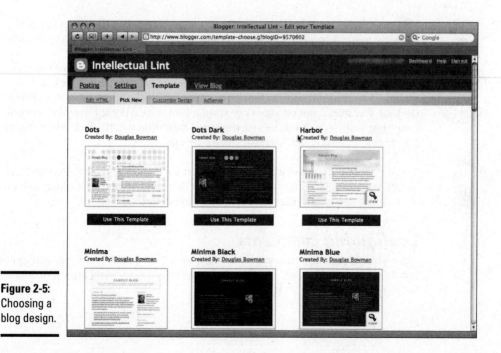

Figure 2-5:
Choosing a
blog design.

Intermediate: Download a new template and install it

Hundreds of free blog templates are available. You just have to download and install them on your blog.

On most hosted blog systems, this task is a relatively straightforward cut-and-paste operation. On an installed blog, you might have to download some files and then upload them to your server.

Whatever you do, if you use a free template, *provide a credit to the author.* The author gave you a great design for free — give him something in return.

Hard: Download a new template, install it, and customize it

You can also find a template that's close to what you want, install it on your blog, and then tweak it until it's just right.

In most cases, completing this task requires a solid knowledge of HTML and style sheets.

Superhard: Create your own

If you're truly determined, you can create your own fully customized template. Every blogging platform, from Blogger to WordPress, offers ways to customize the look and feel of your blog.

So, you can create your own, perfect look and then use the blogging platform's special template language or system to build the look into your site.

Creating your own template requires a lot of HTML expertise and the patience of a saint. It's challenging; however, it can also be a heck of a lot of fun and an excellent way to learn your way around your own site. Just realize that you might spend days creating a template. Having the perfect look (one that's perfect in your eyes, anyway) might be worth your while. Figure 2-6 shows off a blog with a customized design.

Many qualified professionals can help you with this type of customization. Check your blogging platform's site for a list of specialists. Chances are good that one of them can refer you to a developer.

Configuring comments

After your blog looks the way you want, make sure that you're handling comments the way you want. The key is moderation, reviewing comments before they're published.

Book VI
Chapter 2

Getting Yer Blog On

Figure 2-6:
A cus-
tomized
design.

Most blogs provide a few options for comment moderation:

+ **Don't**

  • *Let anyone publish a comment with no moderation.* Bad idea. Don't use this option unless you want your blog stuffed with links to sites hawking pharmaceuticals.

  • *Refuse to allow anyone to publish comments.* That's also a bad idea. A blog without comments isn't really a blog.

+ **Do**

  • *Review all comments before publishing.* This option keeps things simple. You review every comment before you click Publish, which helps you understand the process.

  • *Allow trusted commenters to publish without approval.* If you set a specific commenter as Trusted, your blog publishes that person's comments without moderation. As your site receives increasingly more visitors — and more folks writing comments — this option might make your life a lot easier.

Pick the option that makes the most sense for you. Consider starting with reviewing all comments before publishing because it gives you the most flexibility.

Setting up pinging

When you write a new post on your blog, your blogging software can send a ping. A *ping* is a short message sent to major blogging search engines and directories that says, "Hey, I have a new story here!"

Pinging isn't what it used to be. However, it's still a great way to push content to search engines and blog syndication services. It's almost no effort, so it's still worth doing.

A timely ping sends the basic information about your new post to sites such as Technorati and Weblogs.com. Those sites then publish the post title and a short snippet from the post itself.

Pings can be an effective traffic generator, and they involve zero effort after you set them up.

Your blogging software probably includes a ping configuration page, such as the one shown in Figure 2-7. Note that it might be called Web Services Settings or Pinging, depending on the blog software.

XML-RPC ☑ Enable the WordPress, Movable Type, MetaWeblog and Blog

Update Services

When you publish a new post, WordPress automatically notifies the following site update services. For more
Separate multiple service URLs with line breaks.

http://rpc.pingomatic.com/

Save Changes

Figure 2-7:
Setting up pinging in Movable Type.

Paste the pinging service addresses you want to have included. From then on, your blog automatically pings those services when you publish. Here's a good starting list of pinging services:

```
http://rpc.pingomatic.com
http://ping.blo.gs
```

```
http://ping.feedburner.com
http://rpc.blogrolling.com/pinger
http://rpc.technorati.com/rpc/ping
http://rpc.icerocket.com:10080
```

Ping sites change all the time, so you'll want to check these addresses before you enter them into your blog's pinging configuration.

If you don't have a pinging tool built into your blog, that's okay. Visit www. pingomatic.com and use its simple form to ping new posts. It takes only a moment, and the instant exposure is an excellent traffic generator.

Creating your RSS feed

Every blog should have at least one RSS feed.

RSS stands for (among other things) *really simple syndication.* It's not a technology; it's a format: a common way to publish the headlines and a summary of each post on your blog or the complete post. If you looked at an RSS feed in raw text format, it would look like the nonsense shown in Figure 2-8.

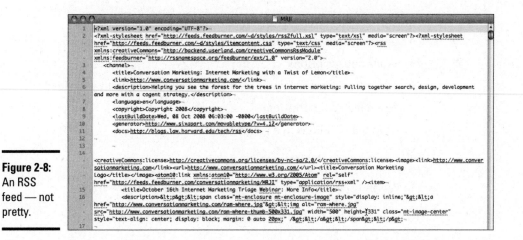

Figure 2-8: An RSS feed — not pretty.

Look at the same text with any standard RSS feed reader, and — *voilà!* — you see what's shown in Figure 2-9.

Figure 2-9:
Ah, that makes more sense.

Visitors can subscribe to your RSS feed by using one of hundreds of easy-to-use RSS feed readers, including Google Reader (`www.google.com/reader`) and Microsoft Outlook. They then see an updated list of recent articles on your blog, without having to visit the blog. It's a helpful way for visitors to keep track of lots of blogs at one time.

You *can* use your blog's built-in RSS generation to provide the RSS feed. That strategy works fine. But the FeedBurner service (now owned by Google) lets you take it a step further. FeedBurner lets you turn your single simple feed into a marketing tool. Using FeedBurner, you can

✦ Add advertising to your RSS feed

✦ Deliver your feed in multiple formats for best compatibility

✦ Track subscriptions

✦ Add nifty features, such as E-mail a Friend, directly in your feed

✦ Add e-mail subscriptions

✦ Leap tall buildings in a single bound

Okay, maybe not the last one.

But FeedBurner can truly make your life easier. And, it's free.

To burn your feed using FeedBurner, follow these steps:

1. **Visit** `www.feedburner.com`.

2. **Create an account and log in.**

3. **Find your blog's feed address.**

Check your blog documentation if you're stumped.

4. **Paste that address into the Burn a Feed Right This Instant field and then click Next.**

   FeedBurner provides a new address for your feed.

5. **In your blog, replace the old feed address with the new FeedBurner address.**

   Your blogging tool now points subscribers to the FeedBurner feed instead.

Writing Your First Post

Phew. The blog is set up. Your RSS feed is set up. It's time to take a break!

Not so fast. Didn't you forget something? Oh, yeah — a post!

Writing your first post can be difficult. You want it to be perfect, of course. You want to explode onto the blogging scene and into stardom.

But, because that's not going to happen (sorry, it's just not), you should have some fun instead and have a stress-free launch. Here are tips for a first post:

✦ **Don't aim for perfection.** Aim for from-the-heart writing instead. Just say what your aspirations are for your blog.

✦ **Don't write about how you don't know what to write.** Everyone knows what writer's block is like. You don't need to remind us.

✦ **Do create a time capsule.** Write a first post that you can look back on later to create a sense of why you started this project in the first place.

✦ **Do publish it right away.** It's always good to edit. But don't spend days or even weeks trying to make that post *just right.* You have to go live sometime.

The most important thing about that first post, though, is getting it done. It won't be your best, and that's totally okay. Blogging is about practice and improvement. Get started!

Chapter 3: Writing Like a Blogger

In This Chapter

✔ Blog writing style and structure

✔ Writing content for online readers

✔ Setting a blogging schedule (and sticking to it)

✔ Battling bloggage

No single *blog style* of writing exists. However, you can try out different techniques to make your blog easier to read (and write), such as using bullets to make more-scannable pages and using images to grab the reader's attention.

For most people, reading online is hard — far harder than reading a print page. You need to take that into account when you write your blog posts. And that's what this chapter is about: how to write posts that are easy for your readers to scan and read, how to write posts that they'll love, and how to write consistently over a long period of time.

All these efforts add up to a blog that firmly connects readers to your blog and your business. That, in turn, translates to a better connection with potential customers and a more successful Internet marketing campaign.

Following the Three Blog S's

The ideal blog post (and blog) creates an image of you, the writer, in the reader's mind. That image is consistent, and it's one with which the reader can identify.

To reach that point, though, you have to know how to structure your posts, eliminate roadblocks to readers, and make sure that they get your point. If you want to achieve that, all blog posts you write must follow the three S's:

✦ **Simplicity:** Your writing should be clear and easy to read. Flowery language is a helpful way to show off your vocabulary, but it doesn't necessarily communicate. Keep your writing simple. For example:

- *Okay:* The steak was the epitome of flavor and texture.

- *Better:* The steak was delicious.

✦ **Scannability:** People don't read online; they scan. Use bullets, photos, and other techniques to break up your writing and make it easy to skim. For example:

- *Okay:* You'll love this website because it has simple lessons, great tips you can act on right away, and no sales pitch.

- *Better:* You'll love this website because it has
  Simple lessons
  Great tips you can act on right away
  No sales pitch

✦ **Sharpness:** Your writing should get to the point — right away. For example:

- *Okay:* I wrote for hours. Then I pondered a bit. And wondered some more. And then I realized that 1 + 1 = 2.

- *Better:* 1 + 1 = 2. I realized this after I wrote for hours, pondered a bit, and then wondered some more.

The rest of this chapter offers techniques for following the three S's and then describes the logistics of consistently publishing a blog.

Writing for simplicity

Mark Twain once wrote, "If I had more time, I would have written a shorter letter." You would think that writing simple prose would be the easiest method, but it takes practice. Follow these tips every time you write, though, and you'll be off to a good start:

✦ **Shred the thesaurus.** Nothing breeds complex writing like a thesaurus. Throw it away. Use a dictionary if you need better words. And, never replace a perfectly appropriate two-syllable word with a four-syllable one. For example, *melancholy* is a great word, but if *sad* will work just as well, why not use it instead?

✦ **Write, think, revise.** Don't try to produce the perfect sentence in your head before you write. Just write down what you're trying to say. You can always improve it later.

✦ **Count syllables.** Make a game for yourself. Read a sentence in your post and see whether you can reduce the number of syllables by 20 percent without changing its impact or meaning. Do this for at least four sentences per day. The practice will help you write shorter, clearer prose. For example:

- *Okay:* I pedaled my bicycle to the grocery store.

- *Better:* I rode my bike to the store.

✦ **Minimize prepositions.** Prepositions, words such as *about, in,* and *from,* can give readers headaches (see the third bullet in this list):

- *Okay:* If you end up with a sentence that has too many prepositions in it, it might be from overediting.

- *Better:* Overediting often creates sentences with too many prepositions.

✦ **Use active voice, not passive.** If you find yourself using *was* or *have been* or similar wording, you might be using passive voice. Grammatically, it's okay, but it's more difficult to read and leads to overly complex sentences:

- *Okay (passive):* The boy was bitten by the dog.

- *Better (active):* The dog bit the boy.

✦ **Minimize parentheticals.** If you use parentheses or an em dash (—), you're creating a *parenthetical,* which can be a handy literary tool that helps you explain something. It's easy to use parentheticals far too much — you can quickly become attached to them — and you may have a hard time getting rid of them. There — see that? Just keep them to a minimum.

✦ **Break up compound sentences.** Whenever you combine sentences using conjunctions, commas, and so on, you create a sentence that's hard to read online.

- *Okay:* Writing simply is a must, because it invites readers in, while complex writing, though fancier, drives readers away.

- *Better:* Writing simply is a must. It invites readers in. Complex writing, though fancier, drives them away.

✦ **Blow away fluff.** It's hard to resist adding words such as *really* or *extremely.* Resist it anyway.

✦ **Be confident.** Make your statement with authority. Don't dilute it with "I think" and "I feel." Obviously, this blog should offer your take on the topic at hand.

- *Okay:* I think simple writing is best.

- *Better:* Simple writing is best.

✦ **Don't get cute.** It's hard to resist writing "$ave dollar$ and ¢ent$." It's also hard to read it. Don't use cutesy punctuation. Don't use texting shorthand like LOL, either, unless it fits your audience.

✦ **Don't! Use! Too! Many! Exclamation! Points!!!!!** Hopefully, you get the point.

✦ **Practice!** Writing is not a talent. It's a skill. The more you write, the better you get. Practice doesn't help you only with blogging. The work you put in on your blog pays off anytime you sit down to write.

Writing for scannability

Online, people don't read; they scan. Typical readers rapidly scroll down the page, looking for words, pictures, and ideas that catch their attention.

Change makes the eye pause: Paragraph breaks, photos, and boldface or italicized text all draw attention. Used properly, these devices help readers get your point before they dive into reading every word of your post.

Before people read your article from start to finish, they want content that

✦ Has no paragraphs longer than four or five lines

✦ Lists important points in numbered or bulleted lists

✦ Breaks up major points with headlines

✦ Includes images to emphasize points and give the eye a break

✦ Includes only one idea per paragraph

✦ Is short and concise

   See the previous section in this chapter.

✦ Includes headlines that explain the subsequent copy on their own

   You should be able to write a headline on a blank sheet of paper and immediately understand it:

   • *Okay:* Overview

   • *Better:* Overview of Online Writing

✦ Includes links that follow the same rule

✦ Uses line spacing of at least 1.5 lines

✦ Places headlines closer to the paragraphs that come after them than to the paragraphs that come before

Figure 3-1 shows an example of a blog post that uses at least a few of these principles: images to break up the page, subheadings and numbered lists, and short paragraphs.

Here's another advantage to scannable posts: Many readers skim through countless posts from multiple blogs using their RSS feed readers. When they do, elements such as headlines and images catch their eyes.

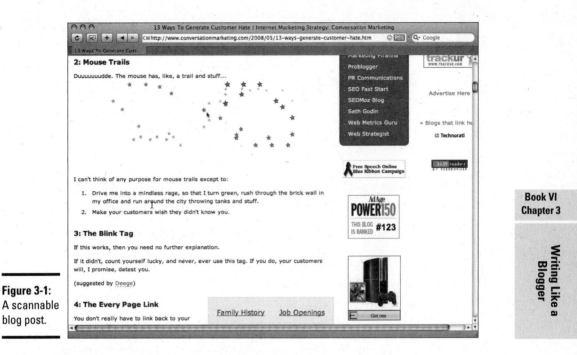

Figure 3-1:
A scannable blog post.

In the example shown in Figure 3-2, you can see a couple of differences in the posts:

✦ **Left post:** It's more scannable and therefore catches your eye. You're more likely to read it.

✦ **Right post:** The lines in this post run together somewhat and are less likely to draw the reader's eye.

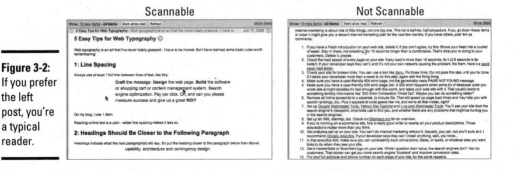

Figure 3-2:
If you prefer the left post, you're a typical reader.

Scannable content gets a chance to be read: The text you write is more likely to be read by visitors to your site.

Writing sharp

Get to the point!

In grammar school, we're taught the funnel writing style: Start broad and then narrow your focus until you draw a conclusion at the end of your essay.

Forget that method. Instead, adopt a more journalistic, *upside down* style. Lead with your conclusion. Tell readers why they should continue reading, and tell them what benefits they'll see if they do.

The first paragraph (or paragraphs) of your blog post should include

✦ What the reader will find

✦ Why she needs to find out about it

✦ How it will benefit her

This isn't a hard-and-fast rule. (No rule ever is.) You can always add a little extra introduction for entertainment value. If you start by writing the sharpest possible text and get to the point, however, the result is always a more readable post.

Clearing Bloggage

If you're avoiding writing on your blog, or staring at your computer screen for an hour without writing a word, you have blogger's block or *bloggage*.

Here are a few ways to clear bloggage:

✦ **Read instead of write.** Find something that someone else wrote, said, or did that makes you laugh, scream, or cry. Responding is sometimes easier than writing from scratch.

✦ **Request ideas.** Ask your audience what they want to read. They may give you some helpful ideas.

✦ **Go wild.** Write something in a tone that's nothing like your normal style. Pretend that you're a new guest author on your blog and write under a pseudonym. It's fun!

✦ **Take a break.** If you're jammed up, it may be your brain's way of saying, "I need a vacation." Walk away from your blog for a few hours or days. Read a book. Come back refreshed and see whether the ideas flow more easily.

✦ **Start talking.** Rather than write, start talking about your subject matter. Use a recording device and pretend that you're teaching a class. Transcribe what you said after five or ten minutes, and you'll likely have some interesting ideas for a post.

Keep reading for more on bloggage-blockage removal techniques that you may find helpful.

Setting your editorial calendar

Using — and sticking to — an editorial calendar can help you avoid bloggage. Dedicate a few days each week to a specific type of article.

For example, Monday might be book review day. Or, Wednesday might be list-of-photos day. You can have a site review day, when you ask readers to submit their sites for review and you write recommendations as a post.

You don't always have to follow your editorial calendar. Use it when you're running low on ideas.

Keeping an idea list

Always keep a pad or file at your computer where you can compile a list of potential blog posts. This idea list is your resource when you're running out of ideas. It also ensures that you don't forget any outstanding ideas when they pop into your head.

Here are some types of information that you can keep on your list:

✦ Interesting websites that inspire you

✦ Ideas that just pop into your head

✦ Questions your clients or customers ask

✦ The title of a book or magazine article that made you think

✦ A quote or comment from you or someone else that might make an interesting topic

✦ Anything else that occurs to you

Get in the habit of keeping a small notebook with you at all times. You can transcribe any new ideas from your notebook to your computer for future blog posts. Or go the geeky way: Use a notes app on your smartphone or tablet and sync with your computer.

Writing ahead

No rule stipulates that you must write one complete blog post, publish it, and then move on to the next.

If you have a half-formed idea, start writing. Save it as a draft in your blogging software. That way, you can return to it later.

If you're inspired and suddenly want to write a series of related blog posts, all at one time, do it! Publish the first one and schedule or save the rest to publish later. Writing ahead in this way creates a library of material that you can publish at any time.

Finding guest bloggers

Letting another blogger write on your blog can give you a break when you need it. It can also attract attention (if the blogger is well known) and bring that blogger's audience to your blog. And, it can get you invited to post as a guest on that person's blog, too.

If you know of a blog that complements yours, or if you comment regularly on a particular blog, consider contacting that blog's author. Ask that person whether she's interested in guest-posting on your blog.

Your invitee doesn't need to guest-post right away. Just keep a list of bloggers who indicate an interest in guest-posting. If you're stumped for an idea, if you're going on vacation, or if you have an interesting idea that requires guest posts, contact a potential contributor.

Chapter 4: Tracking Other Blogs

In This Chapter

✔ **Understanding RSS and feed readers**

✔ **Setting up Google Reader**

✔ **Reviewing your feeds fast with hot keys**

✔ **Getting organized with folders and tags**

Two things power the blogging world: writers and the community in which they function. The earlier chapters of this minibook talk about you, the writer. But that's only half the equation.

Somehow, you need to get involved with the larger community, that is, the many bloggers and readers out there already talking about your subject. That involvement leads to links and references to you by other, more influential bloggers. If you want that kind of involvement, want to be noticed, and want to become a respected member of the community, you need to do one or more of the following:

✦ Connect with other bloggers via social media (see Book VII).

✦ Leave a pithy comment on an influential blog.

✦ Reference another blogger's post in one of your own and link to that post.

✦ Write something highly relevant to current events.

All these methods require that you know what's going on in your industry or community, as well as related news. To that end, you need to know how to track blogs. With that knowledge, you can then "listen" to the conversation that's going on among related blogs and join in with useful information in the form of blog posts of your own. That's what this chapter holds.

Note: This chapter is very similar to Book VII, Chapter 2. If you've already read that chapter, you can skim through this one. This chapter might also seem similar to Chapter 1 of this minibook, but it's not. That chapter shows you how to find the right topic. This chapter focuses on how to track relevant blogs on an ongoing basis.

Understanding Feeds and Feed Readers

Geekery ahead! This section is filled with terms like *RSS* and *XML*. These terms can help you understand how this stuff all works. If you got hives in computer class in high school, you might want to skip ahead.

All blogs (at least within the accepted definition of a blog) generate a list of updates in an *RSS feed*. RSS stands for *really simple syndication,* a standard way of delivering a list of headlines and articles or article summaries as a streamlined text file.

RSS is built using Extensible Markup Language (XML), if you care about that sort of thing.

The raw content of an RSS feed looks like what you see in Figure 4-1.

Figure 4-1:
Raw RSS.
Blech.

Information in this format isn't very useful, is it? Well, not for the average humanoid, at least. However, this format allows a type of computer software — *feed readers* — to retrieve headlines and summaries from just about every blog on the Internet, and deliver them to you in a pretty, easy-to-read format, as shown in Figure 4-2. Much better!

Every time a blogger publishes a new post, the blogging software adds that post to the RSS feed. When you sign in to your feed reader, it checks the RSS feed for updates. Your feed reader then alerts you to the new post.

Here's the first takeaway for convenience and expediency: When you use an RSS feed reader, you can subscribe to the RSS feeds from websites you like and review the latest headlines in the reader instead of having to visit the website itself.

Figure 4-2:
The same
RSS feed,
in Google
Reader.

Here's a bigger takeaway, which explains the power of feed readers: They enable you to collect information from many different websites, blogs, and other news sources (many nonblog sites publish RSS feeds, too). Then you can sort through it all, keep and organize the information you need, and ignore the rest.

Setting Up Google Reader

One of the most popular feed readers is Google Reader. It's easy to use but includes powerful features for reviewing and organizing lots of information at once.

Although this section focuses on Google Reader, many other great tools are available. Regardless of the feed reader you use, though, the basic principles are the same, and you should be able to transfer the lessons from one feed reader to another.

If you have a Google account, you already have a Google Reader account, too. Visit www.google.com/reader and log in using your username and password.

If you don't already have a Google account, set one up and then visit www.google.com/reader. See Book VII, Chapter 2 for more about setting up a Google account.

You see the Google Reader welcome page, as shown in the upcoming Figure 4-3.

Subscribing to feeds in Google Reader is easy. Follow these steps:

1. **Click the Subscribe button, as shown in Figure 4-3.**

A small box opens, right below the button.

Figure 4-3:
Google
Reader, the
first time
you log in.

2. **Type the web address of the blog to which you want to subscribe.**

3. **Click Add.**

   Google Reader detects the blog's RSS feed and subscribes to it.

If a blog's RSS feed isn't set up correctly, Google Reader might not find the feed. No problem. Move on to the following set of steps, where you subscribe to a blog's RSS feed from the blog's homepage.

First, look for the RSS subscription icon or link. It'll look something like the link shown in Figure 4-4.

RSS subscription icon

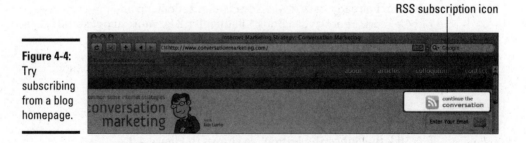

Figure 4-4:
Try
subscribing
from a blog
homepage.

After you find the RSS subscription link or icon, follow these steps:

1. **Click the link or icon.**

2. **Choose Google Reader.**

3. **Click OK.**

Google Reader adds the feed.

If a blog's RSS feed is *really* stubborn, you might have to add it to Google Reader manually. Don't worry! It's not as difficult as it sounds. Follow these steps:

1. **On the blog's homepage, find the RSS link or icon; refer to Figure 4-4.**

2. **Right-click the link.**

3. **From the menu that appears, choose Copy Link or whatever similar option your browser shows you.**

4. **Log in to Google Reader.**

5. **Click Add Subscription; refer to Figure 4-3.**

6. **Paste the link into the subscription field and then click Add.**

Google Reader grabs the feed and adds it to your subscriptions.

If these methods don't work, contact the blog author. Something's wrong, and chances are that the author will appreciate the note (because he's losing subscribers).

Google Reader saves all your subscriptions in your account. When you next log in to Google Reader, you'll see those feeds, updated with the latest headlines from those sites and blogs.

Using Folders and Tags to Organize Your Feeds

If you have only five or six feeds to review, you can keep them all lumped together in a single folder, with no categorization. But you'll probably end up with too many to keep organized in one folder, and you'll rapidly lose track of different feeds. The best tools to aid you in organization, in any feed reader, are

✦ **Folders:** Use folders to group content into broad topics, such as *search engine optimization* or *local news*.

✦ **Tags:** Use tags to group articles, even if they're in different folders.

Using folders to organize feeds

You *could* leave all your feeds mashed into one folder. But that'll make one heck of a mess, as you can see in Figure 4-5.

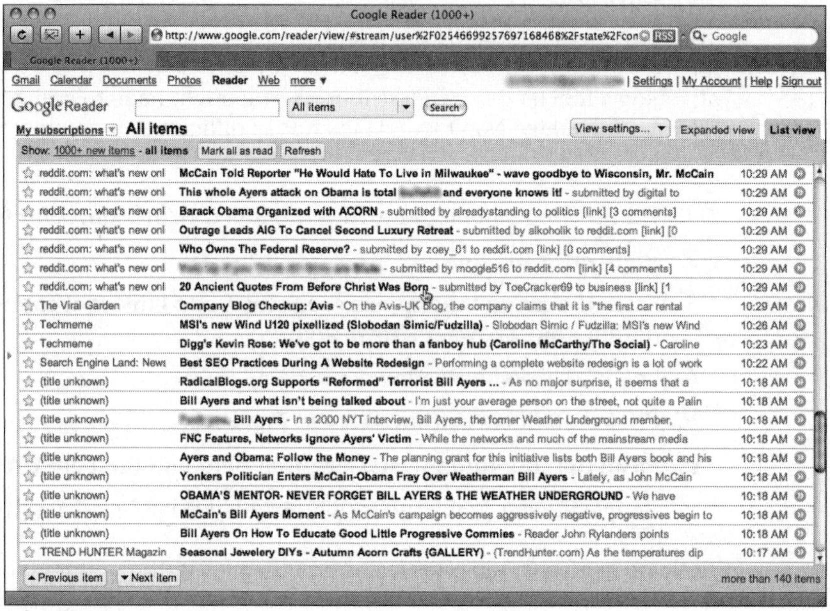

Figure 4-5: Total feed higgledy-piggledy.

It's hard to find want you need. So, to be neat, tidy, and organized, file those feeds in a folder.

When you organize all your feeds like this — grouping them into relevant folders — you get a much more usable feed environment, as you can see in Figure 4-6.

To create a folder and then add a feed to that folder, follow these steps:

1. **Log in to Google Reader.**

If you don't have a Google Reader account, see the earlier section "Setting Up Google Reader."

2. **Click the feed that you want to place in a folder.**

3. **At the upper right, open the Feed Settings drop-down box, as shown in Figure 4-7.**

4. **Click New Folder. Name the folder and click Save.**

The folders appear on the left-hand side of the screen. You can rearrange folder order by clicking and dragging, too.

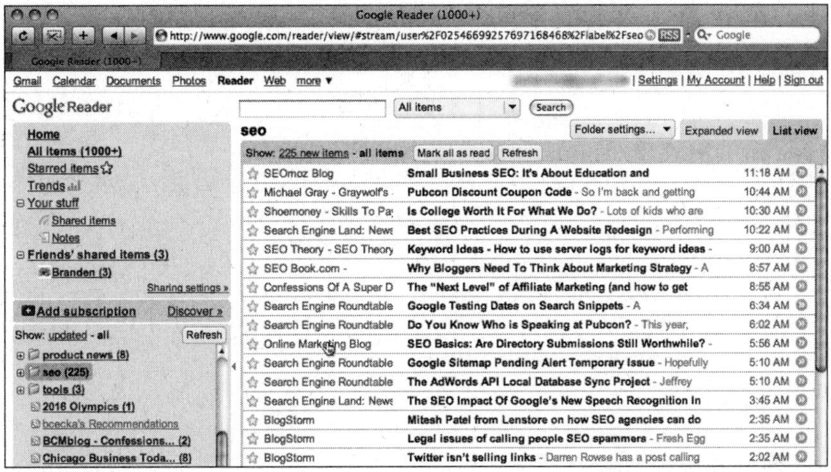

Figure 4-6:
A more organized set of feeds, using folders.

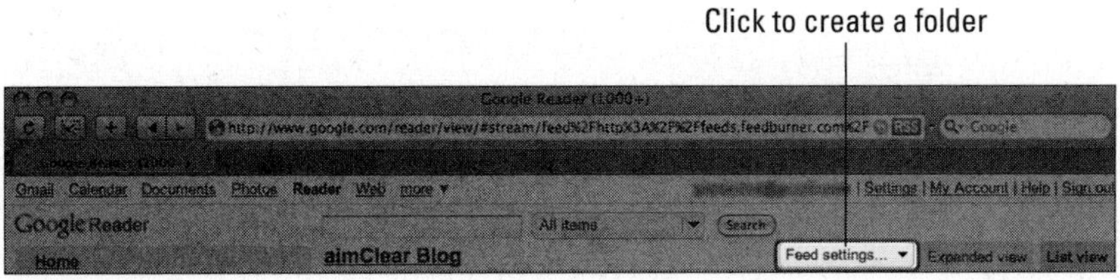

Click to create a folder

Figure 4-7:
Open Feed Settings to create a folder.

Speed demon that you are now, you can also create many folders at once:

1. **Log in to Google Reader.**

2. **At the top right, click the settings button, then select Reader settings, as shown in Figure 4-8.**

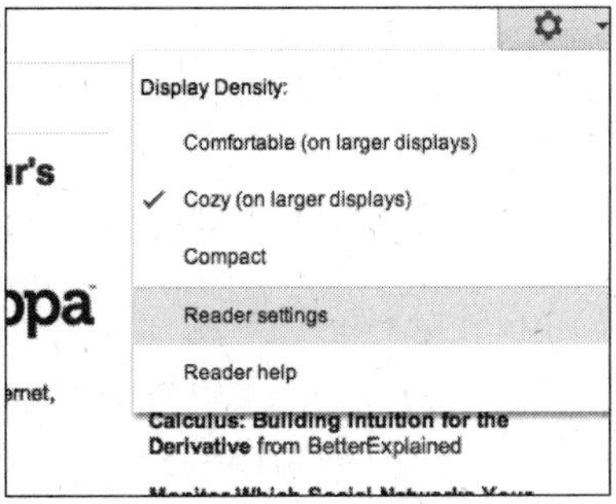

Figure 4-8:
Reader settings access.

3. **Click the Subscriptions tab.**

You see a list of every feed you have as well as the feed's folder assignment. Each feed that's assigned to a folder shows the folder name on the right, as shown in Figure 4-9.

To add, change, or delete folders, select the Folders and Tags tab.

Folders are indeed fantastic tools, getting you halfway to a totally organized blogging radar screen, as it were. Try to use simple, clear folder names that you'll recognize later. It's tempting to just type **New Folder** for now, thinking you'll come back and fix it later. Odds are, you won't. Use a good label now, and you'll be happier for it.

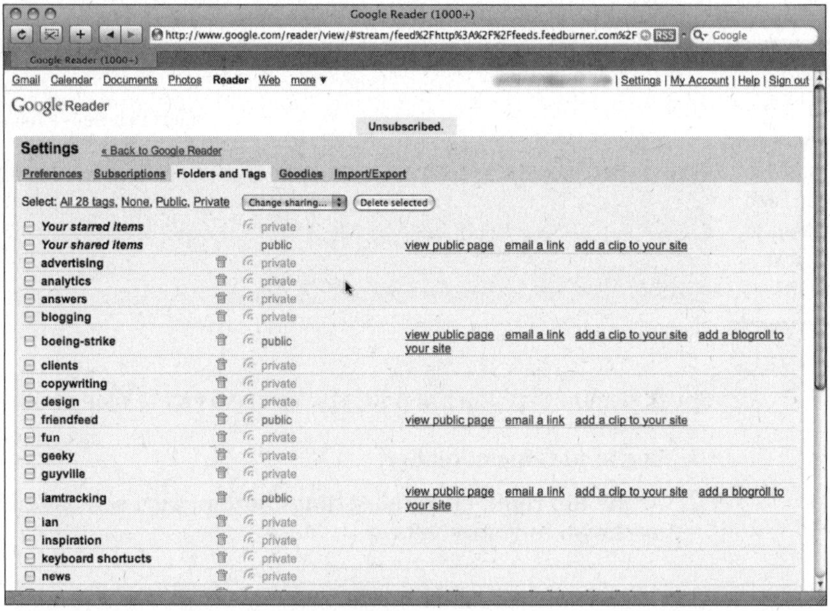

Figure 4-9:
The Manage Subscriptions page.

Using tags to organize feeds

Here's where the real world bumps heads a little with your new organizational system. What if you store two different articles in two categories, but those articles are still related? Say that you have a newspaper article about search engine optimization that ends up in your News folder, and a blog post with a great SEO tip that's related to the newspaper article. You want to link the two somehow so that you can see them in the same "bucket" and remind yourself that they're related. However, you don't want to put their feeds in the same folder. The business section of the newspaper doesn't always talk SEO. The SEO blog doesn't always talk news.

This is where tags can be a great tool.

Tags are keywords or phrases that you assign to a single post instead of an entire feed. You could tag both the newspaper article and the blog post with *SEO*. Then you'd see both articles when you view the hits on your SEO tag.

Here's how you add a tag to a post:

1. **Click the post you want to tag.**

2. **Click Add Tags at the bottom of the post.**

   The Add Tags box appears right above the link.

3. **Type the tags you want, separated by commas, and then click Save.**

   That's it! You tagged your post.

Here's how to tag posts without touching your mouse. While viewing the post in Google Reader, press T. You enter your tags in the Edit Tags field that appears.

You can view all articles with a given tag by either

✦ Clicking that tag at the bottom of the article

✦ Clicking the tag name in the lower-left corner of your Google Reader window. See Figure 4-10.

**Book VI
Chapter 4**

**Tracking
Other Blogs**

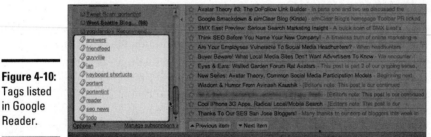

Figure 4-10:
Tags listed
in Google
Reader.

When you use tags and folders together, you can save and organize a lot of information — fast.

Reviewing Feeds Fast with Hot Keys

Phew. All that tedious housekeeping is done (for now, at least). The question before you is how to skim through all your feeds every day. Answer: with hot keys!

Google Reader and most standard feed readers include hot keys, which allow you to use your mouse to rapidly view, tag, or manipulate each post.

In Google Reader, you want to know six critical hot keys:

Pressing This	Does This
J	Moves you down to the next item
K	Moves you up to the previous item
Shift+N	Moves you to the next folder
Shift+P	Moves you up to the previous folder
T	Opens the tagging menu
Shift+S	Shares an item on your Shared Items page

More on the Shared Items page in a bit.

To find many other hot keys, look in the Google Reader Help center by searching for *keyboard shortcuts.*

The most important thing to remember is that you're not here to read the details on every item. You're here to build a reference library. More on that in the upcoming section "Avoiding Information Insanity."

Sharing with a Bundle

If you work on a team, you might want to make interesting items available to team members. Google Reader allows you to do this via Bundles.

The easiest way to share items is to create a *bundle,* a unique page listing all items in a folder or assigned a tag. You can bundle any feed items that are grouped under a tag or a folder.

Here's how you create a bundle:

1. **Create a tag and tag a few items.**

   See the earlier section "Using tags to organize feeds" to see how.

2. **Hover your mouse over the tag you want to bundle.**

3. **Click the small black arrow that appears.**

4. **Click Create a Bundle, as shown in Figure 4-11.**

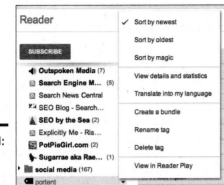

Figure 4-11:
Creating a
bundle.

The page that appears lets you customize and save the bundle, as shown in Figure 4-12. You can add other tags, folders, or individual subscriptions by clicking-and-dragging them into the bundle, or delete them by dragging them to the trash can.

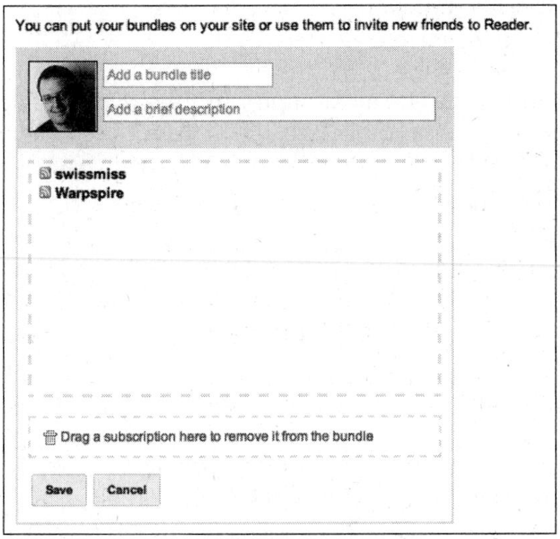

Figure 4-12:
Editing a
bundle.

5. **Click Save.**

Figure 4-13 shows the result. You can e-mail the link to those with whom you want to share posts, and they'll be able to subscribe to all the items to which you add this now-public tag. You can also embed the bundle in your website or blog, or export it for reuse in other tools.

Figure 4-13:
Share your
bundle.

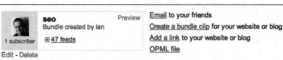

Bundles are doubly handy because they

✦ Create a page that folks can visit to see items you consider important.

✦ Create an RSS feed.

Now your team has two options for finding what they want.

Avoiding Information Insanity

You can easily get buried in articles, posts, and random information. You don't want to end up with a pile of hundreds or thousands of items that's so huge you throw up your hands and give up.

To avoid information insanity, try these rules:

✦ **Organize; don't read.** The most important thing you can do is find interesting stuff and organize it for later. If you want to read a full article, go ahead! But don't force yourself. Tag it and file it. That way, you can retrieve it later.

✦ **Declare bankruptcy.** Every now and then, if you're so hopelessly behind in reviewing your feeds, you can just declare feed bankruptcy. Mark everything as read and start over. Something really compelling will likely be mentioned in future articles, so don't worry about missing anything.

✦ **Be picky.** Don't keep any feed subscriptions that you never read. Clean out your feed reader ruthlessly at least once per month.

With these tips and Google Reader in hand, you're now armed and ready to start getting involved in the blogging world.

Chapter 5: Getting Involved on Other Blogs

In This Chapter

✔ **Why connecting with other bloggers is important**

✔ **Seeing how to connect with other bloggers**

✔ **Minding your manners**

✔ **Blog carnivals: The good and the bad**

Your blog will grow if more people find it and like it. But, for your blog to grow, more people will have to find it and like it. An Internet marketing Catch-22, if you will.

You have a pretty simple solution, though. Other bloggers have already gone through this process. They've attracted the readers and have a loyal audience. If you strike up a conversation with them and they like what you have to say, they'll pass you along to their audience. Instant publicity. ✱

This approach might sound manipulative or cynical, but it's not. Established bloggers keep their audience by presenting great information. Some of that information is stuff they write on their own; some of it, though, is new stuff — quite possibly your stuff — they find in day-to-day research. (See Chapter 4 of this minibook to read about tracking other blogs.)

So, think of this progression as a kind of online social compact: You present content with great value. Other bloggers find it and pass it along to their audience by writing about it and linking to your post. They get some credit for finding what you wrote. In exchange, you get more visitors and more links.

Your job, then, when you first launch your blog, is to connect with some of those bloggers.

Connecting with Other Bloggers

Step 1: Find the bloggers with whom you want to connect. You might have already done this, or put some thought to it, if you've been through Chapter

4 of this minibook. If you haven't, use a Google blog search, Alltop, or the search engine of your choice to locate a few really authoritative blogs.

Step 2: Make contact. However, you can't just start sending those bloggers unsolicited e-mails in hopes that one of them will respond. They might, but you probably won't like their reply of *Stop e-mailing me.*

Instead, have a quick look at Book VII, which covers social media marketing. Set up a Twitter account and "follow" bloggers there. (No, that doesn't involve stalking. *Following* has a very legit meaning in the world of social media, so read all about it in Book VII.) Write about their posts on your blog and link to them. Introduce yourself with your content and your comments on their content.

Take your time with this. No blogger likes to be harassed with "Hey, link to me!" e-mails and comments.

Leaving Great Comments

The best way to first introduce yourself to a blogger is by contributing to her posts. The easiest way to do that is through comments. A well-written, well-thought-out comment can lend a lot to a blog post. It prompts discussion in a way that only audience participation can, and bloggers appreciate it. For example, readers can turn a post about Internet marketing tips into something more: a public discussion of the value of Internet marketing, with a live, growing list of tips and details about the topic.

Here are a few tips for writing a good comment:

+ **Read the whole post first.** Otherwise, you might jump to incorrect conclusions.

+ **Read all the other comments left before yours.** See whether you want to reply to those.

+ **Don't be afraid to bring up a conflicting viewpoint.** Just make sure that you present it well. Being ornery won't make you any friends.

+ **Don't link to your site unless there's truly something relevant there.**

And, a few ideas for responses to a post:

+ Agreeing and adding another idea/point/tip

> *I totally agree with your post. You might also want to consider flipping the pancakes right before you serve them.*

✦ Agreeing, but with a qualification about one tip or another

> *I totally agree with your post. But regarding butter in the pan: Folks can use a little nonstick cooking spray, instead, if they're calorie conscious.*

✦ Politely disagreeing with one point, and offering an alternative

> *Great post. One other viewpoint, though: Buckwheat pancakes can taste just as good if they're not overmixed.*

✦ Following up to someone else's comment

> *Frank's point about chocolate chips is a good one. I'd add that you can use dark chocolate chips and make your pancakes a good cough suppressant, too.*

Write truly useful comments! Don't slap a two-sentence comment that contributes nothing on someone's blog and expect him to publish it. The best test: After you write the comment, read it. Does it add something to the post that wasn't there before? Or does it just restate something and say you agree? The former is great. The latter is a waste of bits.

Come back to the same blog and comment on different posts, too. The blog author will notice that you're a contributor.

Avoiding foot-in-mouth syndrome

When you're speaking to someone in person, your body language, tone of voice, and expression tell her whether you're kidding, angry, or trying to be nice. When you type a comment on a blog, though, you can't communicate those emotions.

Thus, a comment that seems innocent to you could offend the blog author, another commenter, or every single person who happens to read what you wrote. That's a big deal.

You can't avoid every misunderstanding. However, you can minimize the risks. Here are some pointers on how to stay out of the doghouse:

✦ **Don't be sarcastic.** Sarcasm relies on tone of voice. A 50-word comment can't communicate it.

✦ **Don't be nasty.** Ever. If you have nothing nice or helpful to say, don't say anything. It's okay to disagree, but you can do that without being nasty.

✦ **Don't make jokes** unless they're really clear.

Make smart, polite, and helpful comments, and you've taken the first step toward building a blogging relationship.

Sharing Other Blog Posts

If you have a well-followed Twitter, Google+, or Facebook account, consider resharing great posts you find on other blogs. This kind of content curation increases your value to your readers. It's also something that bloggers notice. If you share their stuff, a time will probably come when they'll share yours.

Linking to Other Blog Posts

The next step is linking to other bloggers. Links are the lifeblood of the blogging world. When you link to someone's post, she will appreciate it.

If a post really catches your attention, you can post to your own blog in response. Here are a few styles of response posts:

✦ **Use the link list.** Pick three or four related posts that impressed you and write a short summary of each post, write why you like it, and post a link.

✦ **Cite another post as support for an argument** you're making in your post, and use a link.

✦ **Cite another post as an additional resource** and link to it.

✦ **Use the step-by-step review and critique.** Write a post reviewing each point in another blogger's piece. Add your own clarifications, changes, and additions.

Most bloggers are obsessive. They check their web analytics reports to see which sites are sending them visitors. If they see you're one of those sites, they'll look at your blog. If they like what you're saying, they'll reciprocate. Those links help you move up in the search engines. More importantly, links are like a reference: The blogger who links to you is saying you've made an impact with him. That will get you visitors.

Giving Credit Where Credit Is Due

One quick note: You must always give credit! If you reference another post, link to it and give the author's name.

That's a given — or, it should be a given. But plagiarism is common online, and bloggers are always on the lookout for it. So never quote a blog without giving a link and a reference.

Also, don't use `nofollow` links to deny links from your blog to another. Many blogging tools will automatically have `nofollow` links in comments. That means search engines will ignore those links. You're using `nofollow` if your links look like this:

```
<a href=http://www.mysite.com rel="nofollow">link here</a>
```

You're denying the other blogger the search engine optimization benefits of the link. So give credit where credit is due: Remove the `nofollow`.

Writing a Guest Post

One great way to build traffic to your blog is to guest-post on another blog. In essence, you can offer to write a piece for another person's blog. Bloggers want great content. Guest posts help them build that content, even if they're on vacation, taking a break, or are too busy writing a book to post to their blog. While you build relationships with other bloggers, be on the lookout for guest-posting opportunities.

Bloggers look for guest authors to cover when they go on vacation, to help expand their coverage, or to lend extra expertise.

You can't really invite yourself to guest-post, but you can offer to trade guest posts with another blogger. He writes a post on your site, and you write a post on his.

Here are a few points to remember when guest-posting:

✦ **The blog owner gets some control over what you write.** The blog owner will review what you write, and he'll probably suggest a few ideas that he'd like you to write about. That's his right.

✦ **Put in extra time on the writing.** When you're posting to another blog, it's like you're going to a car show. A little extra polish never hurts.

✦ **Be clear with the blog owner about linking.** Is it okay to link back to your own site? Will he likewise do it for you?

✦ **Provide a little biography of yourself.** Chances are that the blog owner will want to include it with your post.

The Art of Asking Nicely

You undoubtedly hate it when your neighbor starts using his turbo-charged leaf blower at 8 a.m. on Sunday. That's just bad manners. Blogging communities dislike those kinds of disruptions, too. If you want to become a valued member of the community, you need to mind your manners. Ultimately, that's great for your blog and your company's image.

✦ **Never**

- Ask a blogger for a link more than once.✗
- Ask a blogger for a link if you haven't already corresponded ✗ with him.

✦ **Always**

- Say please. ✓
- Say thank you. ✓

- Reciprocate. If a blogger links to you, link back at some point. If the blogger comments on your blog, check in on his blog once in a while and see whether you can comment there, too.

Chapter 6: Promoting Your Posts

In This Chapter

✓ Publishing your post

✓ Using pinging to let the world know about a new post

✓ Submitting your posts to social media sites

✓ Letting other bloggers know when you write a new post

You spent hours writing that perfect post. Or you got inspired and hammered one out in a few minutes. Either way, you want to let the world know that something is new on your blog.

Closing that loop and promoting yourself are those essential last steps that turn your blog from a collection of great writing to a real Internet marketing tool.

Just clicking that Publish button in WordPress isn't enough. A whole online ecosystem has sprung up to help spread the word about new blog posts. This chapter introduces you to it.

Publishing Your Post

In most blogging software, when you click Publish, a lot more happens than you might think. The blog software

✦ Publishes your post on the blog ✓

✦ Updates the blog RSS feed to show the new post ✓

✦ Alerts relevant sites via services like ping and PubSubHubbub ✓

   See Chapter 2 of this minibook for more information on how to set up pinging.

Publishing is really more like "pushing." When you publish, your blog alerts many other blogs and websites about the new post. So, publishing a new post affects more than your own blog. It potentially alerts many other websites, as well as everyone who subscribes to your blog's RSS feed.

You shouldn't get stage fright because you're alerting thousands (or more) people about a new post. Just remember the real, underlying power of blogging: the connection to a vast network of other blogs and sites.

You *can* accomplish the same thing on a standard website by going to each website and manually pinging it. Ugh. However, blogging evolved in a way that makes this process far easier. That's why your blog should be a part of your Internet marketing strategy.

Letting the World Know: Using Pinging

Chapter 2 of this minibook focuses on how you configure your blog to ping relevant sites and services. This section talks more about what pinging can do for your blog.

A *ping* is a short message, typically sent automatically by your blogging software. When a blog sends a ping, here's what happens:

1. When you publish a new post, your blog sends the ping to specific sites, such as Technorati.

2. Technorati receives the ping, and its software retrieves the new post.

3. Technorati adds the new post to its index.

4. Technorati users have access to your new post, minutes after you publish it.

Pinging is really just one way your blog can alert services and search engines about new content. Other services like PubSubHubbub are technically different but functionally the same: They help you get your new posts pushed to all the services folks use to find you. If you're set up for pinging, you're almost certainly set up for PubSub and those services as well. If you've tried everything, and your new posts never show up on Google, Pubsub.com, or other sites, check whether you're actually set up for PubSub. If you're not, use FeedBurner and it'll take care of the problem for you.

You can't take back a ping. After you publish and ping, the sites you ping retrieve your post. If you made a horrific typo, it's published for all to see. *Some* services update retrieved posts when you re-ping, but not all. So it pays to proofread before you publish.

Because pinging is such a powerful way to keep the rest of the Internet up to date about your blog, make sure that your ping list is up to date. See Chapter 2 in this minibook for detailed instructions on setting up pinging as well as for what to do if your blog software doesn't support pinging.

Submitting Your Post to StumbleUpon

StumbleUpon is a huge, addictive bookmarking service. Members can install a toolbar in their browser and simply click a Stumble button. The toolbar then takes them to a site selected based on the member's previous thumbs-up or thumbs-down preferences (also handled in the toolbar). See Book VII, Chapter 4 for more about StumbleUpon.

You need to have the StumbleUpon toolbar installed, and have a StumbleUpon account set up, to follow this section. See Book VII, Chapter 2 for instructions. Or just visit `www.stumbleupon.com` and follow the directions there. It's an easy setup.

Members can also submit new content to the StumbleUpon directory. That content is then added to the available sites, and users have a chance of, um, stumbling upon it.

The more folks stumble upon and give a thumbs-up to a particular page, the more often the page is sent to other stumblers with related interests. So a well-written blog post can generate an unbelievable number of visits, in a very short time. Figure 6-1 shows what happened when one post got more than 10,000 visits from StumbleUpon in just a day.

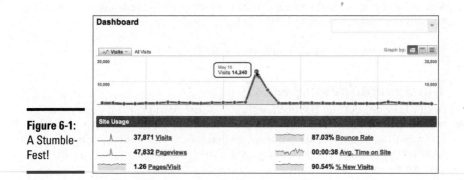

Figure 6-1:
A Stumble-
Fest!

Do not treat StumbleUpon as a PR service! It's tempting to submit your own blog posts to the service and do nothing else. Don't. You need to build a solid profile by stumbling other content from other sites, too. When you're a good citizen and contribute to the community, StumbleUpon will reward you. If you don't contribute, StumbleUpon might penalize or even ban your account. See Book VII to find out more.

When you submit any new content to StumbleUpon, you'll get a pop-up window — the Discovery dialog box. There, you can type in the title of the content, a description, and relevant keywords.

When you complete that form, follow a few basic rules:

✦ **Write a good comment.** StumbleUpon likely uses the description when it decides what your post is about.

✦ **Use good tags.** Tags are just keywords. Use words and phrases that describe the content you're adding to StumbleUpon.

✦ **Pick your first tag from the Interest list.** Then add more specific ones after that.

✦ **Send your post to StumbleUpon friends if you think they'll like it.** Don't abuse this, or you'll lose your friends.

Don't expect StumbleUpon to generate scads of traffic every time. Building your profile takes a while. Plus, not every submission will become popular. However, StumbleUpon is a great community, and you never know when a new post will get huge coverage across the network.

Also, sometimes a post you submitted a year ago will be discovered by an influential stumbler. So your effort might pay off later.

Submitting Your Post on reddit (Once in a While)

reddit is a huge social voting site. If you can get noticed there, you'll end up with a *lot* of traffic. Just realize that the chances of success are slim. reddit can deliver server-crushing traffic in a matter of hours.

For more about how reddit works, read Book VII.

The submadness of reddit

reddit is about getting featured within a "subreddit" or, even better, on the front page of the entire site. reddit is divided into subtopics (subreddits). Folks tend to subscribe to those, as well as to check the first page. So, if you can just get enough votes to show up on the front page of a subreddit, you can get a nice burst of traffic.

The problem with reddit, though: It can generate a lot of traffic, but much of the time that traffic will be of very low quality.

It's worth it to keep trying on reddit. Worst case, you get lots of visitors in a short period and a few new blogs link to you, so your rankings go up.

Knowing when you're reddit-worthy

You need to be picky about what you submit to reddit. Your post has the best chance of competing on reddit.com if it

✦ **Fits well into a niche subreddit that gets steady attention but few posts**

✦ **Has high production standards:** Put in the time to write super-scannable content (see Chapter 4 of this minibook), and don't forget to include lots of images.

✦ **Has a high sneeze factor:** See Book VII, Chapter 1 to read about this.

✦ **Has a high geek value:** If it's content that'll make someone say, "Ooooh, aaaaah," that's a good choice. News about a newly discovered solar system is good. News about the weekend football game is not.

✱ Other social voting sites ✱

You can find other sites similar to reddit. Here are a few and some reasons why or when you might choose them:

✦ **Hacker News** (http://news.ycombinator.com)**:** More nerd-focused

✦ **Newsvine** (www.newsvine.com)**:** In decline but still a good source of links and traffic

✦ **Fark** (www.fark.com)**:** Fun for bizarre stories

Submitting Your Post to Bookmarking Sites

Another promotion resource you can use is bookmarking sites. Sites like del.icio.us and Alltop offer you a way to get your blog posts noticed.

Here are a few tips for submitting your posts to these sites:

✦ **Like StumbleUpon, these sites reward good citizenship.** Don't just bookmark your own posts. Bookmark other useful content, too.

✦ **Accurately and completely tag your bookmarks.** That way, other users can more easily find relevant content on your blog.

✦ **Connect with other users on these sites and share bookmarks.** That kind of networking can spread your posts more rapidly, as some might follow what you bookmark.

Sending a Polite E-Mail

Nothing is wrong with sending a polite e-mail asking folks to take a look at your new post.

You can send an e-mail to

✦ **Other bloggers:** If you think a fellow blogger might want to follow up on your post with one of his own, or if you cited his post in yours, send him a note.

✦ **Subscribers:** Many blogs have e-mail sign-up as well as RSS subscriptions. Notify those folks via e-mail.

✦ **Other contacts:** If you've been in contact with reporters, clients, or others who might be interested in this post, notify them, too.

Be conservative. Send e-mails regarding posts that are only directly relevant to the recipient's interests. For example, if you read a post about guinea pigs that you really liked, and wrote a review with a link back to that post, you might e-mail the author. Or, if you chat with someone at a conference about SEO and you write a post about SEO, you might e-mail that person, too.

Participating in Online Communities

Finally, don't rule out sites like Facebook and microblogging communities like Twitter. A simple announcement similar to the one shown in Figure 6-2 can generate an initial burst of interest that leads to StumbleUpon traffic, reddit submissions, or just lots of readers.

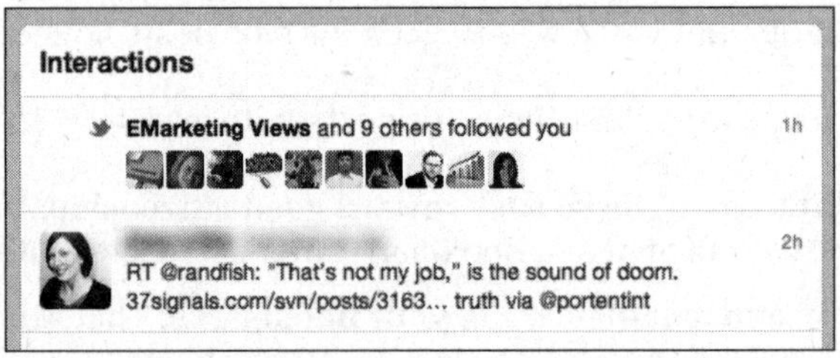

Figure 6-2:
A Twitter announcement of a new post.

Interactions

🐦 **EMarketing Views** and 9 others followed you   1h

RT @randfish: "That's not my job," is the sound of doom. 37signals.com/svn/posts/3163… truth via @portentint   2h

You can be a little freer with your announcements in these communities. When you write a new post, always announce it on Twitter, Facebook, and other social media.

Chapter 7: Introducing Podcasting

In This Chapter

✔ **Setting up an inexpensive production studio**

✔ **Preparing a podcast**

✔ **Recording a podcast**

✔ **Distributing your creation**

*B*logging puts words on a page. Podcasting puts your voice directly on the web in the form of audio files that your readers can download and play back at their leisure. That creates a kind of direct connection with your audience, as they hear your tone and inflection.

Because of that, podcasting is a great supplement to your blogging strategy as part of your Internet marketing campaign.

This chapter is a *very* high-level view of podcasting. If you're going to try it once or twice, the information here will get you through the initial throes. If you're going to get serious, though, read *Podcasting For Dummies,* by Tee Morris, Chuck Tomasi, Evo Terra, and Kreg Steppe (published by John Wiley & Sons, Inc.). It covers everything from using special mics to advanced promotion techniques.

Podcasts do require some extra technology as well as a few extra steps on your part. That's what this chapter is about: getting your blog to a podcast.

Podcasting 101

Podcasting is no longer the realm of audiophiles and sound engineers. Recording, producing, and distributing your very own online audio show has become relatively easy.

A *podcast* is an audio or video recording you make and then distribute by using a special RSS feed. Don't let the word *special* scare you. You can find out more later in the section "Supporting Podcasting on Your Blog."

Podcasts are always fun to produce, but they're best when used to deliver

✦ Training or tutorials

✦ Interviews

✦ Any topic where you need to communicate more subtly than you can with writing

✦ A blog entry when you're sick of writing

Podcast listeners can then subscribe to your podcast via their favorite RSS feed reader, or audio software such as Windows Media Player or iTunes. That software then downloads the audio and video files and transfers them to listeners' iPods, iPads, tablets, or other media players so that they can listen to them on the go.

So, obviously, because podcasts are portable, folks can listen to them when and how they like. And because they're audio/video (compared with print, a visual medium), they provide another way for readers to connect to you, by becoming listeners.

Setting Up Your Podcasting Studio

Setting up a podcasting studio is remarkably similar to setting up a home recording studio. (Go figure.) Think recording device, software, input device, and then (of course) some vehicle for broadcasting. For podcasting, your studio consists of

✦ **Recording device:** A laptop or desktop computer.

You can use any newer PC or Mac to record and edit your podcast. Chances are that if you're reading this book, you already have one of those. So the most expensive tool you need is already in place.

You *do* want a computer with a fair amount of hard drive space (at least 20 gigabytes) and enough processor oomph to edit audio files. You'll also likely need an available USB port for your microphone. If your computer is a creaky 8-year-old machine, it probably can't handle podcasting. But any computer made in the last few years can do the job.

✦ **Software:** Software to record and edit (such as GarageBand or Audacity). You can read more about these in the following section.

✦ **Input device:** Um, a microphone. Read more about your options in the section "Getting a good microphone," later in this chapter.

✦ **Broadcasting vehicle:** A FeedBurner account with SmartCast (www. feedburner.com).

Oh, and you need a place to record and work. That's covered later, too.

Getting the right recording software

You can find many software options for podcasting. Search for *podcasting software* on your favorite search engine to find others if these don't work out for you.

You can, of course, use higher-end audio software, such as Adobe Audition or Logic Studio Pro. Feel free. These are basic software packages that can get the job done, per OS platform.

If you're on a Mac running OS X

✦ **GarageBand** (www.apple.com/ilife/garageband) comes with everything you need to record, edit, and distribute a podcast. It also allows you to do quite a bit of post-recording editing as well as setting up your podcast feed. GarageBand costs $14.99 and is available in the App Store.

✦ **Übercaster** (www.ubercaster.com) is the easiest-to-use podcasting program on the planet. See Figure 7-1 for the Übercaster recording screen. It doesn't offer the same post-recording editing features as GarageBand, but it's very streamlined for podcasting. It has exactly the features you need, and it's easier to figure out. It's no longer available for purchase, but you can download a demo version.

✦ **Audacity** (http://audacity.sourceforge.net) is free and straightforward.

✦ **Adobe Audition** (www.adobe.com/products/audition.html) is a cross-platform solution that works well with Windows and Macs.

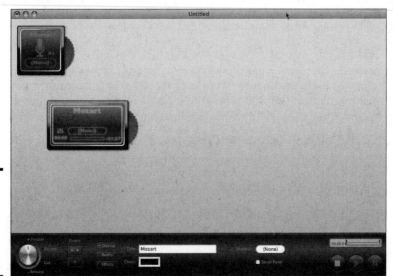

Figure 7-1: Übercaster offers a nice, intuitive interface.

If you're on a Windows PC running either Windows XP or later

✦ **Audacity** is your first choice. See Figure 7-2 for a look at Audacity in action. Audacity is free (in life, as well as this software). It's also easy to use and is a very refined tool for podcasters.

✦ **Adobe Audition** (`www.adobe.com/products/audition.html`) is a professional-grade toolset for sound editing. It's expensive, but integrates with all of Adobe's other tools, and gives you dozens of effects and editing tools.

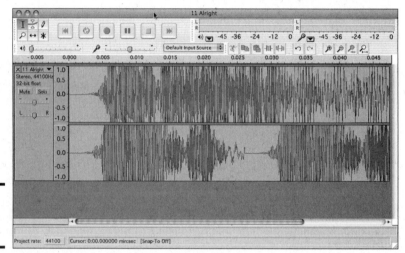

Figure 7-2:
Audacity in action.

Pick one program and stick with it for a while. Get comfortable with the ins and outs of audio editing.

Read. The. Documentation. Sure, you *can* record audio by pushing a button and talking, but just a little time spent discovering how to tune and tweak your microphone and software will make a huge difference in quality.

Getting a good microphone

The microphone makes or breaks the podcast. The better the mic, the better the audio quality. No software on earth can improve a recording if it was recorded with a lousy mic.

By the way, the mic that comes on the computer is synonymous with *lousy*. Don't rely on it for podcasting.

The real problem with choosing a microphone, though, is the thousands of options. Search for *podcasting microphones* on your favorite search engine if you want to get the whole story.

Try these microphones:

✦ **Internal:** If you use a laptop, your laptop's internal mic *might* be okay to start. It's free, and it's already configured. But the sound quality will be tinny at best, and you'll sound like you're talking through a paper cup.

✦ **A USB headset:** Headset mics — like the many made by Plantronics (www.plantronics.com) — are great. They're inexpensive (they start at less than $30) and easy to set up. However, they won't work if you're interviewing someone or if you want more radio-style sound.

✦ **The Blue Snowball** (www.bluemic.com): This is a fantastic USB microphone for about $120. It can work as a unidirectional or omnidirectional mic (omnidirectional is great for interviews), produces great sound quality, and looks cool to boot. But, it does cost $100.

✦ **The Zoom H4n** (www.samsontech.com): This can function as a USB microphone or as a standalone audio recorder. That makes it very flexible. It's also the best omnidirectional microphone for less than $300. But it costs the most of any microphone in this category, and you'll want to read the manual before you start recording.

Nothing beats Blue Snowball for ease of use and audio quality. However, you can squeeze better sound quality out of a professional mic, if you really need to.

✦ **The Griffin iMic** (www.griffintechnology.com): The Griffin isn't actually a mic but rather a device with which you can connect most microphones to your computer. It filters a lot of the noise that a computer might add to your recording. It costs $39.99, and despite the *i* notation, it works on both Mac and PC.

When setting up your mic, follow the instructions that come with your microphone. And read the entire manual! The manual contains tips for getting the best-quality sound.

Setting Up Your Studio

You need a quiet place to record: your studio. A room where the dog isn't barking doesn't count. Background noise — such as appliances, noisy air conditioning, or ticking clocks — will leap out in a recording. And pay attention to how the room is configured and dressed: A room with bare walls or floors might produce echoes.

If you're really concerned about echoes and other acoustics, you can buy damping tiles. Or, hang a few blankets on the walls. Audiophiles reading this just cringed, but it works.

Here are a few tips for setting up a quiet recording space:

+ **Close the windows.** It never fails. If you leave the windows open, ten minutes into your recording, a train, garbage truck, car with no muffler, or murder of crows will position itself right outside and start rumbling, honking, roaring, or cawing away.

+ **Stay away from appliances.** Even a small office refrigerator produces a *lot* of noise.

+ **Unplug the phone.**

+ **Turn off your cellphone and/or PDA.**

+ **Move your microphone as far away from the computer as possible.** Your computer's fans, hard drives, and such can produce quite a racket.

+ **Exit any instant messaging or other software that produces bells, whistles, or other sound effects.**

+ **Put your microphone *at eye level.*** Use a stack of books, if nothing else. When you look up when you speak, your voice has a much clearer quality. Looking down when you speak makes you mutter.

Most important, stay sane. It's easy to spend a lot of money setting up a room in your house to be the perfect sound studio. Remember, the audio you record will be compressed and sent over the web. So a professional studio isn't necessary. Some people record their podcasts in their living room, their car, or the middle of crowded airports.

Testing Your Setup

Before you spend an hour scripting and recording your first podcast, test your setup! Here's how you do it:

1. **Get a passage of text as a test.**

   Make sure that the sentence mixes in most of the typical consonant and vowel sounds so that you get a good sample.

2. **Record the passage a few times using different microphone positions (at eye level, sitting on the desk, held in your hand) and software configurations as suggested by your software's documentation.**

   Eye level is almost always best, but it's possible that your mic works better in a different position.

   You *did* read the documentation, right?!

3. **Encode the audio as you would when you upload your podcast to the web.**

   You can read more about this in the upcoming section "Encoding and Uploading Your Podcast."

4. **Listen to each version and choose the best combination of settings and microphone position and setup.**

   Listen for background noise, volume, clarity of speech, and overall quality.

A little advance work like this will save you from the heartbreak: You don't want to record a 20-minute interview using two Blue Snowball microphones, only to discover that you left one of the microphones turned off.

Supporting Podcasting on Your Blog

Podcasting works because the audio you create is inserted right into an RSS feed. You also can set up and edit a separate, custom podcasting RSS feed from your blog and group all your podcasts.

Creating a separate podcast feed has advantages. If, for example, you want to add your podcast to iTunes or other major podcast directories, it's best to have a separate feed. Remember, though, you can always do this later.

By far the easiest way to generate a podcast feed is to use FeedBurner. Just select the I Am a Podcaster! check box when you add your feed, and FeedBurner includes iTunes podcast data, "rich" media data, and all the other elements necessary to generate your feed.

You can also find separate tools for generating feeds, like Podcast Maker (for Mac; www.lemonzdream.com/podcastmaker) or the tools built into many audio editors. If you're really a glutton for punishment, you can generate the feed by hand. Don't.

Preparing Your Podcast Script

Writing for a podcast is a little different than writing a blog post. You'll almost never write down, word for word, what you're going to say in your podcast. Instead, you'll make a list of the items for discussion with an opening sentence or two and then a list of *talking points* — stuff you absolutely want to mention.

Write at least an outline of your podcast. Go one step further and write a rough draft of everything you want to say as a blog post. You can rehearse your script at least once, have all your thoughts organized, and post the rough draft as a transcript.

If you're comfortable going the outline route, include — at a minimum — the following:

- ✦ **Your introduction:** "Hi, I'm Harrison and you're listening to The Sci-Fi Kids' Podcast. Today is September 20th. . . ."
- ✦ **The topics you'll be discussing**
- ✦ **Your closing:** "You've been listening to The Sci-Fi Kids' Podcast. I'm Harrison, and I'll see you next week. . . ."

If you're doing an interview, write down the questions you'll ask, as well as follow-up questions if you think you know what the answers will be to the first questions.

Try to aim for a 10- to 20-minute podcast. Scripts tend to expand after you start recording. Unless you have a really dense topic, 30 minutes will be your audience's maximum attention span.

Making Your First Podcast

You're ready to go! Time to record your first podcast. Before the rubber really hits the road, though (or, your dulcet tones tickle the airwaves), make sure to take care of the following nuts and bolts:

1. **Do a test.**

   Yes, do it again! Check sound levels and make sure that everything's working.

2. **Double-check that your phone's unplugged, all noisy appliances are squelched, the neighbor's dog has a mouth full of peanut butter, and so on.**

3. **Make sure that your notes are easily visible.**

Here are the broad steps to follow when creating your podcast:

1. Click Record and start speaking.

   You might feel a little nervous. It happens. Just relax and focus on your topic. Be sure to speak slowly and clearly, and remember to look up while speaking so that you don't start mumbling.

2. Keep one eye on your recording levels, just in case something goes wrong.

   Better to find out halfway through the podcast than when you're done.

3. After you're done, save the recording.

4. Listen through the podcast to check for sound quality and so on.

5. If you find any places where you stumbled or stuttered and don't like how it sounds, use your sound editor to select and cut the guilty seconds, as shown in Figure 7-3.

Figure 7-3:
Using
GarageBand
to erase a
sneeze.

6. Add a title and other information to your podcast, as shown in Figure 7-4.

Many podcasting programs, such as GarageBand and Podcast Maker, let you add artwork as well as the date, author name, and title.

Artwork is a chance for you to include your logo or otherwise reinforce your brand in the podcast. That artwork will appear in the listener's media player and on any podcast directories that support it.

After you're happy with the audio and the podcast description, it's time to encode and upload it.

Figure 7-4:
Adding descriptive information to a podcast in GarageBand.

Encoding and Uploading Your Podcast

Whatever software you use, you have to *encode* your recording. The audio you just recorded is stored on your computer in an uncompressed format. It's a huge file. By encoding it, you store it in (encoded) MP3 format, which is the standard for audio delivery over the Internet. Figure 7-5 shows an edited podcast in GarageBand.

After you encode your podcast, listen to it again. Whenever you compress an audio file, you're reducing the quality. The sacrifice you make for the file-size reduction is worth it. Just watch that you don't overdo it, or it will sound awful: Try encoding a bit of the podcast and listening to it first. Make sure that you've used the right balance of sound quality and faster downloading.

Most audio/video software comes with default podcast encoding settings now. Use those and you should be just fine.

The final result of your encoding process will be an MP3 file for audio, or MP4 for video. That's your podcast.

One step is left: Upload the podcast. If you're including it in a blog post, attach the file to the post itself using your blog editor, as shown in Figure 7-6.

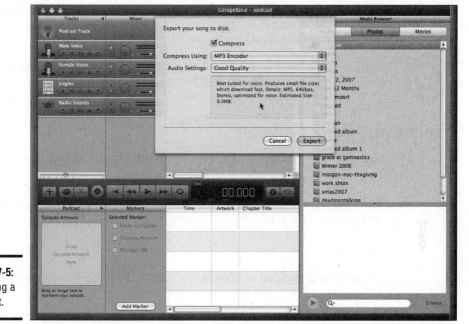

Figure 7-5:
Encoding a
podcast.

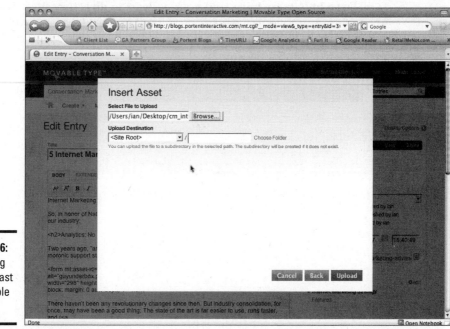

Figure 7-6:
Uploading
the podcast
in Movable
Type.

If you're doing a manual upload, you'll need to use some kind of file transfer software, such as an FTP client, to upload your MP3 file. On a Mac, you can use Transmit. On a PC, you can use CuteFTP or FileZilla.

If you're not sure how to use an FTP client, use your blogging software to upload your podcast. Don't start messing with a manual upload.

Promoting Your Podcast

Now your podcast is live. How do you get people to listen to it?

You can promote your podcast the same way that you promote blog posts (see Chapter 6 of this minibook) by using pinging, blogger networking, and social media sites.

And here are a few additional (free) opportunities:

✦ **Add your podcast to iTunes.** Visit the iTunes Store via your iTunes software (it's free), and then find Submit Podcasts to the iTunes Directory.

✦ **Blackberry Podcasts.** If you want to access a highly focused business audience, submit to Blackberry Podcasts.

✦ **For a little extra juice, add your podcast to directory sites.** Try Podcast Alley (www.podcastalley.com), Podcast.com (www.podcast.com), and PodcastBlaster (www.podcastblaster.com).

Book VII

Social Media Marketing

The 5th Wave   By Rich Tennant

"Guess who found a Kiss merchandise site on the web while you were gone?"

Contents at a Glance

Chapter 1: Understanding Social Media

In This Chapter

✔ Discovering what social media is

✔ Checking out key social media sites

✔ Adding social media to your web marketing strategy

What in the world is social media (as opposed to "antisocial" media) — and what's it have to do with web marketing? Good questions. Social media (as a concept) traces its roots back to the first bulletin board systems, discussion forums, IRC (Internet Relay Chat), and newsgroups. (It might also trace its roots back to the first time when two particularly advanced apes grunted at each other. But for Internet marketing purposes, you can ignore the animal world.)

Today, social media is a complex web of sites and software that allows you to bookmark, discuss, vent, and then share with other people. Social media users represent an enormous market. Facebook alone has over 800 million active users. That number is according to Facebook, but hey! — even if it's exaggerated and you divide that number in half, it's still a lot of people.

You need to understand this space of social media. Even if you're not doing any social media marketing, your customers are there, talking about you. Knowing where they talk and how to answer them is critical.

This chapter introduces you to popular social media sites and terminology. You find out how you can use social media to grow your business, build an interested audience, and keep in touch with your customers in a way that everyone appreciates.

Why social media is so important: The sneeze principle

Here's one critical lesson of social media: the *sneeze principle.* Any social media allows a visitor to watch a video, read an article, or see some other content. Then it lets the visitor *sneeze:* That is, a visitor can somehow indicate that he agrees (or disagrees) with that content by leaving a comment, posting a bookmark, selecting an I'm a Fan check box, or doing something else.

That's the sneeze effect. When that first visitor sneezes, others see it. They go and look at the same content. Then they might sneeze, too. So *their* circle of friends sees the same thing and has the option of transmitting the message even further.

Imagine that you read a funny blog post and give it a thumbs-up on StumbleUpon. Your 50 fans on StumbleUpon, seeing that you liked the post, read it too. A few of them really like it, too, so they give it a thumbs-up. They each have 40–400 fans, who then see that someone they follow liked the post. In a matter of hours, this one blog post has been sneezed to <u>thousands</u> of visitors.

It's not as easy as it sounds, but if you understand the sneeze principle, you understand why social media can be so powerful.

Marketing, Social Media Style

Social media sites and tools enable you to build your reputation and audience over time. Every friend you add on Facebook, every bookmark you add to StumbleUpon, and every post you make on a microblog increases your profile. You can read more about bookmarking in the later section "Bookmarking sites."

If you spend this capital wisely, you can use it to

+ Announce a new product.
+ Ask everyone for feedback about a new idea or blog post.
+ Build some buzz and get others talking about you — and your online presence.

The catch? If the networks or their members think you're abusing them to promote yourself, they'll penalize you or ban you altogether.

As you gain experience with social media, you'll find out how to walk that fine line between market research and promotion and self-aggrandizement to help you find your way around — and exploit — this diverse and expanding marketing medium.

Beware of social network spam

Social network operators do not like spammers! Don't use a social network to make friends with hundreds of strangers and then start sending them coupons or other offers. Chances are you'll end up getting kicked off the network. Instead, approach them like you would a party. Say hello. Shake hands. Chat a bit. Make your sales pitch only when someone states that he's looking for the product or service you provide. ⁄

Exploring Social Media

Social media umbrellas any website or web application that allows your audience to interact with your site and each other, directly or indirectly. Table 1-1 shows the basic categories of social media sites.

Table 1-1	Social Media Sites by Category	
Social Media Type	*Description*	*Examples*
Blogs	Allow you to write, journal-style, and then invite comments from your readers	Blogger WordPress
Social networks	Where people can interact and connect online	Facebook Google+
Bookmarking sites	Allow you to save bookmarks, just like you would in your browser, but on a site that you can access from any computer	Delicious StumbleUpon
Microblogging sites	Allow you to blog one or two sentences at a time	Twitter Tumblr
Media-sharing sites	Where you can upload and share video, audio, and photographs	YouTube Vimeo Flickr Pinterest
Popularity sites	Where you can collect bookmarks and then let visitors vote on them	Digg reddit
Q&A sites	Where you can ask and answer questions on almost any topic	Quora Stack Overflow

All these categories are important for you to explore because they're all interconnected: A Facebook member may also have a YouTube account. If someone forwards her a funny video via Facebook, she can zip over to YouTube to review it. Then, she might tell her Facebook friends. If one of those friends has a Twitter account and posts, his 540 Twitter friends might see it, too.

Social media, more than any other vehicle, has the potential to spread a message far and fast.

You also need to know what sites are social media hot spots and what each site's specialty is so that you can successfully use social media to spread the word about your products or services online.

The following sections explain each category and explore the benefits so that you can begin to formulate your social media strategy.

Posting and commenting on blogs

Blogs are probably the first thing you think of regarding social media. A *blog* (short for *weblog*) is a set of regularly published entries by one or more authors that allows visitors to post their comments on each entry. The word *blog* can refer to

Social Media – Allows Comments

✦ **The software that's used to publish a website:** For example, WordPress is a blogging software.

✦ **A writing and publishing style:** For example, blog *posts* (the articles on a blog) typically appear in chronological order, and the tone is usually very casual compared with, say, a business report.

✦ **Something as simple as a set of journal entries on a web page:** For example, someone who writes a daily memoir.

Most blogs are social media sites — although not all are. If a site calls itself a blog but doesn't allow comments, it's not social media. Think about it: How can you be social if you're the only one talking? You can read more about effective blogging in Book VI.

For the purposes of this discussion, a blog includes regularly published entries by one or more authors and also allows visitors to post their comments on each entry.

Some blogs are major businesses. For example, Engadget (www.engadget.com) and Gizmodo (http://gizmodo.com) — blogs catering to gadget geeks worldwide — are big business. They publish many posts per day, have multiple editors, and support themselves based on considerable advertising income. Figure 1-1 shows just how polished some of the big blog sites look.

Figure 1-1:
Major blogs have a polished look and a huge number of posts in a single day.

Big or small, though, all blogs have these two standard hallmarks:

✦ Comments ✓

✦ A serial publishing style, where posts are shown sequentially ✓

To see examples of the many blogs on the Internet, visit Technorati (`http://technorati.com`) or Alltop.com and look through their listings. They each have a great set of examples.

If you're looking to make that first step in social marketing, a blog is the place to start. Blogs offer a terrific way to

✦ Talk directly to your customers by posting and commenting on your blog

✦ Explain your business philosophy by writing in your own style and exposing your ideas to the public at large

✦ Demonstrate your expertise by commenting on other blogs or creating your own expert blog

✦ Win over potential customers by driving the people who read your blog toward your business

Blogs are your most powerful social marketing tool. The rest of the social media world has grown up around blogs to help bloggers get the word out: Bookmarking sites, social networks, and all their derivatives draw from thousands of blog entries, authors, and discussions. You can use that infrastructure to find the right readers and grow your online presence.

Finally, using a blog can help you move up in the search engine rankings. A blog's text-focused style, regular publishing, and capability to attract links can give you a much-needed boost by building your authority in the search engines. See Book II, which covers search engine optimization (SEO), for more about that.

For the ins and outs of writing a successful blog, see Book VI.

Connecting via social networks

Social networks are sites that let you create your own profile, seek out and connect with other members, and talk to your friends from a single profile page. Social networks also let you share photos, images, links, and other tidbits of information within your circle of friends.

Facebook, Google+, LinkedIn, and hundreds (if not thousands) of other sites all qualify as social networks.

At their simplest, they offer you — and your online presence — a great opportunity to

+ **Get a feel for your potential customers:** Social networks help you find friends and users by interests, geography, and hobbies.

+ **Get advice from colleagues:** Services like LinkedIn offer special Answers networks, where you can ask and answer questions from other members.

+ **Demonstrate your expertise:** You can tell your social network friends about recent accomplishments, answer their questions, and provide the occasional tip.

After you start using the more advanced features on the major social networks, you can also

+ **Distribute custom tools** by using these networks' special development kits

+ **Create targeted discussion groups** by using features like Facebook Groups

Here is a list of social networks that you should be familiar with. They've been around for a while, have thousands or millions of users, and offer access to the widest audience:

✦ **Facebook:** One of the dominant sites, Facebook (www.facebook.com) allows you to create your own profile pages, as shown in Figure 1-2. More important for us marketers, Facebook lets you create business pages and then build a fan base for your company. Facebook also allows custom applications: games, puzzles, utilities, and other little widgets created by third-party developers. You can join for free by creating an account in just a few minutes.

✦ **Google+:** At the time of this writing, Google+ (https://plus.google.com) is the upstart. Google's network uses "circles" to organize your friends and offers a clean, easy-to-use set of tools. Google+ also reached 100 million users in under three months and will definitely be a force to reckon with. Don't ignore this network. Google+ lets you create business pages.

✦ **LinkedIn:** A members-only, pay-to-register network for businesspeople, LinkedIn (www.linkedin.com) is business networking on steroids. After you create a detailed profile, other businesspeople worldwide can connect with you based on common interests, previous work together, or networking groups. Members can create networks of literally hundreds of people.

Figure 1-2:
Use Facebook to create a profile page and share it with millions.

Book VII Chapter 1

Understanding Social Media

✦ **Discussion forums:** Forums are still out there. Sites like WebmasterWorld.com (`www.webmasterworld.com`) and Google Groups (`http://groups.google.com`) are basically enormous collections of discussion threads where you create your membership and then join the fray. Most discussion forums are free to join.

There are thousands upon thousands of niche networks, too. Use your favorite search engine to find them.

All social networking sites offer a rare opportunity to spread the word about yourself or your company to thousands or even millions of people. The trick is doing it politely. See Chapters 5 and 6 of this minibook for advice on doing just that.

Conducting promotions on social media sites can be tricky. Read the terms of services (TOS) of each service to find out what kind of promotion is and isn't allowed. Even if you don't take the time to read the TOS, remember that spamming is not recommended on any social media sites. Your account will most likely be disabled.

Bookmarking sites

Bookmarking sites are applications that let you move your bookmarks from your computer to a single, central account that you can access from any Internet connection. You don't have to worry about losing your bookmarks in a computer crash.

Bookmarking sites are a handy utility and a community at the same time. Members can connect with other members who have similar interests and share bookmark recommendations. You can use bookmarking sites to

✦ Share bookmarks with others

✦ Review each other's choices

✦ Generally gossip about your most recent finds

Examples of bookmarking sites that are worth exploring include the following:

✦ **StumbleUpon:** Install the StumbleUpon toolbar on your computer and then click a button. StumbleUpon (`www.stumbleupon.com`) takes you to sites marked as thumbs-up by folks who share your interests. You can submit additional pages, review them, and follow other members as they bookmark sites. Warning: Highly addictive!

✦ **Delicious:** Clever name, huh? Use Delicious (`http://delicious.com`) to save bookmarks on its server instead of on your browser so that you can access them from any computer. You can also add notes, automatically publish your bookmarks to your blog, and subscribe to other members' bookmark lists. Figure 1-3 shows the unique Delicious homepage.

✦ **Pocket:** This site (`getpocket.com`) provides a quick way to save things you want to read later.

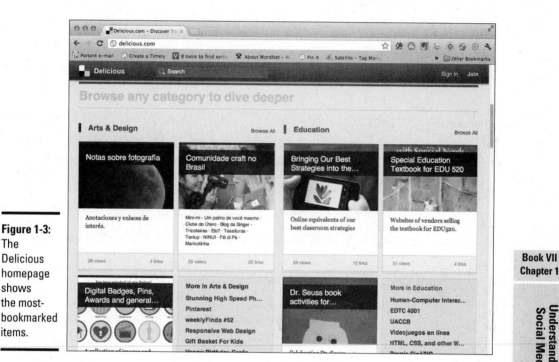

Figure 1-3:
The Delicious homepage shows the most-bookmarked items.

**Book VII
Chapter 1**

Understanding
Social Media

Some sites, such as StumbleUpon, even recommend bookmarks based on their popularity, as shown in Figure 1-4. So, if many StumbleUpon users all "stumble" onto your site in a short period of time, you can get thousands or even hundreds of thousands of visitors.

As an Internet marketer, you can also use bookmarking sites to drive traffic toward your business. If you or someone else bookmarks an article or page on your website with one of these services, and then others do the same, you can gain a lot of traffic from people who *want* what you're offering.

Plus, search engines often *crawl* — read through all the content — these sites looking for important, relevant content. Again, bookmarking sites offer a great benefit for your search engine optimization efforts. See Book II for more about SEO.

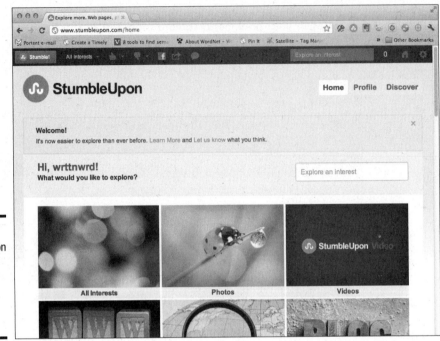

Figure 1-4:
StumbleUpon uses a toolbar installed in your web browser.

Microblogging

Microblog sites allow members to make lots of short blog posts. Short means *short* — often less than 140 characters. Microblogs are fast and easy and can be updated from a cellphone, from a computer, or even via voice mail.

Microblogs look and feel more like old-fashioned chat rooms than blogs. Participants post statements, which are visible in a common *public timeline,* which everyone can see and read. See Figure 1-5.

You might think that microblogging is just like a social network, but microblogs tend to be more "real time," with some participants posting every few minutes, so they allow more of an ongoing conversation. But yes, the lines do get blurry at times.

More importantly, participants can follow fellow microbloggers whom they find interesting. After you make friends on a microblog, you follow them and they follow you. Then their friends see you and follow you, and so on. On most microblogs, you mark people as friends by clicking Friend or Follow. Then they confirm, and you're friends. It's that easy.

Therefore, microblogging is a great way to build a focused audience to which you can pose questions, make suggestions, or announce a new blog post.

Make friends → they then friends see your friends etc.

Figure 1-5:
The public
timeline on
Twitter.

Book VII
Chapter 1

Understanding
Social Media

You'll find a lot of microblogging sites out there, but here are the two biggest:

- ✦ **Twitter:** Half addiction, half publicity platform, Twitter (`http://twitter.com`) is a microblogging tool with which you can enter 140-character messages. By following other people you find interesting, you'll receive their messages. Think of it as a huge chat room that remembers what you said. It's free to join. Like most social networks, you sign up and start posting right away.

    In Figure 1-6, notice that Twitter allows you to see the most recent posts on the network and the statistics regarding who's following you. When you post, your followers' Twitter timeline automatically updates to show the post.

- ✦ **Tumblr:** A more free-form site, Tumblr (`www.tumblr.com`) allows longer posts (as long as you want) and images embedded into your posts. Other Tumblr users can also upvote your posts, highlight them, and favorite them. Tumblr is more blog-like than Twitter, and it's gained a lot of popularity over the last few years.

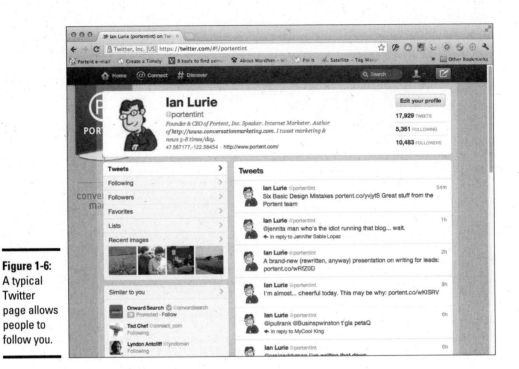

Figure 1-6:
A typical
Twitter
page allows
people to
follow you.

The real power of microblogging lies in your ability to get many followers and then announce things to them. Because the entire purpose of micro-blogs is to make short announcements, try using the following examples as a guide:

Announcement: You just finished writing a new book or white paper.

Post: "Just finished writing my new book!"

Announcement: You just got home from a business trip to New York.

Post: "Just got home from New York."

Announcement: I have a new product.

Post: "Check out this new product I'm selling." (Be sure to add a link to your product.)

Media sharing sites

Media sharing sites allow you to upload videos, photographs, and audio to a single directory. Then visitors can browse through and see your master-piece. If you've been online in the last four years, you know a few of these sites. Examples include

✦ **YouTube:** This is the biggest video-sharing site out there. Upload your video (ten minutes or less, although YouTube's been testing higher limits), and visitors can view and comment on it. Garnering more views and favorites ratings moves you up in the directory. Whole careers have been launched on YouTube (www.youtube.com). YouTube is free and lets you upload video in a wide array of formats.

✦ **Flickr:** Use Flickr (www.flickr.com) to upload and manage photographs. You can divide them into groups, organize them by tags, and restrict access as desired. Flickr also lets you publish your photos individually or as a stream on other websites. Flickr just started supporting video as well. Be careful using Flickr to promote yourself, though; it has strict policies about promotional materials.

✦ **Pinterest:** Build a virtual scrapbook with Pinterest (www.pinterest.com). Find images of stuff you like, click Pin It, and you instantly add the images to categories called "boards." It's literally an online pinboard. The site is invite only, but you can obtain an invite by simply requesting one on the Pinterest home page.

As an Internet marketer, you can post your videos, photos, and illustrations on these sites. It's hardly a sure thing, but the right content at the right time can get you hundreds, thousands, or even hundreds of thousands of new visitors. That's why you want to put your photos and videos on third-party sites: They get a lot of traffic and put you in front of an enormous audience.

Social voting sites

Half social networks, half bookmarking sites, *social voting sites* allow members to submit new content and then vote on other submissions. Items that get enough votes move up in the listings and get more traffic. Social voting sites include

✦ **reddit:** reddit is the dominant force, with everything from images to video to cartoons to random writing by members. Members submit, vote, and comment on items. If an item gets enough votes in a short time, it moves to the front page, and a flood of traffic ensues. Focus your efforts here first. Browse reddit at www.reddit.com.

✦ **Digg:** A front-page listing on Digg (http://digg.com) has been known to crash servers and bring websites to their knees. Digg is a *very* busy site focusing on technology and the funny/odd/bizarre. In Figure 1-7, you can see that the Diggs badges show the number of votes about each article. The left side shows the most recent items to get significant votes.

Posting on popularity sites is a gamble. You can't ignore them because a front-page listing on a site like Digg can bring you the biggest possible burst of new visitors. But that kind of listing can prove very difficult to achieve.

Figure 1-7:
The Digg homepage is total chaos — and a lot of fun.

Q&A sites

If you have a question, the Internet has the answer. But how do you know if it's the right one?

Q&A sites help you by giving you a place where you can post a question, look at the answers that folks provide, and watch as others vote those answers up or down

- **Quora:** Have a question? Visit http://quora.com. Thousands of help-ful members offer answers to questions on topics ranging from Internet marketing to wedding planning to pet care, as shown in Figure 1-8. It's free to join, and answering questions is easy.

- **Stack Overflow:** More focused on the developer and geek community, Stack Overflow (http://stackoverflow.com) is a lifeline for thou-sands of developers and technology users worldwide. If you can estab-lish yourself as an authority here, you know you've arrived.

- **Stack Exchange:** Stack Exchange (http://stackexchange.com) is a broader-interest site than Stack Overflow, similar to Quora.

Figure 1-8:
Quora.

Chapter 2: Creating Your Social Media Desktop

In This Chapter

✔ **Setting up your social media desktop**

✔ **Adding updates to your tracking center**

✔ **Deciding which information to track**

*O*ne of the first problems you encounter in any social media campaign is information overload, or how to keep track of what people are saying on dozens of different sites.

If you create and use a *social media desktop*, however, you have one central place where you can easily monitor

✦ The things that people say about you or your organization

✦ Any stories or themes that you want to track

The best part of having a social media desktop is that you don't have to type the web address for every site and search result you're trying to track, because it's all in one place.

In this chapter, you build your social media desktop. Note: If you haven't read Chapter 1 of this minibook, hop over there and find out about the sneeze principle. (Gesundheit.) You need a social media desktop so that you can know when other people, um, *sneeze* (spread along) your content. You also need a social media desktop so that you can find and pass along other people's great content. That makes you a more valuable member of the community — giving you more authority and making your messages more contagious. Being contagious, so to speak, can boost all your Internet marketing efforts — you'll get more links (which helps search engine optimization), get more fans (which helps in blogging), and build your brand (which helps with everything).

Setting Up Your Social Media Desktop with RSS

Take a deep breath. Relax. Dry your palms. Setting up your social media desktop is easy — honest!

Your *social media desktop* is just an account that you set up using one of the many services that let you track various search results, blogs, and news stories with a few clicks of the mouse. Check out the iGoogle example shown in Figure 2-1. At a glance, you can see what folks are saying about your company and what your favorite blogs are talking about.

The key to your social media desktop is *really simple syndication,* or *RSS,* in which you build your desktop by subscribing to several RSS feeds for websites, blogs, or search results. That way, you can stay up to date without visiting the site, blog, or search result. By putting all those subscriptions in one place, you create your social media desktop: a single place where you can keep an eye on what folks are saying about you, your company, and your competitors.

RSS is a simple way for websites to deliver a list of the latest headlines, articles, or content. An RSS feed is the actual list of headlines. You don't need to worry about the technical details.

You can use any RSS feed reader or organizing service you like, but in this chapter, you find out how to use iGoogle and Netvibes. Both of them are free and offer a broad feature set.

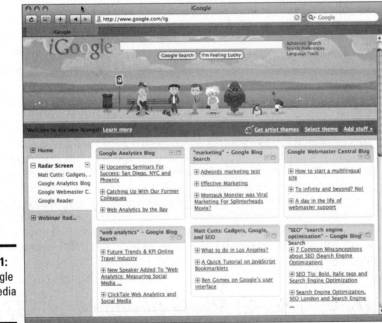

Figure 2-1:
The iGoogle social media desktop.

Setting Up Your Social Media Desktop in iGoogle

iGoogle is one of the simplest social media desktop tools. If you already have Gmail or use another Google service, you can simply add it to your existing account. Plus, it integrates with Google's various other services.

The only downside about iGoogle is this: You don't have much control over how your page looks. If you're not a fan of the Google aesthetic for pages that have a lot of text on them, iGoogle may not be for you. As you'll soon see, your social media desktop will have a lot of text on it.

Setting up an iGoogle homepage

You can set up an iGoogle homepage as your social media desktop in just a few simple steps:

1. **In your web browser, go to** `www.google.com/ig`.

2. **If you already have a Google account:**

- *But you aren't logged in:* Sign in, and then skip to Step 4.

- *And you're already logged in:* Accept the offer on the iGoogle splash page to make it your homepage, and then skip to Step 4.

If you have a Gmail account, you already have a Google account. Sign in using your Gmail address and password. You'll see the iGoogle setup page (see Figure 2-2).

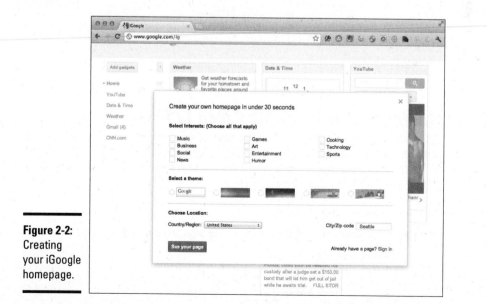

Figure 2-2:
Creating
your iGoogle
homepage.

3. **Select a theme, but leave your interests blank. Enter your location.**

   You'll fill your page with other widgets that bring you news feeds, headlines, and content related to your interests, from blogs, news websites, and search engines.

   When your iGoogle homepage appears (see Figure 2-3), with a bunch of preselected items (such as Google News, weather, and the current time), you can remove them, too.

Figure 2-3:
Your
iGoogle
homepage.

You're ready to start adding items, such as search results and your favorite blogs.

Adding a website or blog feed to iGoogle

After you create your iGoogle homepage, you can start tracking news feeds and getting up-to-date information. You might already have a few blogs or websites that you read regularly. If you do, you can watch their updates on your iGoogle homepage. Here's how:

1. **Go to the website or blog.**

2. **Click the RSS subscription button or link, as shown in Figure 2-4.**

Figure 2-4:
Typical RSS
subscription
options on a
website.

The Add to Google page appears. If your web browser is set up to add
RSS feeds to a different program, the Google page may not appear —
your browser will open a different web page instead. If that happens,
skip to the later section "Adding feeds to iGoogle manually" to work
around this issue.

3. **Click the Add to Google Homepage button.**

You see the latest headlines from that website or blog, as shown in
Figure 2-5.

From now on, when the website to which you just subscribed updates, the
widget on your iGoogle homepage will immediately update.

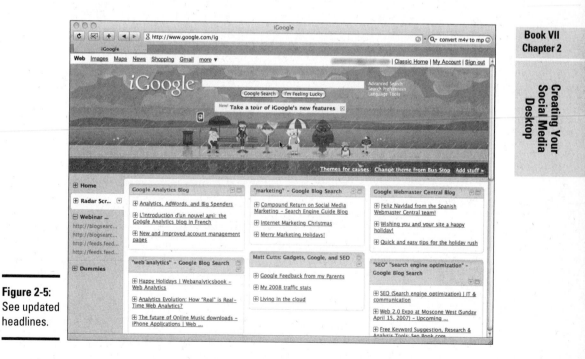

Figure 2-5:
See updated
headlines.

Adding a blog search result to iGoogle

Rather than follow just one specific blog, you can track what most blogs are saying, all at one time, by using Google Blog Search. Running a search for your company name, for example, shows every blog entry mentioning your company. Here's how to subscribe:

1. **Go to** www.google.com.

2. **Click the More link on the left-hand side of the page and then choose Blogs; see Figure 2-6.**

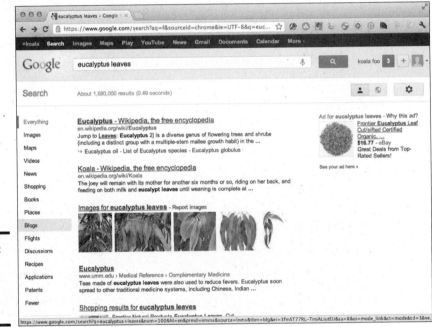

Figure 2-6:
The Blogs search option on Google.

3. **Search for your organization's name.**

   Enclose the name in double quotes. Using quotes narrows your search result to search for a phrase match on the words you entered, whether you have a one-word or a ten-word name.

4. **Click the magnifying glass icon.**

   To see the most recent results first, click the Sort by Date link, in the middle of the left-hand navigation bar. See Figure 2-7.

5. **Click the RSS link at the bottom of the page.**

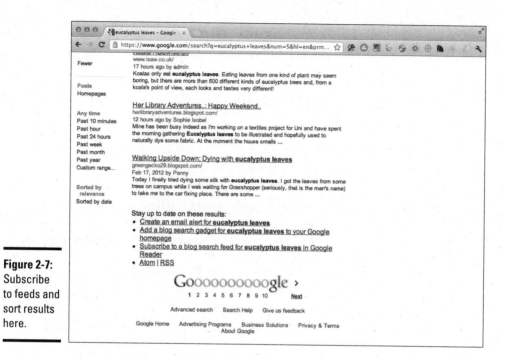

Figure 2-7:
Subscribe
to feeds and
sort results
here.

6. Go back to your iGoogle homepage.

You see the search result in a nice, neat box. When iGoogle adds a new
blog post to this search result, you see it there, as shown in Figure 2-8.

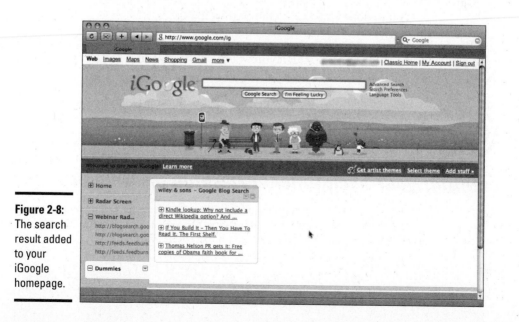

Figure 2-8:
The search
result added
to your
iGoogle
homepage.

You can add other search results, too. Examples include

✦ Competitor names

✦ Names of individuals in your company

✦ Names of individuals at competitors

✦ Product names

✦ Your web address

✦ Common typographical errors for all elements in this list

Adding feeds to iGoogle manually

If iGoogle isn't the default RSS feed reader for your browser, you'll need to add the feed to iGoogle by hand. Only a few steps are added, though, so don't worry:

1. **Click the RSS link on the website you want to follow.**

2. **Copy the feed URL in the address bar.**

3. **Go to your iGoogle homepage and click the Add Gadgets link.**

4. **In the lower-left corner of the Add Gadgets page, click Add Feed or Gadget.**

5. **In the box that appears right below the Add Feed or Gadget link, paste the feed URL.**

6. **Click Add.**

   You're done — you added a feed by hand.

You can try using a shortcut for adding feeds to iGoogle: Type the web address of the site to which you want to subscribe. If it has a correctly configured feed, Google detects and adds it.

To see more or fewer results in a specific content box on the iGoogle homepage, click the gear menu for that content box, click the Edit Settings, and select the number of items you want to see.

Creating Your Social Media Desktop on Netvibes

If you like a slightly more polished interface, want more customization options, or aren't comfortable using Google because of privacy concerns (some folks just aren't), Netvibes is an excellent choice.

Setting up a Netvibes homepage

Setting up a Netvibes homepage takes only five steps:

1. **In your web browser, go to** www.netvibes.com **and sign in or create an account.**

The basic option works well for your purposes.

2. **Enter a topic you'd like to track.**

Now you've got a Dashboard, but it isn't assigned to an account.

3. **To set up your account, click the Sign Up in the upper-right corner.**

4. **Enter your account information, or sign in using Facebook.**

5. **Follow the activation instructions for e-mail activation or via Facebook.**

You're logged in to your new account; see Figure 2-9.

In Netvibes, you have two pages: your public page and your private page. When you first sign up, your public page is turned off. If you turn it on, just be careful that you don't put any widgets you don't want anyone else to see on your public page.

Click to add content

Figure 2-9:
Your new
Netvibes
homepage.

You're now ready to start adding widgets that display RSS feeds and other content.

Adding content to a Netvibes homepage

Adding content to Netvibes is similar to adding content to iGoogle manually. Follow these steps:

1. **Go to the site, blog search, or other page to which you want to subscribe.**

2. **Right-click the RSS or Subscribe to RSS link.**

3. **From the shortcut menu that appears, choose the Copy Link Location command (or a similar one).**

4. **Go to Netvibes and log in (if you aren't already logged in).**

5. **Click the Add Content button; refer to Figure 2-9.**

6. **In the page that opens, click the Add a Feed button, as shown in Figure 2-10.**

7. **Paste the feed URL and then click Add Feed.**

Click to add a feed

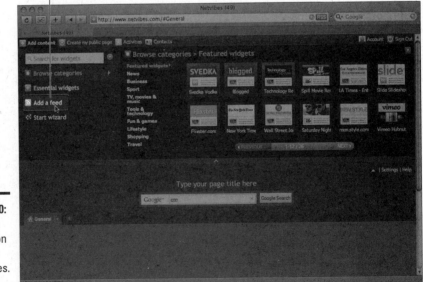

Figure 2-10:
The Add a
Feed button
and menu
on Netvibes.

Netvibes presents options, if necessary. Options are determined by the specific widget. The kind of content you want or don't want, whether to include photographs, or whether to play video automatically are possible options.

8. Click the Add to My Page button.

The feed is now on your Netvibes homepage.

Here are a couple of shortcuts for adding feeds to Netvibes:

✦ **Simply click Add Feed and then, in the field that appears, type the web address of a site.** If the site has a feed, Netvibes finds and adds it automatically.

✦ **Use a Firefox plug-in or a Chrome extension** (if you use Firefox or Chrome as your web browser). Be sure to read about those items when you start using Netvibes. Plug-ins are great and easy to install, but do a little research to find the ones that have been around for a while and are proven to work.

Netvibes offers a few additional options with which you can

✦ Change the number of items shown in the feed box.

✦ Color-code the content boxes; see Figure 2-11.

Color-coding might seem silly at first, but it can make your social media desktop much easier to review.

✦ Show more information about each post.

**Book VII
Chapter 2**

**Creating Your
Social Media
Desktop**

Figure 2-11:
Use color-
coding
on your
homepage
to help sort
content.

Using tabs to stay organized

When you start tracking innumerable different searches and sites, you might find that your social media desktop can get a bit out of control, not unlike a cluttered closet; see the figure. (Talk about info overload!)

When that happens, organize your homepage by creating separate tabs and using them to divide your content accordingly. Netvibes and iGoogle both have an Add Tab (or New Tab) link that you can use.

To access these options and others, click the Edit or the Options button at the top of each content box.

Deciding What to Track

You can start adding content to your social media desktop by tracking a few blog search results and websites or blogs of interest. Later, you might want to add

✦ Twitter feeds or search results

✦ News search results from Google and Bing

✦ Stock data

✦ A Flickr or YouTube channel

The sky's the limit. As you get comfortable using the tools, you might want to add all manner of feeds and information to the page. Some truly advanced marketers even create tools that generate their own readouts of search rankings and other data.

You need to be judicious — okay, picky — though. Otherwise, your social media desktop will leave you just as buried in information as you were before you created it. As a rule, add a feed only if

✦ You need to check it daily or more often.

✦ The information doesn't show up in another feed.

✦ You can skim it.

Your social media desktop should be something you can quickly skim in a matter of minutes. Anything that can't be digested in a list doesn't belong there.

**Book VII
Chapter 2**

**Creating Your
Social Media
Desktop**

Chapter 3: Creating Your Social Media Plan

In This Chapter

↙ **Researching your audience**

↙ **Reviewing your site for social skills**

↙ **Preparing for social media greatness**

↙ **Finding your message**

↙ **Setting your routine**

In this chapter, you find out how to research your audience and pick the message and style that work for you. You also select target sites accordingly as well as prepare a profile that you can use repeatedly. After you make those decisions, it's time to set your social media schedule.

Researching Your Audience

Social media is unique enough that you'll want to analyze your audience there separately from other vehicles, such as search engines. For example, you might expect instant sales from a paid search ad or an e-mail marketing campaign. But when it comes to social media, you're looking for evidence of steady inroads with your audience, such as increased blog mentions about your company, which won't lead to sales for weeks or months. When you research your audience, you need to answer five basic questions:

✦ **What kinds of people are in your audience?** You need to know whom you're speaking to.

✦ **Why does your audience participate in the community?** What do they want from it? If they're participating so that they can trade pictures of their pet bunny rabbit with friends and you suddenly show up selling hunting rifles, they won't appreciate it.

✦ **What communities and sites does your audience use most often?** It's best to focus your efforts where your audience goes.

✦ **How big is this audience?** If a social media campaign on Facebook is going to reach 20 people in six months, for example, Facebook might not be your ideal venue.

✦ **How often does your audience participate?** This, combined with audience size, helps you determine how often you need to participate. It lets you be more efficient.

Write all five questions down so that you can take notes while you research. Use a spreadsheet to keep track of your research, similar to the one shown in Figure 3-1.

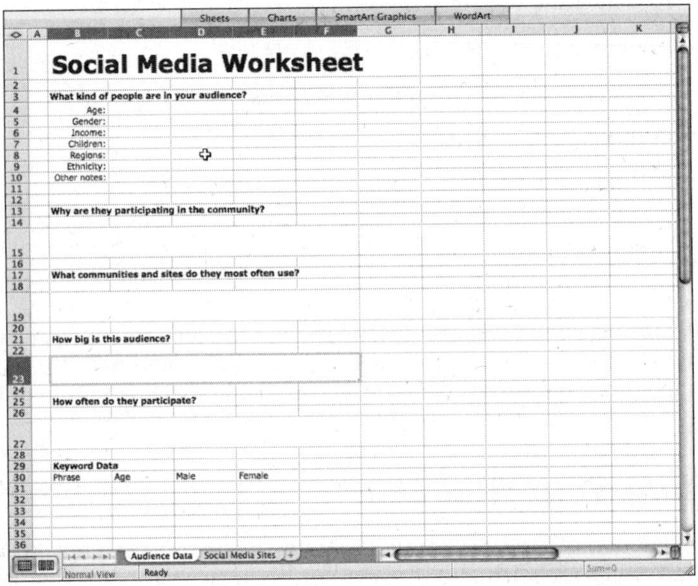

Figure 3-1:
Start with a social media research worksheet.

The worksheet is your central storage for research, so keep it handy.

Now where do you find this information? The Internet offers some great resources.

Starting with online communities

Most important, you have to spend some time exploring a few communities to see what your potential audience is saying and doing. Try these:

✦ **Google Groups** (http://groups.google.com): Search for your product or service and then look into the discussions that you find. What are people asking? See whether you could contribute to the discussion. How active are the discussions? If participants are posting every hour, this is a very active community — you'll need to follow closely if you're going to participate.

Sign up for e-mail updates. That way you'll receive Groups updates in your inbox, and you can respond quickly.

✦ **Facebook** (www.facebook.com): Facebook is so big, and so busy, that groups exist for nearly every imaginable interest. Search Facebook Groups for the topics that relate to your business. See how many members these groups have: Having more members means a bigger audience for you. And don't forget to look at how often participants post to groups because frequent posts mean a more active community.

✦ **reddit** (www.reddit.com): Search for topics, products, people, or ideas related to your business. If people are submitting relevant stories, how are they received? If relevant stories get a lot of votes, social news sites are a potential venue for you, and there's an interested community of readers. If relevant stories are received with sarcastic comments and a handful of votes, you'll want to avoid social news sites — or find a different way to approach the topic. YouTube videos are a great example of this: Blenders don't make good reddit material. But shoving an iPod into a blender? Pure gold!

✦ **Blogs:** Use Google Blog Search (http://blogsearch.google.com), Technorati (www.technorati.com), and Icerocket (www.icerocket.com). Search again for topics relevant to your business. How many bloggers are writing about the topic? The more bloggers, and the more often they're posting, the larger and potentially receptive your audience. What do the bloggers focus on? Their interests may indicate your audience's interests, too.

Audience research is the most important research you can do. Data is great; hard numbers are tremendously helpful, too. But social media marketing is not easily quantified — the general feel you get by checking out the communities is essential, too.

When you look at each community, note what you find on your social media research worksheet.

Researching with Facebook

The Facebook segmentation tool, part of its ads platform, is a great research tool.

Facebook's ad creation tool lets you test different *segments* — potential members of your audience grouped by interest or trait — and see how many people fit into each one. That lets you see which segments you should speak to through social media.

To use the segmentation tool, follow these steps:

1. **Sign in to your Facebook account.**

2. **Click the Advertising link at the bottom of the page.**

3. **Click the Create an Ad button in the upper-right corner.**

   Skip the Design Your Ad section. For the purpose of these steps, you're just using the segmentation tool and won't be building an actual ad.

4. **Scroll to section 2, Targeting.**

5. **Select the attributes that you think match your audience.**

   - *Demographics*: Segment your research by gender and age range.

   - *Location:* Geo-target your research.

   - *Connections on Facebook:* Target people who are already fans of pages you manage, or are not fans of pages you manage. That lets you further segment your research to avoid double-targeting or missing people.

   - *Interests:* Match activities and things folks say they like or follow.

6. **Look at the Estimated Reach number on the right side of the page.**

   That tells you the size of your prospective audience.

Voila! Instant audience membership. Try different combinations of interests and demographics to find the "sweet spot": targeted topics that are big enough to provide useful information and potential followers.

Getting more data with Quantcast

If you want demographic data on a site-by-site basis that's more detailed, Quantcast is a great free resource.

On Quantcast, you can get site demographics, including

- ✦ Visitors by age group
- ✦ Visitor ethnicity
- ✦ Household income
- ✦ Children in household
- ✦ Visitor education level
- ✦ Gender
- ✦ Other sites and categories of sites visited by a site's typical user

Why isn't this site showing up?

Some sites don't get enough traffic to register in the Quantcast database. Well, those sites *can* get into Quantcast data, but the site owner has to add a special snippet of code to his site. You can find the code and instructions on the Quantcast website (www.quantcast.com).

Site owners also need to permit Quantcast to collect some statistics, such as lifestyle or geographic information. You may also want to disclose that you're using the code snippet in the privacy statement on your site.

Using Quantcast is easy. Go to www.quantcast.com, type the web address of the site you want to check, and click the Search button. You should see something similar to Figure 3-2.

WARNING!

Ever hear the expression that 50 percent of statistics are true and 60 percent are lies? Yeah. Be careful when you use any data collected by sites like Quantcast. They're great resources, but we humans have a funny way of screwing up carefully written measurement tools. If the data makes zero sense based on your gut instinct, listen to your gut, at least a little.

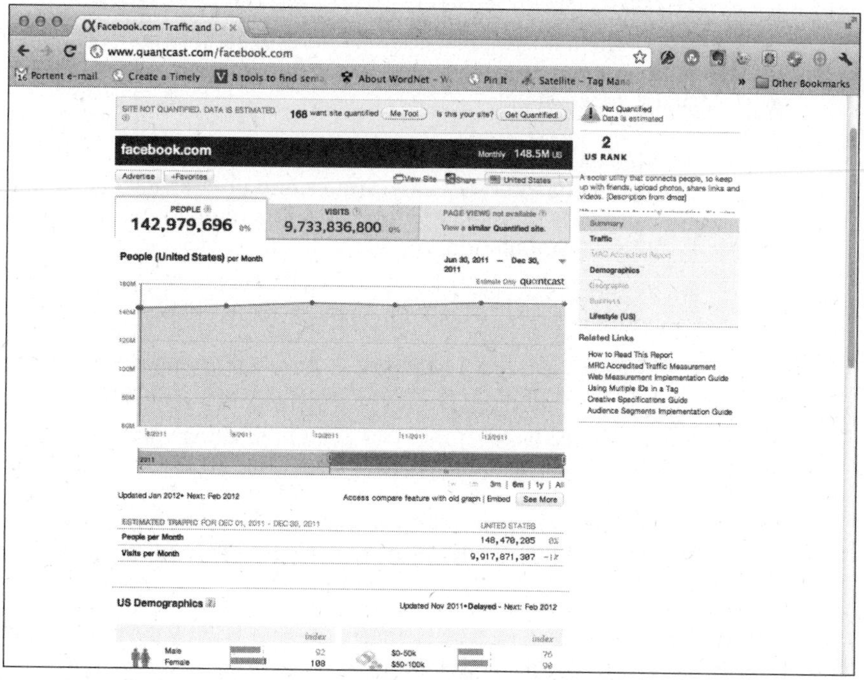

Figure 3-2:
A Quantcast report.

Again, add this data to your social media worksheet. (Refer to Figure 3-1.) Supplement what you already have for each of these sites. By now, your worksheet should have a solid picture of each site, as shown in Figure 3-3.

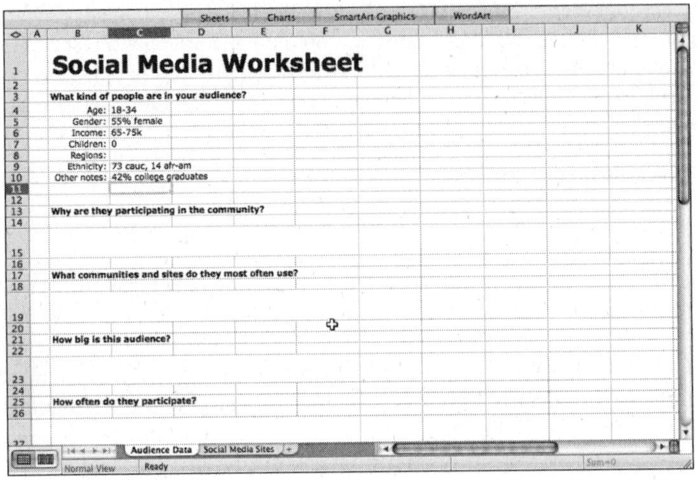

Figure 3-3: Social media research worksheet with Quantcast data.

Getting fancy with paid data services

A lot of the data you can collect comes from free sources. But if you have some dollars to spend on research, though, a number of services can give you far more detail:

✦ **Nielsen** (http://www.nielsen.com) **NetView** lets you create custom reports based on demographics and online viewing habits. Reports are incredibly detailed comparisons between your audience and the entire Internet population.

✦ **Experian Hitwise** (www.hitwise.com) provides in-depth reporting on entire industries or online categories, or specific sites.

✦ **Compete** (http://compete.com) delivers search and site-usage analytics. Site data is free, but the search reports are not.

✦ **comScore** (www.comscore.com) provides a wide range of advertising and site-usage analysis tools.

Expect Compete.com, Nielsen, and comScore to require an ongoing subscription. Hitwise offers individual reports or an ongoing subscription.

Try one or more of these services if you

+ **Have a large social media budget and want to make sure that you allocate it effectively.** If spending a few thousand dollars on reports will mean you can better spend tens of thousands of dollars later, it's worth it.

+ **Can't afford to spend a month or two testing your campaign.** The detail you get from these paid services can eliminate a lot of trial and error.

+ **Have other uses for this data.** If you're also doing a pay-per-click (PPC) campaign and a banner ad buy, you might need this data anyway.

+ **Have the time and interest to dig deep into statistics and create an ultra-detailed picture of your audience.**

Social media marketing is an emerging field. No one has the ideal toolset for campaign planning, so you end up engaging in some trial and error no matter how much data you get. Invest in paid reports to paint a more complete picture, but don't expect a photograph.

ClearVue
Honest Affordable *Comprehensive* *Service*

Crafting Your Social Media Message

You need a message for your social media campaign. Yes, social media is informal. And yes, it's supposed to be spontaneous. But social media is also like standing in front of 50 million reporters. It's best to have some guidelines to prevent foot-in-mouth syndrome.

Your social media marketing message is a little different, though, insofar as it's more about the kind of person or organization you are than it is about the benefits of a particular product or service. It's not so much a message as a guide: a Jiminy Cricket for your social media participation.

Here's how you set your message: Write down three or four words that you want to associate with you and your company — words like *honest, funny, annoying* (hopefully not), and *smart.*

Those words are your message. That doesn't mean that every word you write on a social network has to fit every characteristic. But any time you're about to post anything, anywhere, think of those three or four words and consider whether they fit with what you're about to post.

Write down the message on your social media worksheet, too. Compare it against the sites, audiences, and keyword data you already have. Does your message fit the audience to which each site caters? Use this comparison to further narrow where you're going to concentrate your efforts.

REAL WORLD

Keep it real

Don't forget Sony!

You might remember that Sony got caught publishing fake blogs by supposed fans of its new PS3 gaming console. *Oops* probably wasn't one of the words Sony had in its social media message.

Setting Your Social Media Style

Style is different from message. Here are a few archetypal social media styles. You won't fit totally into any of them, but you can probably find a few favorites. Your style can really guide where and how you participate in social media.

+ The **troublemaker** loves to poke people a little bit, all the time. She's not mean or evil. She just wants to make sure that everyone questions assumptions. Opt to be a troublemaker *only if you know for certain* that you know a *lot* about the topic about which you're going to stir up trouble. Troublemakers can get a lot of attention and admiration. Always be courteous, and poke a little fun at yourself. Troublemakers end up spending a lot of time on microblogging networks and discussion forums, as well commenting on blogs.

+ The **maven** is an expert who loves to help others, thereby demonstrating her knowledge and expertise. You'll seek out folks who are asking questions. If you're a consultant, it's great to be a maven. Spend a lot of time on Yahoo! Answers, LinkedIn, and your blog. Use microblogs to let folks know when and how you're providing information.

+ The **new kid** is polite and tends to keep a low profile, learning his way around. If you're the new kid, you're not necessarily silent, but you're definitely self-effacing. You're getting to know everyone. Be the new kid if you're striking out in a new industry, or if you're going into a social network where the demographic is totally different from your own. Be sure to tell folks why you're there: "I want to help," "I'm starting a business," or "I want to learn." Focus on big social networks like Facebook, as well as microblogs like Twitter. Stay away from answers networks unless you know enough to separate good answers from bad.

+ Everyone knows the **rock star.** If his name shows up on a social network, he instantly attracts dozens or even hundreds of friends and followers. Be the rock star if you're well known in your industry or field. Use Facebook Groups, microblogs, your blog, and any niche sites to keep in touch.

Assuming a fake persona when you start a social media campaign isn't a good idea. Far from it. But you should put serious thought into your strengths and weaknesses as a member of the community. Then play to your strengths.

Preparing Your Social Media Profile

Every social media site asks you to create a *profile* that includes basic information, such as your name, your website (if you have one), and so on.

Every social media site also asks for info that's harder for you to come by, so you might as well collect it all now.

Open your social media worksheet. Then add the following:

✦ **Your avatar:** Just about every social media site will want a photo of you, a symbol, or some graphic to represent yourself. This is your *avatar*. (Skip ahead to the upcoming Figure 3-5 to see one in action.) Find an image or graphic you like (it doesn't have to be a photo of you) and save it. Most services will resize it automatically, but if you know how, you can resize the image to about 200 x 200 pixels to save yourself some time later.

✦ **A short description of yourself:** This can be funny, serious, or anything in between. Write three to four sentences and save it to reuse. You might want to write more than one for different purposes. For example, you can have a serious bio, a funny one, and a few others.

✦ **Separate, short lists of activities and interests:** Also write down your favorite books, foods, TV shows, and music. Sites like Facebook will ask for this info again and again.

✦ **(Optional) Basic contact information:** Gather your e-mail address, mailing address (if you want to share), and any instant messaging (IM) addresses. And, of course, your social media profiles: Twitter username, Facebook page address, Google+ address, and any others you have. It's easier to cut and paste this static info than it is to rewrite it every time.

Now it's time to figure out where to put all this information.

Choosing Your Target Social Media Sites

You'll find a lot of social media sites — more than a hundred. Chances are you don't have 20 hours per day to spend patrolling social media sites for new connections.

So you need to make a few choices. Here are a few guidelines:

✦ **Check the logic.** Go to your social media worksheet. While you select sites, check the answers you wrote to each of the five questions. Do the sites you're picking make sense?

✦ **Think big.** If you need to reach consumers, look at the big social networking sites: Facebook and Google+. These are huge sites and it's hard to stand out, but they're your best potential venue.

✦ **Think business.** If you're more business to business (B2B), look at business-focused social networks such as LinkedIn. Also look at microblogs, such as Twitter and Tumblr.

✦ **Think media.** If you have video, PowerPoint, or photos to post and you want lots of folks to see them, you're definitely going to need the big media-sharing sites: YouTube, Flickr, SlideShare, and iTunes. (Yes, iTunes lets you upload your own media.) Just be careful that you don't violate these sites' terms of service.

✦ **Remember bookmarking.** If you care about search engine rankings (and you'd better), put the major social bookmarking sites on your list: Delicious, Pocket, and StumbleUpon, to name a few.

✦ **Make the news — maybe.** If you have something that could be Really Big News, consider the social news sites like Digg and reddit. Otherwise, don't waste your time on these networks. The audiences on these sites are big, noisy, and very difficult to win over.

✦ **Find your niche.** Consider whether any niche social sites cater directly to your audience. Sites like Gooruze (marketing), AutoSpies (cars), and QoolSqool.com (education) offer focused audiences. See Figure 3-4 for a great example of a niche social media site.

While you create your list of target sites, remember to keep asking yourself: Will this site help you realize your marketing goals? That doesn't mean that the site has to generate sales or leads directly. It may just offer you a chance to improve your brand, talk to customers, or find out what your customers want. But make sure that the site can help somehow.

After you pick your sites, set up your accounts. Be sure to subscribe to each one and put it on your social media desktop.

Figure 3-4:
Don't
overlook
a niche
audience.

Reviewing Your Site for Social Skills

Now it's time to determine whether your site is ready to get social. Here are some things you need to line up before you're good to go for any social media–ready site:

- ✦ **Great bait:** At least some of the content on your site should be the kind that gets folks talking and passing the page to their friends.

- ✳✦ **RSS (really simple syndication) subscriptions:** Visitors must be able to subscribe to an RSS feed for your site! Without this, you're shouting from a soundproof room. See Book VI, Chapter 2 for more information.

- ✦ **Easy sharing:** Visitors should also be able to bookmark, Digg, and other-✳ wise link or pass your pages to their favorite social networks.

Creating great bait

You don't need yet another book telling you to "write compelling content." If it were as easy as saying that, everyone would write it. Here are a few specific ways to write content that attracts readers:

✦ **Answer specific questions.** If one question pops up again and again in discussions, answer it in an article.

✦ **Write lists.** Who knows why, but lists always get attention.

✦ **Use graphics.** Great photography and informational images will always attract attention.

✦ **Write about things that make you angry.** A little passion never hurt a writer.

✦ **Write about things that make you laugh.** It's a great way to entertain and bring back visitors.

✦ **Write for scannability.** Use bullets, short paragraphs of no more than three lines, and subheadings so that a reader can quickly scan the page.

Put all these tips together, and you can get great results. The page in Figure 3-5 generated 22,000 page views in two days, and continues to attract comments and attention. That kind of anchor content makes a site social-friendly.

You can find more about writing great content in Book II, Chapter 7. The same techniques that work for search engine optimization work for social media. Bonus!

Figure 3-5: Generate traffic by creating great bait.

Using RSS subscriptions

RSS (really simple syndication) is a standard way to deliver the latest headlines from your website to any browser, software, or device that's set up to read it. *RSS feeds* drive much of the social media world, and any functional blog has one. They're a wonderful tool. With a *feed reader* — such as Google Reader — web surfers can subscribe to dozens of blogs and sites and then quickly skim down the latest headlines, reading what they find interesting.

Think of an RSS feed as a kind of news ticker that you deliver to anyone who wants it. Your audience can check this ticker any time they want. Many users prefer this to e-mail updates because they don't want to give you their e-mail address or deal with the hassle of finding your e-mail in their spam folder.

RSS feeds are part of the reason why headlines are so important. The headline is usually what visitors see when they skim through their RSS feed reader. Write a good headline.

But RSS feeds aren't just for blogs. You can and should use them anywhere you have content that updates. For example

+ A Special Offers page in your store

+ A News page on your site

+ A Tips or Advice section

+ Any part of your site that includes articles or other serial content

You can tell whether a site has an RSS feed by looking for the well-known RSS chicklet. The RSS button is known as a chicklet because it's shaped like the gum of the same name.

Make sure that your site has at least one RSS feed available and is *auto-discoverable.* When a site is auto-discoverable, a visiting web browser, search engine, or other software can automatically find the RSS feed and tell a visitor that he can subscribe to the feed. The technical details of doing this are beyond the scope of this book.

Let folks subscribe via e-mail, too, if they want to. Send them updates just as you always have.

Make sharing easy

Sharing is the essence of social media. Your ultimate goal is to have visitors to your site grab links and pass them along to friends and connections in their favorite communities. With that in mind, make this task easy for them:

Building work schedule

✦ **Easy buttons:** Make sure that the most popular pages on your site have buttons that let visitors post the page on their favorite social networks. Services such as AddThis (`www.addthis.com`) provide easy, reusable buttons that you can cut and paste onto your site. If you're using WordPress, plug-ins like Digg make it even easier to add a customized set of share buttons with a count of shares to date. That kind of social proof gets more people clicking.

✦ **Easy address:** If possible, keep your page addresses as simple as possible. For example, you can see how much easier it is to remember

    MySite.com/shoes

than

    MySite.com/index.aspx?product=2&category=321

Which one would you rather cut and paste to your Facebook page?

✦ **Easy contact info:** If you have a Twitter or other microblogging account, or accounts on other social networks, make sure to list your contact information for those networks on your site. Visitors might pass those around, too.

Setting Your Social Media Marketing Routine

Three-quarters of social media marketing is consistency. You need to set a routine and stick with it. Your routine centers around the social media desktop. You need to regularly check the desktop and respond to messages, react to posts, or just keep track of what's going on.

How you define *regularly* depends on your time and your goals:

✦ **If you're being aggressive and looking to become a major authority in your space,** spend five minutes scanning and responding via your social media desktop every hour.

✦ **If you're looking to maintain your reputation and gain some authority over time,** spend five minutes two or three times per day.

✦ **If you're just getting your feet wet,** spend five minutes once per day.

Schedule this time! Use a timer running on your desktop if you need to. For example, you can spend five minutes checking your e-mail and another five minutes doing your social media chores every hour.

Keeping to a schedule helps you keep to a social media routine without distracting you from all the other requirements of your day.

Planning for the Long Social Media Marketing Haul

Big caveat here: Social media marketing is *not a quick thing*. It takes a long time to gain the trust of a community, and even longer to parlay that trust into an asset for your business. Your time and effort spent are worth it because you'll get the best customers you've ever had. But it does take a long time.

Therefore, you need to plan for the long haul. Make sure that you consider the following:

✦ **Substitutes:** Do you need someone to stand in for you while you're on vacation or away on business? That person doesn't need to pretend to be you. But if you're blogging, for instance, it's great to have a guest keep things going while you're offline.

✦ **Convenience:** For this to become part of your daily routine, it needs to be convenient. Use a browser, such as Firefox, and have it memorize your various logins. Bookmark all the social media sites that you need to visit.

✦ **Fun:** Make sure that it stays fun! If one network or another becomes a pain in the neck, take a vacation from it. Go where you find people that you enjoy talking to. Those people will be your best audience anyway.

✦ **Promotions:** Plan a few special promotions that you'll offer just to your social media audience.

✦ **Measure:** Make sure that you have a solid web analytics plan in place so that you can measure whether these efforts are paying off. See Book III to read more about web analytics.

If you haven't done so already, go to Chapter 1 of this minibook and read (and reread) about the sneeze principle. Your social media plan should put you amidst the most susceptible audience so that your content passes from person to person.

web Analytics

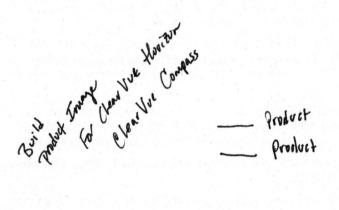

Build
Product Image
For ClearVue Horizon
ClearVue Compass

—— Product
—— Product

Big
Facebook
Google Plus
LinkedIn

↓

Niches
Twitter
Instagram

Chapter 4: Navigating Top Social Media Sites

In This Chapter

✔ Networking with Facebook, Google+, and more

✔ Growing your business with multimedia

✔ Talking in discussion forums

✔ Using Twitter as a launchpad

✔ Building your reputation with Quora

✔ Using the power of niche sites

267 networking

From earlier chapters of this minibook, you set the foundation for a social media campaign that will attract the right audience to your site: You profiled your audience, set up your profiles, and targeted your sites. Now it's time to get to work — *net*work, that is.

This chapter walks you through specific examples of networking on each of the major social networks, as well as shows you how to use bookmarking sites, microblogs, and other social media centers. You also get a few examples of niche sites and discussion forums. And don't skip over the information about how to build your reputation on Quora.

Chapters 5 and 6 of this minibook go into more detail on these topics. The most important thing you need to understand at the end of this chapter is how the various social media sites fit: say, how you can use Twitter to announce a new video on YouTube and then have the video direct folks to a blog. That's the real gold in social media.

The major social networks are a great starting point. Facebook, Google+, and LinkedIn can help you find your audience and let them know you're available.

You can apply what you learn on the big networks to the small, niche ones, too. Look for more information in the upcoming section "Unleashing the Power of Niche Sites."

Clear Vue Insight

Starting with Facebook

Facebook is the current social networking leader. With hundreds of millions of users, Facebook offers an audience for nearly any business.

Read this section even if you're going to focus on using Google+. Many similarities exist between the two services.

If you're using the Internet to market your business, you should use Facebook. Facebook used to be considered consumer-centric. It still is, but any business can benefit from the boost the world's largest social network can provide.

Don't rule out Facebook if your audience is older than 44. Facebook membership covers ages 13–55 and older, and as of this writing the average user age is 39 and rising.

If you haven't read Chapter 1 of this minibook, go there to check out the discussion of the sneeze principle. Facebook is particularly good at spreading a message like a virus. Any two connected Facebook users know whether their friend posted something, joined a new group, became a fan of a Page, installed a new Facebook application, or otherwise acted within the community. Word can spread fast.

From a marketing perspective, you can break Facebook into three types of tools:

✦ Networking

✦ Branding and publicity

✦ Custom applications

Building your Facebook Page

Facebook has a lot of marketing tools, and you use them on your company's Facebook Page. The page is your central switchboard, customer service center, and water cooler, all in one. Almost any content you share as your company will link back to your company Page. It's also where you can update your entire Facebook community.

Before you build your Page, take a look at a few existing ones. Facebook brand Pages have changed since Facebook first rolled out Pages. They now use the Facebook Timeline — a chronological page with most recent events at the top, and older events further down on a continuous scroll.

Here are the basic page components, as you scroll down:

✓ ✦ **A cover image as your opening statement:** Use something eye-catching and relevant, but not a sales pitch or a branded image, as shown in Figure 4-1. Facebook's Terms of Service doesn't allow a sales pitch in the cover image.

✓ ✦ **A profile picture:** This image gets superimposed over the cover image. This is a good place to use your company logo; it provides the branding you need for the top page area.

✦ **Basic company information and your latest photos:** You can also place events listings or highlights in that space. More on this in a moment.

✦ **The Timeline:** The Timeline shows any updates, events, photos or other content you post, and any mentions of your brand by others, as shown in Figure 4-2.

✦ **Update area:** This is a Facebook mainstay. The Write Something area lets you post updates.

You can also see posts, mentions by others, and shares.

Figure 4-1:
The cover image, business information, and highlights on a Facebook company Page.

Figure 4-2:
The
Timeline.

Setting up your company Facebook Page

To create a Facebook brand Page:

1. **Log into your Facebook personal account.**

   Only someone with a personal Facebook account can create a Facebook business Page. You can then assign someone else admin access for that Page, but you must have a personal account to get started. If you don't have one, now's a good time to get one.

2. **Go to** `https://www.facebook.com/pages/create.php`.

3. **Choose the page category:**

   - *Local Business or Place:* If you're a local business who depends on walk-in traffic

   - *Company:* If you're a company that does business over a wider area

   - *Brand or Product:* If you're going to be marketing a single brand or product that's part of a larger company

   - *Artist, Band, or Public Figure:* If you're selling your own presence or art — performers, speakers, trainers and others

   - *Entertainment:* If you're marketing one creation or project

So, if you're a scriptwriter, you create an Artist page to represent yourself. Then you create an Entertainment page to represent your new movie.

- *Cause or Community:* If you're a community organization, represent a political party, or are otherwise seeking to build a following for something non-commercial

You can change the page category later by clicking the Edit Page link.

4. **Select a subcategory and enter your address.**

   The subcategory is the *kind* of business you're in, such as Shopping/ Retail.

5. **Agree to the terms of service and click the Get Started button.**

   The setup wizard starts.

6. **Upload a profile picture. Then click Next.**

   The profile picture is what appears when you post or otherwise interact on Facebook. If you're not sure what to use, you can use your company logo. You can upload the image from your computer, or import it from your company website. It should be 180 x 180 pixels; if it's larger, Facebook resizes and crops it for you.

7. **Enter information about your company.**

   Enter a short description of your business, your website address, and links to your other relevant social media profiles and listings (Twitter, Google+, and Google Places). Click the Add Another Site to add additional links.

8. **Click the Save Info button.**

9. **Select your Facebook web address.**

   The first part of your Page address is www.facebook.com. But you can choose the rest of the address. Any unique text will work.

   It is *very, very* difficult to change your Facebook Page address once you select it, so be sure you have one you like.

10. **Click the Set Address button.**

After that final step, Facebook reserves your Page address and sets up the Page. Take a look at the Page, as shown in Figure 4-3. At the top is the admin panel. That lets you change your Page, view statistics, add updates, and generally check in on how things are going.

Figure 4-3:
Your new
Page, with
admin
panel.

Polishing the Page

Your Page is pretty bare. Time to give it some life. First add a cover image:

1. **Click the Add a Cover button.**

It's right under the admin panel.

2. **Select a photo.**

You can select a photo by uploading from your computer or choosing from among photos you've already uploaded. The cover image is 851 x 315 pixels. For the best result, resize it before you upload.

Choose something relevant to your business but *not a sales pitch*.

3. **Drag the image to reposition it.**

If your image is larger than the cover size, you can drag it to reposition it in the cover area.

4. **Click the Save Changes button.**

Your Page now has a cover image, as shown in Figure 4-4.

Figure 4-4:
Spoke 'n
Spoke with
a cover
image.

Now that you have a cover image, you can build your Timeline. Start by
adding status updates, photos, events, and past milestones. Showing your history gives customers a sense of your business, and gives them another way to
connect on a personal level — if a potential customer sees you were both at
the same bike rally in 1998, they're that much more inclined to stop by.

Think over your company's history, as well as your own. Add things like the
following:

*Book VII
Chapter 4*

*Navigating Top
Social Media Sites*

✦ **When you started the company:** In the Write Something area (refer to
   Figure 4-4), click the Event, Milestone icon. Then click Milestone and
   complete the small form that appears.

✦ **A first for your company:** Add when you hired your first employee,
   moved into a new office, or other events. To add a status, click in the
   Write Something area and type a description. Then click the small clock
   at the bottom left-hand corner of the status field and select the year.

✦ **Great photos and video:** If you have great photography or video that
   you'd like the world to see, add that, too. Click in the Write Something
   area, then upload a new image or video, use your webcam to shoot
   video, or upload several photos to create an album. Click the small clock
   to select the year.

Be creative! Provide as complete a narration as you can. See Figure 4-5 for the Spoke 'n Spoke Page with just a few items added to the Timeline.

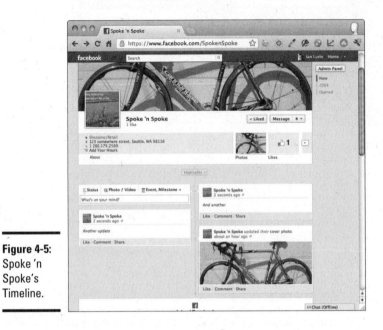

Figure 4-5:
Spoke 'n
Spoke's
Timeline.

Customizing your Page

You may, at times, want to customize your Page. Here are a few scenarios and how you can customize accordingly:

+ **You want one particular post to stay at the top of the Timeline.** Hover over the post you want to stay at the top. Click the Edit or Remove link and then click Pin to Top. Your post remains at the top for 7 days or until you unpin it.

+ **You want one post to span the entire page.** Maybe you have a single photograph that you want to show full width. Or maybe you have a post that you want to get special emphasis. One way to achieve that is to highlight the post. A highlighted post spans the entire page, instead of occupying a single column. To highlight a post, hover over it, then click the star that appears at the upper-right corner of the post.

+ **You want to change permissions.** You may want to restrict who can post to the Page's Timeline, block certain words, or change age restrictions. To do so, choose Manage⇨Edit Page in the admin panel.

✦ **You want to change your page category, description, or other basic settings.** Choose Manage⊃Edit Page⊃Basic Information in the admin panel.

✦ **You want to add other Page admins.** If you want other people to help you manage the page, you need to make them admins. Click choose Manage⊃Edit Page⊃Manage Admins in the admin panel.

Creating your own audience with Facebook applications

Facebook also lets you create custom applications, using a toolbox that Facebook provides. You can then make those applications available via the Applications area.

Examples of applications include

✦ To-do list managers

✦ Trivia tests and quizzes where you compete against other members

✦ Photo-display tools

✦ Widgets that display your latest blog or Twitter post

You can also find recipe collections, music listings, travel maps, file sharing, and applications for just about any other purpose you can think of.

Here's the gold to pan: If you can create a really fun or useful application — and then get a lot of people to use it — you can build a huge audience quickly. Successful applications can accrue 300,000 users and more. And, because you're permitted to link to your own website or Facebook Page in the application itself, the marketing opportunity is big. Sweet!

Facebook holds thousands of applications. Don't expect overnight success. It'll take persistence and a really cool little program to get the attention you want.

Again, the sneeze principle is important If one user selects a Facebook application, her Facebook friends will know and might look, too. A successful application spreads fast.

If you have a yen to create your own Facebook app, here are several tips:

+ **Hire a developer!** Unless you're a programmer yourself, you'll end up tearing your hair out using the Facebook toolset. It's good, but you need to understand basic programming to use it.

+ **Don't imitate.** You need to come up with something really unique if you're going to succeed.

+ **Test some ideas.** If you have a few close friends on Facebook, test your application with them first. If you launch it system-wide, only to discover that it doesn't work or drives users nuts, it'll be too late to recover.

+ **Include your brand.** Nothing is wrong with including your logo and a link back to your site.

+ **Integrate with your brand.** The application you build should somehow relate to your business. If you make wagons, create a little wagon-wheel game. If you make telescopes, make a constellation flash-card game.

+ **Integrate sneezability.** Include something in your application that entices users to send their score or something else to their friends. Some applications are built purely to send around.

+ **Market it.** If you have close friends on Facebook, send them a message letting them know about the new application. Install it on your profile page. And announce it on your Facebook Page. Finally, have a launch event! (Read about Facebook Events earlier in this chapter.)

Facebook is a very complex world with a lot of ways to network. This section gives you the basics. Take a look at *Facebook Marketing All-in-One For Dummies,* by Amy Porterfield, Phyllis Khare, and Andrea Vahl (published by John Wiley & Sons, Inc.), if you want a more detailed tour.

Promoting yourself with Facebook Advertising

Facebook offers a wide range of paid advertising options that you can use to build your audience. Paid ads are a little bit outside the scope of this section. But here are a few quick tips:

+ **Use ads!** Facebook ads, done right, are a fantastic deal. In the Admin panel, choose Build Audience⇨Create an Ad.

+ **Buy PPC.** Buy Facebook ads on a pay-per-click, or PPC, basis. Don't buy them on a per-impression basis. The click-through rates on Facebook tend to be very low. So PPC is far less expensive, but it will effectively get you free display ads.

+ **Use Facebook segments.** Facebook's segmentation tool is a great research tool. See the previous chapter for more information.

To find out more about Facebook ads, check out *Facebook Advertising For Dummies,* by Paul Dunay, Richard Krueger, and Joel Elad (published by John Wiley & Sons, Inc.).

Using Google+ to Rate and Rank

Google+ is a relative newcomer on the social networking scene. But unlike a bunch of false starts that Google has had in this space, Google+ seems here to stay: It's gained 100 million users in months, and Google's promoting the network using its dominance of search.

Like Facebook, Google+ lets you post photos, videos, and text. It has both profiles and pages. But it has a couple of unique features:

✦ **Circles:** You can create and share *circles,* which are groups of similar people that you follow.

✦ **Search results:** Google displays Google+ results from folks you follow right in Google search results, *and* displays relevant pages and people in the upper-right corner of some search results pages.

That last item is crucial. If you read the SEO minibook (Book II), you know how important, and how difficult, SEO can be. Google+ may offer you a shortcut past ranking pages and into the top 10, as shown in Figure 4-6.

**Book VII
Chapter 4**

**Navigating Top
Social Media Sites**

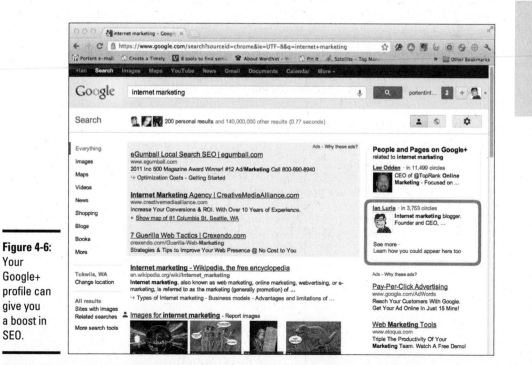

Figure 4-6:
Your
Google+
profile can
give you
a boost in
SEO.

To get started on Google+, log into your Google account, click your user-name in the top-right corner and click the Join Google+ button. Enter your name and click the Upgrade button. Then follow these steps to set up your profile:

1. **Log in to your Google account.**

2. **Click your username link at the top left-hand corner of the screen.**

3. **Click Profile and then Edit Profile.**

4. **Click the About tab.**

   The About page holds all your essential information: Other sites to which you contribute, where you went to school, where you work, a description of yourself, and settings for who can or cannot find you in Google+.

5. **Write a detailed description of yourself, your interests, and what you're going to write about most often.**

   Google+ provides prompts for information. Provide links to all your other pages and social media profiles, and fully describe yourself. Google uses this information when determining whether to show you in search results.

6. **Click Done Editing to save your work.**

Google+ has a company page feature. You can create a page for your brand or company. However, these pages can't circle other people the way personal profiles do. Start with a personal Google+ profile where you can talk about what you do in your business. Use that to build a network first. Then you can build a company page later. Note that building a company page on Google+ is nearly identical to building a personal profile.

Now you have a profile. It's time to do something with it.

Circling friends on Google+

Google+ is built around the idea of circles. A *circle* is a group of related pro-files or brand pages. You can create circles around any topics or ideas you want and then put profiles into one or more of those circles. You can make posts visible to a single circle, all your circles, or the public.

If you're running a bicycle shop, you might create a circle of other folks interesting in cycling. Then, when you post something about cycling or your shop, you can send it to that circle, and they'll all receive the update. It's a great way to contact colleagues and customers in a conversational way.

To add someone to a circle, follow these steps:

1. **Find someone you want to follow.**

   Go to your home Google+ page. Search for a favorite topic, or use the Suggestions list on the right side of your screen.

2. **Hover over Add to Circles under the person or page name.**

3. **Choose a circle:**

   • *Add to an existing circle:* Select the circle to which you want to add this profile or page. You can add one person to multiple circles. These circles are yours alone. Unless you share them, no one else can see who's in them.

   • *To create a new circle,* click the Create New circle link, as shown in Figure 4-7. Type the circle name and click the Create button. Google+ creates the new circle and adds the profile or page to it.

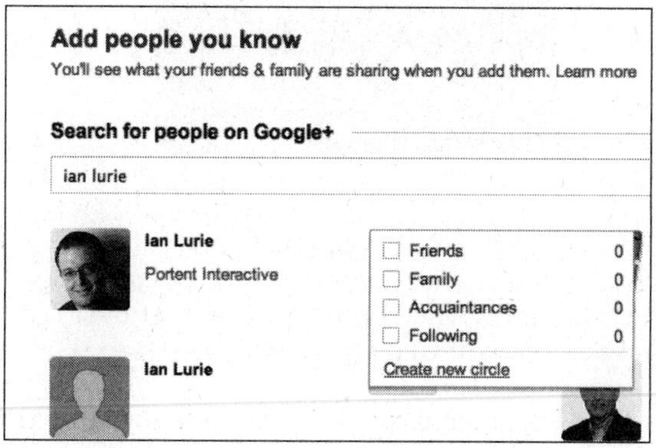

Add people you know

You'll see what your friends & family are sharing when you add them. Learn more

Search for people on Google+

ian lurie

	Ian Lurie Portent Interactive	☐ Friends	0
		☐ Family	0
		☐ Acquaintances	0
		☐ Following	0
	Ian Lurie	Create new circle	

Figure 4-7: Creating a circle on Google+.

Book VII Chapter 4

Navigating Top Social Media Sites

Watching your Google+ stream

Posts from profiles you've circled show up in your *stream.* That's the first page you see when you log in to Google+, as shown in Figure 4-8.

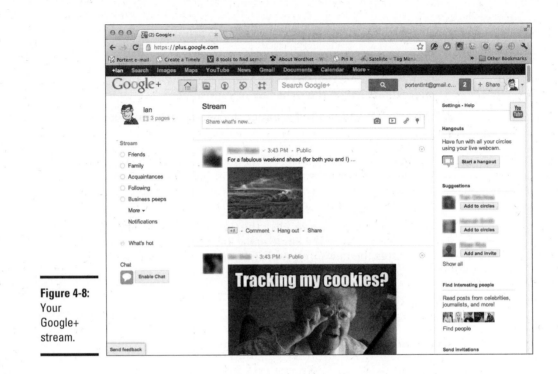

Figure 4-8:
Your
Google+
stream.

You can comment on, share, or +1 posts that appear in your stream. When you do, the person who posted the content receives a notification. If you comment, all the other folks who commented on that post receive a notification via their Google+ account that you commented, too.

That tends to lead to long discussions over interesting stuff. Often, you see thousands of comments on a single post. It's a very powerful toolset for interacting with other people.

Posting content to Google+

If you want to grow your Google+ audience, though, you need to post. Like Facebook, Google+ lets you post text, links to other content on the web, photos, and videos.

To post, follow these steps:

1. **Click in the Share What's New field at the top of your stream.**
2. **Type your message.**
3. **Select the circles that you want to share this message with.**

4. **Click the Share button.**

   Your shared content appears in the home streams of everyone within the circles you selected, as well as on your profile page.

The Google+ interface is still changing daily. Click around and explore. You'll probably find a bunch of new tools that didn't exist when this was written.

Networking for Business on LinkedIn

LinkedIn is an entirely different kind of social network. Built entirely as a vehicle with which businesspeople connect and interact, it functions based on connections rather than friends. Although this might sound like a purely semantic difference, it's not, and here's why:

✦ **LinkedIn restricts whom you can add as a connection.** You need to be able to indicate how you know that person before you can even attempt to connect.

✦ **LinkedIn includes recommendations that you can get from colleagues and clients.** Those recommendations show on your profile page.

✦ **Your profile includes your work history.**

✦ **People are automatically grouped by company.**

✦ **You can't contact people who aren't in your network directly except through InMail,** for which LinkedIn charges a fee.

✦ **Companies can get their own separate profile pages.**

Use LinkedIn if

✦ Your company provides professional services.

✗ Your clients are other companies.

✦ You're a consultant of almost any kind.

✦ You want to focus on quality connections, not quantity.

You can't customize the look and feel of your profile page on LinkedIn. However, completeness is important — even more important than on Facebook — because LinkedIn is driven by one-to-one connections between individuals, and those connections are typically formed based on work history, location, and so on. It's a pure business-networking environment.

Figure 4-9 shows a completed LinkedIn page. It includes work history, recent updates, recent presentations, connections, and recommendations.

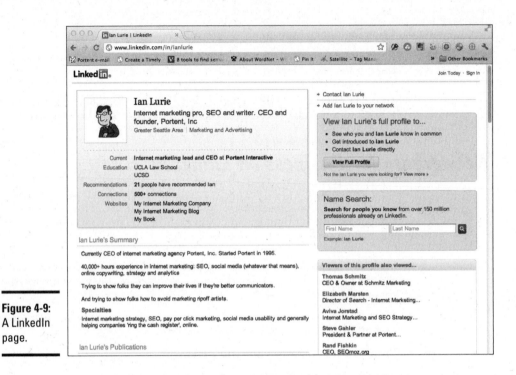

Figure 4-9:
A LinkedIn
page.

To give yourself the best chance of succeeding on LinkedIn, remember these five items:

✦ **Quality:** A few quality connections will take you a lot farther than dozens of lousy ones. Connect with folks you already know, or have someone else introduce you using the Introduction feature on LinkedIn.

✦ **Recommendations:** Get recommendations when you can. They look great on your profile page, and many potential clients will research you via LinkedIn.

✦ **Applications:** Use LinkedIn applications to integrate other social networks (like SlideShare) into your profile page.

✦ **Groups:** The LinkedIn Groups feature works much like Facebook, but LinkedIn groups focus entirely on professional networking.

✦ **Answers:** Use LinkedIn Answers to provide or seek advice. If you provide great information, folks will mark your answer as best. Get enough of those, and you'll be tagged as having expertise in a particular subject.

LinkedIn is a very specialized network. Don't go in there expecting to sell 400 insurance policies. Set up your profile with the expectation that you can make valuable, long-lasting business connections.

↳ *Business Connections*
with young profession

Playing the Social News Game

If any social media makes you grind your teeth down to the nubs, social news sites are the ones. Sites such as Digg and reddit can generate an avalanche of visitors. Stories that make the first page on social news sites aren't just sneezed; they become a full-on epidemic.

Great, you say. Sign me up!

Not so fast. *Everyone* knows the power these sites have. When you submit a story to a social news site, you're joining thousands of others who, at that very moment, are taking their shot at social media stardom, too.

If you're going to try to get a hit in social news, bear in mind the following tenets:

+ **Assume that you're going to fail.** A lot. You need to keep trying.

+ **Commit the time.** Count on spending at least a half-hour per day, for at least a few weeks, just submitting content you find. By submitting lots of content, you can build your reputation on the network, just like on bookmarking sites.

+ **Build a very complete profile page.** When you submit content, other site participants might want to check you out to make sure that you're a real person. Spammers abound on social news sites, so folks are bound to be suspicious. A complete profile puts their minds at ease.

+ **Be prepared for a lot of traffic.** If you succeed, you could get server-crushing traffic. Make sure you're on a web hosting provider that can handle a burst of traffic, and have a backup plan just in case your site is overwhelmed.

+ **Build a network of friends** whom you can directly contact when you submit something new to say, "Hey, what do you think?"

Getting "reddited"

reddit.com is a phenomenon all its own. Making a hit on reddit requires special care:

+ **Build your reputation first.** Spend a *lot* of time building your reputation first. Seek out and submit new news, hilarious videos, and other content the community will appreciate.

+ **Get some friends.** Build a good circle of fans to whom you can shout when you submit something really juicy.

   ✦ **Copywrite creatively.** Write a great title for your reddit submission. *Bicycle breaks 60 mph* isn't as good as *Flaming tires: A really fast bike.*

   ✦ **Use link bait.** Write content that's so compelling that folks feel they have to link to it and share it. Obey all the rules of link bait as described in Book II, Chapter 7.

Even if you do everything right, reddit's first page might prove impossible to crack. After all, it is one of the busiest social voting sites on the web. However, the potential traffic often makes trying worth it.

Submit your content to reddit if any of the following are true:

   ✦ You have truly newsworthy content.

   ✦ You have truly funny content.

   ✦ The story you're submitting is breaking news.

If you want examples of successful stories, look no further than the reddit homepage.

Behaving yourself

Trying to fool the social news sites by having everyone in your office vote at once or by setting up 20 different accounts so that you can vote for yourself more than once is tempting. Believe it or not, though, you're not the first person to have thought of that. It's not a smooth move, and here's why: The users on social news and voting sites *hate* anything resembling inauthentic content. They will react strongly, and they'll give you more negative press than you thought possible. It's not worth a few thousand extra visits.

Avoid doing anything that seems like cheating. These sites are very savvy and will likely ban you the moment you misbehave.

Social news is all about the sneeze principle. You don't have to do any additional work: The whole point of social news sites is to separate the sneezable from the not-so-contagious content.

Growing Your Business with Media Sharing

Media-sharing sites allow you to upload videos, photos, or audio files to a single location where others can see them. These sites offer a chance to put your work in front of large audiences, prompt discussion, and drive traffic to your business.

Use media-sharing sites if the following items pertain to you:

✦ You create any form of video or shoot photos in the course of your business.

✦ You're comfortable putting that content in front of hundreds, thousands, or hundreds of thousands of viewers.

✦ You don't mind that content being reused or redistributed. Although you can control this to some extent, it's bound to happen.

Spreading the word on YouTube

YouTube works a lot like Flickr, only for video. You upload a video to the site, give it a description, and tag it with keywords, and then the rest of the community gets to take a look.

A popular video on YouTube can get tens of thousands of views (or even hundreds of thousands). But, as you've likely figured out by now, getting a big hit on any social network, YouTube included, takes a lot of work.

Use YouTube if you

✦ Have preexisting video content, and all you have to do is upload it

✦ Have entertainment-based content

✦ Want to introduce a wide audience to training, branding, or other video

✦ Are going to produce a series of short videos

YouTube has a few rules you should know about, too:

✦ Videos must be ten minutes or shorter.

✦ Videos must be 20GB or smaller.

✦ You must have permission to publish the video on YouTube!

Here are some tips for YouTube success:

✦ **Keep it short.** The most successful videos on YouTube are two to three minutes long. Obviously, if you're doing a training piece, your video might have to be longer, but try to create a series of short videos instead if you can.

✦ **Make friends.** It's easy to forget that YouTube is a social network and just start uploading videos. Find folks who create great content, make friends with them, and comment on their videos. They'll reciprocate.

✦ **Complete your profile.** Just like on any other social network, a complete profile will establish trust when other users come looking.

✦ **Respond to comments!** If someone comments on your video, reply. Say, "Thanks" or "Good point" or whatever's relevant. It's called *social* media for a reason.

✦ **Write a good title for your video.** The title is what gets folks to watch. *My road trip* isn't as good as *Pulled Over in Louisiana.*

✦ **Write a good description.** A keyword-rich description increases your chance of a good ranking in Google's blended search results. See Book II, Chapter 5 for more about keywords and blended search.

✦ **When you post a new video, let your friends know.** YouTube partly ranks videos according to the number of views and view *velocity* (the rate at which you're getting those views). If you can get a little mob watching the video, it'll give you a boost.

There are other great video sharing services. Take a look at Vimeo (`http://vimeo.com`). Vimeo is second only to YouTube, and provides enhanced pro accounts that let you control who can see your video, customize the embedding tool, and do a few other things that can provide a more professional result.

Sharing content on presentation-sharing services

Presentation-sharing services let you publish your best slideshows in the same way that you might post videos of your speeches on a video site. Examples include SlideShare (`www.slideshare.com`), SlideSnack (`www.slidesnack.com`), and SecondSlide (`www.secondslide.com`).

What sets these tools apart is that they let you upload your slides directly from PowerPoint, Keynote, or Adobe PDF and then turn them into online slideshows that folks can page through. Then, you can embed those presentations in your blog, your website, or social media profiles on sites like LinkedIn.

These services turn your slides into sharable social media content. Give them a try.

Talking in Discussion Forums

Discussion forums have been around for a long time. They predate the Internet, in fact, forming the backbone of many bulletin board services (BBS) that people connected to using a phone modem that looked like two huge suction cups.

Include discussion forums in your marketing plan if *(young family)*

✦ You have a small, concentrated niche audience

✦ You're a leading expert and want to demonstrate that fact

✦ You want to reach and contact individuals based on their questions

Forums don't have the same sneeze potential that Facebook might. That's okay. To their advantage, forums let you talk one on one with your most interested audience.

Forums are versatile, cover a huge array of topics, and often offer the most receptive audience. Sites like WebmasterWorld.com (in Figure 4-10) focus on Internet topics. Others, like CyclingForums.com (in Figure 4-11), focus on a single sport or hobby.

Finally, forums such as Google and Yahoo! Groups cater to every imaginable topic.

Forums are also very tight communities. If you barge in and start promoting your product or service, you'll receive a healthy serving of scorn and dislike.

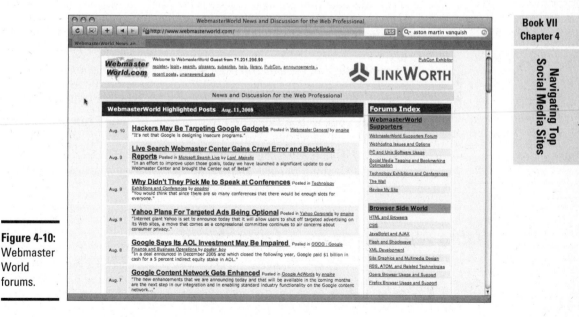

Figure 4-10: Webmaster World forums.

Figure 4-11:
Cycling
Forums.
com.

You can succeed, though, if you follow a few basic rules:

✦ **Choose relevant forums.** Don't select a discussion forum based on traffic potential or page rank. Pick one in which you'll enjoy participating.

✦ **Contribute; don't spam.** You need to spend some time *lurking,* that is, seeing what folks are saying and what's okay or not okay behavior on that forum. Then you can post messages that other members will appreciate.

✦ **Include your web address and information in your signature line.** Also include your Facebook, Twitter, or other addresses if permitted. That way, every post can provide a way for readers to contact you.

✦ **Start by replying to existing threads,** not creating new ones. It's a good way to get introduced to the community.

Using Microblogs as a Launchpad

Microblogs are a social media vehicle by which you can post lots of short statements (usually a 140-character limit) about what you're doing, interesting links, and other trivia as you go about your day.

Typical microblogs support posting from your cellphone or your computer, so it's easy to send an occasional message.

Twitter, shown in Figure 4-12, is currently the best-known microblogging platform.

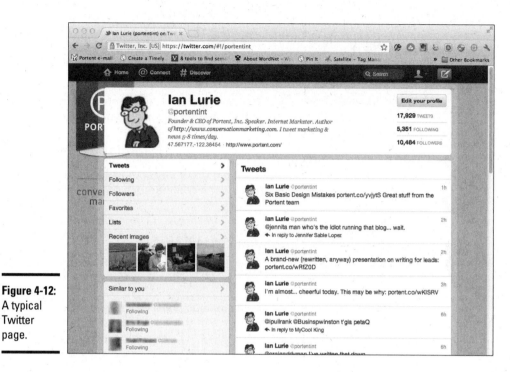

Book VII
Chapter 4

Navigating Top
Social Media Sites

Figure 4-12:
A typical
Twitter
page.

Other microblogs include Tumblr (www.tumblr.com), FriendFeed (http://friendfeed.com), and Identi.ca (http://identi.ca).

In addition, networking sites like LinkedIn integrate microblogging into your profile: You can do short, Twitter-like posts right to your profile page, providing your followers and friends with short updates.

Building a microblog following

You need to accumulate a lot of followers. Then you can capitalize on that to launch a new product, blog post, or site if you follow a few basic steps:

✦ **Set up a complete profile.** The more detail you provide, the more easily others can decide whether they want to keep in touch.

✦ **Follow others.** Look around. Who are some of the biggest participants in the community? Follow them by clicking Follow or a similar button in their profile. They'll likely follow you, too, at some point.

✦ **Announce that you joined.** If you have a blog, let everyone know that you just joined the microblog and provide your account name. Existing members who see that will probably follow you, too.

✦ **Contribute.** If you find an interesting link, have a bit of trivia, or just make a funny observation, post it! Microblogs are very informal. Make sure that if your cellphone has a web browser, you set up mobile access as well.

✦ **Reply.** If someone you're following posts something that catches your attention, let him know.

✦ **Be consistent.** Set a goal to make four to six microblog posts daily. This takes about two minutes, *total,* and you can accumulate a nice following with that goal.

After you accumulate a following, make sure that you announce new blog posts or other important news — and don't forget to include a link. If you announce one or two items per day, the community won't just respond — they'll appreciate it!

Avoiding microblogging overload

Microblogging *can* become a huge time-waster. It's easy to idly flip through posts with no real aim.

Avoid this kind of overload by disciplining yourself to stick with the routine you set. (Read about this in Chapter 3 of this minibook.) Set times when you'll post. Then keep Twitter (or whatever other site you're using) closed the rest of the time.

If you find that you post a lot, try a tool that lets you post without logging into the microblog. HootSuite (www.hootsuite.com), for example, lets you post to multiple microblogs using its toolset. Figure 4-13 shows HootSuite, as well as an example of sending a post to Twitter and LinkedIn using HootSuite.

Figure 4-13: Using HootSuite to post.

Don't let microblogging disrupt the rest of your work. It's exactly the kind of small task that can really sap your efficiency if you let it. Try to be efficient.

Building a Good Reputation on Social Q&A Sites

Q&A sites are a great place to build your reputation around a specific discipline. Figure 4-14 shows a typical Quora answer page, with a list of questions begging for answers.

Figure 4-14:
Quora.

**Book VII
Chapter 4**

**Navigating Top
Social Media Sites**

Include a Q&A site like Quora or Stack Overflow in your social media marketing plan if you

+ **Like answering questions.** This sounds painfully obvious, but that's all you'll do on Quora, so make sure that you're going to enjoy it.

+ **Have expertise to offer.**

+ **Have an hour a week to dedicate to answering questions.**

Pick your topics carefully. Answer if and only if you have what you think is a good answer. If you just throw up a useless answer, you'll draw the ire of the community.

Here are some tips for Quora success:

+ **Set aside an hour a week to answer questions.** This seems like a lot, but you'll need the time if you're going to build a good profile.

+ **Vary the topics where you answer questions.** If you're a consultant, you can answer questions in your area of expertise. But you can also offer advice about owning your own business or about your favorite sport. Mix things up a bit.

✦ **When appropriate, include a link to relevant resources.** Try to reference your own content occasionally if it will really help the reader. Those links will drive traffic, support your statements, and add authority to your answers.

✦ **Ask questions, too!** It's always a good idea to ask an occasional question. If nothing else, you experience the other side of Quora, and those lessons can be valuable when you're answering.

✦ **Don't be glib or nasty.** If someone asks a question and you think it's silly, *don't answer it.* Also, don't be nasty. Bad social media karma will come back around on you.

Unleashing the Power of Niche Sites

This chapter covers some of the major social media sites. Don't overlook, though, the many sites devoted to individual professions, hobbies, sports, and lifestyles.

Use the search engines to track down other niche sites: Type your topic, followed by *social network, bookmarking,* or *forums,* and you'll probably find quite a few sites.

Niche sites may be a better use of your time than the larger social sites. Apply what you read in this chapter to those sites, and you'll reach a smaller but more focused audience.

How do you know whether to use niche sites? Ask yourself these questions:

✦ Is my market very small? If yes, check for niche sites.

✦ Am I finding my audience on major social media sites? If no, start looking to see whether you can find a relevant niche site somewhere.

✦ Is my time really tight? If you can't even find a few minutes a day for social media marketing, a niche site might let you make more efficient use of your limited time.

Don't neglect the major sites if you don't have to. But keep in mind that you always have options, and remember that new social media sites are springing up every day.

Chapter 5: Building Your Network

In This Chapter

✔ **Finding and keeping friends**

✔ **Expanding your network with questions and answers**

✔ **Behaving yourself in social media**

To this point in this minibook, a lot of the mechanics of social media have been covered: setting up profiles, talking to your friends and followers, and posting new items. In this chapter, you see how to actually meet and keep friends — and how to deal with the occasional foot-in-mouth incident.

Finding Friends

All social media websites work on the principle of friends. In social media, a *friend* is someone who keeps tabs on what you're doing on that particular site. The mechanism might vary, as you can see in Figure 5-1, but the principle remains the same. More friends means a bigger network, which means more people to pass your message along. That means more people to sell to, of course. But more importantly, it means that you have a larger audience of potential fans of you and your brand. They can tell other folks about you and multiply the number of people you can reach directly and indirectly.

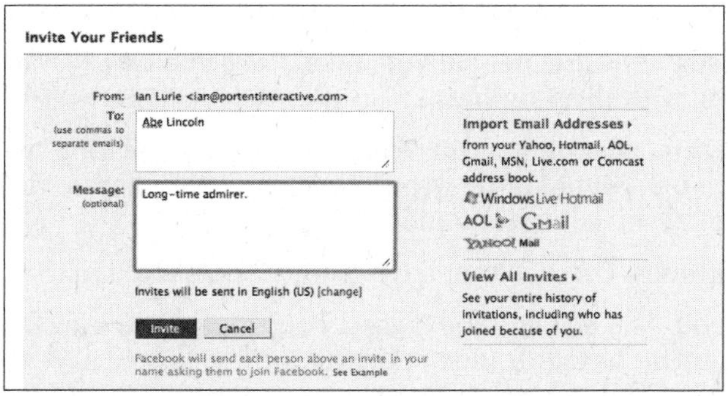

Figure 5-1:
Adding friends on Facebook.

Invite Your Friends

From: Ian Lurie <ian@portentinteractive.com>
To: Abe Lincoln
(use commas to separate emails)

Message: Long-time admirer.
(optional)

Invites will be sent in English (US) [change]

Invite   Cancel

Facebook will send each person above an invite in your name asking them to join Facebook. See Example

Import Email Addresses ›
from your Yahoo, Hotmail, AOL, Gmail, MSN, Live.com or Comcast address book.

Windows Live Hotmail
AOL Gmail
Yahoo! Mail

View All Invites ›
See your entire history of invitations, including who has joined because of you.

✦ **On social networks, such as Facebook,** friends receive updates when their friends write a note, make a blog post, or take some other action. They can also send messages to each other.

✦ **On bookmarking sites, such as StumbleUpon or Delicious,** friends can share bookmarks and pass really interesting bookmarks to each other.

✦ **On social news sites, such as Digg,** friends can "shout" to each other about interesting stories.

✦ **On microblogs, such as Twitter,** friends (*followers*) see other friends' posts.

✦ **On media-sharing sites, such as YouTube and Flickr,** friends can send each other videos.

You can read about all the preceding sites in Chapter 1 of this minibook.

Having a network of friends is how you really make social media marketing work. Friends are your "sneezers," which you can also read about in Chapter 1 of this minibook: They pass along your message. Here's how you find friends on any social media site:

✦ **After you set up your profile, search for groups or content on the site that matches your interests or marketing goals.** For example, you can look for Internet marketing groups or advertising and marketing posts. You're interested in marketing your business, and these groups are a great resource.

✦ **Invite the people who are participating in groups of interest to be your friends.** On microblogs, follow the people you find interesting.

✦ **Check your social media desktop.** When stories, articles, or posts catch your eye, see whether the authors are members of the social media sites that you work on. If they are, invite them to be your friends or follow them.

✦ **Get used to asking people you meet, "Are you on ___?" and then connecting with them online.**

✦ **Post early, post often.** You're probably tired of hearing "write interesting stuff," but it's true. When you post great photos, videos, and thoughts, you get friends and followers.

✦ **Join groups.** On sites that have groups, you should join.

✦ **Latch on.** You *can* find the biggest contributors on a given network and try to friend or follow them, too. But they will likely have thousands, if not tens of thousands, of messages and friends. You'll have to get through the clutter.

How many friends do you need?

You can't know how many friends you need to accumulate before you can really spread a message. One friend who has 1,200 other friends might have more than enough. Just take it a step at a time, and try to accumulate and keep friends who'll stick around.

Keeping Friends

After you get friends, how do you keep them? Some friends might stay with you because they're simply too busy to remove you from their list. But you can take positive steps to keep friends around:

✦ **Update.** Remember your social media routine? Stick to it. Make a post, even if it's just a sentence or two, or a link that you came across. Those contributions will show up in your friends' updates, and these friends will remember who you are. And of course, they might pass the updates along, getting you even more friends.

✦ **Reply.** If friends send you something — a link, note, photo, or something else — reply to them. Make sure that they know you received it, and what you thought.

✦ **Remember.** If you're on a social network, you likely have tools that report others' birthdays and other special dates. A quick Happy Birthday note can go a long way to cementing a social media friendship.

✦ **Curate.** If you see something on another website or blog, or shared by someone in your network, and you think it'll be useful to your followers, share it. This is *content curation,* and it's one of social media's most powerful uses. Do it right and you'll gain a huge following — you'll become a librarian and commentator for thousands of people.

✦ **Behave.** Read the rest of this chapter for more information about this, but you must respect others.

Expanding Your Network with Questions and Answers

You can attract a lot of followers and friends by asking the right questions. Sites and services (such as LinkedIn, Twitter, Plurk, and Yahoo! Answers) are particularly good places to try this strategy. A good question can be as interesting as a good answer. Just remember the sneeze principle; hop to

Chapter 1 of this minibook if you haven't read about this yet. You need to write the question in such a way that it encourages folks to pass it along.

> **Sniffle.** "Does anyone know about Internet marketing?"
>
> [**A-CHOO!** "I own a bicycle shop and want to market it online. Anyone]
> have advice or know someone who does?"

Suddenly you have a winner. This question is crafted well because it

✦ **Is specific to an interest**

Cyclists, other shop owners, and even other small business owners will pay attention.

✦ **Invites others to respond**

✦ **Invites others to pass it along**

By hitting these three points, you're enhancing the community *and* attracting others at the same time. Win-win.

Don't become a question machine. Ask questions when you have them, rather than from some need to attract attention. Remember what it's like when a little kid keeps asking, "Why?" every time you speak? That's how other users feel when you start deluging them with questions.

Of course, another great way to grow your network is to provide answers to some of those great questions. You have to accomplish two things if you're going to answer questions and win friends:

✦ **Find questions that need answering,** even if the questioner isn't your friend. Yahoo! Answers and LinkedIn do this for you. Other sites, such as Twitter and Facebook, aren't as easy.

✦ **Provide a really great answer.** Also provide a way for the questioner to follow up if necessary.

Finding questions

Sites that aren't specifically designed for question and answer don't necessarily hide questions, but they can make them hard to find. Here are a few tips for finding questions:

✦ **Facebook:** Join groups and look in the discussions for each group. That's where most will go looking for answers.

✦ **Twitter:** Use Twitter's search service, `search.twitter.com`, to search for key terms. For example, searching for *seo question* can net you 10 to 20 good questions right away.

✦ **YouTube:** Search the comments on the site by using YouTube's built-in search tool. Then answer questions with another comment.

Make great answers

Your answer should be very clear, offer steps to a solution, and/or invite the questioner to contact you directly if you can't easily answer the question without more information or without more room for text. Twitter, for example, allows only 140 characters per post. Here's a good example of an answer that has a good chance of gaining you a friend:

> *Hi John – I suggest starting out with a Kevlar-belted road tire first. They're a little slower, but they're nearly flat-proof. Try the Armadillo, or maybe the ReallyFlatProof106. If you have other questions, let me know: Bikerguy123*

Don't take it personally when someone doesn't say, "Thanks." It's okay, in terms of Internet etiquette; accept the answer and move on.

Obeying the (Unspoken) Rules

Here are a few unspoken social media rules:

Don't Use Crass Promotion

If you find yourself writing something like "10% off sale on my site! Come now!" pinch yourself and delete your post. This kind of thing will only alienate your friends. It might even lead to penalties from the site owners.

Promoting yourself is okay. Just keep it a bit lower-key. Something like the following is generally acceptable:

> *Shameless plug: I just published a new book about Internet marketing. Please have a look at www.mybookwebsite.com.*

The following is not acceptable, especially if you repeat it ten times per day:

> *Buy my new book! Learn how to earn millions online! www.mybook website.com.*

Don't Post Angry

No one can follow this rule 100 percent of the time. Eventually, someone will say something that really makes you angry, and you'll retort and click Submit before you can stop yourself.

If you snap back at someone, *everyone sees it.* It can reflect on you, your company, and your entire online identity.

Wherever possible, avoid the angry post. If you're inexorably drawn into an online shouting match, try these strategies:

✦ **Take 5. Take 10. Take 100.** Turn off the computer. Go outside. You'll be surprised how minor the offending post or comment seems later.

✦ **Go to the source.** Contact the person via private or direct message. Instead of a slap fight, try asking, "Hey, did I just misunderstand?" or "What'd I do?"

✦ **Vent in private.** Get it out of your system by first writing any angry reply in a word processor. Then step back, take a breath, and edit it to be more diplomatic. Only then, post it.

Do Apologize

No matter what you do, at some point, you're going to shove your foot firmly into your mouth. Social media is still *social* — you're often talking to people all over the planet, and misunderstandings happen. If you offend, overreact, or just forget about a request someone made, just let him know that you're sorry. Social media is all about online karma: The community will generally remember how you behave, but no one expects perfection. A little humility goes a long way.

Do Be a Good Citizen

Help others if they have questions about how to use the site or network. Lend a hand, just as others probably helped you when you signed up.

Do Add Value

Contribute to the community. If you're microblogging, contribution can be as simple as an interesting link or video. On social networks, support the groups to which you belong by answering questions and inviting others to join. You don't have to be the top expert in your field to add value. Value can mean humor, a sympathetic ear, or an interesting link, or just pointing a few people in the right direction.

Knowing When to Stop

Sometimes you can overstay your welcome. Here are a few sure signs that you should take a break and stop sending a specific person or group messages:

✦ **The individual stops replying.** Don't take it personally, but do leave that person alone for a few days.

✦ **A lot of friends or followers start unsubscribing or otherwise going away.** Again, take a break. Look at what you're writing. Any chance that a change is in order?

✦ **You get a warning.** This *should* be obvious: If a site moderator or other person in authority says, "Cool it!" you should listen.

✦ **You feel like you're working really hard to come up with something to say.** Conversations can get strained and uncomfortable online, too. But you can walk away without offending anyone.

Social media communities are very tolerant. It's unlikely that you'll ever overstay your welcome. Just try to be somewhat self-aware, and take a break when you need it.

Chapter 6: Creating a Winning Social Media Campaign

In This Chapter

✔ **Marketing by providing tools**

✔ **Marketing by providing content**

✔ **Marketing by providing entertainment**

✔ **Leveraging your network**

✔ **Addressing harm to your reputation**

Social media marketing is more than making friends and expanding your network. At some point, you need to get your message out.

The balance between marketing and not alienating the community can be tricky. Social network participants don't like it when one of their supposed friends suddenly starts hawking items for sale or charging for answers to questions.

The key to social media marketing success is to treat the social network how you would any other community. To that end, you need to

✦ Provide compelling tools, content, and entertainment that entice others to spread the word

✦ Use your[existing network]to help kick-start your efforts

✦ Correct false rumors or statements about your company, without getting defensive

And that's what this chapter covers.

The Importance of Creating a Winning Social Media Campaign

Compare these two scenarios. Think about what kind of web marketer you want to be — and which results you want.

Scenario 1

You're walking down the street. Someone wearing a sandwich board steps in front of you and shoves a flyer in your face, advertising a new *a cappella* singing group that's just released a CD.

There you were, walking along and minding your own business, and now this stranger is trying to pressure you into buying a CD or going to a performance. You were just walking down the street, enjoying a nice day. So, how do you feel? Intruded upon, probably.

Scenario 2

You're walking down the same street, enjoying the weather. A small knot of people ahead catches your interest. You walk up. In the middle of the crowd, you see three performers singing *a cappella.* They're brilliant. You listen, and more people show up because of the growing crowd. The group has its CD on display, right there. Even though you don't buy a copy, you walk away smiling, and you might even mention the group to your friends later that day.

Scenario 1 is, in many ways, traditional interruption-based marketing, which works to a point but generally alienates those who aren't really in buying mode. Even worse, this type of marketing especially alienates folks who feel they're part of a community that doesn't include any agreement to buy.

Scenario 2 is the classic social media–marketing technique. The *a cappella* trio gave a free performance. Passersby could stop and listen or ignore them. Those who enjoyed the music stuck around, which caught the attention of others. The crowd that grew enjoyed the music without obligation. *Some* of the crowd certainly bought the CD. And others told their friends about the group. That's social media marketing at its best.

Social media marketing has been around a lot longer than the Internet. Scenario 2 really is social media, which has been around since we could speak to each other in grunts.

Marketing by Providing Tools

Social media is the perfect place to help your company by helping others. Say that a bicycle shop is located in your community called Harrison's Bikes. In the summer, the bike shop does a brisk business selling bikes and helmets, and doing repairs. As fall approaches, though, business slows. People are still riding their bikes, but they don't think the bike shop has anything to offer them when they get ready for the long, cold winter.

Harrison could stand out on the street, stapling flyers to telephone poles. He could also buy an ad in the local newspaper advertising a sale on rain fenders (with free installation, even!).

Instead, Harrison starts riding with a few of the local bicycle clubs. He puts his best rain fender on his bike. He doesn't blurt out, "Hey! Look at my cool rain fender!" But other riders see the fender, which really is pretty cool looking. They ask him about it. They already know who he is and that he owns a bike shop. He explains that this new fender is for serious riders (like them) who don't want to look ridiculous but still want to commute to work and end up not splattered with mud. He lets them know he's installing them for free this week.

The next day, a few riders show up at Harrison's shop. They buy the new fenders and let him install them. While they're there, they notice some good rain gear and buy that, too. (Cyclists are like that.) More importantly, when they ride into work that Monday, their cycling coworkers ask about the fender. Harrison's new customers spread the word.

This is a perfect example of marketing by providing tools. Although providing free tools sometimes helps, you can do just fine by providing solutions and tools that cost money if you make the offer compelling enough.

What's important here is that Harrison didn't push his product. He simply went into the community and *used* the product.

A successful tools-based campaign should

+ **Offer a tool that's simple to use:** The whole community should be able to understand the value and use it. That's why Harrison installed the fenders for his customers.

+ **Have very few barriers to entry:** Having few barriers might mean that the tool is free or that it's immediately available. Just don't make the community work for it. Again, Harrison installed the fenders for customers. That eliminated any excuse for not participating.

+ **Be contagious:** If you haven't been there already, skip to Chapter 1 of this minibook to read about the sneeze principle. Something about the tool must be spread (disseminated) easily. In Harrison's case, every customer who bought the fenders became an advertisement. Other cyclists saw them, and when asked, the new fender owner told them to go to Harrison's shop.

+ **Be honest and straightforward:** Any tools that appear to have an ulterior motive —(such as harvesting e-mails for an unrelated campaign or getting people's contact information when it's not necessary — will fail.]

Email lists

Here's a real-world example of a free tool that helped launch a blog to a large community: In a nutshell, it's a simple online calculator that lets visitors figure the value of a click to their website; see Figure 6-1.

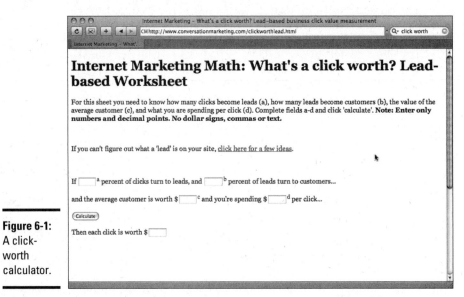

Figure 6-1:
A click-worth calculator.

Notice a few things about this tool:

✦ **It's very simple.** Plug in a few numbers, and you're all set.

✦ **It has no barriers to entry.** The user doesn't have to log in, provide any information, or do anything else to use this tool.

✦ **It's contagious (in a good way).** It's easy to forward a link to this page, and it offers a tool (albeit simple) that's something every online marketer needs.

✦ **It's straightforward.** No tricks here. Plug in your data and get the result. Come back as often as you want.

Don't have any tools in mind? If not, that's okay. You can do the same thing with content. Keep reading.

Social Media Marketing with Content

The *a cappella* singers described at the beginning of the chapter didn't offer any tools, per se. Instead, they put their content in front of the audience.

You can do the same thing: Create informative or entertaining content, put it in front of a community, and then let those folks spread the word.

If you haven't read about Harrison and his bike shop, hop back to the preceding section and then come back here. The fender-installation campaign (via a tool) was successful, but a lot of cyclists simply pack up their bicycles for the winter. They don't need fenders. Their primary concern is staying in shape during the winter.

So, Harrison creates a small booklet, entitled "Summer Fitness, Winter Months," that tells cyclists how they can stay in shape during the winter by doing a few simple exercises and also by buying a stationary trainer. (The stationary trainer turns a regular bicycle into a stationary bike so that you can ride your bike indoors.)

He sets a small stack of the booklets next to the cash register in his store. He also attends the monthly meetings of a few local bicycle clubs and does a few free lunch-hour classes at his shop. Harrison tells the community members how they can stay in shape during the winter, points out the equipment they need, and explains why this is a good alternative to the gym for those who don't like lifting weights.

As a result, he sells stationary trainers. He also gets a reputation among local cyclists as someone who genuinely knows them and helps out.

All this was done without creating a tool. All Harrison did was deliver some useful content.

The hallmarks of a successful content campaign

Not all content is made for social media. In the preceding example of Harrison and his booklet, Harrison stuck to some basic principles:

✦ **Don't sell!** Your content shouldn't be an overt advertisement for one product or your services. Inform and teach, but don't advertise. Harrison demonstrated relevant equipment, but he never told folks where or how to buy.

✦ **Be relevant.** Focus on your audience's immediate needs. Harrison focused on indoor training because winter is coming. In May, this training won't help.

✦ **Be available.** Your content has to be easy to find and access. Harrison went to other people's places of work and bicycle clubs. He offered training at his shop during lunch.

✦ **Don't try tricks.** Don't try to get information that's not required. It's tempting to collect e-mail addresses, but that's not your mission here.

(Handwritten margin notes: "Inform r / Teach Do no AD", "immediate", "immediate needs")

A bike shop is great, you say, but we're talking about the Internet. Fair enough. Here's a real-world online example. This blog post, shown in Figure 6-2, is about a sneaky way to trap plagiarists.

common sense internet strategies
conversation marketing
with Ian Lurie

Stop Plagiarism in 3 Easy Steps

October 30, 2008 by Ian

I recommend the death penalty for plagiarism. Until that happy day arrives, I'll share a technique that at least makes life harder for thieving scumbags.

Step One: Trap Your Post

First, you need to add a trap to your blog post. Usually that means an invisible GIF image. Use your image editing software to create a 10x10 pixel image that matches the background of your blog or that's transparent.

Insert that into your blog somewhere where no one will notice. Use the absolute address for the image. So:

http://www.conversationmarketing.com/images/trap.gif

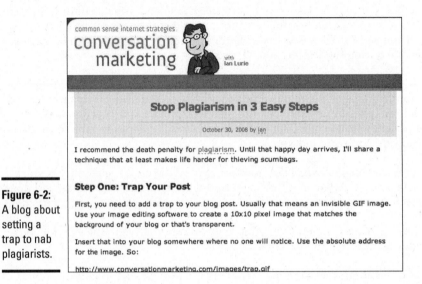

Figure 6-2: A blog about setting a trap to nab plagiarists.

Word of this post spread. A few people added it to Digg, and within a few hours, more than 2,000 people had "Dugg" the article. (See Chapter 2 of this minibook for more about Digg.) Traffic, shown in Figure 6-3, spiked: 60,000 visitors in one day, with a healthy 30 percent more subscribers and daily visitors.

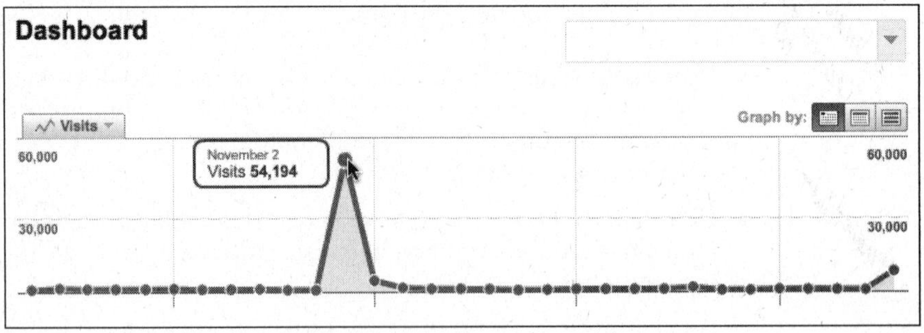

Figure 6-3: Whoa! That's a lot of traffic.

This post stuck to the rules:

+ **No sales pitch was given.** It was, in fact, 100 percent pure rant.

+ **It was very relevant.** Any blogger, writer, or other content producer hates plagiarism. It's enormously frustrating. So any example of someone putting one over on the thieves is going to be popular.

+ **The article was easily available.** It's just a blog post — no login or purchase required.

+ **It didn't contain any tricks.** Readers could go straight to the content without any hurdles, such as e-mail sign-ups.

Providing entertainment with a content campaign

Including some entertainment in your content has value. Whether you're using written text, video, or photos, your chances of producing truly sneezable content are far higher when you can teach and entertain at the same time.

Sometimes, the entertainment value is built in: Inserting ridiculous photos into the websites of unwitting thieves is *funny.* Sometimes you'll want to add entertainment value to subjects that aren't overtly fun or funny.

Humor increases the chances that someone will carry your content to her friends.

Leveraging Networks to Create a Winning Social Media Campaign

You can produce the coolest tool or the best content on the planet. If no one knows about it, though, it won't help.

Now is the time to use the social media network that you've built. After you post your article or tool, send a quick note to your Twitter followers, your Facebook friends, and your other audiences in the social media world. Don't push it: Just a single note will do.

Try to write a note that will catch attention. This probably won't help:

New blog post about plagiarism.

This approach is better because it catches folks' attention:

⌈I wreak horrific vengeance upon plagiarists. Mwahahahahaha!⌉

Obviously, be conscious of your audience. They might not like to read *Mwahahahahaha!* Write appropriately.

Addressing Harm to Your Reputation

Sometimes, folks will misinterpret what you write, disagree with you, or resort to plain ol' name calling. That's the nature of any community.

If readers misinterpret what you write, *don't snap at them*. Reply to them via whatever network they're using and explain what you meant. Even better, thank them for pointing out something that wasn't clear about your content or tool and then explain how you fixed it.

If readers disagree, just grin and bear it. If you want everyone to agree with you, don't publish anything online. Disagreements are in the nature of any community. Tastes and opinions vary. Don't take it personally, and again, don't snap at anyone.

Finally, if someone just starts calling you names (it does happen), don't take the bait. Sure signs that you shouldn't bother replying are when folks call you an idiot or a cretin, or say that you're clueless. Ignore such taunts, respond with humor, or let your community handle it for you.

In all these cases, responding in anger or pointing out that the dissident is dumb, wrong, or silly will only pour gas on the fire. That's the most important lesson in managing your reputation: Respond only when you can do so in a positive manner.

By the way, no one's perfect. Everyone loses his temper a few times and publishes things he regrets. The best thing you can do then is admit you're human, apologize to the community, and move on.

Applying These Lessons Everywhere

Compelling social media–marketing campaigns succeed because you show a genuine interest in helping the community. Help might mean providing a tool, valuable information, or a laugh. Help does not mean a sales pitch.

It also requires patience and a little faith in your community. You have to trust that they have the judgment to know what's legitimate and good and what's not.

And, it requires persistence. If you're lucky, one in ten of your social media–marketing campaigns will succeed when you start.

All these lessons hold true in all Internet marketing. Deliver value, be patient, trust your community, and be persistent. Success is nearly inevitable if you do.

Book VIII

Mobile Marketing

Contents at a Glance

Chapter 1: Getting Started with Mobile Marketing

In This Chapter

- ✔ Discovering mobile marketing and its key elements
- ✔ Exploring the myriad mobile devices and networks
- ✔ Finding out about the two approaches to mobile marketing
- ✔ Complying with rules, regulations, and best practices

*L*ife is mobile. People around the world are on the go, and nearly everyone has a mobile phone or a mobile device of some kind to help him or her get through the day. Users are connecting with other people, being entertained, gathering relevant information, and interacting with businesses anywhere, anytime, and for nearly any purpose. Today's mobile device has become an all-purpose utility. People are still making and receiving phone calls with their mobile device albeit maybe to a lesser degree. Today they're texting, searching the web, downloading applications, consuming and creating content (weather, radio, television, social media posts, deal of the day), interacting with and responding to advertisements, scanning codes, checking in with friends and at places via social media, finding stores, buying stuff, and so much more.

Today, mobile devices (phones, tablets, e-readers, game terminals) are increasingly becoming a cornerstone of society and indispensable to marketing. In fact, for many people around the globe, a mobile device has become their primary communication and commerce tool. The world has changed, and whenever the world changes, so must your practice of marketing.

This chapter is all about showing you how to embrace mobility, the impact it is having on marketing, and how you can integrate mobile elements into your own marketing efforts. You find out how to embrace mobile marketing and engage your customers through and with myriad mobile devices, networks, and mobile services. You also find all the rules and regulations that pertain to mobile marketing.

Understanding Mobile Marketing

Mobile marketing is simply using the capabilities of mobile (devices, networks, and channels) to market your business with your customers.

Mobile marketing, according to the Mobile Marketing Association (www.mmaglobal.com), is "a set of practices that enable organizations to communicate and engage with their audience in an interactive and relevant manner through any mobile device or network." This definition contains just 26 words, but it packs in a lot of meaningful terminology.

In the following sections, and through this entire minibook, you find out what these 26 words really mean and how they can be used to engage your customer in a manner that generates meaningful results that are mutually beneficial for you, your business, your customers, and potential customers — essentially, everyone!

The days of mass-market marketing are waning. Today is an age of connectedness — an age of hyperfragmentation of communication/media channels and market segmentation down to individual members of the audience. With mobile marketing, you're not broadcasting messages to the masses. Rather, you use mass media and the mobile channel to engage individuals in a relevant, one-to-one, interactive exchange of value.

Mobile marketing has five key elements:

✦ **Organizations:** Organizations are commercial entities — brands, agencies, marketers, nonprofits, enterprises (including individuals), and so on — with products, services, and offerings they want to deliver to the market. In other words, organizations are you and your companies. Mobile marketing works for any type of business.

✦ **Practices:** Practices consist of the many faces and facets of marketing activities, institutional processes, industry player partnerships, standards making, advertising and media placing and buying, direct response managing, promotional engagements, relationship management, customer services, loyalty management, and social media stewardship. In other words, practices include all the things that you want to use to engage your customers. All types of marketing practices can be applied to mobile marketing.

✦ **Engagement:** This is the heart of marketing today, the process by which you and your customers interact with each other in a two-way (push-and-pull) dialogue to build awareness, conduct transactions, provide support, and nurture each other. Mobile marketing is one of the most engaging forms of marketing because it's done through and with such a personal device.

✦ **Relevancy:** Mobile interactions can provide information (for example, a user's location, the time of day, activity, and so on). You can use this information to understand the context of your customer's current environment to tailor and to create an appropriate experience that is closely linked (even maybe relevant) to his current context. For example, if someone in New York is doing a search on the mobile Internet for pizza, you want to show him listings for pizza shops nearby and not send him to Lima, Ohio, to get his pizza. Mobile marketing is highly relevant.

✦ **Mobile devices and networks:** These terms refer to any wireless-enabled device, regardless of form factor or network. Although certain types of devices have their limitations, you can execute some type of marketing campaign on every type of mobile device.

The Two Approaches to Mobile Marketing

You should consider two approaches when integrating mobile marketing into your marketing strategy and mix (your marketing mix is all the activities you undertake to engage and deliver value to your customer):

✦ Direct mobile marketing

✦ Indirect or mobile-enabled traditional and digital media marketing

The next sections give you an overview of the two approaches so that you can decide how to use both approaches and when.

Direct mobile marketing

One of the really special things about mobile marketing is that it provides you with the opportunity to interact directly with a person — not a household address, a post office, or a television network — because mobile devices are personal and generally used by a specific individual.

Direct mobile marketing involves engaging an individual on a one-to-one level. The mobile channel provides you with three basic ways to practice direct mobile marketing:

✦ **Marketer-initiated communication:** This occurs when you start an engagement with the consumer — for example, you send a message, place a call, or push an application alert. It is sometimes referred to as *push marketing.*

✦ **Consumer-initiated communication:** This occurs when the consumer starts the engagement with you — for example, visits your mobile website, places a call, downloads an application, and so on. It is sometimes referred to as *pull marketing.*

✦ **Mobile advertising:** This occurs when you place advertising messages in one or more of the eight mobile media paths (see Chapter 4 in this minibook for an overview of mobile advertising).

Mobile marketing is an extremely effective direct marketing practice. Marketers consistently see response rates of 8–14 percent to their initiated communication (compared to less than 1 percent for most direct marketing channels), and mobile advertising consistently ranks higher in brand favorability, purchase intent, brand recall, and awareness versus other advertising media. Finally, in what is referred to as the cross-media effect, consumer engagement has been known to increase by as much as 21 times when mobile marketing is tightly integrated with traditional marketing like Internet, television, and print.

Make sure that the customer contacts you first! With marketer-initiated direct mobile marketing, keep in mind that this is a personal medium. What that means is that you must first get a consumer's explicit permission prior to initiating communication, like sending her a text message, making a call, or pushing a download. Because you need permission, you can't engage in marketer-initiated direct mobile marketing without first using mobile advertising, by having the customer engage you and give you permission for ongoing communication, or by combining your mobile marketing programs with other forms of marketing to gain the permission in the first place.

Mobile-enabled traditional and digital media mobile marketing

Mobile-enabled traditional and digital media mobile marketing refers to the practice of mobile-enhancing your traditional and new-media programs (TV, radio, print, outdoor media, Internet, e-mail, voice, and so on) and inviting individual members of your audience to pull out a phone or connected device and respond to your mobile call to action.

For example, within your television advertising, you can have your viewers text a keyword to a Short Code to receive a coupon. Or, you can ask them to fill out a form on the web or mobile Internet, including their mobile phone number, to participate in the program. One of the most common places for mobile-enabled traditional media, however, is within retail. Figure 1-1 illustrates how a retailer may use signs in-store to invite people to participate in its promotional offerings.

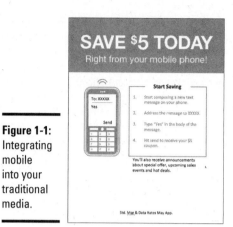

Figure 1-1:
Integrating mobile into your traditional media.

Adding Mobile to Your Marketing Strategy

Developing a mobile marketing strategy can be straightforward. However, the task does involve reviewing a lot of data (the current and future trends and needs of your customers, your industry experience, the competitive landscape, and industry rules and regulations), sifting through your business marketing objective, technology trends, and the engagement details that are unique to mobile marketing. After you've done all this, you then need to integrate these details with your overall marketing strategy. Developing and executing an effective mobile marketing strategy takes time, attention, and a keen understanding of every aspect of your market, your business, and even other businesses that provide the mobile services and connections you need.

An effective marketing strategy doesn't rely on a single channel or tactic. In marketing, the rule is that a consumer must see your promotional message three to seven times across multiple channels for awareness of your offering to stick.

You can make your mobile marketing strategic processes as detailed and complex (or as simple) as you like, but keep in mind that developing a strategy is an iterative process. In other words, you try something, learn, adjust, and try again to see what works best. And, when the market shifts and what you've been doing stops working, you must learn, adjust, and try again.

The key to any plan, however, is to clearly understand what it is you want to accomplish and how and what you'll do to accomplish it. When building a marketing plan that includes mobile, consider these four things:

✦ **Strategy:** Understand what the objectives are for your overall marketing efforts and your individual marketing and mobile marketing campaigns. You'll need to understand what resources you have available (for example, time, money, people), which channels and tactics you want to use, and whether you have enough resources to get the job done. If your objectives are not clear, your channel and tactical plans are not clear, and if you don't know what kind of resources you have, take a step back and reconsider your plan until you are clear. Figure 1-2 aligns a number of mobile marketing tactics to a variety of marketing objectives. This framework may help you with your planning.

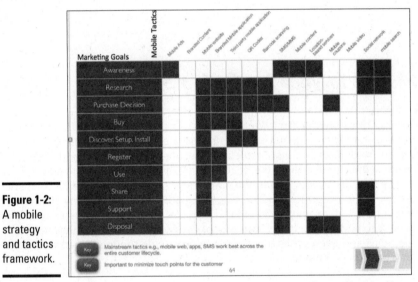

Figure 1-2:
A mobile strategy and tactics framework.

Courtesy of the-dark-matter.com

✦ **Creative:** Develop a plan for what you want your programs to look and feel like, including word choice, color schemes, and other design elements.

✦ **Technology:** Assess your technology and consider what you need to launch and run your programs — not just your mobile programs but your traditional programs as well. Consider how they might interact with each other.

✦ **Report:** Consider how you'll monitor and report on your programs. Reporting is key; without it, you won't know if and when you've met your goal.

In choosing how you'll go about executing your mobile marketing efforts, you can take four basic strategies to build your plan:

✦ **Do-it-yourself:** With this approach, you go it alone: You develop your own strategies, create and execute your own programs, and build all your own technology. This takes a massive commitment and investment — think things through before taking on this approach.

✦ **Agency:** With an agency approach, you contract with one or more marketing agencies or specialized mobile agencies or service providers to handle everything for you.

✦ **Platform:** With the platform approach, you handle the strategy, creation, and execution of programs yourself, and you use a mobile service provider's licensed software application or a platform for your technology and measurement.

✦ **Hybrid:** With the hybrid approach, you choose elements of each of the aforementioned approaches. For example, you may outsource creative work to a mobile service provider or agency and keep strategy for yourself, or license a platform for one part of a campaign.

Picking the right strategy for you and your firm is a very personal decision. You need to consider your resources and the type of company you are and want to be. See Chapter 4 in this minibook for an in-depth analysis on finding resources.

Which approach you select depends on how much of the overall mobile marketing process you want to personally take on and what pieces you see as being critical to your company's competitive advantage and core business offerings.

Exploring Mobile Devices

When most people think about mobile marketing, the first thing that comes to their mind is a mobile phone. But you need to ask yourself, what is a phone today? You find two types, feature phones and smartphones.

Don't disregard the other mobile devices (like tablets, game terminals, e-readers, and GPS devices) that people carry with them as not being pertinent for mobile marketing.

For the purposes of mobile marketing, you should be familiar with three categories of mobile devices:

✦ **The feature phone:** The feature phone (see Figure 1-3) is the most common phone in the market. As of December 2011, about 60 percent of the phones carried in the United States are feature phones. These phones run a real-time operating system (RTOS), which is a *closed operating system* — one in which you can't make modifications such as adding functionality to a mobile browser or changing the user experience on the phone. With feature phones, you're limited to SMS, MMS, voice, and limited mobile Internet.

Figure 1-3: Feature phones are the most common type of phone today.

✦ **The smartphone:** The smartphone (see Figure 1-4) is a mobile device that integrates mobile phone capabilities with the more common features typically associated with a personal computer, including Internet, applications, e-mail, entertainment, and rich-media services. Moreover, smartphones increasingly include location, motion and related sensors, touchscreens, and full keyboards. Smartphones are categorized by the operating system they use. The top smartphone operating systems (OS) are the Apple iOS, Google Android, Microsoft Windows Phone, Research In Motion BlackBerry OS, HP Palm webOS, Samsung Baba, Nokia Symbian, and Linux-based operating systems such as the MeeGo, which is used in Nokia high-end phones. Smartphones account for approximately 35 percent of the U.S. market today. In the United States, by the end of 2011, nearly 40 percent of consumers have a smartphone, a number that is surely to rise. Worldwide, however, smartphone penetration is still in the 6 to 10 percent range.

More and more people will have smartphones and tablet computers and be able surf the Internet, use e-mail, and download applications. In fact, analysts estimate that by 2015 more people will access the Internet through a mobile device than through a traditional desktop or laptop personal computer.

Figure 1-4:
The
smartphone.

- ✦ **Connected devices:** The connected device category is the industry catchall term for all nonphone, mobile-enabled devices. This includes tablets (the Apple iPad, Cisco Cius, Samsung Galaxy, Research In Motion BlackBerry Playbook, Amazon Kindle Fire), e-readers (Amazon Kindle, Barnes and Noble Nook), portable gaming devices (PlayStation Portable), and so on.

Smartphones and tablets tend to run the same operating system, but for marketing purposes, you must treat them as very different mediums. Tablets, with larger screens, are used to consume content (books, articles, movies), while smartphones are used to take actions (search, scan, find stores, and offers).

Getting to Know Mobile Networks

The basic premise of mobile marketing is that you're engaging the consumer over *mobile networks.* You find three basic mobile networks:

- ✦ **Mobile carrier network:** The mobile carrier network (also referred to as the operator network) consists of a series of radio towers (so-called *cell towers*) that transmit and receive radio signals that talk with a mobile device. All kinds of technologies and acronyms go into making all this work — CMDA, TDMA, GSM, LTE, EDGE, and so on — but you really don't need to know anything about these. You'll also hear terms like *2G, 3G,* and *4G,* with the higher numbers referring to faster data speeds over the network. A 4G network is pretty close to broadband Internet speeds over mobile carrier networks (for example, it will enable things like real-time, interactive videoconferencing and social media).

✦ **Wi-Fi and WiMAX:** *Wi-Fi,* or wireless fidelity, more commonly referred to as a wireless local-area network, is a wireless network powered by a small terminal connected to an Internet connection. You see them most often in homes, coffee shops, and airports. WiMAX is a Wi-Fi network on steroids. A WiMAX network is a Wi-Fi network that is broadcast over miles rather than a few hundred feet like Wi-Fi. Most smartphones and connected devices can connect to Wi-Fi and WiMAX networks to access the Internet. A huge amount of mobile marketing (ad serving, application downloading, and mobile Internet browsing) happens over these faster networks.

✦ **Local frequency:** A number of low-frequency channels can be used to exchange data and interact with the mobile device, like Bluetooth, Radio Frequency Identification (RFID), and Near Field Communication (NFC). *Bluetooth* is a low-bandwidth radio spectrum that has a reach of about 1 to 109 yards, depending on the power of the device. RFID and NFC systems are similar in concept to Bluetooth in that they're both short-range communication systems, but they have unique identification and commerce capabilities.

Bluetooth and Wi-Fi may be used to engage consumers in what is referred to as *proximity marketing,* or the localized distribution of content to a mobile device. The *Bluetooth path* refers to the use of the Bluetooth communication channel on the phone.

That little blue icon on your phone represents Bluetooth capability. If you use Bluetooth, you probably use it to pair your phone with a peripheral device such as a wireless headset or hands-free car kit. You also may use it to sync your phone with your laptop computer or to send pictures from your phone to your printer. Wi-Fi is the channel that connects your phone to the Internet via a Wi-Fi access point.

In addition to working with peripheral devices, both Bluetooth and Wi-Fi can be used for mobile marketing — a practice called *Bluecasting.* You place Bluetooth access points and a Bluetooth transmitter in a public area (such as a mall, airport lounge, bus stop, or movie theater) or at a live event. When a consumer walks by the access point, if his phone is set to receive Bluetooth requests automatically, his phone beeps, and he's asked to accept a pairing request from the Bluetooth access point. If he accepts the request, the Bluetooth access point sends an image, ringtone, game, or other communication to his phone.

Leading Bluecasting providers include BLIP Systems (`www.blipsystems.com`), Ace Marketing (`www.acemarketing.net`), Aura Interactive (`www.aura.net.au`), and ProximityMedia (`www.proximitymedia.com`). Also, a new type of proximity marketing has been recently spearheaded by shopkick (`www.shopkick.com`), a retail loyalty solution. It has developed a proprietary audio signal for proximity marketing that is taking the retail market by storm.

Make sure that you're clear with your Bluecasting permission statements. Pushing content to consumers' phones without the consumers' solicitation or consent is a modern-day discourtesy sometimes termed *Bluejacking*. Make sure to look into standards and the code of ethics to ensure that you are helping your customers, not annoying them. Also, *never* engage in *Bluesnarfing*, which is the unauthorized access of information from a wireless device through a Bluetooth connection. Bluesnarfing is illegal in many countries due to privacy issues involved with unauthorized access to personal information such as contacts and calendars.

Understanding the Many Paths within the Mobile Channel

Marketing paths are the combination of the tools, technologies, and media used to communicate messages and reach consumers. For example, advertising on a billboard is often referred to as outdoor advertising, which is one type of marketing path. When it comes to mobile, many different types of paths can be used to reach consumers (see Figure 1-5).

The eight different mobile paths can be organized into six broad buckets:

✦ **Messaging** consists of the three messaging channels: SMS, MMS, and e-mail. SMS messaging contains up to 160 alphanumeric characters, while MMS and e-mail may contain more characters and rich media (image, audio, and text).

✦ **Browsing** refers to mobile Internet access through a browser.

✦ **Downloading** refers to the software applications downloaded to the mobile device.

✦ **Proximity** refers to engagements that can be had through local radio and audio channels.

✦ **Voice** refers to the voice and audio channels of the phone.

✦ **Content** refers to any type of content, text, video, and so on.

Although each of the mobile paths can work all by themselves, they are more effective when combined together. For example, a text message can deliver a mobile website link, which when clicked may include a phone number link. When that phone number link is clicked, it places a call. The call may present a prompt for the user to say or press 1. When the 1 key is pressed, an application or content download may begin. Granted, this string of linkages would present a terrible user experience, but hopefully it demonstrates that all the paths can work together.

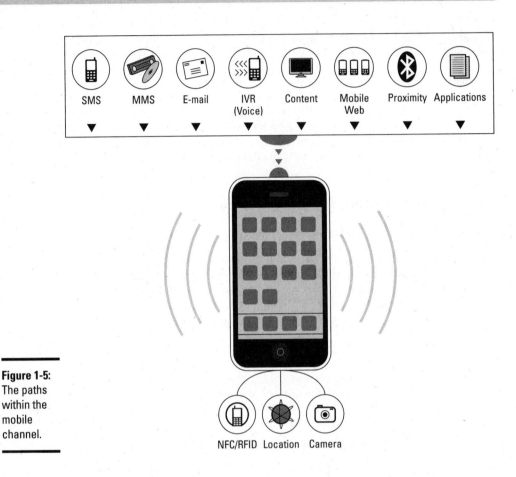

Figure 1-5:
The paths
within the
mobile
channel.

The next chapter goes into depth on each of these paths.

Creating Your Company's Mobile Marketing Policy

Every company engaging in mobile marketing should have its own mobile marketing policy to ensure compliance with laws, regulations, and other standards in the marketplace. Your *mobile marketing policy* is a written document that outlines your company's position on key regulatory issues in mobile marketing and how you expect your employees and partners to react to these issues.

Regulations refer to government-mandated rules and laws that must be followed on both the state and federal levels in the United States, throughout a particular region, or in other parts of the world. *Best practices* and *guidelines* are a compilation of accepted industry practices, wireless carrier policies, and regulatory guidance that have been agreed upon by representative members of a particular industry.

The following sections walk you through the components of a thorough policy that will give you the security and confidence you need anytime you run a mobile marketing campaign.

Adopting a code of conduct

A *company code of conduct* is a collection of statements within a mobile marketing policy that clearly states what you believe to be right and wrong when it comes to mobile marketing and consumer engagement in general. Think of your code as all the following rolled up into one:

✦ **A statement of your intent:** For example, "Our goal is to engage our customers through the mobile channel in a safe, easy, consumer-friendly way so that they ultimately will consider their mobile devices as a seamless and natural medium through which they can interact with our brand."

✦ **Your framework within which you engage consumers and protect their data:** For example, "We ensure that consumers interact with our brand strictly on a voluntary basis and in a highly secure environment using state-of-the-art encryption and other security protocols to protect against inadvertent disclosure, misappropriation, and external attack."

✦ **Your treatise for complying with laws and regulations:** For example, "We commit ourselves to ensuring that our mobile marketing programs are in compliance with current and future laws, regulations, and industry best practices. We will work with the governing bodies, our partners, and regulators to evaluate our program no less often than quarterly and will establish a communication policy to advise our employees, clients, and partners of any changes to our programs that are necessary to be in compliance with these regulations. Moreover, we will promptly address any industry audits conducted by the mobile carriers, application store, or related parties."

The Mobile Marketing Association maintains a recommended code of conduct that can be downloaded at www.mmaglobal.com/codeof conduct.pdf.

Publishing your privacy policy

A privacy policy is absolutely critical if you want to collect information from consumers. Although privacy policies are not required in the United States, consumers expect them when your business is engaged in electronic commerce and collecting consumer data. Not only does a privacy policy help to inform and please consumers, but you also save yourself a lot of legal headaches later if you can demonstrate your adherence to a publicly available privacy policy if someone complains about your privacy practices.

Your mobile marketing policy should clearly spell out how your company plans to

✦ Obtain permission when you want to engage someone in your mobile marketing programs

✦ Keep a record of someone's permission after you obtain it

You should take the security of consumers' information very seriously. If you don't, you may ruin any possible future relationship with a consumer at the very least. At worst, you could pay a severe fine and even end up in jail (especially in Europe, which has incredibly stringent consumer protection laws).

To find out more about privacy statements, go to `http://mmaglobal.com/privacy-policy`.

Stating your permission practices

The use of consumer information and most forms of outbound mobile communications require opt-in permission from the recipient before they are legal or permitted by mobile carriers. Your mobile marketing policy should include a statement of your permission practices so that you can ensure that your information is usable and your messages will be deliverable and legal.

You must obtain prior opt-in permission from consumers before you can initiate engagement on their mobile devices. The following are examples of cases where opt-in permission is needed and examples of how opt-in might be applied in the interest of the best consumer discloser:

✦ **Be upfront about the cost.** The marketing material you use to invite the consumer to engage in your mobile program must contain opt-in information about the cost of engagement. For example, adding *Std Txt&Data rates may apply* (which stands for *Standard text and data rates may apply*) as part of the legal information near the call to action to participate means that the consumer would be charged a fee by his carrier for all text messaging, multimedia messaging, and data — application downloads, website views, and so on — in accordance with the contract that he has entered into with his mobile carrier. You can find even more detailed versions of this language as detailed in the Mobile Marketing Association Consumer Best Practices (`www.mmaglobal.com/best practices.pdf`).

- **Send text messages on an ongoing basis.** Your permission statement needs to outline the steps for obtaining prior permission. For example, your statement might require new customers to reply *yes* to all your text-message prompts before they can receive future messages.

- **Charge for content or services on a phone.**

- **Ask for donations through mobile devices.** Your statement should detail the process for confirming present and future donations.

- **Track physical location.** Some mobile applications can serve pertinent information to consumers based on their physical location. Before activating any location usage application, consumers must be prompted with the specific request for permission. Your statement should include a process for gaining permission, such as a check box or online form that asks users whether they want to allow you to use their location.

Securing and managing consumer data

Personal information can take many forms, including a consumer's mobile phone number, address, health and financial data, current location, and behavioral data. In marketing, personal information is divided into two classes:

- **Personally identifiable information (PII):** PII is any and all information that can be used to identify a person.

- **Nonpersonally identifiable information (non-PII):** Non-PII is information collected through the course of the marketing process, such as clicks on a website, that can't immediately be linked to a specific person.

  California is the only state that actually requires businesses collecting PII from California residents to have and post a privacy policy. The Online Privacy Protection Act has quite a few requirements, so if your business collects PII from residents, you should definitely consult with an attorney who is knowledgeable in this area.

Both PII and non-PII are collected in mobile marketing interactions. The information may simply be a person's phone number, as when someone text-messages into a program, or it may include additional details such as age, name, and address. The information may be provided by the consumer during the course of his interaction with you or obtained later by combining data from multiple public and private data sources.

Regardless of how the information is collected, you *must* protect and safeguard all information that you collect during your interactions with consumers. You should collect only information that you really need. Frankly, why assume the liability of having it if you don't have to?

Your customer data is very valuable to your company, but keep in mind that it's even more valuable to identity thieves. These days, governments not only go after those who steal it. They also go after companies who allowed the data to be stolen.

As a general rule, if you include the follow four steps in your mobile marketing policy and adhere to them, you'll usually be in compliance with data security laws:

✦ **Collect only the data that you absolutely need.** If you collect your customers' Social Security numbers, but don't do anything with them, you've created unnecessary risk.

✦ **Limit internal access to customer data to only those people who absolutely need it.** Some businesses give everyone in their IT department access to all information out of convenience in case someone from IT has to fix something. But if you allow an employee who sets up e-mail accounts for new employees to have access to a customer's payment history, you've created unnecessary risk.

✦ **Store data in highly secure form.** Encryption has become standard of care.

✦ **As soon as you're done with a customer's data and have no further need for it, destroy it.** If you retain customers' data after they have closed their accounts, you've created unnecessary risk.

After you have a plan for storing your data, you should document your data management policy and make sure that it spells out the logistics of all the concerns mentioned previously. Your data management policy should answer questions such as where is the data; how is it secured; who has access to it; what are the protocols for accessing, retaining, or deleting it; and so on.

If you hire a third-party agency to manage the engagement and collect data, ensure that an agreement is in place regarding the PII obtained and stored on your behalf. It should be managed, shared, and disposed of based on the security you require. It's wise not to make assumptions here; an agency might have a different viewpoint on this issue that is not in accordance with your policies.

Creating policies for special programs

Some mobile marketing campaigns have the potential to create unique legal and regulatory implications, so you need to address them individually in your mobile marketing policy. These special programs include

✦ **Winner data in prize promotions:** Talk with your attorney to make sure that your policy addresses state and local laws in addition to national laws for contests and promotions.

✦ **Incentives:** If you're using gifts, prizes, or other incentives to engage your customers, make sure that your policy complies with local, state, and federal laws. These laws can be extremely complicated; consult your attorney or a specialist firm like ePrize (`www.eprize.com`).

✦ **Social media:** If your business has a social media presence, give some thought to whether your policies or procedures should treat those who interact through their mobile device differently from those who access through laptops or desktops. For example, if you want to use mobile social media technology to utilize consumers' location data, you may run into legal issues with publicly posting the physical location of individuals. Allowing the general public to know where specific individuals are (or that they aren't home right now) can present safety and privacy concerns.

Special program policies are often specific to your business, industry, or local jurisdiction. Get help from your attorney before you address them in your policy or in practice.

Complying with Trade Association Guidelines

Following industry guidelines is always important. Even though the mobile marketing industry is young, you still have practices to follow. You need to follow these guidelines if you want to be effective in marketing through mobile channels. The following sections show you what you need to know.

Getting to know the influencers

You'll find a number of trade associations whose guidelines and best practices are well respected when it comes to mobile marketing. It's a good idea to become familiar with each association and its guidelines:

✦ **The Mobile Marketing Association (MMA):** The MMA is the leading worldwide trade organization whose members include agencies, advertisers, hand-held device manufacturers, carriers and operators, retailers, software providers, and service providers, as well as any company focused on the potential of marketing through and with mobile devices. The MMA's Consumer Best Practices Guidelines (`www.mmaglobal.com/bestpractices.pdf`) is a good place to start learning about accepted industry practices, wireless carrier policies, and regulatory guidelines that have been agreed on by representative member companies from all parts of the industry. Check its website every six months or so for updates.

✦ **The Direct Marketing Association (DMA):** The DMA is a leading trade organization in both the United States and the United Kingdom that focuses on direct marketing practices, including mobile marketing. In 2009, the DMA included a mobile marketing section in its Guidelines for Ethical Business Practice (`www.dmaresponsibility.org/Guidelines`), which is designed to help you execute your mobile marketing programs properly.

✦ **CTIA — The Wireless Association:** The CTIA (`www.ctia.org`) is an international nonprofit membership organization that has represented the wireless communications industry. Its membership includes wireless carriers and their suppliers, as well as providers and manufacturers of wireless data services and products. Participating wireless carriers, in conjunction with CTIA, have voluntarily adopted the Wireless Carrier Content Classification & Internet Access Control Guidelines. This is another critical resource you should consult if you want to market to consumers through the mobile channel.

✦ **Interactive Advertising Bureau (IAB):** The IAB is an organization that includes more than 375 leading media and technology companies that are responsible for selling 86 percent of the online advertising in the United States. Among the IAB's core objectives are sharing best practices and educating industry members in responsible marketing methods to help fend off adverse governmental legislation and regulation. The IAB mobile committee produces best practices and mobile advertising guidelines, which are available at `www.iab.net/iab_products_and_industry_services/1421/1488/mobileplatform`.

✦ **Groupe Speciale Mobile Association (GSMA):** The GSMA is a global association spanning 220 countries and uniting nearly 800 of the world's mobile operators, as well as more than 200 companies in the broader mobile ecosystem, including handset makers, software companies, equipment providers, Internet companies, and media and entertainment organizations. This organization is focused on innovating, incubating, and creating new opportunities for its membership and the growth of the mobile communications industry. Information on the GSMA is available at `www.gsmworld.com`.

In addition to the five most influential trade associations, an increasing number of guidelines and best practices are set by installed application providers. These guidelines aren't set by an association, but rather are set by the application stores. For example, the Apple App Store requires that any iPhone application that offers location-based services must notify and obtain consent from an individual before his location data is collected, transmitted, or otherwise used by the application. Make sure that you are aware of any and all individual provider guidelines before going through the trouble of building an application, website, or other program involving a partner.

Complying with U.S. Government Regulations

The U.S. government and individual states have managed to pass a few laws specifying what you can and cannot do with mobile marketing. The following sections highlight key laws, statutes, and regulatory activities that intersect with mobile marketing. As with all legal analysis, consult with your attorney before setting your company policies or taking any action with legal implications.

Steering clear of mobile spam

Mobile spam is unsolicited, unwanted communications in the form of e-mail, text messages, multimedia messages, and so on. As you might imagine by looking at your e-mail inbox or junk folder, spam is one of the more heavily regulated activities. Different laws apply, depending on the specific technology used to send communications. Most communication practices fall under these federal statutes:

✦ **CAN-SPAM:** CAN-SPAM is a U.S. federal statute that regulates the senders of commercial electronic mail. Electronic mail messages regulated under CAN-SPAM include e-mail and other electronic messages sent through social networking sites, but do not include text messages. (Text messages are governed by the TCPA, discussed in the following bullet point.) To comply with CAN-SPAM, check the current law at http://business.ftc.gov/documents/bus61-can-spam-act-compliance-guide-business. If you violate any of the CAN-SPAM laws, the U.S. Federal Trade Commission (FTC) can prosecute you.

In addition to FTC involvement in spam, the Federal Communications Commission (FCC) has imposed a ban on sending unwanted commercial e-mail messages to wireless devices if the e-mail address receiving the e-mail includes a wireless domain e-mail address listed at www.fcc.gov/cgb/policy/DomainNameDownload.html. This is a special rule designed to prohibit marketers from sending commercial e-mail to mobile devices.

✦ **Telephone Consumer Protection Act (TCPA):** The TCPA was passed by Congress in 1991 — long before SMS technology existed. The TCPA generally applies to telephone solicitations and other calls made to phone numbers, including wireless numbers. The FCC has noted that the law encompasses both voice calls and text calls to wireless numbers,

Book VIII Chapter 1

Getting Started with Mobile Marketing

including SMS messages. One of the things the TCPA prohibits is the use of autodialers — computers that dial phone numbers — without prior express consent from the owner of the mobile number or account. Without getting into all the legal mumbo jumbo, the TCPA's application to text messages gets pretty convoluted. To be on the safe side, don't send unsolicited text messages to anyone.

The best practice with any of the preceding regulations is to make sure that you get consumers' consent before you contact them through mobile channels.

In addition to CAN-SPAM and TCPA, the FTC issued the Telephone Sales Rule and has revised it on several occasions to update its applicability to the evolving climate of the mobile channel. The TSR consists of four general requirements for telemarketers:

✦ **National Do Not Call Registry:** On October 1, 2003, the TSR gave consumers a choice about receiving most telemarketing calls by establishing the National Do Not Call Registry. Telephone solicitors are required to ensure that they do not make telephone solicitation calls to any number listed not only on the National Do Not Call list, but also various lists containing those numbers that have changed from landline to wireless accounts and numbers that have been set aside for wireless service. Consumers can register their home and mobile phone numbers with the Do Not Call Registry at `www.donotcall.gov`. Most marketers are forbidden to place telemarketing calls to any phone number listed in the registry, but some exceptions exist, such as political organizations, charities, telephone surveyors, and companies that have preestablished business relationships with a consumer. Marketers are required to check the registry at least once every 31 days to clean their internal lists. Text messaging and e-mail also fall under the umbrella of the Do Not Call Registry.

✦ **Standards for telemarketers:** The TSR prohibits deceptive and abusive telemarketing acts and practices and sets forth standards of conduct for telemarketing calls:

  • Calling times are restricted to the hours between 8 a.m. and 9 p.m., specific to the time zone you are calling, such as Eastern Standard Time (EST).

  • Telemarketers must promptly tell you the identity of the seller or charitable organization and that the call is a sales call or a charitable solicitation.

  • Telemarketers must disclose all material information about the goods or services they are offering and the terms of the sale. They are prohibited from lying about any terms of their offer.

✦ **Predictive dialers:** A *predictive dialer* is a computerized dialing system that automatically calls a batch of phone numbers within a given range. Telemarketers who use predictive dialers must connect the call to a live representative within two seconds of the consumer's completed greeting. If they don't, the call is considered abandoned, even if it's answered by a live representative after the two seconds. Abandoned calls are generally prohibited, meaning that you cannot keep someone waiting on a line longer than two seconds before he is connected to a live attendant.

✦ **Caller ID:** To be in compliance with the Caller ID component of the TSR, a marketer may not block Caller ID and must list a company name and telephone number that can be called by the consumer for company Do Not Call requests. The callback number must be answered with the same company name listed on the Caller ID.

All the rules and requirements surrounding contacting wireless devices seem like a virtual landmine. The DMA has come out with a very useful Wireless Marketing Compliance chart that helps you navigate through the rules and requirements surrounding contacting wireless devices. Check it out at www.dmaresponsibility.org/WirelessChart.

Chapter 2: Planning a Mobile Marketing Campaign

In This Chapter

✔ Counting the costs

✔ Using Common Short Codes

✔ Handling opt-ins and opt-outs

The process of thinking things through before you act usually leads to success. You need to set objectives, and you need to calculate the costs of achieving them so that you can decide whether your ideas are financially feasible and achievable before you spend money and time on them.

You also need a plan to reach the members of your audience — both before you contact them using mobile, because of legal issues with permission, and after you have their permission, because of the wide variety of mobile marketing solutions and communication methods available.

The chapter provides strategies for planning your objectives, estimating your financial and time investments, coordinating your use of Short Codes, and inviting people to participate in your mobile marketing programs.

Understanding the Costs of Mobile Marketing

Mobile marketing involves both up-front and variable costs that you need to be aware of before you plan and eventually execute your strategy. The following sections explain how to include costs in your plan.

How you absorb these costs depends on the approach you take to executing your mobile marketing program. If you're simply going to run one-off campaigns and don't plan to strategically invest in mobile marketing (which given the pervasive of mobile in society today isn't advisable), you need to simply consider the variable costs. If you plan to strategically integrate mobile marketing into your business, however, you want to consider the up-front costs as well.

Calculating up-front costs and estimated timelines

Some mobile marketing costs apply at the outset of your mobile marketing practice. Following are some common up-front costs to consider:

✦ **Strategic resources:** You need to estimate the costs for your team members, consultant retainers (including your marketing agency), and their training, as well as the costs for the development and maintenance of your strategy. This activity can take as little or as much time to complete as you want, depending on the nature of your program and your partners.

✦ **Mobile marking platform and development fees:** You pay these fees to gain access to the application platforms that power your mobile marketing programs (messaging, applications, websites, voice, location, social, advertising, and commerce) and the software developers you hire to build your mobile programs if you choose to bring one or more of your program elements in house (for example, mobile websites and applications). Trying to build a mobile marketing platform or mobile websites and applications yourself can become quite expensive and time consuming. Moreover, it may take some time to find an individual mobile web and application developer you're comfortable working with.

In addition to monthly fees, you should budget for account setup and training fees when you sign up with an application provider.

✦ **Connection aggregator fees:** These fees apply if you decide to go it alone and build your own mobile marketing platform software for sending text messages, enabling direct-to-carrier billing or related services. You need to connect your application to a messaging connection aggregator, and this setup will cost you between $1,000 and many thousands of dollars per month, depending on the aggregator you use. Connection aggregators' fees typically are included in mobile marketing application fees (discussed earlier in this section), which is one of the many benefits of working with an application provider. (You can read more about connection aggregators in Chapter 1 in this minibook.) Like working with an application provider, contracting with a connection aggregator can take a few days to weeks.

If you have *high-throughput* requirements — that is, you need to send and receive hundreds or thousands of text or e-mail messages per second — you should expect to pay extra to the connection aggregator or application provider for this higher-than-average throughput.

✦ **Short-code leases:** A Common Short Code (CSC) is a phone number that is only five to six digits long. If you're going to run any text-messaging mobile marketing programs, you must lease a CSC. In the United States, short-code leases cost $500 to $1,000 per month and are billed quarterly.

You may be able to rent a Short Code from your application provider or connection aggregator, but you'll probably pay a similar fee.

Leasing a CSC takes about an hour, but then you must work with your application provider to have the Short Code activated and approved for use. It takes 8 to 15 weeks (or more) to obtain approval across all participating wireless carriers. You can read more about Short Codes in the section "Working with Common Short Codes," later in this chapter.

Over the last year, the use of a Long Code (10-digit phone numbers) rather than a Common Short Code has been increasing. Long Codes are much cheaper to use than CSCs and have reduced carrier oversight. However, in the United States especially, the industry is evaluating their practice and use. To find out more about using Long Codes, contact a leading service provider, like Twilio (www.twilio.com).

Accounting for variable costs

Following are the variable costs of a typical mobile marketing program:

✦ **Program strategy development:** These costs include all the activities needed to conceive your campaign and lay out the plan. This activity can take as little or as much time to complete as you want, depending on the nature of your program and your partners.

✦ **Creative concept development:** These costs include all the design activities associated with your campaign. This activity can take as little or as much time to complete as you want, depending on the nature of your program and your partners.

✦ **Content licensing and/or creation:** These costs include licensing fees or design fees for any content you may use for the campaign (such as images, ringtones, videos, or news feeds). This activity can take anywhere from a few minutes to a few weeks, depending on the type of content and who you're working with.

✦ **Mobile marketing platform application licensing fees:** These costs are the fees you pay a service provider for hosting and reporting on your campaign — that is, if you're not already licensing an application or haven't built it yourself.

On average, depending on the functionality you license, mobile marketing platform fees range from a few hundred to thousands of dollars per month. Licensing access to a mobile marketing application can take a few minutes to many weeks or even longer, depending on your licensing and procurement procedures and on the number of providers you evaluate and ultimately select.

**Book VIII
Chapter 2**

**Planning a
Mobile Marketing
Campaign**

✦ **Tactical execution of the program:** These costs include creative program certifications (as needed), technical implementation, legal fees (if you're running a sweepstakes program, for example), and any custom nonrecurring software development that may be needed to tailor the application(s) to your specific campaign. This activity can take as little or as much time to complete as you want, depending on the nature of your program and your partners.

✦ **Transactional items:** These costs include messaging traffic via Short Message Service (SMS), Multimedia Messaging Service (MMS), or e-mail; Internet and mobile Internet page views; advertising page views and click-throughs; application downloads; interactive voice response (IVR) minutes; content royalties; images recognized; and individual wireless-carrier tariffs.

✦ **Program certification:** In the United States, all text-messaging mobile marketing programs must be precertified by the wireless carriers, and downloadable applications are approved by application stores, like the Apple App Store. For text-messaging programs, an application form must be completed and submitted through your application provider or connection aggregator to each carrier. Costs for this activity vary (from free to thousands of dollars), as does the timing (typically, 8 to 15 weeks or more, depending on the nature of the program). For downloadable applications, each application store has its own process and registration fees that range from free to a few hundred dollars.

✦ **Campaign auditing:** Wireless carriers in the United States regularly audit text-messaging mobile marketing programs running over their networks. Although no up-front cost is involved when a carrier audits your program, you may incur a cost for updating your program if, after an audit, a carrier finds that your program doesn't comply with current industry guidelines.

✦ **Traditional media and retail channels:** These costs are the fees you pay to promote the program in any traditional-media, new-mediator retail channel.

Depending on the provider you're working with, you might be quoted a single price for your entire mobile marketing program plus fees for traditional media buys and retail promotions. Or, you may get a detailed breakdown of the costs. Often, it's helpful to ask for the breakdown if you're not provided one so that you can adjust your plans and strategies accordingly.

You can often reuse portions of your strategy, creative elements, and any custom software and content development in future campaigns, as well as in your broader strategic mobile marketing program. This multiple-use strategy can end up saving you quite a bit of money and time down the road.

Estimating your timeline

The last step is to plan your timeline. You have to consider several activities when you develop your program, and each of these activities takes time. Some activities can be done in parallel; others need to be done in a serial manner. The time you actually need depends on the nature of your program and the partners you're working with:

✦ **Certification for and launching a typical text-messaging mobile marketing program:** This can take 8 to 15 weeks, in addition to the time required to design the program, develop its creative elements, and coordinate media channels.

✦ **Receiving approval from an application store:** Plan to take one to four weeks after the development of your application is complete.

Mobile websites, IVR Long Code messaging, or mobile advertising programs need no approval or auditing, so those can go live as you're ready to release them.

You may be able to speed your timeline if you're working with a platform provider or mobile website and application developer that takes care of precertified programs and other elements, in addition to having templated services that streamline the setup of your programs. Consult your platform and development providers or connection aggregator to see what can be done if you're on a tight timeline.

Working with Common Short Codes

When it comes to commercially addressing text messages, your Common Short Code means everything. In the United States, all commercial text messages (text messages for the purpose of mobile marketing) must be addressed and sent via Common Short Codes.

A *Common Short Code (CSC)* is simply a short (five- or six-digit) phone number used to address and route commercial text or multimedia messages through wireless operator networks (see Figure 2-1). CSCs are critical because nearly all effective mobile marketing programs leverage text messaging in one way or another.

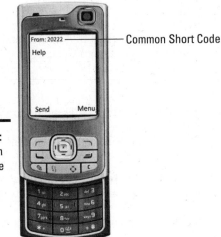

— Common Short Code

From: 20222

Help

Send   Menu

Figure 2-1:
A Common
Short Code
(CSC) is a
shortened
phone
number.

Common Short Codes are effective for mobile marketing because they're all of the following things:

+ **Bidirectional messaging:** Messaging traffic can be addressed both ways with CSCs, both to and from the mobile subscriber and you.

+ **Cross-carrier enabled:** After they're activated on a carrier network, CSCs work across most of the leading U.S. carriers, extending a marketer's reach to more than 235 million mobile subscribers in the United States.

CSCs are country specific, unlike Internet domains, which work world-wide. You need to lease a CSC in each country where you want to run your mobile marketing (see the next section in this chapter).

+ **Billing engines:** You can use premium Short Message Service (SMS) and charge people for participation in your programs. (For more information about premium SMS, also called PSMS, see Chapter 6 of this minibook.)

+ **Effective mechanisms for permissions marketing:** CSCs are the primary means of obtaining opt-ins in mobile marketing.

+ **Useful:** CSCs are useful for a wide range of marketing campaigns and services.

The following sections show you how to acquire and use CSCs for your text-messaging campaigns. Chapter 3 of this minibook shows you how to launch and run those campaigns.

Acquiring a Common Short Code

You have two ways to gain access to a CSC for your mobile marketing program:

+ **You can lease a CSC directly.** Choose this option when you want to run lots of different campaigns with no limit to the complexity of the campaigns.

+ **You can rent access to an existing CSC.** Choose this option when you're on a budget or you need to run a minimum number of simple campaigns.

Many countries don't have a centralized Short Code administration body, in which case you must rent access to a Short Code. Although this approach may get you up and running faster, at less expense, you should take care when using this model. Depending on the relationship you forge with the application provider, the provider may end up owning all your customers (all the opt-ins) on the code. Also, if the application provider does not pay the Short Code lease or if a program on the code in a shared model runs afoul of the carrier requirement, the carriers may turn off the code and your programs along with all the other programs running on the code. If you're going to be doing any mobile marketing beyond one-off campaigns here and there, make the investment and lease your own CSC.

If you'd like to lease your own CSC directly, you can obtain it from one of the few Short Code administration bodies:

+ **United States:** Common Short Code Administration (www.usshort codes.com)

+ **Canada:** Canadian Wireless Telecommunications Association Common Codes Administration (www.txt.ca)

+ **Latin America:** Administracion de Codigos (www.latinshort codes.com)

+ **United Kingdom:** U.K. Mobile Network Operators (www.short-codes.com)

+ **France:** Association Française du Multimédia Mobile (www.smsplus.org/index.php)

To lease a Short Code or obtain access to one in other countries, you need to go through your application provider or a local aggregator. Ask your mobile marketing provider or local aggregator for assistance.

If you decide to lease a Short Code, it's a pretty easy process. The following are the steps for doing so in the United States. Remember that every registry may have a slightly different process:

1. **Go to the Common Short Code Administration website at** www.us shortcodes.com.

2. **Click the Get an Account Now button, complete the form that appears (create a user ID and password, enter your address, and so on), and register your account.**

   If you're the marketer (as opposed to the application provider), select the role of content provider and click Create Account.

3. **Log in with your user ID and password, click the Apply for a New CSC link (on the left), and fill out the form that appears. Click Submit.**

   If you're having your application provider do this for you, be sure that he puts your contact info in as the content provider. That way, if you leave your application provider, you are the leaser of record for the Common Short Code, as opposed to him. In addition, you need to specify whether you want to lease the code for 3, 6, or 12 months, as well as indicate the type of code (random or vanity) that you'd like. (See the following section for an explanation of random and vanity codes.)

4. **Read the terms and conditions and select the I Agree check box.**

5. **After you've accepted the terms and conditions, confirm your purchase.**

   Your code is e-mailed to you. If you do not complete the payment for the Common Short Code immediately, the administration will hold it for 60 days. If you do not pay within 60 days, the code goes back into the pool of available codes.

Leasing your CSC is just the first step. After you've leased your CSC, you then need to have it activated on the mobile operator networks and have it bound to an aggregator, who in turn binds it to a mobile marketing application. After this binding is complete and your CSC is registered in the carrier networks, all messaging traffic addressed to the CSC must be routed through a carrier network, who hands it to the registered aggregator, who in turn routes it to your specified application provider's text-messaging platform.

Leasing your own CSC can cost anywhere from $500 to $1,000 per month, and it takes many months to get a new CSC approved. If you're not prepared to get your own Short Code — due to the expense or due to the time it takes to activate one — you can ask an application provider or connection aggregator to rent you access to one of its CSCs.

Deciding what type of CSC to use

When you lease or rent access for your CSC, you have some other choices to make — namely, choosing the type of CSC to use. Here are the options you have and some tips for making the right choice:

✦ **Choosing random or vanity codes:** You need to choose between two Short Code schemas:

- *Random*: The code-administration body gives you a random number sequence.

- *Vanity*: You pick the numbers for your CSC. An example of a vanity Short Code would be 46445, purchased specifically to spell *googl.* Choose to lease a vanity code when you want easy recall (77777) or to build your brand (57238 = kraft).

✦ **Deciding on five or six digits:** In the United States, you can lease five-digit codes as either random or vanity Short Codes, but six-digit codes can be leased only as vanity codes.

You may see four-digit Short Codes, but these codes tend to be reserved for the sole use of wireless carriers. Codes greater than six digits are called *Long Codes,* and they're primarily used for running cross-border international programs.

Going dedicated or shared

You can choose to run multiple mobile initiatives on a single Short Code simultaneously or to run only one at any given time. When multiple mobile marketing campaigns are run on a single Short Code, the code is referred to as *shared.* When only one service is running on the code at any given time, the code is referred to as *dedicated.*

In Short Code terms, *dedicated* and *shared* have nothing to do with who owns or leases the Short Code; they apply solely to how the Short Code is being used. Therefore, you can use your own dedicated code, rent a dedicated code, use your own Short Code in a shared model, or rent access to a shared code.

Both dedicated and shared Short Code models have pros and cons, as you see in Table 2-1.

The shared and dedicated models are not cast in stone. As part of your CSC strategy, a Short Code can be used as dedicated for a certain period and then used as shared with multiple initiatives running on it. Consult your application or connection aggregator partner for details.

Table 2-1		Short Code Models
Model	*Pros*	*Cons*
Shared	Multiple initiatives can be run under one Short Code for a lower cost per initiative.	You need to include keywords in SMS messages to identify the initiative. User flow and instructions for initiatives are more complex. One noncertified "outlaw" initiative could shut down all other initiatives on a shared Short Code.
Dedicated	End-user task flow is easy. End users can text without having to include keywords to identify the initiative. You have more flexibility in initiative tactics. Reporting is easier.	The company is not amortizing Short Code costs over multiple initiatives. All metric data can belong only to the initiative on the dedicated Short Code.

Managing Opt-Ins

Mobile marketing is about reach and establishing a dialogue with the members of your audience through and with the mobile channel. Sometimes, this interaction occurs only one time: A customer reaches out to you to request some information via your website. At other times, you invite a customer to receive ongoing communication from you via text messaging, e-mail, or downloadable application alerts. If the customer gives you consent to contact him in the future, you have the right to contact him again via the same channel. This process is often referred to as *obtaining an opt-in*. As a result, the process of obtaining opt-ins is crucial to your long-term success in mobile marketing.

The following sections help you determine how to obtain opt-ins. You can read more about the legalities of obtaining permissions in Chapter 1 of this minibook.

Industry best practices and regulations require all text messages to contain opt-out instructions, such as a *stop* keyword. For more information about opt-out instructions, see the section "Handling Opt-Outs," later in this chapter.

Placing an opt-in call to action in media

A request for an opt-in is called an *opt-in call to action.* You can place an opt-in call to action in any traditional, new, and mobile media channel, including the following:

+ Television

+ Print

+ Radio

+ Point-of-sale displays

+ Face-to-face encounters

+ Outdoor advertising

+ A web or mobile Internet site

+ An e-mail

+ A customer-care call

+ Online advertising

+ A dialog pop-up setting in a downloadable application

Figure 2-2 shows the seven primary calls to action you can use to enhance your media. The following sections explain these calls to action in more detail.

All the following opt-in methods can be monetized. For details, see Chapter 6 of this minibook.

Dialing and pressing

Dialing and pressing is all about using the voice channel of the mobile phone. You can encourage people to call a phone number by asking them to "Dial 1-800-XXX-XXXX to experience the sounds of the movie" or "Call 408-XXX-XXXX to listen in on the game," for example.

You don't have to answer the calls yourself; you can use an IVR system to ask the caller to make selections. Selection options in an IVR session could be "Press 1 to receive a ringtone," "Press 2 to get your last five transactions," or "Press 3 to get the movie listings sent to your phone."

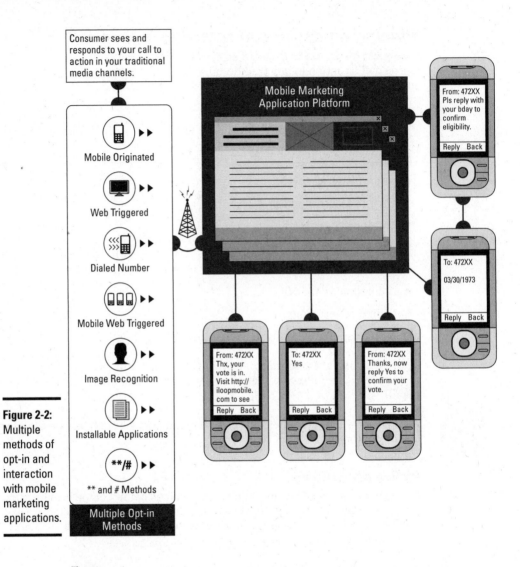

Figure 2-2: Multiple methods of opt-in and interaction with mobile marketing applications.

Texting

Texting simply means sending and replying to a standard alphanumeric or multimedia message. You can place the call to action in traditional, new, and mobile media by saying something like "Text *win* to 12345 to enter the sweepstakes." You can also obtain a mobile subscriber's opt-in via texting.

Mobile marketing programs and any other programs that use text messaging (such as IVR, Internet, mobile Internet, or applications) must use a CSC to address and route text or multimedia message traffic. For details on CSCs, refer to the section "Working with Common Short Codes," earlier in this chapter.

Snapping and scanning

Snapping and scanning means taking a picture and scanning a bar code — nearly every phone today has a camera on it.

The camera is a wonderful tool for gathering opt-ins. You can instruct audience members to take a picture of an object — a soft-drink can, a magazine ad, a movie poster, an action code (quick response or QR code), or almost anything else that has clearly defined edges — and then instruct them to use a scanning application (like Scanbuy's Scanlife application for action code scanning) or have them e-mail or text (via MMS) the picture to your mobile marketing program. When your program receives a picture, it processes the picture and then opts the mobile subscriber in to your program.

Submitting

Another great way to invite someone into your mobile marketing program is to present a form on an Internet page or a mobile Internet page, or in an installed application.

Dialing an abbreviated code

Two companies — Zoove under the brand StarStar (www.zoove.com) and Single Touch (www.singletouch.net) — have developed two alternative opt-in channels; they invite you to place calls prefaced with ** and ##.

Zoove's method uses the star (*) key on the mobile phone. A mobile subscriber on the Sprint network, for example, can press **267 — that is, **AOL — and the Send/Talk button on his phone (typically, the green button). In return, an AOL promotional mobile Internet site is sent to the phone. Single Touch's solution works the same way but uses the pound (#) key instead.

Both services are still limited in their deployment across wireless carriers, but you can see the possibilities of these methods of opt-in.

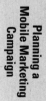

Executing opt-ins

To leverage text messaging, you need to be familiar with two important text-messaging opt-in classifications:

✦ **Mobile originated (MO):** A mobile subscriber composes (*originates*) a message on her phone and sends it to you.

✦ **Mobile terminated (MT):** A message goes from an application provider's service to a mobile phone, so the message ends (*terminates*) on the phone.

When someone opts in to your mobile campaign with an MO message, you return an MT, discussed in the following sections.

Executing a single opt-in

In a *single opt-in,* someone sends in an MO and you send an MT back confirming the opt-in. For subscription alerts or ongoing programs, very few carriers support single opt-ins. Mostly, this process is used for one-time interactions; when the initial interaction is done, no future interactions will occur.

Executing a double opt-in

A *double opt-in* is typically used to gather an individual's confirmation. The flow is straightforward:

1. The user opts in to the program.

2. The mobile marketing application responds with a text message that asks for confirmation ("Reply *y* to 12345," for example).

3. The user sends the confirmation.

4. The mobile marketing application processes the request and sends back a welcome message (such as "Thank you. You're now in the group. To opt out, reply *stop,* or for help, reply *help*").

Executing a multistep opt-in

You use *multistep opt-in* when you want to challenge consumers with additional questions before they can participate in your program. You may ask users for their ages if you're running a program suitable only for users 17 and older, or you may ask a series of questions to collect additional *metadata* (data about themselves). After a user responds to the additional challenges, the interaction may end, or you may follow up by triggering a double opt-in as well to get expressed consent for future marketing.

Handling Opt-Outs

Sometimes people just want to leave — opt out and stop interacting with you. Maybe they'll come back, and maybe they won't, but you need to handle their requests with grace. Accept each request, reply politely, and *never contact the person again*. Otherwise, you'll become a spammer, and you don't want that.

Every best practice guideline on calls to action covers opt-outs. You'll want to include opt-out instructions in your media and in the legal terms and conditions that explain your program.

You can use any of the opt-in methods discussed earlier in this chapter to capture opt-outs. But the most convenient way to gather an opt-out is simply to have the mobile subscriber send the mobile marketing application a text message that includes the keyword *stop* (or any other reserved opt-out keyword, such as *end, quit,* or *cancel*), or in the case of application alerts, include a disable alerts option within the application's settings. In the case of text-messaging opt-outs, when you receive the opt-out request, you'll want to send a final reply, such as this: "Thank you. Your opt-out request has been processed. We'll miss you. If you'd like to join again, reply *join* to 12345."

Chapter 3: Running Mobile Communication Campaigns

In This Chapter

✔ **Setting up mobile communication user flows**

✔ **Interacting with users through text quizzes, surveys, and polls**

✔ **Giving users incentives**

✔ **Encouraging user-generated content**

A mandate of marketing is to communicate — and oh, boy, can you communicate with mobile marketing. You can use mobile marketing to generate consumer responses to your queries, disseminate information, collect information, entertain your audience, and conduct commerce.

This chapter focuses on showing you how to set up and run interactive text-messaging communications programs — including promotion services, quizzes, polls, and surveys — as well as the various ways you can get consumers into the game by generating and sharing their own content.

In the following pages, you discover how to create program text-messaging user flows, documenting all the steps for text-messaging communication between your company and the mobile customer so that you can significantly enhance your marketing programs. You find out about the common elements of mobile marketing text-messaging communication programs (such as opt-in/opt-out management and error/response messaging) and about the unique elements of common mobile marketing communication programs (such as trivia games, polls, and surveys).

When you're done with this chapter, you'll have a clear, concise picture of exactly what it takes to run a mobile marketing communication program.

Planning Your Communication Flow

Launching a mobile text-messaging campaign takes more planning than you may expect. One of the most important aspects of planning is creating text-messaging *user flows* — documents that show as thoroughly as possible how your users engage in your campaign. User flows are critically important for two reasons:

✦ **They help you design and execute your program.** You'll save time and money by planning early in the program-development process instead of fixing mistakes later. Moreover, a detailed text-messaging user flow clarifies any ambiguity about interactions between mobile subscribers and your program. It also helps streamline communication among members of your marketing team and any partners and vendors you may be working with to launch the program.

✦ **They're required for certification of your program.** As part of the certification process (see Chapter 1 of this minibook), you're required to submit your text-messaging program's user flows to your mobile marketing platform provider or connection aggregator. Wireless carriers test your program against your documented user flows. If the program works as described, your carrier can certify your program; if not, your carrier will reject it. Also, carriers use submitted user flows for future campaign audits to make sure that your program still meets the original certification criteria.

Creating a user-flow diagram

The best way to plan your text-messaging communication campaign flow is to use *a user-flow diagram* — an image that outlines the user flow and details all the interactions that may occur between a mobile subscriber and your mobile marketing program (see Figure 3-1).

Create your text-messaging user-flow diagram with any software application such as Microsoft Word, Excel, PowerPoint, or Visio. Some people use standard flow-charting techniques (refer to Figure 3-1); others use images of phones to map the user flow (look ahead to Figure 3-2). The method you choose depends on which one is more useful for documenting all the possible interactions that a mobile subscriber may have with your program.

Your application provider or connection aggregator typically has the most common user flows already designed — as well as the not-so-common ones. Rather than start with a blank piece of paper, ask the provider to give you a few examples. Then you can tailor an existing user-flow diagram to your individual needs.

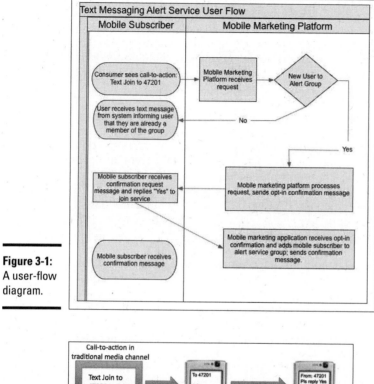

Figure 3-1:
A user-flow
diagram.

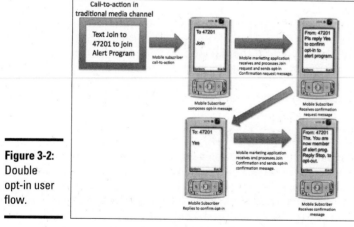

Figure 3-2:
Double
opt-in user
flow.

Step 1: Paint a positive picture

Start by imagining what you want to have happen when everything works
flawlessly. Picture what you want the perfect consumer experience to be.
How do you want the opt-in flow to work, for example? What will the con-
tent-download experience look like?

Step 2: Map your opt-in flow

List the steps that a mobile subscriber must take to opt in to your program. Single opt-in is appropriate for programs that don't charge the consumer for participation or programs in which you're picking up the user's share of the text-messaging costs. These programs typically are called *free to the end user (FTEU)* or standard-rate, text-messaging programs.

If you're going to have ongoing interactions with mobile subscribers, however, or plan to charge them a premium for participation, the industry's consumer best practices and regulations require you to get a double opt-in from all subscribers, so you need to include that requirement in your user flow. (See Figure 3-2 for an example.) You can read more about managing opt-ins in Chapter 2 of this minibook. For more information about industry best practices and regulations, turn to Chapter 1 of this minibook.

Step 3: Map your opt-out flow

List the steps a mobile subscriber must take to opt out of your program. At any time, a subscriber should be able to send *stop, end, quit,* or any related reserved keyword to your program to opt out of it. *Reserved keywords* are keywords reserved by industry best practices, meaning that they're designated to perform a specific function. The reserved keyword *stop* must opt someone out, for example, and *help* must elicit a help message.

After you receive an opt-out request from a mobile subscriber, you must cease all interactions with the mobile subscriber with regard to the specific program. If you don't, you run the risk of being fined by the wireless carrier (at best) or being fined *and* having your programs shut down.

You can read more about managing opt-outs in Chapter 2 of this minibook.

Step 4: Map your help user flow

How will participants in your program get help if they have a question? At a minimum, according to the Mobile Marketing Association's Consumer Best Practices Guidelines (www.mmaglobal.com/bestpractices.pdf), if a user needs help and sends the text *help* to your program, your program must respond accordingly. You should also refer to the CTIA playbook (www.wmcglobal.com/images/CTIA_playbook.pdf), which contains the rules that WMC Global relies on to audit programs on behalf of the carriers and the CTIA (Cellular Telephone Internet Association).

If your program's keyword is *win* and its Short Code is 12345, for example, anyone who's interested in getting help with your program should be able to text *win help* or *help win* to 12345. Your mobile marketing application must respond by returning a text message that includes information about the campaign's terms and conditions, along with details on how to get help. (For more information about Short Codes, see Chapter 2 of this minibook.)

You might want to include in this message a link to a website where the user can get detailed program terms and conditions, as well as a phone number that the user can call to talk to someone or interact with your automated customer-care system. (In the United Kingdom, this number must be a toll-free number.)

Step 5: Map your error response

How will your mobile marketing application respond if the mobile subscriber does something wrong, and what instructions will the application provide automatically to help the subscriber? If the program requires the subscriber to submit a redemption code (*abc123*) along with the program keyword (*win*), and the mobile subscriber text-messages only *win* to the Short Code, the mobile marketing application should reply automatically with a help message (such as "Sorry, we did not understand. Pls txt *win* to *<your code>* to opt in to this program.").

Step 6: Map your final message

When the mobile subscriber is done interacting with your program, what will you say in the final message? Common final messages include "Thank you" (or "Thx") and an invitation to participate and opt in to other programs. You could send a final message like this one: "Thx. The survey is complete. To join our messaging alert service, pls reply *join* to 12345."

Considering optional user flows

You also might want to consider several common optional user flows that don't apply to all mobile communication campaigns:

✦ **Age verification:** To augment the opt-in process, you may provide the mobile subscriber with an age-verification challenge — that is, require him to reply with his birth date before he can move on to the next step of the program. If you're promoting an R-rated movie or have other content that's not suitable for children, you may want to make sure that you have the mobile subscriber's proffered birth date in your campaign's customer database.

✦ **Instant win:** You may want to award loyalty points, free content, a coupon, or some other form of incentive to participants. You could configure your mobile marketing application to award an instant prize to every third participant in the program, for example, or set it so that one in three participants wins. Ask your application provider how to configure this user flow in your system.

✦ **Grand prize:** A grand-prize winner is selected from the pool of participants at the end of the campaign. The mobile marketing application can be set up to draw the specified number of grand-prize winners automatically at the end of the campaign, or you can make the drawing manually from the list of participants, based on whatever selection criteria you choose.

Make sure that your rules are in line with both state and federal regulations.

✦ **Couponing:** Couponing is a very powerful incentive for participation in mobile programs. You may consider adding coupons within any message in your user flow to encourage continued participation in your programs as well as to encourage users to purchase your offerings.

When you send a message, a coupon — either generated by the mobile marketing application or supplied by you to the application — can be appended to or inserted into the message.

✦ **Personalization:** If your mobile marketing program is integrated with an internal or external customer relationship management (CRM) system (see Chapter 7 of this minibook), you may be able to pull data from this system to personalize the messages in the program. You could insert a participant's first name in a message, such as "Hi, Mike. Pls reply *yes* to confirm."

Considering what could go wrong

In addition to mapping the best-case interaction scenarios for your program, you want to map the worst-case scenarios and edge cases for your program — that is, try to think through all the things that could go wrong with your program, even the most outlandish possibilities (the edge cases), and then map them in your user-flow diagram.

Document how both you and your mobile marketing application will react if one or more of

these scenarios comes to pass. What if some of your potential customers speak French instead of English, for example? Your mobile subscriber may respond to your program's opt-in call to action by sending *oui* instead of *yes* as instructed. To prepare for that possibility, you need to configure your mobile marketing application to accept *oui, si, yup, ok, yse, yes, y,* and so on as synonyms of *yes.*

Providing Text Promotions

One of the most basic mobile marketing communication programs you may want to run is a text promotion. In a *text promotion,* a mobile subscriber sends a text message to a mobile marketing application, and the application sends a message back. The content of the message depends on the nature of your program, but it may include details about a new movie or a recipe and coupon.

Setting up a text promotion service in your mobile marketing application can be as straightforward as filling out a form on the web.

Using quizzes to gather information and entertain

Mobile subscribers interact with quizzes by responding to questions sent to their phones. You can use text messaging in quiz programs to gather feedback, consumer opinions, or votes, as well as to inform and entertain. Your customers can have a great time with trivia programs, for example.

A *closed-ended* quiz is a program that gives mobile subscribers a fixed set of response options, such as *a, b, c,* and *d* or *true* and *false.* If a user gets the answer right, you can send a response message saying, "You're correct" or "You win." But if the user sends an answer that doesn't match any of the predefined answers, you should send back an error-response message with instructions for answering the question correctly. If the user tries to answer a question twice, you could send a reply like "I'm sorry, you've already answered that question" or "We did not understand your answer."

Setting quiz options

In addition to the typical user-flow program elements listed in the section "Planning Your Communication Flow," earlier in this chapter, your mobile marketing application provider should be able to provide the following configurable options for a quiz program:

✦ **Question-response format:** Decide which format you'll use for user responses, such as alphanumeric selection (*a, b, c,* and *d* or *1, 2, 3,* and *4*), binary choice (*true* and *false* or *yes* and *no*), or individual items (*red, green, blue,* and so on).

✦ **Question order:** Decide whether questions should be delivered in a fixed linear order or pulled randomly from a pool of questions. You may want your audience to answer the same five questions in a specific order, or you may have the service pull five questions randomly from a pool of 500, generating a random set of questions for each participant.

✦ **Question count:** Decide how many questions a user must answer to complete the program. If the quiz is configured so that the user has to answer five questions, for example, the mobile marketing application will send the next question in the sequence or pull one randomly (see the preceding item) until all the questions in the campaign sequence are sent and/or the user opts out of the service.

✦ **Autoresponse format:** Decide whether each question has a correct answer or is simply being used to collect user input (see the next section in this chapter). In either case, you also need to decide when to send an individual text message to the mobile subscriber: after each answer (correct or incorrect) or upon completion of the quiz, for example.

Setting response options

You may run a quiz that doesn't have correct or incorrect answers; you just want a response. In this case, you don't have to specify the response options as being correct or incorrect. All responses are simply accepted and recorded. Following are a few examples of response options you can set:

✦ **Clue:** If your program supports a clue element, users can request a clue to answer a question. Suppose that a user is stuck on question 3. If he texts *clue* or *hint* to the mobile marketing application, the application sends back a clue for the question — in this case, question 3.

✦ **Action on incorrect response:** Decide what happens when users give incorrect responses. If a user gets question 3 wrong, for example, does she simply start over or move on to the next question until the campaign question count is reached? (For more information about question count, refer to the previous section in this chapter.)

✦ **Response timing:** You can choose to run a speed quiz that measures the speed of user responses. The fastest responder may win, for example.

✦ **Participation cap:** You may want to set a participation cap to limit how many times users can participate in the program during a given period — one to ten times a day, once a week, once a month, one time only, or unlimited times through the entire program, for example.

✦ **Repeat questions:** Decide whether to configure the service so that users receive some questions more than once or whether they always get different questions.

✦ **Premium billing:** Decide whether to bill mobile subscribers for participation in the program. (For details on making money with your mobile marketing programs, see Chapter 6 in this minibook.)

Figure 3-3 shows some example quiz-response settings within a mobile marketing platform.

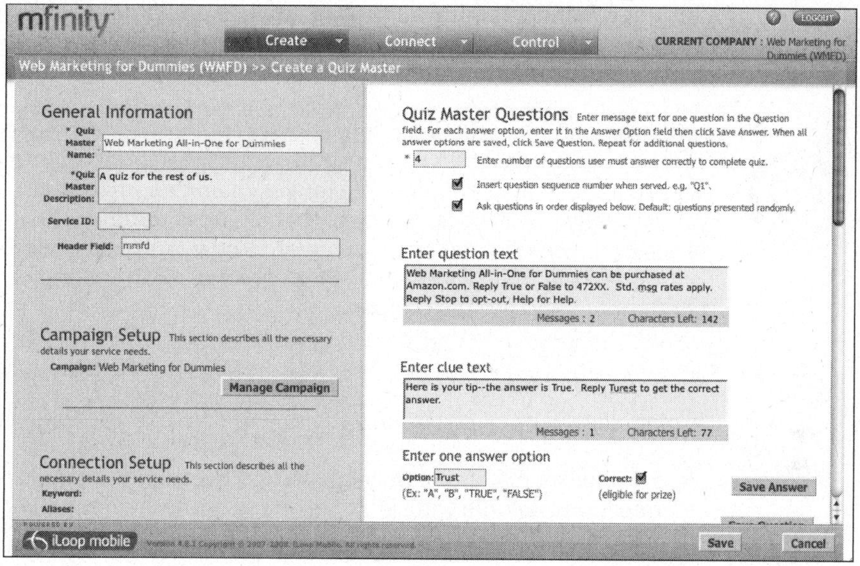

Figure 3-3:
Quiz
template
in a mobile
marketing
application.

You can also use the application for quizzes to direct mobile subscribers to a particular next step in an application's user flow, such as a product offering (a content storefront, for example) or another text-messaging campaign or service. You can use the response to a question to initiate a mobile subscriber into a horoscope program, for example. When the subscriber answers the question, his response is used to configure the next question to be sent to his phone.

Gathering input with open-ended survey questions

You can use open-ended, text-messaging survey programs to gather information such as consumer, candidate, or employee feedback. After a job interview, for example, you could send the candidate a text message like this: "Please give us your feedback on the interview process. Reply to this message with your feedback."

Unlike questions in quizzes (refer to the section "Using quizzes to gather information and entertain," earlier in this chapter), survey questions sent to mobile subscribers' phones don't have preconfigured response options, such as multiple choice or true/false. Rather, subscribers are asked a question and invited to send free-form responses. You may ask a mobile subscriber "What's your e-mail address?" for example. When he answers

**Book VIII
Chapter 3**

**Running Mobile
Communication
Campaigns**

this question, the mobile marketing application automatically sends the next question, and the process repeats until all the required questions have been sent and answered.

Ask your mobile marketing application provider whether you can chain your survey program, or even your quiz programs, with any other mobile marketing programs you're running. When you chain one program to another, you can do really cool things. Suppose that a user is opting in to your couponing program. If you chain a survey template to the coupon service, you can collect the user's preferences and other personal information before you allow her to opt in and get the coupon.

Planning the survey

In planning a survey program, you need to consider the following points:

+ **How many questions to ask:** Don't go overboard. If you ask too many questions, people will simply drop out without completing their participation in your program.

+ **The order in which questions will be asked:** Think about the order in which you ask the questions. Does some flow make particular sense?

+ **The required length of answers:** Remember that most people don't have mobile phones with full keyboards, and pecking out long messages can be tedious for them. Try to limit the information you need to short responses.

Setting survey options

In addition to the typical user-flow program elements listed in the section "Planning Your Communication Flow," earlier in this chapter, your mobile marketing application provider should be able to provide the following configurable options for your survey program:

+ **Question count:** Decide how many questions a user must answer to complete the program.

+ **Question order:** Decide whether questions are always delivered in a fixed linear order or pulled randomly from a pool of questions.

+ **Question labels:** Make sure that your mobile marketing application allows you to use a configuration tool to label your survey questions. Later, when you data-mine and report on the survey responses, the labels help you sort and organize the data. (For details on reporting on your programs, see Chapter 7 of this minibook.)

Calling People to Action: Polling

In *polls* (also referred to as *votes*), unlike quizzes and surveys, the questions you want your audience members to answer are placed in media: billboards; in-store end caps; newspapers; television, e-mail, and radio programs; and so on. Like quizzes and surveys, however, polling allows you to gather audience members' opinions and feedback as well as to inform and entertain.

Mobile subscribers see or hear the call to action (such as "Text *a* or *b* to cast your vote"), and when they respond, the mobile marketing application sends a reply (such as "Thanks. You voted *a*. Total tally: *a* 35%, *b* 6%, *c* 59%"). See Figure 3-4 for a poll user flow.

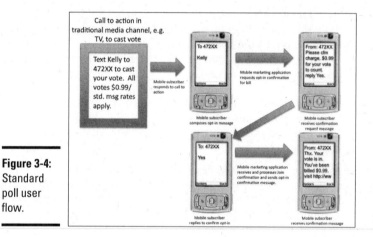

Figure 3-4: Standard poll user flow.

Choosing a poll type

Following are some of the most common uses of mobile polling and voting:

✦ **Television voting/polling:** The CBS Show *Survivor* uses texts to have viewer vote on the player of the week, with those that vote having the chance to win $10,000. Millions of people participate every week.

✦ **Live-event polling and voting:** Increasingly, polling and voting are being used in live events such as sporting events, keynote speeches, and radio broadcasts. The call to action for the poll is placed in traditional media, and people respond. Then the results of the poll are displayed on the stadium's in-venue display screens, on a screen behind the speaker, or on the radio station's website.

If you expect high-volume interactions — hundreds of thousands or even millions of messages in just a few hours — be sure to consult your mobile marketing application provider and connection aggregator. They can fine-tune their systems to ensure that high-volume traffic is processed efficiently. Often, in the case of high-volume programs, the marketer opts to turn off the poll's immediate-message-response feature so that the mobile marketing application can spend all its time processing poll responses. Responses can be sent after all the poll responses are processed.

Be sure to take time zones into account when you decide when the delayed responses should be sent. You don't want to wake people up in the middle of the night.

Setting poll options

In addition to the typical user-flow program elements listed in the section "Planning Your Communication Flow," earlier in this chapter, your mobile marketing application provider should be able to provide the following configurable options for your poll program:

✦ **Question-response format:** Decide which format you'll use for user responses, such as alphanumeric selection (*a, b, c,* and *d* or *1, 2, 3,* and *4*), binary choice (*true* and *false* or *yes* and *no*), or individual items (*red, green, blue,* and so on).

✦ **Response message:** Decide whether you want to include poll statistics in your response message (such as "Thank you. You voted *a,* and so did 60% of the other participants"). Ask your mobile marketing application provider whether it can support real-time results in your response messages.

Offering Incentives: Gifts, Freebies, Samples, and Coupons

It should come as no surprise to you that people respond to incentives. Offer them something of value, and they'll be more inclined to participate in your program and initiate communication with you. Continue offering them value, and they may become customers. Keep offering them value, and they'll become loyal customers. Keep offering them value after that, and you'll turn them into evangelists who'll start doing your marketing for you. This process starts with the first engagement, and an incentive is a great way to kick-start the interaction.

The most common forms of incentives are

✦ **Money:** Coupons, discounts on services, or even hard cash

✦ **Content:** Free ringtones, wallpapers, images, and so on

✦ **Free stuff and experiences:** Tickets for trial and sample products, free movie admissions, a chance to go backstage and meet the star, and so on

In the United States, wireless carriers tend to frown on your offering free content such as ringtones and wallpapers, especially if they're selling the same content via their branded content storefronts on the phone. Free content programs must be preapproved and certified with the wireless carriers, and your best shot at getting approval is offering content that isn't available anywhere else.

Not surprisingly, offering this type of content is also your best shot at getting mobile subscriber participation; many subscribers value unique and/or personalized content.

Managing prize promos, contests, and giveaways

It's common practice in marketing to offer prize promotions, run contests, and give stuff away as incentives to encourage people to participate in marketing programs. You could run a program that gives small prizes instantly throughout the campaign period and ends by awarding one lucky participant a grand prize, such as a new car or a vacation trip. This format works well in traditional marketing programs, and it works well in mobile marketing programs too.

You can enhance any of your mobile marketing promotions — text-based communication programs, voice programs, mobile Internet programs, and so on — with incentives. The process is simple:

1. **Promote the incentive along with the call to action to participate.**

2. **Set the odds of winning (often a configurable element) in the mobile marketing application.**

   If you're going to have an instant-win component or a grand prize, configure the odds for that too.

3. **Coordinate with your prize fulfillment house if you're going to be giving away physical goods or services, or configure your mobile marketing application to award content (such as a ringtone) to be consumed on a mobile phone.**

Giving people a taste: Product-sampling programs

Sampling is another fantastic tool you should consider using in your marketing communications programs. For many products, all it takes to get a consumer hooked is that first use. Mobile marketing is a good vehicle for sampling. For digital content, you can deliver a clipped version of the song, a photo with *Preview* stamped on it, and so on. You can't get physical goods (such as a new sports drink) into a phone, however, so your best bet is to mail product samples to program participants or mail them a card that they can use to get the samples free at a local store.

To run a sampling program, promote it in traditional media. When a mobile subscriber responds, you can query him for his address via interactive voice response (IVR; see Chapter 6 of this minibook) or text messaging. (You could use a survey for this purpose.) When you have all the information, you can thank the user and send him a text message saying that he'll get his sample in a few days (barring any delays in shipping).

The mobile marketing company ShopText (www.shoptext.com) has refined this process to an art. With ShopText, you can set up not only sampling programs but also commerce programs.

When you run any type of contest, sweepstakes, or giveaway program, you must work with your legal team to document the rules and the related terms and conditions of your program. The law requires you to provide this documentation. Every state has its own laws about these types of programs; if you're running a campaign, make sure that you're compliant with all the individual state laws. You can read more about the legalities of mobile campaigns in Chapter 1 of this minibook.

Offering mobile coupons

Coupons are very effective tools for driving participation in mobile marketing. The following sections discuss three common ways to deliver coupons to a mobile phone: text messaging, applications downloaded to the phone, and bar codes.

Coupons by text messaging

Text messaging (see Figure 3-5) is by far the most ubiquitous way to deliver coupons to mobile phones. As in any mobile marketing program, users can request the coupons by responding to your promos in traditional media, or if they've given you consent, you can push a coupon to them.

Figure 3-5:
Coupon
in text
message.

Text coupons are alphanumeric codes consisting of letters, symbols, and/or numbers (*a23bcs-win,* for example). Your mobile marketing application can generate the coupon codes automatically. Alternatively, the application can generate the codes from a spreadsheet containing your own coupons — coupons that are compatible with your point-of-sale (POS) system or website. All the mobile subscriber needs to do to redeem the coupon is show the coupon code to a store employee (if you're using a POS system) or complete a form on your website.

The most challenging part of closing the loop of coupon marketing is point-of-sale redemptions. Make sure that you train your people, or your client's people, so that they know what to do when a mobile subscriber brings a mobile coupon into the store.

Coupons through bar codes

Another emerging method of couponing (and ticketing, by the way) is the use of actions codes, traditional 1D bar codes, and QR codes (another form of a bar code). When you use this method, you deliver a 2D or 3D bar code to a user's phone; a special POS scanner reads the bar code and starts the coupon/ticket redemption process. (Traditional in-store scanners can't read a mobile phone's screen reliably, and phone screens are very small, so bar-code data footprints are limited.)

Incentives through offer networks

Text messaging is not the only medium for couponing. Offer networks are emerging that are capable of delivering an incentive across all networks. Offer networks are services that distribute coupons and related incentives through mobile websites, applications, and mobile advertisements. An offer network aggregates an audience outside a company's owned digital media channels and, on behalf of the company, presents offers where users are living their digital lives — in games, on social networking sites, and in online communities.

mphoria (www.mphoria.com) is a great example of a leading offer network in the market today, and companies like Omaha Steaks have generated stellar results by working with it. By partnering with mphoria, Omaha Steaks has successfully reached consumers through new channels and redirected them to Omaha's website or retail stores for direct purchase. Shoppers can redeem offers by linking them to their credit card or by purchasing online through a custom discounted order link.

One challenge with this method, however, is that the 2D and 3D scanners can be quite expensive. Although they're common in some countries, such as Japan, they're not widely deployed in the United States. Another challenge is that mobile phones and networks must be configured to support 2D and 3D bar codes, which will be a while before this method becomes popular.

Applying User-Generated Content

The mobile phone is an extremely personal device for communicating, gathering information, and conducting commerce and exchange, as well as for personal expression. The past few years have seen a groundswell of user-generated content (UGC, for short). *UGC* is any type of content — videos, pictures, text, news, stories, and so on — that people create and share with their own communities and society at large. In fact, it is estimated that 70 percent of all the content on the Internet is created by the user.

Mobile is a perfect tool for UGC. People use mobile phones to send text messages, take videos, place calls, snap pictures, send e-mail, post status updates, check in, and so on. Mobile subscribers also use every one of these capabilities to create content.

The following sections provide an overview of some of the most common forms of UGC.

Mobile posting and social networking

Posting is the practice of maintaining or contributing to a community website, blog, or social media portal. Through these, updated commentary is featured on any number of topics, event descriptions, and UGC (videos, pictures, and so on). People commonly use mobile phones for blogging.

From a marketing prospective, you can take advantage of social services by encouraging mobile subscribers to like, comment, or provide some related comment or attribution about your product service. You should encourage people to:

✦ Send comments, notes, thoughts, and observations to social sites via text messaging, e-mail, or Multimedia Messaging Service (MMS)

✦ Send pictures and videos

✦ Send audio posts

✦ Like and/or otherwise provide a comment

All you need to do is connect your mobile marketing application with the various social media services. This feature is available on all the major social media platforms, including Twitter, YouTube, and Facebook. As your audience members submit content, the content is sent to the service.

It's a really good idea — if not imperative — to have a moderation step between UGC submission and UGC display on the site. You should use both an automated filter system and a real person to look at all user-submitted content and evaluate its suitability. If the moderator accepts the content, it gets posted on the site immediately. If the moderator deems the content to be unsuitable, she can reject it, and the content isn't displayed.

Text-to-screen and experiential campaigns

Another popular form of consumer interaction via text is text-to-screen, a simple idea that can create a lot of interaction with live audiences at sporting events, concerts, television broadcasts, and so on. In a text-to-screen program, you place a call to action in traditional media (the giant video screens at a sporting event, a public-address announcement at a concert, or a ticker at the bottom of the TV screen, for example), inviting mobile subscribers to send a text message (such as encouragement for the team or a shout-out to a friend), a photo (such as a picture of a group of friends watching the event), or some other content. When it receives a message of this type, the mobile marketing application places the message in a moderation queue.

Then, after the message has been moderated by an automated system or a live person, it's displayed on-screen at the event for a few seconds.

Another useful application of text-to-screen is to poll audience members during live presentations. Unlike mobile polls, in which mobile subscribers answer questions, in text-to-screen programs, mobile subscribers ask the questions. You present the call to action during the event, and subscribers text their question, which you moderate and display on-screen. Then the presenter can look at the screen and provide answers to the audience. This same capability has been used in live events to provide real-time feedback to speakers, but as you might expect, feedback sometimes distracts the speaker, especially if the feedback is negative. Leading text-to-screen applications providers include Mozes (`www.mozes.com`), Vibes (`www.vibes.com`), and so on.

This chapter just scratches the surface of what is possible with SMS. A lot of topics aren't covered, including customer relationship management loyalty programs, customer support and care programs, more advanced secure SMS programs, and "intelligent" programs like those offered by iLoop Mobile and its Smart SMS solution (`www.iloopmobile.com`).

Tell-a-friend (word-of-mouth) programs

It's generally understood that we're more likely to accept a message coming from a friend, a colleague, or someone we know and trust than from an anonymous person or group. In a *tell-a-friend* program (also referred to as *word of mouth* and *viral marketing*), you can have people share your message with friends rather than communicate it yourself, thereby leveraging existing bonds of trust. You may want to encourage your subscribers to forward mobile coupons or website links to their friends in the hope that the community will help you get out your message about your offerings.

Most of the time, people will forward your message simply for the love of sharing interesting things with their friends. If you're running a loyalty program, however, you may want to offer loyalty points or some other form of incentive each time a user forwards a message.

Chapter 4: Displaying Your Advertising on Mobile Devices

In This Chapter

✓ Leveraging buyers, publishers, and networks

✓ Understanding how to buy mobile advertising

✓ Discovering how to monetize your sites with advertising

✓ Placing mobile ads in front of mobile users

*W*ith the proliferation of mobile devices and the increased consumer adoption of services like the mobile Internet and mobile applications, marketers are turning to mobile advertising, and like them, you can too to:

✦ Generate brand awareness. Increase the number of people who know about your company and its products and services.

✦ Increase the likelihood that consumers may want to buy your products.

✦ Increase sales by driving traffic directly to a transaction.

✦ Generate new revenue streams by including advertising in your messaging, mobile Internet sites, and applications.

If you've never bought an advertisement in your life, or even if you're not sure how you can use mobile advertising, don't worry. You've come to the right place. In this chapter, you get up to speed about mobile advertising: what it is, who to work with, and how to buy and sell it.

Squeezing the Advantages Out of Mobile Advertising

Mobile advertising is the practice of a marketer (also referred to as a buyer) placing paid-for promotional content and sponsorship messages within a publisher's mobile media property as supported by a mobile advertising network or search provider (see Figure 4-1). For example:

✦ Text messages, multimedia messages, and e-mail messages

✦ Mobile Internet sites, both your own and others

> ✦ Mobile applications that people download through application stores
>
> ✦ Mobile audio and video content that plays on a mobile device

For a compressive list of all the different types of mobile advertising players, see the Mobile LUMAscape at `www.lumapartners.com/lumascapes/mobile-lumascape`.

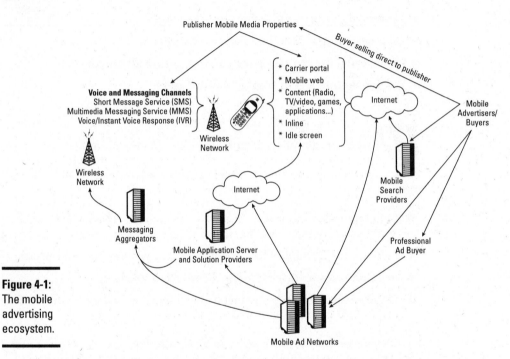

Figure 4-1:
The mobile advertising ecosystem.

Mobile advertising is a lot like online advertising, but with three key advantages over traditional online advertising. You should become familiar with each advantage so that you can include them in your marketing plans:

✦ **Reach:** *Reach* is defined as the number of unique individuals seeing an ad at least one time during a specific period. To get the best results for the least amount of money, you want your ad to be exposed to as many people (in other words, to have as broad a reach) as possible.

Mobile has the potential of greater reach than any other medium because a lot of people are carrying a mobile device or tablet and increasingly using mobile media like SMS, mobile Internet, and applications. Research firms like InsightExpress (`www.insightexpress.com`) also point out that mobile generates better brand awareness and overall purchase intent than online media advertising. You can find out more about increasing your reach in the next section.

✦ **Relevancy:** *Relevancy* refers to an ad or advertised product being pertinent to the target audience. If your product or message within your ad campaign is not targeted to a relevant audience, the ad campaign will be ineffective. Increasingly, ad networks are able to adjust the content and type of ad to take many factors into account, such as the consumer's physical location, type of phone, direction of travel (and speed), stated preferences and interests, demographic profile, and past and current behaviors (like what he owns or is reading). By taking all this information into account in real time, advertisers are able to ensure that your ad is placed in front of people who are interested in what you have to offer.

✦ **Immediacy:** Mobile offers the best "in the moment" engagement. Given the personal nature, the uncluttered space (most pages have only one or two ads), and the, well, mobile nature of the mobile medium, when they're presented with a relevant ad, mobile users are often inclined to respond immediately. Unlike other forms of advertising, mobile advertising can reach a user while she is interacting with a brand or product. For example, an ad for laundry detergent is much more relevant to someone standing in the grocery store than someone sitting at work in front of a computer.

Leveraging Different Types of Mobile Advertising

Mobile advertising can take a variety of forms. You should be aware of each so that you can know your options and think about advertising across multiple channels and formats, which broadens your reach.

Given the rich diversity of mobile media and devices, mobile advertising has a lot of potential. The following sections help you become acquainted with the different types of mobile advertising and its advantages.

Using multiple ad units and placements

The first thing to consider when building a mobile advertising strategy is the type of advertising you want to do. The type of advertising you want to do is known as an *ad unit*. Because each type of mobile advertising space and device supports a different type of advertising, you need to format your advertising using the ad units that make the most sense for each opportunity. Here are the most common types of ad units:

✦ **Text:** Text ads consist of alphanumeric text, including mobile Internet URLs and phone numbers.

✦ **Banner ads:** Banner ads refer to both static and animated images displayed on mobile Internet pages, in applications, in video, and in animated content (see Figure 4-2).

**Book VIII
Chapter 4**

Displaying Your
Advertising on
Mobile Devices

Chevron sponsorship
ad in an application

Text link in mobile web page

Mobile web link
in a text message

Figure 4-2:
Banner
ads are
not limited
to mobile
Internet or
application
pages.

Different formats of display advertising

Rich media advertising

+ **Audio ads:** Audio ads refer to advertisements inserted into audio content, music and radio, directory services, and event text-to-speech services (for example, when a service reads a mobile web page to you, advertisements may be interlaced into the content).

+ **Rich-media ads:** Rich-media ads take banner advertising to the next level and are supported on only the latest smartphones and mobile devices. A rich-media ad unit may include text, images, video, animation, and audio that may expand to full-screen, float on the screen, or perform any number of other interactive and visual gymnastics. In addition, rich-media ad units may leverage the advanced capabilities of the latest mobile devices, like location detection, interaction through the touchscreen, or unique motions of the device (like shaking it).

Almost any mobile advertisement may appear at different places with mobile media, including

+ **Pre-appended or post-appended to a text message, MMS message, or mobile Internet site:** That is, at the beginning or end of the message or site.

✦ **Inline:** The ad is placed in line within a message, a page, or application.

✦ **Pre-roll or post-roll:** In this case, the ad is placed at the start or end of a video or audio clip.

✦ **Interstitial (or bumper ad unit):** The ad is displayed when pages are loading or when applications are downloading.

✦ **Idle screen:** The ad is displayed on the home screen of the device when it sits idle for a period of time, maybe a few seconds or minutes.

Each type of ad unit and placement decision is valuable in and of itself, but advertising is most effective when a variety of messages get in front of the same consumer. Make sure that you're familiar with all the advertisement types and placements before you come up with your strategy. You also have to think about the device platforms: iPhone versus Android and tablet versus smartphone are two to consider. Consumers respond to different advertising on the different platforms. Be sure to include three or more ad units and placements in any given advertising campaign. Visit the Mobile Marketing Association (`http://mmaglobal.com/main`) to find out more.

Placing ads in mobile search

Everyone who browses the web uses search engines to find websites, and advertisers place ads on search engines like Google or Yahoo! to attract clicks from the people who are searching for things. Mobile search is a practice similar to Internet search, but with mobile search, people use their mobile phones to conduct the searches.

Most people who engage in mobile search still go to the most familiar search engines, but you should be aware of some key differences in the way that mobile search advertisements work so that you can alter any of your search engine advertisements that are targeted at mobile searchers. (If you want to learn the basics of placing search engine ads in general, turn to Book IV.) Here are the key factors to remember about mobile search:

✦ **Mobile searches are usually optimized for location.** Search providers like Google, oneSearch, AT&T Interactive (`www.attinteractive.com`), and Microsoft with its Bing service have optimized search programs to take into account a user's location. Local search providers can be very effective as well, such as Yelp (`www.yelp.com`), Marchex (`www.marchex.com`), Citysearch (`www.citysearch.com`), Where (`www.where.com`), Poynt (`www.poynt.com`), and others. For example, if you're in San Jose, California, and you're using your mobile browser to look for a pizza place, Google starts by showing you the results for pizza places near where you are standing.

✦ **Mobile users have access to mobile question-and-answer services.** These services allow users to post questions to the service. Automated or live agents (meaning real people) answer the questions. Some of the leading providers of this service include Snackable Media (www.snack ablemedia.com), ChaCha (www.chacha.com), and MobileBits (www.mobilebits.com). These services don't own the whole search market, but it's a good idea to be on one or more of them so that your business can be the answer to someone's question about your products or services.

✦ **Mobile directories are friendlier than web directories.** Mobile directory search, like the local yellow pages, helps people find local services nearby. Mobile directories sell listings and are optimized for smaller screens. When listing on a mobile search directory, make sure that your listing points to a mobile website.

Working with mobile search providers to place search engine advertising is pretty easy. For most solutions, you don't have to do anything technically different from your web-based search advertising to get your search engine advertisements to appear on mobile screens.

In addition to placing paid search advertisements, make sure that your mobile websites are optimized for search engines so that your site appears in organic search results.

Grasping the Basics of Buying and Selling Mobile Advertisements

Mobile advertising involves two primary players — the buyer and the publisher — either or both of which may be your company or another company, depending on the situation. Here's how it works:

✦ The company that pays to place a marketing message in an available mobile space is called the mobile *ad buyer*. For example, you're the ad buyer when you buy an ad on someone else's mobile website. Another company can be the ad buyer when it buys an ad on your behalf. You may also hear ad buyers referred to as media buyers.

✦ The company that provides the space for an ad and takes the money from the buyer is called the *ad publisher*. For example, you're the ad publisher when you sell ad space on your own mobile website to an ad buyer, and another company is the ad publisher when you buy advertising space from it.

Buying and publishing mobile advertising require a combination of technology, connections, and expertise. If you have all three, you might be able to buy and publish your own mobile advertisements. Chances are, however, that you'll need at least one of the companies described in the following sections to be successful with all your mobile advertising.

Partnering with media agencies

If buying mobile advertising is not within your area of expertise, you may choose to work with an outside ad buyer (also called a *media agency*). Media agencies are ad buyers that negotiate and purchase mobile advertising space or inventory on your behalf. Buyers work with you to plan and spend advertising budgets so that you can maximize the return on investment for a given ad campaign.

Here are some scenarios where you might want to consider using a professional mobile media buyer:

✦ **You want to advertise on premium sites, such as MTV, CNN, The Tribune Company, ESPN, the Weather Channel, Disney, and others.** These organizations tend to sell their own ad inventory or work with a specialist group. Moreover, they often want to work through a media buyer, meaning that they don't want to work with you (the buyer) directly, unless your budgets are fairly large and your needs are unique.

✦ **You have a large budget.** When you have a large budget, the buyer can help you draw up a strategy to ensure that your advertisements are spread across all the appropriate mobile media, with the right reach and frequency (the number of times an ad is displayed in a given period). A lot of work goes into this, and you definitely ought to leverage the buyer's expertise.

✦ **You need to place ads across several mobile mediums.** If you want to advertise across mobile mediums, such as SMS, MMS, mobile Internet, applications, and so on, realize that a lot of work goes into understanding how to buy the media as well as deliver it. You shouldn't try to become an expert in all of them — let the buyer do that. If you're buying in only one medium, however, you can go directly to companies like 4INFO (www.4info.com) for text-messaging advertising or Google (www.google.com/ads/mobile) for display advertising.

✦ **You need several inventory sources.** *Inventory* refers to all the possible locations where your advertisement may be placed in all the different forms of mobile media. Even the biggest media properties such as CNN or ESPN may not be able to get you the reach and the exposure you're looking to achieve with your advertising. You may need to go to many media companies and use many mobile mediums to get the reach you're looking for. A buyer can help you with this.

Book VIII Chapter 4

Displaying Your Advertising on Mobile Devices

✦ **You want a discount.** An ad buyer can negotiate discounted rates due to prior relationships and bulk rates. He also knows the best sources of inventory. He saves you time and money and delivers better results by managing the different allocations of spending across inventory sources where the ROI (return on investment) is highest.

✦ **You want to reach a specific audience.** If you're looking to reach a specific audience, a practice referred to as *targeting,* you'll want to work with a specialist in hyperlocal advertising like Where (www.where.com) or Poynt (www.poynt.com), or a premium network like Pandora (www.pandora.com), which intersperses audio advertisements throughout its programming. These organizations can help you reach people based on demographics, location, time of day, past and current activity, preferences and interests, and any number of other factors.

✦ **You're short on time.** You should use an ad buyer when you can't dedicate resources to real-time campaign management, monetization, and the negotiations for getting the best price for your advertising buys.

✦ **You need an expert.** For big-spending clients new to the advertising space, buyers can provide more expert industry knowledge and resources to invest in the most relevant products and targeting methods.

Resources such as the Mobile Marketing Association (www.mmaglobal.com) and *Advertising Age* (http://adage.com/datacenter) can provide lists of the most popular ad-buying agencies. The choice of which to use is a personal one and can depend on your product, the size of the ad, and the resources that an agency can dedicate to an ad campaign. You really have no easy way to figure out which one is best for you. You simply need to call a few candidates to see whether they know anything about your market and whether their pricing is competitive. If they've been in the industry a long time, you probably can trust that they can do a good job, but be sure to look at smaller firms that may be hungry for your business or have a unique specialty in serving your market. Sometimes the larger firms won't understand the nuances of your business, in which case a smaller firm may do a better job for you.

Because every ad needs a space to be seen by consumers and because advertising generally works better when it's placed in lots of spaces, every ad buyer needs to buy space from *multiple* publishers. If you're working through a formal ad buyer or agency, however, you won't have to interact with mobile publishers directly. The agency will work on your behalf to purchase relevant inventory on placements to obtain the highest ROI.

Another advantage of using media agencies to buy ads for you is that they can also work with multiple publishers to provide data that shows how your ads are performing on their sites in aggregate.

Working with mobile advertising enablers

Mobile advertising enablers are companies that help advertisements get distributed to mobile devices. You'll find mobile advertising networks, exchanges, demand- and supply-side platforms, real-time building providers, search solutions, and so much more.

This section focuses on *mobile advertising networks,* companies that aggregate supply and demand for advertisers and publishers by buying inventory from multiple publishers and by providing different types of ad units. They allow buyers and agencies to reach groups of people who use different mobile sites without needing to work with a different publisher for each site. For example, if an advertiser would like to target females age 25–54, the ad network can target multiple sites that attract a large number of women within this age range. Women from the category who use different websites see the same ads, and the women from the category who use multiple websites see the ads multiple times. Millennial Media, shown in Figure 4-3, is one of the industry's leading mobile advertising networks.

Figure 4-3: Millennial Media, an industry-leading mobile advertising network.

Advertising with crosses

When ad networks target ads, they usually base them on several crosses. *Crosses* are characteristics of the ad and the audience that intersect, such as the intersection of age, interests, location, and gender. Examples include the type of handset, demographics, geography, gender, and so on.

The people at mobile advertising networks use a lot of geek-speak to describe the different programs they offer. Here are some of the ways mobile advertising networks can help you target consumers and the terminology you need to be familiar with if you want to get your point across:

- **Run of network:** Your ad runs on sites across the mobile ad network's full list of publisher sites, at a frequency set by you. When placing run-of-network ads, make sure that you know your network's reach in terms of number of audience members and audience makeup. Your network should have these numbers, but Nielsen also issues a monthly custom rollup of the mobile advertising networks that indicates the reach capabilities of each ad network. The Nielsen numbers may be licensed for a fee. (See www.nielsen. com.) Sometimes, however, you can find Nielsen summary reports available for free at www.slideshare.net and www. marketingcharts.com.

- **Channel:** You can choose to target your ad by content affinity, such as advertising on all-sports sites, female sites, or automobile enthusiast sites.

  When targeting channels, don't be afraid to cross channels to hit an intersection of your target, for example, crossing the female and sports channel to hit only females within sports sites.

- **Custom subnet or subnetwork:** Your mobile ad network sets up a two-tier custom affinity site list. Examples include female sports sites or working mothers.

  Make sure to tell the network the specifics of your demographics, but do not narrow it too much or you will ultimately limit the total reach of your campaign. For example, if you are marketing an expensive electronics sale, don't target only users with an annual household income of more than $150,000. Instead, be a bit more broad, say, to $100,000. You're advertising your brand to this larger demographic and also hitting users more likely to buy as well, with the specific message of a sale.

- **Takeovers or network blocks:** A *takeover* or *network block* is also commonly referred to in the online space as a *roadblock*. Ultimately, these refer to large ad campaigns (in terms of budget and target impressions) delivered in a short time frame (typically less than a day or two). A takeover simply means fully taking over inventory (typically only one mobile site or a segment of one site), owning every ad on that particular target within the specific time. A network block is used only by networks and targets a large amount of impressions within a target audience (based on geographic location, demographics, gender, channel, and so on) across a group of sites.

  Typically, any type of block has two goals: reach (to hit as many unique people as possible within your target) and frequency (to hit all users as many times as they access the inventory). You can only maximize one of these goals within one campaign because they are inversely related. Given that blocks are not performance geared (driving traffic or having a user complete an action), they are typically only sold on a CPM (cost-per-thousand) or flat-rate basis. These are a "must-buy" component of an advertiser's ad strategy mix.

If you work with a sophisticated ad network, chances are that it can uniquely identify users and therefore create custom audiences based on affinity and behavior. Keep in mind that the more targeted your ads, the higher your advertising costs. For a full list of the global mobile ad networks, their attributes, and how they stack up against other similar mobile ad nets, visit mobiThinking at `www.mobithinking.com`.

Additionally, mobile advertising networks allow an advertiser to target multiple audiences with one or more specific characteristics that span the entire audience. For example, you might want to advertise to people who live in Boston, love sports, and own iPhones. Your advertising network can place your ads on mobile sports sites and display the ads only to people in Boston using an iPhone. Networks can also allow you to target by behavior, so someone who loves the Yankees won't see your ads when they visit a sports site while they happen to be visiting Boston.

If you decide to work with an advertising network, some of these organizations have HTML script (software code) that they'll give to you to paste into your site. Google is one such network.

After the code is in your site, everyone who visits your mobile web page (or application) sees the ads that your advertising network pulls based on relevancy to the page or application being viewed.

Buying ads directly from publishers

If you choose not to advertise through an advertising network, you need to reach out directly to the sales staff that sells the space for the publisher to buy space for your mobile advertising. You can get a list of top mobile ad sites by looking at Nielsen (`www.nielsen.com`) — a top data-collection and research firm with specific outlets for mobile data. Visit its website to find out how to license its data.

Some publishers can also be aggregators that work with several inventory sources at once. These aggregate publishers can help you simplify what would otherwise be a very complex process of ad placements because mobile handsets, carriers, and diversity in the types of ad space tend to require many different creative and technical capabilities. Strong mobile publishers also have best practices to ensure creative compatibility.

When you go directly to a publisher to make ad placements, ask your publisher for advice so that you can decide how much to spend. Mobile publishers should be able to evaluate the best placement for ads. They do this based on their audience and traffic and by choosing when and how often to show ads to optimize the user experience on the site and maximize interactions with ads. If your mobile publisher can't show you lots of useful data, don't buy space from him!

Advertising with mobile carriers

Mobile carriers such as Verizon, AT&T, Sprint, and T-Mobile offer advertising space on their proprietary mobile sites, also known as *on-deck inventory*. Carrier sites are a good choice when your goal is to reach only the customers using a specific carrier, but keep in mind that you'll need to also consider other characteristics of the people who use that carrier.

Understanding all the carrier's devices, users, geographic coverage, and data plans can become cumbersome, especially when you're trying to run a single ad campaign on more than one carrier's inventory. Unless you really need to reach the customers of a specific carrier, choose a mobile advertising network instead.

Paying publishers and billing buyers for mobile ads

Mobile advertising is purchased on terms that are based on the level of interaction with the ad — just like online advertising. The terms can dictate the cost of each ad displayed or the cost of various actions taken in response to an ad. Here are the most common payment terms for mobile advertising, followed by some advice for choosing the right method:

✦ **Cost-per-thousand (CPM):** CPM means that you pay a fee based on the cost of 1,000 *impressions* (every time the ad appears in front of someone). For example, a CPM of $5 means that you pay $5.00 for every 1,000 times your ad appears. Keep in mind that CPM does not require anyone to click the ad or even to look at the ad. It just means it was displayed when someone visited the page where the ad is placed. That's why CPM is typically used as a way to compare impressions to clicks or other actions rather than a way to bill you for advertisements.

✦ **Cost-per-click (CPC):** CPC means that you pay a fee every time someone clicks an ad (or, in the case of mobile, every time someone taps the ad). For example, a CPC of $5 means that you'll pay $5.00 every time someone taps one of your ads. Use this method when your main concern is driving traffic to a mobile website and you are trying to convert visitors to customers.

✦ **Cost-per-action (CPA):** CPA means that you pay a fee every time some-one completes a specific action as a result of tapping an ad, such as visiting a website, filling in a form, or sending a text message with a secret code word found in the ad. Use this method when your agency or another partner is responsible for driving traffic to a mobile website and converting visitors to customers for you.

✦ **Sponsorship:** Sponsorship means that buyers can also simply pay a pub-lisher a lump sum and sponsor the inventory in a media property for a fixed period of time. For example, you may sponsor the development of an application and pay a little extra to have your logo on the *launch screen* (the screen that appears when the app is loading) for a number of months.

You can't have a meaningful discussion about paying your mobile buyer, publisher, or network until you know what actions you want to pay for. Make sure that everyone involved understands your goals so that you can build a payment strategy that charges you no sooner than the moment you get value in return.

Getting a Return on Your Mobile Ad Buying

If you want to get a return on the money you spend buying mobile advertis-ing, make sure to pay attention to the purpose of your advertising in relation to the costs of your advertising. If you spend too much, it's probably not because you paid too much, but rather because

✦ You failed to effectively target your ads to the right audience.

✦ You paid the agency, network, or publisher for the wrong deliverable.

✦ You failed to invite your audience to take the right action on your ads.

The next sections explain how to target your ads and set them up to invite actions that lead to sales.

Choosing targets and formats for your mobile ads

Before placing any mobile advertisements, make sure that your ads are going to reach the right people — the people who are most likely to buy from you! Here are the questions you need to answer before you talk to an agency, make any placement decisions, or spend any money:

✦ **Am I trying to reach everyone or a specific group?** If you're targeting a specific group of people, you'll need to know which websites, applica-tions, and phones they use. Publishers can give you this information. Make sure to ask for it before placing any ads.

✦ **How do I want people to engage with my ad?** If you just want people to see your ads, you have more choices than if you need people to be able to click through and complete a purchase or share the ad through social media. You should choose actions that move your audience closer to completing one of your goals. Actions are discussed in more detail in the section "Inviting action on your mobile ads," later in this chapter.

✦ **How will I know that my ads achieved my goals?** Decide from the onset how you'll measure success and how you'll track and quantify your results. Your publisher or network can give you a variety of data points that demonstrate your advertising performance. Many of the ad networks allow you to create predictive models so that you can make your initial placement decisions and make changes afterward if you aren't getting the results you want.

After you have answered these questions, you should have a good idea of your target audience and target goals. The next step is to share these targets and goals with your publisher or agency or apply the goals to your network by including them in your ad parameters. Then you can begin creating your ads.

Creating banner ads for mobile properties

When creating banner ads for mobile properties — whether they're for mobile websites or applications — you need to make sure that your ads are sized and formatted correctly. If you're working with an agency or network, it usually has creative services to help you. If you're buying directly from a publisher, you need to do the creative work yourself in some cases. Even if you're outsourcing your creative work on some level, you need to keep the following in mind so that you can get the results you need:

✦ **Size:** You'll find many standard sizes for different screens. The Mobile Marketing Association (www.mmaglobal.com) in December 2011 released its MMA Universal Mobile Ad Package Whitepaper, a document that details the six universal ad sizes based on width and height most used across the world's leading networks and publishers. These include 120x20, 168x28, 216x36, 300x250, 300x50, and 320x50 pixels.

✦ **Format:** The format of the ad depends on the type of phone the ad is being served to and the network it's going over. It's best to work with an expert when deciding on a format because so many variations exist. For example, iPhones don't support Flash (Adobe's multimedia platform used to add video, animation, and interactivity to web pages), and most phones don't support JavaScript or other rich media.

✦ **Creative:** Your creative style matters, including the size of fonts, colors, and animation. For example, Dynamic Logic (www.dynamiclogic.com), a leading research firm, notes how often a simple static image may perform better than a more dynamic presentation.

✦ **Analytics:** Make sure that you've integrated a mobile analytics package such as Google Analytics (www.google.com/analytics), Abode Omniture (www.omniture.com), Webtrends (www.webtrends.com), or Bango (www.bango.com) to track the traffic on your properties and the success of your programs. The data from these tools helps you optimize your strategy.

Every media platform has a different setup of sizes, formats, and reporting capabilities, not to mention best practices. For example, Pandora (www.pandora.com) recommends through the MMA Universal Mobile Advertising Package (www.mmaglobal.com/files/umap.pdf) that streaming audio ads are accompanied by a full-screen companion banner (500x500) displayed for the duration of audio message (15 or 30 seconds long).

Inviting action on your mobile ads

Whether you use publishers, agencies, or networks to place your mobile ads, you need to decide what you want people to do, if anything, when they see your ads. Making your ads clickable or tappable is not enough. If you want people to take action on your ads, the ads need to suggest or invite those actions, and then those actions need to meet two criteria:

✦ **Your actions must be mobile friendly.** For example, if your mobile ad asks someone to tap or click the ad to visit your website, your website had better work properly on the mobile phone that person used to tap or click the ad.

✦ **Your actions must help you reach your goals.** For example, if your mobile ad asks someone to watch a video, that video had better include enough information and incentives to invite a purchase if you want to sell a product.

Mobile is a location-aware media. That means your ads can invite location-based actions without requiring a click or tap, such as asking someone to walk into a store and show the ad to a salesperson.

Here are some ways you can invite action from people using your mobile ads as the starting point, and some tips to make sure that those actions are friendly to mobile users. (Mobile advertisers call these *postclick actions.*)

✦ **Ask them to submit a form.** Use a mobile form to enlarge your mailing lists, take orders, or collect survey information. Mobile forms shouldn't be too long because screens and keyboards are small. The simpler, the better.

✦ **Invite click-to-call.** Click-to-call can happen two ways — directly from an ad or redirecting to a landing page that customers opt to dial. For an immediate response, click-to-call from the ad is the way to go because it immediately asks a user to tap and automatically dial the phone number. For a secondary opt-in to ensure that the user really wants to connect with someone live about the product, redirect the user to the landing page and give him the choice to dial there. This essentially acts like a double opt-in, which could lead to better caller quality, but could lead to drop-off (users getting impatient and moving away from the process before they make the call). In either case, make sure that your ad copy asks the caller to mention the ad so that you can track the number of calls resulting from your ads.

✦ **Display a coupon.** Use mobile ads as coupons to capture comparison shoppers on the go or to enable a discounted purchase on a mobile website.

✦ **Promote a store locator or map.** Mobile ads can be set up to utilize GPS so that you can direct shoppers to specific locations such as product displays or VIP parking lots.

✦ **Offer an application download.** If you've built an application, mobile ads are a great way to drive people to install the application on their phones.

✦ **Show a video.** Only certain phones are capable of displaying video on the handset. Typically publishers and ad networks are able to tell clients which handsets are video capable. The video must be formatted to fit mobile specifications. The videos can be created by an in-house mobile creative staff, or they can be outsourced to mobile creative agencies or ad networks with a creative department. Users have the option to inter-act with the ad campaign through streaming video, either through the ad unit or as a call to action on your mobile site or landing page. (The action could be to watch a movie preview, demo a product, watch an interview, and so on.) If a client doesn't have a video specifically built on her homepage, a link to a YouTube video works as well but is limited in the devices it can play on — at this time, mostly only smartphones.

Mobile enablers (like Rhythm, `www.rhythmnewmedia.com`; Smith Micro Software, `www.smithmicro.com`; Brightcove, `www.bright cove.com`; and VMIX, `www.vmix.com`) can help with video optimization and help you reach the largest audience able to view a video.

✦ **Make mobile commerce.** Allowing an immediate purchase as part of your call to action requires the consumer to provide credit card or pay-ment information. To enable this action, you need a mobile application or a secure mobile site.

✦ **Go social.** Direct people to your social media site to become fans or ask people to share your mobile ad with friends.

Mobile audio advertising

Don't forget the mobile phone is just that, a phone, and that voice calls can be made with it. Moreover, with the proliferation of smartphones, more and more users are streaming audio over the data channel (the Internet) over their phones, like with Pandora radio (www. pandora.com). Recently, a number of companies have emerged to make it possible to serve advertising into these audio channels. Here are a few examples:

✔ **Click-to-call audio advertising:** Buyers promote phone numbers in text messages, mobile websites, and applications, as shown in the following figure. When the ad is clicked, the phone dials and the ad plays.

The leading provider of this form of advertising is UpSNAP (www.upsnap.com).

✔ **Directory services:** Marchex (www. marchex.com) deploys a robust advertising-supported directory service. Consumers may receive free directory services and forgo the carrier charges by calling 1-800-Free411. To receive the free directory services, all they need to do is to listen to a few ads. This is a great place for buyers to research.

✔ **Internet radio:** As radio and related audio services go mobile, leading firms like TargetSpot (www.targetspot.com) are making it possible to buy advertising within mobile radio broadcasts.

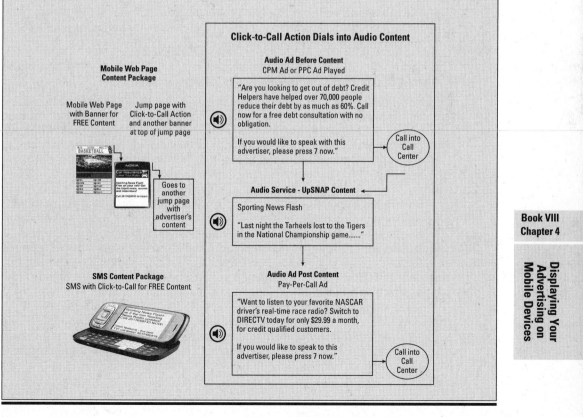

Click-to-Call Action Dials into Audio Content

Mobile Web Page Content Package

Mobile Web Page with Banner for FREE Content — Jump page with Click-to-Call Action and another banner at top of jump page

Goes to another jump page with advertiser's content

Audio Ad Before Content
CPM Ad or PPC Ad Played

"Are you looking to get out of debt? Credit Helpers have helped over 70,000 people reduce their debt by as much as 60%. Call now for a free debt consultation with no obligation.

If you would like to speak with this advertiser, please press 7 now."

Call into Call Center

Audio Service - UpSNAP Content

Sporting News Flash

"Last night the Tarheels lost to the Tigers in the National Championship game......."

SMS Content Package
SMS with Click-to-Call for FREE Content

Audio Ad Post Content
Pay-Per-Call Ad

"Want to listen to your favorite NASCAR driver's real-time race radio? Switch to DIRECTV today for only $29.99 a month, for credit qualified customers.

If you would like to speak to this advertiser, please press 7 now."

Call into Call Center

Book VIII Chapter 4

Displaying Your Advertising on Mobile Devices

Of course, if you just want people to see and remember your ads, that's okay too. Lots of companies use mobile advertising to increase recall or loyalty, and that doesn't necessarily require a click or tap. Just make sure that you're measuring recall and loyalty by taking surveys or doing research before and after you run your advertising campaigns.

Placing Ads in Your Own Mobile Properties

If you want to be an ad publisher and sell your own space to other ad buyers, or if you want to advertise your own products or services in the mobile properties you already own, you can use the available space in your mobile properties to place advertising as a publisher. For example, you could place advertisements in

✦ Your own mobile website

✦ Text messages and multimedia messages you send

✦ Mobile applications and downloadable content you own

Placing ads on your own mobile properties allows you to make money on those properties or pay for the costs to create them. Either way, mobile advertising is a great way to make money.

Placing ads on your own mobile site

If you're placing your own ads on your own site, or if you have a simple mobile website and only a few advertisers buying space from you, you can simply cut and paste the ads you create into the appropriate space on your mobile site. If you really want to make money selling mobile ads, use an advertising network so that you can sell your inventory to multiple buyers and allow them to bid for the price on your space.

If you want to publish with a network, you need to verify that your mobile marketing website application is integrated with one or more mobile advertising networks. If it's not, have a member of your technical team or your mobile applications provider contact a mobile advertising network aggregator to ask what it would take to integrate your application(s) with the ad network. After you have verified network integration, you can use one of two methods to include advertising network ads in your mobile web Internet sites and pages:

✦ **Use a mobile Internet visual editor.** Mobile Internet visual editors make placing ads on your mobile Internet site a snap. These editors are integrated with the leading mobile advertising networks. You simply need to get your account credentials (such as username and password) from the mobile advertising aggregator, paste this information into the editor, and click Save to insert an ad placeholder into your site. When a mobile subscriber visits your site, the mobile marketing application reaches out to the aggregator's system, requests an ad, places the ad on the site, and displays it to the mobile subscriber — all in a matter of seconds. See Figure 4-4 for an example of a mobile Internet site visual editor, like iLoop Mobile (www.iloopmobile.com), Mad Mobile (www.madmobile.com), DudaMobile (www.dudamobile.com), and others.

Figure 4-4:
Inserting ads into a mobile Internet site with a visual editor.

Courtesy of iLoop Mobile, Inc.

✦ **Paste ad network code into your pages.** If you're not using a visual editor and are simply working in code, getting an ad onto your mobile Internet site may take a few more steps, but is definitely doable. See the section "Working with mobile advertising enablers," earlier in this chapter.

Placing ads in your messaging

Text advertisements can be inserted into Short Message Service (SMS) messages to advertise products, services, or special offers. The ads are usually placed at the end of standard SMS messages as links, or the ads can stand as text alone. SMS ads are not display ads because they are made up of text only. SMS ads can be linked to display ads, however, as shown in Figure 4-5.

Figure 4-5:
SMS ads
can include
links to
display ads
placed on
mobile sites.

MMS (Multimedia Messaging Service) ads can be formatted with images, text, audio, and video, which makes them great for delivering richer ads, as shown in Figure 4-6.

Figure 4-6:
MMS ads
can contain
pictures or
videos.

Courtesy of Mogreet

Format is important here to allow the greatest number of viewers. Service providers can compress content like videos in your MMS advertising and use their unique application to make your content work across more carriers and handsets.

In most cases, MMS and SMS ads need to be sent through an MMS or SMS service as opposed to an advertising network because it's impossible to dynamically add advertising into MMS and SMS messages through code insertion.

Not all carriers support MMS messages. Using them may reduce the number of people you are able reach if rich content is the only communication you offer.

Advertising in applications and downloadable content

In-application or *in-app* refers to advertisements placed in free or paid applications installed on a mobile device. Ads can be sold within applications to make money or to help offset the cost of building and maintaining the applications. Ads can also be placed by the application owner to increase the brand recall or confidence of the people who use the applications. Ads can also be placed in downloadable content, such as videos, ringtones, or podcasts, to achieve the same goals as in-app advertising.

Placing ads in mobile applications and downloads requires forethought because you need to include the ability to display advertising when you're building the applications or downloads. Talk to your programmers or application providers about including dynamic ad network servers or static display ads and make sure that your agency is aware of your goals and target audience.

Chapter 5: Delivering Valuable Mobile Content

In This Chapter

✔ Developing and distributing mobile content

✔ Adding value with mobile applications, enhancements, and games

✔ Setting up a mobile Internet site

Customers are looking for value — that is, they want to acquire content, goods, and services, as well as engage in experiences that they find to be genuinely useful, informative, educational, enriching, delightful, or entertaining when they interact with you. The mobile channel is an ideal medium for value exchange.

Perhaps you want to send content produced by your business, use content as a promotional offer to create awareness for your business, or offer points and coupons that can be redeemed for content, experiences, or products and services. Or maybe you want to generate brand utility by offering store locators, nutrition or financial calculators, shopping-comparison widgets, and similar services. If so, you've come to the right chapter.

When you're done with this chapter, you'll understand what it takes to create, manage, and deliver content to mobile subscribers via mobile marketing services: alerts, installed applications, websites, the mobile Internet, loyalty programs, and so on.

Sourcing Your Mobile Content

You can create your own content, or you can license it from third-party content providers and/or content aggregators. For details on working with content providers, see Chapter 4 in this minibook.

Before you use content created by someone else as the basis of your own mobile content, be sure to check with the content rights holder about any licensing or use restrictions. Don't get yourself into trouble by using someone else's content without all the necessary rights and licenses. Just because the content is out on the web doesn't mean that you have the right to use it or create a derivative work from it (change and/or rebrand someone else's content for your own purposes).

The safest, but not necessarily easiest, way to obtain mobile content is to create it yourself or contract someone to do it for you.

Here are some tips to remember before you create your content or prepare to use someone's third-party content:

+ **Get permission.** You must always have permission (also referred to as *expressed* or *prior consent*) from mobile subscribers before you can send them a text message. See Chapter 1 in this minibook for details on industry best practices and regulations.

+ **Be relevant.** Send your audience members only information that is relevant to them. The mobile phone is a very personal device. If customers find that you're abusing their trust — such as sending them messages about some new hot product when the subscribers didn't opt in for that information — they're likely to perceive your message as irrelevant at best or spam at worst and to opt out of your program faster than you can text *stop*.

Relevance involves many factors. Don't look just at audience demographics, but also look at subscriber preferences, the times when messages are sent, subscribers' locations when receiving messages, and so on. Relevance is about taking the time to understand your customers and their needs and wants.

Sending Content via Messaging

Using the messaging paths, including Short Message Service (SMS), Multimedia Messaging Service (MMS), and e-mail, can be a very effective means of delivering content. The following sections describe how you can use text-messaging alert services to send content.

Sending messaging alerts

Mobile text alerts are very common content programs, broadcasting SMS or MMS text messages to people who have given the marketer permission to send those messages. (For details about these technologies, see Chapter 1 in this minibook.) You can send the same content to an entire group or a tailored message to each person.

Sourcing text content

To send text alerts as content, you need to create or acquire your text content and ensure that it's formatted properly for text messaging.

Creating text content is easy. All you need are a text editor (such as Notepad or Microsoft Word), your computer keyboard, and some creativity to create compelling messages of no more than 160 characters — the maximum number you can use in a single text message. Remember that spaces and carriage returns count as characters.

You can try to spread your alerts across multiple text messages, but don't exceed two or three messages; otherwise, you'll simply annoy your audience.

Make sure that you have the right compliance language, you don't use special characters, the content is encoded properly in your messages, and you maintain alignment with the best practices and regulations of each country you'll be delivering messages to. Ask your application provider for help with this.

Setting up the service

After you amass the ingredients of your messaging campaign, the next step is setting up your messaging service. Figure 5-1 shows the application interface of the mobile messaging platform from iLoop Mobile (www.iloop mobile.com). You can use this application to set up and configure your text-messaging alert service, including the opt-in, opt-out, help, and privacy elements. (If you're not doing the work yourself, your agency or partner will use an application like this one to run your messaging campaign.)

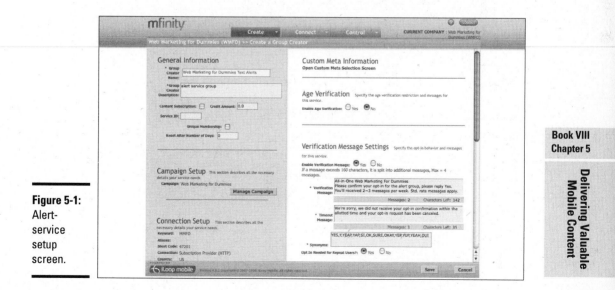

Figure 5-1: Alert-service setup screen.

Book VIII Chapter 5

Delivering Valuable Mobile Content

To set up your program, simply fill out the form and click Save. Then you're ready to start promoting your program in traditional media and messaging the subscribers who have opted in to your programs. See Chapter 2 in this minibook for information on gathering opt-ins. For details on setting up communication-program user flows, refer to Chapter 3 in this minibook.

Sending the content

You typically have two ways to send a message to your opt-in list:

✦ **Manually:** To publish your message(s) manually, log in to your mobile marketing application and select the groups to which you want to send the message. Filter the selected groups, if you want, by age, location, carrier, preferences, or other criteria and then enter the message.

You can send the message immediately or schedule it so that the mobile marketing application sends it later. (Figure 5-2 shows an alert message being scheduled in the iLoop Mobile platform.) You can schedule messages hours, days, weeks, or months in advance. If you have a horoscope service, for example, you can queue up six months' worth of horoscope messages before they're due to be sent.

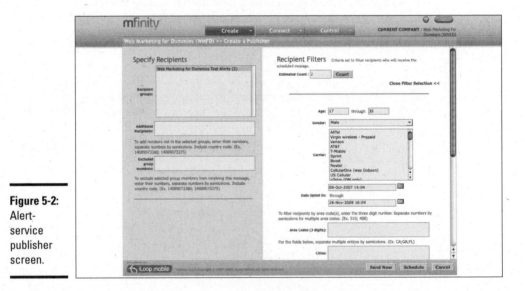

Figure 5-2:
Alert-service publisher screen.

Mind your timing

Taking time zones into consideration when sending or scheduling your messages is important. You don't want to wake up someone at 3 a.m.

Also, if you're sending a lot of messages, processing all of them may take time, so you'll want to know the *throughput* of the application you're using — that is, how many messages it can process per second. Add up the total messages you want to send, divide that total by the application throughput, and multiply the result by 60 to find out how many minutes it will take to process and send all your messages.

✦ **Via an automated data feed:** Instead of, or in addition to, sending or scheduling messages manually, you may want to have messages sent to your audience automatically on a regular basis. Typically, you work with a content provider (such as a news vendor or weather service) and your mobile marketing application provider to set up and schedule automatic alert programs. Then you set up a messaging alert schedule. When the content management system is ready to publish a message, it simply pushes the message to the mobile marketing application, which sends the message.

Be sure to test content feeds coming from a content management system before launching your service commercially. You need to check the feeds to make sure that the messages are within the character limit specified by your service (135 to 160 characters per text message, depending on carrier and country) and that the feeds don't contain special characters or encoding that won't display properly on mobile phones.

Sending personalized text alerts

You may want to deliver a tailored message to an individual customer. You may want to remind him that his car payment is due or that he has a dentist appointment tomorrow, for example, or to provide a coupon tailored to him.

To send personalized text alerts, you use all the systems and processes listed in the section "Sending messaging alerts," earlier in this chapter. The only difference is that instead of messaging a large group of people, you're messaging a single person. You can message the person manually, schedule message delivery, or have your content management system prepare a personalized message and send it to that person's phone number.

E-mailing informative messages

E-mail can be an effective way to deliver information to consumers, and it is increasingly becoming a mass market solution. At this writing, 40 percent of consumers access their personal e-mail, and 20 percent their work e-mail, in any given month (this is up from only about 10 percent of consumers in 2008). The main driver of this is the adoption of smartphones. Today in the United States, 50 percent of consumers have a smartphone, and the number is climbing.

For mobile marketing purposes, e-mail isn't always reliable; however, it is getting better. You have little control of how your content is viewed. E-mail services often reformat content to optimize its readability on mobile phones, and much of your message can be lost in translation. Also, many e-mail clients for mobile phones don't support attachments, and many types of data files are difficult to render on mobile phones, so e-mail attachments are unreliable means of broadcasting your marketing content to a mass audience.

You can use either of two methods to deliver e-mail to a phone (but keep in mind that they're not viable for mobile marketing):

✦ **Traditional e-mail:** The traditional e-mail route is simple. You send a message to an e-mail address (such as XYZ@gmail.com) just as you would in any traditional e-mail marketing program. Alternatively, you may want to consider using a service such as Constant Contact (www.constantcontact.com) or mobileStorm (www.mobilestorm.com). If your mobile subscribers have access to e-mail on their phones, and if they've opted in to your campaign, they'll get the message.

✦ **Mobile-phone e-mail:** This method uses the e-mail channels provided by mobile carriers (such as 555-555-5555@t-mobile) to send short bursts of text, similar to text messaging. This system is designed for personal use, not for commercial use, and shouldn't be used for commercial mobile marketing. You can find a list of restricted mobile e-mail domains at www.fcc.gov/cgb/policy/DomainNameDownload.html.

You can reach out to a number of mobile e-mail solution providers for help, including ExactTarget (www.exacttarget.com), mobileStorm (www.mobilestorm.com), CheetahMail (www.cheetahmail.com), and others.

Providing Mobile Enhancements and Applications

Mobile enhancements (also referred to as *personalization content*) are extremely common types of mobile content, as are mobile games and a host of other applications. The following sections review various content-distribution strategies for your branded mobile content.

If you lack artistic talent and can't create compelling wallpapers, screen savers, or ringtones on your own, you can hire someone else to create the content or tap your friends and family members to do it. Outsourcing content development to a third party is common and needn't cost much. A professional marketing agency can help you and probably will provide great service, but you can also go to a local art school college or high school — or even an elementary school — and ask a student to produce your artwork. You can find a lot of talented people out there!

Providing branded wallpapers and screen savers

Mobile wallpapers and screen savers are wonderful ways to personalize mobile phones and are conceptually identical to personal-computer wallpapers and screen savers.

A *mobile wallpaper* is the still image displayed on a mobile phone's main screen, and a *mobile screen saver* is the still and/or animated image that's displayed on the mobile phone's screen when the phone is idle. The image you use for wallpapers and screen savers can be your company's logo or any other image that represents your business or the objectives of your marketing campaign: a character, artistic scene, cityscape, landscape, and so on.

Delivering ringtones and other system sounds

The term *ringtone* refers to the sound a mobile phone makes when it is being called. Ringtones are immensely popular with all consumer segments and can be a great way to offer value to customers. Your subscribers can get ringtones from many places, including their mobile carriers, sounds built into their phones, and third parties like you.

Ringtones help personalize a user's phone. Unlike wallpapers, however, ringtones are public, because everyone around can hear them when the phone rings. Therefore, ringtones are a great way for a mobile subscriber to demonstrate affinity for a brand, campaign, or cause.

Making Mobile Games and Applications

Since the launch of the iPhone in 2007, mobile applications (especially games) have become an increasingly important element with mobile marketing. Over 1 million applications are circulating in the marketplace, roughly 400,000 on the Google Play Store (http://play.google.com), 550,000 in the Apple App Store, and hundreds of thousands of apps for the other leading mobile operating systems and connected devices like the Apple iPad, Samsung Galaxy, Amazon Kindle Fire and Barnes & Noble Nook.

You need to make a lot of decisions before you can even start building a mobile application because apps are so customizable. You can develop apps for specific functions, specific phones, and for an almost unlimited variety of tasks. The next sections show you how to think through your mobile app strategy so you have all the information you need to get started building your app.

Deciding whether a mobile app is the best choice

Mobile apps are cool. You can have so many unique and interactive experiences with them. For example, you can create exciting and fun games, entertainment services, social media and community experiences, financial services programs (for example, find the nearest ATM, transfer money, or even deposit checks through Chase's iPhone app), retail storefronts, picture galleries, broadcast media portals (like those offered by CNN), and so much more.

An app can be a very powerful consumer engagement medium. However, before you start building a mobile application, it's a good idea to consider that mobile apps are not necessarily the right choice for *every* business or business need. Before you jump into the world of mobile app development just because it seems like everyone else is, ask yourself the following questions about your business and your goals:

✦ **Are you trying to reach the most people possible?** If you're trying to reach as many people as possible, a mobile application may not be the right choice. For example, today in the U.S. market, about 50 percent of consumers have a smartphone. It is less than 10 percent worldwide, so the reach of a mobile app is limited to that audience.

✦ **Do you need a mobile app or mobile website?** For the most part, if your customers need to use the native device functions (for example, a device's camera, address book, location-detection capabilities, motion sensors, and so on) of the mobile device to accomplish whatever task you want them to accomplish, a mobile app is the right choice. If you just want to deliver content to your customers, a mobile website is probably a better choice. You can read more about building mobile websites in the later section "Serving Up Mobile Websites."

✦ **Do you have the time to do the care and feeding of a mobile app?** Successful apps, like popular websites, require care and feeding. If you struggle to find time to update your business website, you will likely encounter the same challenge in keeping your app fresh and exciting.

✦ **What phones do your customers use?** Different smartphones and related tablets like the Apple iPad require different development, have differing screen sizes, and in some instances, require completely unique development for each. If your customers use a wide variety of phones, you need to develop a variety of apps, or you need to justify the fact that you'll only be reaching a portion of your customer base by developing a single app.

✦ **How will you develop your app?** Unless you're a programmer, or you have a team of app developers who work at your company, go with an expert app development company to build your apps. Whether you use your own programmers or hire an outside developer, be sure you budget for the entire app lifecycle: concept and design, development and iteration, quality assurance and user experience testing, and distribution and promotion. Work with your development teams to scope out a complete budget. Remember, it will take longer than you may think to do it right.

You must develop several versions of each app to work with the various operating systems on your customers' mobile phones (the iPhone, the Android, and so on), or you need to realize that you'll only be reaching a portion of your customer base if you develop a single app.

Distributing mobile apps

The most popular route for distributing applications is via the app stores of the various smart device companies. Although you have other means to distribute apps, think of the app stores as the swankiest department store in the mall with a big neon sign. They typically carry the endorsement, if not the name, of the smart device manufacturer and enjoy a high level of trust on the part of the device user.

In addition to offering easy, immediate distribution, app stores provide billing flexibility. You can choose to distribute an application for free, a one-time premium charge, or a recurring or subscription-based charge.

Alas, nothing in life is *truly* free. Although most device app stores allow free apps to be made available at no cost (about 80 percent of all apps are offered for free), they keep a share of any premium charges if and when the application is sold. Known as a *revenue share,* the retail fee of the application kept by the smart device company is generally around 30 percent. So, even though the app store will help you distribute the application, you get to keep only about 70 cents of every dollar charged to your users. Keep in mind, whether your application is sold or offered for free, you can also make money with your application through mobile advertising (see Chapter 4 in this minibook) and through mobile commerce (see Chapter 6 in this minibook) strategies.

Which app store you choose depends on two key qualifiers:

✦ **What environment you developed your app for:** You can't distribute an app to an app store not built for it. BlackBerry App World doesn't take apps built for Android, for example.

✦ **Which store provides your app the greatest visibility:** You can determine this in a number of ways, including the number of apps in the app store or how many downloads the app store enjoys.

App stores require that you submit your application via a clearance process before an app is posted to the catalog. Some of these approval processes can take months to be completed, so don't go printing flyers with your launch date on them until you know an app has been approved.

Check out the app store websites for more information:

✦ **Google Play (for Google Android devices):** `https://play.google.com/apps/publish/signup`

✦ **BlackBerry App World:** `http://na.blackberry.com/eng/developers/resources`

✦ **iPhone Developer Program (for iPhone, iPod touch, and iPad):** `http://developer.apple.com/programs/iphone`. To get your app into the App Store, you must go the route of the developer program.

✦ **Windows Phone App Hub:** `http://create.msdn.com/de-DE`

For a fairly complete list of application stores and application resources. see the Wireless Industry Partnership website at `www.wipconnector.com/appstores`.

Serving Up Mobile Websites

The mobile web implies an intimate one-to-one experience, often with a user who is on the go or visiting your website for a specific purpose (like checking sports scores and the weather forecast or looking to buy a specific item). The mobile web is a completely different animal than the traditional Internet, which was and is developed for stationary consumption.

When building your mobile site, put yourself in the user's mind-set. People on the go or with a specific agenda in mind have little time to dig through menus, scroll left or right, or wait for pages to load. They're frequently multitasking — walking down the street or drinking a cup of coffee with one hand while browsing with the other. Keep in mind that about 90 percent of the population is right-handed, so you may want to optimize one-hand use with the idea that the right thumb can reach the primary features. See Figure 5-3 for a mobile app that puts its navigation at the bottom of the screen. It's critical that you think through what people will want to do on your site and make sure that your site lets them perform these actions quickly and easily.

Figure 5-3:
This app includes links at the bottom for easy navigation.

One common mistake is trying to give mobile web visitors quick access to your entire broadband website experience. A more prudent plan is to develop a simple, clean homepage that loads quickly on a mobile device over the wide range of mobile networks and puts key information a click or two away. Simplifying makes sense. Creating a short, descriptive page title, using simple language, and providing order to the content you present are all great ways to stay on track. It is also a good idea to put a link on the bottom of the page to your full website so that visitors can go there if they choose.

Considering the purpose of your mobile site

A traditional website is usually the destination for all your company's information, including everything from products for sale to job postings. Mobile sites need to be established with a specific purpose in mind because people who view mobile sites aren't going to dig through hundreds of links to find the task-oriented information they need.

The next sections help you to establish a purpose for your mobile site so that you can serve your customers and prospects with only the most relevant information.

Identifying the needs of your mobile audience

Establishing a purpose for your mobile website should take the needs of your prospective visitors into account, not the needs of your company. Answering the following key questions can ultimately help lead to a solution that works for you and your customers:

✦ **What are your customers most likely trying to accomplish with your site?** Make a list of all the tasks that your customers need to accomplish on the go. Examples include finding your phone number or directions to your store, looking up in-stock availability of an item, or making a reservation.

✦ **What functionality do you need to give customers on your site?** You can serve up content like text, images, videos, and audio, or you can give them interactive functions such as chatting with customer support.

✦ **Will your audience be buying things through your mobile site?** If so, make sure that your site can accommodate payment gateways and security. If not, your site can act as a source of information for making purchases through another means, such as on a computer or in a store. Remember that people can phone in a purchase too. After all, it's still a phone!

✦ **Will social media be a consideration?** Social media interaction on mobile devices is getting a lot more popular and familiar to mobile users. Make sure to build social media into your site if you have social media users among your customers and prospects.

These are just a few of the questions you should ask and answer for yourself. You know your business best, so think through them all.

Choosing from three types of mobile Internet sites

Before you head off to design and develop your mobile website, consider that many different types of sites exist, all of which have their uses. Among the many permutations, you need to be aware of three basic types of mobile websites:

✦ **Basic landing page:** This is generally a simple, one-page site built to deliver basic information fast. Traffic frequently comes from online ads. Restaurants, small retailers, and service companies are often well served by this type of site. Populate the basic site with

- Key contact information

- Operating hours

- Map/locator

- Special events

- Any other information important to people on the go

✦ **Promotional site:** Promotional sites are built around a specific product, event, or limited-time promotion. For example, a music festival would likely build a promotional site to provide festivalgoers with the lineup/ schedule, sponsorship information, maps, special events, and links to local happenings and restaurants. After the event is over, the site may go away.

✦ **Persistent site:** Persistent sites are permanent, evolving sites designed to meet the ongoing needs of mobile website visitors. Businesses expecting constant customer traffic — from airlines and banks to social media and on-the-go information portals — build persistent sites to provide easy access to information that mobile web visitors constantly need. An airline company, for example, may create such a site to make it easy for visitors to check departure and arrival status, view reservations, and check in online.

Your mobile web marketing strategy may involve building and maintaining more than one type of mobile site at a time. To avoid confusing your audience as to which site to visit, choose a domain name strategy that differentiates your mobile sites.

Designing and building your mobile site

Websites designed to be viewed by PCs are developed in a number of different programming languages, including HTML, Flash, XML, Ajax, PHP, and more. Your browser is designed to read and understand the instructions written in these languages, as well as to learn new languages. The same concept holds for your mobile Internet browser. Languages have been developed to improve your experience when viewing the mobile web — including WAP, XHTML, cHTML, and KHTML — but they are all device and operator dependent, meaning that they don't work on all phones or networks. Because fewer than 1 percent of websites today can be viewed properly on a mobile phone, the mobile web is far from a finished product.

One strategic decision that's sure to have ramifications for how you build your mobile site is what types of handsets you plan to support. Because handsets are not standardized, you need to determine which type of site to build:

✦ **A default site that renders the same on all mobile devices:** A default site should be designed for the lowest common denominator, to render the same on practically all mobile handsets. A default site is generally a basic, low-effort text site free of bells and whistles that gives visitors easy access to key information on your site using simple HTML, CSS, and semantic markup. When designing a default site

- Choose a readable font and size
- Use a single-column format
- Minimize scrolling

✦ **A medium site that increases functionality and design possibilities:** If a basic default site isn't enough, the next step up is a site designed to provide more functionality and a richer user experience. Using style sheets, forms, and map integration, for example, you can ensure that visitors can access a professional-looking site to get the information they need and take advantage of advanced handset capabilities. For more details on style sheets, forms, and maps, see *Mobile Web Design For Dummies,* by Janine Warner (published by John Wiley & Sons, Inc.).

When designing this type of site, determine what specific phone capabilities you want to take advantage of or enable before you get started. Testing is very important, as even the same handsets react differently depending on the network.

✦ **A high-end site that provides an optimal experience for people on feature-rich devices:** This type of site gives users access to videos, forms, maps, and other features and functionality enabled by iPhones, BlackBerrys, and Windows Mobile phones, among others. If you want to ensure an optimal experience for customers on smartphones, this is the way to go. Although it takes more effort to build your site, it also provides considerably more benefit and improves usability for more sophisticated mobile users.

Take a good look at your audience. Who is coming to your site and what do they need to do on it? Site analytics can give you a very clear idea of what type of handsets access your site and what kind of site might be your best bet.

Choosing tools to build your mobile site

Building a simple mobile version of a website isn't difficult. Building a mobile site that looks good on multiple mobile-phone models and browsers is an entirely different story. Your options depend on your site's complexity, your expertise, and your budget. You have four primary options:

✦ **Working with an agency:** If you have a budget, high expectations, a demanding timeline, and little expertise in mobile site building, working with an agency to develop a mobile website is a smart approach. Working with an agency offers many advantages, including brand consistency, ease of maintenance, and a single and trusted point of contact for updates. An agency can help you identify and answer all the key issues involved in your mobile site build. Check to be sure that the agency you choose has the specific skills you need, plus broad expertise in the mobile space, website design, and development, as well as the content development, database, and back-end IT capacity you require.

✦ **Using automatic transcoders:** *Automatic transcoders* are software tools that look at the HTML code in an existing website and translate the code into a mobile-friendly version on the fly or to produce a static mobile site. Transcoders work well for simple HTML websites. Buyer beware, however. Although they're a nice, simple solution, they are far from perfect. Pages are rendered based on templates, which can lead to a far less visually appealing site. dotMobi, the leading mobile domain registrar, offers a great free transcoder with the purchase of a .mobi domain. Usablenet offers high-end transcoding of existing sites at www.usablenet.com.

✦ **Using visual editors (see Figure 5-4):** If you are creating a mobile site from scratch, or maybe just using assets from an existing wired site, a visual editor tool is a good choice. Visual editors are usually web-based, drag-and-drop or WYSIWYG (What You See Is What You Get) site-building tools. They make it fairly simple to create a basic site. You can upload images and create and format pages simply. Some visual editors even have advanced features, such as the ability to pull in dynamic content from an RSS (Really Simple Syndication) feed and populate databases with user information (RSS is the industry standard for converting web content into data feeds, like news stories, so that the content can be easily shared across the Internet).

Visual editors are a great choice if you want to build a basic site that renders correctly on almost all phones and includes some complex features (RSS feeds and so on), but don't want to bother with designer or developer expenses. However, use caution. Aside from a few templates, visual editors give you little freedom to customize your site. Most sites created with a visual editor will be menu driven, with copy and links stacked on top of each other. Many visual editors don't have the ability to arrange links horizontally, for example, and type, image, and color options are limited. Some of the leading providers include iLoop Mobile (www.iloopmobile.com), Mad Mobile (www.madmobile.com), DudaMobile (www.dudamobile.com), and Siteminis (www.siteminis.com).

Figure 5-4: Visual editors allow you to build your mobile site with a minimum of coding.

**Book VIII
Chapter 5**

Delivering Valuable Mobile Content

✦ **Using code editors:** If you understand web software coding and development, a code editor may make the most sense for you. Code editors allow you to upload your own code into a tool that ensures that your site renders correctly on a mobile device. A code editor can solve some of the issues with customization that often arise when using a visual editor. Many visual-editing tools have a code editor feature. If you have a large organization and multiple developers with different mobile skill levels, you should probably license a tool that has both a code and visual editor. Because many editors let you switch back and forth between code and visual editors, the visual editor/code editor combination can serve as a learning aid as your developers get comfortable with mobile development.

See Google's GoMo (www.howtogomo.com) site for additional resource and testing tools to help you build your mobile presence.

The mobile web versus apps and the role of HTML 5

While you're grasping all of the new and exciting things you can accomplish with a mobile website, keep in mind that one of the many moving parts of the mobile web is the software language that is used to structure, create, and present mobile web pages on a mobile device. The goal of a mobile web software language is to provide a good experience for the mobile consumer: to display content in a legible manner, to be fast (loading pages quickly from all the possible data sources, including content management systems, static pages, image repositories, commerce systems, and so on), and to be secure (protecting the consumer's personal information, commerce transactions, and so on from being monitored by someone who shouldn't be monitoring them).

A new entrant in the web page software development lingo has recently emerged that should not be ignored: HTML 5.0. It was first developed in 2007 by the W3C (Worldwide Web Consortium, www.w3c.org), the standards body for the web. Just recently, more and more companies are launching mobile websites using HTML 5.0. HTML 5.0 offers many advantages. It's fast, provides a good experience, is secure, and, most importantly, can increasingly be used to provide an experience that is more like an application than a traditional website.

Chapter 6: Getting Paid for Your Mobile Marketing Efforts

In This Chapter

✔ Making money through the mobile channel

✔ Distinguishing among mobile payment models

✔ Cashing in on carrier billing relationships

✔ Building out your own commercial presence

The mobile channel is unique. It is a personal, location- and time-independent, interactive marketing medium that can be used to enable commerce. You can use it to process transactions and as a storefront, as well as a tool to interact with and turn your once-inert print, television, radio, outdoor, advertising, and related marketing media into immediate retail engagement mediums. In 2012, eBay estimates that between its auction site and PayPal, it will process over $8 billion in transactions through mobile. Worldwide, mobile commerce transactions are expected to exceed $1 trillion by 2015, up from $24 billion in 2011.

This chapter reviews the many ways you can leverage mobile as a medium of commerce. It explains how you can commercialize physical and virtual goods through and with mobile, including music, movies, tickets, parking, televisions, and clothes for your virtual avatar within a game. And most importantly, it explains the different ways to consider mobile commerce and the various payment methods you can use to make money with mobile.

Methods of Monetizing the Mobile Channel

When considering mobile commerce, it is important to recognize that the term *mobile commerce,* or *mCommerce,* can be confusing. It's like trying to measure sunlight; depending on the tool used for measurement, it will either be perceived as a particle or a waveform. Depending on how you look at mobile commerce, you'll either perceive it one of two ways:

✦ **Receiving payment via mobile** is the activity of processing a transaction through the mobile device, that is, exchanging money or stored value (such as a rebate or prepaid card) via one of the mobile paths, including SMS, applications, mobile web, and voice. See Chapter 1 of this minibook for more details on all the mobile paths.

✦ **Mobile-influenced transaction** is the use of the mobile device to engage people and influence their awareness, interest, and relationship with your business to eventually encourage them to make a purchase, whether through your brick-and-mortar store or your website. For example, people may use the mobile phone to search for a local store, check for discounts, or compare products but complete their transaction at your store's traditionally manned or self-service checkout counter. They may even just go home and buy the product from your website and have it shipped.

Figure 6-1 illustrates this idea, putting mobile commerce as a unique process/event within the context of mobile marketing.

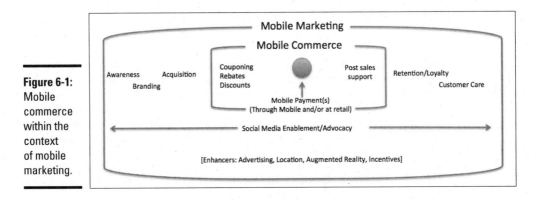

Figure 6-1: Mobile commerce within the context of mobile marketing.

Understanding mobile payments

When thinking about taking a payment for a transaction through mobile, it is important to consider what kind of goods and services you're looking to sell and to understand the flow of money between the consumer and you.

In the mobile world, people tend to consider two billing models:

✦ **Direct carrier:** In this model, the charges for items being bought are billed directly to the consumer's mobile carrier bill, and the consumer pays for the services each month when he pays his phone bill.

Two methods exist for direct-to-carrier billing:

• *Premium SMS:* The practice of using text messaging as a billing method. See the section "Making Money through Premium Text Messaging," later in this chapter.

• *Internet-based carrier-billing models:* Billing solution providers supply the developer of your mobile Internet or applications with software to include in your mobile websites and applications (see Chapter 5 of this minibook) to support carrier billing.

Leading carrier-billing solution providers include Zong (www.
zong.com), BilltoMobile (www.billtomobile.com), BOKU
(www.boku.com), Payfone (www.payfone.com), and OpenMarket
(www.openmarket.com).

✦ **Internet-based:** In this model, you manage the billing in the cloud
(online servers) and through your mobile payment solutions providers with the charge going directly to the carrier bill as opposed to your
credit card. See the section "Selling Your Content and Services via
Mobile," later in this chapter.

Offering Your Content through a Carrier's Portal

With the growth of smartphones and the ability to engage a consumer
directly, it may come as a surprise that the mobile carrier itself is still an
incredibly valuable channel to reach your audience. Every mobile carrier
offers a branded portal on the mobile phone. This portal features content
and services created by the carrier and its partners. You too can offer content through a carrier portal. To offer your content and services for sale
through a carrier's portal and ensure that you ultimately get paid, you must
follow one or more of the paths described in the following sections.

Mobile carriers today typically are not enabling the physical goods and services through their portals. It is one thing to take on the sale of a ringtone,
image, or movie. It is a completely different thing to take on the liability of
physical goods.

Developing a direct relationship

Many companies establish a direct relationship with each individual carrier
for the purposes of promoting content and services directly on the carrier's
portal. The deals that you can strike can vary greatly, but here are some
common ways to develop revenue opportunities with a carrier:

✦ The carrier gives you a lump-sum payment for access to your content
for a certain period.

✦ The carrier provides you minimum sales guarantees.

✦ You and the carrier enter into a revenue-sharing relationship in which
you share the revenue (often not equally).

Direct carrier relationships take time to develop and negotiate — often 12 to
18 months or more — and this time frame assumes that you already have a
head start and generally know who to talk to.

Entering into a channel relationship

Many carriers offer developer and content-channel relationship portals that you can sign up for on the Internet. The channel relationship business model differs from the direct carrier relationship discussed in the preceding section in that you're not negotiating a direct deal. Instead, with a channel relationship, you get access to the carrier portal, business terms that are easy to adopt and employ, royalty payments for the sale of your content, access to the carrier's marketing education materials, and more. Table 6-1 lists various carrier content and developer programs.

Table 6-1	Carrier Developer Programs
Name of Carrier	*Contact Information*
Sprint	http://developer.sprint.com
Verizon	www.vzwdevelopers.com/aims
T-Mobile	http://developer.t-mobile.com
AT&T Wireless	http://developer.att.com

Here's how to get started with channel relationships:

1. **Go to the carrier's website, and sign up for a standard third-party service program.**

2. **Have your content or service certified.**

   This step is important, because you must be certified before the carrier puts your content on its portal. Every carrier's certification process is different, based on the type of content or service you're offering. You'll need to review the details of the process on the carrier's website.

3. **Accept the terms and conditions of the program.**

   The terms include how much and when you get paid for your services. In very rare situations, you may be able to obtain minor adjustments in the standard program terms.

Contracting with an intermediate company

Some intermediary companies have direct relationships with mobile carriers that have been forged over many years. The intermediary firms sublicense your content to get it on a mobile carrier's portal. Some of the leading players include BilltoMobile (www.billtomobile.com), Zong (www.zong.com), Mocapay (www.mocapay.com), PayOne (http://payone.com) and others.

TIP

Intermediaries are great channels because they enjoy economies of scale and greater reach than you can get on your own by going to each carrier individually.

Making Money through Premium Text Messaging

Premium text messaging, or PSMS (*P* for *premium* and *SMS* for *Short Message Service,* or text messaging — yes, all the jargon can be confusing), is an extremely common, fast, and versatile way to monetize a mobile marketing campaign by charging mobile subscribers for content you sell via the mobile channel. When you use PSMS, the price you charge for access to your content — 99¢, $1.99, $9.99, and so on — is billed to the consumer's mobile phone bill, and after carrier collection of payments and deduction of carrier fees, you get a check.

PSMS can be used only for content and services that can be consumed (read, viewed, played, and so on) on a mobile phone or tablet, such as a text message, wallpaper, or ringtone. You can't charge for physical goods or nonmobile services by using PSMS.

PSMS charges are billed in the mobile subscriber's local currency. In the United States, for example, numerous fixed-price points between 10¢ and $29 are available for charging mobile subscribers via PSMS. A *price point* means that you can't make up a price; you have to choose among the various price tiers that are available for you to use. Contact your application provider or messaging aggregator for a list of all the PSMS price points that you can use in each country.

You might consider using PSMS to charge your subscribers for the following:

✦ Entering a sweepstakes

✦ Voting in a poll, quiz, or survey

✦ Purchasing your content, such as text (news, horoscopes, sports alerts, and so on), wallpapers, screen savers, ringtones, applications, and games

See Figure 6-2 for how a PSMS charge appears on a mobile phone bill.

**Book VIII
Chapter 6**

**Getting Paid for
Your Mobile
Marketing Efforts**

Figure 6-2:
PSMS
charge on
a Verizon
Wireless
bill.

Description	Date	Time	Usage Type	Application Price	Total
Prem_sms 76278 Papa ver 2	06/11	02:58P	Q2	$.99	$.99

PSMS can be used for one-time purchases and donations as well as for recurring (weekly or monthly) billing. The versatility of this method comes from the fact that you can initiate the PSMS billing process from any marketing channel, including the following:

✦ Mobile-originated (MO) text messaging — that is, a message originated by consumers and sent from their mobile phones. MO messaging is used in all programs in which you're mobile-enhancing traditional media and retail with a text-messaging call to action (see Chapter 2 of this minibook).

✦ A website or mobile Internet site.

✦ A widget, such as a plug-in for use on a social networking site.

✦ An interactive voice response (IVR) session. (See Chapter 2 of this minibook for more details on IVR.)

Putting PSMS to work: An example campaign

Suppose that you're trying to sell a ringtone called BestSong and want to let everyone know about it. If you use PSMS, the process works as follows:

1. You promote the ringtone in various media:

    • *Traditional media:* In flyers, on billboards, in store displays, and so on, you place a call to action like this one: "Text *tone* to 12345 to buy BestSong for $1.99. Standard messaging and other data rates apply."

    • *Digital media:* On a web or mobile website, in a widget, or in other digital media, you place a message like this one: "Enter your mobile number in the field below and click Submit to buy BestSong for $1.99. You'll receive a text message asking you to confirm your purchase. Standard messaging and other data rates apply."

    • *IVR:* In an IVR session, the singer records a sultry prompt such as this one: "Preview and get the latest track I've laid down, BestSong, for $1.99. Say or press 1. You'll get to hear the preview and then receive a text to confirm your purchase. Standard messaging and other data rates apply."

2. The consumer responds to your call to action.

3. You send a text message to the consumer's phone, asking him to confirm his purchase request. Your message may say something like this: "Please confirm your purchase of BestSong for $1.99 by replying *yes*. Standard messaging and other data rates apply. Reply *help* and/or *stop*."

4. The consumer responds to your purchase request.

5. You send a text message with a download link to the consumer's phone. Your message may say something like this: "Thanks. To download BestSong, click `http://c4d.com/1212fas`."

6. The consumer downloads the ringtone.

7. You send the consumer a final text message to initiate billing (see Figure 6-3).

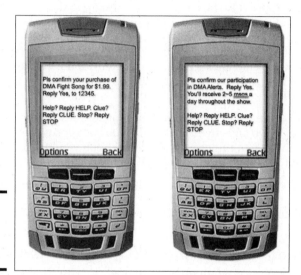

Figure 6-3:
Initiating
billing via
PSMS.

The actual billing event happens after the content or service has been delivered — not before. Make sure that your application provider is handling this step properly.

Setting up a premium messaging program

Setting up a PSMS program is similar to setting up an SMS program (which is covered in Chapter 3 of this minibook), but you need to complete a few extra steps. To set up and run a PSMS program, you need the following elements:

✦ **A Common Short Code (CSC) approved to run your premium program:** This code must be certified for each price point you want to use it for. (For details on CSCs, flip to Chapter 2 of this minibook, and for more information about price points, refer to the section "Making Money through Premium Text Messaging," earlier in this chapter.)

✦ **A mobile marketing messaging application solution:** You need a solution that's compliant with carrier and messaging aggregator requirements in each country in which you plan to run the PSMS program.

If you want to bill through PSMS, make sure that you work with an experienced mobile services application provider. You must meet many rules, regulations, and technical requirements before mobile carriers allow you to bill via their networks using PSMS.

✦ **Campaign approval:** The carrier has to review and approve your program and all its user flows, including ensuring that you receive text-message purchase confirmation from the consumer — known as a double opt-in. The carrier also must determine that your program meets all other requirements, such as opt-out, help, and privacy. (For more details on best practices and guidelines, refer to Chapter 1 of this minibook.)

If your program isn't preapproved, the carriers won't turn on billing support. If you have an active Short Code, your unapproved program may run, but one of two things will happen: (1) You won't get paid, or (2) Your CSCs will be shut off, and you'll be blacklisted.

Don't skip the approval process, which takes 8 to 15 weeks. Ask your application or messaging aggregator provider (see Chapter 4 of this minibook for details on providers) to help you get certification.

Determining how much you'll get paid and when

When you have your program up and running, you can start getting paid for your content and services. Typically, PSMS revenue is split among the following parties:

✦ **Carrier and aggregator:** Messaging aggregators and carriers retain a percentage of the gross receipts from PSMS billing events — combined, typically 40 to 60 percent. The percentage depends on the price points of the transactions, the total volume of transactions, and the carriers that the mobile subscribers are using. Payouts typically are made 12 to 15 weeks after the sale.

✦ **Application and billing providers:** Some application and billing providers will negotiate with you to share in a percentage of the revenue in lieu of or in addition to software licensing fees, download fees, or messaging transaction fees.

✦ **Content rights holder:** If you've licensed content from a third party, or if you're using content licensed by your application provider, the content rights holder must be paid from the proceeds of the sale.

Processing PSMS refunds

Refunds are tricky things to manage in the world of PSMS. If you have a customer who calls to complain, you can give her a refund by cutting her a check, but you may be losing out. The customer may already have requested and received a refund from the mobile carrier, in which case the carrier will deduct this refund from your payout. Alternatively, if the consumer went to you for the refund, not to the carrier, you'll refund the entire amount to the consumer. But you'll receive only that amount less any carrier, aggregator, and application provider fees. You'll probably owe the content rights holder a royalty, too, because the content was delivered and can't be revoked.

Be sure to get a rate card from the content rights holder before selling the content. You need to determine how much you can expect to earn — which may be less than you think. Suppose that you're selling — in moderate volume — a ringtone for $1.99. The mobile carrier and aggregator retain 50 percent of the sale price, leaving 99.5¢. If you have a 20 percent revenue share with the application provider, and the cost of the ringtone from the content rights owner is 50¢, you'll receive a payout of 29.6¢ per sale. And if you're reselling leading-artist ringtones (referred to as *master* tones), you'll receive 1 to 3 percent of the gross receipts after all the fees are deducted. Furthermore, carriers reserve the right to provide credit to customers who complain about a premium charge. Any such credits will be deducted from your receivables before they are paid.

Selling Your Content and Services via Mobile

The mobile phone is an incredible payment platform, because mobile subscribers almost always have their phones with them. In fact, most of us are never more than a few feet away from our phones.

Entire industries are looking to use the mobile phone for payment — not just for mobile-consumable goods and services, as discussed in the preceding sections — but in the last 18 months, the opportunity to sell physical goods and services with Internet-based billing methods has emerged. The following sections discuss the most common alternative billing methods you can use to get paid via the mobile phone.

Using mobile Internet link billing

One alternative method of promoting and selling mobile-consumable content and services is the mobile Internet. In industry jargon, this practice is often

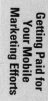

referred to as Wireless Application Protocol (WAP) billing, a legacy term for the mobile Internet. To continue the example from the section "Putting PSMS to work: An example campaign," earlier in this chapter, you can promote your Hot New Ringtone track with a Purchase link on a mobile Internet page. But instead of using the PSMS channel, which uses text messaging to capture consumers' consent to the charge, you can use mobile Internet link billing.

In mobile Internet link billing, mobile subscribers click a link on a mobile Internet page to initiate and then confirm their purchase of the content or service.

Billing via mobile Internet links is not something anyone can do; it requires special relationships with wireless carriers. If you want to use this method of billing on your mobile Internet site, you need to make sure that you're work- ing with a mobile application service provider that has mobile Internet link billing relationships with the connection aggregators, such as Ericsson IPX (www.ericsson.com/solutions/ipx) or OpenMarket (www.open market.com), or with mobile billing firms such as Bango (www.bango.com) or Buck (www.gobuck.com).

Internet-based billing solutions

Internet-based billing solutions leverage the Internet infrastructure to pro- cess payments. You have to rely on your payment-processing partners to help you pull all the pieces together. *Payment-processing partners* are com- panies that help you take in and process payments and then distribute the money with you after taking off a prearranged processing fee (typically 2.5 to 5 percent plus a per-transaction fee).

You can find numerous solution providers to assist you with integrating bill- ing into your messaging, voice, mobile websites, and applications, including any number of e-commerce solution providers for the web and then mobile commerce specialists such as Visa (www.visa.com), MasterCard (www. mastercard.com), Google (www.google.com/Wallet), Buck (www.gobuck. com), PayPal (www.paypal.com), and Mocapay (www.mocapay.com).

You'll also find all kinds of other types of mobile payments, specifically mobile banding and commercial and personal money transfers. These types of mobile payments are highly regulated by the government.

Using a mobile wallet

Money does not simply appear. Many people think that with mobile com- merce, cash, checks, or credit cards are not needed. It may be true from a customer experience prospective, but you still need to have the customer get the money to you. Anytime someone stores money or links accounts, it's a *mobile wallet*. The generally understood concept of the mobile wallet is that it is used to easily associate the consumer's Internet-based billing account to her online credit, banking, or stored-value accounts. Here are a few options you can offer customers:

✦ **Prepaid cards:** The customer puts money on a card and then uses the card to purchase products with it. A prepaid card is similar to a debit card.

✦ **Through an app:** A customer can link an account (which has money in it) to a store with an app. He can then pay for purchases and add more money to his account through the app. (See the Starbucks example in the "Using mobile as a point-of-sale solution" sidebar.)

✦ **A loyalty program:** Customers can sign up for a loyalty program, giving a bank account or debit or credit card information to automatically pay for purchases through the program. (See the PayPal example in the "Using mobile as a point-of-sale solution" sidebar.)

Alternatively, if the consumer is not using a prepaid card, he often has the option of linking his bank account or debit or credit cards to the mobile payment service.

Using mobile as a point-of-sale solution

For many businesses, both large and small, mobile devices are increasingly used as a payment and redemption tool at the point of sale. Here are a few:

✔ Inmar, the industry-leading processor of paper coupons (to name just one of its many services), has a mobile solution that is integrated with many grocery stores. Users can scan coupons and associate their loyalty accounts with the Inmar system, and when they check out at the register, they simply need to scan their phone and/or enter their mobile phone number at the checkout keypad for the system to access their stored coupons, previous purchase history, rewards, and so on. All this information is then considered and applied to the consumer's current transaction and added to his history.

✔ K&G Brands has also integrated its mobile programs, specifically its text-messaging-powered coupon program, with its point-of-sale system. Consumers simply need to text in to the text program, which is prompted in-store, to receive a coupon. They then can show the store associate their phone at the store to redeem the coupon.

✔ Starbucks offers an app that allows customers to scan a phone at the register to pay for items with money stored in a Starbucks account. The customer can also use the app to reload the account with more money.

✔ PayPal gives customers the choice to link one or more bank, debit, or credit card accounts to their PayPal account. Therefore, when they use PayPal to buy something, they don't need their bank or credit card information.

Book VIII
Chapter 6

Getting Paid for
Your Mobile
Marketing Efforts

No universal mobile wallet exists. Today's implementations require that a consumer have her account information duplicated across every Internet-based billing solution she chooses to work with. This information may include not just the consumer's desired payment methods, but can also include — just like her physical wallet — coupons, receipts, and loyalty and reward cards.

If you are not ready to integrate your mobile programs into your stores' point-of-sale system yet, not to worry; you can always leverage stand-alone mobile point-of-sale solutions:

✦ You can scan a phone screen and charge the consumer's registered account. Check out LevelUp (`www.thelevelup.com`).

✦ Attach a small device to your phone, and it will act as a credit card scanner. The leading solution for this is Square (`www.squareup.com`). However, Intuit and PayPal are also coming out with their own offerings.

Mobile commerce solutions are innovating every day. Just keep looking around. For example, shopkick (`www.shopkick.com`) is an in-store loyalty engagement solution. People receive loyalty points for checking in at the store and scanning products. foursquare, the leading check-in social media solution, has partnered with American Express. If you check in via four-square to a participating establishment, you can receive a discount, and if you pay with your American Express card, you'll automatically receive the discount on your next credit card bill. Also, keep an eye out for contactless payment solutions like Near Field Communication (NFC), RFID, and SIM RFID. Future phones will be embedded with chips using these local-frequency technologies, which will link to the consumer's mobile wallet. All a consumer will need to do is wave his phone over a scanner that can detect the NFC, RFID, or SIM RFID signal and a transaction is complete. No need for any messy credit cards, wallets, or keypads.

Chapter 7: Tracking a Mobile Marketing Campaign

In This Chapter

✔ Understanding the measurement and analysis of mobile marketing campaigns

✔ Setting up databases, profiles, and CRM systems

✔ Collecting data and analyzing reports

✔ Calculating return on investment (ROI)

*M*easuring and tracking the results of your marketing programs, including both your direct and mobile-enabled traditional marketing programs, are an essential part of your job as a marketer. Over the last few years, marketers have been put under a significant amount of pressure to demonstrate a return on investment for the organizational resources they consume. *Return on investment (ROI)* is the measurement of dollars received for every dollar invested. Moreover, lately, marketers are starting to measure *return on engagement,* that is, how much value is created with each interaction with a person. In other words, you need to show the value of your effort and demonstrate how those efforts contribute to meeting the company's goals and objectives.

Mobile analytics provide valuable insights into the performance of your mobile campaigns. *Mobile analytics* refers to the process of measuring, monitoring, and tracking your mobile marketing campaigns. With mobile marketing analytics, you can

✦ Track individual user participation in all your programs by time, frequency, location, and other measurements

✦ Measure and compare all your mobile marketing campaigns, in some cases in real time, so that you can make immediate adjustments to your programs

✦ Use data to calculate your ROI to see whether you're making more than you spend (a positive ROI) or whether you're losing money on your programs (a negative ROI)

This chapter shows you a number of ways you can collect information and analyze it to improve your mobile marketing programs.

Determining What to Track and Analyze

Mobile analytics is the process of collecting data from your mobile marketing efforts so that you can compare a change in a single metric over time and compare multiple sets of data to each other. Mobile analytics impacts your mobile strategy in two ways:

✦ Analytics help you plan your mobile campaign strategy

✦ Analytics help you evaluate the success of your strategy

To gauge your mobile marketing success, you need to analyze which parts of your strategy work and which parts don't. Measurable data collected for the purpose of analysis are often called *metrics*. A metric is any number expressed in a scale, used to quantify how much you have of something. (Think temperature in degrees Fahrenheit, or speed limits in miles per hour, for example.)

Marketers use metrics all the time in other media, especially digital, direct, and retail. Although you could track literally hundreds of metrics, Table 7-1 shows you a list of the main mobile campaign interactions and the metrics you should be prepared to track and analyze.

Table 7-1	Mobile Interactions and Associated Metrics
Interaction	*Metrics Worth Paying Attention To*
SMS	Unique participants in a campaign Number of respondents, opt-ins, opt-outs, and total churn (percent of people who opt out compared to the total list) Successfully and unsuccessfully delivered messages Carrier participation and which mobile carriers drove the most participation Participation by geography Count of embedded URLs visited Average revenue per user (ARPU) Total revenue per campaign
MMS	All the SMS metrics listed previously Number of unsupported devices Mobile operator MMS policy rejections
Content downloads	Unique downloads Total downloads Failed downloads Total revenue

Interaction	Metrics Worth Paying Attention To
Mobile websites	Unique visitors Repeat visitors Entry and exit points Bounce rates (number of visitors who see only one page) Number of page views Geographic location of visitors Devices used by visitors Mobile operators used by visitors Average time spent on a site, on a page Conversion rate
Mobile advertising	Cost per impression (CPI) Cost per click (CPC) Cost per conversion (CPC) or cost per acquisition (CPA) Total number of click-throughs (the number of times an ad is clicked on)
Voice campaigns	Date and time of incoming calls Number of calls Total minutes per call Billable minutes Average call length Number of transactions per call Revenue per call Error messages processed
Mobile applications	Number of downloads Download count by handset type Unique active users Failed downloads Time to download Total revenue Location of download User reviews of your application Time spent using application
Mobile e-mail	Click-through rate (CTR) Conversion rate Opt-ins and opt-outs Open rate Unsubscribe rate Forwards and shares
Bluetooth and Wi-Fi	Total delivered sessions Total content downloads Frequency and time spent per location The type of phone interacting with the system The mobile carrier used Location access point by location

The metrics in Table 7-1 are by no means an exhaustive list; they simply highlight some of the more prominent measures tracked.

Metrics aren't just about measuring success. In fact, just as often, metrics help you recognize that parts of your mobile marketing are *not* working so that you can fix them.

Preparing Your Database to Collect Information

A *mobile marketing database* (see Figure 7-1) is simply a database that houses all the information about each and every mobile customer you have and all the campaigns and programs you run. A mobile marketing database allows you to link your mobile marketing campaign interactions with the people in your database and apply metrics to individuals and groups of individuals.

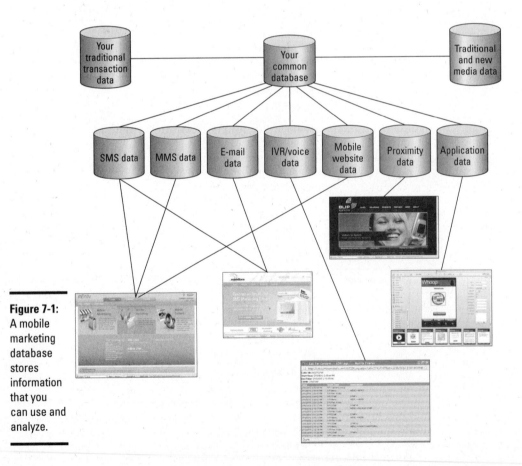

Figure 7-1: A mobile marketing database stores information that you can use and analyze.

You'll probably end up working with a number of databases, depending on how many mobile marketing companies you work with. Many companies support multiple mobile media paths, but no one supports them all. For a specific setup of programs, a database is typically built and hosted by your mobile marketing application provider. Or, you may already have your own customer relationship management (CRM) system or database that you work with.

In any event, whether your mobile marketing database is hosted by your application provider, is integrated with your CRM solution, or is some hybrid model, you need to set up your database files to accept the data you need to collect and analyze from each type of interaction.

The following sections show you the types of information to consider adding to your database for each customer or prospect who interacts with your mobile marketing campaigns.

Outlining demographic data

Demography is all about studying populations; consequently, demographic data are the data points that detail a population's characteristics. You want to think about the various demographic data points you'll find helpful for your business (every business is different). Data you might consider including in your database include

✦ Age (either in the form of a birth date or age range, for example, 14–24, and so on)

✦ Sex (male/female)

✦ Marital status (single, married, divorced, domestic partnership, and so on)

✦ Number of children (zero, one, two, three, more than you can handle)

✦ Level of education (high school, some college, college graduate, doctorate, life experience)

✦ Occupation (there simply are too many to list — isn't that a great thing?)

✦ Income (typically presented in monetary ranges, for example, $50,000–$75,000 per year)

✦ Nationality (American, French, British, Chinese, and so on)

✦ Geography (residence, place of work, or if you're a road warrior, American Airlines, seat B17)

In tech speak, all this data is commonly referred to as *metadata*, or "data about" something. When your engineer asks you, "What kind of metadata do you want to capture?" you can say, "I need demographic metadata — age, geography, and psychographic data (that is, information about your preferences, attitude, intention, and so on)." Now you're cooking!

Book VIII
Chapter 7

Tracking a
Mobile Marketing
Campaign

Organizing psychographic data

You may want to capture and organize psychographic data about members of your audience. *Psychographic data* is qualitative data used to measure an individual's lifestyle. Examples could include

+ Behaviors such as frequent travel

+ Attitudes, interests, and beliefs

+ Values and opinions

+ Personality

+ Purchasing motivation

+ Usage behavior

You can include psychographic information in your database to help you describe and identify customers and prospective customers in more detail and to aid in developing promotion strategies designed to appeal to specific psychographic segments of the market for a product or service.

Planning for preferences data

Preference data is data volunteered by a member of your audience regarding his preferences, for example, and his likes and dislikes (favorite food, music, and so on). Other preference criteria may include the days of the week and the times the consumer prefers to be messaged or called, or how many times the consumer is willing to let you contact him within a particular timeframe (for example, ten times a month, but no more than three times per week).

By setting up your database to include preferences information and using it appropriately, you have a much better chance of pleasing the customers and prospects who interact with your mobile marketing campaigns.

Planning for behavioral data

Behavioral data includes information about past behavior or expected behavior based on past interactions or predictions based on other data. Including behavioral data in your database can tell you whether someone is likely or unlikely to respond to a specific campaign. For example, people with a behavioral profile that indicates procrastination might not respond to a limited-time offer.

You can get some great mobile subscriber behavior data from comScore (www.comscore.com) and Nielsen (www.nielsen.com), two research firms that track user behavior on mobile phones.

Behavioral data is an emerging field in marketing. Talk to your application provider and connection aggregator to get a sense of what they're doing in this area or with whom they're working.

Looking out for location data

Location is a dynamic data point that can be used to adjust your interaction with members of your audience so that those interactions are contextually relevant to their location. For example, if they're browsing a mobile Internet site and your database knows a user's location, you can display location-relevant advertising or guide her to the nearest location. You can also track location in real time and use that information to deliver location-based messages when your customers give you permission to use their location data.

Mining syndicated data

Syndicated data is consumer purchasing data compiled from individually scanned consumer transactions from thousands of purchase locations. The data is collected by market research firms, cleansed, and put into aggregate to protect the privacy of individuals. It's then used by marketers to better understand the purchasing behavior of their target audience. Marketers use syndicated data to

✦ Improve sales tracking of their products and their competitors

✦ Monitor marketing promotions and merchandising for both their own products as well as those of their competitors

✦ Determine which distributors are using their products

✦ Segment customers effectively, identifying their best and worst prospects

✦ Perform market basket analysis, understanding what other products are typically purchased at the same time as theirs

Syndicated data can be very useful. In fact, it can often be better than data you collect yourself because it amasses information not just about your own client interactions but also those of your competitors as well.

Although data and information collection may give you knowledge and power, with this knowledge and power come great responsibility and liability. You must protect the data you collect. If you don't protect it (if you misuse it, or if it gets in the hands of someone else), you may face many commercial and legal challenges. Seriously think through all the liabilities before you collect and use data. Be sure to consult your legal counsel. You can read more about the laws governing mobile marketing in Chapter 1 of this minibook.

**Book VIII
Chapter 7**

Tracking a
Mobile Marketing
Campaign

Populating a Mobile Database

After you've identified the types of customer and prospect data that you're going to collect and you've worked with your own internal team or mobile marketing application provider to build a database, you're ready to start populating the database, that is, loading it up with all the information about your campaigns and your customers.

The following sections show you how to collect profile information about your customers when they interact with your campaigns. Then in the next section, you track the details of each interaction with your campaigns.

Collecting data through SMS

With SMS, you can collect some data automatically as well as request that participants of your campaigns provide the data. When a consumer opts in to your campaign via SMS, the mobile marketing application captures the participant's mobile phone number. From this mobile phone number, your application provider can identify the following:

✦ **Previous participation in other programs you've run:** You can match the number to see whether the number has been used in other campaigns.

✦ **Wireless carrier:** Discover which wireless carrier the subscriber is using.

✦ **Crude location:** Using the country code and area code of the number, you can make a crude estimate of location (country, state, city, and time zone). This method should not be used for real-time location detection because it does not tell you where the person is, just where their phone was registered.

✦ **Porting history:** Find out whether the number has ever been moved from one wireless carrier to another.

✦ **Technical bits:** Discover whether the phone supports binary data (for example, pictures and video), text messaging, or WAP push. (*WAP push* is a method of delivering content and mobile Internet sites. Ask your mobile marketing application provider about this.)

In addition to the preceding data, you can request the user to submit any number of different types of data points, including demographic, psychographic, and preference data via SMS. For example, you may ask the user to submit her birth date as an opt-in challenge if you're marketing a program not suitable for children. You simply need to make sure that your text messaging application supports the ability to collect the data you're asking for and in the manner you're asking for it.

Collecting through the mobile Internet and installed applications

You can use Internet and mobile Internet browser forms or forms in an application that you've downloaded to your mobile device to collect information from your prospects and customers by requesting that the visitor to the site complete the form. Upon submission, you capture the requested data.

For example, you can use web forms that can capture different consumer preference attributes, as shown in Figure 7-2.

Figure 7-2: A consumer retail-focused preference opt-in form via the Internet.

You can use forms on mobile Internet sites, but be sure to keep them short. Mobile subscribers do not have the patience to complete long forms via their phone, so ask only the basics. If you need more info, augment the experience with another mobile (for example, voice) or traditional (for example, the Internet) path. But be careful. Make sure that you understand your audience. For example, not all demographics use all mobile technology.

Be sure to ask your application provider whether you can create your data schema and forms. Companies like iLoop Mobile (www.iloopmobile.com) have robust mobile customer relationship management elements that give you this capability.

Integrating CRM with mobile campaigns

A time may come when you want to merge your mobile campaign data with that data stored in your company's customer relationship management

(CRM) system. This is easy to do and typically can be handled in one of three ways:

✦ **Manually:** You can ask your mobile marketing application provider to give you a manual report (in Microsoft Excel or in an XML data structure) so that you can combine your data with that of the mobile marketing campaign database manually.

✦ **Via data feed:** Your mobile marketing application provider should be able to give you access to an XML data feed that you can pull from on a regular basis (once a day, every five minutes — the timing depends on your application needs) so that you can combine your data with that of the mobile marketing campaign database automatically per the set schedule.

✦ **In real time:** You can also ask your mobile marketing application provider whether it can pass you data in real time as your participants interact with the system (see Figure 7-3). For example, maybe you need to know immediately if someone opts out of your mobile marketing campaign so that you can update the other permission marketing management system in other parts of your company.

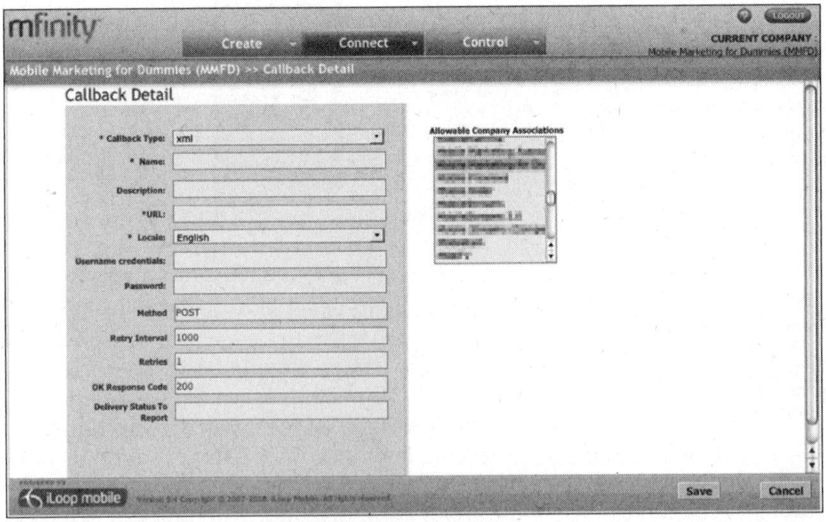

Figure 7-3: The real-time data transfer configuration screen in the iLoop Mobile mfinity platform.

Tracking Interactions: Clicks, Calls, Votes, and More

Your mobile marketing application is capable of tracking most, if not all, interactions a mobile subscriber has with it. That includes any calls, text clicks, snaps, scans, StarStars (**), pounds (#), presses, pictures taken, acceptances, submits, votes, requests, replies, and more.

How this information is tracked and reported on, however, varies significantly by the type of mobile method you're using. Moreover, you should consult with your mobile application provider prior to running your campaigns(s) to ensure that the data you need (that is, the data you want to use to measure and report on the efficacy of your program(s)) is being tracked and retained.

Using third-party tracking tools

You have your choice of a number of mobile analytics providers to track consumer interactions on your mobile websites and applications. For example, if you want to track interactions on your mobile websites, you can consider using Google Analytics (www.google.com/analytics). Google Analytics allows users to get rich website information, and the account creation process is simple:

See Figure 7-4 for mobile web report from another tracking tool, Bango (http://bango.com).

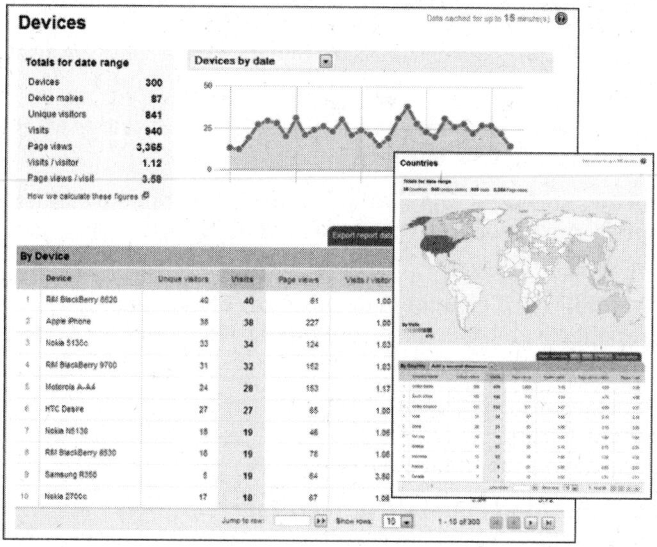

Figure 7-4:
A Bango mobile behavior multi-channel meeting report.

Courtesy of Bango

**Book VIII
Chapter 7**

Tracking a
Mobile Marketing
Campaign

You can choose among a number of application provider reporting tools, including Flurry (www.flurry.com), Medialets (www.medialets.com), Motally (www.motally.com), Bango (www.bango.com), Adobe Omniture's

SiteCatalyst (`www.omniture.com/en/products/online_analytics/
sitecatalyst`), Webtrends (`www.webtrends.com`), and others.

If your mobile application provider won't let you integrate a third-party reporting tool, find another vendor. Third-party validation is incredibly important.

Obtaining metrics from partners and service providers

You should be able to obtain from your mobile application service provider a wealth of operational and business metrics from your campaigns. In general, obtaining metrics is a straightforward process, and as a marketer, you have to assess what mobile metrics are appropriate for you to measure.

Here is a list of the common metrics, tools, and questions you should be asking your provider about so that you can develop your mobile analytics strategy:

✦ **Frequency of data available:** How often are the reports updated? (Many providers only provide previous-day snapshots, not real-time data.)

✦ **Summary levels of data (in addition to detailed transactional data from the mobile campaign):** For example, does it provide you with a total SMS message count or mobile web page view count in a summary report?

✦ **Specific data elements available:** Ask your provider what data elements it can provide you, like those listed in Table 7-1.

✦ **Sorting and selecting data capability:** Can you sort and filter the data online, or do you need to export it and do it in a spreadsheet program like Microsoft Excel?

✦ **Availability of campaign dashboard tools:** Campaign dashboards are graphical web-based tools provided to marketers for manipulating and visualizing data.

✦ **Charts and graphs availability:** Similar to summary level data, can you get bar charts, pie charts, timeline graphs, and other visual representations of your campaign data?

✦ **Customization options (alarms, triggers, views):** In other words, can the system send you an e-mail notifying you whether your opt-out rate exceeds a threshold that concerns you, or if your text-message campaigns hit previously unreached heights?

✦ **Integration capability:** Do you have the ability to integrate with databases or other proprietary tools for data delivery?

✦ **Help support availability:** Is both business and technical help available?

✦ **Privacy controls:** Can you administer privacy controls, such as masking a user's phone number out of reports?

✦ **Process analysis (for user flows and consumer acquisition):** Can you evaluate consumer engagement across different types of campaigns, such as moving from initial acquisition into a loyalty or customer service program?

If your mobile service provider cannot comply or provide the majority of these items, either as a standard offering or by developing a custom report or tools for you, you may want to consider finding another vendor who can help you.

Before you set up a custom report with a service provider or agency, be sure that you're clear about who owns the information gathered. Also, be sure that you understand and are comfortable with its process for data security. You want to make sure that you own the data and that you can take the information with you if you choose to move on to another service, even if the information is collected through its platform.

Understanding analytics reports

An *analytics report* is a collection of mobile metrics presented to you in a single report so that you can see all your data as a whole and begin to gather insights from it. You can then use these insights to make decisions on how to best move forward with your business (see Figure 7-5). In other words, reporting and analyzing the data generated from your programs are absolutely critical components to your mobile marketing efforts. What good is the best mobile marketing campaign if you do not have strong insights in exactly how it performed or is performing?

Many of the companies in the mobile marketing space today can provide a high level of reporting sophistication. Campaign dashboards are often configurable so that you can see the metrics that matter to you and see them in a variety of formats.

Reports typically are summary views of a mobile campaign on a daily, weekly, or monthly basis, but they can also be unprocessed and unformatted data files that require additional work to arrange and present the data.

Every mobile application provider has a different user interface for pulling its reports. Ask about the reporting feature in the application as well as the mobile website reports available when you're selecting a mobile service provider.

Figure 7-5:
Analytics
reports
quantify the
interactions
with your
mobile
campaigns.

Courtesy of Mobile Behavior

You'd be amazed by how quickly data can be amassed as mobile subscribers interact with a mobile marketing application. Every click, snap, and call can be, for the most part, tracked.

Your application provider(s) no doubt has a lot of experience with collecting and analyzing transaction data. However, more often than not, the application provider is not in your business and doesn't know exactly how you want to look at the data or what analysis of the data is meaningful. Rather than assuming that it knows what you need, tell it the type of results and data you want to see in the transaction reports. Have this discussion before your campaign launches; otherwise, you may have some late nights slogging through log files to get the answers you need. If you plan and coordinate with your application provider prior to the launch of your program(s), the application provider can give you the answers you seek in a perfectly packaged report, often in real time.

From log files to readable reports

In addition to all the reports your application provider shares with you, you should keep in mind that more information may be stored in an application provider's server log files. Application providers capture a lot of data within their systems; however, due to time constraints, technical challenges, or their own failure to realize that the information is valuable, they may not immediately share it with you. All you need to do is ask for it. They may be able to provide you with custom reports and data access or start tracking additional information that they were not tracking before. For example, during an SMS interaction, the mobile marketing application may record the following transaction: abcvote yes 4085551212 543221. In this example,

- ✔ abcvote is the keyword associated with a particular text-messaging voting campaign

- ✔ yes is the vote response

- ✔ 4085551212 is the mobile subscriber's phone number

- ✔ 543221 is the wireless carrier's CarrierID, which is a number that tells the mobile marketing application that the phone number is on Verizon Wireless, T-Mobile, or Sprint, for example.

It takes a lot of computer power to analyze data, so a mobile marketing application often processes the data externally to its core applications and/or late or early in the day, say, every morning at 4:00 a.m. Be sure to ask your mobile marketing application provider to show you what data is available in real time versus what data is processed later. You should also find out what data is available upon request, that is, in the log files, but not readily available in the system for general consumption.

The preceding example is very simple. Log files include lots of other data, including success and error codes, serverIDs, time stamps, and so on. Converting the log file data — data that is often unintelligible to the common reader (log files are written in another language, engineering-speak) — into actionable results is another matter entirely. Your mobile marketing application provider needs to map the log file codes to a series of database tables that help translate the numbers in the log file. For example, 543221 equals AT&T Wireless. The provider then maps this data to reports.

Transaction reports can come in two flavors: raw data dumps and analyzed reports. With raw data dumps, you receive a report that provides a line item for every transaction. You can use spreadsheet software like Microsoft Excel to analyze the data and report on it. For analyzed reports, the mobile application provider gives you calculated statistics in an analysis report. For this example, the report provider displays not just the votes but also how many votes occurred and which option received the most votes.

Mobile marketing reports can often contain both graphs and data for the metrics and be made available in a variety of formats (such as Microsoft Excel spreadsheets, Adobe Acrobat PDFs, or other formats). A current trend is to provide a visual representation, typically in graph form, so that a user can quickly see how his campaign is doing. Figure 7-6 shows a sample trend graph on the effectiveness of mobile advertising.

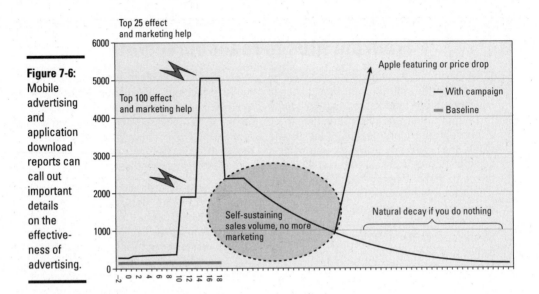

Figure 7-6:
Mobile advertising and application download reports can call out important details on the effectiveness of advertising.

Calculating Your Return on Mobile Marketing Investment

Return on mobile marketing investment (ROMMI) is an important measure to keep track of because it lets you know whether you're achieving your objectives and getting more out of your mobile marketing than you're putting into it. You'll find two basic ROMMI measures: a ROMMI against direct revenue–generating programs and a ROMMI against indirect revenue–generating programs. Both are discussed in the following sections.

Calculating expected ROMMI for direct revenue programs

Calculating your ROMMI for revenue-generating mobile marketing programs is a simple math exercise. The ROMMI for revenue-generating programs compares the sales you generated, or expect to generate, in revenue terms against your mobile marketing spending, or expected spending, that helped generate those revenues.

Here's the formula to calculate your ROMMI for direct revenue programs:

[Incremental revenue attributed to mobile marketing (in dollars) * Sales contribution margin – Mobile marketing spending (in dollars)] / Mobile marketing spending (in dollars)

Here's an explanation of each variable:

✦ **Incremental revenue attributed to mobile marketing (IRAMM)** is the total additional revenue, in monetary terms (for example, in dollars) you generate by running the mobile marketing program as opposed to the revenue you'd receive if you did not run the mobile marketing program. For example, if your revenues were going to be $22,000 before running the mobile marketing program and you estimate they'll be $30,000 by adding the mobile marketing element to your marketing program, your IRAMM is the difference, $8,000.

✦ **Marketing spending** is the total cost for running the mobile marketing program, including all strategy, creative, tactical execution, and technology elements.

✦ **Contribution margin** is the calculation of the marginal profit (a percentage) generated from the product or service being sold. To calculate this, you need to know the selling price of the product(s) or service(s) that is contributing to the revenues being tracked and the variable cost it takes to produce it. With this information, you can use the following formulas to calculate your contribution margin. The calculation is a two-step process. You first must calculate the contribution per unit, and then you can calculate the contribution margin:

   • *Contribution per unit (in dollars):* Selling price per unit (in dollars) – Variable cost per unit (in dollars)

   • *Contribution margin (percentage):* Contribution per unit (in dollars) / Selling price per unit (in dollars)

Here is an example: Say that you're selling T-shirts. The shirt sells for $10 and it costs you $1.50 to make it.

The contribution per unit (in dollars) is $10.00 – $1.50, which equals $8.50. The contribution margin is $8.50/$10.00, which equals 85%.

If you plan to use mobile marketing for the promotion and sales of multiple products, you can use the same model. You simply have to run the math for each product and add things up.

For example, say that you own a chain of retail outlets and you want to use mobile marketing to drive traffic to your store to generate T-shirt sales. You're already spending money on a direct-mail campaign, and you want to include a mobile component by adding a mobile coupon call to action. The total cost of the mobile marketing element to enhance your existing marketing campaign is $5,000. You expect the mobile marketing element of the campaign to increase revenues from $22,000 to $30,000. You previously calculated that the contribution margin of the T-shirts sales averages out at 85%.

Leveraging industry data as a baseline

As a keen mobile marketer, you should read industry reports, websites, and blogs that denote trending or typical mobile marketing statistics. Several of these services have mountains of data and reports readily available. These include Keynote Systems (www.keynote.com), comScore (www.comscore.com), Nielsen (www.nielsen.com), eMarketer (www.emarketer.com), Marketing Charts (www.marketingcharts.com),

and other third-party data sources. These services can be used to establish performance baselines for better understanding the relative performance of a mobile marketing campaign.

Leading mobile marketing case studies that highlight campaign results and best practices can also be pulled from free sources like Mobile Marketer (www.mobilemarketer.com) and other companies by doing a web search for *mobile marketing case studies*.

In this case, your ROMMI would be

$$[(\$8,000 * 85\%) - \$5,000] / \$5,000 = 36\%$$

In this case, your mobile marketing program is estimated to generate $0.36 per every dollar of spending. Not bad!

Calculating expected ROMMI for indirect revenue programs

Calculating your ROMMI for indirect revenue programs can be a bit harder than doing so for direct programs, but it is not impossible. The same premise applies as for direct revenue programs: You want to estimate the overall value of the mobile marketing program to your achievement of the company's objectives.

Your goal for indirect revenue objectives is not sales, but rather some other trackable measure (opt-ins, impressions, clicks, traffic, redemptions, and so on). For example, maybe you want to measure the number of new leads in the opt-in database (opt-ins), total mobile advertising impressions generated (impressions), increased traffic in the store or on Internet or mobile Internet sites (traffic), the number of loyalty points redeemed by customers (redemptions), and so on. To calculate your ROMMI, you need to know what each of these measures means to you. Look at your historical data and calculate how much additional revenue an opt-in, impression, redemption, or traffic means to you in terms of real revenue. You can then compare the value of an indirect measure, like an impression, against the estimated/actual costs of running the marketing program to estimate your indirect ROMMI and see whether the program is worth doing.

Here's the formula to calculate your ROMMI for indirect programs:

[Estimated value of measure – Mobile marketing spending (in dollars)] / Mobile marketing spending (in dollars)

Here's an explanation for each variable:

✦ **Estimated value of measure** is the total revenue you'd expect from the metric. For example, say historically that you've calculated that every new impression on your website, on average, is worth $0.20 in expected revenue.

✦ **Mobile marketing spending** is the total cost for running the mobile marketing program, including all strategy, creative, tactical execution, and technology elements.

As an example, say that a travel agency wants to sponsor a live event. The sponsorship costs $35,000 (including the mobile marketing program costs). The agency assumes that the sponsorships will generate 250,000 impressions, which results in a cost of $0.14/impression ($35,000/250,000). The agency knows that historically an impression is worth, on average, $0.20 in future revenues.

The ROMMI for these indirect programs is

($0.20 – $0.14) / $0.14 = 43%

Based on these estimates, the sponsorship is worth the expense.

Index

B

C

E

1

J

K

N

R

pple & Mac

Pad 2 For Dummies,
rd Edition
78-1-118-17679-5

Phone 4S For Dummies,
th Edition
78-1-118-03671-6

Pod touch For Dummies,
rd Edition
78-1-118-12960-9

Mac OS X Lion
or Dummies
78-1-118-02205-4

logging & Social Media

ityVille For Dummies
78-1-118-08337-6

acebook For Dummies,
th Edition
78-1-118-09562-1

Mom Blogging
or Dummies
78-1-118-03843-7

witter For Dummies,
nd Edition
78-0-470-76879-2

WordPress For Dummies,
th Edition
78-1-118-07342-1

usiness

ash Flow For Dummies
78-1-118-01850-7

nvesting For Dummies,
th Edition
78-0-470-90545-6

Job Searching with Social Media For Dummies
978-0-470-93072-4

QuickBooks 2012
For Dummies
978-1-118-09120-3

Resumes For Dummies,
6th Edition
978-0-470-87361-8

Starting an Etsy Business
For Dummies
978-0-470-93067-0

Cooking & Entertaining

Cooking Basics
For Dummies, 4th Edition
978-0-470-91388-8

Wine For Dummies,
4th Edition
978-0-470-04579-4

Diet & Nutrition

Kettlebells For Dummies
978-0-470-59929-7

Nutrition For Dummies,
5th Edition
978-0-470-93231-5

Restaurant Calorie Counter
For Dummies,
2nd Edition
978-0-470-64405-8

Digital Photography

Digital SLR Cameras &
Photography For Dummies,
4th Edition
978-1-118-14489-3

Digital SLR Settings & Shortcuts
For Dummies
978-0-470-91763-3

Photoshop Elements 10
For Dummies
978-1-118-10742-3

Gardening

Gardening Basics
For Dummies
978-0-470-03749-2

Vegetable Gardening
For Dummies,
2nd Edition
978-0-470-49870-5

Green/Sustainable

Raising Chickens
For Dummies
978-0-470-46544-8

Green Cleaning
For Dummies
978-0-470-39106-8

Health

Diabetes For Dummies,
3rd Edition
978-0-470-27086-8

Food Allergies
For Dummies
978-0-470-09584-3

Living Gluten-Free
For Dummies,
2nd Edition
978-0-470-58589-4

Hobbies

Beekeeping
For Dummies,
2nd Edition
978-0-470-43065-1

Chess For Dummies,
3rd Edition
978-1-118-01695-4

Drawing For Dummies,
2nd Edition
978-0-470-61842-4

eBay For Dummies,
7th Edition
978-1-118-09806-6

Knitting For Dummies,
2nd Edition
978-0-470-28747-7

Language & Foreign Language

English Grammar
For Dummies,
2nd Edition
978-0-470-54664-2

French For Dummies,
2nd Edition
978-1-118-00464-7

German For Dummies,
2nd Edition
978-0-470-90101-4

Spanish Essentials
For Dummies
978-0-470-63751-7

Spanish For Dummies,
2nd Edition
978-0-470-87855-2